SOCIALIST THOUGHT:
MARXISM AND ANARCHISM
1850–1890

SOCIALIST THOUGHT
MARXISM AND ANARCHISM
1850-1890

BY

G. D. H. COLE

LONDON

MACMILLAN & CO LTD

NEW YORK · ST MARTIN'S PRESS

1964

MACMILLAN AND COMPANY LIMITED
St Martin's Street London WC 2
also Bombay Calcutta Madras Melbourne

THE MACMILLAN COMPANY OF CANADA LIMITED
70 Bond Street Toronto 2

ST MARTIN'S PRESS INC
175 Fifth Avenue New York 10 NY

PRINTED IN GREAT BRITAIN

PREFACE

SEVERAL reviewers objected to the arrangement of the first volume of this work, because they held that it should have been grouped round ideas or general movements of thought rather than round the attitudes and projects of particular thinkers. Such reviewers will probably prefer this second volume, which comes nearer to the arrangement they favoured. I cannot, however, say that they converted me; for this second volume was completely planned and largely written before the reviews of the first volume appeared. It was, in my opinion, necessary, in dealing with the period up to 1848, to group the account of developments in Socialist thought round individual thinkers and the movements they inspired; for in effect there was, in the first half of the nineteenth century, no such thing as a Socialist movement possessing a unity and a central point of focus. Such a movement came into being only after 1848, and to a great extent after 1860, with the International Working Men's Association and the struggles within it between the rival tendencies I have described in the present volume. These struggles were indeed the birth-pangs of Socialism as an international force acting upon the working classes of all the economically advanced countries. The contest between Marxists and Anarchists — which was in fact a confused conflict of many rival tendencies — occupied a key position in the development of Socialism as a movement; and at the same time the struggle in Germany between Lassallians and Eisenachers, though the points at issue were essentially different, gave to the Marxists, after the destruction of French Socialism in the Paris Commune, a commanding lead in the creation of the new Socialist movements of the 1880s. The record of these events, and of the thought which influenced them, lends itself to a much more coherent account than was possible in dealing with the welter of theories and movements that confronts the student of Socialism up to 1848.

Of course, the main reason for the difference is that, in its revival in the 1860s, Socialism became for the first time decisively a working-class movement resting on the support of a large proletariat of industrial wage-earners in factories, mines, railways, and other relatively large-scale employments. Theorists no longer made theories in a vacuum, or in relation to a mainly unorganised mass of victims of oppression. They had to take increasing account of Trade Unions as established bodies, and of political parties to which the enlargement of electorates gave an impetus towards parliamentary activities, and away from mass revolts or revolutionary plottings. They had to turn more of their attention to the problems of bringing large-scale industry under social control and to the uses to be made of parliamentary action either as a new means of propaganda or for the winning of reforms within the structure of capitalist society. This question, of reform *versus* revolution, was not fully fought out until a later period ; and the main account of it will be given only in my third volume. But it had already presented itself, by the 1860s, in both Great Britain and the United States, as well as in Switzerland, though hardly in France or Belgium, or in Germany, barely in Italy, and not at all in Spain. Marxism, as well as the various brands of Anarchism, Anarchist-Communism, and Federalism, still presented itself mainly as a revolutionary force, in hostility to the various kinds of reformism, from Christian Social movements to *bourgeois*-led Radicalism and 'Liberal-Labourism'. But it was significant that, in the First International, Marxists no longer formed the extreme left.

I have again been hampered in writing this volume by my linguistic limitations — by knowing no Russian, very little German, and practically no Spanish or Italian. This means that I tend to rely as much as possible on sources in English or French, including translations, and that my Russian and Spanish information, in particular, comes largely at second hand. My third volume, which will cover the period, approximately, from the birth of the Second International in 1889 to the Russian Revolution of 1917, is already fully planned, and partly drafted. I hope to round off the work in a final volume, and then, possibly, to go back and deal with the antecedents of Socialism in the period before 1789.

PREFACE

My obligations for help with this second volume are great. Mr. Isaiah Berlin has again aided me generously, especially in relation to Russia; and I have profited very much from the criticism and advice of Mr. H. N. Brailsford and of Mr. Morris Pearl, who both read the whole volume in typescript and gave me most valuable suggestions for improving it. Mr. John Plamenatz was kind enough to read three chapters — VI-VIII — and made useful suggestions. Mr. Arthur Lehning and Dr. Rüter, of the International Institute for Social History, both helped me with book references for the Belgian chapter. Mr. H. M. Pelling kindly lent me the proofs of his book, *The Origins of the Labour Party*, which has since been published. I have again to thank my brother-in-law, Raymond Postgate, and Mr. H. L. Beales for lending me books from their collections, and in addition to these Mr. Pearl and Mr. James Joll. My secretary, Rosamund Broadley, has again coped nobly with a mass of difficulties.

G. D. H. COLE

ALL SOULS COLLEGE, OXFORD
September 1953

CONTENTS

		PAGE
PREFACE		V
THE PRINCIPAL CHARACTERS		xi

CHAP.

I. INTRODUCTORY : SOCIALISM AFTER 1848 1

II. GERMAN SOCIALISM IN THE 1850s — RODBERTUS AND MARLO 14

III. THE DAWN OF SOCIALISM IN RUSSIA — BELINSKY, HERZEN, AND CHERNYSHEVSKY 32

IV. BELGIAN SOCIALISM IN THE 1850s — COLINS, KATS, AND DE KEYSER 57

V. LASSALLE 71

VI. THE FIRST INTERNATIONAL IN THE 'SIXTIES 88

VII. THE PARIS COMMUNE 134

VIII. DECLINE AND FALL OF THE FIRST INTERNATIONAL 174

IX. BAKUNIN 213

X. GERMAN SOCIALISM AFTER LASSALLE — 'CHRISTIAN SOCIALISTS' AND 'STATE SOCIALISTS' — THE *KULTURKAMPF* AND THE ANTI-SOCIALIST LAWS 237

XI. MARX AND ENGELS — *DAS KAPITAL* AND *ANTI-DÜHRING* 267

XII. ANARCHISTS AND ANARCHIST-COMMUNISTS — KROPOTKIN 315

XIII. AMERICAN SOCIALISM IN THE SECOND HALF OF THE NINETEENTH CENTURY — HENRY GEORGE AND DANIEL DE LEON 361

XIV. THE REVIVAL OF BRITISH SOCIALISM — WILLIAM MORRIS 379

CHAP.   PAGE
XV. SOCIALISM IN THE EARLY 1890S. CONCLUSION   425

SELECT BIBLIOGRAPHY   445

INDEX OF NAMES   465

INDEX   473

THE PRINCIPAL CHARACTERS

	CHAP. REF.		CHAP. REF.
COLINS, 1783–1859	4	MALON, 1841–1893	7, 12
WARREN, 1798–1874	13	DE PAEPE, 1842–1890	6, 8
RODBERTUS, 1805–1875	2	KROPOTKIN, 1842–1921	12
[BLANQUI, 1805–1881] [1]	—	HYNDMAN, 1842–1921	14
[PROUDHON, 1809–1865] [1]	—	BROUSSE, 1844–1912	12
DELESCLUZE, 1809–1871	7	GUILLAUME, 1844–1916	6, 8
MARLO, 1810–1865	2	GUESDE, 1845–1922	12
BELINSKY, 1811–1848	3	MOST, 1846–1906	12
KETTELER, 1811–1877	10	NECHAIEV, 1848–1882	8, 9
HERZEN, 1812–1870	3	POWDERLY, 1849–1924	13
BAKUNIN, 1814–1876	6, 8, 9	BELLAMY, 1850–1898	13
MARX, 1818–1883	6, 8, 10, 11	ZHELYABOV, 1850–1881	12
RUSKIN, 1819–1900	14	BERNSTEIN, 1850–1932	15
ENGELS, 1820–1895	6, 8, 10, 11	DE LEON, 1852–1914	13
STEPHENS, U., 1821–1882	13	CUNNINGHAME GRAHAM,	
LAVROV, 1823–1900	3	1852–1936	14
LASSALLE, 1825–1864	5	MALATESTA, 1853–1932	12
LIEBKNECHT, W., 1826–1900	10	BAX, 1854–1926	14
SORGE, 1827–1906	8	KAUTSKY, 1854–1938	15
SYLVIS, 1828–1869	13	DEBS, 1855–1926	13
DIETZGEN, 1828–1888	11	[HARDIE, 1856–1915] [2]	—
CHERNYSHEVSKY, 1828–1889	3	[MANN, 1856–1941] [2]	—
RÉCLUS, ÉLISÉE, 1830–1905	12	[SHAW, 1856–1950] [2]	—
SCHWEITZER, 1833–1875	10	[PLEKHANOV, 1857–1918] [2]	—
DÜHRING, 1833–1921	11	[WEBB, BEATRICE,	
MORRIS, 1834–1896	14	1858–1943] [2]	—
APPLEGARTH, 1834–1924	6	[JAURÈS, 1859–1914] [2]	—
VARLIN, 1839–1871	7	CHAMPION, 1859–1928	14
GEORGE, HENRY, 1839–1897	13	BURNS, J., 1859–1941	14
BEBEL, 1840–1913	10	[WEBB, SIDNEY, 1859–1947] [2]	—

[1] Discussed in Volume I.
[2] To be discussed in Volume III.

CHAPTER I

INTRODUCTORY: SOCIALISM AFTER 1848

THE 1850s were almost a dead period for Socialist thought. The defeat of the European Revolutions of 1848 and the repressive police régimes which thereafter re-established themselves over most of Europe left for some time little scope either for open agitation or even for free discussion of Socialist ideas. Wherever freedom of speech did exist — in England, in the United States, and in parts of Switzerland — exiles from France, Italy, Germany, and Austria-Hungary took refuge and, after the manner of exiles, fell out among themselves. Most of them — at any rate, most who remained in Europe and had no skilled trade which they could follow — were very poor, as well as frustrated and lonely. For a while many of them refused to believe that the Revolution had been defeated more than momentarily, and waited and intrigued eagerly for a renewed explosion which would allow them to return to their own countries and renew the struggle. This mood, as long as it lasted, kept up their courage ; but it also made them the readier to denounce anyone among them who doubted the imminence of the revolutionary second coming. As hopes faded, more and more of the exiles either made their peace, if they could, and slunk back home, or left Europe for America, where they had more chance of making a tolerable living and establishing themselves as citizens of a new country, and also, if they so wished, of carrying on propaganda for the 'cause' — chiefly among their fellow-migrants.

Among the exiles who found refuge in London were Marx and Engels and a number of their fellow-members of the Communist League. The League, moreover, was able for a short time to maintain an underground existence in Germany itself, or at least in the Rhineland, which had been its principal centre during the Revolution. Marx and Engels were even able to issue through a Hamburg publisher a few numbers of a *New*

Rhenish Review in which they began an analysis of the revolution and of the causes of its defeat. It was already clear to them that the hopes of a speedy revival of the revolutionary movement were baseless. 'In face of the general prosperity now prevailing, which allows the productive powers of *bourgeois* society to develop as fast as they can possibly do within the framework of such a society, there can be no question of any real revolution. Real revolution is possible only at a time when two factors are in collision — when the modern powers of production are in collision with the *bourgeois* mode of production. . . . A new revolution will be rendered possible only as the result of a new crisis, but it is no less certain than the coming of that very crisis.'

Thus Marx and Engels, recognising that the Revolutions of 1848 had been precipitated by the economic depression, were reconciled to waiting for the next economic crisis before attempting a new revolutionary *putsch* ; and they were soon angrily denouncing their more impatient colleagues who were already issuing fresh manifestoes calling for a new uprising. They had, indeed, at this time no idea how long their wait would have to be; and for the rest of their lives they continued to scan the economic horizon in eager expectation of further and more devastating manifestations of the contradictions of capitalism. They had, however, at any rate the sense to understand in good time that there must be a period of waiting — though even to them the realisation of the Revolution's defeat did not come at once. In March 1850 they drafted for the Central Committee of the Communist League, already re-established in London, a manifesto which rested on the assumption that a fresh wave of revolution was on the way, and that this wave would sweep on far enough to carry the *petit-bourgeois* democrats into power with the proletariat's help. The manifesto, after urging the workers to help the 'democrats' to win, proceeded to instruct the proletariat how to act when the *petit-bourgeois* victors attempted to halt the Revolution at a point convenient to themselves. As against this attempt, Marx and Engels argued, it would be the task of the proletariat to make the Revolution 'permanent' until all the owning classes had been driven from power and the state-power taken over by the workers. This would involve, they said, that 'the association of the workers, not merely in one country, but in all the most important countries throughout the world, shall have so far advanced that competition between the workers of these countries shall have ceased, and at any rate the most essential instruments of production shall be in their hands'. In this passage we can see a foreshadowing of the hopes with which Marx set out to build up the International Working Men's Association fourteen years later.

These hopes soon waned, as political reaction and economic recovery advanced hand in hand to destroy what was left of the revolutionary movement in the leading countries. By September 1850 Marx and Engels, though they could command a majority on the London Committee of the Communist League, were faced there with a minority which, still calling for renewed attempts at revolution, made a stronger appeal to the main body of the Communist exiles. In these circumstances Marx, using the same strategy as he was to apply more than twenty years later in the First International, took advantage of his precarious majority to transfer the headquarters of the Communist League from London to Cologne. The London group split into two : the dissidents, headed by August Willich (1810–78) [1] and Karl Schapper (1813–70), formed a rival organisation, and the London part of the League before long ceased to exist save as a tiny and impotent group.

In Germany the League could operate, in face of the growing repression, only underground, and before long it ceased to operate at all. One of its leading members, the tailor Peter Nothjung, was arrested in May 1851, and papers found on him enabled the Prussian Government to lay hands on the entire Central Committee. They lay in gaol untried until October 1852 ; and in the meantime a number of Germans who had taken refuge in Paris were arrested there by the French police and sentenced as participants in a Franco-German plot of insurrection which appears to have been largely manufactured by the police. This Paris group had no connection with the Cologne Communist League, and attempts by the Prussian

[1] Willich, a former Prussian artillery officer, fought in the German Revolution of 1848, and escaped to London in 1849. He was an active member of the Communist League. In 1853, after his projects for a further rising had failed, he went to the United States. There he fought in the Civil War on the side of the North and became a general.

police authorities to establish such a connection broke down. But the exposure, organised by Marx himself, of the forgeries carried out by the police in the hope of implicating the Cologne Communists did not save them. Even though the forgeries had to be admitted at the trial, when it was at last held after repeated delays, most of the accused men were convicted to long terms of imprisonment. The Communist League was dissolved ; and its insurrectionary rival also disappeared. Willich emigrated to the United States : Schapper rejoined the small group in London which still accepted Marx's leadership.

Marx wrote in German a short book, *Materials, Elucidations and Writings concerning the Communist Trial in Cologne*, exposing the methods used by the police ; and this was printed in Switzerland for smuggling into Germany, a separate edition being issued almost simultaneously in the United States. But the Swiss edition was seized in Germany by the police, and few copies of the book found their way into that country. Nor could it have made much difference had Marx's exposure been more widely circulated : reaction was too firmly in the saddle for even the most convincing exposure to shake its power. As early as February 1851 Marx and Engels had been making the best of a bad job by congratulating each other on their isolation, on the ground that it would remove all need for watering down their doctrine to suit the imperfect comprehension or the idealistic foibles of those with whom they had been compelled to act, and would give them time and means to work out more completely their fundamental principles. Marx was already hoping soon to publish his work on Political Economy, of which the first part (*A Critique of Political Economy*) did not in fact appear until 1859. The great obstacle in their way was the dire poverty to which Marx found himself reduced. It was in order to be able to help his friend that Engels reluctantly went back to Manchester and resumed his place in the English branch of his family firm. To this physical severance posterity owes the long series of letters which passed between the two almost continuously till Engels came back to live in London nearly twenty years later.

In the 1850s Great Britain was the unquestioned leader in the field of industrial development. Large-scale production, the factory system, and the means of transport were all a long way ahead of the stage reached in other countries. Foreign trade was growing fast and already included a considerable export both of capital for investment and of capital goods — especially railway equipment. The cotton industry still stood easily first in the value of its exports — roughly three times that of woollens, which disputed the second place with iron and steel. But both iron and steel and other metal goods — machinery, hardware, implements, etc. — were being exported in rapidly increasing quantities. On the other side of the account, food imports were rising fast — especially grain, but also meat, butter, cheese, and fruit. The number and tonnage of steamships were growing at a great pace, while those of sailing ships had not yet begun to decline. Though there were economic recessions during the 1850s, including a financial crisis in 1857 — ten years after the last — the whole tendency was one of rapid expansion, and the crisis of 1857 was much less devastating in its social effects than that of 1847, which had helped to precipitate the Revolution in Europe. In 1857 the crisis was again international and started in the United States ; but it had no political repercussions similar to those of ten years before. Neither in France nor in Germany was the upper *bourgeoisie* still a potentially revolutionary force ; and in Great Britain it had, of course, ceased to be one in 1832. The *petite bourgeoisie* showed no sign of taking the initiative Marx and Engels had hoped for in 1850 : the workers were mostly unorganised and, in any case, much too weak to move alone. In Great Britain the skilled workers were busily organising themselves in Trade Unions, and did begin in the later 'fifties that movement towards parliamentary reform which was to lead up to their enfranchisement in 1867 ; and the more radical wing of the middle classes, led by John Bright, also began to stir.

Chartism, as we saw in the first volume of this survey, had been dying away even before 1848 ; and despite the efforts of Ernest Jones its decline continued throughout the 'fifties at an increasing rate. By the end of the decade it was extinct as a movement, and its place was being taken by the new and more moderate reform movement which found its mainstay in the developing Trade Unions of the skilled workers. The renewed agitation for Manhood Suffrage did not become really active or widespread until the 'sixties. During the 'fifties, though the

Trade Unions were growing fast, the main preoccupation of their leaders was still that of consolidating their position in the several trades rather than of taking concerted action over a wider field. The Amalgamated Society of Engineers, founded in 1851, had to allow itself time to rebuild its strength after the great lock-out which had come near to breaking it in 1852. The National Miners' Union, powerful in the 1840s, had worn itself out in a decade of ceaseless struggle ; and the miners did not succeed in building a new national movement until the 1860s. The cotton operatives made, thanks partly to booming exports, the most continuous gains, winning in one district after another the right of collective bargaining, and establishing their status as skilled workers with the aid afforded them by the Ten Hours Act of 1847. The cotton spinners became perhaps the most highly organised of all the major skilled crafts : with the skilled engineers they came to count as the aristocrats of large-scale industry. Finally, at the end of the decade, the establishment of the London Trades Council, with a membership including the principal officials of a number of the leading Unions, was the first sign of a recognition of the need for action over a wider field. The London Trades Council arose largely out of the extemporised agencies set up to help the London builders in their struggle of 1859, and its main purpose was mutual aid in industrial disputes. But it had from the first a wider function as well, and it partly filled the place of a central agency for taking up working-class claims and grievances until the need for representative bodies more closely connected with the northern and midland industrial centres led to the establishment of the National Reform League and the Trades Union Congress during the following decade.

The new Trade Unionism that was developing fast among the engineers and other operatives in the 1850s and was to spread during the 1860s over a much wider field was, then, primarily a movement of skilled workers to whom the benefits of high British productivity were beginning at length to filter down. Their gains were, however, precarious, and seemed to depend on their ability to prevent the employers from either admitting too many newcomers to the trades they represented or finding means of doing without their skills. Accordingly, the craftsmen's Unions tended to follow restrictive policies, seeking to keep a tight control over apprenticeship or its equivalents, and refusing to admit unqualified workers to membership. This did not mean that they were unprepared to fight the battles of the working class as a whole in the political field ; for when it came to voting they clearly needed the less skilled workers' help. But it did mean that industrially they tended to be unsympathetic to organisation on a wide basis, because they were afraid of being swamped by the unqualified mass. It was to a great extent the same with the developing Co-operative movement, in which the consumers' societies were rapidly outstripping all other types. It is a mistake to suppose that either the Rochdale Pioneers or the numerous societies founded after 1844 on the 'Rochdale model' had any considerable following among the worse-paid members of the working class. Their appeal was predominantly to the relatively well-to-do and thrifty, who could afford to pay cash for what they bought and to set aside a little for saving out of their weekly earnings. Consumers' Co-operation went ahead rapidly in the 1850s and 1860s precisely because there was a considerable increase, among factory workers, miners, and other groups of skilled labourers, in the numbers who had just enough money coming in, not too irregularly, to make cash dealings and thrifty investment possible, and also because the Consumers' Societies offered the outlet for savings that came easiest and provided the best security for the frugal and industrious members of the working class. It is not surprising that when, in the 'sixties and 'seventies, the Socialists in the First International came to debate their attitudes towards the rising Co-operative movement, a good deal of suspicion was expressed that the Consumers' Societies were helping to create a labour aristocracy set apart from the main body of the proletariat and, with their payments of interest on share-capital and dividends on purchase, were teaching this aristocracy the ways of capitalism and turning it into a defender of the system of exploitation of 'labour-power'.

The Christian Socialists, although they did their best to help Co-operative Societies of all sorts to win secure legal foundations through the Industrial and Provident Societies Acts, to some extent shared these fears, and kept their main enthusiasm for the Producers' Societies which they attempted

7

to establish on a basis of Christian service. But by the middle 'fifties the Christian Socialists' experiments in Working Associations had mostly run their course, and Producers' Co-operation languished till its revival in the great upward movement of the late 'sixties and early 'seventies. Consumers' Co-operation, on the other hand, prospered, but lost all connection with the Owenite Socialism out of which the Rochdale Pioneers had sprung. The new members who flocked into the 'Co-ops' in increasing numbers, especially in the north and midlands, joined mainly for the direct benefits — unadulterated goods, fair prices, dividends on purchases, reasonably safe investment opportunities for small savings — rather than for any idealistic reason or because they saw in the Co-operative Society any foreshadowing of a new social system. The idealists — Edward Vansittart Neale, George Jacob Holyoake, William Cooper, and many others — were still active ; but in the practical working of the movement their voices were being drowned by the thrifty newcomers who increasingly dominated the boardrooms and quarterly meetings where policies were decided.

Thus, in the 1850s, the most advanced industrial country in the world seemed to have turned its back firmly on Socialism and on revolution, and to have settled down to making the best of capitalism. Meanwhile, on the Continent, Co-operation was being more and more advocated as a means whereby the workers — or rather the thrifty and industrious among them — could be weaned from notions of revolution and class-war and given scope to win both an improved economic position and greater freedom without challenge or harm to the established social order. In both France and Germany — and above all in Germany — Co-operation found advocates both among socially-minded Conservatives and among socially-minded 'liberal' progressives — the Conservatives hoping to consummate an alliance between the old order and the sober-minded workers against the political claims of the *bourgeoisie*, while the liberal advocates of Co-operation believed that the forces of 'free enterprise' would be strengthened by the advent of a manageable contingent of working-class entrepreneurs and that the workmen Co-operators could be turned into allies of the *bourgeoisie* in its struggle for constitutional, responsible government. In Germany, Victor Aimé Huber (1800–1869) stood for conservative, and Hermann Schulze-Delitzsch (1808–83) for 'liberal', advocacy of Co-operation as a voluntary movement calculated to improve working-class conditions without endangering social peace ; and Wilhelm Emmanuel von Ketteler (1811–77), the Christian Social Bishop of Mainz, did his best to enlist the Catholic Church on the side of Co-operation as a reconciler of classes. In France, where Consumers' Co-operation was weak, the Government of Napoleon III was hesitantly favourable to Producers' Co-operatives, provided that they were prepared to shed their Trade Union and revolutionary associations and to serve the State as agencies for the execution of a limited number of public contracts, in competition with other forms of business enterprise.

Co-operation, then, under a variety of influences, was cutting its socialistic connections during the 1850s, on the Continent as well as in Great Britain, and was to some extent receiving encouragement as a means of channelling working-class activity into unrevolutionary and non-political courses. Trade Unionism, in most of the continental countries, had been broken up in connection with the political defeat ; and the local craft Unions which managed to maintain their existence were reduced in the main to friendly society work or to maintaining loose connections through journeymen travelling from place to place in search of employment. Only in Great Britain was the Trade Union movement able to develop steadily ; and this development was limited to the skilled workers and still had to encounter, in the 1860s, a further challenge to its right to exist.

In these circumstances, there was a sharp break in the development of Socialist thought. The great period of the utopian projectors had definitely finished in 1848, though its after-effects were still being manifested in the United States, where American Fourierism remained an active force and Cabet, as well as Fourier's disciple, Considérant, was trying to demonstrate the practical working of a utopian society. America was still at a stage which made such community-making possible, with the frontier being pushed continually forward and new settlements still springing up in the interstices of the already developed areas. In the Old World, such community-making was no longer practicable save in the more backward countries — Russia, Spain, and Portugal, for example, where

Fourierism still had some hold. But in these countries, as well as in Western Europe, the political conditions after 1848 were highly unfavourable to utopian experiments, except where a landlord chose to develop his estate on entirely patriarchal lines. In Western Europe, no such experiments were likely to be made after 1848. The most that was attempted was profit-sharing, of which the pioneer was Edmé Jean Leclaire (1801–72), a self-made Parisian house-painter, who had started to share profits with his more skilled workers as early as 1842. Leclaire's experiment became widely known only after 1850, when he published his pamphlet, *De la misère, et des moyens de la faire cesser*. Leclaire had considerable trouble with the French police : he wanted to bind himself down by a definite profit-sharing contract with his employees, but was forbidden to do this, as the law forbade contracts between masters and workmen. Leclaire had therefore to work on an extra-legal basis ; but he persisted, and gradually extended profit-sharing to cover all his employees, while preserving differential wages according to skill and merit. Leclaire's work was followed up by that of Jean Baptiste André Godin (1817–88), another self-made man, who had become a follower of Fourier. Godin gave Victor Considérant 100,000 francs to help in the establishment of Considérant's Fourierist colony in the United States ; and he also set about turning his own works at Guise, where he made stoves, grates, and other hardware, into a patriarchal settlement, including co-operative provision for the needs of his community. Houses, institutes for recreation and common services, store-keeping, and other activities were all organised under his auspices and gradually converted to co-operative forms. In the 1850s this experiment was still at an early stage : the famous Familistère of Guise was not given a formal constitution until 1859, and did not turn into a fully co-operative affair until the 'seventies. The final form, in which the share capital became the workers' property, was not reached until 1880. But already in the 1850s the work of Leclaire and of Godin was becoming known, and was attracting supporters. In France Charles Robert became the leading theoretical advocate of profit-sharing, and in Germany the gospel was spread by Viktor Böhmert (1829–1918), who held a professorship at Zürich in the 1860s, but later returned to Germany and there continued his work.

The famous Zeiss works at Jena were not put on a co-partnership basis until later — not completely until 1896. But Ernst Abbe (1840-1905), the proprietor who was responsible for this remarkable experiment, came out of the tradition set on foot by Godin.

Profit-sharing and full co-partnership are of course two different things ; for co-partnership involves at any rate some transfer of ownership to the workers, whereas profit-sharing does not. The actual developments of the 1850s seldom advanced beyond profit-sharing, and even so encountered legal difficulties, as we have seen. Neither movement spread to Great Britain until the 1860s, when they appeared side by side in a revived activity of Christian Socialists and old Owenites, in close connection with a renewed movement for Co-operative Production in the Trade Unions — a development which became extensive in the early 'seventies, only to be snuffed out by the great depression a few years later.[1]

Such, then, was the situation when the European revolutionary movements of 1848 had run their course, and the more advanced countries settled down to a period of very rapid economic development under conditions of political reaction and, on the Continent, of actual and severe repression of working-class organisations. The gap between the movements of 1848 and the revival of the 1860s, which was marked by the emergence of the First International, was filled by a considerable amount of Socialist and near-Socialist speculation, especially in Germany, and, also mainly in Germany, by the rise of a new kind of 'Christian Socialism' which for a time seemed likely to develop along liberal Catholic lines, but later, as we shall see, turned largely into a reactionary force. In France, after an interval of prostration, the revival of the working-class movement took place largely under the influence of Proudhon, who, dying in 1865, left behind in his book on *The Political Capacity of the Working Classes*, a legacy that has not ceased to be influential to-day. Marx thought to have settled accounts with Proudhon in 1847, when he replied to *La Philosophie de la misère* with *La Misère de la philosophie*. But Proudhon was by no means done with. In the 1850s, his gospel of Mutualism

[1] For an account of this movement, see my book *A Century of Co-operation*.

fitted in much better with the restrictive conditions of the Second Empire than any other form of the Socialist gospel ; and the renewed French working-class movement, based mainly on mutual or friendly societies in the various crafts, grew up mainly under Proudhon's influence. The French workers' delegates who took part in the formation of the First International were, as we shall see, mainly Proudhonists and opponents both of socialisation and of centralisation of political and economic power. This, however, will come up for discussion later : in the 1850s French Proudhonism, though already active, was still only beginning to take shape.[1]

Thus, in the 1850s, Socialism slumbered ; and Marx, deprived of all chance of acting, spent his days in the British Museum accumulating materials for the forthcoming great work which was to put materialist Socialism on firm foundations as a scientific doctrine. The *Communist Manifesto* had been a clarion-call to action, not a systematic treatise ; if it stated a theory as well as a summons to war, it left this theory unproven and at many points unclear. During the actual period of revolution, it had been almost without influence on the course of events : with the Revolution's eclipse it looked like being altogether forgotten. Looking back on it from the vantage-point of the present, we are apt to think of it as having given the Socialist movement, from 1848 onwards, a new foundation and a new gospel. But the plain truth is that nobody, except Marx and Engels, thought of it in these terms either in 1848 or for a long time afterwards. It was nobody's bible even in the days of the First International. It was not reprinted, even in German, until 1872, when the International was already collapsing ; and it did not become a best-seller until the rise of Social Democratic Parties provided it with an almost world-wide public.

If Utopian Socialism perished in the European conflagration of 1848, Marxian Socialism did not immediately replace it. Indeed, what new Socialist thought there was in the 1850s was for the most part singularly untouched by Marx's influence and was fully as ethical in its inspiration as the utopianism which the *Manifesto* had denounced as obsolete. It is fair to say that no contemporary observer guessed, or could have guessed, that a

[1] For Proudhon see the first volume of this work, Chapter XIX.

century later the most living and often-quoted document of the European revolutionary uprisings would be this pamphlet, issued by a small and obscure German sect, of whom most people — even most of the revolutionaries — had never even heard.

CHAPTER II

GERMAN SOCIALISM IN THE 1850s —
RODBERTUS AND MARLO

IN Germany, after the collapse of the revolutionary move-ments of 1848, there was for some time no possibility of an active Socialist movement. The leaders who had been active in 1848 were in exile or in prison : Marx himself had broken with those who believed in the desirability of a further imme-diate revolutionary attempt. The movement which was thus snuffed out accepted defeat the more easily because it had never in reality had any considerable activist following. There was in Germany no dearth of philosophers affected by socialistic ideas ; but there was hardly any organised working-class movement with which they could connect themselves, even if they so desired ; and what there was consisted mainly of journeymen who belonged to small artisan clubs, mostly much more of the nature of friendly societies than of Trade Unions.

German Socialism could thus fall back fairly easily in the hour of defeat of what had been, from start to finish, essentially a *bourgeois* revolutionary movement, into a mood of philo-sophical contemplation. As we saw in the previous volume of this work, this had been the prevailing mood before 1848 — often to the extent of refusal by those who were affected by Socialism as an ideal to have anything to do with practical movements aiming at mere social improvements, rather than at a comprehensive change of system. Marx and Engels had attacked this tendency in their *German Ideology* and in other writings, and had endeavoured to push the socialistic intellec-tuals towards action as the inseparable companion of creative thought. But they had not met with much success outside the narrow circle of the Communist League ; and even there they found after the defeat of the Revolution that their success in indoctrinating the Leaguers with the teachings of the *Communist Manifesto* had been less than they had hoped.

In Germany, then, in the 1850s there hardly was a Socialist movement. But there were a good many intellectuals and middle-class individuals who, without being quite Socialists in any usual sense of the term, were well aware of the existence of a 'social question' which needed to be resolved and had a feeling that the French Socialists from Saint-Simon and Fourier to Louis Blanc and Proudhon — not to mention Lamennais — had found at any rate some of the ingredients needed for a solution. They had read Lorenz von Stein's *History of the Social Movement in France*, first published under another title in 1843, and reissued in a revised and expanded form in 1850–1851 ; and some of them had read Engels's *Condition of the Working Classes in England* and the numerous controversial articles published in the various *Yearbooks* on the 1840s. Many of them felt both a strong dislike of the rising power of the German *bourgeoisie* and a keen fear of the effects of industrialism on the German way of life. They were ready to believe that the rise of the factory system, which threw women and children into employment outside the home, was undermining the basis of family life and that the advance of large-scale enterprise in both mining and manufacturing was bringing with it the pauperisation of the artisan and the destruction of economic security by reason of the inherent instability of the new capitalist system. True, these developments had not yet gone very far in most parts of Germany in the 1850s ; but they could be seen as already well on the way.

Of course, not all the German intellectuals regretted these tendencies. Indeed, there was a party in Germany which pushed the doctrine of *laissez-faire* to an extreme, and outdid the apostles of the 'Manchester School' in declaiming against all interference by the State with the natural workings of 'economic law'. This party had strong support among the 'progressive' groups in most of the lesser German States, as well as in Prussia ; but in Prussia especially they came up against strong intellectual resistance. Belief in the State and in its unifying mission went deep, not only among the conservative defenders of autocracy and paternalistic landlordism, but also among the Hegelians, 'Young' as well as 'Old', and among those who built rather upon Fichte than upon Hegel. Neither Hegel's view of the State nor Fichte's, nor any view even remotely resembling either, was any more reconcilable than feudal monarchism with the doctrine that the economic part of the national life ought to be let alone, to regulate itself by its own laws quite apart from the laws of the State. The notion of separate political and economic orders in society, operating under the guidance of essentially different principles, not only ran counter to the general tendency of German philosophical and juristic thought, but also offended against the deep-seated desire for national unity, which was felt to require social as well as political unification.

There was, moreover, long before Bismarck's great struggle with the Roman Catholic Church, a Catholic social tendency which opposed the doctrines of the Manchester School no less energetically than the 'Statists', to whose views it was equally in opposition. The Catholics in Germany feared the rising power of the State, especially where it was under Protestant control ; but they saw that they could make their Church an effective counterpoise to the State only if they could enlist under its banner, in social as well as in religious matters, a large following among the people ; and they were disposed to see in 'the social question' the means of establishing this influence by espousing certain of the workers' claims against the rising 'liberal' *bourgeoisie*. We shall see later how this reaching out for popular support took shape in a movement which came to be known for a time as 'Christian Socialism', though it was nothing like Socialism in any modern sense of the word and soon became involved in bitter struggles with the Social Democratic movement which began to take shape in the 1860s. But before we come to 'Christian Socialism', either in the Catholic form given to it by Bishop von Ketteler and his follower Moufang, or in the bastard Protestant imitation of Pastors Todt and Stocker, we must consider more closely the forms of 'State Socialism' which were formulated, chiefly in the 1850s, by Rodbertus and Marlo, and helped to prepare the way for the movement known as 'Professorial Socialism' (or 'Socialism of the Chair') which gained widespread influence in intellectual circles during the 'sixties and 'seventies.

Fichte, as we saw in the previous volume, had worked out early in the nineteenth century a social theory which involved the active participation of the State in the organisation of economic life, as part of a general doctrine of functional organisation of society as a unified system. Fichte's theory had indeed been centred originally upon the claims of the individual in society, and had involved no such totalitarian notion of the State as was proclaimed by Hegel. But in his later writings he had gone almost as far as Hegel in exalting the State to the position of the highest reality as against the individual, whose life he came to see as without meaning apart from it. Hegel had also drawn a sharp distinction between the State and that 'Civil Society' which its mission was to unify and endow with a higher reality. Thus, Hegel's doctrine had left room for the operation in 'Civil Society' of practices based on utilitarian considerations, subject only to the right of the State to enforce the conformity of these practices with its overriding claims. Hegel, when he wrote about economic affairs at the level of 'Civil Society', used many phrases reminiscent of the classical economists ; and it was possible for a follower of Hegel to be also a devotee of Ricardo *at this level*, but always subject to the assertion that 'economic laws' could be of no validity against the needs of the 'whole', as represented by the State. Thus, both Hegel's doctrine and Fichte's were fundamentally inconsistent with economic individualism and with the 'liberalism' of the *bourgeois* progressives who were in revolt against the autocratic State in the cause of *laissez-faire*.

In effect, 'Statism' was part of the basic philosophy of a large part of the intellectual classes in Germany, and above all in Prussia ; and this attitude opened the door for the reception both of proposals that the State should intervene in economic affairs as the regulator of class-relations and the planner of economic development and even of projects involving actual public ownership of the means of production. The idea of the paternalistic State, ruling the people for their good, which was identified with the good of the whole society, had a wide appeal ; and this idea involved the notion that all property in private hands must be held subject to the right of the State to determine its use in accordance with the interest of the whole society. This interest was conceived of as fully consistent with the maintenance and reinforcement of autocratic rule : there was nothing in it of belief in the right of the citizen to determine by democratic voting what the general interest was. The State, through its ruler taking counsel with his loyal subjects, was to settle this, with powers wide enough to safeguard the solidarity of the whole society against anything that threatened to disrupt its traditional values. The advance of *bourgeois* enterprise, and of the individualistic, *laissez-faire* attitude which so often accompanied it, was widely felt to involve this peril of disruption ; and accordingly it was held to be entirely legitimate for the State to arm itself with whatever powers of intervention and control might be needed to avert the danger. The threat came from two quarters — from the developing money-power of the *bourgeoisie*, armed with the new techniques of banking and of large-scale production, and from the revolt among the workers engendered by the conditions of employment to which they were being subjected by the rising capitalist class. It was therefore felt to be right, on the one hand to affirm the power of the State to regulate capitalist enterprise and to resist demands for responsible government put forward on behalf of the *bourgeoisie*, and on the other hand to do what could be done to protect the working classes against *bourgeois* exploitation, by regulating the conditions of employment in mines and factories and by giving the various trades and professions some sort of status, inferior but assured, which would link them to the old order and range them on the side of autocracy against the economic tyranny of the *bourgeois* profit-seekers. It was in this spirit that Bismarck was induced to introduce manhood suffrage in the North German Confederation, and later in the Reichstag, as a counter-move to the demands of the *bourgeois* progressives for a limited franchise coupled with responsible government, and to coquet with ideas of State help to workers' productive associations in an attempt to detach the workers' movement from its tendency to make common cause with the *bourgeoisie* in its attacks on autocracy and on the privileges of the old aristocratic order. Thus arose the peculiar attitude known as 'Feudal' or 'Conservative' Socialism, which Marx and Engels singled out as early as 1848 for attack in the *Communist Manifesto*.

But side by side with this 'Feudal' Socialism, which was at once anti-capitalist and pro-landlord, because the landed aristocracy and its privileges were regarded as essential parts of the traditional order that was to be defended against *bourgeois* attack, there was a second tendency critical of landlordism as well as of industrial and financial capitalism. This tendency emerged out of, or was closely connected with, the movement for constitutional nationalism, but its protagonists fell foul of the rival school of *bourgeois* nationalism in that they repudiated the individualism of the rising capitalist class. The exponents of this attitude were no less hostile to the conferment of political power on the *bourgeoisie* than the 'feudalists'; and they laid even greater stress on the evil effects of industrial capitalism on the status and economic condition of the workers. But they saw also the evil effects of landlordism and believed these to be getting worse as the growth of commercialism exposed the peasant as well as the industrial worker to the machinations of the bankers and to the increasing uncertainties of a 'free' market economy. Regarding the State as the authority responsible for the security and well-being of all its subjects, these 'Statist Liberals' denounced the rival liberals of the *laissez-faire* school, and demanded that the State should so control the economy as to ensure the security and stability of the conditions of living. They did not for the most part suggest that the people should democratically control the State : they did hold, however, that the State could not do its duty towards the people without placing itself in a position to control the productive forces of society ; and some of them went so far as to assert that this could be done only by making the State the actual owner, and not merely the external regulator, of the essential means of production. Their proposals did not, as a rule, involve any revolutionary change in the basis of society, such as Marx envisaged. They were indeed for the most part insistent that nothing should be done in haste to upset the traditional ways of living. They put forward, not so much projects for immediate adoption, as criticisms of the working of the actual society of their own day, and theories of the long-term transformations which social institutions would need to undergo in order to adapt them to the changing conditions of production — with the proviso that the requisite transformations could be brought about without disaster only as results of a gradual alteration in social attitudes. Rodbertus, for example, contemplated that it would take centuries — 'five hundred years', he said in an oft-quoted passage — to carry through the changes in the economic structure of society which he believed to be necessary in order to bring social arrangements into line with the conditions of the modern era. He hardly considered what further technological and economic developments might occur during these centuries to make his proposed remedies out of date long before they had been applied.

Of the theorists who came, in the 1850s, to advocate a sort of State Socialism resting on these intellectual foundations the most important were Rodbertus and the benevolent professor who wrote under the name of Karl Marlo. Of the two, Rodbertus is much the more important, because his influence was considerable during his lifetime, whereas Marlo was little known until the Austrian, Schaeffle, revived the knowledge of his doctrines in 1870.

Karl Johann Rodbertus (1805–75), sometimes called Rodbertus-Jagetzow from the name of the estate of Jagetzow, in Pomerania, which he bought in 1835, was the son of a professor of law, and himself studied law at Göttingen and Berlin. From these studies he went on to Heidelberg, where he took up philosophy. He then travelled extensively in Holland, France, and Switzerland before returning to settle down on his newly purchased estate. In 1837 he produced his first work, a large pamphlet entitled *The Claims of the Working Classes*, in which he clearly adumbrated many of his leading ideas, under the influence of what he had learnt during his foreign travels. At Jagetzow he practised scientific agriculture and began to play a part in politics as a supporter of German unity on a basis of constitutional monarchy. In 1842 he published a second work, *On the Explanation of our National Economic Situation* (*Zur Erkentniss unserer Staatswirthschaftlichen Zustände*). In 1847 he became a member of the provincial Diet, and in the following year he played an active part in the national movement for constitutional government, and served for a short period as Prussian Minister of Public Worship and Education, but soon resigned because he fell into disagreement with his colleagues. On the collapse of the constitutionalist movement he retired into private life, and spent the remainder of his days between writing and farming. His writings included, besides the formulation of his economic theories, studies of the economic foundation of society in the Roman Republic and Empire and some attempt to formulate a general theory of sociological development ; and he also conducted with some of his contemporaries a voluminous correspondence in which many of his most interesting ideas are to be found. One of his most regular correspondents was Ferdinand Lassalle.

The clearest general exposition of Rodbertus's ideas is contained in his *Social Letters*, addressed to his friend von Kirchmann and published in 1850 and 1851 (to which must be added a further Letter to von Kirchmann on *Capital*, published only after his death.) These were reissued in two volumes in 1875 and 1885, under the title *Light on the Social Question (Zur Beleuchtung der sozialen Frage)*. The dates of his writings are of importance chiefly because of the great amount of controversy there has been on the question whether he had a major influence on the doctrines of Karl Marx. Opponents of Marxism have repeatedly alleged that Marx stole a high proportion of his ideas from Rodbertus. This assertion was vigorously rebutted by Friedrich Engels, and seems to have been made in the first instance by writers who knew little of the earlier sources on which both alike drew ; but there is some reason for holding that Marx, though he developed his main ideas without owing anything to Rodbertus, was influenced by him in their formulation in his later writings, especially in dealing with the problems of 'over-production' and business crises. What is quite certain is that Rodbertus greatly influenced Lassalle, especially in the formulation of his 'iron law of wages', and that Marx's sharpest differences with the Lassallians on this question — and on the closely related question of the power of Trade Unions to affect wages under capitalism — arose at points where Lassalle followed Rodbertus as against Marx.

Rodbertus, in his economic theory, set out from the conception of labour as the sole source and true measure of value. But he held this theory, not in its Marxian form, but in the form in which it had been advanced by earlier writers such as William Thompson and John Francis Bray, and echoed by Proudhon. That is to say, he proclaimed that in justice each individual ought to receive back from society the full equivalent of his contribution to its common stock of valuable products ; whereas Marx contended that, under modern economic conditions, the individual had as a rule no ascertainable product, and that the claim to the 'whole product' could be advanced only on behalf of the class of labourers as a whole and not of the individual labourer, and was further subject to necessary deductions for capital accumulation and for the maintenance of public services and of those who were not in a position to provide for their own support. Rodbertus, in working out his form of the labour theory, proposed the substitution for money as the medium of exchange of a labour currency based on socially necessary labour-time — an idea which, of course, had been put forward long before by Robert Owen in his *Report to the County of Lanark* (1820) and re-echoed by many subsequent writers. Rodbertus, indeed, elaborated the proposal to a greater extent than any of these predecessors ; but the work in which he did this most fully, *The Normal Working Day*, did not appear until 1871. Broadly, what he proposed was that there should be fixed an artificial normal working day which would consist of different numbers of actual working hours varying with the arduousness of different occupations, so that a miner's normal day would consist of fewer working hours than a textile operative's. For each such normal day he proposed to calculate a standard output, based on what an average, or a normal, worker could produce in the time. The wage payable to the worker was to be based on these two factors, the remuneration of the individual varying above or below the standard according to his output. These standard wages were to be fixed by law in such a way as to ensure that the workers should receive the advantages of rising productivity — advantages which, Rodbertus held, accrued under the existing system to the capitalist classes. Rodbertus also insisted that the law should be amended to give the worker greater security of employment. He argued that, under the existing conditions, wages were held down to subsistence level, so that the benefits of higher productivity were denied to the workers, and that accordingly the share of the workers in the total product tended to fall continually as output increased. He regarded the consequent limitation of the purchasing power of the workers as the essential cause of business crises, which he attributed to over-production of commodities destined for the limited consumers' market. Accordingly, he looked to his plan of wage-regulation, by giving the workers the benefit of increasing productive power, to put an end to crises and to the exploitation of labour-power for the benefit of the non-producers. He also put forward a series of proposals for the State provision of credit to the agricultural producers in order to relieve them from the pressure of exploitation by land-owners and usurers and to allow them to receive the whole produce of their labour.

These were Rodbertus's suggestions for reforms that could be carried through by stages without any revolutionary upset. But he also looked forward, in the long run — the very long run — to much more extensive changes, which would include the passing of land and capital instruments of production under public ownership, and would leave in private ownership only the 'labour-time' incomes that could be spent in buying con-sumers' goods and services. At this point, Rodbertus's eco-nomic theories link up with his conception of historical develop-ment. According to him, human history fell into three great stages, each containing within it a number of secondary phases. The first stage, which he called the 'Heathen-Ancient', was marked by the existence of private ownership not only of things, but also of men. The second, the 'Christian-Germanic', retained private ownership of land and capital, but discarded the ownership of man by man. This was the stage through which contemporary society was still working its way, and would be for some time to come. After it would come the 'Christian-Social' stage, at which land and capital would pass under collective ownership, and the only form of private owner-ship would be that of labour. At this stage, labour would be the sole title to a share in the product, and each labourer would receive a share corresponding to his productive service.

Rodbertus thus looked forward to a future socialistic society ; but he would have nothing to do with any attempt to hasten the advent of this society by rousing the workers to revolt. He believed, as we have seen, that it would take hundreds of years to prepare men for the successful working of such a society, and that in the meantime only gradual advances could be made towards it by improving the labourers' position through the regulative action of the State. Holding that, in the absence of State intervention, wages were kept down inexorably to subsistence level, and that Trade Unions could do nothing to prevent this exploitation, he saw the only available remedy in laws which would compel the employing classes to pass on to their employees the benefits of rising productivity. He also contended that, because of the inexorable workings of the 'iron law', Co-operative Societies could do nothing appreciable to improve the workers' condition, whether they were started on a voluntary basis, as advocated by Schulze-Delitzsch, or aided with State credit, as was demanded by Lassalle. Under either arrangement, he held, the competition of capitalist industry would continue to keep the workers' wage at subsistence level. Only State action to fix wages and limit profits could achieve any real effect.

Rodbertus, moreover, thought of the State which was to confer these benefits on the workers as monarchical, with the monarch continuing to control the executive power. He favoured the growth of a representative system, collaborating with the monarchy, and wanted the monarchy to take sides with the people against the oligarchs. But he did not believe the people themselves to be ready to take control of their own destinies. His writings therefore fitted in with the social policies of Bismarckian 'State Socialism' — so-called — rather than of Social Democracy. He refused to join Lassalle's German Workmen's Association, to which he addressed, in 1863, an *Open Letter* expounding his objections, while expressing his sympathy. He did not believe, with Lassalle, that manhood suffrage would open the door to the achievement of Socialism, or even to a rapid advance towards it. After the disillusionment of 1848, he had little faith in political movements : he became the detached observer, seeking to look forward into the future and to persuade intelligent men to recognise the tendency of world development and to do what they could, without undue disturbance to the existing order, to advance towards a juster social system. But he would have nothing to do with agitation or class-war. He looked to reason, not to force, to bring men to an acceptance of his ideas. This helps to explain why Engels so strongly repudiated the notion that he and Marx had been influenced by Rodbertus, and makes the essential difference between their views. The notion of the class as a driving force in history was quite foreign to Rodbertus's way of thinking, whereas it was right at the centre of Marx's theory well before the *Communist Manifesto* was written.

The other principal exponent in Germany, during the 1850s,

of a socialistic theory which had no connection with any working-class movement was the scientist and technician, Karl
Georg Winkelblech (1810–65), who wrote under the name of
Karl Marlo. Marlo, who was Professor of Chemistry at the
Higher Trade School at Cassel, produced only a single work,
which was left unfinished at his death. The three volumes
which he did publish between 1850 and 1859 were issued under
the general title *Enquiries concerning the Organisation of Labour,
or, System of World Economy*. They contained the whole of his
theory, but not the detailed working out of his practical proposals. They were not widely read, and seem to have been
almost forgotten when the Austrian economist, Albert Schaeffle,
made favourable mention of them in his book on *Capitalism
and Socialism*, published in 1870. Thereafter Marlo's views
were summarised in histories of Socialism — for example, by
Émile de Laveleye and by John Rae in the 1880s. But Marlo
neither founded any school nor exercised any such influence as
Rodbertus. His work was prompted by a spirit of pure philan-
thropy : a casual conversation in Norway with a German
workman about the privations and insecurities of working-class
life set him to study conditions for himself, and he seems to
have reached his conclusions almost in isolation, and to have
been but little influenced by any contemporary thinker. His
observations of industry and of the effects of advancing capitalism led him to the conclusion that a process of 'proletarianisation' was rapidly taking effect, that the smaller entrepreneurs
were being crushed out by the great capitalists, and that under
the developing industrial system wages were held down to
subsistence level and the workers subjected to increasing risks
of recurrent unemployment. He also stressed the bad physical
effects of factory employment and overcrowded, insanitary
housing, the growth of drunkenness and immorality in the
expanding industrial towns, and the evil consequences of the
employment of women outside the home on family life and
morals. Mechanisation, he said, was also rendering the
workers' tasks more monotonous and uninteresting ; and the
combined consequence of all these factors was a *malaise* which
found expression in revolt and revolution.

Nevertheless, Marlo was an optimist. He believed the
French Revolution of 1789 to have been the starting-point of a

new era of human progress. Indeed, he sweepingly divided all human history into two periods, the second of which had barely begun. The whole history of mankind up to 1789 had been dominated by the principle of 'Paganism' or 'Monopolism'. During this epoch it had been regarded as 'natural' that the many should be sacrificed to the few, and that the few should 'monopolise' the control of the means of production. This régime of monopoly had taken successive shapes in the institutions of slavery, serfdom, and wage-labour, which were all forms of exploitation of the many by the few. Christ had proclaimed many centuries ago the rival principle of human equality ; but it had not been translated into political terms capable of being applied until the French Revolution had proclaimed the 'Rights of Man'. The *Declaration of the Rights of Man* was, then, to be regarded as the starting-point of the era of true Christianity ; and the task of the nineteenth century was to work out the social implications of the Christian principle. This principle, Marlo held, had since 1789 been acceptable to the conscience of society, without the support of which it could not be applied. But even when it had come to be thus acceptable in theory, its application had to wait on the discovery of the appropriate means. There had been, so far, two rival attempts to apply the principle — Liberalism and Communism — but these were both fatally one-sided and therefore unacceptable. By 'Liberalism' Marlo meant primarily economic liberalism in the continental sense — that is, *laissez-faire* — resting on the belief in a 'natural order' that would come into its own if the State and other regulative bodies ceased to interfere with its working. Liberalism in this sense, said Marlo, had shown itself to be 'the parent of plutocracy', and, far from leading towards equality, merely to transfer the power of exploitation into different hands. On the other side Communism — by which he meant mainly the equalitarian Communism of Babeuf and Cabet — was no less astray from the right course. It would disastrously weaken the incentives to exertion, and would impoverish the people in the process of equalising their rights.

Marlo's own proposed system, which he called 'Panpolism', was meant to effect a reconciliation between Liberalism and Communism, with the dual purpose of accomplishing the greatest self-development and the greatest happiness of all. It would seek both freedom and plenty. At its foundation would be the universal obligation to labour for every able-bodied man ; and with this would go the universal right of access to the means of production, which was to be assured by the State. Every worker, freed from exploitation by landlords, employers, or credit monopolists, was to enjoy the whole product of his labour in the form of a full equivalent for his contribution to the common stock. In order to achieve all this, the State was to take over the direct running and ownership of all essential utility services — Marlo enumerated among these railways, ports, water, gas, banking, and education — and over and above these other large-scale forms of economic activity, including forestry, mining, fishing, foreign trade, and all forms of whole-sale trade in raw and partly finished materials and in manufac-tures which did not pass either directly from producer to con-sumer or from producer to retailer. Marlo proposed that agriculture, small-scale production, retail trading, and local transport should be left in private hands, but that all such occupations should be organised in guilds (*Zünfte*) under State regulation. He was prepared to leave existing accumulations of private capital untouched, until they died out of themselves. All fresh accumulations of capital were to be forbidden by law : the means of production were to become public property. In order to guard the society thus organised and to ensure the payment of adequate incomes to the producers, there were to be protective barriers against the introduction from abroad of goods produced under unfair conditions.

Marlo was of the opinion that the plan which he put forward would prove unworkable unless population could be stabilised, so as to prevent it from outrunning, or at least offsetting, the increase in production. He wished to impose stringent restric-tions on the right to marry, regarding Malthus's 'prudential checks' and 'moral restraint' as likely to prove quite inadequate. No one, he argued, should be allowed to have children unless he could show that he had the means to maintain them. His proposals included a general system of contributory insurance for provision in sickness, accident, and old age, and for the maintenance of widows and orphans. The right to marry, he held, should be made conditional on paid-up membership of the social insurance fund. Marlo thus propounded, but with the marriage condition attached, a plan of compulsory insurance not unlike that which Bismarck was to institute later ; but his project was of course much more comprehensive.

Marlo was in his general attitude a philanthropic 'State Socialist', with strongly equalitarian sympathies, but with no disposition to advocate the introduction of his projects by militant means. Therein he and Rodbertus stand together as keen critics of the rising capitalist system and as believers in the necessity for State action to procure the workers the means of decent living. They are both 'anti-liberals' in the economic sense because they are themselves liberal in a political sense. They both put first the claim of the individual to the means of well-being and enjoyment, subject only to his willingness to accept his responsibility for contributing by labour to the common stock. They are both led, in pursuance of these principles, to advocacy of public ownership of the means of production, including the sources of money capital and credit ; and they both think of the problem in terms of the claims of common humanity rather than of a particular class. They differ, as far as they do differ, in that Marlo shows no such caution as Rodbertus in being ready to spread over centuries the change from the existing order to the new. Marlo, indeed, perhaps because he never produced his final volume, was quite unexplicit about the pace at which he expected the change to occur — or, perhaps, failed to produce this volume because he could not make up his mind what to say on that important issue.

The kind of detached socialistic speculation for which Marlo and Rodbertus stood has, as we shall see, many later echoes in Germany. It was the direct forerunner of the 'Professorial Socialism' of the 1870s and 1880s, which challenged the orthodox Political Economy and proclaimed the function of the State as including the regulation of the nation's economic life. But the economists' challenge to *laissez-faire* was being made, in the 1850s, not only by the 'State Socialists', but also by the leader of the so-called 'Historical School'. Wilhelm Roscher (1817–1894), the initiator of this school, had published his *Foundations of Political Economy* as early as 1843 ; and the most challenging works of Bruno Hildebrand and of Karl Knies, his principal supporters, had appeared in 1847 and in 1853 respectively. The movement exemplified in the work of Rodbertus and Marlo was in effect part of a much wider movement of challenge to the dominance of the classical school of Political Economy. This movement, which found congenial soil in Germany, rested, as Sismondi's earlier criticism had done, on an attack on the entire conception of a body of 'economic laws', deducible from the very nature of the process of exchange and advanced as valid absolutely in their own right, without any apparent admission of their relativity to the conditions of place and time. In opposition to this absolute, deductive system, the 'Historical School' denied the existence, not so much of absolute economic laws as of absolute practical precepts deducible from such laws. They argued that the economic factor was only one among a number of which particular societies had at all times to take account in shaping their collective ways of living, and that what laws there were could be made to operate very differently according to the institutions which societies adopted for the regulation of their working. This institutional and historical approach to Economics did not, of course, lead necessarily to any socialistic conclusions : it was entirely reconcilable with belief in class differences and unequal rights for different social groups. It did, however, exclude any general presuppositions in favour of *laissez-faire* ; and in practice those who adopted it during the nineteenth century usually drew from it either socialistic or conservative (often combined with imperialist) conclusions.

To this point we shall have to come back later : at this stage we are concerned only to indicate that the speculations of such men as Rodbertus and Marlo, remote though they were from any contact with working-class Socialist movements, did contribute to weaken the intellectual foundations of capitalism at the very time when it was making, in practice, the most rapid and triumphant advance. These men's disturbing thoughts expressed a deep discontent with the human effects of the rising capitalist system, different from, but similar in its effects, to the vaticinations of Thomas Carlyle and of John Ruskin — or, earlier, of Samuel Taylor Coleridge and Robert Southey — in Great Britain. Marx, intent on demonstrating his theorem of the class as the agency of social revolution, had no use for these ethical opponents of capitalism, save to borrow from them an occasional argument when it served. Nor had most continental intellectuals, in the 1850s, any great readiness to listen to the

voices of the critics ; for the eclipse of the revolutionary movement seemed to have taken away the practical urgency of what
they had to say. They came back into their own only when, in
the 1860s, the working classes began to reorganise their forces
and again to trouble the surface of a more developed capitalist
society.

In the meantime, these humanitarian critics of the rising
capitalist system served a double function. They did something
to qualify the intellectual claims of capitalist liberalism by
asserting the counter-claim of the Welfare State ; and they also
provided a new version of the gospel of economic planning
which had been preached in the earlier part of the century by
Saint-Simon and his school. In economic matters both Rodbertus and Marlo came down unequivocally on the workers'
side, giving expression to the view that capitalism involved
exploitation and poverty, and therewith disastrous insecurity,
for its victims ; and they both looked forward to a planned
society in which the welfare of the whole people would be the
essential principle of public policy. This led them both to
the advocacy of socialisation ; but it did not make them
Socialists in any ordinary sense of the term because in their
minds the Welfare State would not necessarily depend for its
existence on political democracy. They both thought of the
State as an ethical instrument for the promotion of social
well-being, but not as an instrument to be wielded by the
workers themselves. Because of this, their doctrines were
equally at the service of democrats and of believers in autocratic
or aristocratic paternalism ; and Rodbertus at any rate influenced Bismarck fully as much as he influenced Lassalle.
Roscher and his fellow-members of the 'Historical School'
were even less Socialists than Rodbertus ; and their doctrines
were chiefly important in promoting, not State Socialism, but
rather a State Capitalism under which industry would accept the
regulative rôle of the State in the interests of national or imperial
development. In the German situation of the 1850s and 1860s
the two groups were intellectually powerful enough to prevent
laissez-faire from becoming the common creed of the German
employers and to help in preparing the way for Bismarck's
imperial policy. For this reason there has been the greater
reluctance among Social Democrats to accept the importance

of Rodbertus as a social thinker ; but his contribution was by no means insignificant, and both he and Marlo are links in the chain of ethical socialistic thinking, which, pushed for a time into the background by the spread of Marxism in the 1860s and 1870s, was nevertheless continually reasserting itself within the ranks of Social Democracy, and has been a main ingredient in the making of the Western Socialism of to-day.

CHAPTER III

THE DAWN OF SOCIALISM IN RUSSIA— BELINSKY, HERZEN, AND CHERNYSHEVSKY

UP to the middle of the nineteenth century Socialism, in all its forms, was almost exclusively a West European doctrine. It had indeed been carried across the Atlantic both by American visitors to Europe and by European settlers in the United States ; but the Americans had made no specific contribution to it — unless we are to count J. F. Bray, who was living in England when he wrote his well-known book.[1] There had been American followers of Robert Owen and of Fourier ; and in 1848 Étienne Cabet had set out from France to found his 'Icaria' in Texas. America was full of community-makers, religious as well as socialistic ; but they were mostly working on the basis of imported ideas, and largely with imported human beings. After 1848 the stream of emigrants in search of a new world in which they could find the means to living and freedom greatly increased. But Socialism struck no deep roots in American soil : indeed, it became less influential as the older utopian enthusiasms grew weaker and as European Socialism itself lay prostrate after its great defeat.

It was, however, precisely during this period of stagnation in Western Europe that Socialism first showed signs of becoming a force in Russia, not as a popular movement, but as the cult of a section of the intellectuals. The death of Nicholas I in 1855 and the accession of Alexander II brought with them for a time a relaxation of the extremely repressive régime instituted after the crushing of the Decembrist conspiracy of 1825. There was a great increase in the number of newspapers and journals ; and for a time, under the guise of literary or philosophical criticism, rather more open writing about social questions

---

[1] *Labour's Wrongs and Labour's Remedies* (1839). Bray, born in the United States, had been taken to England as a boy and was working in Leeds as a compositor when his book was written. See Vol. I of this History, Chapter XII.

became possible. It also became easier to smuggle in foreign books and journals ; and Alexander Herzen's famous *Kolokol* (The Bell), printed in Russian in London, was widely circulated among the intellectual classes in Russia — the first uncensored journal ever to reach the Russian public. Of course, *Kolokol* could circulate only clandestinely ; but circulate it did, quite widely, for the few years before the repression descended again with almost its previous rigour after the Polish revolt and the attempted peasant risings of 1863.

There had, of course, been movements of liberal thought in Russia long before this period. Catherine II had encouraged speculation based on the ideas of the French enlightenment until she was scared first by Pugachov's peasant rising and then by the French Revolution ; and it had been impossible to keep the ideas spread abroad by the French Revolution from exerting some influence on the Russian intellectuals. But this influence, in its political and social aspects, did not go deep ; and the struggle with Napoleon and thereafter the part played by Alexander I in the Holy Alliance after 1815 made against its persistence. It survived most strongly in South Russia, where its protagonist was Pavel Ivanovich Pestel (1793–1826), the inspirer of the more extreme party among the military leaders and aristocrats who took part in the Decembrist risings at the time of the accession of Nicholas I. Pestel stood for the emancipation of the serfs and their endowment with half the land of Russia — the other half to be held by the State for leasing to progressive farm entrepreneurs. He advocated universal manhood suffrage and the establishment of a centralised democratic Republic. His views were far ahead of those of the Northern Decembrists, headed by Nikite Muraviev, who wanted decentralised constitutional monarchy and a restricted franchise, or of the economist Nikolai Ivanovich Turgenev (1789–1871), who as an imperial official had been urging Alexander I to emancipate the serfs and institute large reforms in the tax and administrative systems. Turgenev — the economist, not the novelist — lucky enough to be abroad at the time of the Decembrist rising, was condemned to death together with its overt leaders, and spent the rest of his life outside Russia, coming nearer in exile to Pestel's views on land reform. He differed, however, from Pestel in proposing only small allot-

ments of free land to the individual peasants and in looking
forward to the development of an agricultural proletariat compelled to work for wages in order to earn a living. Such a body
of agricultural workers, he thought, would be necessary to
provide a basis for improved land-cultivation by advanced
capitalistic techniques, and would constitute, for Russia, a kind
of proletariat analogous to the industrial proletariat of the West.
These views were worked out during his years of exile and
published in 1847 in Paris (*La Russie et les Russes*, 3 volumes).

After the crushing of the Decembrist movement there was
little scope for the expression of democratic or libertarian
opinions. But there was still room for controversy on the
literary and philosophical plane between the rival schools of
'Slavophils' and 'Westernisers' — that is, between those who
looked to the development of Russian society on the basis of
the historical traditions of the past and the distinctive national
character of the Russian people, and those who held that the
country could advance towards a higher civilisation only by
learning and assimilating the culture of the West. These rival
attitudes could both lead to a variety of views. Thus, among
the 'Westernisers', one school of thought, represented by Peter
Chaädaev, looked, under the influence of von Baader and
Bonald and de Maistre, to the Catholic Church as the great
unifying and civilising force, whereas others, such as V. G.
Belinsky and Alexander Herzen, were influenced in their several
ways by Western Radical and Socialist ideas. The Slavophils,
for their part, ranged from extreme advocacy of autocracy and
religious orthodoxy, combined with complete scorn for Western
notions of parliamentary government and democracy, to liberal
advocacy of land reform and emancipation of the serfs, coupled
with demands for the preservation and development of the
communal elements in the traditional systems of village economy. Moreover, the Slavophils, though they repudiated
Western ways of living as unsuitable to the Russian character
and tradition, were themselves greatly influenced by Western
philosophy. They built on Herder and on Schelling and also
largely upon Hegel, in whom they found both a conception of
the State which fitted in with their defence of autocracy and,
in his account of 'Civil Society', an insistence on the vital
importance of *Sittlichkeit* as the foundation of national sociality

and as the material which it was the State's task to unify and raise to a higher plane of rational reality. Naturally, the Slavophils did not accept Hegel's view that German culture, unified by the Prussian State, stood for the highest rationality. On the contrary, they found in the life of the Russian people a no less mystical foundation for the highest achievement, and held — or rather most of them held — that the Russians had been happy in escaping the contaminations which were destroying the civilisation of the West. Many of them were acutely hostile to industrialism, as well as to constitutional government, which they saw as its twin ; and most of them exalted the mystical virtues of the Orthodox Church as against the undue intellectualism of Catholicism and the utilitarian individualism which they regarded as characteristic of the Protestant Churches.

The Slavophils, I have said, were influenced by Hegel, and favoured Czarist autocracy against any form of representative government. They were, however, by no means favourable to State action. They thought of the relation between the Czar and his people in terms of a paternalistic mysticism which had nothing to do with political activity : indeed, they stressed the nothingness of politics in comparison with the freedom of man's inner life. This Slavophil movement was quite different from the Russian Pan-Slavism which developed in the 1860s and set Russians to dreaming of a vast Slav empire based on the unity of all the Slav peoples. Slavophilism was a cultural rather than a political movement : it acquired a political quality only because of its hostility to politics. For this reason, despite its support of Czarism, it was even mildly persecuted under Nicholas I.

The Slavophil doctrines were not fully developed for some time after 1825 ; but they were then already in the air. They are not to be identified with the early — any more than with the later — movement of Pan-Slavism, which grew up side by side with them, but had its strongholds largely among the Slav peoples under the rule of Austria or of Turkey. These Pan-Slav movements, though they looked to Russia, had a pronounced democratic tinge, because they were concerned with the issues of national liberation from autocratic alien rule, and found themselves in many places opposed by aristocratic elements which had been partly assimilated to the governing elements in the ruling powers. The Slavophils were, indeed, divided between those who supported movements of liberation in Slav countries outside Russia and those who, regarding Russia as the representative of the Slav spirit, favoured Russi-fication of all the peoples under Czarist rule — including the Poles — in the cause of 'Greater Russian' unity. Bakunin, in 1848, took part in the first Pan-Slav Congress, held in Prague in the heat of the European Revolution. Herzen lost much of his popularity in Russian intellectual circles when he defended the Polish Insurrection of 1863. Slavophil tendencies could be combined with a wide variety of attitudes on current political and social issues. The only common characteristics were a belief in the need for Slavs to work out their own salvation on the basis of their own cultural history, and therewith a deep dislike, and often a no less deep contempt, for the political and social institutions of the capitalistic, liberal-parliamentary West.

The three men who stand out as the earliest apostles of some sort of Socialism in Russia are Belinsky, Herzen, and Bakunin, who were all born during the final stages of the Napoleonic Wars, and were in their earlier teens at the time of the Decem-brist conspiracy. In adolescence and early manhood they were all 'Westernisers', and all under the spell of the prevailing German philosophy. In the 1840s they all came under the influence of the leftward trend of Hegelianism and more par-ticularly of Feuerbach ; and through German writers, as well as directly, they came into touch with French Socialist ideas. Vissarion Grigorievich Belinsky (1811–48) in particular passed during his brief career as literary critic and philosopher with great rapidity from romanticism through a sort of left Hegelian-ism to a materialistic radicalism which has enabled Soviet writers to make much of him as a forerunner of Russian Marx-ism. This interpretation of his attitude rests on very slender foundations, and is, to say the least, suspect. No doubt Belinsky became a materialist and a determinist in much the same sense as Feuerbach was both these things ; but that does not make him a Marxist or, in any real sense, a Socialist of any sort. He was primarily a Westerniser, an opponent of Czarism, and a radical literary critic who in the last year or two of his short life showed a growing awareness of the 'social question'. Writing in a period of exceedingly severe censorship, he had to avoid openly political allusions, and to say what he wanted to say in the guise of literary criticism of contemporary opinion. His earlier work was almost pure Hegelianism. 'A people is not an abstract concept : a people is a living individuality whose vital diversities serve a single end. A people is an individual like a separate man.' Accordingly the State, as representing this unity, 'is the highest form of associated life and its only rational form. Only by becoming a member of the State does a man cease to be a slave to nature, and only as a member of the State does he appear as a truly rational being.' But when he had come into contact with French Socialism his tune changed. The 'social question' then began to take a prominent place in his writings, and he argued vehemently that art and literature could not be appraised without regard to their social content, though he never fell in relation to them into the extreme utilitarianism which Chernyshevsky professed. The writer, he said, is the incarnation of the people's conscience, and his task is to arouse the social consciousness of the mass of the people. Literature must be realistic — Belinsky was an ardent champion of Gogol, whom he treated as a realistic novelist of the people — and its account of reality must be inspired by clear social purpose. This is the aspect of Belinsky's writings that has caused Russian Marxists, without much warrant, to acclaim him as a forerunner. He died before he had been able to do more than adumbrate his changed views, and it is very doubtful whether they would have led him, had he lived, to any sort of Marxist, or even pre-Marxist, theory. He was a revolutionary democrat who admired Western radicalism and hoped for the development of industry and of an industrial middle class to rescue the Russians from barbarism and to create the conditions for a popular revolt. It is because he took this line that Russian Marxists have been able to build up a Belinsky legend, and to credit him with ideas that he never possessed.

Alexander Ivanovich Herzen (1812–70), a year younger than Belinsky, was by temperament and upbringing under the influence of French much more than of German ideas. The illegitimate son of a wealthy Russian aristocrat and a German mother, he grew up under the spell of his father's Voltairian rationalism and of the Revolution of 1789 as its logical outcome. German metaphysics did not really attract him, though he fell for a while under their spell : French utopian Socialism did. Both ways of thought were under the ban of the authorities, as soon as they took any political form ; and Herzen was banished from the University of Moscow to the town of Vladimir, where he spent three years of enforced absence from student politics. During this period he married his cousin Nathalie, an illegitimate daughter of his father's brother. After three years he was allowed back to Moscow through his father's influence and given a post in the civil service. There he stayed till 1841, when he was dismissed and sent for a year to Novgorod. He made no attempt to resume his official career. In 1846 his father died, leaving him an ample fortune, and the following year he and his family left Russia for good and settled in Paris — the city of his dreams. 'I entered it', he says, 'with reverence, as men used to enter Jerusalem and Rome.'

From Paris the Herzens made a journey to Italy. They were there when the Revolution of 1848 broke out. Herzen hurried back to Paris, in time to be a witness of the defeat of Blanqui and Barbès in May and of the crushing of the workers by General Cavaignac in the 'Days of June'. He was by this time thoroughly disillusioned with Paris, and indeed with much else in the Western civilisation he had admired from afar. He had hated the atmosphere of Paris under the '*bourgeois* monarchy' of Louis-Philippe ; and he liked still less the *bourgeois* Republic which replaced it. Aristocrat by temperament and idealist by conviction, he loathed the rising capitalism of Western Europe and denounced the freedom and democracy which it proclaimed as mere shams and disguises for sordid self-interest. He became a revolutionary against Western reformism as well as against Russian repression, at the very moment when, in the West, the revolution was undergoing for the time being an utter defeat.

The next few years were filled with personal tragedy — his wife was unfaithful to him, and there were disturbing quarrels up to her death in 1852. Herzen then migrated from Switzerland, where he had been living, to England. There, after the death of Nicholas I had been followed, under Alexander II, by a relaxation of the repression, he founded *Kolokol* (The Bell) in 1857, with Nicholas Ogarev, his lifelong friend from student days, as collaborator. *Kolokol* began as a monthly, but was later issued every fortnight. Printed in London in Russian and smuggled into Russia to the extent before long of several thousand copies, it became the principal inspiration of the new generation of Russian intellectuals who were hoping great things now that the strong hand of Nicholas had been removed. Some of Herzen's readers looked forward to revolution as the only hope : others had hopes of reform led by the new Czar and beginning with the emancipation of the serfs and the abolition of the censorship and of political persecution. Alexander II, as we have seen, did for the time being appear as a reformer, though not as ready to alter the autocratic basis of the régime. Plans were set on foot for the emancipation of the serfs ; and there were hopes that the terms of emancipation would be liberal enough to give the peasants a fair start, and that other liberal measures would follow. Herzen had been from the first deeply mistrustful of those Russians who in their hatred of Czarism were prepared to put their hopes in a blind peasant revolt and were eager to sweep the old, bad system away and trust that a better social order would spring from the ruins. He hated cruelty, and had no confidence that good could come out of mass violence directed against the oppressors, however justified the revolt might be. Perhaps, too, living for a number of years in a Western Europe from which all prospect of revolution seemed to have taken flight had strengthened his mistrust. At all events, he welcomed the coming of the new Czar, and was prepared to cheer on Alexander as the great reformer doing battle with the entrenched battalions of privilege and bureaucracy. *Kolokol*, in issue after issue, called on the new Czar to constitute himself the crusading leader of the Russian people and to guide them, in accordance with their national genius and deeply-seated communal traditions, into a way of life entirely different from that of the capitalist-ridden, money-grubbing West.

Kolokol lasted from 1857 until 1868. It was transferred from London to Geneva in 1865 ; but by that time it had lost much of its early support. The emancipation of the serfs in 1861 had been accompanied by such onerous conditions of compensation to the landowners and had allowed such small holdings to the peasants as to disillusion the most ardent of its supporters ; and the Polish Insurrection of 1863 and the peasant risings which accompanied it had broken up the united front of the reformers whose spokesman Herzen had been. The westernising liberals in Russia were largely satisfied with the reform, which they saw as preparing the way for a gradual liberalisation of the entire régime and for the growth of a social system more closely akin to that of Western Europe. The Slavophils who had favoured emancipation were largely alienated by Herzen's defence of the Polish insurgents. Moreover, the resumption of the repression in face of these disturbances and the Czar's abandonment of the reforming rôle which he had assumed at the beginning of his reign drove the radicals underground again, and set them a-seeking for new leaders and prophets more revolutionary than Herzen.

For Herzen could not adapt himself to the changed situation in Russia or accept the return to the destructive revolutionism which had aroused his mistrust even before 1848. To the radicals inside Russia he seemed cautious, even cynical ; and they passed him by, and followed after other prophets. Moreover, Herzen was by this time a sick man ; he outlasted *Kolokol* by only two years.

Mr. E. H. Carr has given a somewhat exaggerated picture of Herzen's private life in *The Romantic Exiles*, or there would be no need for me to discuss it here. It lends itself to sensational treatment : from the quarrel with Herwegh and the troubles of his first Nathalie the unfortunate Herzen was set free only to become entangled with a second, infinitely more difficult Nathalie, who had the further disadvantage of being the wife of his closest friend and collaborator. The *ménage à trois* that continued to contain Herzen, Ogarev, and the Nathalie who was Ogarev's wife and Herzen's mistress was certainly curious ; but it has to be realised both that the advanced Russian intelligentsia of Herzen's day considered it an act of tyranny to insist on the marriage-tie and that Ogarev loved his friend a good deal more deeply than he loved his wife. Even so, Ogarev drank himself into a sort of insensibility, and took to himself by way of consolation a prostitute who with her child — not by Ogarev — was presently added to the remarkable group that centred round Herzen. It would all have been a great deal more awkward had Herzen not been a wealthy man ; but it was not, in practice, nearly so *outré* as Mr. Carr's biography suggests. It did not prevent Herzen's children from being brought up in a quite normal way ; nor did it upset his friendships or close his home to countless visitors who seem to have taken it all as a matter of course.

The only writings of Herzen that are much read in Great Britain are his memoirs, translated into English as *My Past and Thoughts* (six volumes, 1924-7), which are widely quoted for their portraits of European revolutionary leaders and for their running commentary on the course of affairs. These memoirs had been available in French long before they appeared in English ; and a good deal of Herzen's best writing appeared in French during his own lifetime, including his *From Another Shore*, in which he set down his disillusioned impressions of Western Europe as he found it after his emigration in 1847. To the same period belong his well-known *Letters from France and Italy* (1850), the record of his sense of bitter disappointment at the victory of reaction in the West. His essay, *Du développe-ment des idées révolutionnaires en Russie*, also appeared first in French. After his removal to London in 1852 he set up a Free Russian Press, from which he issued numerous booklets and pamphlets both before and after the beginning of *Kolokol*. After 1855 much of his best writing appeared in *Kolokol*. Of his later writings not in periodicals the most important are his essay, *Le Peuple russe et le socialisme* (1855), in the form of an open letter to the historian Michelet, and the *Letters to an Old Comrade* (1869), which he addressed to Bakunin in the last year of his life.

Marx had a great dislike for Herzen, as he had for most Russians. Lenin, on the other hand, in a study written for the centenary of Herzen's birth, praised him highly as 'the first to raise the standard of battle by turning to the masses with the free Russian word'. Marx, at any rate until in his last years he began to find disciples in Russia, had nothing good to say of a man who denounced Western civilisation as decadent and exalted the claim of the backward peasants of Russia to be the standard-bearers of the coming Socialist society. In Marx's view Russia was the great barbarian danger that threatened to overwhelm Europe and, in alliance with Prussian reaction, impose its iron heel on the rising proletariat of the West. To Lenin, on the other hand, Herzen, though misguided in many respects, was the first powerful voice of Russian Socialism, the forerunner of the Narodniks, and the first clear exponent of the view that the Russians, despite their backwardness, could yet have a masterful part to play in the coming world revolution. Lenin wrote particularly in order to answer those who were praising Herzen as the apostle of moderation, basing their eulogies on what he had written in hope of Alexander II putting himself at the head of a great reforming movement and also on his critical reception of Bakunin's extreme revolutionism in the later 'sixties, when Bakunin had fallen for a time under the influence of Nechaiev. Against these aspects of Herzen's teaching, Lenin could set the sharply revolutionary temper of his writings in 1848, his defence of the Polish Insurrection, and his faithfulness, despite all his doubts, to the cause of revolution in Russia. It would, however, have been a long stretch of the truth to say that Herzen had 'turned to the masses' if this had meant that the Russian masses ever saw *Kolokol* or read any of his books and pamphlets. Herzen's appeal in Russia was to students and intellectuals : nor could it have been otherwise when the masses could not have obtained access to his writings — or been able to read them if they had.

Herzen's view of Socialism and of the Russians' part in it can be summarised quite briefly. In the West, he saw the industrial proletariat as the essential revolutionary force, but, after 1848, had not much hope of its early victory. Indeed, he was inclined to regard the entire civilisation of Western Europe as poisoned by capitalism, perhaps beyond hope of recovery. He agreed with de Tocqueville in thinking that the development of parliamentary democracy as the accompaniment of *laissez-faire* capitalism meant the rule of mediocrity and short-sighted egoism, and was inconsistent with the human greatness after which he romantically yearned. But he was not prepared, with de Tocqueville, to make the best of a poor job. He intensely wanted to find a way of escape from his disillusionment, and, finding none in the West, turned to Russia as the last hope. For a time, he studied America in order to discover whether greatness could be found in its rapidly expanding synthetic culture. His conclusion was that the emigrant from Western Europe had a better chance of finding in the United States, if not happiness, at any rate a moderate contentment with his lot. But that quite failed to satisfy his yearning. 'Their contentment', he wrote, 'will be poorer, more commonplace, more sapless than that which was dreamed of in the ideals of romantic Europe'; but, if that was enough for the emigrants, let them go. He could see nothing worth staying for in the decaying and decadent societies of Western Europe, which deemed themselves the advance-guard of human progress.

Herzen turned, then, to the Russians, and convinced himself that it lay within their power to make a revolution in which the peasant would play the part assigned to the industrial worker in the socialistic theories of the West, and that this peasant revolution could take on a socialistic character because of the elements of primitive communalism still alive in the rural sections of Russian society. Not that Herzen either romanticised the peasant or repudiated the West to the same extent as some of his successors. He remained a 'Westerniser', despite his abhorrence of the mess the West had made of its vast power over natural forces. He wanted the Russians to take over the good elements in Western society without the bad ones — to adopt Western productive techniques for the improvement of agriculture and small-scale industry without adopting capitalism with them or accepting the rule of the *bourgeoisie*, even as a transitional form of social organisation. He wanted Russia to go back to the forms of communal ownership of the land which, still surviving in some areas where the land had been neither taken over by the State nor appropriated by the nobility, had once prevailed over most of Russia, and fitted in with the natural 'communism' of the Russian popular spirit. There was no need, he argued, for Socialism to rest on foundations of industrialism and urbanisation: it could rest much better on advanced agriculture, using the best techniques under a system of communal ownership and co-operative labour.

Of this structure the *mir*, the form of village community which existed in a vestigial form in the contemporary Russian village, was to provide the essential foundation. Even under serfdom the Russian village retained to a considerable extent its collective institutions for dealing with the landowner and his agents and for the provision of communal services. Between 1847 and 1852 the German social historian August von Haxthausen (1792–1866), following his earlier studies of Slavic elements in the land systems of Eastern Germany, had published his researches into the systems of landholding and village organisation in Russia ; and Georg Ludwig von Maurer (1790–1872) produced in 1856 the first of his great works on the German mediaeval village structure of the *mark*. These works did not originate the study of village communities, which was carried on by Sir Henry Maine chiefly in India (*Ancient Law*, 1861 ; *Village Communities*, 1871), and by many other social historians. The Decembrist and Slavophil writers had already stressed the communal elements in Russian village life. But Haxthausen's work in particular threw a wealth of new light on the past of the Russian peasant community ; and round the issues which he raised arose an immense controversy between those who believed that there had been at one time, both throughout Europe and in other continents, a system of communal or clan ownership and collective direction of the village economy, on which private property and land-owner-rule had been superimposed. The extent to which this primitive village democracy did ever exist as an almost universal phase in social development has been hotly disputed ever since, and this is not the place for any attempt to settle the issue. What is beyond dispute is that in Russia serfdom had been widely superimposed on much more free village institutions, and that the collective organisation of the village, albeit in decay, kept a greater vitality among the Slav peoples than in Western Europe. The *mir* did exist as a point of focus for collective village sentiment and not merely as an administrative device for disciplining the villagers ; and to Herzen and many others it seemed that emancipation of the serfs would enable the *mir* to regain its vitality, and that its influence would prevent, or could be used to prevent, the development of an individualist, capitalistic village structure. Believing in the past existence of a village democracy collectively owning and managing the village lands, the advocates of peasant Socialism also believed in the possibility of a return to the peasant collective as the basis of rural economic and social life. On this they built their hopes of a socialistic society uncorrupted by the vices of industrialisation and capitalistic control as manifested in the economies of Western Europe.

Herzen shared this faith in the potentialities of the Russian people for democratic self-government based on the institutions of the village community; but he made no attempt to work out in any detail the structure of the new order: equally with Marx he rejected such schematising in advance. Till his last years he trusted almost as much as Bakunin to the creative genius of liberated humanity to work out what was best for itself, provided that its liberators remained true to their ideals and did not allow themselves, out of hatred, to become mere destroyers, and provided also that no authoritarian State was set over men to direct them along the wrong road. Later, he did not so much modify these views as insist that a long period would be needed before they could be fully acted on. In the early 'fifties he had sometimes written almost as anarchistically as Bakunin that the immediate task was that of destroying the existing order and its values, and then leaving the new generations to build on the ruins. But, even then, he was not prepared to encourage blind revolt and the unloosing of indiscriminate brutality. Later, in the 'sixties, and especially in his *Letters to an Old Comrade* in 1869, he stressed the necessity of a slow growth of the new values on which society would have to be re-built and the danger of overthrowing everything too speedily, before there could be anything ready to be put in its place. This caution did not, however, carry with it any concession to reformism or to Western parliamentary democracy. Herzen remained a revolutionary to the last, looking for the impetus towards the new society to come from the heart of the people rather than from parliamentarians or from any reformers tainted with the decadent values of Western capitalism.

Indeed, Herzen, fully as much as Bakunin, whose attitude will be considered in a later chapter, hated the authoritarian State and anything that savoured of its *de haut en bas* philosophy. He wrote of Communism — the Communism of the *Manifesto* of 1848 — 'I think there is a certain basis of truth in the fear which the Russian Government is beginning to have of Communism: Communism is Russian autocracy turned upside down' — a fear mentioned, and attributed to 'certain western liberals' by Benoît Malon in writing of Herzen in his *History of Socialism* in the 1880s. Malon there speaks of the stress on the communal elements in Russian society as having caused fears in the West 'that Russia might impose on Europe some sort of despotic Communism'. It was not a centralised

Communism that Herzen wanted for Russia, but a system of decentralisation in which the restored commune, as owner of the soil, would play the master part. He wrote in 1866 these sentences, expressing his essential thought :

> We bring a new relation between man and soil : our people seeks to develop individual liberty without letting the right to the land be lost, to limit the sovereign right of real property by the sovereign right of each man to individual possession. As colonists who have cleared for ourselves our soil and are accustomed to a certain agricultural redistribution, with no overlay of conquerors on our shoulders, it is easier for us than for the other peoples of Europe to solve the problem in a social sense. The relation of man to soil, as we understand it, is not a new invention in Russia : it is a primordial fact, a *natural* fact so to speak : we wish now, with a sincere remorse, to develop it with the aid of western science and experience.

Thus Herzen, the Westerniser, set out to apply Western science without at the same time applying the values which had accompanied its progress. He was out of love with Western revolutionism because, as he said, in 1848 and again in the 'sixties, it advanced to battle 'without a flag' — without any creative idea or organic thought. He called, at this late stage in his public career, for new thinking, which must be in terms not of some privately-conceived utopia, but of the needs of the whole man. Among the utopians, he praised the Fourierists for having attempted to think in these terms. 'We can make of our world neither a Sparta nor a Benedictine convent. The coming revolution must reconcile all the elements of social life for the general good, as the Fourierists dreamed of doing : we must not stifle some elements for the advantage of others.'

Herzen, it will be seen, was too much the cultured idealist to give free rein to revolutionary fervour, but he remained to the last a romantic, in search of human greatness and hating the mediocrity of the world in which he was, and always felt, an exile. But by the middle 'sixties, when he wrote in this strain, he had lost his formerly immense hold on the Russian youth. The challenge to his influence came mainly from two sources — from the so-called 'Nihilism' of which Pisarev was the principal literary exponent, and from the development of his own ideas by Chernyshevsky and other writers who worked inside Russia and, not needing to smuggle in their writings from abroad, were in closer touch with the changing moods of the intellectual classes.

The name 'Nihilist' was immortalised and spread abroad by Turgenev in his novel, *Fathers and Children* (1862). Nihilism was not primarily a political or social movement : indeed, with its extreme emphasis on the individual and its challenge to all socially based values, it was in sharp antagonism to the communalistic philosophy of Herzen. Its principal apostle was the literary critic Dmitri Ivanovich Pisarev (1840–68), who in his few years of activity made a prodigious impact on a generation which had been first uplifted by the movement for the abolition of serfdom and then utterly cast down by the conditions attached to the emancipation and by the failure to make it the starting-point for further reforms. Pisarev himself was not interested in politics : he was concerned only to stress the claims of the individual and to repudiate all the values of a society which denied the individual his right to free development. But this personal repudiation of traditional values was capable of taking on a political colour, as it did in the revolutionary Nihilism of Nechaiev [1] and of the extreme revolutionary groups which formed themselves, chiefly among students, in the later 'sixties. Pisarev had been the apostle of a gospel of self-realisation akin to Max Stirner's. He admired what has been called 'rugged individualism' wherever he could find it. Nechaiev and the groups which followed Pisarev's doctrines and attempted to apply them to the politics of contemporary Russia added to the repudiation of all traditional values the belief that devotion to the cause of the Revolution, as a means to individual emancipation, justified every act : it converted a gospel of individual self-realisation into a gospel of uninhibited revolutionary action for the destruction of *bourgeois* morality and of the institutions through which that morality was upheld. We shall see in a later chapter how Bakunin came for a time under the spell of this Social Nihilism. In Russia it took shape, not only in a repudiation of all idealistic notions, except the notion of the Revolution as a destroyer, but also in a cult of unpolite manners which was designed to cut its adherents adrift from social conformity, but helped besides to prepare the

[1] For further discussion of Nechaiev see pages 194 ff. and 228 ff.

way for the Narodnik movement of going among the peasants, whereby the intellectuals tried to identify themselves with the people and to educate them for the revolutionary overthrow of the existing society.

Side by side with this growth of Nihilism, but on an essentially different plane of thought, went the development of social criticism which came to be chiefly associated with the work of Chernyshevsky and Dobrolubov in the periodical *Sovremennik* (The Contemporary). Nikolay Gavrilovich Chernyshevsky (1828–89) began his association with *Sovremennik* in 1853 as a literary critic. He followed up and developed much further Belinsky's ideas on the relation of the arts to life, not only insisting on the proper function of art as social criticism, but also accepting Feuerbach's identification of the beautiful with the real and advancing an entirely utilitarian view which has been reflected in recent Soviet theory and practice. From 1858 he handed over the literary department of the journal to Dobrolubov (1836–61) and concentrated on social and economic criticism. He translated John Stuart Mill's *Principles of Political Economy* (1848) into Russian, adding notes and essays of his own concerning applications to Russian social history and institutions. He defended the materialistic philosophy of Feuerbach and his disciple Büchner, and strongly combated Hegelian ideas about the real personality of the State, or of any collective body. His social philosophy was utilitarian, much influenced by Bentham and Mill ; but his utilitarianism was essentially social. He attacked violently the views of the 'Social Darwinians' who believed in the 'survival of the fittest' ; and he developed out of Mill's discussion of French Socialist ideas a gospel of social co-operation which also showed strongly the influence of Louis Blanc. Chernyshevsky looked forward to a society based on democratic producers' associations helped by a reformed democratic State and protected against the advance of 'proletarianisation' after the manner of the West by the revived power of the commune as the essential collective institution of an emancipated Russian people. Chernyshevsky did not commit the error of regarding the village commune as a specifically Russian institution. He thought of it as a type of social organisation which had been everywhere characteristic of primitive societies, but had partly survived in Russia after its extinction in Western Europe because of Russia's economic and social stagnation. Thus, like Herzen, he regarded Russia's industrial backwardness as a positive help towards the establishment of a new order in which primitive communalism would be raised to a higher plane. The Russians, he believed, could make a revolution which would enable them to skip the stage of industrial capitalism and to advance directly to a free society based on the emancipated peasant class.

Chernyshevsky wrote unmolested during the years of comparative freedom from censorship which followed the accession of Alexander II. But as soon as the new repression set in he became a victim. Imprisoned in a fortress in 1862, he used his enforced leisure to write his social novel, *What is to be Done?*, which was soon translated into a number of European languages. After nine years in prison he was exiled to Siberia, where he spent twelve more years in enforced segregation from the main centres of Russian intellectual life. But his influence remained : he was one of the principal inspirers of the Narodnik (Popular) movement and of the new generation which ceased to follow Herzen as the hopes founded on the emancipation of the serfs faded away and in desperation took to a violence out of tune with the critical, gradualist outlook of that fine romantic exile.

Chernyshevsky was not without influence on the development of ideas in Western Europe. His work on Political Economy (*L'Économie politique jugée par la science*) was translated into French by A. Tvertinov in collaboration with the Belgian Socialist, César de Paepe, in 1874, and helped to reinforce the arguments of those Western Socialists who stood for decentralisation and communal supremacy against the advocates of centralised State authority. Therewith, his hostility to industrialism placed him among the formative influences of Anarchist-Communism. Chernyshevsky was a strong opponent of the extreme division of labour characteristic of capitalist society. He regarded the specialisation of work as inconsistent with the human claim to happiness and satisfaction in labour, and looked on the commune as an institution by means of which such division could be kept down to the minimum needed for efficient production. In this part of his doctrine he was influenced by Fourier, who had insisted that every man should be free and equipped to practise a number of trades, in order to escape the monotony of repetitive labour and to be able to vary his occupation to fit his mood. Fourier had, indeed, won a considerable following in Russia in the 1840s, and his Russian disciples, of whom the most important was Petrashevsky, conducted an active propaganda during the years before 1848. It was on account of his participation in Petrashevsky's group that the novelist Feodor Dostoievsky was sent to a fortress and exiled to Siberia in 1847. The Russian Fourierists provided the basis for his novel, *The Possessed*, which appeared in 1871, long after he had lost all sympathy with the revolutionary movement.

Fourier has to be counted among the main influences which went into the making of Russian Narodnik Socialism. The *phalanstère*, transplanted to Russia, seemed a possible development of the peasant commune into a society of social equals, employing advanced methods of intensive cultivation and escaping the evils of capitalist industrialisation. Chernyshevsky saw in capitalist production a dehumanising tendency, not only because of its progressive supersession of craft skills by the use of labour-simplifying machinery, but also because, in treating the human being as a mere 'commodity', it eliminated the human factor from the economic process. Man, Chernyshevsky held, could be treated as a man, with proper regard for his individual human nature, only in a small-scale organisation in which he could co-operate freely with his fellows on terms of mutual understanding and respect.

The purpose of this chapter has been simply to outline the development of Russian Socialism in the 1850s and early 1860s, stopping short of the rise of the Narodnik movement inside Russia and of the activities of Bakunin outside Russia after his escape from Siberia in 1861. Of Bakunin there will be much to say in a subsequent chapter, and also something of Nechaiev as the political exponent of the extreme Nihilist creed. In this chapter Alexander Herzen has been the central figure, because he was the first, despite his fundamental 'westernism', to tackle the problem of a specifically Russian approach to the questions posed by the socialistic creed of co-operative equality, and to suggest that there might be a solution in terms essentially different from those in which the problem was being stated, and the solution offered, in relation to the more developed industrial societies of the West. Herzen had, of course, no prevision of the actual course of events when Russia had at last to face the long-awaited collapse of Czarist autocracy and the task of building a new society on the ruins of the old. He had no inkling that this building would take the form of a gigantic industrialisation, based on an imitation of the most advanced capitalistic techniques of mass-production. What he did foresee was that it would not be necessary for the Russians, in creating their new society, to pass through the same stages of capitalistic domination as were being experienced under his eyes in the Western Europe of his exile. Herzen was no Marxist and no Leninist : he hated dictatorship and violence from the bottom of his heart ; but his blend of Western and Slavophil ideas nevertheless has much to make it appeal to the Russia of more recent years. Not that Herzen would have liked Stalinism : he would have been utterly opposed both to its ruthlessness and its centralised authoritarianism and, hardly less, to its eager promotion of mass-production on the American model. Indeed, he would undoubtedly have regarded Stalinist Russia with the utmost aversion and disgust. Nor would Chernyshevsky have been much more ready to accept these tendencies as consistent with the freedom in co-operation which he regarded as the essential of the Socialist idea. Nevertheless, it cannot be denied that Stalin's idea of 'Socialism in one country' owes much to these apostles of the belief that it was the mission of the Russians to work out their own kind of Socialism on foundations essentially Russian and not borrowed ready-made from the West. Moreover, if not in industry, at any rate in agriculture, the Soviet Union has drawn heavily on the ideas of these pioneers of agrarian Socialism, though it has diverted them to very different ends. From one point of view, the *kolkhoz*, or collective farm, can be regarded as a kind of realisation of the communalistic conception of Herzen and Chernyshevsky, though it has been created from above by force and has not arisen naturally out of the peasants' will, and is controlled after a fashion which they were very far from anticipating or desiring. This partly explains why, despite Marx's extreme dislike of Herzen, his name, as well as Chernyshevsky's, is held in honour in contemporary Russia — with the emphasis laid, of course, on his disdain of Western capitalism and parliamentarianism and on the revolutionary aspect of his writings rather than on the gradualism which, always present, grew more pronounced in his later years. His very gradualism is, however, the less unacceptable because it was advanced largely as a criticism of Bakunin's anarchistic gospel of sheer destruction as the necessary precursor to the work of social re-creation. To have sided against Bakunin during the titanic struggle which rent asunder the First International is no small merit in Marxist eyes ; and Herzen, though he and Marx disliked each other cordially and were poles apart in thought — and though he was dead before the contest reached its climax — at all events devoted his last work of importance to taking his old revolutionary comrade, Bakunin, somewhat seriously to task.

Chernyshevsky presents no less of a problem to those who would wish to regard him as a forerunner of modern Communist doctrine ; for, though a materialist, he can by no stretch of fancy be regarded as a determinist in the Marxian sense. Chernyshevsky was, indeed, a 'realist' in the sense that he rebelled against the idealism of those Russian radicals who had been most deeply influenced by Western idealistic Socialism and by Western conceptions of democracy. He repeatedly insisted that it was futile to appeal to the Russian peoples with notions of civil liberty, human rights, and democratic government. The people, he said, wanted, not votes, but enough to eat, not liberty, but boots and good, warm clothing. These were the gifts the practising revolutionary should offer them, if he really meant business. The rest could wait. This was the aspect of his thought that Lenin admired and invoked as a weapon against the liberal Socialists of his own day.

Chernyshevsky insisted, too, on the need for a scientific approach to social problems and on the domination of law in social affairs ; but he treated the laws governing human history as at bottom laws of thought, beside which, save at the early stages of social evolution, the material environment is no more than secondary. 'Climate, soil, resources of capital, even the strength of physical force — all these are negligible', he writes, 'in comparison with the development of thought.' He gives the greatest importance in social development to the institutions under which men live in societies, and regards these institutions as man-made and as greatly affected by powerful personalities who give direction to the chaotic impulses by which the mass of men are moved. In the last resort, he does indeed regard human history as the expression of a law of necessity, so that the great men can shape its course only within the general conditions presented by a determined order of development. Human progress, he says, is 'simply the law of growth' — a purely natural phenomenon which does not need to be explained. But this law is not, in his conception, economic in its fundamental character : it is simply an expression of the process of organic growth. The revolutionary aspect of this theory of natural evolution comes out when Chernyshevsky insists that, though human progress is slow, 'nine-tenths of it is brought about in short periods of intense activity. History moves slowly, and yet almost all its advance takes place by sudden leaps.' But even here his conception of the cause is far away from Marx's ; for he attributes the speeding up and retardation of progress chiefly to the presence or absence of great men, rather than to the changes in the material conditions of production. This tunes in with his final stress on the individual and his repudiation of all supra-individual social ends. 'I hold nothing on earth higher', he wrote, 'than the human individual.'

There is one other Russian Socialist of whom it is necessary to say a little in this chapter, though it does not set out to discuss the Narodnik movement with which his name is most closely connected. Peter Lavrovich Lavrov (1823–1900), son of an army colonel, taught mathematics at the Military Academy of St. Petersburg from 1844 to 1867, and became known as a frequent contributor to journals of a liberal tendency. He was not, however, a Socialist, much less a revolutionary ; and he had done nothing to call for the attentions of the police when, in the general persecution which followed on Karakazov's attempt to kill Alexander II, he was arrested and banished to Vologda. During his three years' stay he wrote anonymously, and got past the censorship, his famous *Historical Letters*, which at once began to circulate widely among the young Russian intellectuals. Escaping abroad in 1870, he took part in the Paris Commune, which sent him to Brussels and London to organise help. But, being abroad at the time of its defeat, he escaped persecution, and was able to settle down in Paris, where he founded in 1873 his journal *Vpered* (Forward), and developed his sociological doctrines. By this time he had become a convinced Socialist ; but he differed from both Bakunin and Chernyshevsky in that he was opposed to immediate revolutionary attempts and urged the need for a long period of education and ethical propaganda to prepare the way for the new society. His doctrine of Socialism was essentially evolutionary ; and he would have nothing to do with the followers of Nechaiev or Bakunin. Still less would he have any dealings with his fellow-exile Tkachev, who in his *Nabat* (The Alarm Bell), published in Geneva, denounced Bakunin as a *bourgeois* reactionary, and preached a pure Blanquist doctrine of insurrection to be organised by a disciplined *élite* in terms so violent as to earn the denunciations of the terrorists inside Russia, including Zhelyabov's Narodnaya Volya itself.[1] Lenin expressed admiration for Tkachev as a true revolutionary ; and attempts have been made in recent years to build him up as a revolutionary thinker who foreshadowed Communist doctrines. But he was in reality a follower of Blanqui and Babeuf, who insisted that the revolution must be made by a trained *élite* before the mass had been brought over to its side ; whereas Lavrov stood consistently for the need for mass-propaganda and education to precede the actual revolution, and to serve as the necessary foundation for its success. Lavrov, because of this conviction, stood apart from the Russian revolutionary movement during the years of the main terrorist campaign up to 1881. He then rallied to Narodnaya Volya in its years of rebuilding in exile, and from 1884 to 1886 was joint editor with Leo Tikhomirov (1850–1922) of its journal, *Vestnik Narodnoy Voli* (People's Will), in London. This Tikhomirov had been prominent in Narodnaya Volya with Zhelyabov, and had edited its clandestine journal in Russia before 1881. In exile, he wrote lives of Zhelyabov, Perovskaya, and other terrorist leaders, but subsequently changed his politics and, returning to Russia, became a leading journalist of the extreme reactionary party. Lavrov, on the other hand, never changed his opinions. He was indeed throughout his life by temperament a thinker, rather than a man of action ; and his lasting importance lies in the field of historical sociology.

Lavrov's sociological doctrine is based on a strong belief in

[1] For Zhelyabov and Narodnaya Volya see pages 319 ff.

the creative power of the individual. He sees human societies as developing out of forms of society similar to those which exist among animals. Primitive man, he says, like his animal forerunners, begins with a simple pursuit of pleasure and avoidance of pain in accordance with the prompting of elementary needs. But in human societies the process of living together gives rise to the development of altruistic as well as egoistic behaviour. The sense of justice is born ; and so is the sense of mercy and reciprocal fellowship. Moreover, the growth of the intellectual powers brings with it a faculty of criticism and a rationalisation of these impulses into ethical imperatives. The domination of sheer custom is modified by the use of reason ; and men learn to formulate ideals and to make moral choices. In these developments, Lavrov insists, it is always the individual who leads the way, and gradually wins converts by precept and by example. The advance of civilisation is thus always the work of minorities gifted with superior intelligence and moral insight : it is the mission of these minorities to lead the people towards higher ways of living. Therefore, the duty of the intellectual is to devote his life to giving back to the people some part of the debt he owes them for his own superior opportunities.

The individual, says Lavrov, makes history in the image of his own ideals. The growth of civilisation, far from being determined by material forces, is the work of great men who impose the pattern of their subjective ideas upon society, not by force but by persuasion. Lavrov nevertheless accepts the view that the movement of history is objectively determined, but only in the sense that the subjective ideas of the great innovators are facts no less objective from the historical standpoint than the material environment.

Naturally, these views have laid Lavrov open to strong attack from every generation of Marxists. In Russian Communist accounts he is taken as the very type of *petit-bourgeois* Socialism. He is accused of treating the working class, not as a creative force in history, but as mere crude material to be manipulated by the superior class of *petit-bourgeois* intellectuals, as well as of committing the cardinal sin of making thought, rather than material conditions, the main motive force in human development.

An ideal [Lavrov writes] is born in the brains of individuals ; it grows qualitatively in the measure in which the intellectual and moral value of these individuals increases ; and it grows quantitatively in the measure in which their numbers increase. It becomes a social force when these individuals become conscious of their unity of purpose and resolve on concerted action.

The main mass of mankind, on the other hand, being condemned to a life of monotonous and deadening toil for the advantage of others, is deprived of the possibility of taking the lead in moral and intellectual innovation, and can at most but follow those among the more fortunate who realise their duty to serve the people. This was the basis of the Narodnik doctrine as elaborated later in Russia by Nikolai Mikhailovsky (1842–1904), who is usually linked with Lavrov as the theoretical inspirer of Narodinism and of the Social Revolutionary movement which succeeded it. It is easy to see how Lavrov's conception of service as the duty of the intellectual could be developed from the original insistence on propaganda by peaceful example and persuasion into the activist doctrine of 'propaganda by deed' which took hold of the Russian intellectuals when every other means of action seemed to have been closed by the repression.

This, however, is not the place for any full account of Lavrov or of Mikhailovsky, who belong essentially to a period later than this chapter is meant to cover. Lavrov is dealt with at all at this point only because with the removal of Chernyshevsky from the scene near the beginning of the 1860s and with the waning of Herzen's influence there was left a void which his *Letters on History* helped to fill before the decade ended.

CHAPTER IV

BELGIAN SOCIALISM IN THE 1850s — COLINS, KATS, AND DE KEYSER

THE heroic age of 'Utopian Socialism' was over by the middle of the nineteenth century. Thereafter, though Owen, Fourier, Cabet, and other projectors had still their faithful followers, and the influence of the Saint-Simonians was by no means entirely spent, no fresh major prophet appeared with the offer of a universal system that would set the world's affairs to rights by virtue of its manifest superiority over all others. There did, however, appear one solitary minor prophet with a gospel as all-embracing as Saint-Simon's — or as Comte's — and with an equal assurance of the absolute rightness both of his principles and of the practical deductions to be derived from them. This late-born utopian was a Belgian — by name Colins — whose principal works were all published in the 'fifties, during the last few years of a long and varied life. Outside Belgium their influence was never wide ; but Colins had some following in France and Switzerland as well as in his native country, and even enlisted a small number of supporters in England and as far afield as Spain and Portugal. His system, expounded in several treatises each of which ran into a number of volumes, went by the name of 'Rational Socialism'. In terms of practical policy its corner-stone was public ownership — of the land first and foremost, but also of other large-scale instruments of production ; but in the 'Colinsian' system, this policy appeared as a rational deduction from a general theory of man's nature and place in the universal scheme of things.

Colins — or, to give him his full title, Baron Jean Hippolyte de Colins (1783–1859) — claiming descent from Charles the Bold, was born in Brussels in 1783. At the age of 17 he went to Paris, with the intention of becoming a student at the École Polytechnique ; but instead, hoping to take part in Napoleon's projected invasion of Great Britain, he joined the French army, serving at first in the ranks. He became a non-commissioned and then a commissioned officer, rising at length in 1815, in the hour of Napoleon's final defeat, to the rank of colonel. Under the Restoration, he is said to have been offered the position of general ; but he remained faithful to Napoleon and left France, first for Belgium and then for America, where he attempted to devise a plan for rescuing the ex-emperor by means of a submarine or a balloon. His studies, pursued with this object, caused him to become a member of the scientific Academy of Philadelphia ; and he also studied medicine and qualified as a doctor. He then went to Havana, where he developed a large agricultural estate and also practised medicine. There he remained until the Revolution of 1830 called him back to Europe. Settling in Paris, he attempted to organise a Bona-partist conspiracy ; but on the death of the second Napoleon he abandoned politics and set to work on the formulation of his ideas for publication. He had already written, as early as 1813, a *Memorial on Rural Economy*, which had been awarded the gold medal of the French Society of Agriculture ; but between then and 1834 he had published nothing of substance. In the latter year he issued anonymously a book, *Le Pacte social*, in which he clearly set down his advocacy of land nationalisation. This work, though little noticed, gained him his first disciples, among whom was his chief Belgian expositor, Louis de Potter. Thereafter he devoted himself for fifteen years to intensive study, interrupted only by the Revolution of 1848, in the course of which he was arrested and narrowly escaped being shot by General Cavaignac's soldiers in the 'Days of June'. Through all these years he remained an ardent Bonapartist, holding that only under the autocratic rule of one enlightened man could his 'Rational Socialism' ever be put into effect. But Napoleon III showed no inclination to act on his proposals, which, from 1851 to his death in 1859, he poured out in a succession of volumes in which he reiterated the same ideas. *Qu'est-ce que la science sociale?*, in four volumes, appeared between 1851 and 1854. In 1856 he published *L'Économie politique, source des révolutions et des utopies prétendues socialistes*, in three volumes, and also *Société nouvelle, sa nécessité*, in two. The following year came *De la souveraineté*, in two volumes, and *Science sociale*, in five. The three volumes of

De la justice dans la science hors l'Église et la Révolution appeared in 1861, after his death ; and he left in manuscript a number of other works — on Descartes, on Bacon, on Religion and Materialism, on the *bourgeoisie*, and on eclectic philosophy — some of which were edited by his disciples after his death.

Colins, as a philosopher, was at one and the same time atheist and anti-materialist. He believed that the individual human soul was eternal and indestructible, self-subsistent and not the creation of any superior being. This eternal soul, he held, was reincarnated in a succession of bodies, not merely in this world, but in the countless worlds of which the universe was composed ; and each soul carried into each new life what it had made of itself in its previous incarnations. He drew an absolute line between man and the animals, to whom he denied all 'sensibility'. Everything in the universe, except man, he regarded as merely material, determined, and void of thought and feeling : man alone had the dual nature of corporeality and 'immaterial sensibility', the union of these two constituting 'real intelligence or liberty'. Colins insisted that this soulhood of man involved the possession of free will, of moral values, and of responsibility for right conduct.

His utopianism appears most plainly in his remarkably simplified theory of history. He distinguished in the whole past and present of the human race only two historical epochs — to be followed by a third in which man was destined to enter into the realm of true freedom and felicity. In the first of these epochs men lived in ignorance of the existence of any right (*droit*), knowing no other rule of action than the law imposed by the strong upon the weak. But, the operation of this rule involving the continual threat of anarchy and the danger of the sheer destruction of the human race, the stronger found it necessary to secure the obedience of the weaker voluntarily, and not by sheer force. This, says Colins, was the social origin of religion. The strong took command of the processes of education and indoctrinated the weak with a belief that the rule of the strong rested on a law revealed to man by a super-human being. They made themselves priests for the interpretation of this supposed revelation, and lawgivers for the interpretation of 'the terrestrial part' of the same doctrine. 'Force is thus transformed into right, and obedience into duty.'

The strong, as priests and lawgivers, decree severe penalties against any of the weak who question their law, and use their power to keep the masses in a state of complete brutishness, by denying them all intellectual culture and all leisure, and by imposing on them heavy labour of which the benefits accrue to the strong. They also deliberately keep the weak of each society isolated from other societies, because if there were to be contacts and knowledge of national differences of laws and customs, the critical spirit of the masses would inevitably be aroused, and they would learn to question the dogmas instilled into them by the priests and lawgivers of their own societies. In order to achieve these results, the strong alienate the land, from which all wealth finally proceeds, from the cultivators into their own hands. This first phase of human history is characterised as the rule of force 'masked by fraud' (*sophismes*).

This situation cannot, however, endure indefinitely ; for it is impossible to maintain for ever the isolation of one society from another. The development of invention prevents this. The mariner's compass breaks down the isolation of continent from continent : the discovery of gunpowder transforms the art of war into a matter of the exercise of intelligence based on scientific knowledge and overthrows the dominance of brute force : the invention of printing makes it impossible to prevent the dissemination of knowledge : finally, railways and the electric telegraph, by making distances in effect less, break down the intellectual frontiers between the peoples and make for the growth of an international spirit of criticism, against which the old systems of pretended rights cannot stand.

But this breakdown of the old order does not suffice to create the new. The growth of criticism leads rather to a new anarchy — this time of conflicting and ever-changing opinions. Men do not *know* the real law of reason ; they only *believe* different things. There is still no 'social science' ; for, if there were, everyone would agree about it, just as everyone agrees about the fundamental propositions of mathematics and the fundamental laws of natural science. 'Right would become *one*, as science is *one*.'

What, then, is to happen to humanity ? A chaos, in which, Colins declares, 'riches and pauperism increase together along parallel lines', the rich becoming ever richer, and the poor poorer, in accordance with the anarchy men call 'the laws of political economy'. Such a situation is entirely inconsistent with the maintenance of order, which is essential to social survival. The poor come to see that their poverty is the result of the property system : they see through the sophisms of religion, and come to the conclusion that words such as 'duty' and 'right' are mere empty sounds void of meaning : they reach the conclusion that they are poor only because they have not had the sense to make themselves the stronger party. Accordingly, the age of revolutions begins : the poor revolt against the rich and, because of their numbers, are able to win the day. But the mere victory of the poor settles nothing : it only establishes a different, and equally unstable, rule of the strong. Revolution succeeds to revolution in an unending series.

How, then, can the age of revolutions be brought to a close ? Only, Colins asserts, by ending pauperism in both a material and an intellectual sense — that is, by restoring to men the material means of free existence, above all the land, and by educating them in the understanding of the true rational law of right, which is that 'sensibility' is a regenerating power in man, independent of force, on which a just social order can rest. But no such lesson will ever be learnt by the mass of men by themselves : nor will the strong, who rule the many, ever wish to teach it to their subjects. The sole hope of the advent of the new order rests on the appearance, somewhere on the face of the earth, of a single autocrat who, cutting himself away from the privileged classes, will devote himself to the task of human enlightenment. Even such an autocrat could not hope to act effectively on the minds of his own generation ; but he could, by laying hands on the schools and using them to teach the true knowledge to the young, make the society over which he had presided so signal a success in the ensuing generation that all other societies would hasten to follow in its footsteps. This would involve the autocrat in using his authority to prevent the adult members of his society from wrecking his educational experiment in their blindness. The benevolent autocrat would have in addition to prevent the children thus educated in the true science from being blinded when they went from school out into the world through subjection to the stultifying influences of the old order. He would accordingly have to take the land of his country into collective ownership, and by doing so and placing the means of production at the disposal of everyone able to put them to good use, 'annihilate *bourgeoisie* and *proletariat* together, leaving only a single class, humanity, in existence'.

This curious doctrine evidently owes a good deal to Saint-Simon and his followers, and also to Comte ; but the blend is essentially Colins's own. On it he and his disciples built a considerable superstructure of practical proposals. They demanded collective ownership not only of the land but also of other capital factors of production. But they did not wish the collectivity itself to till the land or to organise the general run of industrial operations. Like Thomas Spence and other earlier 'land nationalisers', they wanted the publicly-owned land to be let out for cultivation by small-scale agencies of public administration — the communes — to individuals or to groups of producers, on payment of rents corresponding to its productive value. They wanted the public authorities to divide the land into suitable units for leasing, with the requisite buildings and equipment ; and in the same way they wanted industrial buildings and equipment to be rented to the highest bidders, individual or co-operative. Only in cases of really large-scale operation, such as railways and some mining enterprises, and in the public services, did they stand for public operation as well as ownership. As a means of making access to the means of production fairly and equally open to all, they wanted public Credit Banks, after the manner of those which Proudhon was advocating ; but they also contemplated that the working capital of the individual and co-operative producers would be provided in part by the producers themselves. In order that everyone should have a fair opportunity to participate in this way they proposed that everyone, on finishing his education, should be provided by the State with an endowment (*dot*) which he would be free to invest in the enterprise in which he went to work, but not elsewhere. All private ownership of fixed capital was to be forbidden by law ; and all existing companies and corporations resting on joint-stock ownership were to be dissolved.

In order to bring about this comprehensive transfer of

property to public ownership, the Colinsians proposed to levy a 25 per cent tax on all property passing at death by the will of the owner. They further proposed to abolish all collateral rights of inheritance and to cause all estates, in cases of intestacy, to pass to the State unless there were direct legal heirs. Direct inheritance in the family line they wished to leave intact, as providing a necessary incentive to labour ; and they also wished to allow any owner of property to leave it, subject to death duty, to whom he pleased, on the ground that this too was a necessary incentive. But it must be borne in mind that these survivals of private property were to apply only to property actually used by the owner : if the heir of a property-owner did not make use of what he inherited as an adjunct to his personal labour his right was to lapse to the State — for ownership in such cases could not serve as an incentive to production.

As a means of preparing the people for life in such a society as these arrangements would produce, Colins and his followers proposed the absolute control of education by the State. All children, on reaching the age of 2, were to be handed over by their parents to the State's care. The State, without charge to the parents, was to lodge, clothe, and feed the children, as well as to educate them intellectually and instruct them for their future careers ; and this system was to continue until they reached their majority. There was to be complete separation of the sexes throughout the educational process. On leaving this communal schooling, every male was to spend five years working for a wage, under the orders of the State, on some form of public works, but was to be maintained by the State during this period, receiving his accumulated wages, *plus* his social *dot*, at the end, when he would be free to take up the occupation of his choice and to contribute his quota of working capital to whatever enterprise he decided to enter.

The Colinsians had also their own views about government. Legislation, in a strict sense, they held would no longer be needed when human affairs were regulated scientifically in accordance with the laws of reason. There would remain only administration of the law, which would have been made once for all by the establishment of the rational order. To the tasks of administration they held that every rational man ought to make a personal contribution, in accordance with his capacities as recognised by his peers. They insisted, however, on marriage as a necessary qualification for active citizenship. 'The collective family', said Hugentobler, Colins's leading Swiss disciple, 'ought not to be administered by either eunuchs or sultans.'

Colins and his disciples again and again insisted that society should be regarded as a collective family. Its administration, they said, should be based on a combination of centralisation and decentralisation. The primary unit was to be the commune, which they called 'city of the first order' : it was to be administered by a mayor and council, elected by universal suffrage. The communes were to be grouped into 'cities of the second order' — that is, regions — with mayors and councils chosen by the assembled mayors and councils of the communes. At a higher level were to be cities of the third and fourth orders and, finally, a single 'city of the fifth order' — the 'Universal Republic', embracing the entire world. Each of these 'cities' was to have its mayor and council, chosen by the mayors and councils of the order immediately below it. But in conjunction with this 'decentralisation' there was to be a system of 'centralisation', in the form of nomination from above. The mayor of the 'city of the fifth order' was to nominate a commissar to serve in each 'city of the fourth order' as supervisor of the execution of the 'absolute law' and of the general administrative regulations applicable to the entire world. This process of nomination was to be repeated at each lower stage, the commissars of the 'cities of the fourth order' nominating commissars to serve in the 'cities of the third order', and so on, down to the commune itself. This combination of election from below with nomination from above was held to constitute the right foundation for a well-balanced administration ; but no great effort was made to work out the respective powers of mayors and councils on the one hand and commissars on the other, or to say what functions should be assigned to the various 'orders' of 'cities'. These questions were considerably discussed later among the Colinsians, as well as by César de Paepe, who was much influenced by Colins, though he rejected the general Colinsian philosophy. But there was on these issues no recognised orthodoxy, each advocate of the system making his own choice between a high degree of local or regional autonomy and a more centralised régime. Colins himself, insisting on the completely scientific character of his system, tended to regard these matters as due to settle themselves when the fundamental laws based on the lessons of science had once been clearly laid down ; for he held that it would then appear plainly where uniformity was needed, and where local variations were called for by the different conditions and economic structures of the areas subject to the unified world system.

It is, of course, easy to dismiss this vast pseudo-scientific construction as mere nonsense. Critics of Colins were quick to point out that his system rested on pure dogma, and that his sole proof of its validity was reiteration. The Colinsians, and their master, had an inveterate habit of proclaiming that whatever they wanted to affirm was 'as certain as that two and two make four' ; but what they meant by this was that the truth of their basic propositions seemed to them self-evident and therefore in no need of proof.

They were not alone in proclaiming their devotion to 'science', declaring the universal application of its laws, and ignoring altogether the hypothetical procedures which are characteristic of the methods of the natural sciences. The entire work of Colins is a characteristic product of the isolated thinker, who devises a complete system of his own as the expression of his desires and sentiments, and is satisfied of its truth because it corresponds to the shape of his own thought and hangs together by the thread of his own personality.

Nevertheless, it would be a mistake to dismiss Colins as altogether unimportant in the history of Socialist thought. He was of considerable influence in bringing into the main stream of Socialist development the theme of collective ownership of land and capital and in emphasising the idea that every citizen should be educated and trained by the State both in order to endow him with the equipment, intellectual and moral, needed for the consolidation of a just and rational social order, and to prepare him for the work that society needed to get done. He was also an important pioneer of the idea of 'industrial armies' of young men for the execution of desirable public works ; and he was original in the way in which he linked together material and intellectual 'pauperism' as twin evils to be eradicated before the new social order could be established on firm foundations of reason and justice.

As against these merits, Colins's curious notions about souls and bodies and his ardent belief in the necessity for the inauguration of the new order by an autocrat who would set to work to train up a new generation in right social attitudes and knowledge of the laws of 'social science' inevitably antagonised the main body of the working-class advocates of comprehensive social change. The antagonism was the greater because Colins, having begun — as Saint-Simon did — by entertaining high hopes of Napoleon I, went on to transfer his enthusiasm to the second and to the third Napoleons. Bonapartism had, no doubt, a popular following after 1848 ; indeed Louis Bonaparte deliberately set out to enlist against the dominant *bourgeoisie* the support of the proletarians whose comrades had been shot down by General Cavaignac in the 'Days of June'. But at any rate after the *coup d'état* Napoleon III gave the organised workers, who were the backbone of the political clubs and trade societies, no reason for loving him ; and Colins's call for a benevolent autocrat to inaugurate his new system greatly limited his influence. He won support, like Comte — and indeed in keen competition with Comte — chiefly among professional men. His disciples were doctors, lawyers, architects, *fonctionnaires*, and cranky business men, rather than manual workers. Within these limited groups the Colinsian doctrine showed considerable vitality in both France and Belgium and to a smaller extent in Switzerland. It had even a substantial intellectual revival in the 1880s, under the leadership of Frédéric Borde, who edited the Colinsian journal, *Philosophie de l'avenir*. Colins's first important followers were the Belgian, Louis de Potter,[1] and the Swiss Hugentobler, who edited certain of his works and produced a condensed version of his system. Agathon de Potter,[2] the doctor-son of Louis, and the Parisian architect Delaporte, were other leading advocates ; and, as we have seen, César de Paepe, the principal theorist of Belgian Socialism in the First International, owed a great deal to his influence. This will come out plainly when we consider the discussions that took place within the International on the

[1] Louis de Potter (1786–1859) took a leading part in the Belgian Revolution of 1830. His principal writings appeared before those of Colins, whose influence on him was felt mainly during the last years of his life.

[2] Agathon de Potter also produced, in 1881, a work summarising and expounding Colins's social system.

problems of collectivisation and administration of collective property.

It would, however, be misleading to treat Colins as the sole original source of the specifically Belgian contribution to the growth of Socialist ideas. Colins was indeed, though Belgian by birth and upbringing, more French than Belgian in his intellectual development and in his social affiliations. Well before Colins had written anything of substance under his own name, the Fleming Jacob Kats (1804–86), son of a Dutch republican officer who had taken refuge in Brussels after 1830, had helped to lay the theoretical foundations of Belgian Socialism. Kats was at first a weaver : he then became a schoolmaster and later a tobacconist, and in his leisure wrote a number of popular plays with a propagandist twist. As a social thinker, he wrote extensively concerning the influence of the arts on the life of the people, emphasising the need for opportunities for satisfying creative work as a foundation for a democratic social order. As early as Louis Blanc in France, he was crying out in the 1830s for 'organisation of labour' as the State's duty towards the mass of the people. He was a strong advocate of universal free education for democracy, and of complete religious and political liberty. Again like Blanc, he demanded universal suffrage as a means towards changing the State into an agency for the promotion of the general welfare, and advocated the levying of taxation exclusively on the surplus incomes of the rich.

The third contributor to early Belgian Socialist thought was the farmer-geometrician, Napoléon de Keyser (1806–?), who took an active part in the Belgian Revolution of 1830 and worked closely with Kats during the next few years. Apart from journalism, he published little : the big book on which his reputation depends, *Het natuer in regt*, appeared only in 1854, at a time when Colins was pouring out his books at a great rate. Most of it, however, had been written much earlier. De Keyser's main theme was a forthright attack on what he called 'the two feudalisms' — the landowning interest and industrialism. These he described as the twin enemies against which the workers had to do battle. Like Colins, de Keyser asserted that every man had a right to a share in the land, and that this right — a 'natural right' in his view — could be made effective only by communal ownership. He wanted the communes to own the land and to let it out for a rent either to family tenants or to Co-operative associations, and he also proposed that the communes should supply the working capital needed for its effective use. Small industrial enterprises were to be similarly financed by the communes, while those which needed large-scale operation were to be carried on under the auspices of federations of communes covering suitable areas. These proposals are practically identical with those of Colins, and it is not easy to say who thought of them first. Where de Keyser differed from Colins was in being a much more determined upholder of communal independence and opponent of centralised control. He put forward no theory of a 'rational law' under which every question would be settled 'scientifically', beyond the possibility of disagreement among rational men : nor did he at all share Colins's view that an autocrat would be needed to introduce the new system. He was prepared for the independent communes to federate over appropriate areas for the joint conduct or supervision of large-scale services ; but he was as firm as the followers of Bakunin were later in insisting that the local communes must be the basis of all social and economic organisation and must be free from all control by any Government imposed on them from above. For the establishment of the new order de Keyser regarded revolution as the necessary means. He attacked the notion that re-distribution of incomes or property could be achieved by taxing the rich while the means of production remained in private ownership. He also attacked religious institutions as upholders of the unjust social order based on privilege, but believed the religious impulse to be natural to men, and tried to work out a 'natural religion' divested of theological trappings.

Not the least important part of de Keyser's work was his account of what was happening to the *bourgeoisie* under developing capitalism. In his terminology, the *bourgeoisie* meant, not the greater capitalists, but the small masters, traders, small farmers, and other intermediate groups which Marx always designated as the *petite bourgeoisie*. These middle classes, de Keyser showed, were being remorselessly crushed out by the advance of large-scale capitalist enterprise. Their interest, he argued, was to take sides with the workers in the struggle against the combined forces of the feudal landowners and the increasing class of great capitalist investors, merchants and money-lenders. He was opposed to the view that the workers should help the capitalists against the feudalists as a step on the road to Socialism — influenced, no doubt, by the fact that in Belgium, with its relatively advanced industrialisation, the feudalists and the *grande bourgeoisie* had already to a great extent joined forces to control the new State established by the Revolution of 1830. The Belgian social and political situation was indeed much closer to the British than to the German, or even the French ; and de Keyser's analysis fitted it in many respects better than Marx's.

The situation in Belgium was, however, always complicated by the mixed composition of Belgian society. Kats and de Keyser were Flemings : Colins was a Walloon. Industrialism, broadly speaking, was further advanced in the Walloon than in the Flemish districts ; and the French-speaking workers and intellectuals were much more open to French influence than the Flemings.

The relations between French and Belgian Socialism were indeed close from the very beginning. Buonarroti, Babeuf's colleague and historian, lived in Belgium for a great part of his life and published in Brussels his account of the Conspiracy of the Equals. Brussels was second only to Paris as a centre for German exiles in the 1840s, when Marx spent some time there before his removal to London. Under Napoleon III many Frenchmen found refuge in Belgium, and journals and books which could not be safely published in France were issued from Brussels or Ghent. French-speaking Belgians worked in France in substantial numbers ; and there was much coming and going across the frontier.

Up to 1848, despite the German exiles, France, as the principal centre of revolutionary movements and ideas, exerted a pervasive influence, whereas the Flemings were comparatively little affected by either German or Dutch radical thinking. Holland indeed made until considerably later hardly any contribution to the stream of Socialist thought, playing only a very small part in the First International, and that mainly as a reflection of Belgian-Flemish activity. The relative intellectual isolation of the Flemings makes it the more remarkable that they should have poured into the Socialist stream two contributions as substantial as those of Kats and de Keyser ; whereas Colins is to be reckoned rather as the last of the French-inspired utopian system-makers than as a distinctively Belgian thinker. In de Paepe, as we shall see, these French and Flemish influences were synthesised ; but in the subsequent development of Belgian Socialism in the hands of Louis Bertrand the French influence again preponderated, whereas the two continued to be combined in the development of the Co-operative movement under Eduard Anseele. In Holland, the first figure of importance was H. Gerhard (1829–86), who organised the cloth-workers and wrote a pamphlet on the International in 1872. But Flemings from Belgium, such as Van den Abeele, played the leading part in spreading Internationalist ideas among the Dutch. These phases belong, however, to a later chapter. At this point, I have been seeking only to make clear that among the intellectual forces that went into the making of the great European Socialist revival of the 1860s and 1870s the Belgian contribution ought not to be ignored, as it so often has been.

CHAPTER V

LASSALLE

IN the development of German Socialism after the collapse of 1848 pride of place must be conceded, not to Marx, but to Ferdinand Lassalle. Marx, in exile, was not in a position to act directly on German opinion, nor had he in fact the qualities required for popular leadership. After the few issues of the *Neue Rheinische Zeitung* in 1850 and the single volume of his *Collected Works* issued by Hermann Becker in Cologne in 1851 — the second never appeared — no work of Marx was published in Germany until the *Critique of Political Economy* appeared in Berlin in 1859 ; and even his booklet on the Cologne Communist trials, printed in Switzerland in 1853 for circulation in Germany, failed to reach those for whom it was intended.[1] Marx had a few faithful friends and admirers in Germany throughout these years ; but he had no popular following, even after the publication of the *Critique*. Not until Wilhelm Liebknecht returned to Germany in 1862 had he an emissary there capable of expounding his essential doctrines in popular form ; and not till the International Working Men's Association had become a challenging force did Marx's name come to mean anything to the majority even of the leaders of the growing German Socialist movement.

The man who became the leading figure in German Socialism and the effective creator of the first considerable Socialist movement in that country was Lassalle. Lassalle was indeed well acquainted with Marx's writings and again and again referred, and deferred, to Marx as his master. But Lassalle was far too much a natural leader of men, and too conscious of his own intellectual qualities, ever really to accept another's leadership, either in practice or in theory ; and although Marx

[1] *The Eighteenth Brumaire of Napoleon Bonaparte* was published in German in New York. It appeared in J. Weydemeyer's *Die Revolution* in 1852. Marx's pamphlet against Willich, *Der Ritter vom edelmüthigen Bewusstsein*, also appeared in New York and London in 1853.

was at first attracted by Lassalle's brilliance and hopeful of being able to guide him into the right course, it is inconceivable that, had they been both in Germany, they could have worked together. In practical politics Lassalle would have expected to lead, not to follow, in the assurance that he had the *flair* ; and in matters of theory, whatever deference he might have been prepared to pay to Marx as a thinker, he would have gone his own way regardless of Marx's objections. No doubt there was much, in theory, that they had in common ; and the issues which divided them seemed unimportant to most of their followers. But in practical politics they were poles apart, because Marx was for the *bourgeoisie* against the Prussian State, whereas Lassalle was fully prepared to side with the Prussian State against the *bourgeoisie*. Behind this difference, moreover, lay a theoretical difference which was much more fundamental than their rival doctrines about the forces determining wages or about the value of Co-operative enterprise. Lassalle, with all his taste for personal ascendancy, had a deep belief in universal suffrage as a means of transforming the State into an instrument of democracy : Marx, with all his readiness to help the *bourgeoisie* to power and all his insistence on the need for parliamentary action, had none. But this came out clearly only at a much later stage, long after Lassalle's premature death : in the 1850s their differences appeared to turn rather on economics than on politics, and even more on the contrast in their circumstances than on either. Marx, the exile living in poverty, resented Lassalle's opulence and profusion, even while he was putting himself about to entertain him when he visited London ; and Lassalle's homage to Marx's intellectual eminence was touched with a suspicion of patronage which Marx was not the man to forgive.

Nevertheless, till 1859 there was no open breach. It was Lassalle who found a Berlin publisher for the *Critique of Political Economy* and negotiated favourable financial terms. Lassalle sent Marx a copy of his revolutionary verse drama, *Franz von Sickingen*, published in the same year as the *Critique*, and, though he was in complete disagreement with it, arranged for the issue in Berlin of Engels's pamphlet, *Po and Rhine*, which dealt with the attitude which Prussia ought to take up in face of Napoleon III's attempt to intervene in the dispute between Austria and Italy over Lombardy. Engels, fully supported by Marx, favoured Prussian intervention on the Austrian side against Napoleon. Lassalle, on the other hand, held that Prussia had no vital interest in defending Austrian control in North Italy, and regarded war between France and Germany on such an issue as a danger to European culture and to the prospects of European Socialism. On this question, of which it would take too long to consider the rights and wrongs, the uneasy alliance which had been maintained between Marx and Lassalle began to fall apart. Marx even accused Lassalle, quite mistakenly, of having deliberately obstructed the publication of the *Critique*, and thereafter he regarded Lassalle's every move with a distrust which sharpened into deeper antagonism as Lassalle established his position of leadership in the German working-class movement. This, however, did not prevent Marx from continuing his relations with Lassalle, with whom he could not afford to break openly without isolating himself from the growing Socialist movement in the German States.

Ferdinand Lassalle was born in 1825 and died in 1864, having crowded into his brief life an immense amount of activity, not only as the outstanding figure in the German working-class movement, but also as philosopher and lawyer, as the defender of Countess Hatzfeldt in her protracted struggle with her husband,[1] and, last but not least, as an amorous adventurer whose advances a remarkably large number of women seem to have been unable to resist. Lassalle's career

---

[1] The Hatzfeldt case has nothing whatsoever to do with Socialism, and is connected with Lassalle's politics only in the sense that it enabled him to appear as the champion of a wronged wife against a German aristocrat who was abusing his wealth and power in refusing her justice. When Lassalle first met the Countess in 1845, at the age of 20, she had already been long separated from her husband and was involved in a complicated legal dispute with him concerning both her property rights and the custody of the children. Lassalle seems to have taken up her case in a spirit of romantic quixotry. It led him into a ten years' struggle, interrupted only by the Revolution of 1848-9, for his part in which at Düsseldorf he suffered a year's imprisonment. The Hatzfeldt case was fought in all before thirty-six courts of law, with an incredible amount of publicity and a great variety of incident — including that of the famous casket stolen from the Count's mistress, Baroness Meyendorf, in order to get possession of a deed required for the establishment of the Countess's claims. The case ended in victory for the Countess, who in gratitude settled on her champion a handsome annuity and became his eager supporter in the political crusade to which he turned his energies when it had been won.

has exercised an unfailing appeal to biographers, and there are so many Lives of him that it is quite unnecessary in a work of this kind to go over the oft-trodden ground again. Yet Lassalle's personality is so intimately connected with his contribution to the development of German Socialism that it is impossible to leave out altogether those parts of his activities which seem, on the face of the matter, to have little or no connection with his Socialism. The most that can be done is to deal with these aspects as briefly as possible and only where their relevance to his importance in Socialist development is manifestly high.

Lassalle was a Silesian Jew, born in Breslau at a time when Jews in Prussia still suffered the disabilities of unequal citizenship and still more the stigma of social inferiority. From his childhood Lassalle deeply resented the dis-esteem in which he was held on account of his race, and this resentment aggravated his ambition, which even without it would have known few enough bounds. He was determined from the very beginning of his career to make a resounding impression and to force his way to some sort of leadership, despite the handicaps under which he laboured. In whatever he set his hand to he was determined to brook no defeat. Just as he fought on year after year in the apparently hopeless cause of Countess Hatzfeldt and brought it after all to a triumphant conclusion, so he spared no labour to achieve recognition as a great philosopher, a great jurist, and latterly a great political leader of the German nation. Hampered throughout his brief career by ill health he conquered his physical as well as his racial disabilities by sheer power of will, packing into his life so great a variety of activities and experiences as to astonish both his contemporaries and his biographers. As both writer and politician he had the advantage of a distinctive, though often unduly flamboyant, literary style, which he could turn with ease from philosophical abstractions to pamphlet appeals couched in plain language which the ordinary man could readily understand. He was certainly both vain and egotistic, but there was also in his nature an element of quixotry which allowed him to throw himself wholeheartedly into a cause on the sole condition that his way of doing so would resound to his own glory. Having a great belief in himself and in the virtues of leadership, he had in him the makings of a *Führer*, and undoubtedly fancied himself in his final years as the prospective unquestioned leader of a revitalised German nation. There was only one man to whom he behaved over a considerable number of years as pupil to master, and that man singularly enough was Karl Marx.

Much has been written about the relations between Marx and Engels and Lassalle. There are a great many references to Lassalle in the letters of Marx and Engels, and many of them are uncomplimentary. Engels greatly disliked Lassalle from the first, and continued his dislike to the end, though even he recognised that Lassalle had done more than any other man towards creating a national movement of the German working class. Marx, on the other hand, seems clearly to have begun by liking Lassalle, despite the extreme difference of their temperaments, and to have turned round only gradually as he saw Lassalle establishing over the workers of Germany an influence hostile to his own, and, as he thought, against the interests of the workers' revolution. At all events, it is certain that Marx for a considerable time regarded Lassalle as the most valued of his informants in Germany after the collapse of the revolutionary movements of 1848, that he repeatedly borrowed money from him (and repaid it), and that as late as 1861 he quite seriously contemplated collaborating with Lassalle in the production of a new Socialist journal, which was to provide a point of focus for the development of the German movement. Marx, however, even while he was in close relations with Lassalle over German affairs, was keenly conscious of the ideological differences between them, and we find him in his letters to Engels complaining that Lassalle had plagiarised and distorted many of his ideas. The letters leave a clear impression that Marx was growingly jealous of Lassalle's position and influence in Germany ; nor was this at all unnatural in one conscious of great powers of organisation as well as of theorising, who was compelled to live in exile and in poverty while his rival for the leadership had both plenty of money at his disposal and the advantage of being able to lead the German workers' movement in Germany itself and not in exile.

Lassalle's name was not really Lassalle ; it was Lassal. He himself added the two final letters, thus Frenchifying the name, either because it sounded more aristocratic that way, or perhaps because it sounded more revolutionary — for France was then still the unquestioned centre of European Socialist thought. Either motive fits Lassalle's curious personality, for he was at one and the same time an aspirant to aristocratic friendships and ways of behaviour, and a quite genuinely revolutionary leader. His father was well-to-do in an economic sense, and Lassalle himself was never seriously pressed for money, though he was a great spender, both on himself and as the champion of the Countess Hatzfeldt during the long period of litigation on her behalf. His father was incredibly indulgent to him. Again and again we find him writing for money and getting it, even when the older Lassal had to borrow it. The father greatly worshipped the clever and ambitious son, and was prepared to sacrifice anything for him, and Lassalle, despite juvenile escapades, received the best education that money could buy. His university career turned him into an ardent Hegelian, as it had turned so many earlier leaders of the German Left, including Marx himself. Lassalle, however, unlike Marx, remained a Hegelian idealist to the end of his life ; he neither accepted nor fully understood Marx's inverted Hegelianism as expressed in the *Communist Manifesto* and later in many other writings. The awareness of this unrepentant idealism of Lassalle's was one of the factors that turned Marx against him, especially when Lassalle most seemed to be echoing some of Marx's leading ideas. This idealism comes out very clearly in both of the two major books which Lassalle produced — *Heraclitus the Obscure*, published in 1857, and his *System of Acquired Rights*, published four years later. In both these works his method is entirely that of Hegel, with no trace of Marxian influence. What he learned from Marx comes out only in his political speeches and pamphlets, and even in these, when he appears to be echoing Marx, he is quite often in fact echoing rather Marx's predecessors in the formulation of the theory of surplus value, or his personal friend Rodbertus, to whom in a number of respects he was much more akin in ideas than he was to Marx. Thus, in the *System of Acquired Rights* Lassalle sets out to discuss the entire basis on which the inheritance of property rests in different types of civilisation. In the enormous excursus on the main work which forms the second volume he formulates a theory that different systems of inheritance rest on different national conceptions of the survival of man after death. The Roman conception, as developed in Roman law, he believed to rest on the notion of the will of the dead man as persisting after his death, so that the acts of his heir were regarded as acts carried out in pursuance of the dead man's will. As against this, Lassalle sets the Germanic conception of inheritance which he regards as resting on the notion not of the survival of the individual as a source of will, but rather of the family as persisting beyond the death of any individual member. This explanation of the differences between Roman and Germanic law in respect of inheritance is not likely to be accepted by anyone to-day. Its importance for the present purpose lies not in its truth or falsehood but in the account which Lassalle gives of the origin of the two discrepant ideals. Instead of seeking to explain the different systems of inheritance in relation to either the economic conditions in which they arose in early Roman and early Germanic systems, or indeed in any terms of historical environment, Lassalle simply attributes the two views to the different *Volksgeist* of the Roman and Germanic peoples, leaving entirely unexplained why one people should have had one *Volksgeist* and another a quite different one.

This attempt to explain social institutions in terms of the spirit of the people was, of course, a part of Lassalle's essentially Hegelian attitude. In his opinion, history was at bottom the history of ideas in the minds of nations, which, like Hegel, he regarded as more real than the minds of individual men. These ideological 'realities' were the true moving forces in history, of which the external events were only manifestations. No view could be more sharply in contrast with that of Marx, whose sociological doctrine was that ideas were always to be explained in terms of concrete conditions which had given rise to them and not *vice versa*.

There seems no need for the purposes of this book to delve more deeply into the doctrines expounded by Lassalle in his *System of Acquired Rights*, for the only relevance which these have to Socialism is that Lassalle does bring an immense array of legal acumen and Hegelian logic-chopping to the demonstration of the proposition that society is under no obligation to accept as irreversible rights which have in fact been recognised in the past but have ceased, as he puts it, to correspond any longer to the 'spirit of the people'. A man has a right, Lassalle argues, only to that which is the outcome of his own voluntary action. All other rights are merely contingent on their correspondence with the claims recognised by the *Volksgeist* — claims which are bound to change as the *Volksgeist* itself alters its content. Accordingly, there is no true legal barrier in the way of legislation that does away with prescriptive rights. The only correct test of the validity of such rights is to be found in the popular consciousness. In relation to the institutions of Germany in Lassalle's day and to the claims of the privileged classes this line of argument had no doubt its temporary importance. Lassalle was arguing against a type of governing class of which only the relics are left in the advanced societies of to-day, though the old mentality still keeps its force in many backward societies in which social revolution has still to occur. In Western thought, or at any rate in any part of the Western thought with which we need to concern ourselves in dealing with the history of Socialism, no elaborate argument is needed to demonstrate that there is nothing sacred about the prescriptive claims of privileged classes.

Lassalle's importance as a Socialist thinker must rest not on the elaborately argued sociological jurisprudence of his *System of Acquired Rights* but on his more directly political and economic writings. Of these there is not a great deal — a number of speeches, some of them elaborately written for publication as pamphlets, a small polemical book directed against the Co-operative projects of the Liberal Schulze-Delitzsch, and much that is interesting in letters addressed to various correspondents, including Marx and especially Rodbertus. This does not add up to a very formidable total. Nor is there much that is original in the content of Lassalle's political and economic thought. He expressed more than once the intention of writing a large work on Political Economy, but he never did write it or, as far as can be seen, even begin writing it. Lassalle's central political idea was that the German working class must organise itself into a powerful nation-wide association with universal direct suffrage as its first demand. Without universal suffrage [1]

---

[1] I use the phrase 'universal suffrage', rather than 'manhood suffrage', because both Lassalle and Blanc in common with most of their contemporaries used it, even though they were not thinking of it as involving votes for women.

nothing, he thought, or at any rate nothing of substance, could be done to improve the economic position of the workers. As soon, however, as the workers got the right to vote, they would get therewith the power to make the State subservient to their desires. The State would become, in fact, what Lassalle always insisted that it necessarily was, always and everywhere — as far as it was legitimate at all — the instrument for the further-ance of the general good of the entire people. Lassalle went on to urge the workers, having won the vote, to use it for the purpose of insisting that the State should enable them to become their own masters by placing at their disposal the capital and credit that would allow them to dispense with capitalist employers and to reserve for themselves the whole product of their collective production. In other words, Lassalle was putting forward a programme which very closely resembled what Louis Blanc had been advocating in France during the decade before the Revolution of 1848. Blanc, too, had demanded universal suffrage as the basis for 'the organisation of labour'. He had called on the workers to win universal suffrage and to use their power to compel the State to set up national workshops which would thereafter be conducted not by the State but by self-governing workers' corporations in such a way as to ensure to all men both the 'right to work' and the enjoyment of the full product of their labours. There was no essential difference between what Louis Blanc had advocated in France in the 1840s and what Lassalle was advocating in the Germany of the 1860s, though of course the political environment in which these doctrines were preached was very different in the two cases. Moreover, Lassalle like Louis Blanc stressed the indis-pensability of manhood suffrage and of State action because he held it impossible for the workers to achieve their economic emancipation by means of voluntary Co-operative effort without State aid. Louis Blanc had been arguing against the Fourierists and various other advocates of Co-operative enterprise that, in the nature of things, voluntary Co-operation, even if it could be used to improve the position of small groups of workers, could do nothing to affect the general exploitation of the working classes as long as private property in land and capital remained intact.

In the Germany of Lassalle's day Schulze-Delitzsch, closely

associated with the Liberal Progressive Party in Germany, had been advocating voluntary credit unions and Co-operative Societies as means of escape for the workers from their subjection to capitalist exploitation. The Christian Socialists in Great Britain had been doing the same thing, as the Owenites had done it before them on a much larger scale. Lassalle's answer to Schulze-Delitzsch, to the extent to which it was valid, struck equally at all attempts to advance towards the new society by means of voluntary Co-operation either of the producers or of the consumers. Lassalle rested his attack on Schulze-Delitzsch's policy on his conception of 'the iron law of wages'. This he took over from the pre-Marxian economists, who had discovered a foundation for it in Ricardo's economic doctrines, and from Rodbertus, who had put forward much the same notion independently, though later, in Germany. There is, of course, a doctrine closely similar to Lassalle's doctrine of the iron law to be found in Marx's *Communist Manifesto*, but Marx insisted that Lassalle's conception of the nature of the law of wages and his own were fundamentally different. Lassalle, like Marx, and also like Ricardo, in advancing a theory that the wages of labour under capitalism tended always and everywhere towards subsistence level, admitted that 'subsistence level' was not something invariable but depended on the conception of the minimum standard of living existing in a society at a particular time. Neither Ricardo nor Marx nor Lassalle said that under all conditions the labourer was necessarily ground down to an unvarying physical minimum of existence. They all regarded 'subsistence level' as something that was bound to change over long periods with changing conditions of production and social organisation. Lassalle did, however, hold that, subject to such long-term changes, the actual wages paid under capitalism were continually oscillating round a level of physical subsistence which remained unchanged over long periods, and that fluctuations above or below this level depended on the relative conditions of the supply of and demand for labour. These fluctuations of supply in relation to demand he believed to depend primarily on the Malthusian law of subsistence, that is, on the tendency of population to press continually on the means of subsistence in such a way that any rise in real wages would be followed by an increase of population, which would in due course, through the increased supply of labour, bring wages down again to or below subsistence level, whereas any fall of real wages below the current subsistence level would be reflected in a reduction in population, and, through the fall in the number of workers seeking jobs, would bring wages back to or above the current level of subsistence.

Marx, recognising the apparent similarity of this theory of wages to his own, nevertheless dissented from it sharply on a number of counts. In the first place, what Lassalle said about the inefficacy of voluntary Co-operation in improving the workers' position under capitalism applied to Trade Unionism fully as much as to Co-operation. If, because of the operation of the iron law of wages, it was impossible for the workers to better their economic condition by means of Co-operation, was it not equally out of the question for Trade Unions to achieve any real advantages for their members until the capitalist system had been destroyed ? Lassalle and his followers were inclined to argue that it was impossible for Trade Unions to achieve really beneficial results within a capitalist society, though later they did attempt to organise Trade Unions in connection with the General Union of German Workmen, mainly as auxiliaries to the movement for political emancipation. Marx, on the other hand, believed strongly in the value of Trade Unions and of efforts to better the workers' conditions, even while capitalism continued in being. He pointed again and again to the positive achievement by the British workers of factory legislation limiting the working day to ten hours in the textile factories, and in his connections with the British working-class movement he was always seeking to identify his policy with the immediate demands of the Trade Union movement — a policy which he also endeavoured to make the basis of the International Working Men's Association. Thus Marx and Lassalle differed sharply about the utility of Trade Unions and their relation to the working-class struggle. Secondly, Marx's theory of wages, though like Lassalle's it emphasised the tendency for wages under capitalism to be prevented from rising above subsistence level, did not explain this tendency mainly in terms of the Malthusian law of population. On Marx's showing wages were kept down in a capitalist society primarily because of the capitalist monopoly of the means of production, which enabled the owners of capital to appropriate the benefits of increasing productivity. Marx held that wages tended to be pressed down below existing conventional levels of subsistence because of the inherent 'contradictions' of capitalism — by which in this connection he meant primarily the tendency of capitalism to enlarge production faster than the means of consumption in the hands of the main body of the people. Thus, whereas Lassalle presented a picture of wages oscillating continually round a subsistence level which was fixed over long periods, Marx stressed the tendency under capitalism for the working classes to fall into 'increasing misery' as the more skilled workers and the displaced members of the *petite bourgeoisie* were flung down into the general mass of labourers by the increasing concentration of capital and the development of mass-production techniques. Marx further stressed the importance of capitalist crises in depressing working-class standards. His view was in general even more pessimistic than Lassalle's, but it was also less inflexible and made larger allowances for the possibilities of successful working-class action in resisting the capitalist forces which were driving the workers into a condition of increasing misery. In effect, whereas Lassalle argued that nothing could be done to help the workers without the capture of the State machine and its use to enable the working class to become its own master, Marx, laying emphasis on the value of the day-to-day struggle, looked forward rather to a revolution based on the development of the workers' movement as an economic force than to a predominantly political agitation for universal suffrage.

Underlying this difference about the utility of Trade Unions was a much more fundamental difference concerning the value of universal suffrage and the nature of the State itself. Lassalle always assumed that the workers, if they could but win the vote, would be able without difficulty to convert the State into an instrument of their purposes. Marx, on the other hand, was sceptical about the effects of universal suffrage, which he thought of as more likely to lead to some form of Caesarist dictatorship than to the execution of the workers' will. Marx never regarded the State as primarily a legislative machine for grinding out whatever kind of legislation the electors wanted. He regarded it rather as an essentially coercive instrument of class power, the character of which could not be changed by a mere widening of the franchise. Accordingly, although he supported the movement of the English Trade Unions for political reform which led up to the Reform Act of 1867, he regarded success in widening the franchise as merely a means of increasing the power of the working class to act upon the State and not as a means whereby the State itself could be converted into an instrument of the workers. Lassalle, on the other hand, dominated as he was by the Hegelian view of *Staatsrecht*, thought of the State as not in its essence a class institution at all but an agency for properly expressing the will of the whole people — an agency which had been perverted through the ages from its true purpose but could be brought into the right path by means of universal suffrage. To Marx it seemed absurd, and indeed treasonable, that the whole working-class movement should be invited to look to the State as the means of emancipating the workers or of securing to them the whole produce of their collective labour. Marx was also critical of Lassalle's State-financed workers' Co-operatives on the ground which Lassalle himself had urged against Schulze-Delitzsch, namely that such associations armed with State capital and credit could easily turn into privileged bodies still pursuing private profit at the expense of less privileged groups. Lassalle's doctrine seemed to Marx to rest on the idea that the worker, if not individually, yet as a member of a limited group, had an identifiable product to the value of which he was entitled as the reward of his labour, whereas in Marx's view the increasingly co-ordinated character of production was fast depriving both individual workers and limited groups of any specific product of their own, and was constituting the whole mass of social labour the creator of a class social product to which the workers' claim was essentially collective in the fullest sense. The notion of the unity of the class counted for much in Marx's economic theory, as was made manifest in the treatment of value and surplus value both in his *Critique of Political Economy* (1859) and in the opening volume of *Capital* (1867). Lassalle's belief in the virtues of State-financed workers' Co-operatives, accordingly, appeared to Marx as yet another instance of *petit-bourgeois* illusion.

But most of all was Marx antagonistic to the entire Lassallian conception of the State as an ideological expression of the *Volksgeist*. In Lassalle this notion of the State was closely linked with that of the national unity of the German people. Marx's Socialism was essentially international, often though he stressed the special quality of the contribution which the Germans were equipped to make to the consciousness of the world proletariat. Lassalle, on the other hand, thought primarily in German terms, and set out to build up the German working class as a political power in close connection with the achievement of German political unity. Both Marx and Lassalle were opposed to the *klein-deutsch* notion of German unity, and looked for a movement of the German people as a whole against the existing forms of government in the German State. But in practice Lassalle was far more disposed than Marx to accept Prussia as the main instrument through which German unity would have to be achieved. Marx, as a Rhinelander, belonged essentially to the cultural tradition of the West. Lassalle, as a Silesian, thought much more in terms of a Germany pivoted upon Berlin. Marx was always inclined to regard Bismarck and the Prussian Government as the allies of Czarist Russia against the West, and to insist accordingly on a strong opposition to Prussian hegemony. Lassalle, on the other hand, much less Russophobe than Marx, was prepared to coquet with Bismarck in the hope of persuading the 'Iron Chancellor' to espouse some of his plans in order to enlist the nationalism of the German proletariat on the side of his endeavours towards the unification of Germany under Prussian leadership ; and Bismarck, for his part, was not unwilling to listen to Lassalle, though there is no evidence that he had ever the smallest intention of making a real concession. It was after all Bismarck who adopted manhood suffrage as a basis first for the Assembly of the North German Confederation and subsequently for the Reichstag in the new German Empire of 1870, well understanding that universal suffrage by no means involved a worker-controlled State in a country still predominantly agricultural, or as long as the power of the elected Chamber was restricted by the existence both of an Upper House chosen on a quite different basis and of an executive authority mainly immune from control by the popular Chamber.

Bismarck was able to think in these terms because for him the problem was to enlist as much popular support as possible behind a system of autocratic monarchical government in opposition to the demands of the German middle classes as represented in Lassalle's day by the Progressive Party. Lassalle, in attempting to build up an independent workers' political party, found himself in sharp opposition to the Progressives, with whom the existing workers' associations over most of Germany had been co-operating in the campaign for constitutional government. These German Progressives, representing mainly the merchant and trading classes and the professional groups in German society, for the most part combined opposition to autocratic government with a fervent belief in the virtues of economic *laissez-faire*. They were, therefore, acutely hostile to any forms of working-class combination which threatened to demand economic intervention by the State in the interests of the poorer classes. On this account Lassalle regarded them, rather than the defenders of political autocracy, as the workers' worst enemies, and far from being prepared to co-operate with the *bourgeoisie* in wresting political concessions from the reactionary governing classes, he set out to build up an independent working-class movement in fervent hostility to the Progressives and to detach the workers who had been acting under Progressive leadership from their allegiance. He was even prepared, as his letters to Bismarck show, to contemplate the possibility of an alliance between the Prussian monarchy and the workers against the *bourgeoisie*, just as Bakunin and other Russians had cherished hopes of the Czar putting himself at the head of the people against their exploiters. How seriously Lassalle entertained such hopes must always remain in doubt : that he held them at all suffices to explain Marx's strong suspicions and hostility to his political line. For Marx, insistent though he was on the establishment of an independent working-class political movement, was bitterly hostile to Prussianism, and held that such a movement should for the time being co-operate with the *bourgeoisie* in attacking the government of the old privileged classes and should turn on its allies only when the Revolution had successfully overthrown the old order. This had been Marx's policy in the Revolution of 1848, and it continued to be his policy through the ensuing period. He was accordingly in strong opposition to Lassalle's attitude towards the *bourgeois* constitutional reformers, and was very ready to suspect Lassalle of going even further than he had actually gone towards allying himself with the Prussian autocracy against the Progressives. This difference in practical and immediate political strategy was closely entwined with the more theoretical differences between the Marxist and the Lassallian theories of the State.

Lassalle's meteoric career was cut short before he reached the age of 40. He died, as everyone knows, in a duel arising out of a love affair with a young woman nearly twenty years his junior, who had first promised to marry him and then, under pressure from her aristocratic parents, renounced him in favour of a rival lover. Outraged at the treatment of his beloved, and half beside himself with thwarted passion and fury, Lassalle challenged his rival to combat, and was mortally wounded. George Meredith made use of the affair in his novel *The Tragic Comedians*, and it is altogether too well known to need recounting again in this book. What concerns us is that death prematurely took Lassalle away hardly more than two years after he had launched his great political crusade, and before there had been time to give it any solid foundations. His missionary tours in 1863 and 1864 had been astonishingly successful and had given him an unchallenged personal ascendancy. But the whole movement had been to so great an extent his personal creation that its capacity to survive the loss of its leader was far from assured. Survive it did, however, despite the quarrels which beset it under the ineffective leadership of Lassalle's immediate successor, Bernhard Becker. Before long, it found in J. B. von Schweitzer a new leader of considerable capacity, who did much to raise its fortunes ; and it lasted on until 1875, when it was merged with the rival Social Democratic Party of Bebel and Liebknecht which had been founded at Eisenach in 1869.

To these developments, which followed Lassalle's untimely death, we shall come back in a subsequent chapter. At this point it is necessary only to observe that the removal of Lassalle's outstanding personality cleared the way for the development of Marxism under Liebknecht's leadership, and thus gave the German Socialist movement a character essentially different from that which it might have assumed had Lassalle been alive and active at the time of the Franco-Prussian War and the establishment of the German Reich with Bismarck in control. Perhaps it would have come to the same thing in the long run : who can say ? At all events, Marxism filled the void left by Lassalle's removal, and was able, by way of Germany, to impress itself on European Socialism as a whole very much more easily than it could have done had Lassalle not been a romantic lover as well as a Socialist agitator of genius.

CHAPTER VI

THE FIRST INTERNATIONAL
IN THE 'SIXTIES

THE International Working Men's Association, set up in London in 1864, began as a joint affair of the British and French Trade Unions, with the participation of a number of exiles from other parts of Europe who were then living in London. It is important to understand that it began primarily as a Trade Union affair — as an expression of the solidarity of the organised workers of France and Great Britain — and not as a political movement, although it had from the first political interests. There was indeed no other way in which it could have begun, in the two countries responsible for setting it on foot. In France, under the Second Empire, almost no political organisation of the workers could exist openly, though the first working-class candidates since the establishment of the Empire had made their appearance the year before — in 1863. Trade Unionism itself was only just achieving a very restricted toleration as Napoleon III, threatened by increasing *bourgeois* opposition to his régime, began very hesitantly to try out the possibilities of using the working class, or part of it, as a counterpoise to his *bourgeois* assailants. Even in 1864 Trade Unions were still illegal in France, though allowed to exist under the guise of friendly societies as long as they did not cause too much trouble. The Frenchmen who took part in setting up the International had come to London first, in 1862, not as Trade Unionists, but as members of an elected workers' delegation to the London International Exhibition. They had been sent, no doubt, with the idea that they would return impressed by the moderation and good sense of the New Unionists and Co-operators of the most advanced capitalist country in the world, and in a mood to discard the revolutionary traditions which still lived on in the underground sentiment of French working-class society.

In London these Frenchmen had found, in 1862, as the principal organiser of their welcome, the London Trades Council, set up only two years before as an outcome of the London building dispute of 1859. There was still, in Great Britain, no central organisation representing the Trade Union movement as a whole — much less any organised working-class party. Chartism had completely died out ; and with it had perished the International Association which, as successor to the Fraternal Democrats, had tried to maintain the links with continental Radicalism after the defeat of the Revolutions of 1848–9. The London Trades Council, as the most representative agency available, had to some extent taken over the functions of the older bodies and was giving them a new basis of Trade Union support. It took a leading part in supporting the cause of the North against the slave-owners in the American Civil War ; it arranged the welcome for the Italian as well as for the French working-class visitors to the International Exhibition of 1862 ; and it collaborated in the great reception organised for Garibaldi when he visited England in 1864. The London Trades Council also participated actively in 1862 in setting up the Trade Union Political Union, which developed into the National Reform League and became the principal working-class instrument in the struggle for parliamentary reform. But even in 1864, when the French delegates again visited London and put forward plans for an international organisation, these developments were still at an early stage.

Up to this point there had been closer relations between the British workers and the Italians than between the British and the French. There were strong sympathies between British Radicals, of the middle class as well as of the working class, and the Italian Nationalists headed by Mazzini and Garibaldi ; and the latter especially ranked as a popular hero, as was shown by the ovation given to him when he visited England in 1864. But the Italian societies formed under Mazzini's influence were not Trade Unions, or led mainly by workers. Though they were called workers' societies they were composed largely of intellectuals, and had little in common with the Trade Unionists who welcomed them when their delegates came to England in 1862. Nevertheless, the original idea of the English leaders was that they should form part of the International ; and the first draft of the proposed statutes for that body was drawn up by Garibaldi's lieutenant, Major Wolff, on the model of Mazzini's Italian Workmen's Associations. This was among the drafts that were thrust aside in favour of Marx's when it came to the point ; and the Mazzinists played no further part in the I.W.M.A. The French visitors were of an entirely different sort. They were workmen actually at the head of real Trade Unions which were fighting for recognition and for improved wages and working conditions. The English Trade Unionists recognised them as men and brothers, with whom they could make common cause. The I.W.M.A. was founded primarily as a joint British-French Trade Union movement, in which it was hoped to secure the co-operation of like-minded groups in other countries : and as a first step a selected band of exiles living in London was invited to take part in the proceedings. Marx owed his invitation mainly to the fact that two friends of his — the German tailor, George Eccarius (1818–89), and the Swiss watchmaker, Hermann Jung (1830–1901) — had won for themselves a place in the British Trade Union movement, and were able to get him in at the very start.

The Frenchmen who took part in the proceedings of 1864 — Henri Louis Tolain (1828–97), Charles Limousin, E. C. Fribourg, Eugène Varlin (1839–71), and Eugène Dupont (1831–81) — were respectively a carver, a lace-factory machinist, an engraver, a bookbinder, and a musical instrument maker. They were all, except Dupont, who lived in London, Parisian craftsmen, representing the small-scale industries which still held pride of place. Three of them — Tolain, Limousin, and Fribourg — were followers of Proudhon and opponents of collectivist Socialism, though not of working-class political action. The fourth Parisian, Eugène Varlin, was the principal organiser of the French Trade Union movement, and stood a long way to the left of the others : in modern language he would be called a Syndicalist. Dupont, the London resident, was more under the influence of Marx and his friends. But for the time being they were all agreed upon the necessity of building up a vigorous Trade Union movement, of taking independent working-class political action, and of emphasising the separation of the workers from the revolutionary radicalism both of the *bourgeoisie* and of the followers of Auguste Blanqui, between whom and the Proudhonists (Proudhon himself died in 1865) the conscious elements among the French workers divided their allegiance.

Marx himself, in 1864, spoke highly of Tolain and thought well of the whole group, though he was before long to fall foul of them all — except Dupont. In drawing up the Inaugural Address and Statutes of the International, Marx was careful to say nothing that might antagonise the two main groups which had to be induced to accept them if the new body was to be effectively set up. The greater part of the Inaugural Address was taken up by a sharp presentation of the contrast between the rapid growth of material wealth and income in the leading industrial countries and the continuing dire poverty of the main mass of the workers. As against this Marx dwelt on the great victory of the political economy of the working class over that of the *bourgeoisie* embodied in the Ten Hours Act of 1847 and in the factory legislation of other countries ; and he also greeted the successful establishment of Co-operative factories under the workers' control as a demonstration of working-class capacity and a foreshadowing of the industrial democracy of the future. At the same time he asserted the impossibility of the workers in general achieving their emancipation by means of voluntary Co-operation and the need for national action to bring the new industrial order into being. To this end, he said, the workers must organise for the achievement of political power. At the same time, they must build up their Trade Union movements both nationally and internationally for protection and resistance and as instruments for the creation of the new order. The Address ended with a paragraph in which the barbarous tyranny of Russia, the wrongs of Poland, and the sympathy shown by the governing classes of Europe for the American slave-owners were eloquently denounced, and the workers were called upon 'to master themselves the mysteries of international politics' and 'to vindicate the simple laws of morals and justice, which ought to govern the relations of private individuals, as the rules paramount of the intercourse of nations'.

All this, of course, could be read in more than one sense. Marx, in 1864, had not ceased to be a revolutionary Socialist, or abandoned the standpoint which he had taken up in the

Communist Manifesto sixteen years earlier. He had, however, become much more aware, after the experiences of 1848 and the following years, of the difficulties in the way of giving the revolution the required Socialist direction and of the dangers of mere revolutionism without the backing of a well-organised working-class movement. After 1850 Marx had ceased to belong to the extreme left of the revolutionary movement and had become acutely suspicious of mere *émeutisme*, which he saw as presenting unnecessary opportunities to the enemy to destroy the workers' organisations and deprive them of their leaders by imprisonment or exile. What he wanted to do in founding the International was to take the workers' movement as it was and to build up its strength in the day-to-day struggle, in the belief that it could thus be led into the right courses and develop, under ideological leadership, a revolutionary outlook arising out of the experience of the struggle for partial reforms, economic and political. He told Engels, in half-jesting regret, that he had been compelled to introduce into the International's Inaugural Address some phrases about right and justice, which would do no harm ; but it may be doubted whether the use of these phrases really jarred on him, for they were part and parcel of the driving force of the movement he was seeking to harness to his purposes, and the entire text of the Address bears witness to the strength of his own feeling about the crass injustice of the capitalist system as it had developed during the period which he passed under review.

In effect, Marx in 1864 saw revolution again approaching in Europe, and especially in France, but was less concerned to foment it than to do all he could to build up the power of the working-class movement in readiness for the situations to which it would give rise. In his correspondence we find him saying again and again that Great Britain, as the one great country in which large-scale capitalism had already driven out the older forms of production and destroyed the peasantry as an effective force, was the only country in which the real Socialist revolution could take place. But he was not expecting an early British revolution. He argued that revolution in Ireland, which would undermine the power of the British landowning aristocracy, was a necessary pre-condition of revolution in Great Britain ; and on that account he built large hopes on the Fenian movement, which rose to its height in the later 'sixties.[1] He did hope that the developing struggle of the British Trade Unions and the accompanying movement for parliamentary and social reform would lead to the establishment of a British working-class party sharply separate from Liberalism and growing in militancy as it came to grips with capitalism in both the economic and the political fields. This indeed might well have happened had not the British governing classes, Liberals and Tories alike, seen the danger and made large concessions in good time. As things turned out, the Irish revolt was easily suppressed ; while the Reform Act of 1867 and the full legalisation of Trade Unions in 1871 and 1875, the amendment of the Master and Servant Laws in 1867 and 1875, and the spate of social legislation which accompanied these concessions to the workers, effectively prevented the intensified class-struggle to which Marx had looked forward. But in 1864 all these developments were still in the future, and it was reasonable to expect that the British workers, even if they did not become revolutionaries, would at any rate become much more militantly class-conscious, and to hope that with Marx at hand to lend them the ideological power which he always regarded as mainly a prerogative of the Germans, this class-consciousness would take increasingly a Socialist colour. In the meantime, the immediate task was to create an international movement based directly on the British and French Trade Unions, to establish its headquarters in England, where it would be secure from embroilment in the sectarian quarrels of the French and from domination by Proudhon's influence, and to keep it open to the participation of the German exiles in

[1] The Irish Fenian Brotherhood (from '*fianna*', soldiers) was founded in 1858, with sections in Ireland and in the United States. Its leaders were James Stephens and John O'Mahony. It was a secret, oath-bound revolutionary society, with the object of bringing about a rebellion in Ireland accompanied by an attack on Canada from the United States and by disturbances among the Irish in Great Britain. The Irish rising was planned for 1865, but was forestalled by widespread arrests ; and the actual outbreak in 1867 was easily quelled. This outbreak was accompanied by the planned movements in England — the attack on Chester and Clerkenwell gaols, and the successful rescue of prisoners in Manchester. There were a number of executions and many Fenians were gaoled for long periods in connection with the events of 1867 ; and thereafter the Fenian movement took to political rather than insurrectionary methods. Marx's hopes of an Irish Rebellion were based on the rapid growth of Fenianism during the early 'sixties.

London, who had in his view the right ideology, though they had no national movement in Germany of a solidity comparable with that of the British, or even of the French.

It should be noted that neither in the Inaugural Address nor in the Preamble to the Rules of the International did Marx say anything at all about socialisation of the means of production. He spoke of Co-operative production as showing that large-scale industries could 'be carried on without the existence of a class of masters employing a class of hands'; and in stressing the limitations of voluntary Co-operative enterprise he urged that 'to serve the industrious masses, Co-operative labour ought to be developed to national dimensions, and consequently to be fostered by national means'. On this account and because the owning classes could be expected to resist their supersession, he argued that 'to conquer political power has become the great duty of the working classes'. He could not, even if he had wished to do so, have contended for the socialisation of the means of production in any more definite terms, because to do so would have brought him into sharp opposition to most of the French delegates, and probably to the leading British delegates as well. Tolain and his group were *mutuellistes*. The society to which they looked forward was one in which every man would own property and receive the full fruit of his own labour, either individually or as a member of a Co-operative producing group. The Proudhonists put their faith, as a means to this end, in a system of 'gratuitous credit' — that is, capital advances free of interest — to be made to producers, individually or in groups, through a People's Credit Bank which was to be an autonomous public institution, written into the Constitution, but in no respect under State control. They were strong opponents of economic equality, holding that each man should be rewarded according to his services, and strong upholders of a reformed system of property, freed from class-exploitation, because they regarded the family as the essential basis of society, and property in the land and other means of production as the necessary condition of the family's social existence. With this went an active hostility to women's labour, as destructive of family life, and to women's rights, as destructive of the patriarchal foundations of the family as an institution.

As for the English, who had no such dogmatic belief in

Proudhon's social doctrine, they might have been induced to accept socialisation of the land ; [1] but for them the socialisation of industry had hardly presented itself as an issue, except in the form of a traditional friendliness towards the idea of Co-operative production, which was undergoing in the 1860s a notable revival and was receiving considerable Trade Unionist support.

Marx, then, could not have come out as a collectivist without wrecking the International at the very start. But there is no indication in his correspondence that he even wished to do so. It was no part of his policy to persuade the existing States to take over the ownership and control of industry. He wanted, in due course, to overthrow these States and to replace them by States controlled and refashioned by the victorious workers. How precisely the workers would set about organising industry after the Revolution there is no sign that he had even considered: certainly he had no wish to make any pronouncement on the matter or to put it into the programme of the International. The tasks he envisaged for the International, in the immediate future, were to fight for improved conditions both by Trade Union methods and by agitation for further laws on the lines of the Ten Hours Act — and, at the same time, to build up a workers' party with a view to the conquest of political power. The question of organising industry under the workers' authority could be left over until after the workers had won power. In the meantime, the Co-operative producers' societies existed to foreshadow how it could be done.

The question of Co-operation, rather than that of socialisation, was uppermost in Marx's mind in 1864 for several sufficient reasons. First and foremost, it was the leading issue in the developing German Socialist movement. Ferdinand Lassalle had launched two years before his General German Workmen's Association, of which the outstanding demand was that the State should place capital and credit at the disposal of workers' Co-operatives and should thus enable them to replace capitalist industry. This was a revival of the programme which Louis

---

[1] Actually, a considerable controversy developed in Great Britain in the late 'sixties and early 'seventies over the question of land nationalisation. The Land and Labour League, which Marx regarded as one of his principal auxiliaries, advocated nationalisation of the land. Marx's lieutenant, Eccarius, was joint secretary, and the Owenite, John Weston, treasurer.

Blanc had launched in France in 1839, in his *Organisation du travail* ; and it was put forward as the Socialist answer to the many who urged the workers, instead of chasing political phantoms, to put their whole effort into the founding of voluntary Co-operative producing societies as means to the emancipation of labour. Such ideas, which went back to Fourier and to Owen, as we have seen had been taken up, shorn of their more revolutionary aspects, by many Conservative and Liberal social reformers as counterblasts to Radical Socialism. In Germany in the 1860s they were advocated especially by the progressive Liberal, Hermann Schulze-Delitzsch, against whom Lassalle directed his main attack. Lassalle, as we saw, argued against Schulze-Delitzsch, first that as wages under capitalism were held down to subsistence level by an 'iron law', any advantages the workers might have reaped from consumers' Co-operation would be wrested from them by means of wage reductions, and secondly that producers' Co-operatives set up by voluntary action could do no more than create small privileged groups of workers, who would be withdrawn from the class-struggle without doing anything to help the general emancipation of labour. It was necessary, he argued, for the workers' Co-operatives to have the support of the State, and to be in possession of sufficient capital resources to enable them to withdraw all the best labour from the capitalists, so as to compel the latter either to raise wages and improve conditions or to go out of business — which, indeed, he thought was what would happen to them in the long run if the State took the workers' part. In effect, Lassalle was challenging the entire *laissez-faire* doctrine, and was arguing that the 'iron law of wages' would cease to operate if the State intervened to regulate the conditions of production in the workers' interests. Accordingly, borrowing an idea from Proudhon as well as from Louis Blanc, he advocated a system of State credit on a scale sufficient to enable the entire working class to become its own master. This, he held, required the establishment of universal suffrage, which would convert the State into the guardian of the workers' interests ; and accordingly universal suffrage was made the first plank in the programme of the General German Workmen's Association, as the means towards the establishment of the new system of State-financed Co-operative production.

Marx, as we have seen, was at many points highly critical of these views of Lassalle's. He did not believe in the 'iron law of wages', in the form in which Lassalle held it ; and the difference was of practical importance because Lassalle's doctrine implied that Trade Unions could do nothing to improve conditions under capitalism, whereas Marx held strongly that they could do a good deal. Moreover, Marx entirely disapproved of asking help from any State except a workers' State set up on the ruins of the State of the exploiters. He accused Lassalle, not without justice, of coquetting with Bismarck, and of being misled by his hatred of the *bourgeois* Progressives into a readiness to ally himself against them with the most reactionary forces in Germany. Marx had no love for the Progressives ; but he nevertheless held that they should be supported by the workers in their struggle against Prussian and other forms of German feudal autocracy. His own followers in Germany, headed by Wilhelm Liebknecht, were at that time working in uneasy alliance with the more advanced *bourgeois* democrats in many parts of Germany ; and Lassalle's policy seemed to him a betrayal of the Socialist cause. But he was opposed, not to State-financed Co-operatives as such, but to any proposal to seek the aid of the existing State, which he regarded as an essentially reactionary institution.

In France, the Proudhonists were also for the most part advocates of Co-operative enterprise, as an alternative to individual production, in the new order. But, as fierce opponents of the Second Empire, they would have nothing to do with proposals for State aid to Co-operatives from so tainted a source. They favoured voluntary workers' Co-operative productive societies, many of which were set up in France during the 'sixties ; but their proposals for 'gratuitous credit', after the collapse of Proudhon's attempt to found a Credit Bank on a voluntary footing, were regarded as appropriate only after the revolution which they expected soon to overthrow Napoleon's Empire. Thus, they were on Marx's side against Lassalle. In Great Britain, where the Co-operatives were developing on a purely voluntary basis, the question of State aid had not arisen since the early days of Robert Owen's propaganda, when he had called on the local poor law authorities to play their part in establishing 'Villages of Co-operation'. The climate of British opinion was wholly unfavourable to such ideas, because it was dominated by notions of *laissez-faire*, whereas neither Bismarck's Germany nor Napoleon's France had any theoretical objection to State intervention in economic affairs — though of course French and German *bourgeois* 'Liberals' did object most strongly. They, however, were in the opposition : they did not control the Governments.

At the Inaugural Conference of the International Working Men's Association, four countries were represented — not counting those which were nominally represented by exiles resident in London. These four were Great Britain, France, Belgium, and Switzerland — or rather Geneva, for no delegates came from other parts of Switzerland. Of these, Belgium had one delegate — César de Paepe — and Geneva two — the German J. P. Becker and the French refugee François Dupleix. Apart from Becker, Germany was represented only by exiles living in London — Marx himself, and his friends Eccarius, Friedrich Lessner, and Karl Schapper. France sent Tolain, Limousin, Fribourg, and Varlin — all from Paris ; and Dupont attended on behalf of the London French refugees. Great Britain was represented by George Odger, then President of the London Trades Council and on the point of becoming its Secretary, George Howell, its actual Secretary, W. R. Cremer, of the Carpenters' Union, who became the first Secretary of the International, and Marx's friend George Eccarius, the German tailor working in London. The contingent of the Congress was completed by the Polish exile, Bobczynski, the London-Swiss watchmaker, Hermann Jung, and the Italian, Major Wolff, who dropped out at an early stage.

There were no real representatives from Germany for two reasons. The one given, that the laws of Germany prohibited affiliation to international bodies, was hardly the real one — for it certainly did not apply to all the German States. The real reason was that the only large organised body of German workers in 1864, apart from local trade societies, was Lassalle's General German Workmen's Association — a body to which Marx by no means desired to extend an invitation. He preferred to wait, in the hope that Liebknecht would be able before long to build up a rival German workers' movement more suceptible to his influence and less suspect of a willingness to ally itself with the reactionary Government against the *bourgeois* Progressives. Marx's support in Germany came mainly from the Rhineland, whereas Lassalle's centre of operations had been Berlin, which Marx regarded as the home of eastern barbarism in comparison with the intellectual enlightenment of the German West. If he had summoned any of his own friends in Germany, they would have represented nobody except themselves, and the consequence would have been an absolute break with the Lassallians, which at that stage he did not want. Lassalle himself was killed in the famous duel in August 1864 ; and the future of his movement was thereafter for some time in doubt. In the circumstances the Lassallians could hardly have attended the London Congress, even if they had been invited — which in fact they were not.

As the Pole in effect represented nobody and the Italians whom Major Wolff represented were quite out of sympathy with an International resting mainly on Trade Unions, there remain to be considered, at this stage, only two countries — Belgium and Switzerland. Between these two a preliminary attempt to form an International had actually been made the previous year, when the Swiss, Dr. Pierre Coullery, had visited Belgium in pursuance of the project. Belgium, it should be emphasised, was at this time, next to Great Britain, the most highly industrialised country in Europe, with a developed capitalist structure and a continuous history of industrial warfare, especially in the coal-mining and metal-working areas. In the realm of ideas it was very open to French influence, which was strengthened by the presence of a large number of French refugees. But it had also a considerable tradition of Socialist thought of its own, both Walloon and Flemish. As we have seen, Jacob Kats, Napoléon de Keyser, and the Baron Colins had been its outstanding pioneers. In the 1860s its leading theorist was the young printer-doctor, César de Paepe (1842–90), who was to play a large part in the policy controversies within the International during the next few years. In 1864 he was only twenty-two, but already prominent. No other delegate from Belgium appeared at the gatherings of the International until the Brussels Congress of 1868, when the Belgians attended in force ; but de Paepe came again to the London Conference of 1865 and to the Lausanne Congress of 1867. At

London he was still something of a dark horse : his special contribution came only when the International settled down to discuss the problems of socialisation and control of industry.

Switzerland, we saw, sent to the Inaugural Conference J. P. Becker (1800–86), a German, an old Socialist and a friend of Marx, long settled in Geneva, and a Frenchman, Dupleix, also resident in Geneva, who became the editor of the International's first Swiss journal. The movement in Switzerland was still, in 1864, in an embryonic stage. The best-known exponents of Socialism were Becker and the reformist doctor, Pierre Coullery, who had a considerable following in the French cantons. The Swiss had more political liberty than existed anywhere else in continental Europe, and also a considerable movement of local Trade Unions in the leading towns. They had, however, no nation-wide organisation — none, even, that bound together the various districts of either French or German Switzerland. In the German districts there was not much movement of any sort, though there were groups of German exiles in some of the towns. In the French areas, Geneva, the most active centre, was dominated by the trade societies of the skilled crafts, most of whose members were citizens enjoying full electoral rights and acting politically in association with the middle-class Radicals. As against this, the building workers were mostly not citizens of Geneva, and had no votes ; and this group provided most of the working-class backing for the rival faction, which strongly opposed all collaboration with the Radicals and stood for a policy of direct action for the redress of grievances. In the rest of French Switzerland — the Jura — the predominant type of industry was domestic employment, especially in watch-making, in the service of capitalist merchants. These branches of small-scale production were already being threatened by the development of factory industries in Great Britain and the United States ; and conditions were getting worse. Many of the domestic workers were ready to rally behind any militant movement that would take up their grievances ; and the home-workers of Le Locle, La Chaux-de-Fonds, and other centres in or near the Jura became, with the Genevese building workers, the main basis for the Swiss following of Bakunin in the quarrel which finally rent the International asunder. Their outstanding local leader was soon to be James Guillaume

(1884–1916), the schoolmaster-printer-journalist who has left behind him by far the most informative of the many histories of the International.

These anarchistic groups did not make their appearance in the Congresses of the International till it met in Geneva in 1866. In the meantime Becker and Dupleix on the whole followed Marx's lead. At the Inaugural Congress Marx needed to bother only about the British and the French ; and these were in agreement in wishing to establish the International primarily on a Trade Union basis and not as a federation of political parties or as a primarily political body.

In the Preamble to the Rules, as adopted at the Inaugural Congress, appeared the following clause, which was destined to give rise to violent controversies at a later stage.

> That the economical emancipation of the working classes is therefore [1] the great end to which every political movement ought to be subordinated as a means.

This, like much else in the Address and Preamble, could be interpreted in different ways. It could be taken, as on the whole both the French and the English Trade Unionists took it, to involve the primacy of Trade Union action and the relative unimportance of political activity, except on a Trade Union basis. It could even be taken, as some of the French took it, as a warning against any form of political action that might involve the working-class movement in compromises with the existing State or with the political parties of the *bourgeoisie*. But it could also be taken, as Marx undoubtedly meant it, as an assertion of the necessity of political action by the workers as a means to their economic emancipation.

Confusion was made worse by the fact that when the Rules of the International were translated into French by the Paris Council, the words 'as a means' were dropped in the French version, which read simply as follows :

> Que l'assujetissement du travail au capital est la source de toute servitude : politique, morale et matérielle ;

[1] 'Therefore' refers back to the previous clause, which reads as follows : 'That the economical subjection of the man of labour to the monopoliser of the means of labour, that is, the sources of life, lies at the bottom of servitude in all its forms, of all social misery, mental degradation, and political dependence'.

Que, pour cette raison, l'émancipation économique des travailleurs est le grand but auquel doit être subordonné tout mouvement politique.

This undoubtedly has a different *nuance*, whether deliberately or not who shall say ? It emphasises much more unequivocally than the English version the subordinate nature of political action, and is quite consistent with ruling it out altogether. Marx, when he read it, went into a fury, and accused the Anarchists of having done it in order to falsify the purposes of the International. But it is quite possible that, even if the wish was father to the translator's phrasing, he was quite unconscious of altering the meaning. Whatever the truth on this point, the clause became a bone of high contention between the Marxists and the Anarchists in the later years of the International, when the struggle between the rival factions had been fully joined.

The International was launched at a moment when Europe was from end to end in a condition of acute disquiet, and it developed during the next few years in an environment of spreading wars and revolutions. In general, up to the outbreak of the Franco-Prussian War of 1870, these conditions favoured its growth ; and they certainly increased its stature in the eyes of its enemies, who were very ready to attribute to it every manifestation of popular unrest. The International also got the credit — or the blame — for the great increase in strikes, which was in fact largely the outcome of the economic crisis of 1866–7 and of the ensuing revival. It is probable that the existence of the International was a factor in stimulating the rapid growth of Trade Unionism in a number of countries during these years ; but to a considerable extent this growth would have occurred without it, as a natural reaction to the prevailing economic conditions. Certainly the course of Trade Union development in both Great Britain and France, and also in Belgium, can be explained without much reference to the International ; and in Germany the International had almost no influence on the course of events. In Spain, the great development of working-class organisation took place mainly in its name, but quite independently of any direction from the General Council in London ; and in Italy the movement was influenced much more by Bakunin than by Marx or the General Council, and never owed more than the barest allegiance to the

I.W.M.A. It is indeed difficult to point to any country in which the International as an organisation really supplied the main driving force. For the most part, the working-class movement in each country went its own way, whether or not it acted mainly in the International's name. The International gave some help in strikes, both by collecting money and by preventing the transport of strike-breakers across national frontiers ; but beyond this it could do little to guide the course of events. It was able to make a great deal of stir, and to arouse large fears in the minds of its opponents, as well as large hopes among its supporters. But its real power was always narrowly limited ; and the foundations of what power it had ever possessed had been undermined well before the doctrinal disputes within it had reached their head.

It is a point of some importance that the First International was neither, like its successor, the Second International, a federation of national parties, nor a body based on the affiliation of Trade Unions or other working-class bodies. It was made up, in each country, of *individual* members, who joined its branches and sections, paying contributions directly. The national Sections, where they existed, linked together local branches, and had to some extent a federal structure ; but the Trade Unions which were influenced and in some cases inspired by the International were not, as such, members of it. In France, for example, the organisation of the International in Paris and other cities existed side by side with, and independently of, the federal Trade Union structure. This separation was doubtless partly due to legal restrictions on both federal Trade Union combination and federal political organisation ; but it was also designed to constitute the branches and Sections as the organs of a militant working-class party leading and inspiring the mass movement.

It had been intended that the second Congress of the International, at which its constitution was to be definitely ratified, should meet in Belgium in 1865. But when the time came to make the arrangements, Belgium was regarded as unsuitable as a place of meeting because of a new law regulating the admission of foreigners, and apart from this it seemed unlikely that many delegates would be sent. The General Council therefore postponed the Congress for a year and convened instead a small

Conference in London to transact only pressing business. At this stage Marx was in a state of great enthusiasm about the development of the International in Great Britain and seems to have believed that he was pulling the strings of the British movement much more than he really was. The General Council set up in 1864, with its seat in London, had been given the double function of presiding over the International as a whole and of organising the British Section of the movement; and Marx readily attributed to its influence the action of the Trade Unions in launching their own Reform League to press for manhood suffrage and the ballot and also the movement towards linking up the Trade Unions into a comprehensive national organisation. It is true that at this time a number of the most influential leaders of the British Trade Unions were sitting on the International's General Council and playing an active part in its work ; but it hardly follows that they were following its leadership in the conduct of their domestic affairs. Indeed, the movement which brought the Trades Union Congress into being in 1868 owed much more to the initiative of the Miners and of the Trades Councils in Glasgow and the North of England than to the London Trades Council or to the group of Amalgamated Societies with headquarters in London ; and the Londoners, though the most active in the struggle for parliamentary Reform, were far from representing the most militant elements in the industrial movement. It is unlikely that the course of events in Great Britain would have been different in any important respect if the International had not existed. Marx undoubtedly induced the London Trade Union leaders to put their names to a number of documents which they would never have thought of drawing up without him, and it is beyond question that the prestige of the British movement made the apparent support given by its leaders a considerable factor in increasing its influence of the International in other countries. But these leaders were not at all disposed to let Marx or any other outsider run their movement for them. They went on building up their own organisation for the conduct of their home affairs, treating the International as a side-line ; and the very magnitude of the successes they achieved in 1867, both in the extension of the franchise to the urban workers and in the amendment of the Master and Servant Laws, made them less and not more revolutionary. Moreover, the Sheffield outrages of 1866 and the legal judgment in the case of Hornby *v.* Close the following year threw the Trade Unions on to the defensive and made the leaders less disposed to take any action calculated to frighten the British *bourgeoisie* even before they had themselves been thoroughly scared by the explosion of the Commune in Paris.

In France, meanwhile, the Internationalists also went their own way, governed much more by the course of events at home than by any directions from London. The restricted toleration accorded to the Trade Unions by Napoleon III from 1864 onwards by no means produced the hoped-for result of converting the working class to support of the Empire. On the contrary, the influence in the French movement passed by stages from Tolain and his fellow-moderates to a more militant group headed by Eugène Varlin. In 1868 the Paris workers set up a central Trade Union Federation independent of the Paris Council of the I.W.M.A., but living in the same building and in close relations with it ; and similar Federations soon came into being in a number of other towns, such as Lyons, Marseilles, Rouen, and Brest. Varlin went all over the country organising such Federations side by side with local Sections of the International ; and for the most part they turned out to be a good deal to the left of the original Proudhonist group. Tolain continued to be the leading French spokesman at the Congresses and Conferences of the International ; but in France itself he was losing ground to such men as Varlin and Benoît Malon in Paris, André Bastelica in Marseilles, and Albert Richard in Lyons, whose outlook was more Syndicalist than *mutuelliste* and who were soon to take sides against Tolain in the dispute over collective ownership and at the same time against Marx on the question of political action and what they called his 'authoritarian Communist' policy.

At the Geneva Congress of 1866 these issues had not yet come to a head. The main business of the Congress was to give the International a definite Constitution by ratifying or amending the Constitution adopted at the Inaugural Congress of 1864. This did not prove a highly controversial matter — the less so because the divergence between the English and French texts of the Preamble, which was endorsed without discussion, had not yet come to light. In the debate on the Constitution, the only sharp dispute arose out of the desire of a majority of the French delegates to restrict membership of the International entirely to manual workers — which would have excluded Marx — and, when that proposal had been defeated with the aid of the British and Swiss delegates, to allow only manual workers to sit on the General Council or to hold office. This too was voted down ; and it was then decided that the seat of the Council should remain in London for the ensuing year.

This question about the composition of the International was of key importance, but bore different connotations for the delegations from the various countries. For the British it was simply a matter of accepting the help of a few outsiders, such as Marx and the small group of middle-class sympathisers with whom the Trade Unions were collaborating in the National Reform League. No one in Great Britain was under any doubt that the main support of the International in Great Britain must rest on the Trade Unions : nor, in view of the eclipse of Chartism, was there any other group on which it could rest. For the French, on the other hand, the question was whether the large and active body of revolutionary republicans, mainly under middle-class leadership, was to be admitted into the International, which, if they were admitted, they could almost certainly proceed to dominate, at least in Paris. The French group which took part in founding the International was aiming, above all else, at building up a distinctively Trade Union movement, based on the federation into local unions of the *sociétés de résistance* which were being built up in the various trades. This group wanted to make these purely Trade Union bodies a counterpoise to the revolutionary republican movement of the middle-class intellectuals and to the sheer *émeutisme* of the Blanquist and other revolutionary clubs ; and the latter retorted by accusing the Trade Unionists of being in secret alliance with Napoleon III against the Revolution. The International itself had to enquire into this charge, and dismissed it as baseless — which it was. But it was true that the French leaders of the International were much more interested in strikes and in economic movements than in politics, and were determined to prevent their movement from being captured by the Radical politicians. They were, however, divided among themselves between the moderates, headed by Tolain, who wished to build up a working-class political movement on a Trade Union basis and to fight elections in complete independence of the middle-class Radicals, and the Trade Unionist left wing, headed by Eugène Varlin, which had no faith in parliamentary action and hoped to build up the Trade Unions, through local and regional federations, into an independent revolutionary force strong enough to wrest the control of the revolution from the middle-class Radicals. For the moment, these groups were united in wishing to make the International a definitely working-class body and to reject participation of middle-class politicians in its control. But before long they were to fall out among themselves, and the main power in the French Sections was to pass from Tolain's to Varlin's group.

The other delegations mainly concerned, in 1866, with the question of middle-class participation were the Swiss and the Belgians. The Swiss, who held the numerical domination at the Geneva Congress, mostly voted against the French. In Switzerland class-relationships were a good deal more complicated than elsewhere, because, especially at Geneva, the line between small masters and skilled craftsmen was not at all sharply drawn and many of the craftsmen had voting rights. There was accordingly a traditional attachment to the Radical parties, which were not, like the French Radicals, revolutionary, and were intensely local in their main interests. As against this there were, especially in the small towns and country districts of the Jura, large numbers of domestic workers who were suffering under very bad conditions, and in Geneva itself, as we have seen, the building workers were largely immigrants without civic rights. There was thus a large section on one side which favoured moderate policies and collaboration with the middle-class Radicals, and on the other a left wing made up mainly of the Genevese non-citizens and of the home-workers in the country areas. These latter, unable to influence the elections to any great extent, tended to rely on industrial action and to denounce the corrupting influence of politics on working-class leaders. They had not, however, any such hostility as the French towards the intellectual left ; for there was no middle-class revolutionary Radical movement to dispute the leadership with them. They were fully prepared to accept non-working-class support and rallied round Bakunin when he proclaimed a gospel of revolution which, far from setting out to capture the State, required its abolition and looked to the revolutionary instinct of the workers to create the new society on a basis of free, local association.

Thus on the immediate issue raised by the French delegates, the Swiss were united in welcoming middle-class helpers into the International. The Belgians, who would have had views of their own, were not represented at all at the Geneva Congress; and the Germans were a small and unrepresentative group, as the Lassallians sent no delegates and the German Marxists were only beginning to organise on independent lines.

Marx, who did not attend the Geneva Congress, was uneasy about its outcome. He briefed Eccarius, as representing the General Council, with a report on the events of the past two years and with detailed instructions for handling the Proud-honist Frenchmen, who were to be present in force. When the Congress was over he was much relieved, not because anything in particular had been accomplished beyond getting the statutes ratified, but because nothing that really mattered had been done to commit the International to Proudhonist ideas. The Congress had indeed carried a resolution in favour of an International Credit Bank to be established on Proudhon's principle of 'gratuitous credit' and had pronounced emphatically in favour of the promotion of producers' Co-operative Societies. But it had also proclaimed the inadequacy of voluntary Co-operation to change the basis of the social system, and had endorsed a report by Marx which put great emphasis on strikes and Trade Union organisation and advocated the use of Trade Unions not only for the day-to-day struggle against the employers but also for the more fundamental purpose of uprooting the wage-system and creating a new social order based on the power of the working class. At the same time the Congress had been induced, against some French and Swiss opposition, to declare for the legislative enactment of the eight hours day and for a public system of education for all children. These two decisions committed the Congress to political action and to the use of the State power as a means of enforcing social reforms. Marx regarded them as a victory over the Proudhonist form of Anarchism : the Bakuninist form, which was soon to offer a more fundamental challenge to his leadership, had not yet become vocal in the Congress.

The Geneva Congress of 1866 was mainly a Franco-Swiss gathering, with the Swiss groups providing more than half the total number of delegates — 33 out of at most 60 in all — and the French 16. The others included three Germans and six from Great Britain — but only three of the six were British — Odger, W. R. Cremer, and James Carter — the others being the German Eccarius, the Swiss Jung, and the Frenchman Dupont, all from London. There was no one from Belgium or Italy ; and the Spaniards and Dutch had not yet entered the International.

The following year's Congress, which was held at Lausanne, was again mainly Franco-Swiss. It is difficult to be quite sure about the number of delegates ; but the recorded names include 37 Swiss and 20 Frenchmen, out of a total of 72. This time there were six from Germany, still not representing any considerable German movement ; two from Italy, where Bakunin's influence was being felt ; one Belgian — de Paepe ; and six from London — three British, two Germans, and a Frenchman — but not this time any outstanding British Trade Union leader. The British Trade Union leaders, deeply occupied with the double struggle for the Reform Act and for Trade Union rights, could not get away, and Eccarius was left to act as their main representative, with the perfumer, James Carter, and Alfred Walton, the builder-architect, of the National Reform League.

At the Lausanne Congress, the International, in matters of policy, was still feeling its way. It was, indeed, quite uncertain how far it was meant to be a policy-making body, and how far it should leave each national or regional group free to work out its own methods in accordance with varying conditions. It was taken for granted that in the day-to-day economic struggle the workers in each country should help those in other countries as much as they could, both with money and by doing their best to prevent the breaking of strikes by blacklegs imported from a distance. It was also a matter of general agreement that Trade Unions should be federated on the widest possible basis, both into regional and national federations of all trades within a single country and into international federations in each trade or industry. There was also fairly general agreement that Co-operative production should be encouraged and the Trade Unions called up to support it by investing in it as well as by moral help. But there were considerable differences concerning the kinds of Co-operative activity that deserved support. A good many delegates were strongly critical of consumers' Co-operation, on the two grounds that it involved exploitation of the employees by the consumer shareholders and tended to create a privileged labour aristocracy, and also that its success, under capitalist conditions with wages determined by an 'iron law', would merely make it easier for employers to reduce wages. Co-operative producers' societies found more favour, as foreshadowing workers' control of industry; but in this case, too, some of the delegates objected that such societies would only create privileged groups of self-employed workers without doing anything to emancipate the great majority. The resolution finally accepted at the Lausanne Congress admitted this danger, but argued that it could be avoided if the proletariat was aware of it. The report submitted to the Congress by the commission set up to consider the matter urged that there must be full equality among the members of the producers' societies and no class of privileged shareholders drawing a profit from their labours. This point was stressed by the Proudhonists, who also secured a further endorsement of their project of 'gratuitous credit' to be placed at the disposal of any worker or group of workers through a system of Credit Banks. Some of those who voted for the resolution dealing with Co-operative production did so in the belief that the spread of voluntary Co-operation with Trade Union support could in course of time oust capitalism without the need for a political revolution; some — the Proudhonists — regarded a social revolution which would abolish the State and institute 'gratuitous credit' as a necessary prerequisite of the Co-operative Commonwealth; yet others held, in accordance with the teachings of Louis Blanc and of Lassalle, that the State, democratised by means of universal suffrage, would be required to become the financier of producers' Co-operation before it could escape from its existing limitations or shake off the danger of emancipating only a section of the working-class and at the same time leaving in existence an exploited proletariat of non-Co-operators — a 'fifth estate'.

These differences became more apparent as the Lausanne Congress proceeded to the later items on its agenda. Deep-seated differences of attitude concerning the 'State' and the workers' policy in relation to it then made their appearance. The first sharp difference arose over the question of education. It was generally accepted that education ought to be regarded as a universal human right: the difficulty was to say how the enjoyment of this right should be enforced. Some delegates wanted a general system of compulsory education to be set up by law and operated by the State on a strictly secular basis. Others contended that it would be wrong and dangerous to place education in the hands of the State, even if its secular character could be ensured — for was not the State essentially the organ of the ruling class, and would it not use the control of education to indoctrinate the workers with wrong social ideas ? Some — the Proudhonists — went further and asserted not only that the State was an inherently reactionary agent, but also that education was properly the parents' business, which no public agency had any right to take out of their hands. The differences were finally patched up in a resolution which began by asserting the universal need for education and insisting that it must be secular, and then went on to say that the State had no right to interfere except where the parents were not in a position to give the child the education it ought to have — a phrase which left it open to the advocates of collective action to contend that as no working-class parents could afford this, the State was authorised to take the matter into its own hands. The Proud-honists, having got the phrase they wanted put into the resolu-tion, swallowed the rest ; and the references to the State were accepted without their real meaning being at all fully considered.

The question of the 'State' had, however, to come up more directly in the next item on the agenda, which raised the issue frontally in the form of a report on the rôle of the State in relation to the workers' movement. The Congress passed a resolution declaring for the public ownership of the means of transport and exchange, but refused to accept an amendment by César de Paepe calling for the public ownership of land as well, remitting this further issue for fuller discussion at the

International's next Congress. This was the beginning of an immense debate on the subject of collective ownership that lasted throughout the rest of the International's existence. The proposal to socialise banks and transport services arose out of the radical difficulty of organising such agencies as producers' Co-operatives, these being thought of as essentially local groups of co-partners working together in single establishments. The British had been calling for nationalisation of railways and other large-scale services on the ground that these were necessarily monopolistic and must be wrested from the capitalists who controlled them by some agency larger than a Co-operative working group. The Proudhonists on their side denounced the capitalist banking monopoly and demanded in its stead public Credit Banks worked on a non-profit basis ; and they were prepared to vote for public ownership of other monopolies as well, provided that they were not asked to declare explicitly for *State* ownership — that is, provided the form of public ownership was left undefined. They would, however, on no account vote for public ownership of the land ; for they were strong upholders of peasant ownership and regarded the peasant's property as an essential part of his personal right to liberty. The Swiss being divided on this issue, the Congress left it over for further consideration by the affiliated Sections.

The decision in favour of public ownership of monopolies was regarded by the collectivists in the Congress as a victory ; but it was in effect still left an open question whether 'public' ownership meant ownership by any sort of 'State'. The next subject on the agenda brought up the same issue in a different connection. The subject was the part to be played by the working class in the 'political struggle', and the relation between 'political' and 'social' liberties. After much debate, the Congress passed these two resolutions : '(1) That the social emancipation of the workers is inseparable from their political emancipation ; and (2) That the establishment of political liberties is a first measure of absolute necessity' — on which de Paepe commented sharply that it was 'putting the cart before the horse'. In the end, almost everybody voted for these resolutions, because anyone could interpret them much as he pleased. They had been meant to serve a double purpose — to condemn those who rejected political action altogether — the

Anarchists and extreme Syndicalists — and also to condemn those who were prepared to work for social amelioration without political revolution, and especially any who were prepared to come to terms either with Napoleon III's Empire or with Bismarck's Prusso-German State. No one, however, at the Congress was prepared to admit any sympathy for these last policies ; and, for the rest, the resolutions were too vaguely worded to divide the delegates. That the Congress nevertheless regarded them as of fundamental importance was plainly indicated by a further decision which laid down that they should be 'solemnly reaffirmed' at every ensuing Congress and should be officially communicated to all members of the International.

The last major question discussed at the Lausanne Congress of the I.W.M.A. concerned the attitude to be taken up by the International towards the International Peace Congress, which was about to meet at Geneva under the auspices of the newly founded League of Peace and Freedom. This body, established on the initiative of the former Saint-Simonian, Charles Lemonnier (1806–91), was an attempt to link the advocacy of peace to that of European union under republican government. Lemonnier proposed at first to convene a Peace Conference at Paris ; but the Government of Napoleon III vetoed the project and the centre was transferred to Geneva. Lemonnier's plan was opposed by many of the older peace societies, especially in Great Britain and the United States, on the ground that it was wrong to link the propaganda for peace with proposals either for republican government or for a union of European States into a sovereign Federation ; but influential committees were formed in a number of countries to support the plan, and over 10,000 signatures were collected for a declaration in its favour. Among those who signed were such outstanding figures as Victor Hugo, John Bright, Garibaldi, John Stuart Mill, Louis Blanc, Edgar Quinet, Herzen, and James Fazy of Geneva. W. R. Cremer, connected also with the International, was secretary of the British organising committee.

Lemonnier's initiative followed on a long period during which the European peace movement had been almost inactive. A World Peace Convention had met in 1843 ; and between 1849 and 1851 a series of World Peace Conferences had been held in London, Brussels, Paris, Frankfurt, and finally

London again, during the International Exhibition of 1851. But after the Crimean War the movement had petered out in Europe ; and in the United States it had been wrecked by the Civil War, which sharply divided its adherents. In 1866, however, a new Universal Peace Union had been started in Baltimore, and the following year there were several separate attempts, besides Lemonnier's, to set up a new organisation in Europe. Most of these new movements concentrated on the advocacy of international arbitration as a means of preventing war, and avoided political proposals that might scare off conservative support. The League of Peace and Freedom, on the other hand, was definitely a movement of the left, backed by a great many professors, literary men, and *bourgeois* radical politicians, and appealing especially for radical and working-class participation. Garibaldi, as the outstanding popular hero, was made the leading figure of the Congress, which he attended in person ; and to it were drawn a great number of the exiles who had been driven from their own countries after the collapse of the European Revolutions of 1848 and the following years. Among these was Michael Bakunin, who at once constituted himself the leader of a left wing among the participants and set out to wrest the control of the movement from its *bourgeois* promoters.

The organisers of the Geneva Peace Congress, eager for working-class support, had invited the co-operation of the International Working Men's Association ; and the delegates at Lausanne had to make up their minds what answer to give. At the meeting of the General Council preceding the Lausanne Congress Marx had come out strongly against having anything to do with the League, which he dismissed as a futile gathering of impotent *bourgeois* ideologues. But he had failed to carry his point ; and at Lausanne the majority of the delegates were in favour of working with the League in its struggle against war, though at the same time insistent on getting the League to face the social question and to agree that war could not be abolished except by a change in the economic system. The Lausanne Congress accordingly adopted a Collective Address to the Geneva Peace Congress, in the following terms :

The Congress of the International Working Men's Association, assembled at Lausanne, considering

That war weighs chiefly on the working class, in that it
not only deprives it of the means of existence, but also
constrains it to shed the workers' blood ;

That armed peace paralyses the powers of production,
demands of labour only useless tasks, and intimidates
production by putting it under the blow of the threats of
war ;

That peace, first condition of general well-being, needs
in its turn to be consolidated by a new order of things that
will no longer know in society two classes, the one of which
is exploited by the other,

Decides to gives its adhesion fully and entirely to the
Peace Congress which is to meet at Geneva on September 9,
to afford it energetic support, and to take part in everything
that it can undertake in order to bring about the abolition of
standing armies and the maintenance of peace, with a view
to arriving as speedily as possible at the emancipation of the
working class and at its liberation from the power and
influence of capital, as well as at the formation of a confederation of free States throughout Europe.[1]

This resolution, supported by most of the Swiss delegates, did
not pass altogether unchallenged. When it was decided to send
a delegation of three from the Lausanne Congress to present the
Address at Geneva, Tolain, suspicious of the proposed collaboration with the middle-class Radicals, moved and carried
a rider, supported by de Paepe, making the adherence of the
International conditional on the acceptance by the Peace Congress of the terms of the Address. This rider, which presented
a sharp challenge, was worded as follows :

The Congress, considering that war has as its first and
principal cause pauperism and the lack of economic equilibrium, and that, to achieve the suppression of war, it is not
enough to disband armies, but that it is also necessary to
modify social organisation by ensuring an increasingly more
equitable distribution of production, makes its adherence
subject to the acceptance by the Peace Congress of the
declaration set forth above.

This, of course, was meant to put the cat among the pigeons ;
and it duly achieved its effect. The Geneva Peace Congress was
much too heterogeneous an assembly to be prepared to range

[1] Translated by me from the French text.

itself on the side of the International on the social issue ; and accordingly Marx got his way. James Guillaume, who more than shared Marx's distrust of Radical politicians, was the person who acted as the International's official spokesman at Geneva, where the Address was not directly debated. But the League of Peace and Freedom did not endorse it ; and after the Congress a struggle speedily developed on the Council which it had set up. Bakunin, not yet connected with the International, after taking an energetic part in the Geneva Congress, continued to act inside the League as leader of a left wing which pressed for the adoption of a comprehensive and revolutionary social programme ; and the following year, at the League's second Congress, held at Berne, the dispute came to a head. Bakunin and his followers seceded from the League and decided to throw in their lot with the International Working Men's Association.

This brings the story to the point at which began the great contest inside the International — a contest which in the end destroyed what was left of it after the hard knocks it had taken in 1870 and 1871. Up to 1868 the internal dispute among the Internationalists had appeared to be mainly a matter of the Proudhonists versus the rest, with Marx passing from the stage of describing Tolain and his associates as 'good fellows' to his contemptuous repudiation of their 'Proudhonist nonsense'. But from 1868 the Proudhonist influence ceased to count for much. The effective leadership of the French Sections had passed largely from Tolain to Eugène Varlin ; and the new issues between Marx and the followers of Bakunin over-shadowed everything else.

What were these issues ? In the first place, there was a sharp conflict of temperament. Marx, with all his revolutionary fervour, had an essentially orderly mind, and could not bear Bakunin's conviction that the only thing that mattered was to stir the masses to orgies of revolutionary destruction and to leave to their spontaneous capacity the entire task of creating the new social order. Secondly, Marx's idea of the Internationa. was that of a movement working under central and unified direction, even if a good deal of latitude had to be left to the national Sections to shape their own policies in accordance with varying national conditions; whereas Bakunin, supported in this matter by most of the International's adherents in the Latin countries, insisted that each national — and indeed each local — movement should have complete freedom to shape its own policy without any direction from a controlling centre. This was the issue in the International between the centralisers, or 'authoritarian Communists', as they came to be called, and the 'federalists' or 'autonomists', who called themselves the 'free collectivists', or sometimes the 'Social Democrats' — names not yet appropriated by State Socialists or Marxists, and used at this time as antithetical to 'Communism' as a doctrine of centralised proletarian dictatorship.

Thirdly, Bakunin and the groups whose side he took in the International were out-and-out opponents of the State in all its forms. *God and the State*, Bakunin's best-known work, links these two concepts together as the embodiments of the authoritarian principle — the twin arch-enemies of human freedom. Marx too denounced both God and the State ; but the 'State' he regarded as the enemy was the 'police State' of the feudalists and capitalists, which he was seeking to overthrow and to supersede with a new State — a *Volksstaat* — based directly on the power of the working class. In Bakunin's view, the *Volksstaat* could be only a new instrument of tyranny over the workers : a workers' State was for him a sheer contradiction in terms. He agreed with Marx in advocating a dictatorship of the proletariat over the exploiting classes ; but he held that this dictatorship must be a spontaneous dictatorship of the entire uprisen working class, and not of any body of leaders set in authority over them. Opposition to Bakunin's anti-statism threw Marx for a time into alliance against him with the followers of Blanqui, who stood precisely for the kind of dictatorship of a conscious minority of leaders against which Bakunin railed. But Marx's own conception was neither Bakunin's nor Blanqui's, but something between the two. Marx wanted a dictatorship which would rest on the support of the main body of industrial workers but would be exercised with this support by a closely-knit group of leaders acting under a common discipline — what is called nowadays 'democratic centralism'. He was very insistent that these leaders must not attempt to force the pace unduly and must never allow themselves to get out of touch with the movements of mass working-class opinion. But the anti-authoritarians in the International could not recognise any difference between Marx's and Blanqui's conceptions of the dictatorship. They denounced Marxists and Blanquists alike as authoritarian centralisers, who were seeking to rivet upon the workers the fetters of a new kind of State, instead of making an end of an institution which would be always an instrument of tyrannical power of man over man.

Fourthly, Bakunin, when once he had broken with the League of Peace and Freedom, and most of his supporters in the International, were opposed to every form of collaboration with or support of Radical politicians and *bourgeois* movements ; whereas Marx, liking these elements no better than they, accepted the necessity of supporting them whenever they were pressing for reforms which were in the interests of the working class — for example, extension of the franchise, limitation of the working day, or the enlargement of political liberty. Marx, unsparing though he was in his denunciations of the *bourgeoisie*, was deeply opposed to all those Socialists who reacted through hatred of them into support of political reactionaries or auto-crats. Not a few political reactionaries proclaimed themselves as advocates of social reform and of voluntary Co-operation, and some set out definitely to woo the Trade Unions, or at any rate those Trade Unions which could be persuaded to adopt policies of social peace and class-collaboration. Marx and Bakunin were both active opponents of these tendencies ; but they parted company when it came to defining their attitudes towards the *bourgeois* Radicals. Marx demanded support for policies which made it easier for the workers' movements to operate and to extend their pressure for social reforms within the existing system ; for he considered that such a policy would strengthen the working class for its revolutionary tasks. Bakunin, on the other hand, after his break with the League, rejected all forms of compromise with the existing system, and argued that working for reforms within it would only weaken the revolutionary impulses of the workers and end up in the subjection of the working-class movement to capitalism and to the State.

Marx, in taking up his stand on this issue, was influenced largely by British and German conditions : Bakunin, on the other hand, was influenced mainly by conditions in Russia and Italy. Marx, living in England and regarding Great Britain, because it was the most advanced capitalist country, as the key area for the development of the working-class movement, realised the sheer impossibility of getting the British Trade Unions not to direct their main energies to the establishment of Trade Union rights, the extension of the suffrage, and the improvement of industrial legislation — Factory Acts, Mines Acts, Master and Servant Acts, and so on. He therefore based his tactics in Great Britain on furthering these causes, in the hope and expectation that the effect would be to increase the militancy of the workers' movement and to lead it to more integrated action in the struggle against capitalism. At the same time, watching the development of the workers' movement in Germany, where it had to face both a much more autocratic State system and a *bourgeoisie* much less developed as an economic class and needing, he considered, to be constantly pushed on by the workers to oppose this autocracy, Marx was acutely suspicious of the tendency of Lassalle and his successors to coquet with Bismarck against the *bourgeois* Progressivists — a tendency which he was apt grossly to exaggerate, even to the length of believing, without any warrant, that the Lassallian leaders were actually in Bismarck's pay.

Bakunin, on the other hand, was under no temptation to coquet with the political reactionaries — or indeed with *bourgeois* Radicals either, when once he had broken away from the League of Peace and Freedom. The countries he thought most about in developing his policy were Russia, where it seemed to him sheer absurdity to work for reform within the existing State structure, and Italy, which was in a condition of continuous upheaval on account of the sheer poverty of the working classes and of the stark contrast between the high-souled pretensions of Mazzinist nationalism and the sordid realities of the new State set up in 1860 and, even more, of the still utterly feudal south. In Italy Bakunin, who lived there from 1864 to 1867, had found what working-class movement there was dominated by Mazzinist intellectuals who, true to the master's gospel, though they were republicans and rejected the monarchist State, preached to the poor more about their duties than about their rights ; and he had taken sides with, and helped to organise into a powerful movement, the scattered left wing that was in root and branch opposition to the Mazzinist Republicans as well as to the new State of Cavour. In Italy, and above all in Naples, the only practicable form of working-class resistance was the *émeute* — the armed revolt of the starvelings against misery and oppression ; and such revolts were bound in practice to be local uprisings almost devoid of concerted planning and based on acute local grievances. The only organisation there could be behind them was secret conspiracy, which was wholly in the Italian tradition ; and such methods entirely suited both Bakunin's temperament and his Russian background. When, after 1867, he made his appearance on the wider stage of the International, he carried over into its affairs the fruits of his Italian experience and hoped to induce the workers of all Europe to dance to the same tune. But in fact many of those who worked with him in the International against Marx were far from sharing his fundamentally conspiratorial approach. They agreed with him in objecting strongly to Marx's 'authoritarianism' and to all attempts to impose a centrally directed policy on the International. They shared his hatred of the existing State and of *bourgeois* politics : they looked forward to free, loosely federal societies resting on self-governing local Communes controlled by the workers. But they were also keen advocates of workers' Co-operatives, in which Bakunin was not at all interested ; and they had no such passion as moved him for uprooting the entire social order, so as to leave the emancipated workers to make a totally fresh start. They were indeed for the most part respectable family men, not ill content with the accustomed values and ways of living, except that they wanted to lift the oppression of the rich from the backs of the poor.

Of course, there were many intermediate positions between Bakunin's all-out des ructiveness and the constructive social Anarchism of many of Marx's opponents in the International in Switzerland, France, and Belgium. In France the prevailing anti-authoritarian tendency, after the decline of the Proudhonist group, was Syndicalist rather than completely Anarchist. In French Switzerland it was communalistic and Co-operative. In Belgium there were conflicting tendencies — partly arising out of national differences between Walloons and Flemings, which made Belgium always a battleground of rival ideas. In Germany there was a small Anarchistic group, headed by Johann Most ; but the main battle was between Lassallians and Marxists, which were both authoritarian groups. Bakunin's main following — the groups that most fully shared his outlook — was in Italy and a little later in Spain, where conditions fitted the conspiratorial pattern. In Spain, however, the Syndicalist tendency had also some strength, especially in Catalonia ; and there were close connections between the movement in Barcelona and Valencia and the Syndicalistic movements in Marseilles and Lyons.

Bakunin, during his sojourn in Italy, had organised some sort of secret Revolutionary Brotherhood or Alliance. It is, however, exceedingly difficult to tell how far the various revolutionary bodies of which Bakunin was reputed to be the leader and inspirer really existed in any formal sense. Bakunin hated formal organisation : what he loved was the sense of being bound together with friends and fellow-workers in an association too intimate to need to be made formal or have any rules written down — or indeed any clearly defined membership at all. He loved to enrol by word of mouth in his Brotherhoods and Alliances anyone who seemed willing to further his aims ; and often he left such persons very much in ignorance of what it was they had joined, or even whether they had joined anything at all. Bakunin kept up an enormous correspondence with revolutionaries, or supposed revolutionaries, in many countries. He continually invented, but hardly ever used, secret cyphers for his revolutionary correspondence — cyphers which were quite often captured by the police, but served no other purpose than that of diffusing an air of immense conspiracies afoot. Bakunin's celebrated International Revolutionary Brotherhood, I think, never had any real existence outside his own head, except in the sense that he was personally in correspondence with a large number of persons whom he could regard as members of it when he was so minded. His Italian Alliance of Social Democracy, the forerunner of the Alliance which he set up later in Geneva, does appear to have had a rather less unreal existence.

Outside Italy, there was no real Bakuninist organisation until Bakunin and a group of supporters — mainly exiles — seceded in 1868 from the League of Peace and Freedom and announced the formation of the Alliance of Social Democracy at Geneva. Even then the Alliance, though it claimed to have

Sections and branches in a number of countries, hardly existed in any formal sense outside Switzerland, or indeed outside Geneva. It was, no doubt, supported in a broad sense by considerable groups in Italy, Spain, and Southern France ; but the bodies which supported it in these countries were rather independent organisations than parts of the Alliance. Bakunin, in organising it, announced his intention of allying it to the International Working Men's Association, to which, he informed Marx by letter, he meant henceforward to devote himself heart and soul.

Before the secession took place, Bakunin had attempted, with some success, to persuade the governing Council of the League of Peace and Freedom to enter into a close partnership with the International on the basis of a broadly common programme, but so as to leave the International to deal with economic while the League handled political problems. He had persuaded the League Council to write to the International inviting its collaboration and asking it to be represented at the League's Berne Congress ; but this invitation had not been well received in London, and the International, at its Brussels Congress of 1868, declared that it saw no good reason for the League's existence, and invited it to dissolve, at the same time suggesting that its groups and individual members should transfer their allegiance to the International. The Brussels Congress had indeed repudiated Bakunin's proposal for a division of functions by taking up the question of war and peace, and passing a resolution in which it urged the workers in all countries to take energetic action for the prevention of war between nations — which it declared could properly be regarded only as civil war among the workers — to the extent of 'a complete cessation of labour in the event of war breaking out in their respective countries'. The policy of an international general strike against war thus made its first appearance on the stage of history — much to the annoyance of Marx, who in reviewing the proceedings of the Brussels Congress, denounced the whole idea as absolute nonsense.

The Brussels Congress, having defined its own working-class policy in relation to war, proceeded to consider its attitude to the League of Peace and Freedom in the light of this decision. It did not attempt to prevent its members from attending the

League's Berne Congress, at which a considerable number of them were intending to be present ; but it made clear that they would be attending simply as individuals, with no authority to commit the International ; and it sent to accompany them its own resolution calling upon the League to dissolve. This annoyed Bakunin, who rightly attributed the International's attitude mainly to Marx ; but it did not prevent him from carrying to the Berne Congress his own proposals to commit the League to an advanced economic and social programme. At Berne he moved the following resolution :

> In view of the fact that the question which most imperatively presents itself to us is that of the economic and social equalisation of classes and individuals, this Congress affirms that, without this equalisation — that is to say without justice — freedom and peace are unrealisable. Consequently, this Congress puts on the order of the day the study of the practical means of resolving this question.

In speaking to his resolution, Bakunin declared himself to be a 'collectivist' — a doctrine which he contrasted sharply with Communism. The latter he denounced as a necessarily authoritarian and centralising doctrine. 'I detest Communism', he said, 'because it is the negation of liberty and I can conceive nothing human without liberty. I am no Communist because Communism concentrates and aims at the absorption of all the powers of society in the State, because it leads necessarily to the centralisation of property in the hands of the State, whereas I wish for the abolition of the State — the radical extirpation of that principle of authority and guardianship of the State which, under the pretext of moralising and civilising men, has hitherto enslaved, oppressed, exploited and depraved them. I stand for the organisation of society and of collective or social property from the bottom up, by way of free association, and not from the top down by means of authority of any sort. Standing for the abolition of the State, I stand for the abolition of the individual inheritance of property, which is but a State institution, a consequence of the State principle. Thus you have the sense in which I am collectivist and not at all Communist.'

Bakunin's resolution, opposed by the Proudhonists because of its collectivist tendency and also by some of the German Socialists as well as by most of the *bourgeois* Radicals, was defeated ; and he and a group of followers thereupon seceded from the League of Peace and Freedom and announced the establishment of the Alliance of Social Democracy. The best-known members of this group were the geographer Élisée Réclus, the Russian exile Nicholas Joukovsky, the Pole Valery Mroczowski, the Italians Giuseppe Fanelli and Alberto Tucci, Albert Richard of Lyons, and Aristide Rey, who had been one of the original organisers of the League of Peace and Freedom. The Alliance, announcing its intention to organise itself as an international revolutionary body, applied to the International for affiliation, on the understanding that it should keep its distinct organisation and hold its own delegate Congresses in connection with those of the International as a whole. The General Council of the International not unnaturally rejected this application. The Alliance thereupon decided to dissolve itself as an international body, to urge its Sections to join the national and local Federations of the International, and to reconstitute its own central organisation as a Propaganda Section of the International at Geneva, for which it renewed its application to be accepted by the General Council. On this basis, the General Council rather surprisingly decided to accept the affiliation, while refusing the Alliance's request that it should approve the programme Bakunin had drawn up for it. The General Council said that it did not pass judgment on the programmes of its affiliated associations, but only accepted or rejected the organisations themselves according as they appeared to be genuine or not. Privately, Marx was very scornful of Bakunin's programme — particularly of the importance given in it to the abolition of inheritance, which he denounced as a *petit-bourgeois* sentiment, and of the demand for 'equalisation of classes'. This latter, he said, was mere nonsense, because the purpose of the International was not to equalise classes but to do away with them. This point was taken up by the General Council, and at their insistence the Bakuninists readily agreed to amend their programme so as to make clear that this was what they meant. But the trouble over inheritance, as we shall see, remained.

At Geneva, where the Alliance set up its headquarters, Bakunin did not have an easy time. The majority of the Genevese Internationalists were hostile to his Anarchist views, though there was a Section which favoured him, especially among the building workers, who conducted a big successful strike in 1868, with the International's help. Bakunin's main support in Switzerland came from refugees — Russian, Polish, French, and Italian — and from the French-speaking domestic workers of the Jura valleys — the groups which subsequently formed the separate Jura Federation. The German-Swiss gave him hardly any support, and the Co-operators, headed by Dr. Coullery of La Chaux-de-Fonds, were also hostile. His Alliance fought a running battle with the majority in the Geneva Federation of the International, which refused to accept the local Section of the Alliance as an affiliated body despite the acceptance of this same body by the General Council in London. The local contest in Switzerland went on side by side with the larger contest between Marx and Bakunin in the International as a whole.

To this major struggle we must come back later ; for it is now necessary to pick up the story of the International itself by considering the rest of its proceedings at the Brussels Congress of 1868. This gathering was composed of elements widely different from those which had been brought together at Geneva and at Lausanne the two previous years. Instead of the Swiss having the numerical preponderance, the Belgians now had a clear majority — 56 out of 100 delegates in all. The French came next, with 18. The British, including the members of the General Council, centred in London, had 12, of whom 6 were foreigners. The Swiss had but 8, the Germans 4, and the Italians and Spaniards 1 each. The British contingent included, besides Eccarius, only one prominent Trade Union leader — Benjamin Lucraft. Tolain still headed the French group : Varlin was absent in gaol, whence, after the Congress, he and a number of others sent to the League of Peace and Freedom a protest against the International's unfriendly attitude towards it. De Paepe was the outstanding Belgian and J. P. Becker the leading participant from Switzerland. James Guillaume, the leader of the Swiss Anarchist group, could not attend. Among the Germans the only important delegate was Moses Hess, who actually lived in Paris. The Italian was a Genevese follower of Bakunin : the Spaniard came from Barcelona under a false name.

In such an assembly the last word was with the Belgians, who had prepared for the Congress a number of special reports and had held many preliminary discussions among themselves. The main issue which the Congress was called upon to decide was that of the ownership of land, which de Paepe had brought forward the year before at Lausanne. At his instance, and against the opposition of the dwindling band of French and Belgian Proudhonists and Swiss moderates, the Brussels Congress declared that the land should be brought under collective ownership. The decision, indeed, was more comprehensive than this ; for it included mines and quarries, railways, canals, telegraphs, and other means of communication, and forests, as well as the land itself. Consideration was also given, in a separate resolution, to the question of capital instruments of production ; and the Congress laid down that machines, which had hitherto been used for the exploitation of the workers, could be made of true service to them only when 'a more equitable organisation should have put the machines into the workers' possession', and that 'only by means of Co-operative association and by an organisation of mutual credit can the producer arrive at the possession of the machine'.

Thus at Brussels the International came down definitely on the side of a large measure of collectivism. But the type of collectivism which it envisaged rested, as far as manufacturing industries were concerned, on producers' Co-operatives, aided by a system of 'gratuitous credit' — that is to say, interest-free capital put at their disposal through mutual banks. It was not State ownership or control of industry for which the Congress declared, but Co-operative ownership on a basis of decentralisation, or rather of localisation. In the case of agriculture, a similar solution was envisaged — ownership of the land by the local communes and its cultivation by Co-operative Societies of agricultural workers. It was more difficult, in the view of the delegates, to determine how large-scale services, such as railways and canals, which transcended local boundaries, could be dealt with ; but the majority of those who spoke held that such services would be somehow organised under federations, based on the local communes, covering the areas over which they operated. *State* ownership and control were ruled out by most of the delegates, who regarded the State as an essentially reactionary institution ; but it was agreed that the whole question of the future organisation of large-scale services needed further study, and that it should be considered at a further Congress.

In declaring in favour of Co-operative associations as the most suitable bodies to take over the control of mechanised industries, the Brussels Congress was at pains to make clear what sort of Co-operative bodies it had in mind. The report presented by the commission set up to consider this question stressed the danger of Co-operation taking capitalist forms. It denounced the accumulation of interest-bearing capital and the payment of dividends on purchases as capitalistic practices calculated, instead of replacing capitalism, to continue it in the interests of a part only of the working class, and thus to create a 'fourth estate' of a *bourgeois* and conservative character. The true purpose of workers' Co-operation, the report urged, was to wrest the instruments of production from the capitalists' hands and to place them in the hands of their legitimate proprietors. Accordingly, the Congress carried the following resolution :

Every society based on democratic principles rejects every exaction, in the name of capital, no matter what form it may take — rent, interest or dividend : it thus reserves for labour its entire right, its entire just remuneration.

The Brussels International Congress would have nothing to do either with consumers' Co-operation on the Rochdale model or with producers' Co-operatives which paid interest on capital invested in them or rewarded their workers with a share in profits. It stood only for forms of Co-operation which rested on the principle of social and economic equality, though it had not yet advanced far towards a positive definition of what this principle involved.

The Congress discussed a number of other matters, reported on by the commissions which it set up. The Belgians had prepared a plan for the establishment of a Credit Bank to aid Co-operative enterprise. This was approved in principle, the detailed plan being sent to all the Federations of the International for further consideration.

On the question of Trade Unions the Congress concluded that strikes were necessary, though strike action could not suffice to emancipate labour. It called for comprehensive organisation of the workers in their various trades and for federation into general associations ; and it recommended that in each locality the federated Unions should set up a 'Council of Arbitration', by which was meant, not a joint body of employers and workers, but a body drawn from the Unions of the different trades with the function of deciding whether proposals for strike action should receive general support. This proposal was probably based on what had recently been done in Great Britain, by the setting up in 1866 of the United Kingdom Alliance of Organised Trades.

Education came up again at the Brussels Congress; and this time it was decided to urge the Sections of the International itself to establish public courses of 'scientific, professional and productive instruction' in order to make up as far as possible for the defects of the education which the workers actually received. It was at the same time recognised that such projects could not succeed unless the length of the working day were reduced; and on this question the Congress decided that the time for action had come, and laid it down as the duty of all Sections to undertake campaigns for shorter hours.

Marx, who did not attend the Brussels Congress, expressed much dissatisfaction with its proceedings, partly because of the persistence of mutualist credit ideas, which he regarded as silly, and partly because he disliked the idea of a general strike against war, which he thought impracticable. The Congress was, however, an important landmark in the history of the working-class movement, because it marked the definite acceptance of the idea of socialisation.

1868 was a year of considerable strike activity in a number of countries, as trade began to revive after the depressions and panics of 1866 and 1867. But in 1869, with restored economic prosperity, the strike movement was greatly intensified, and in all the countries belonging to the International there was a great increase in Trade Union membership. In France, and also in Belgium, these movements led to the arrest of many of the leaders: almost every strike was widely attributed to the International's sinister influence, even if it had played no part; and the Internationalists joyfully tried to live up to the rôle their opponents assigned to them. In Spain the constitutional Revolution of 1868 had for the time being opened the door to working-class organisation and agitation, and the International grew fast, mainly under the influence of Anarchist and Syndicalist ideas. There was also a rapid spread of organisation in Italy, in the north as well as in Naples and parts of Sicily. In Germany the Social Democratic Party came into formal existence at the Eisenach Congress of 1869, when a section of the Lassallians broke away and joined hands with Bebel and Liebknecht on a programme which was largely Marxist in inspiration. The new party did not become formally a Section of the International — it could not under German law. But Liebknecht, in effect representing it, came to the Basle Congress of 1869, which was the most representative yet held and showed the International almost at the zenith of its influence.

At Basle there were indeed fewer delegates than at Brussels — 72 as against 100. But the reason for the decline was that the Swiss sent only 24 delegates, whereas the year before the Belgians had sent 56. In 1869 no one country had a majority. There were 25 Frenchmen, 24 Swiss, 5 Belgians, 5 Germans, 2 Austrians, 2 Italians, 2 Spaniards, and 1 American — the first to put in an appearance. From Great Britain, including the General Council, came but 6 — Robert Applegarth, Benjamin Lucraft, and Cowell Stepney, and the three foreigners Eccarius, Lessner, and Jung. Applegarth, outstanding among British Trade Unionists, was an important new recruit. Among the French Varlin, released from prison, was back in his place ; and Tolain was again present despite his defeat on the issue of collectivisation. De Paepe again headed the Belgians ; and most of the leading Swiss were there, except Coullery, who had dropped out when the International went collectivist. One of the two Italian delegates was Bakunin, making his first appearance at a Congress of the International.

The question of landed property came up again at the Basle Congress, though it had been voted on already at Brussels. Tolain and his friends insisted that the vote had been taken without adequate preparation, and it was agreed to reopen the matter. This time the question was divided into two — Had society the right to make the land collective property ? and — Was it expedient to do so ? Both questions received affirmative answers by large majorities ; but differences arose over the correct methods of cultivating the land when it was collectively owned. On the commission which reported on the matter, a majority favoured actual collective farming by the communes.

Eccarius, on behalf of the General Council, advocated the leasing of the land by the State to agricultural Co-operative societies large enough to make full use of mechanised methods of production. De Paepe and some others favoured communal ownership, with leasing of the land either, preferentially, to agricultural Co-operatives or to individual rent-paying tenants. The issue was left undecided.

The most hotly disputed issue at Basle was that of inheritance. Bakunin's group, as we have seen, had made the abolition of inheritance a key question at the Congress of the League of Peace and Freedom ; and after the secession Bakunin continued to press the matter upon the Sections of the International. Some of his French adherents were mainly responsible for placing the question on the agenda of the Basle Congress, much to Marx's annoyance. For, in Marx's view, inheritance of property was no more than a derivative of private appropriation and the correct course was to attack private property directly, as its abolition would automatically do away with inheritance rights. Marx regarded this point as of fundamental importance because he held that to attack inheritance was merely to waste time in dealing with a secondary factor dependent on legal institutions — that is, on the State — whereas the question of property itself was related to the underlying economic structure. Accordingly, he argued, to stress the abolition of inheritance rather than that of private property was to take up a *petit-bourgeois* attitude. Marx nevertheless favoured as a transitional measure higher death duties ; but he was opposed to giving a prominent place in the Socialist programme to anything short of complete socialisation of the means of production.

Marx felt so strongly on this point that he briefed Eccarius — for he did not go to Basle himself — with a report in which his views were set out. Consequently there was a great wrangle, with most of the delegates unable to understand what was really at issue. The commission appointed by the Congress reported in favour of abolishing inheritance : Eccarius produced Marx's rival proposal ; and Bakunin made a great speech in support of the commission's views, admitting in the course of it that for the time being peasant property in land would have to be let alone, but arguing that it would be readily superseded when the right of inheritance had been done away with. Against

Marx Bakunin urged that, though the economic conditions were the fundamental determinants of property relations, the institutions sanctioned by the State, such as inheritance rights, attained in historical development a secondary determinising power of their own, so that it was no less necessary to attack them than to take advantage of the development of the underlying economic forces. The attack on inheritance, Bakunin concluded, was part of the necessary onslaught on the whole institution of the State, and could be used to further the essential objective of abolishing coercive government in all its forms.

Bakunin's argument convinced the majority of the delegates who cast their votes, and the commission's proposal to abolish inheritance was carried by 32 votes to 23, with 13 abstentions and 7 absent. Marx's alternative proposal, moved by Eccarius on behalf of the General Council, was defeated by 37 votes to 19, with 6 abstentions and 13 absentees — for it was near the end of the Congress and the delegates were beginning to melt away. Thus, no proposal had an absolute majority, which was needed for a conclusive decision. Marx, though greatly annoyed, consoled himself that Bakunin had failed to bind the International ; and the General Council in fact did nothing to take the matter any further. It had, however, been shown clearly that the General Council's hold over the International was precarious and that, on this issue at any rate, Bakunin's influence was not to be despised.

The remaining issue of importance discussed at Basle related to the powers of the International's General Council ; and on this issue, surprisingly, Bakunin found himself on the General Council's side. Perhaps he was swayed by the fact that the General Council had accepted the affiliation of the Alliance of Social Democracy, whereas the Geneva Section of the International had rejected it. At all events, he spoke in favour of giving the General Council wide powers — power to admit or refuse admission to the International, subject to final decision by the Congress, and power to suspend any Section accused of acting against the interests of the International, again subject to an appeal to the Congress. In face of this agreement, the Basle Congress gave the General Council the authority it had asked for — an authority which was to be turned before long against Bakunin and was to have increased importance because circumstances prevented the International from holding any further full Congress for three years.

Thus, between its formation in 1864 and its point of greatest development in 1869, the International Working Men's Association had formally travelled a long distance on the road to Socialism. The battle against the followers of Proudhon had been decisively won — for land nationalisation was a notion they were quite unable to accept. The League of Peace and Freedom, which had threatened to establish itself as a rival centre of internationalist activity likely to divert support from the I.W.M.A., had been disrupted. Bakunin's Alliance had been dissolved as an international body, and reduced, at any rate in form, to a mere Propagandist Section of the Swiss Section of the I.W.M.A. There had been a great growth of Trade Unions in a number of countries, and many successful strikes had been fought, if not by the International, at any rate so that it reaped the credit. The name of the International had come to be known, and feared, over a large part of Europe, and its organisation was still spreading fast, especially in Spain and Italy. In Germany a Social Democratic Party had been set up at Eisenach and, though it could not yet formally join the International, was expected to collaborate with it closely. Finally, despite the disputes between centralisers and auto-nomists, the General Council, dominated by Marx, had been given a large, though not very clearly defined, authority between Congresses over the national and local Sections — and this had been done with the support of Bakunin himself.

On the whole, then, Marx, whatever his private grumblings, had on the face of the matter very good reason to be pleased. If he was not so, the causes of his dissatisfaction lay beneath the surface of current events and had not yet reacted seriously on the work of the International. They were none the less already pressing upon his mind and threatening trouble in the future. In the first place, there was no longer any prospect of an early outbreak of rebellion in Ireland, which Marx had said to be a necessary pre-condition of a British revolution. The Fenians had been defeated in Ireland, though they were still active in the security of the United States. Secondly, the British Trade Union leaders had got the parliamentary reform they had demanded — or at any rate a sufficient instalment of it to set them thinking much more about the use to be made of their new political influence than about revolution, either at home or abroad. They were, moreover, well on the way to getting legal recognition of Trade Union rights, and were increasingly absorbed in the parliamentary struggle to make these rights secure ; and they were also receiving plain demonstration that the Reform Act would yield a rich harvest in social and industrial legislation. In these circumstances they were much less disposed to pay attention to Marx's advice than they had been while they were in the heat of the Reform struggle. Marx, for his part, was well aware that his control over the International depended entirely on his ability to manipulate the British members of the General Council. He had, indeed, outside England almost no following in the International, which had no effective German Section. In France he knew he had little support ; for he could rely no more on Varlin than on Tolain to act as an obedient disciple. Spain and Italy, as far as they counted, were Bakuninist — certainly not Marxist. In Switzerland, he thought he could rely on Becker and on a few other German exiles ; but there, too, the Bakuninist influence was strong, and the right wing at Geneva and elsewhere was committed to an alliance with the *bourgeois* Progressives. Belgium had its own line, which was certainly not Marx's — and that was all. Marx, up to 1869, had managed to dominate the International because the British Trade Union leaders were content to give him and his little group of exiled Germans what was practically a blank cheque in continental affairs ; but he could see that this happy spirit of complaisance was not likely to last. Moreover, and above all, Marx must have known full well how illusory the apparent might of the International really was, and how easily the hot breath of war would be able to sweep most of it away.

At this point we must, for the time being, leave the internal history of the I.W.M.A. ; for the story of its decline and fall cannot be told until we have considered the impact on the European working-class movement both of the outbreak of war between France and Prussia and of the sequel to France's defeat — the Paris Commune. We can then come back to relate the further history of the International in the light of these shattering events.

CHAPTER VII

THE PARIS COMMUNE

UP to 1870 Paris had been by far the most active centre of
the International Working Men's Association. Although
Trade Unions had been tolerated there only for a few
years and were still subject to police supervision ; although the
International itself was proscribed as an unlawful society and
its three successive Paris Councils were imprisoned ; although
there were constant prosecutions of Radicals and Socialists and
their journals were heavily censored ; despite all this, Paris in
the 1860s was in a growing ferment of working-class unrest.
There was much economic distress as well as political hostility
to the Second Empire ; and towards the end of the decade
strikes became frequent in the leading provincial towns as well
as in Paris. Lyons, Marseilles, Le Creusot, Brest, St.-Étienne,
Rouen were all centres of lively unrest and active organisation
under the banner of the International.

There were, however, sharp divisions within the ranks of the
Radical and working-class movements. The greatest single
influence among the Trade Unionists, especially in Paris, was
that of Proudhon ; and the aspect of Proudhon's doctrines
which was most to the fore was his 'mutualism'. As we have
seen, his projects of 'gratuitous credit' were much debated at
the Congresses of the International ; and the collapse in 1868
of the Mutual Credit Bank set up by his followers by no means
convinced them that his doctrines were at fault. They considered only that mutualism could not succeed in face of a
hostile State dominated by capitalist finance, and hoped that
the fall of the Empire, which was confidently expected, would
give them their chance. The Proudhonists in the International
were often accused of being in secret league with Napoleon ;
but this charge was nonsense. It was based on two facts — the
one, that Napoleon had indeed attempted to woo the workers'
leaders into courses of peaceful co-operation ; the other, that

the Paris leaders of the International, without accepting his overtures, had tried to take advantage of the relaxation of the laws against combination to organise legally instead of underground. Their critics, headed by Blanqui, who instructed his followers to boycott the International, regarded any such acceptance of legality as treason to the revolutionary cause, and pursued their methods of secret organisation of a revolutionary *élite* side by side with other underground Radical groups which held to the Jacobin traditions of conspiracy. As in the 1830s and 1840s Paris was honeycombed by revolutionary clubs and societies ; and the members of these conducted, with strong support from the University students, a series of short-lived Radical journals which continually led to prosecutions and suppressions by the police authorities. Among the most influential of the radical journalists was Henri Rochefort (1830–1913) who, after attacking the Government of Napoleon III in a succession of journals, founded *La Lanterne* in 1868, and soon found himself in prison for a year. Released in 1869, he renewed his attacks in a new journal, *La Marseillaise*, and was again sent to gaol. He was later to conduct *Le Mot d'ordre* in Paris during the Commune, and to be transported to New Caledonia for his attacks on Thiers. Later still, he was to support General Boulanger and to join in the hunt against Dreyfus. But in the late 'sixties he was reckoned the outstanding journalist of the Republican left.

Most of this out-and-out Radicalism was not Socialist in any definite sense ; and most of its leadership was furnished by intellectuals rather than workers, though Blanqui, working from his base in Brussels, had a substantial working-class following. Among the older Radicals the traditions of 1848 were strong ; and those who remembered the 'Days of June' looked back beyond 1848 and beyond 1830 to the great days of the Revolution of 1789 and especially to its apogee in 1792 and 1793, before it was overthrown by Napoleon I. These veterans of revolution hated Napoleon III both for his own misdeeds and for those of his uncle. They hated the Empire as the destroyer of the Revolution : they were ardent Republicans, to whom the Republic meant not merely the removal of the Emperor and the continued exile of Bourbon and Orleanist pretenders but also the overthrow of the State — of that great centralising power which was the constant enemy of human freedom. They were set on sweeping away the whole apparatus of autocratic power, even if they had only a vague notion of what they wanted to put in its place. Blanqui, with his conception of revolutionary dictatorship and his equalitarian notions derived from Babeuf, thought he knew, at any rate in outline, what kind of new society he was trying to build. But most of the traditional Jacobins were disposed to rest content with knowing their enemy and ready to assume that anything would come right when their enemy had been removed from power and the democratic Republic set up in his place.

This kind of Jacobin Radicalism had a strong egalitarian sentiment, but for the most part no hostility to property as such. It demanded complete political equality — a complete removal of political privileges — but it was hazy about its economic aspirations, except that it hated financiers, large-scale capitalists, and the hosts of corrupt pensioners of the imperial régime. It wanted fairer taxation as well as manhood suffrage and an executive directly and entirely subordinate to the elected legislature. It hated functionaries — above all policemen and the officers of the regular armed forces. It stood for a citizen militia, for an armed people that would take charge of its own defence. It was keenly suspicious of the Liberals and *bourgeois* Radicals who played the part of an official opposition ; but it also found itself to some extent following the lead of the more radical politicians, because there was no other lead to follow, except in underground conspiracy. There was no sharp line between those Radicals who wished to overthrow the Empire in order to put the *bourgeois* Republic in its place and those who, mindful of how the Republic had used them in 1848, hated it, in its *bourgeois* form, only less than they hated the Empire, and set against it the idea of a truly democratic Republic in which the people themselves would hold the power and would not yield it to any authoritative State apparatus — even to one based on manhood suffrage. For the Radical left wing, manhood suffrage had been poisoned by Napoleon III's plebiscites. They wanted manhood suffrage ; but they held that it could not work aright until it had been purged of its connection with the authoritarian State. But when it came to a question of voting, these left-wing Radicals could for the most part only choose between abstaining and voting for the *bourgeois* Radical politicians — or at any rate for those of them who made the most left-wing speeches. Some voted, and some abstained : to put up candidates of their own, under the Empire, seemed to many of them to be a treasonable act of compromise with a régime that could be displaced only by revolutionary action.

As in the course of the 1860s Trade Unions began to develop and to build up connections between trade and trade, a more specifically working-class movement began to detach itself from the radical mass. But here, too, there were difficult problems to be faced. At the one extreme there were a few who were prepared to compromise with the Empire to the extent of trying to keep the Unions out of politics and simply to take full advantage of such toleration as was extended to them by the Napoleonic State. But the vast majority of the industrial workers in the larger towns were much too deeply hostile to the Empire for such an attitude to be possible for them. There were, then, two alternatives : to make the most of the concessions and to organise openly, without renouncing opposition to the régime, or to refuse the concessions and attempt to organise secretly on definitely revolutionary lines. The Blanquists and many of the Jacobins favoured the latter policy ; but most of the active members of the numerous trade clubs of craftsmen very naturally preferred the other. They organised their clubs openly, and before long linked them together in Chambres Syndicales, representing a number of trades ; and then, growing bolder, they began to organise, side by side with these local federations of trade clubs, branches, or sections of the International Working Men's Association, both duplicating the membership of the clubs and enrolling directly large bodies of factory workers, miners, transport workers, and building workers who had not previously been organised at all, and for whom the craft friendly society was not a suitable basis for industrial action. In Paris and in a number of other towns, the Chambres Syndicales and the branches of the International came in the late 'sixties to exist side by side, with partly over-lapping membership and often sharing the same offices and places of reunion.

Under this arrangement the Chambres Syndicales represented chiefly skilled craftsmen, mostly working for small employers or, at any rate, in small workshops, or in their own homes ; whereas the branches of the International contained both a high proportion of less skilled workers and most of those who were employed in large establishments or on extensive works. But the leadership was largely common to the two groups, although there were among the craftsmen substantial numbers of moderates whose chief concern was with the affairs of the recognised skilled trades. Most of the moderates were in a sense revolutionaries — for they too wished to overthrow the Empire and believed in its impending fall. They were, however, more inclined both to support the more advanced *bourgeois* Radical politicians and to attempt to establish a working-class party to fight elections and aim at the building up of the constitutional Republic. It was from the craft clubs that came in 1863 the first group of working-class candidates for the Chamber, headed by Tolain, then their outstanding leader in Paris. From them too, the following year, came the 'Manifesto of the Sixty', signed by the leaders of most of the Parisian trade societies, with its claim for social emancipation as the complement to the political concession of universal suffrage. This movement was strongly influenced by Proudhon's *La Capacité politique des classes ouvrières* ; most of the French Proudhonists of the late 'sixties favoured political action in support of working-class claims, even though they looked forward to the disappearance of the political State when the workers had come into their own. This, too, was the group which came to London and there helped to constitute the First International.

At this stage Trade Union organisation had not yet spread beyond the skilled craftsmen. As we saw, the four French delegates who took part in the International's Inaugural Meeting in 1864 were all artisans, representing small-scale industry. One of them, Eugène Varlin, was soon to make himself the outstanding organiser of the French Trade Union movement, to extend his appeal from the craftsmen to the general body of workers, both in Paris and in the provinces, and to become the real leader of the International in France. But that development was still in the future. Of the others Tolain was an important political figure as well as a Trade Unionist — the leader of the 'Sixty' — but essentially a moderate, who found himself at home with the British Trade Unionists with whom he fraternised in London. The other two were like him, and were to find themselves, when the time came, ranged with Tolain as opponents of the Commune and denounced as traitors by their erstwhile comrades. These two dropped out of the International at a fairly early stage.

Tolain and his friends, however, were not Radical politicians of an orthodox parliamentary kind. They were followers of Proudhon, believers in small-scale private property, in free credit, and in the claim of each producer to be rewarded according to his works. They opposed any sort of collective ownership of the means of production as carrying with it the destruction of individual liberty. They attacked large-scale production and the growth of capitalism as involving the exploitation of the many by the few, and held by the notion that each producer should be entitled to demand, free of interest, the capital needed to enable him to pursue his trade, either individually or in association with others through Co-operative groups. The situation against which they were directly in revolt was one in which the skilled craftsman, unable to work for himself, had to sell his services either to a small-master middleman who was in turn exploited by the merchant-financier or directly to the latter, and had no access to the market except by way of the merchant-financier. Proudhon's idea of a great Central Credit Bank, making, through subsidiary banks, interest-free advances of capital, seemed to them the appropriate means to ensuring to each producer the full product of his labour. Proudhon, as we have seen, looked to the establishment of his proposed Bank, not by the State, which he rejected, but by the direct act of the people in setting it up and giving it an independent constitution quite apart from the State. It was the purpose of the Proudhonists, who stood for election as deputies in 1863 and in subsequent years, not to use the State as an instrument for nationalising banking, but to employ their influence to get the Bank set up independently and at the same time to get rid of the existing State — that is, of the Empire — by revolution. The Parliament of Napoleon was for them only a platform from which they hoped the better to preach their anti-statist doctrine.

Varlin, as far as we can tell, at this stage agreed with them, except that he put much more emphasis than they did both on mass-organisation of the workers in the economic field and on Co-operative association as against individual production. But his outlook was, by virtue of these two things, widely different from theirs, and speedily diverged further, because he thought in terms of large-scale as well as of small-scale industry and of the working class as a whole as well as of the individual artisans and their trade clubs.

This entire group — Varlin as well as Tolain — was, moreover, strongly hostile to centralisation. They were federalists, intent on building up working-class organisation on a local basis and then federating the local federations. The free France to which they looked forward was to be a country made up of locally autonomous communes, freely federated for common purposes which required action over larger areas, but with the local commune as the seat of power and no coercive authority vested in the larger federal groupings. In this sense they were Anarchists — though the name had hardly come into common use — repudiating the political State in all its forms — even the democratic Republic — and hostile to the Blanquists, whose notions of a revolutionary dictatorship seemed to them tainted with authoritarian conceptions. The only authority they were prepared to recognise was that of the people itself, directly expressed in the commune. They repudiated the idea of a revolutionary *élite* claiming to represent the people, and to tell it what to do.

In this matter the Jacobins held an ambiguous position. Often they denounced the Internationalists as 'Girondists' who refused to see the need for a directing revolutionary authority. But they also fell foul of the Blanquists, because they insisted that power must belong to the whole people and not to an *élite*. Moreover, most of the Jacobins also believed in the free commune as the necessary basic structure for a regenerated France, but did not go to the length of insisting that all authority must be vested in the local commune. They looked forward to a powerful revolutionary central authority which would replace the State of the exploiters by a Directory or Committee of Public Safety acting as the executant of the people and using direct legislation — the referendum — as its main law-making instrument. Apart from this, the Jacobins differed from both the Blanquists and the Internationalists in not thinking mainly in terms of class. Their outlook was primarily political, where that of the Internationalists was basically economic : it was based on an attempt to enlist mass support, where the Blanquists put their entire reliance in the revolutionary action of a 'conscious minority'.

Marx in his dealings with the French leaders was always in a difficulty. In the International he was scornful of Tolain's Proudhonism and bitterly opposed to his defence of small property. He was wholeheartedly in sympathy with Varlin's efforts to build up mass Trade Unionism as the foundation for a mass political movement of the workers, but deeply hostile to Varlin's Anarchist federalism, which he regarded as inconsistent with the need for consolidated and centralised class power as an instrument for the defence and construction of the new order. To the Jacobins Marx objected even more strongly, accusing them of being incurable doctrinaires, always harking back to the great days of 1789 and 1793 instead of studying the world around them, of ignoring the patent fact of the class-struggle, and of being only a sect among the *bourgeois* Radicals with no understanding of the social revolution for which they professed to stand. Marx, in effect, was temperamentally out of sympathy with every one of the French groups — despite what he found it in his heart to say of the Paris Commune in the hour of its defeat ; and his lack of sympathy for them all was an important factor in the chequered history of the First International.

By 1867 Varlin, and not Tolain, had become the effective leader of the French Sections of the I.W.M.A. Before long his militant leadership landed him in prison : he was unable to attend the International's Congresses in 1867 and 1868. When he came back, at the Basle Congress of 1869, the struggle about collective ownership was in effect already over. In the International, as well as in that part of the French Trade Union movement which continued to adhere to it,[1] the Proudhonists had been defeated, and the International had turned to the difficult task of defining the character of that collective ownership for which it had already in principle declared. In France,

[1] Proudhonist ideas continued none the less to have a strong hold on many of the French craft societies. The French Internationalists captured the Paris Section and were also dominant in Lyons, Marseilles, Brest, and a few other areas. But Proudhonism was by no means dead ; it remained a powerful influence and, as we shall see, reasserted itself strongly in the 1870s.

Napoleon III's Government had been alarmed by the spread of strikes and the growth of Trade Unions into persecuting the International. At a number of places soldiers were called in to shoot down strikers : the Trade Unions held protest demonstrations and collected funds to help the strikers both in France and in Switzerland and Belgium.

This rising tide of Trade Unionism, which was spreading over Spain as well as over France, Belgium, and Switzerland, and was also making itself felt in Great Britain and in Germany, was abruptly checked in 1870 by the outbreak of the Franco-Prussian War. The war, into which Bismarck had lured Napoleon III, confronted the working-class movements of both countries with a difficult problem. In France there was too deep hostility to the Second Empire for most of the working-class leaders to feel any call to support the war until the invasion of the country and the series of swift defeats which destroyed the armies of Napoleon had turned the issue into one of national defence against the threat of occupation and dismemberment. In Germany, where the Social Democratic Party under the leadership of Wilhelm Liebknecht and August Bebel had just become organised at the Eisenach Congress of 1869 in opposition to the Lassallians, the question of voting for the war credits in the North German Assembly had to be faced. The French Section of the International had sent to the German workers a manifesto calling for peace and international working-class solidarity ; and the Eisenachers had responded with a fraternal declaration. When war actually broke out, Napoleon III appeared to be the aggressor ; and a wave of patriotic feeling swept over Germany. The Lassallians in the North German Assembly voted for the war credits : Liebknecht and Bebel abstained, on the ground that they could not cast their votes in favour of a war waged by the Prussian autocracy, but equally could not vote in such a way as to appear to support Napoleon's aggression. Marx, appealed to for advice, on the whole approved their conduct, though Engels, in his correspondence with Marx on the subject, revealed himself as strongly in hope of a German victory. In the end Marx and Engels agreed that the correct course was to support the war as long as it remained defensive, but to take a strong line against any proposal to annex Alsace-Lorraine and to demand peace as soon as a

German victory had overthrown the Empire and cleared the way for a Republican Government in France.

The swift victories of the Prussian armies, the enforced surrender of Napoleon III at Sedan, and the collapse of the Second Empire left France disorganised and without a Government, and Paris under immediate threat of occupation. The old Government was swept away ; and a new Provisional Government of National Defence, with hardly a vestige of legality and very little popular support, took its place. Gambetta was sent to the country to galvanise resistance and to raise new armies ; and Paris prepared to stand siege. The Government despatched Thiers to tour the European capitals in search of help : in Paris the National Guard was reconstituted and suddenly assumed a major importance because arms were put into the workers' hands. In a military sense the defence of Paris was hopeless : invested by the Prussians, it could be starved out even if it could not be taken by assault. The new armies raised in the country met with speedy defeat : it became plain, at any rate to the Government, that there was no real alternative to capitulation on such terms as Bismarck was prepared to concede. The return of Thiers, empty-handed, and the surrender of Bazaine at Metz, confirmed these views. But the Parisians refused to see matters in the same light as their uneasy rulers. Blanqui himself, in his journal *La Patrie en danger*, and most of the Jacobins became ardent patriots, determined to fight on to the last man and regarding the surrender of Paris as an unbearable humiliation. They blamed the Government for remaining on the defensive, instead of sallying forth to drive the Prussians back. With Bazaine's surrender the murmurings against the Government rose to a height. Blanquist groups — against the advice of Blanqui, who thought the movements premature — twice attempted *coups* with the intention of installing a revolutionary Government, but received little support and were beaten back. In the meantime there were vain and ill-managed sorties, made under pressure by the Government's generals, who knew their futility ; and the food supplies of the isolated city rapidly ran out. The Government opened negotiations with the Prussians, who insisted on occupying the northern and eastern forts and on marching into the centre of the city.

Already the Paris National Guard, still under the command of government-appointed leaders, had set up its own Vigilance Committees in the arrondissements on which its organisation was based ; and most of these committees had sent delegates to a Central Committee representing the twenty arrondissements. This met on the same premises as the Chambre Fédérale of the Paris Trade Unions and the Paris Committee of the International. Paris had at this time no Municipal Council of its own : it was controlled by government-appointed military and civil officials. Each arrondissement had, indeed, a Mayor and two Deputies (Adjoints) with very limited powers ; and these local officers had taken on many new duties during the siege. They were of varied political views, according to the class-character of the different districts : the majority were *bourgeois* Liberals or Radicals, very few proletarians or even middle-class Socialists or revolutionaries. The leadership of the National Guard was more radical, but was made up mainly of unknown men, largely of the lower middle classes, with only a sprinkling of working-class activists.

With no more than a few days' provisions left and no hope of relief from without, the Provisional Government agreed to surrender the city. Under the proposed terms there was to be a truce. The Provisional Government was to resign, and an immediate election was to be held throughout France to choose a National Assembly, which was then to ratify terms of peace. The northern and eastern Paris forts were to be surrendered at once : the soldiers in Paris were to be disarmed, except a limited force of National Guards, which was to keep its weapons for the preservation of order.

The Assembly elected in February 1871 was almost incredibly reactionary. It consisted largely of monarchists — Legitimists and Orléanists in about equal numbers making up nearly two-thirds of the total. There was even a group of Bonapartists: Liberals and Republicans of all complexions were only a sixth of the whole. The Socialist and Jacobin left wing counted a bare 20 out of 630, including Louis Blanc, Delescluze, Victor Hugo, and other veterans of 1848, together with Henry Rochefort, the journalist, and four candidates from the workers' list — Tolain, Benoît Malon, Félix Pyat, and the Blanquist lawyer Charles Frédéric Gambon. The Assembly chose

Thiers to head the new Government that was to make the peace.

Bismarck's terms were hard : the cession of Alsace-Lorraine, a large indemnity, and the occupation of Paris itself by the Prussian army. But there was no real alternative to acceptance, and the Assembly agreed. The question was, how would Paris receive the news ?

Radical Paris received it with furious indignation. There were continual street demonstrations, kept down by the soldiers and police. For the first time revolutionary feeling spread beyond the professing revolutionaries and beyond the ranks of the organised working class. The National Guard, in opposition to the commanders imposed on it by the Government, began to organise on more comprehensive lines under a new and more representative Central Committee. There were seizures of weapons left unguarded : some battalions of the National Guard removed the artillery, which were to have been surrendered to the Prussians, to a place of relative safety. As the cannons had been bought for the National Guard by a public subscription of the Paris people, the attempt to surrender them caused much anger. There was some talk of armed resistance to the Prussians when they attempted to march into the city. In the event, no resistance was offered. The Prussians limited their occupation to a small area, and withdrew after two days to the northern and eastern forts : they made no attempt to enter the working-class areas, into which the advocates of resistance and much of the general population withdrew. Many of the upper- and middle-class Parisians fled from the city. When the Prussians had gone the people emerged, and street demonstrations were renewed. Meanwhile the Assembly, meeting at Bordeaux, passed decrees which created fresh indignation, requiring the immediate payment of overdue rents and bills and thus threatening many shopkeepers and householders with bankruptcy and destitution. Even greater was the fury when the Assembly, fearful of the Paris people, decided against sitting in the capital and, after some hesitation, settled upon Versailles. To the Parisians the 'decapitalisation' of their city appeared the final insult after their heroic defence. The tension grew more acute : Thiers, who had kept sending more troops to Paris to keep order, but could not trust them if it came to an insurrection, gave orders to evacuate the capital — army, Government departments, and all. Paris was left to its own devices, with no authority in charge, except a scratch committee of Mayors and Deputies, with no power behind them — and the new Central Committee of the National Guard. This latter still consisted mainly of men known only in their own districts; but it was in close touch with the Trade Union groups and with the Paris Sections of the International. It constituted, in effect, the only available authority after the withdrawal of the official Government; and the control of Paris passed for the time being into its hands.

This was the genesis of the Paris Commune. Long before, from the very moment of Napoleon's fall, there had been cries raised in Paris for 'the Commune' — cries which harked back to the revolutionary Commune of 1793, but meant different things to different utterers. At one extreme, the demand could mean no more than that Paris wanted municipal self-government, which had been denied to it under successive régimes. At the other, it meant the social revolution long dreamed of by the extreme left — a France made up of co-operating free Communes, each fully self-governing and federated from the bottom upwards to form such larger units of administration as might be needed, but so that the ultimate power would be vested in the Communes as directly representing the people. There were of course intermediate views. During the siege the 'Commune' had come to mean primarily the right of the Parisians to organise their own defence, instead of being subject to the nominees of the despised Provisional Government. But, when Thiers withdrew not only the army, but also the entire administrative machine, the Commune appeared to many who had hitherto opposed it, or been lukewarm, an imperative necessity; for how else was the city to be administered at all?

It is fairly clear by now, in the light of historical study, that Thiers, in ordering the withdrawal, was definitely making up his mind, if not to civil war, at all events to use any means that might be needed to bring the Parisians to heel. He could not hope to persuade the National Guard, outraged by the surrender and by the proceedings of the Assembly, to give up its arms; and he was not ready for an attempt to overcome its resistance by force. He had too few troops at his disposal; and those he had were mostly demoralised by defeat and could not be trusted. In order to overcome Paris he needed a new army and hoped to get it mainly from war prisoners whom he would induce Bismarck to surrender in order to 'restore order' and endow France with the stable Government the Prussians were demanding. By withdrawing and giving the Mayors no help to constitute a moderate administration, he in effect handed over Paris to the revolutionaries and forced the Commune upon them — so that he was committed to drowning it in blood unless it collapsed of its own accord. Thus could he hope to found the new *bourgeois* State with the applause of all respectable persons and to rid France once for all of the traditional revolutionary Paris which had been left as the legacy of 1789.

The Central Committee of the National Guard, left to fend for itself, had no thought of becoming the Government of revolutionary Paris. It had no mandate, its leaders declared ; and many of its members were aghast at the responsibility that had been thrust upon them. It decided immediately to hold elections for a fully representative Government of Paris, to be chosen by manhood suffrage. This body was to be called the 'Commune of Paris', and the Central Committee announced that, as soon as it had been elected, they would hand over their authority to it. The Mayors and Deputies, in the meantime, were endeavouring to mediate between Thiers and the Parisians; but Thiers put them off with words and gave them no help. On March 28th the Commune was elected by a vote of 229,000 electors out of 485,000 on the registers — a heavy vote, as many of the inhabitants had left the city. It was by no means, at the outset, a body composed only of revolutionaries. Quite a number of moderate Liberals and Radicals were elected, mainly from the middle-class areas ; but these either did not take their seats or soon withdrew. The rest were a mixture of well-known Radicals, including many journalists, members of the Central Committee of the National Guard, Blanquists, and Jacobins from the revolutionary clubs, and working-class members and a few others connected with the International. The Internationalists numbered 17 out of 92, of whom 21 soon resigned and were replaced by supplementary elections. The majority, after the changes, was Jacobin-Blanquist, with the Internationalists forming a fairly compact minority.

It is no part of my purpose in this book to re-tell the tragic story of the Paris Commune. My concern is with its place in the history of Socialist thought, and I have had to include so much factual recital of the events which led up to it only because its nature cannot be understood without reference to its origins. I think I have made it clear that the Commune arose, not because a compact body of revolutionary Socialists had planned it in advance, as the model organisation for a new Socialist society, but because events dictated its structure. To be sure, the idea of some sort of revolutionary Commune had been in the minds of the Paris left ever since 1793 ; and the cry for 'the Commune' had been raised in every revolutionary crisis. But there had been no clear idea of the Commune as a new kind of workers' State, resting on proletarian dictatorship or on any basis other than that of free, equal, and universal manhood suffrage. The commune was for Frenchmen the traditional unit of local administration : France was made up of local communes ; and every opponent of centralised State power naturally thought of the commune as the point of focus for a rival power emanating directly from the people. The Paris Commune became a body primarily representing the working classes only because the respectable classes either fled from Paris or elected representatives who, hostile to the Revolution, refused to serve. Even to the end a high proportion of the members were not workmen but middle-class Radicals and Jacobins in sympathy with working-class demands, including many returned exiles of 1848. The Commune included, too, not a few members of the Paris lower-middle class, who had found their way into the Revolution through the National Guard.

Who were the Commune's leaders ? They were too many, and too various, for any coherent leadership to emerge from their debates. No one man stands out as the central figure : there is rather an endless series of 'close-ups' against a background of tangled cross-purposes and confusions. Out of 36 of the principal figures, for whom I have been able to find birth-dates, 7 were under thirty years old, and 21 under thirty-five. Another 5 were under forty, leaving only 10 over that age. Of these latter, 5 were in their forties, 2 in their fifties, 2 in their sixties, and 1, Charles Beslay, seventy-five. They were thus predominantly a group of young men, with half the total number under thirty-two, and a clustering round about thirty, especially of the manual workers connected with the International and of the followers of Blanqui.

Let us consider a number of the outstanding persons, beginning with the oldest. Charles Beslay (1795–1878) was a follower of Proudhon, a credit reformer, and a bit of a crank. He belonged to the International, and was one of its few *bourgeois* members. He was a man of some means, altogether honest, but no leader. After the fall of the Commune he escaped to Switzerland, where he wrote his reminiscences (*Mes Souvenirs*, 1873, and *La Verité sur la Commune*, 1877). His influence on the events of 1871 was not very large.

Next in age was Louis Charles Delescluze (1809–71), a veteran of the 1848 Revolution and a former lieutenant of Ledru-Rollin in exile. Delescluze was an advanced Radical, and a Socialist after the fashion of 1848 rather than of any later school. He had been the editor of several revolutionary journals, from *La Révolution démocratique et sociale* in 1848, to the *Réveil*, which he started in 1868 to attack the Government of Napoleon III. He was the outstanding personality among what can be called the 'old Jacobin' group. He possessed both courage and integrity, and struggled hard to hold the conflicting groups together and to prevent the excesses of the Commune's last days. Against his will, he was made military director during the closing phases of the hopeless struggle : at the very end, when resistance was almost over, he exposed himself deliberately on a barricade, and died not ignobly.

A year younger than Delescluze was Félix Pyat (1810–89), romantic dramatist and orator with a strong taste for self-dramatisation, but no capacity for practical affairs. Pyat could make speeches, or draft proclamations ; but he was of no use in an emergency. He had been a considerable figure in Paris literary circles, an intimate of George Sand and a successful playwright and journalist. In the Commune he was out of his element among the intensely serious-minded young artisans, who thought him rather ridiculous and sometimes accused him of cowardice as well as of vainglory. Like Beslay, he escaped, and survived to come back to France and play some further part in Radical politics in his last years.

Next in age comes Jules Allix (1818–97), the inventor who

had undergone prolonged imprisonment under Napoleon III. He suffered from fits of insanity. The Commune made him a general, but he went off his head and had to be shut up. The Versaillese sent him to an asylum, from which he emerged in his latter years to play an active part in the movement for women's suffrage. Then comes the great painter, Gustave Courbet (1819–77), who became Chairman of the Committee of Revolutionary Artists. He was sentenced to a heavy fine for his share in the destruction of the Vendôme Column, but escaped to Switzerland.

These five were the veterans. Then we come to General Gustave Paul Cluseret (1823–1900), whose disputed title of 'General' came from the American Civil War. As a young soldier, he had fought against the workers in 1848. He is a rather enigmatic figure, boastful and swaggering, with a good deal in him of the adventurer. His military reputation gained him for a brief period the generalship of the Commune's army ; but he was incompetent, and was soon deposed. He was another of those who escaped abroad and survived to write his memoirs. Apart from a general leftism, he had no very clear political views, though he became a member of the I.W.M.A. in 1871.

Gustave Lefrançais (1826–1901) was another who survived to write, in Switzerland, a study of the Commune and, later, to publish his memoirs. He was associated with the Internationalist group, but often acted with Delescluze. He tried to prevent the execution of the Commune's hostages, and showed a fair amount of common sense. Lefrançais took part in the anti-Marxist St.-Imier Congress of 1872 : later, he emigrated to the United States.

Gabriel Ranvier (1828–79) came to the Commune from the Central Committee of the National Guard. He was mayor of Belleville, the only mayor of a Paris arrondissement who was wholeheartedly for the Commune from the first. It was he who uttered the words proclaiming its establishment ; and he also posted its last proclamation, and led the defence of Belleville to the very end. He escaped to England and was a Blanquist delegate at the Hague Congress of the International in 1872.

Next in age were Antoine Magliore Brunel (1830–71), who

played a notable part in the fighting, in which he was killed, and the celebrated Louise Michel (1830–1905), whom we shall meet again as a leader in the Anarchist movement. She took part in the fighting, and was accused of having been active in the burning of buildings. She demanded the death sentence, defying her accusers ; but she was transported to New Caledonia, whence she returned to play a leading part in the reviving Trade Union movement, and to write her memoirs.

Arthur Ranc (1831–1908) was a follower of Gambetta and a Radical journalist. He stood well on the right of the Commune's leadership. He had edited Buonarroti's *History of the Conspiracy of the Equals* and the journal *La Petite République*.

Gustave Flourens (1831–71), the next in seniority, was the son of a professor of science at the Collège de France and had taught there himself. He had been an active revolutionary under Napoleon III, and had been implicated in an attempt on his life. He had been condemned to death for his part in the abortive rising of October 1870, but had been released from prison in January 1871 together with other convicted revolutionaries by a crowd organised by the Blanquist leaders still at large. He was a swashbuckling romantic, with a keen taste for leading forlorn hopes. He was killed in a *sortie* against the Versaillese in the early days of the Commune.

No other leader on my list of 36 was over forty. The next in age was the novelist and journalist Jules Vallès (1832–1885), author of the largely autobiographical trilogy, *Jacques Vintras*. During the 1860s he had written for the *Courrier français*, and during the Commune he continued to conduct his own journal, *Le Cri du peuple*. Vallès was a mordant critic of *bourgeois* society, and an associate of the Blanquist group, though not a member of it. He escaped to London.

A year younger than Vallès was Charles Longuet (1833–1901), soon to become Karl Marx's son-in-law. Longuet had been active in politics from his student days : he had been a follower of Proudhon, but came over to the International. During the Commune he edited the *Journal officiel*. Later, he played a large part in Guesde's Parti Ouvrier and wrote a number of books on Socialism. He and his wife committed suicide together in 1901.

Three years younger was the Pole, Walery Wroblewski

(1836–1908), who served the Commune well as a military leader, and was lucky enough to escape. Next came another Internationalist, Jean Baptiste Clément (1837–1903), who also escaped to play a further part in the movement in London. The other leading Pole, Jaroslaw Dombrowski (1838–71), was probably the best of the Commune's generals. He had taken an active part in the Polish rising of 1863, and, like Wroblewski, was living in Paris as an exile. He was killed in the fighting. Prosper Oliver Lissagaray (1838–1901), who survived to write one of the best histories of the Commune and was thought likely at one time to marry Marx's third daughter, was in the fighting to the end, but got away.

The next in age of the 36 was only thirty-two years old; and with this group we enter on a new and different generation, composed mainly of leaders of the Parisian Trade Unionists and of the Paris Section of the International and of the young men, largely students, who had gathered round Blanqui. These formed a group very close together in age. Of the Internationalists Varlin and Theisz were both thirty-two; Pindy and Camélinat were thirty-one; Assi, Malon, and Duval were all thirty; Jourde and Allemane were twenty-eight, and Frankel only twenty-seven. In the same age-group belonged the Blanquists Protot, who was thirty-two, Vaillant, who was thirty-one, Tridon, who was thirty, and Eudes, who was only twenty-seven. Still younger were the two Blanquists who came into greatest disrepute as successive Chiefs of the Police Department of the Commune — Ferré was twenty-six and Raoul Rigault only twenty-five. To complete the list, the Proudhonist Vermorel was thirty, and Rossel, the regular officer, who for a time took command of the Commune's armed forces, was only twenty-eight. A good many of these younger men either perished in the fighting or were executed or transported to New Caledonia when it was over.

Eugène Varlin (1839–71), who was captured, mutilated, and at last shot at the end of the fighting, was, as we have seen, the principal leader of the Trade Unions and the outstanding figure in the Paris I.W.M.A. During the Commune he undertook a great variety of tasks, first as the delegate to the Bank of France and then in one capacity after another, wherever the need was most urgent. I have said so much of him elsewhere in this volume that no more need be said here. Albert Theisz (1839–81), the wood-carver, who was his close associate in the Trade Union movement and in the I.W.M.A., was Secretary of the Paris Chambre Syndicale and delegate to several Congresses of the I.W.M.A. He served the Commune as delegate for Posts and Telegraphs, and fell wounded in the last stage of the fighting. He was condemned to death, but escaped.

Louis-Jean Pindy (1840–1917) was another of the 'Internationalist' group. He was a joiner. During the Commune he served on the Military Commission. He was lucky enough to escape to Switzerland, where, as we shall see, he took part in the attempt to revive the French Section of the I.W.M.A. and was in close touch with Guillaume and Kropotkin. Rémy Zéphirin Camélinat (1841–1932), another 'Internationalist', was a bronze-worker, and under the Commune was put in charge of the Mint. He had led the Paris metal-workers in their strike in 1866 and had been active with Varlin in the Chambres Syndicales. He was one of the longest-lived of all the Communards, taking an active part in the French Socialist movement from the amnesty up to his death in 1932. He received an impressive public funeral.

Adolphe-Alphonse Assi (1841–86), also of the I.W.M.A., had been the leader of the Le Creusot strike of 1870. He was a skilled mechanic. It fell to him to be chairman of the Commune's sessions during the early stages, and on this account the Commune was sometimes dubbed 'the Government of M. Assi'. He was not, however, a person of any outstanding importance. He was deported to New Caledonia, whence he returned to play some part in the workers' movement in the 1880s.

Benoît Malon (1841–93) began life as a working painter. At the beginning of the Commune he was deputy-mayor (adjoint) of the 17th arrondissement, active in the Paris Trade Union movement and as a journalist — he reported the I.W.M.A.'s doings in Rochefort's *Marseillaise* — and closely associated with the novelist Mme Léodile Champseix, who wrote under the name of André Leo. He and she together wrote an appeal to the agricultural workers to support the Commune. They escaped together to Switzerland after the defeat; and Malon, as we shall see in later chapters, lived not only to produce the first large-scale *History of Socialism*, but also to become the real founder of the Independent Socialists and to establish the *Revue socialiste*. His later career will lap over into the third volume of this work.

Of the same age as Malon was Émile Victor Duval (1841–1871), another member of the International, who fought bravely but was captured and shot by the Versaillese at a fairly early stage in the fighting.

François Jourde (1843–93) was in the last fighting. He was captured and transported to New Caledonia, whence he came back after the amnesty and wrote his memories of the Commune. At the beginning of the Commune he and Varlin shared the responsibility for its finances, and for dealing with the Bank of France. Varlin was soon called away to other duties ; but Jourde remained at his post, keeping a scrupulous account of the Commune's financial affairs, which he produced at his trial. Jourde was a thoroughly competent and most conscientious administrator, who kept his head through all the confusions of the period. He was one of those who came to the Commune from the Central Committee of the National Guard : he was not by nature a politician, but rather a methodical office administrator. Jean Allemane (1843–1935) we shall meet with again as the leader of the left wing of the Possibilist Socialist Party from the 1880s. He was among those transported to New Caledonia.

Leo Frankel (1844–96), youngest of the outstanding leaders of the 'International' group, was a jewellery worker, Hungarian by birth. He had come to France only a few years before the Commune, and before moving to Paris had helped to found the Lyons Section of the I.W.M.A. The Paris Commune made him its delegate for Labour and Industry ; and, as we shall see, he was mainly responsible for such constructive work in the economic field as the Commune found opportunity to begin. Frankel was wounded in the fighting. He escaped to London, where Marx made him I.W.M.A. Corresponding Secretary for Hungary. Later he returned to his birthplace, Budapest, was one of the founders of the Hungarian Social Democratic Party, and took part in the early activities of the Second International.

That finishes the 'Internationalists' — those who figure in

my rather arbitrary list. There remain seven names — five of them followers of Blanqui. The oldest of these young men was Eugène Protot (1839–1921), who had been active in his student days and, as we have seen, had attempted to attend the Congress of the International in connection with the League of Peace and Freedom. Protot was a lawyer and became the Head of the Commune's Department of Justice. He was thought to have perished in the fighting, but survived to a ripe old age.

Next in age among the Blanquists was Édouard Vaillant (1840–1915), civil engineer and physicist, whom the Commune put in charge of education. Vaillant set to work to organise the schools on a basis of *laïcité*, and did the job as well as the conditions allowed. He escaped to Switzerland and was later in London. On the amnesty he returned to France and became the leader of the Blanquists in the Chamber of Deputies, until the Socialist unification of 1905, when he took his place in the Unified Party. He was a man of high ability who remained faithful to the revolutionary and rationalist Republicanism of his youth.

Gustave Tridon (1841–71) was Blanqui's closest associate. He was joint editor with Blanqui of *La Patrie en danger* in 1870, and had previously edited his own journal, *Candide*. A lawyer by training, and a man of some means, he belonged to the left wing of the Blanquists. His brief career ended with the Commune.

Émile Eudes (1844–88), another Blanquist of the left and a notable freethinker, was joint editor with Blanqui of *Ni Dieu ni maître*. During the Commune he was active chiefly on the military side, and was one of the Commune's commanding generals. He escaped to Switzerland and thence to London, where he became the leader of the Blanquist group organised in the Comité Central Révolutionnaire. He continued to collaborate closely with Vaillant, and with him edited *L'Homme libre*. He was one of the principal leaders of Blanquism in France after the amnesty.

The remaining Blanquists, Théophile Ferré (1845–71) and Raoul Rigault (1846–71), who both perished, shared the main responsibility for the Police Department of the Commune and were thus in charge of the hostages arrested when the Versaillese began killing their prisoners as well as of the rest of those arrested and imprisoned under the Commune. It was Ferré who almost at the end authorised the shooting, among other hostages, of Darboy, the Archbishop of Paris. A chemist by profession, he was in politics a cold-blooded terrorist. He was captured and shot by the Versaillese. Rigault was, by comparison, a much less unlovable character — a hot-headed revolutionary, who had been an active Blanquist from his law-student days. As head of the Police Department he made fierce speeches and arrested a great many people, but let most of them go. Only towards the end did he order the killing of a number of prisoners ; but in the latter stages he lost his head, and turned bloodthirsty in revenge. He was caught and shot, unrecognised, in the final fighting, and was subsequently tried in absence and condemned to death. The police continued for some time to chase him in ignorance of his fate.

There remain two persons on my list. The first of these is the Proudhonist journalist Auguste Vermorel (1841–71), who had been the editor of the very effective opposition journal, *Le Courrier français*. He had written important books, too — *Les Hommes de 1848* and *L'Opposition*. He died on the barricades. The other is General Nathaniel Rossel (1843–71), an engineer-captain in the regular army, who had escaped from the defeated army of Bazaine, and was made the Commune's General-in-Chief — a post from which he soon removed himself when his military methods did not meet with the approval of the National Guard. Rossel had no previous connection with the Socialist or working-class movement : he joined the Commune because he was shocked by the collapse of the French forces and opposed to the Provisional Government's surrender to the Prussians. He was captured, tried, and shot after the Commune's fall. He was only 28.

This list is, I admit, arbitrary. It leaves out a number of men who after playing some part in the Commune became important, or at any rate well known, for their later achievements — for example, Paul Brousse, later to be the leader of a party called after him which, rejecting Guesde's Marxist orthodoxy, kept its separate existence up to the unification of 1905. It omits also Kropotkin's ally, Élisée Réclus, the geographer, who was the Commune's library director. But it includes, I think, all the active leaders who played an important part in the Commune's affairs. I have left out Henri de Rochefort because, although he paid the penalty of transportation to New Caledonia, he was never really a Communard.

Out of the 36, exactly half — 18 — escaped abroad, mostly to Switzerland or England; 10 were killed in the fighting, or shot out of hand after capture; 2 were executed after trial, and 5 transported to New Caledonia. One — Allix — was interned in an asylum. Thus, only one-third of these leaders perished — a small proportion, considering the intensity and ferocity of the fighting and of the vengeance taken during the 'Bloody Week' (*la semaine sanglante*) which put an end to the struggle. From the magnitude of the total casualties it is evident that the leaders fared better than the led. No one will ever know accurately how many Parisians perished in that bloody week, or in the subsequent hue and cry. One estimate puts the numbers killed on the barricades at about 2500, and of those killed after the fighting was over at 14,000. Another puts the total at 30,000 killed and 45,000 prisoners. Hanotaux says that there were 35,000 prisoners at Versailles, a good many of whom died, and that the number arrested up to 1875 — for the hue and cry continued — was 43,521. This figure of course excludes the slain. Lists survive showing the occupations of about 20,000 of those who were tried by regular courts. These lists include 2901 labourers, 2664 mechanics and locksmiths, 2293 masons, 1659 joiners, 1598 commercial employees, 1491 shoemakers, 1065 clerical workers, 863 house-painters, 819 compositors, 766 stone-cutters, 681 tailors, 636 cabinet-makers, 528 jewellery workers, 382 carpenters, 347 tanners, 283 monumental sculptors, 227 tinsmiths, and so on, down to 106 teachers, and to a long list of less numerous occupations. The vast majority of the condemned were manual workers, well spread over the trades and industries of Paris.

During its brief existence of two months the Paris Commune had no chance to lay even the foundations of a new society. Its task was to fight — a task which was hopeless from the moment when the idea of a mass *sortie* against Versailles had been given up and Thiers had been left free to build up the military force with which to crush the Revolution. Indeed, it was probably hopeless from the very first; for the Commune's armed force, made up mainly of the National Guard, was better suited to defence than to attack ; and a successful attack, had it been possible, would probably but have provoked Prussian intervention. Had the provincial towns risen and successfully set up their own Communes, the dispersal of the Assembly's weak forces might have given Paris a chance, at least of compromise. But such movements as there were in the provinces — at Lyons, Marseilles, St.-Étienne, Brest, and a few other places — were easily crushed ; and in face of the overwhelming electoral victory of the reaction Paris was entirely isolated. The Commune debated in an atmosphere of inevitable defeat, even if its members could not bring themselves to admit the truth. Their main cares had to be military, and in such a situation a body so heterogeneously composed was bound to fall to quarrelling and to looking for scapegoats when things went wrong. Leo Frankel, in charge of the affairs of Labour and Industry, did his best to get factories and workshops deserted by their owners reopened as Co-operatives, to improve labour conditions, and to collaborate with the Trade Unions. He was able to get a number of workshops into operation, to improve wages on public contracts, to abolish night baking, and to put through some secondary reforms ; but there was no time for much to be done. Édouard Vaillant, who was in charge of Education, made plans for free and compulsory secular instruction, but most of his reforms remained on paper for want of means to put them into effect. François Jourde and Eugène Varlin, who were made mainly responsible for organising the Commune's financial affairs, behaved with remarkable moderation. They let the Bank of France alone, on condition that it provided funds for carrying on the Commune's affairs ; and the Bank, doubtless in consultation with Versailles, doled out enough bank-notes to enable the Communards to make ends meet, with the aid of the taxes they continued to levy and of some special loans. It would not have suited Thiers to have the Bank taken over and the whole financial structure disorganised ; and Jourde and Varlin were not prepared to face, in the midst of the crisis, the task of constructing a new financial system. Later, Varlin transferred his main attention elsewhere : Jourde carried on to the end, keeping the Commune's accounts with scrupulous accuracy and maintaining a strict financial orthodoxy in spite of the clamour of Proudhonists and monetary cranks.

All in all, the Commune had little to show in the way of
socialist construction, unless it be counted to it as Socialism
that it replaced the old bureaucracy with men working at
workmen's wages. A high proportion of the lower officials and
clerks remained at work when their superiors withdrew to
Versailles ; and the Commune seems to have been remarkably
successful in getting the essential public services back into
operation. They continued to work right through the fighting,
until they were disorganised again during the final collapse.

The Commune's great difficulties were military. It changed
its military commanders again and again, imprisoned some of
them when things went wrong, and never gave them any clearly
defined authority. Its main military force, the National Guard,
could never be treated as a regular army. Based on local battalions and legions (groups of battalions from the same arrondissement) it was intensely devoted to the defence of its own
districts. It had, moreover, its own structure of authority ;
for its Central Committee did not disband upon the election of
the Commune, but remained in existence side by side with the
Commune's Military Commission, without any clear demarca-
tion of powers or functions. The first military commander,
Cluseret, was incompetent : Nathaniel Rossel, who succeeded
him, was a regular officer who could never get on terms with
the unmilitary habits of the National Guard, and could not get
his orders carried out. The Commune's best generals were the
Poles Jaroslaw Dombrowski and Walery Wroblewski, who
fought manfully ; but Wroblewsky held only a secondary
position, and Dombrowski became commander too late in any
case to retrieve the Commune's military fortunes. The Blanquist Brunel also did well, but fell into disgrace through no
fault of his own. Émile Victor Duval, a dissident Blanquist
who had joined the International, was killed early in the fighting. As the imminence of defeat became more obvious, the
military leaders' position was further complicated by changes
in the political control. Two successive Committees of Public
Safety, appointed to bring order out of chaos, succeeded only in
making it worse ; for the Commune itself, its Commissions, and
the Central Committee of the National Guard continued in
being side by side with them, issuing conflicting instructions.
Disastrous disaccords arose over the appointment of these

Public Safety Committees, and over other matters, between the Jacobin-Blanquist majority of the Commune and the Internationalists, who objected to Jacobin dictatorship and wanted to give the Commune a more definitely working-class character. For a time the Internationalists even withdrew from the sittings of the Commune, though they continued their work on the various functional Commissions.

In these disputes the Blanquists and old-time Jacobins were in general the extremists, and the Internationalists, headed by Varlin, Frankel, and Jourde, and backed by a number of the National Guard's representatives, the moderates. The Internationalists had a keen sense of the need to keep close to the main body of the workers and to interpret their desires. They had no faith in Blanquist revolutionary *élites* or in Jacobins who were constantly recalling the memories of old revolutions. But inevitably, as the situation became more hopeless, the extremists got more of their way. Even so, till almost the last, the Commune behaved with remarkable humanity towards its enemies. The Versaillese, from the first, shot and maltreated prisoners and uttered daily threats of no quarter to the rebels. The Communards for some time freely allowed their opponents to leave Paris for Versailles, and, even when they imitated Bismarck's example by taking hostages and threatening to shoot them if the Versaillese continued to shoot their prisoners, refrained from carrying out their threats — which were in fact carried out only at the last, and then only in a few cases — when all central control had broken down. Even the fiery Blanquist, Raoul Rigault, in charge of the Police Department, though addicted to violent utterances, did little, till he lost his head at the end, to justify the execrations which have been heaped upon him. It was Ferré, his successor, who signed the order to execute the Archbishop of Paris.

In comparison with the Versaillese, the Commune for the most part was far from brutal. It was indeed strongly criticised by Marx, even while he was defending it, for having shown undue hesitation in attacking the fundamental institutions of the old order. It produced much blood-and-thunder oratory and journalism, as was to be expected ; but its bark was a great deal fiercer than its bite. Most of its Jacobins were at bottom ardent humanitarians, not the ruffians they were taken for by

e horrified *bourgeois* of Europe. Thiers was infinitely more
vage than any leading Communard ; and Thiers himself was
t behind in brutality by many of his Versailles supporters.
iis brutality of the 'right' was no doubt largely the outcome
fear. The French upper classes, humiliated by the Prus-
ins, were in double terror of revolutionary Paris ; and their
irs destroyed all understanding and sense of compassion.
iey became sheer savages, athirst for blood. On their behalf
iiers and his generals carried fire and sword through the
eets of Paris, killing and mutilating their prisoners as they
vanced. On their behalf Thiers and his judges followed up
eir victory with the trials and executions, the mass-deporta-
ins to New Caledonia — all the atrocities that, more than
ything else, made the Paris Commune an undying memory
r the European Socialist movement. In the short run, the
utality succeeded : revolutionary Paris was blotted out for a
neration, and France settled down to the reactionary régime
the Third Republic — Republic only because there was no
inarch on whom the reactionaries could agree.

The fall of the Commune destroyed the First International
already greatly weakened by the outbreak of the Franco-
ussian War. In France itself, almost nothing was left of the
werful working-class movement which Varlin — killed in the
hting — and his comrades had built up. The French
icialist movement survived only in exile ; for the handful of
iderates, such as Louis Blanc and Tolain, who had taken sides
ainst the Commune and tried only to mitigate the severity of
e repression, counted for nothing. They were regarded as
inegades by the surviving working-class leaders and treated
th contempt by the triumphant reactionaries. Of the group
icted to the Assembly just before the Commune, Gambon,
alon, and Pyat had resigned their seats and rallied to the
fence of Paris. Louis Blanc and Tolain alone had remained
Versailles, discredited and helpless. Blanqui himself, the
elong revolutionary, had been out of it all because he was
vay from Paris, ill and with a price on his head, when the
evolution he had been hoping for at last broke out. The
termath found him back in prison, where he had spent most
his adult life.

The exiled Communards and left-wing leaders — those

who escaped the massacre and the transportations — soon fell to quarrelling abroad. The Blanquists, who formed the most coherent group, at first joined the International, which they had hitherto despised, and then, as we shall see, walked out of it in disgust after the Hague Congress of 1872. In Great Britain, meanwhile, the International had been falling to pieces. The Trade Union leaders had for the most part lost interest in it even before the Commune, being heavily preoccupied with their own affairs. They had never sent many delegates to its Congresses : indeed after 1866 the only prominent leaders to appear at all, except Eccarius, were Benjamin Lucraft in 1868 and 1869, and Robert Applegarth in 1869. The other British delegates were either middle-class supporters, such as Cowell Stepney and Alfred Walton, or minor figures, such as James Carter, Thomas Mottershead, and John Hales. Nor had the Trade Union leaders been at all regular in their attendance at the General Council, which was left to be run mainly by Marx, Eccarius, Jung, and a few others — mostly foreigners. Up to 1871, however, the International had been able to count on the nominal adhesion of many of the principal British Trade Union leaders. Marx's impassioned defence of the Commune (known as *The Civil War in France*), issued in the name of the International, brought this situation to an end. Lucraft and George Odger, almost the only outstanding British Trade Unionists remaining on the International's General Council, resigned in protest against Marx's manifesto ;[1] and, as far as Great Britain was concerned, the International ceased from that time to have any real connection with the main body of the working-class movement. Marx, in anger, accused the British leaders of having 'sold the movement to Gladstone' ; but in truth they had never been revolutionaries, and the Paris Commune was much too strong meat for them. They had always regarded the International mainly as a means of organising Trade Unions and promoting mutual help across frontiers in strike action and, to a smaller extent, as an instrument for promoting working-class candidatures and agitating for electoral reform. In 1871, faced with the need to defeat the Criminal Law Amendment

[1] George Howell, who became Secretary to the Trades Union Congress in 1871, also resigned about this time ; but I am not sure exactly when, or for what reason.

Bill and to secure the full legalisation of Trade Unions, they were especially anxious not to antagonise middle-class parliamentary support. To have sided with the Paris Commune would have been to wreck their prospects of success at home, even had they not been genuinely shocked by Marx's defence of it. Socialism and the class-war had but little following in the Great Britain of 1871. Chartism was dead, and no successor to it had yet been born.

The Paris Commune, then, went a long way towards destroying the International, quite apart from the disputes between Marx and Bakunin which were soon to give it the *coup de grâce*. Up to 1870 France, and not either Great Britain or Germany, had been the real centre of the International's activity as a mass workers' movement, with offshoots in Belgium and in French Switzerland. The Germans, busy building up their own movement and torn by the quarrel between Lassalians and Marxists, had played but little part in it : the British, despite appearances to the contrary, in truth even less. In Italy and Spain, even when the workers acted nominally in the International's name, they had always gone their own ways, paying no attention to the wishes of the General Council in London. Moreover, France, or rather Paris, had been in the 1860s still the unquestioned centre of the European revolutionary movement ; and its overthrow meant, fully as much as in 1848, that reaction was back in the saddle. Marx must already have known in 1871, as he had known in 1851, that for the time being the revolutionary game was up. But there were many who were unaware of this : the shadow of the Workers' International remained, even when its substance had melted away.

What, as we look back, are we to characterise as the essential contribution of the Paris Commune to the development of socialist thought ? Marx, in *The Civil War in France*, praised the Communards as having found, by revolutionary instinct rather than by any process of ratiocination, the correct form for the class uprising of the workers — the revolutionary Commune as a working agency combining legislative and executive functions and thus doing away with the separate authority of a State machine superimposed upon the people. He praised the Commune because its members worked for ordinary wages, as fellow-workers with the rest of the proletariat, and not as a higher class to which the people owed obedience. The existing States, as he saw them, were instruments of government vested with authority over a body of subjects, controlled by a privileged minority and supported by a coercive apparatus of army and police subject only to themselves. As against this the Commune, emerging directly from a popular vote, itself not only made the laws but supervised their execution through its delegates, who were responsible to it and to its commissions for the day-to-day working of the various departments. There were no high executive officers vested with authority apart from the Assembled Commune : the entire corps of *fonctionnaires* worked directly under the control of the elected members of the Commune ; and these elected members were in turn directly responsible to the citizens who had chosen them.

In all this there is, of course, a good deal of resemblance to the system of responsible government which has developed since in such countries as Great Britain and Sweden, where the Government departments work directly under the orders of Cabinet Ministers and the Cabinet is responsible to a legislature elected by universal suffrage. But that was not how Marx saw the situation. In 1870 there was no country in which such a system existed. Great Britain came nearest to it in many respects ; but the structure there still rested, even after 1867, on a franchise which left the main power in the hands of the middle classes, and on the still unbroken power of the House of Lords and the Crown. Moreover, the British State still carried in its very being — as to a smaller extent it does even to-day — class-characteristics which made it impossible to think of it as an emanation of the popular — much less of the workers' — will. The army and the civil service, the municipal and county government, the educational system were still firmly in the hands of the upper and upper-middle classes : only in the elected part of the legislature had even the possibility of any direct representation of the workers appeared, and the House of Commons still contained not even one working-class member. It was natural for Marx to think of all existing States as coercive agencies superimposed on the workers, and not as democratic agencies through which the workers could express their will. Moreover, Marx thought of States as essentially class institutions. He could not conceive that existing States could be captured by the workers and used to carry out the changes required for a revolution in the very foundations of society. Such changes, he held, must be the work of the workers themselves, acting as a class and on a basis of class organisation for power. The workers could not hope to carry them through by methods which involved departing from the basis of class-action and collaborating with *bourgeois* or *petit-bourgeois* politicians. Marx believed the workers ought to *support* the more radical sections of the *bourgeoisie* in fighting against the reactionaries ; but *support* and *collaboration* were, in his view, different things. In order to support without being engulfed in *bourgeois* politics, the workers must maintain the strict separateness of their own class organisation and class action. It might suit them to help the *bourgeoisie* to capture the State from the feudalists — the old privileged classes — or to urge on the lesser *bourgeoisie* against the greater. But the purpose of all true proletarian politics must be, not to capture the existing States, but to overthrow them and to put in their place new 'States' constructed to suit the needs of the proletariat raised to the status of a ruling class. Thereafter, the workers' State might be allowed to 'wither away', but only when it had used its authority to remove the danger of counter-revolution by the actual abolition of class differences.

Thus, Marx saw the removal by Thiers from Paris of the entire superstructure of the old State — army, government, upper civil service, and armed police — as the opportunity for the workers to set about the construction of a quite new State of their own. In this light he interpreted the constitutional history of the Paris Commune. True, the Commune rested on a foundation of manhood suffrage, without any exclusion of persons who did not belong to the working class ; but this was all to the good, now that for the first time the electors were in a position to vote freely without being subject to the influence of the privileged classes whose representatives had left the city. Marx always thought of the proletariat as constituting, together with the poor peasants, the great majority of the people — and in the towns the majority without the complication of the peasantry. He was therefore in favour of manhood suffrage, without exclusion of classes which were different from the working class ; but in his view it made all the difference whether the electors were called on to vote for candidates to sit in a Parliament forming part of an existing State machine or for a new kind of assembly free to re-make the entire State in its own image. The essential thing was not that only workers should vote but that whoever voted should vote for delegates to sit in a combined legislature and executive endowed with complete power, subject to the mandate of their constituents, to re-order the society.

The essence, then, of the Commune, as Marx saw it, lay in its unification and centralisation of the power of the majority, freed from class-control, to govern through directly elected delegates to whom they could issue binding instructions — the *mandat impératif* so much spoken of during the Commune. Given such a basic political structure, the workers, organised as a class, would be in a position to impose their collective will. The function of the International, closely integrated with the Trade Unions, was to formulate this will and to provide the indispensable driving force.

That was how Marx, and Lenin after him, interpreted the Paris Commune. But the Commune became an inspiring historical memory not only for Marxists but also for a number of groups acutely hostile to Marxism — in particular for Blanquists and for Anarchists and Syndicalists of various brands. The Blanquists saw the Paris Commune as a working model of the revolutionary *élite* in action, and blamed the Internationalists for having spoilt it by insisting on democratic notions quite inappropriate during a period of revolutionary dictatorship. For the Blanquists the interest of the Commune lay not in its electoral system or its notion of the responsibility of the delegates to the electors, nor in the basis of Trade Union organisation on which it partly rested, but in the dictatorial character enforced on it by the exigencies of civil war. They too were 'democrats', of a sort ; but they conceived of democracy as something to be achieved after the revolutionary dictatorship had destroyed the old order, not as an instrument to be employed in destroying it. For a short time this difference between Marx and the Blanquists was obscured because they agreed on the necessity for dictatorship and centralisation of power and were united against Anarchists, Syndicalists, and 'petty *bourgeois* democrats'. But the union

as short-lived, as it was bound to be, because Marx believed
nd the Blanquists disbelieved in mass-organisation as the
ecessary basis of the Revolution itself.

The Anarchists and Syndicalists saw the Paris Commune in
et another light.   In their view its essence was its localism, its
evolt against centralised authority, its destruction of the
olitical State as a centre of authoritative control.   For them
was the *Paris* Commune, the direct expression of the right
f the people of Paris to govern themselves, and the model for
world-wide system of free local Communes which would rid
he earth of the pests of authoritarian government and central-
sed power.   The Paris Commune was, in their view, not a State
ut the negation of the State ;   and accordingly it had, even in
ace of military exigencies, to maintain its democratic character
nd its basis in the smaller local communities of which Paris
vas made up.   The Anarchists and Syndicalists were essentially
ederalists, in search of a society in which power, as far as it
urvived at all, would be firmly vested in local groups and any
gencies operating over a wider field would have no more than
lelegated functions.   There were, however, among the Com-
nunards Anarchists and Syndicalists of a number of different
•rands.   There were, at one extreme, Proudhonists who
pposed collective ownership of the means of production,
avoured peasant proprietorship and individual craft produc-
ion, regarded Co-operative societies as necessary for the
xecution of the larger works but distrusted all large-scale
•rganisation, opposed the emancipation of women, and wanted
he political State to disappear altogether.   They wanted a
constitution', under which would be set up for all time a
ystem of Credit Banks to finance the producers and ensure to
hem the full fruit of their labours ;   but they did not think of
hese Banks as subject to any sort of State, or as involving the
State's continued existence.   Their theory was a sort of revolu-
ionary version of *laissez-faire* :   everything, they argued, would
vork out all right of itself when the incubus of the State and
he tyranny of rent, profit, and interest had been removed.

Some of the Proudhonists were lukewarm about Trade
Unions, or even opposed to them when they were more than
nere craftsmen's Trade Clubs.   Others, however, regarded
vorkers' organisations, springing out of the Trade Unions, as

the necessary basis for the new order. As we have seen, the
men who took part in the founding of the International in
France were largely Proudhonists of this latter type. But
against the Proudhonists in the French Trade Union movement
were ranged the 'collectivists', headed by Eugène Varlin ; and
by 1871 the collectivists were the dominant group in the Paris
area, as well as at Lyons and Marseilles. Varlin, no doubt, had
at bottom a great deal more in common with Proudhon than
with Marx ; but on the issue that was uppermost in the 1860s
he and his group found themselves on the same side as Marx
because they favoured collective ownership of the means of
production. The question of centralisation versus federalism
had not yet come to the front in the debates of the International :
when it did, the Commune was over, and Varlin and many of
his closest associates were dead. It was, however, already clear
enough before the Commune that Varlin and his associates
were by no means 'collectivists' in the sense of standing for
State ownership of the land and other means of production.
They wanted the land and the instruments of large-scale
production to be owned by the local Communes, or, when
necessary, by federal agencies set up by the Communes. They
wanted the actual operations of production to be carried on as
far as possible by Co-operative societies emanating from the
Trade Unions ; and they regarded such Co-operative operation
as the essence of 'collectivist democracy'. The Trade Unions
were thus of fundamental importance in their vision of the new
society : indeed, they tended, though not very explicitly, to
think of the Commune of the future as resting rather on the
federated *syndicats* of the locality than on any political foundation. With this Syndicalist outlook went a considerable sus-
piciousness of middle-class Jacobins and Radicals, and an
insistence on keeping control of the International firmly in the
hands of actual workers. There were, however, in the ranks
of the Paris I.W.M.A. Marxists as well as Syndicalists, though
it is significant that their leader, Leo Frankel, was not a Frenchman — he was Hungarian by birth, German by race, but
domiciled in Paris. The French 'collectivists' for the most
part were with Marx against the Proudhonists, but hostile to
his 'centralism' and to his views about the State. They too
regarded the Paris Commune as a great historical precedent,

the first independent appearance of the workers on the scene of history ; but their view of the Commune was federalist and anti-authoritarian. They were the ancestors, not of Social Democracy or of modern Communism, but of the Syndicalism of the Confédération Générale du Travail in the period before the first World War.

In face of all this confusion of elements, and of the conditions of stress under which the Paris Commune lived out its brief and troubled existence, it is extremely difficult to present any picture of what it was really like. It had indeed very little chance to show what constructive capacities were behind it, or which way it would have gone had it, by a miracle, survived. The Commune came into being, not because anyone had planned for it in advance, but because when Thiers removed what he could of the governing and administrative machinery of the city there was left a void which had to be filled somehow unless there was to be a complete surrender. In the mood which had seized on a large section of the people of Paris — a mood made up of outraged patriotism, civic pride raised to a great height by the experience of the siege, radical detestation of the reactionaries who dominated the National Assembly, and resentment at the attempt to deprive the citizens of the arms with which they had held the Prussians at bay — surrender was out of the question, not only for the convinced revolutionaries, but also for a large proportion of the local officers and common soldiers of the National Guard. Of those who were unmoved by such feelings a high proportion, including most of the well-to-do citizens, had either fled the city earlier or left it before the Commune entered on its task. There remained the workers, the shopkeepers, the lesser civil servants and municipal functionaries, and such other persons as were unable to get away — the sick, the aged, and the sheer rabble — and also a small host of journalists, artists, students, and other intellectuals, most of whom held leftish opinions of one sort or another.

The siege helped to prepare the way for the Commune : it had forced on Paris an improvised administration, an isolation from the rest of the country and from the Government, and a civic military organisation, which provided both a nucleus and a pattern for the new structure of the resistance. It made the creation of the Commune seem more natural, as well as easier, than it could have been without this recent experience of standing alone. But, of course, the Parisians who set up the Commune had no idea in their minds of constructing a new workers' State to stand lastingly on its own feet. The Paris Commune was meant to be only one among many — a part of the basic structure of a new democratic France, no doubt, but no more than a part. Even the Blanquists, who had the clearest notion of what they were trying to do, envisaged the new Parisian régime mainly as a dictatorship that was to lead the way in a revolution covering all France and to result in the establishment of a new government for the whole country. The Jacobin Radicals similarly — but without the same notion of dictatorship — thought of the Commune as the democratic beginning of a new Republic that was to be extended to all France. The Federalists, whose main strength lay in the Trade Unions, differed from both Blanquists and Jacobins in thinking of the new France as needing to be made up of auto-nomous Communes — of which that of Paris was the first — loosely grouped together in some sort of federation unarmed with coercive power ; and they accordingly came nearest to thinking of the Paris Commune as an alternative to the State, rather than as the forerunner of a new national structure of government within which it would fall into place. But none of these attitudes really counted for much in influencing the immediate course of events. The Commune was not planned : it happened, and then each group framed its own idea of what it was and ought to be in a situation in which the main pre-occupation was necessarily that of mere survival in face of its enemies.

At the outset, when Thiers withdrew from Paris, there were two possible alternative agencies for the task of improvising some means of carrying on the essential services and of organ-ising the resistance — if resistance there was to be. One of these agencies was the National Guard : the other was the joint committee formed by the mayors and adjoints of the arrondissements. But the second of these bodies was too heterogeneous in its composition, and too largely composed of politicians who were quite as much scared of the Paris mob as hostile to the National Assembly, to be a possible candidate for the leadership of the resistance. It devoted itself, instead, to the task of attempted mediation between Paris and the National Assembly — a task hopeless from the outset, because the Assembly was in no mood to come to any terms short of absolute surrender. That left only the Central Committee of the National Guard, a body which at once recognised its incompetence to assume either political or administrative control, but was not at all disposed to surrender its arms or to see Paris ignominiously occupied by the Prussians. Finding itself thrust into a responsibility it was not prepared to shoulder, the Committee of the National Guard decided at once to divest itself of political power by handing the unwanted authority over to the people. It ordered immediate elections for a representative municipal government — to be chosen by the whole people. That seemed the natural, democratic way out of the difficulty ; and that was how the Commune of Paris came to be born.

As we have seen, the elections held under these conditions — with every male adult citizen who remained in Paris entitled to vote — resulted in the choice of a number of representatives who either never took their seats or withdrew at an early stage and needed to be replaced. Of the 92 elected, 21 were of these types, and were mostly replaced within a few weeks by supplementary elections. Even thereafter the Commune was made up of very diverse elements. There were more intellectuals than workers — among them many journalists of varying views ; and there were quite a number of tradesmen and other members of the lower middle classes. Most of the members had no precise affiliations : 22 at least are known to have been members of the International, and 24 either Blanquists or near-Blanquists. Half a dozen were members of the Central Committee of the National Guard about whose political views nothing definite is known. The majority of the remainder were left-wing Radicals, of varying types and colours, with no known Internationalist or Blanquist connections, though of course a number of these may have been in fact conscious Socialists of one school or another.

Among those of definite affiliation, the best-known Internationalists who have not been mentioned already were the following : Victor Clément, Auguste Serraillier, Eugène Pottier the song-writer, Jules Johannard, Paul Vésinier, and

Auguste Avrial — mostly manual workers. Of the Blanquists, or near-Blanquists, the outstanding figures not yet mentioned were Clovis Dupont, the three Da Costas, and Jules Miot. Babick was a follower of Enfantin : Descamps was, or became later, an Anarchist. Y. Y. Pillot was a left-wing priest who harked back to Lamennais : Édouard Alfred Goupil, a well-known doctor in a working-class district ; Paschal Grousset, a hard-hitting journalist who later helped to introduce English sports into France. They were indeed in all a strange mixture of Trade Unionists and intellectuals, of old Radicals and young workers and students, of the declamatory and of the silent who did their best amid the hubbub to get on with the jobs they had been assigned or had taken on for themselves because they needed doing and nobody else seemed to be ready to do them.

From so heterogeneous a gathering, so filled with ready talkers and leaders, no coherent theory of government or of Socialism could have emerged, even if there had been time to make one. Such theoretical lessons as can be got from the Paris Commune have to be read into it : none are to be found in it ready-made. Marx, in *The Civil War in France*, produced a contemporary interpretation, designed to put the best face on the matter because he was concerned to defend the Communards against their enemies. Lenin later strained the facts further in order to extract the lesson he wanted, and was able to make a great deal out of the Commune by way of reinforcing his own theory of dictatorship. But the plain truth is that the Communards had no common theory, and were, during the few months of the Commune's existence, much too busy to make one. This, of course, meant that each group, and each individual, did his best to make the Commune fit the pattern of ideas conceived before it began : their quarrels became to a great extent a conflict between Blanquists, often in alliance with Jacobins, against the elements which wanted either more direct democratic responsibility to the whole body of electors or closer links with the Trade Unions and specifically working-class societies. But across this conflict cut the disputes between military leaders and those who retained the status and outlook of civilians, and, at times, the cross-current of violence versus moderate behaviour even in face of the savage intransigeance of the Versailles Assembly and its partisans. I have said earlier that Raoul Rigault's bark was worse than his bite ; but he had from the first a strong taste for wholesale and spectacular arrests (though many of those whom he arrested were quickly released) and for making a great show of dictatorial authority. Nor had he any scruples about killing his hostages when the final stage of defeat was reached. The Commune was mild in comparison with Thiers ; but its mildness was comparative, not absolute.

Its defeat was certain, practically from the first — that is, from the moment when it became plain that Thiers and the Assembly would not compromise in any way. The Prussians would have acted entirely out of character had they not helped Thiers to crush the Commune by allowing him to build up an army out of the prisoners of war whom they released. Nothing but a mass rising in the other towns of France could have saved the Paris revolution ; and outside Paris the attempts at revolution were put down almost before they had begun. Therefore Thiers was both able to wipe out the Paris revolt in blood, and eager to do so in order to teach all France a lesson. He was acclaimed in every reactionary circle in Europe, because in destroying the Paris Commune he also laid low the International and the revolutionary movement over most of the Continent.

CHAPTER VIII

DECLINE AND FALL OF THE FIRST INTERNATIONAL

THE defeat of the Paris Commune brought the Socialists' hopes of an early general European revolution to an end. Through the 'sixties the eyes of the exiles in Paris, Switzerland, and London had been fixed above all on France, watching eagerly for the expected collapse of the Second Empire. Paris, despite the police régime, was still the centre of revolutionary feeling in the West, and was looked to to give the lead by overthrowing the Emperor and establishing afresh the Republic which had gone so signally to the bad in the Days of June, 1848. France indeed was not the most advanced country in economic development : that distinction belonged to Great Britain, with Belgium holding second place. But in the 1860s nobody supposed Great Britain to be on the verge of revolution. The considerable struggle which was in progress there over the twin issues of Trade Union rights and parliamentary reform was pretty soon to be settled without a violent upheaval, though few expected in the early 'sixties victories for the workers in both fields of the magnitude of those actually won between 1867 and 1875. At any rate, as soon as, in 1867, the Reform Act, the Master and Servant Act, and the new Factory Act had shown the bulk of the ruling classes to be in a mood to make concessions to working-class claims rather than to engage in an out-and-out struggle, it was impossible for anyone, except a tiny handful of fanatics, to believe that a British revolution was impending. Marx had set his hopes on the Irish Fenians, in the faith that revolution in Ireland would lead to intensified class - struggle in Great Britain ; but this was never likely, even if the Fenians had been much stronger than they actually were. The plain truth was that the very elements which formed the bulk of the *bourgeois* oppositions on the Continent belonged in Great Britain to constitutional parties which could alternate in power without appealing to force, and that the working class, or at any rate the more articulate part of it, had been getting fairly continuously better off since the Hungry 'Forties, and was disposed to rest its hopes on Trade Union bargaining and an extended franchise rather than on a renewal of the Chartist demands for an out-and-out conflict with the ruling classes. The British Trade Union and Reform leaders might be induced to give some support to continental revolutionaries who were living under autocratic police régimes ; but nothing was further from their thoughts than the making of a British revolution.

In Belgium, where the ruling classes were much more reactionary and wages and working conditions very bad despite the high development of industry, there was a good deal more revolutionary feeling ; but it was mainly in the Walloon areas, and Belgium was in any case too small a country to take the lead in a general European movement. The French-speaking Belgians, indeed, were waiting for the signal from France and were much under French influence, though they had a considerable body of independent Socialist doctrine already to their credit in the work of Colins and other pioneers. Outside France, the greatest revolutionary possibilities existed in Italy and in Spain. But Italy had already had its national revolution, and though social disturbances were continuous and serious there was no clear purpose or direction behind them and no organised proletariat, except in a few northern cities. Italy was still very backward economically ; and if it did make a revolution such a movement could clearly have little in common with the revolution foreshadowed in the *Communist Manifesto*. Spain, more backward still, had little of a working-class movement outside Catalonia, and its impending revolt was unlikely to have much effect on the course of events in the rest of Europe.

There remained Germany, the Austro-Hungarian Empire, Turkey and its subject countries, and Russia. In Russia underground revolutionary movements had markedly revived since the 'fifties ; but Western Europe had little knowledge of them, and the students and aristocrats who led them still appealed mainly to the peasants rather than to the small urban proletariat. The Poles, still sharply divided between aristocratic and democratic nationalists — the latter in many cases the great apostles of international revolutionary action as their only hope, — were in no position to rise successfully against their Russian masters. In the Turkish dominions there were nationalist revolutionaries in contact chiefly with the extreme left wing of the Italians or with Garibaldian adventurers seeking new fields for battle, or in the case of Bulgaria with the Russians; but there were no working-class movements. Nor was there any considerable working-class movement in Austria-Hungary. The Viennese Socialists looked mainly to Germany and to German Switzerland ; the Hungarian Socialists were too few to matter. Moreover, both Austrians and Hungarians were unable to find common ground with their Slav fellow-subjects : national still took precedence over social questions.

This leaves only Germany, where the first large-scale workers' movement since 1848 had recently made its appearance under the leadership of Ferdinand Lassalle. But Germany was clearly in no state for the workers to give a revolutionary lead. In Prussia, and in North Germany as a whole, Bismarck was steadily consolidating his power and preparing the way for a unified German Reich under Prussian leadership. Against him was an irresolute *bourgeois* opposition which was half-paralysed by sympathy with his expansionist nationalism and deeply hostile to any independent political activity of the working classes. Cutting across the social conflict was the sharp division between those who favoured the unification of Germany under Prussian leadership and those who clung to the independence of the separate German States and were thus apt to find themselves in alliance with some of the most reactionary elements in German society. The leaders of the growing working-class movements were sharply divided between those who wanted, first and foremost, to break away from the *bourgeois* Progressives and create an all-German independent working-class party, even at the cost of siding with Bismarck on the question of German unification under Prussian hegemony, and those who wished to act as the independent allies of the Progressives in the struggle against autocratic rule, and to oppose anything that would strengthen Prussian influence, because Prussia was clearly the power-centre of autocratic and militarist control. The Lassallians, broadly speaking, represented the first of these trends, Liebknecht and Bebel, with Marx's blessing, the second — though Marx was often exceedingly critical of his lieutenants for being too subservient to the *bourgeois* left wing, and for being led into an apparent opposition to German unity by their hatred of Prussian supremacy.

In so tangled a national situation the German Socialists were much too preoccupied with their own problems to have much thought to spare for the European revolution as a whole. Moreover, Bismarck's victory over Austria in 1866 in effect settled the national issue in favour of Prussia ; and the circumstances attending the outbreak of the Franco-Prussian War of 1870, by causing the war to appear one of German national defence against French aggression, made it entirely impossible to rally the German workers against Bismarck — the more so because he was fighting Napoleon III, and everyone on the left agreed in wishing for the overthrow of the Second Empire. Thus, although Liebknecht and Bebel, at the head of the newly organised Eisenach Socialist Party, courageously refused to vote for the war credits and, with other leaders, suffered imprisonment for their opposition to the terms imposed by the victorious Bismarck upon the French, there was never any question of the upheavals of 1870 and 1871 leading to any sort of German revolution.

Even in France the Revolution came to a head only in Paris and was shown by the easy suppression of the attempted Communard movements in Lyons, Marseilles, and elsewhere to have no deep roots in the rest of the country. The rise of the International Workmen's Association, the great strikes which it had waged successfully in a number of countries during its early years, and the apparent support for it in Great Britain during the British Reform struggle, had led its sponsors as well as its enemies to form greatly exaggerated ideas of the power behind it and of the extent of revolutionary feeling among the working classes. It would no doubt have lasted longer as a considerable force and have accomplished more in the industrial field if its chances had not been wrecked by the Franco-Prussian War and by the destruction of its most lively centre of real working-class feeling — Paris. But as soon as it was compelled to pass from strike action to the appeal to sheer force, the odds against it were seen to be overwhelming and its dissolution was unavoidable.

Before we discuss the later history of the International Working Men's Association it is necessary to give some consideration to its position in the two countries in which it continued to spread at a great rate after its progress had come to a stop in France and after the British had to all intents and purposes dropped out. These two countries were Italy and Spain ; and in both the movement developed in entire independence of the wishes and policies of Marx and the General Council in London, and on lines of Bakuninist Anarchism rather than of either French Blanquism or Marxian Socialism.

Italy, as we have seen, had been represented at the start of the International Working Men's Association in London by Major Luigi Wolff, a former officer of Garibaldi and a friend of Mazzini, in close touch with the Mazzinist Workers' Associations which existed all over Italy in the 1860s. Wolff had presented a set of draft statutes for the International based on those of the Mazzinist central body ; but these had been brushed aside in favour of Marx's rival draft. Thereafter the Mazzinists played no further part in the I.W.M.A., in which they would not have found themselves at all at home. Mazzini's organisation had been revolutionary in its beginnings and still kept not only its republicanism, but also something of its revolutionary character in the parts of Italy which had still to be united to the new State ; but the Mazzinist movement had never rested on a class basis or been greatly concerned with the economic struggle. It was a nationalist movement almost exclusively, and its leadership was in the hands and a large part of its following made up of middle class, especially professional, men. Mazzini himself, as we have seen, was mildly socialistic in his views ; but he had a deep hatred of class-conflict, as destructive of national unity, and the emphasis which he laid on the strict correlation between rights and duties and on the moral approach to politics made him a bitter opponent of Socialism in its Marxist form — and indeed no less of the type of Anarchist Socialism of which Bakunin was the outstanding prophet. Mazzini's full hatred of the new Socialism did not become manifest till he rose to heights of outraged denunciation of the Paris Commune ; but from the outset it was clearly out of the question to create an International comprehensive enough to hold both Mazzini and Marx.

The Italians, then, took hardly any part in the International during its first few years. Most of the Italian exiles in London were supporters of Mazzini ; and Marx was not able to find any sufficient numbers for a rival movement. Engels was appointed to act as Corresponding Secretary for Italy by the General Council in London : he managed to establish a few contacts, but reported extreme difficulty in establishing direct relations with workers, as distinct from intellectuals. His principal contact in Italy was Enrico Bignami, of Lodi, whose journal, *La Plebe* (founded in 1867), gave steady support to the General Council against Bakunin and his followers. In 1871, at the height of the quarrel, the General Council sent a delegate from the small London Italian group of the International to Northern Italy in the hope of enlisting support for the coming Congress at the Hague ; but he achieved nothing. At an earlier stage the hopes of Marx and Engels had been fixed on the Marquis Carlo Cafiero (1846–83), who had been an attaché at the Italian Embassy, but had resigned and declared his conversion to Socialism. Cafiero, however, on his return to Italy, fell speedily under the spell of Bakunin and went over to the anti-authoritarian creed.

Until the 1860s Socialism had no real roots in Italy, and no hold on the working class, which was still mainly under Mazzini's influence. There were indeed a number of isolated adherents of particular schools of French Socialism. In Tuscany Leopoldo Campini tried to popularise Fourierism during the 1830s, while Constantino Marmocci preached a doctrine derived from Babeuf and Buonarroti. There was a group of Saint-Simonians at Bologna, headed by Marco Minghetti and Gabrielo Rossi, who were in touch with another Italian Saint-Simonian, Angelo Fava, then living in Paris. There were other Saint-Simonians in the 1830s at Pisa and Florence and in Calabria. All these groups were influenced by the Milanese Princess of Belgiojoso, better known as Christine Trivulzio (1808–71), who emigrated to Paris in 1830 and there set up a *salon* much frequented by the Saint-Simonians. In 1848 many of the Socialist exiles went back to Italy for the time being — for example, Giuseppe Ferrari, who took a leading part in the revolutionary movement in Lombardy, and quite a number of those who were associated with the short-lived

Roman Republic. Much the most important of these was the romantic soldier Carlo Pisacane, Duke of St. Giovanni (1818–1857). Pisacane took part in the 1848 Revolution as Chief of Staff to the army of the Roman Republic, and thereafter served in Algeria in the French Foreign Legion, but remained a romantic adventurer. In 1857 he landed in Italy with a small force of volunteers, in the hope of starting an insurrection, but his force was routed and dispersed and he himself killed in battle. In his lifetime nothing much was known of his Socialist views ; but in 1860 his *Saggi* were published in Paris, and were fairly widely read. Pisacane advocated common ownership of the land and of industrial capital : he wanted the land to be collectively cultivated by the communes and the people to share equally in the consumable product. Living and working outside Italy, he founded no movement : he belonged to that militant left wing which took Garibaldi as its inspirer — and of course Garibaldi himself was in a broad sense a Socialist as well as a republican nationalist whose nationalist sentiments were by no means limited to his own country.

Neither Garibaldi nor Pisacane, however, created any Italian Socialist movement ; and in effect almost none existed till the 'sixties. The establishment of the new Italian State in 1860 was followed by a great stirring among the workers. At the Ninth Workers' Congress, held in Florence in 1861, there was a struggle between those who wished the Workers' Associations to confine themselves to 'friendly society' activities and those who called for a more militant industrial policy to improve wages and working conditions. Strikes were still forbidden by law ; and one of the demands of the left wing was for recognition of the right to organise for mutual defence. But the victorious majority did not break with Mazzini, and the main effort of the movement was still put behind his and Garibaldi's demand for the liberation of the areas left outside the new Kingdom of Italy. The following year, however, the wounding and arrest of Garibaldi by the royal forces at Aspromente caused a ferment. The Workers' Associations mostly declared their support of Garibaldi, and were suspended or dissolved in large numbers by the police. Those which remained held a further Congress at Parma the following year (1863) and, on the motion of Gaspare Stampa of Milan, drew up a 'Federal Compact' for common action, and established a standing commission. The year after that, at the Naples Congress, Giovanni Bovia, of Trani, proposed the holding of periodical International Workers' Congresses representing the workers' movements of all countries. This was just after the I.W.M.A. had been set up in London. This Congress also set up a definite Federation of Italian Workers' Societies in which Stampa was an outstanding figure.

At the time of this Congress Bakunin was in London, in touch with Marx, but was preparing to settle in Italy, where he had been earlier in the year, and had established contacts with Garibaldi and with a number of the leaders of the Workers' Associations in Northern and Central Italy. Early in 1865 he returned to Italy, and soon settled down in Naples, where he gathered round him a group which included Herzen's friend, Carlo Gambuzzi, Saverio Friscia, Alberto Tucci, and Giuseppe Fanelli, later the main organiser of the I.W.M.A. in Spain as well as Italy. During the same year Nicolo Lo Savio founded at Florence *Il Proletario*, commonly regarded as the first definitely Socialist journal to be published in Italy. Lo Savio was, broadly, a follower of Proudhon, and his paper became a rallying point for the moderates against the Bakuninist movement. Two years later Enrico Bignami's *Plebe*, at Lodi, struck a more decisively Marxist note.

In 1866 a series of risings in Sicily provoked a general repression. To meet this, Bakunin and his friends founded at Naples the following year the association called 'Justice and Liberty', and the journal of the same name. They also formed at Naples the first Italian Section of the International Working Men's Association. Stampa of Milan made a report on the situation in Italy to the Lausanne Congress of the International, held later in the year ; and Tanari was present as delegate from Bologna. Stampa's report stated that the Workers' Associations in Italy had upwards of a million members ; but of course this figure included societies of many different tendencies. The next year, at the Brussels Congress of the I.W.M.A., Friscia was the only Italian delegate.

Bakunin, settling at Naples in 1865, found in the appalling economic conditions and endemic peasant unrest of the former Kingdom of Naples and Sicily an opportunity for revolutionary propaganda which he was not likely to miss ; and when he left

Naples in 1867 at any rate the nucleus of a revolutionary
organisation, with an organ *Uguaglianza* (Equality), remained,
and the effects had spread, not only to Sicily, but also to the
Romagna and to parts of Northern Italy, especially Milan.
During these years Bakunin had not been directly connected
with the I.W.M.A. in London : he had been building local
revolutionary groups which owed no formal allegiance to any
central body and had been acting in the name of a mysterious
society which he called the 'International Brotherhood' — a
secret International without rules or formal organisation that
existed mainly in his own head. In 1867, as we have seen, he
for a time transferred his main attention to the League of Peace
and Freedom, which met that year in Geneva. Leaving Italy,
he settled in Switzerland — for the time being in Geneva. But
from Geneva and later from other Swiss centres he kept in
close touch with the development of the revolutionary movement in Italy ; and after his secession in 1868, together with
his friends at Naples, from the League of Peace and Freedom
and the establishment of the Alliance of Socialist Democracy
with its headquarters at Geneva, the Alliance served him as a
link with the Italian movement — though it too had little real
existence apart from its Geneva Section and from Bakunin's
voluminous correspondence with his revolutionary friends in
many countries. From 1868, however, Bakunin at any rate
purported to be acting as an agent of the I.W.M.A. When the
General Council of that body, urged on by Marx, refused to
accept the affiliation of the Alliance of Socialist Democracy on
the terms Bakunin had proposed, the Alliance, except its Geneva
Section (which the I.W.M.A. did accept into affiliation), was
dissolved, and such allegiance as the Italian groups in touch
with Bakunin had professed to the Alliance was transferred to
the International. As we have seen, Italy had already been
represented by two delegates — Gaspare Stampa of Milan and
the Marquis Sebastiano Tanari of Bologna — at the I.W.M.A.'s
Lausanne Congress in 1867, and it was represented at the
Brussels Congress of 1868 by a single delegate, Saverio Friscia
(1813–86), who had been among Bakunin's supporters in the
League of Peace and Freedom. But these delegations had not
been much more than nominal : only Stampa at Milan really
stood for any organised working-class movement. The Italian

movement over most of Italy was still only detaching itself gradually from the Mazzinist organisations and finding a new basis in the workers of the industrial centres of the North. At the Basle Congress of 1869 the two Italian representatives were Stefano Caporusso, a tailor from Naples, and Bakunin himself, then living in Switzerland. The northern areas sent nobody.

During the interval between the Basle Congress and the Hague Congress of 1872 there was a great growth of the International in Italy. In 1870 and 1871 there were secessions from the Mazzinist organisation, and the seceding groups in most cases proclaimed their adherence to the I.W.M.A. The events of the Paris Commune, and Mazzini's impassioned denunciation of it, increased the tension and drove those who had hitherto kept a divided allegiance into the one camp or the other. In December 1871 a Congress held at Bologna formed a new body — *Il Fascio Operaio* — to promote united action by the left wing of the workers' movement against the Mazzinists. 'Fascio' — the bundle of staves tied together, giving strength without full unification — stood, not for what is now known as Fascism, but for the federal unity of the local workers' groups. The movement, ably led by Andrea Costa (1851–1910), later the principal founder of the Italian Socialist Party, soon spread to other centres. It was Anarchist, or at any rate 'federalist', in outlook, and in full sympathy with Bakunin and the Swiss opponents of the I.W.M.A. General Council. Mazzini died in March 1872, and the movement he had led began to dissolve. During the following months there were many further secessions from the Mazzinist Workers' Association. Nabruzzi and Domenico Trombetti went as delegates from the workers' groups associated with the International to solicit Garibaldi's support, and came away with his blessing. Cafiero announced to Engels his definite defection from the Marxist to the Bakuninist side ; and in August 1872, shortly before the Hague Conference, the groups which had given their adhesion to the International held a national Congress at Rimini and there formed an Italian Federation of the I.W.M.A., with Cafiero as President, Nabruzzi as Vice-President, and Andrea Costa as secretary. The Rimini Congress at the same time declared for the complete autonomy of each national constituent of the

I.W.M.A., denounced the General Council in London as guilty of authoritarian and centralising deviations, and took sides strongly with Bakunin and the Jura Federation in the controversy between Marx and the 'Federalists' — a controversy which had by no means been laid to rest by the tragic outcome of the Paris Revolution. The Rimini Congress set up the Italian headquarters of the I.W.M.A. at Imola, near Bologna, in the form of a 'Federal Correspondence Bureau' without executive powers or authority to commit the Italian I.W.M.A. to any central direction. Friendly relations were maintained between the Bologna Bureau and Bakunin's Alliance in Geneva and the Jura Federation ; but the Italians announced that they would refuse to send delegates to any international Congress convened by the I.W.M.A. under the existing statutes, which in their view conferred undue power not only on the General Council but also on the Congress itself.

After the Paris Commune the Italian Government became much less tolerant towards the Italian Sections of the I.W.M.A. and arrested many of the leaders. Violent antagonisms developed between Mazzinists and Internationalists ; and in many parts of the country the International was again driven underground. When preparations began to be made for the Hague Congress of the International — the first since 1869 — the Geneva Alliance and the Jura Federation brought strong pressure on the Italians to be well represented, in order to uphold the anti-authoritarian standpoint ; but after the Rimini Congress the Italian leaders replied that they had received a definite instruction from their own Congress and proposed instead that the elements in the International which disapproved of the General Council's attitude should convene a rival Congress pledged to uphold the complete independence of the constituent national groups. The Hague Congress of 1872 consequently met without a single Italian representative, though the Spaniards, most of whom shared the Italian views, decided to send delegates. Instead, the Italians sent their fraternal representatives to the rival Congress called by the Swiss at St. Imier soon after the Hague meeting.

Thereafter, the Italian I.W.M.A. became involved in the widespread hunger revolts which spread over Italy in 1873 and the following year, and in the Bologna rising of 1874. The easy suppression of that movement was followed by a split in the North Italian Sections of the International. A group in Central Italy, headed by Osvaldo Gnocchi-Viani, secretary of the Rome Section, broke away; and a northern group hostile to Anarchism formed a new Lombard Federation on non-insurrectionary lines, favouring constitutional political action. Benoît Malon, the French advocate of 'integral Socialism', who had changed his place of exile from Switzerland to Italy, also helped to prepare the way for the constitution of an Italian Socialist Party, though this did not come into being until in 1879 Andrea Costa, then in prison in Paris, broke with the Anarchists and took the lead on the Social Democratic side. In the meantime the Anarchists, among whom Errico Malatesta (1853–1932) was already becoming the outstanding figure, had reorganised their forces in Central and South Italy, and in Sicily, and had conducted a series of local *émeutes*, of which the most important was the Benevento rising of 1876.

Italy, of course, was in the 1860s an economically undeveloped country, with a predominantly rural population living at exceedingly low standards and with deep poverty in the crowded towns as well. The south and Sicily were still utterly feudal, with huge landed estates and a peasantry accustomed to bitter repression and to mass-movements of sheer desperation when times were bad. Even the towns, except in the north, were too impoverished and too little industrialised to provide any foundation for stable Trade Unions or to throw up any effective working-class leadership. In Milan and Turin and in a few other northern towns there was at least the nucleus for an organised working-class movement; but even in these centres the leadership still rested mainly with revolutionary aristocrats and professional men who could find no outlet for their capacities. Even so, there was a sharp dividing line between the hunger-revolts of the south and the country areas and the more articulate movements of the northern cities. But in the 1860s and 1870s both sections were united by hostility to the middle- and upper-class nationalists who refused to face the social question; and both were attracted to Anarchism rather than to Socialism because it seemed a hopeless task to wring concessions from the State by any sort of constitutional political action. Marx's policy of aiding the *bourgeois* Radicals o make themselves masters of the State and to destroy feudalism, with the intention of turning upon the *bourgeoisie* in its hour of triumph, seemed to most of the Italian leaders to be quite inapplicable to their own conditions — or rather, it seemed to them that the hour for turning upon the political Radicals had already come, in face of the manifest incapacity of the new Italian State even to master feudalism, much less to do anything to improve the condition of the urban working class.

Spain, of course, was for the most part even more backward economically than Italy and was subject to much more reactionary and repressive government up to the Revolution of 1868, which provided the opportunity for the development of the Spanish Sections of the International. Catalonia, and particularly Barcelona, was the most industrialised area and was most open to influence from Southern France ; and it was in Barcelona that the Spanish movement first gathered strength as the Revolution which dethroned Queen Isabella drew near.

In Spain, until the 1860s, there was practically no Socialist movement, though the doctrines of Fourier and, later, of Proudhon had a considerable influence on individual thinkers. The leading Spanish Fourierist was Fernando Garrido, who was also influenced by Owen and was editing a Fourierist journal, *La Atracción*, in Madrid as early as 1846. Another influential figure was Joaquín Abreu, who lived in France from 1823 to 1834, got to know Fourier, and became an active propagandist of his doctrines after settling in Cadiz in 1834. Other early advocates of Socialism included Sixto Cámara, who edited the Madrid satirical journal *Tarantula* in the 1840s, Roque Barcía, and José Munts, the Barcelona founder of Workers' Mutual Associations from 1840. Ordax Avicella, a deputy to the Cortes, declared his adherence to Socialism in 1848 ; and Narciso Monturiol founded a group of followers of Cabet in Barcelona in the 1840s. The first Socialist programme in Spain was produced in 1858, by a group of which Garrido was the inspirer. At that time the Socialists formed a section inside the Republican Party ; three years later they forced a crisis within the party by attempting to induce it to adopt a Socialist policy. The dispute was, however, patched up. Garrido visited England in the early 'sixties, making a study of the Co-operative movement : he returned an enthusiastic advocate of the

Rochdale system. But Garrido was essentially a moderate, and during the next few years he was swept aside. The Spanish Revolution of 1868 was immediately followed by a sharp quarrel between the Socialists and the victorious Republicans. The Socialists broke away and began an energetic campaign of working-class organisation, partly for strike action and partly for wider political purposes. The International Working Men's Association spread, first into Catalonia and then into the rest of Spain, largely from Marseilles and Lyons. The newly formed workers' associations speedily grouped themselves into Sections and Districts of the International : a Spanish workman delegate appeared at the I.W.M.A.'s Brussels Congress of 1868. He called himself Sarro Magallan : his real name was A. Marsal y Anglosa. He came from Catalonia, and was a metal-worker. The following year two Spaniards were present at the Basle Congress of 1869 — Gaspar Sentiñon and Rafael Farga-Pellicer of Barcelona. The latter was a printer and journalist and a follower of Bakunin. He edited, as organs of the Spanish I.W.M.A., *La Federación* (1869–72) and *El Trabajo* (1872– ?). Another influential figure, Fermín Salvochea (? –1907) of Cadiz, was a member of the Provisional Government set up there in 1868, but was in prison during the critical years of the International's activities in Spain. He took a substantial part in the revival of Spanish Socialism in the 1880s.

The Spanish Sections of the International were from the first mainly Anarchist in outlook. The Frenchmen who played a leading part in building them up — André Bastelica of Marseilles, for example, and Charles Alerini — belonged to the most militant groups in the French I.W.M.A. and those most closely in touch with Bakunin. Most important of all in establishing the International in Spain was the Italian Giuseppe Fanelli, who had worked with Bakunin in the League of Peace and Freedom and had seceded with him from the League to the International. Fanelli was mainly responsible for the spread of the movement beyond Catalonia. He set up the Madrid Section of the I.W.M.A. and there came into sharp conflict with Marx's son-in-law, Paul Lafargue, who, urged on by Marx and Engels, started a rival Madrid Section supported by the General Council in London.

Bakunin himself took no part in the Spanish movement ;

but it developed on lines similar to those which had been followed in Italy under his more direct influence. Its principal organs were *Federación*, published in Barcelona from 1867, and *Solidaridad*, issued in Madrid from 1870 as the official journal of the Spanish Federation of the I.W.M.A. In 1870 the Spanish Federation held a public Congress at Barcelona, and the proceedings made clear the intensely revolutionary character of the organisation. The Co-operative doctrines formerly in favour were condemned as calculated to divide and emasculate the proletariat ; and the Congress also declared against all forms of political collaboration with the Republican politicians.

The Paris Commune was enthusiastically greeted by the Spanish leaders of the International, and the organisation continued to grow at an even greater rate during 1871. But its period of open development was at an end. The I.W.M.A. was proscribed by the Government, and the Congress which had been fixed for Valencia was unable to meet in public. Instead, the leaders held a secret Congress at which it was decided to reorganise the International on a Trade Union basis, and to introduce a central control over strike policy in order to prevent diffusion of resources. The Spanish Cortes in October 1871 decreed its dissolution as an 'immoral' organisation, taking advantage of the only clause in the republican constitution that enabled it to outlaw the I.W.M.A. That body, nevertheless, continued to grow as an underground organisation and operated publicly through the Federal Union of the Manufacturing Workers of Spain which had been set up under its control. There was an epidemic of strikes in the main industrial centres. The Government attempted repression, and many arrests were made. The question arose whether, in order to meet the repression, the Internationalists should seek an alliance with the left wing of the Republicans. A number of the leaders, and especially the Madrid Section of the International founded under the influence of Paul Lafargue, favoured such a policy ; but the great majority of the Spanish Sections rejected it, and in the ensuing split the Anarchists carried almost the whole organisation with them. Lafargue had actually been sent to Spain as the agent of the General Council in London, in the hope of winning over the Spaniards from their allegiance to the Bakuninist policy ; but the entire situation was against him. José Mesa, in *Emancipación*, the Madrid organ of the Marxist Section, could make no headway against *Razón* (Seville and Madrid), edited by Nicolas Alonso Marselau, and *Federación* (Barcelona), the organs of the majority. Anselmo Lorenzo, who came to represent Spain at the London Conference of the I.W.M.A. in 1871, was a leader of the Anarchistic section — author of numerous books expounding the doctrines of 'collectivist' Anarchism. Having rejected co-operation with the Radical politicians, the Spanish I.W.M.A. began to organise for a revolutionary attempt. In 1873 local insurrections broke out — the most serious at Cartagena, where a left-wing revolutionary Government was proclaimed and held power for a time. But the failure of these risings destroyed the Spanish I.W.M.A. as a mass-movement, though it continued to the end of the decade as an underground organisation and passed on its Anarchist traditions to the modern Spanish Anarchist and Anarcho-Syndicalist movements.

These events had taken place against a background of continuous and violent political disturbance. General Prim's bloodless revolution of 1868 had been followed by a period of uncertainty during which the victors scoured Europe for a constitutional monarch to succeed the deposed Isabella. Towards the end of 1870 Amadeus of Savoy was persuaded to accept the throne ; but his troubled reign lasted little more than two years, coinciding with the struggle between the Government and the International. The Republic proclaimed on his abdication endured for less than two years, during which it had four Presidents. One of them was the Socialist leader, Francisco Pi y Margall (1824–1901), whose period of office was one day.[1] Civil war raged between Carlists, supporters of Isabella's son, Alfonso, Republicans, and Anarchists, until in 1874 Alfonso was called to the throne and stamped out the divided opposition. Throughout the years of trouble the Spaniards had shown an entire incapacity to work the various parliamentary régimes that had been attempted and a marked tendency towards regional autonomy as against any form of centralised government. Many of the Republicans were regionalists ; but the markedly anarchistic attitude of the workers' movements

[1] Pi y Margall wrote, besides Socialist works, a *History of Spain in the Nineteenth Century*, published in seven volumes the year after his death.

made it impossible for them to secure mass-support and made the return to monarchy inevitable. Marx saw clearly that the only chance of defeating the reaction in Spain lay in co-operation between the workers and the *bourgeois* Radicals ; but the sole effect of his efforts, through Lafargue, to promote such a policy was that of losing all influence for the General Council in the affairs of Spain.

Switzerland, during the years between the Basle Congress of 1869 and the Hague Congress of 1872, remained the principal centre of the revolt within the International against the leadership of Marx and the General Council in London. Bakunin had been living there since 1867, and had placed there the headquarters of his Alliance of Socialist Democracy and of his continuous correspondence with revolutionaries in many countries. From Switzerland it was easy to keep in close touch with Italy, with Southern France, and with such sympathisers as were to be found in Austria and in Southern Germany. Bakunin's French friends, in Lyons and Marseilles, were in regular touch with the Spaniards in Barcelona and Valencia ; and his Italian associates had connections in Greece and even in the Balkans. There was, moreover, in Geneva and in some other Swiss towns a substantial colony of Russians and the usual band of Polish exiles, to whom was added, in 1871, a large body of refugees from Paris and from other centres of the International in France.

Bakunin had indeed formally dissolved his Alliance of Socialist Democracy, as an international organisation, when the I.W.M.A.'s General Council had refused to accept it as an affiliated body with its own national Sections and independent international congresses. But this dissolution could not in practice mean very much, because internationally the Alliance had possessed practically no formal organisation. When, therefore, Bakunin secured the I.W.M.A.'s recognition of the Geneva Section of Propaganda as an affiliated Section of the International, he and his followers were still well placed for carrying on their propaganda against the centralising and authoritarian tendencies of which they accused the London leadership. The Geneva Section of the Alliance, which came to be widely known simply as the 'Alliance', was itself a thoroughly international body, made up largely of Russian, Polish, Italian, and

French exiles, with enough Swiss sympathisers to prevent it from being simply alien. It had, moreover, in Switzerland the support, against the Londoners, of Guillaume's Federation of the Jura, which had been constituted as a separate Section of the I.W.M.A. and recognised by the General Council. This separate recognition of the Jura Federation had come about as the outcome of a violent internal quarrel among the Swiss. In Geneva, as we saw, the main body of the local trades, except in the building industry, favoured participation in city and cantonal politics and was hostile to the anti-political tendencies which were dominant in the small towns and villages of the Jura. At the outset, Geneva and the Jura had been organised in a single Federation of the International under the leadership of the German veteran of 1848, J. P. Becker. For a time Becker, though in close touch with Marx and usually ready to accept his lead, worked with Bakunin and his Alliance in opposition to the *bourgeois*-radical policies of the followers of Coullery and of the Geneva trades. But when the anti-political groups headed by Bakunin and Guillaume won a majority in the combined Federation, the minority, which was the majority in Geneva itself, seceded and refused to accept the verdict against participation in local politics — and Becker, after some hesitation, went with them, the more readily because the extreme right, under Coullery, had shaken the dust of the International from its feet. The London General Council, confronted with this split, agreed to accept both the Geneva Federation and the Jura Federation as affiliated bodies, provided that they took these separate names. There were thus in Geneva itself two rival bodies — the Geneva Federation and Bakunin's Geneva Propagandist Alliance — and the latter worked in close association with the Jura Federation, led by James Guillaume and Adhemar Schwitzguébel. Bakunin's Alliance, as we saw earlier, had originally applied to be accepted as a constituent Section of the Geneva Federation, but had been rejected, despite its acceptance by London. The Anarchists were thus free to conduct their propaganda through two separate agencies — through the Geneva Alliance when it suited them, and through the Jura Federation when they wished to act as a recognised national constituent of the I.W.M.A. This meant in practice that the Alliance dealt mainly with Italy and Spain and with the left-wing Sections in Southern France, whereas dealings with Belgium, Holland, Paris, and London were conducted mainly by the Jura Federation. Bakunin at first pressed Guillaume to establish a separate Section of the Alliance in the Jura ; but Guillaume refused either to do this or to join the Alliance as a member. He saw the value of acting in the name of a regional Federation of the I.W.M.A. rather than of an openly rebellious fraction.

It was a paradoxical situation that Bakunin himself had voted at the Basle Congress in favour of the extended powers for the General Council against which his Anarchist and Syndicalist followers found themselves increasingly in revolt. In 1869, before the outbreak of the Franco-Prussian War, there had been a widespread belief in the imminence of a new '1848' — of a general revolution which, beginning in France, would spread through Europe and would give the organised workers the chance, which they had been too immature to seize in 1848, of turning it into a movement under proletarian leadership and control. Such a revolution, Bakunin had to agree, would require a central revolutionary direction ; and what body other than the General Council could possibly play the part ? The Italians and Spaniards, intent on their own national revolutions, did not agree even at this stage ; but they then formed only minor groups in the I.W.M.A.'s counsels. The French and the Belgians, and most of the Swiss, did then want a common leadership ; and the British were playing in practice so little part in the International that Marx could on this issue say pretty much what he pleased in their name. But after the outbreak of war in 1870 the prospect of a general European revolution vanished as Germany was swept by a wave of patriotic feeling and as the defeat of France changed the character of revolution in that country by making its outcome subject to Prussian consent. Still more did the defeat of the Commune in Paris make it evident that the day of proletarian revolution in Western Europe was still a long way off.

Marx reacted to the changed situation, as he had done after 1850, by a realistic acceptance of the facts. He was well aware that the chances of the International, as an agency of European revolution, had disappeared, and he was fully prepared to wind it up, if he could, rather than allow it to become the promoter of a series of impracticable and costly *émeutes*. Bakunin, on the other hand, and the Anarchists generally had their eyes much less on the advanced industrial countries than on Italy, Spain, and Russia, and were quite undeterred by the changed state of affairs in the West. It now became for them a matter not of a general European revolution but of seizing every opportunity that occurred anywhere for revolutionary action, almost regardless of the prospects of success — for they held to the idea that every rising was part of the process of revolutionary education of the masses and was accordingly a step towards the desired end of utterly uprooting the existing social structure. The Anarchists, then, saw all centralisation as an obstacle to free local initiative and to the revolutionary *élan* of the masses. Far from wishing to give the General Council extended powers to direct the movement, they wished to sweep it away altogether and to replace it by a mere Correspondence Bureau, which would keep the groups in the various countries in touch one with another but would have no mandate to direct their policies in any respect.

This conflict of views was not the outcome of any 'conspiracy', either on Bakunin's part or on that of Marx. It arose out of real differences both of attitude and in the character of the movements of which the International was made up. Bakunin and Guillaume, and the Spanish and Italian leaders, did carry on an increasingly active propaganda against Marx and the General Council ; but there was nothing particularly conspiratorial about it, unless one counts Bakunin's habitual tendency to give his most commonplace activities a conspiratorial tone. Marx, for his part, intensely irritated by what he regarded as the unrealistic folly of the Anarchists, had developed, by the time the quarrel reached its height, an aggravated form of conspiracy-mania, which led him to see the entire anti-authoritarian movement as a sinister conspiracy directed against himself — an attitude which Engels, in his hero-worship, strongly and unfortunately encouraged. Moreover, Bakunin, who was always a good deal of an ass as well as a volcanic force, committed two disastrous errors which to Marx, in his neurotic condition, appeared to involve highly sinister interpretations.

The first, and by far the less important, of these errors concerned the translation into Russian of the opening volume of

Marx's *Capital*, which had appeared, in Geneva, in 1867. That Bakunin, in 1869, should have undertaken the task of translating *Das Kapital*, and that Marx should have agreed to his doing so, shows that the two were at that stage certainly not enemies. It is no doubt extraordinary that anyone should have supposed that Bakunin would in fact ever finish the translation, or that Marx would be satisfied with it if he did ; for Bakunin left almost everything he started unfinished and was the last person in the world to carry out conscientiously so difficult and wearisome a task. It is on the other hand not at all surprising that Bakunin, who was habitually out of funds and accustomed to raising the wind wherever he could, got an advance payment for the work and showed no disposition to pay it back when it became plain that the translation would never get done. Such were the ways of the Russian giant, who was also a great baby and entirely irresponsible in financial affairs. Marx must have known his Bakunin well enough to have no right to be surprised, however annoyed he might feel, at being let down. But unfortunately this affair of the translation got mixed up with the other, and much more serious, affair which led Marx to declare war *à l'outrance* on Bakunin and on all his friends.

This was the celebrated *affaire* Nechaiev, of which the story has been told so often that I can be content to give the merest outline of it here. Sergei Nechaiev (1847–82), a young Russian who arrived in Switzerland in 1869 and became for a time a close intimate of Bakunin, was clearly a pathological case. Beside his passion for anarchy and destruction, Bakunin's doctrines appear mild and amiable. The genuineness of his revolutionary fervour cannot be doubted — he paid for it by dying at the age of 34 in the Peter-Paul fortress, in which he had been shut up for ten years. But his revolutionism and his application of it in terms of personal behaviour were of a kind to shock any decent-minded person — including even Bakunin, when the facts became known. Repudiating all morality as a *bourgeois* superstition, he acknowledged no limits to revolutionary action. He murdered an associate who had become too inquisitive about the affairs of his mythical 'Revolutionary Committee', and so arranged the murder as to incriminate the other members of his group, and thus ensure their revolutionary solidarity ; and he thought nothing of bringing less uncompromising revolutionaries under police suspicion in order to implicate them more thoroughly in his conspiracies. He lied as freely to his friends as to his enemies ; and he was an inveterate romancer about his own exploits. For Bakunin's delectation he invented a great revolutionary movement that was sweeping over Russia and an underground organisation of which he represented himself as the head. He posed, on his arrival in Switzerland, as having escaped from the Peter-Paul fortress, though he had never been arrested at all. Bakunin for a time swallowed all his stories and came deeply under the influence of this youth of 21, who had in fact no more revolutionary activity to his credit than his leadership of a small student group of no wide influence. He induced Bakunin to co-operate with him in a series of pamphlets of extreme violence for smuggling into Russia : even to-day it is a moot point whether Bakunin was part-author, under Nechaiev's influence, of the notorious *Revolutionary Catechism* in which the doctrine of complete revolutionary amoralism was set down without reserve. Even if Bakunin did not write the *Catechism*, he certainly approved of it, and had often said much the same things himself, though not quite so crudely. Bakunin nicknamed Nechaiev 'the Boy' and became his devotee, flattered by the attention of one he accepted as the emissary of Young Russia to the patriarch of the Revolution. Even when Nechaiev had been exposed, Bakunin could not forget his fondness, though he could not but disapprove of his favourite's behaviour, even if not of his ideas. But before he had found Nechaiev out, and broken off collaboration with him, the mischief had been done.

Nechaiev found Bakunin bored and bogged in his translation of *Das Kapital*, and promised to get him out of his commitment. Characteristically, he did this by threatening the prospective publisher with unspecified vengeance if he insisted on Bakunin either going on with the translation or paying back the advance he had received. Knowledge of this came to Marx, who received the news with fury, and treated it as confirmation of Bakunin's full complicity with Nechaiev and deliberate bad faith and enmity to himself. He scented a conspiracy to prevent his great work from being published in Russian ; and this got mixed up in his mind with his inveterate hatred of Russia and of Russian ways, with his strong disapproval of Nechaiev's Nihilism and repudiation of all principles of human decency, and with the belief that there was a comprehensive plot to ruin the International by setting up Bakunin as its dictator in his stead. In point of fact, Bakunin's correspondence as well as his published writings make it clear that he had a deep, though by no means an unqualified, admiration for Marx's intellectual capacity, despite his disagreement with Marx's policy; and it is also practically certain that Bakunin had nothing to do with the threats made by Nechaiev to the prospective publisher of the Russian version of *Das Kapital*. But Marx was no longer in a state to view the situation reasonably ; and the London Conference of the I.W.M.A., held in 1871 in lieu of the full Congress which it was impossible to convene, wasted a great deal of its time in investigating Marx's charges against Bakunin instead of considering what the International was to do in face of the defeat of the Paris Commune and the eclipse of the movement in France.

Further complications arose out of the activities in Geneva of another Russian exile, Nicholas Utin. Utin had left Russia in 1863 and had been living mainly in Switzerland since that date. He had collaborated, and then quarrelled, with Bakunin, and had become the leader of a group of Russians opposed to the group which belonged to Bakunin's Alliance of Socialist Democracy. Early in 1870 he managed to get control of the Geneva organ of the I.W.M.A., *Égalité*, which had been previously in the hands of Bakunin's friends. He next proceeded to organise at Geneva, in rivalry with the Alliance, a Russian Section of the International, which applied for recognition to the General Council in London, reinforcing its appeal with a request to Marx to become its representative on the Council. Marx, eager to support any move hostile to Bakunin, accepted this office and got the application accepted, remarking in a letter to Engels that it was indeed a queer situation for him to find himself the representative of anything Russian. Thereafter Utin fed Marx steadily with information from Geneva discreditable to Bakunin and his followers, and played a considerable part in working Marx up to a pitch of vindictiveness which made him ready to use any weapon against his antagonist. Utin attended the London Conference of 1871, took part in the discussions about Bakunin and the Anarchists, and was commissioned to prepare an account of the Nechaiev affair, from which the Conference emphatically dissociated the I.W.M.A. After he had played his part in the quarrels which destroyed the International Utin disappeared from the movement. Making his peace with Czardom, he returned to Russia and ended his days as a wealthy and respectable Government contractor.

At the London Conference, held in September 1871, France was represented only by refugees — Vaillant, Frankel, Rochat and Serraillier of Paris, and Bastilica from Marseilles. Switzerland had two delegates — Utin and Henri Perret of Geneva, a former supporter of Bakunin who had changed sides. The General Council, engaged in a procedural quarrel with the Jura Federation, had refused to summon to the conference anyone representing the Swiss opposition. Spain had only one representative, and Italy none ; and the British delegation included only John Hales and the Irishman Thomas Mottershead, unless one counts the London foreigners — Marx, Engels, Eccarius, Jung, Cohn from Denmark, and the Pole, Anton Zabicki. Belgium, the one country in which the International was still really flourishing, had six, headed by César de Paepe ; and this group held a moderating position, but was not able to prevent most of the time being wasted on the question of Bakunin's sins against the General Council and, in particular, against Marx. There were no Germans, for the German movement was largely out of action for the time being as a result of the war.

At this stage and right up to the Hague Congress of the following year, Marx was working in temporary alliance with the French refugees, who were largely Blanquists, against the Anarchists. The British adherents of the International, no longer including any of the major Trade Union leaders, were demanding the establishment of a separate British Federal Council. As long as the principal leaders of the London Trades Council and of the newly established Trades Union Congress were supporters of the I.W.M.A., it could be argued that a separate Council for Great Britain would merely duplicate their work on these bodies and on the National Reform League and its successor, the Labour Representation League of 1869. But when the British leaders had dropped out, some before and the rest in consequence of the I.W.M.A.'s support of the Paris

Commune, it became clear that the International could have no real existence in Great Britain unless it were separately organised under its own Council, as a point of focus for left-wing working-class opinion hostile to the studiously moderate tactics of the Junta of Trade Union leaders. Consequently a British Federal Council of the I.W.M.A., distinct from the General Council, was established immediately after the London Conference ; but it never rallied any mass support. Its advent, however, further narrowed the already exiguous foundation on which the General Council's authority rested ; for it could by no means be guaranteed either to do what Marx wanted or to let him alone, as the more distinguished British members of the General Council had usually done.

Among the decisions taken at the London Conference of the International was one which declared the imperative necessity for the workers in each country to form their own political party, entirely independent of all *bourgeois* parties. The absence of the Anarchists and the predominantly Blanquist complexion of the French contingent made the carrying of such a resolution easy ; but it was not likely to be accepted by the unrepresented opposition, which disputed the competence of the meeting to bind the International. The Swiss groups hostile to Marx at once convened a Congress of their own, repudiated the London decisions, and issued a circular to all the Federations making up the International urging them to demand the calling of a proper Congress for the earliest possible date. It became evident that when such a Congress did meet there was bound to be a struggle without quarter between the Anarchists and Federalists on the one hand and the centralisers and political actionists on the other.

This long-awaited struggle took place at the Hague Congress of 1872 — the last real meeting of the First International in full force. It was indeed, at any rate on paper, by far the most widely representative Congress the International ever held. Of the nations which had played any substantial part in the movement, only the Italians were absent. They, as we have seen, refused to come. The Spaniards, on the other hand, sent five delegates, the Belgians nine, and the Swiss four — representing both the rival groups. There were seven somewhat undistinguished delegates from the British Federal Council and its associated bodies. The Germans, with a complement of ten, were for the first time represented on a substantial scale. The Dutch made a first appearance with four delegates, and the Danes with one. There were three supposed to represent the United States, headed by Marx's friend, F. A. Sorge ; but they were all European immigrants. Single delegates purported to represent Sections in Hungary and in Bohemia. From France came three, under false names — an equivocal group, of whom one at least was a spy. But there were also a number of French exiles attending as representatives of the General Council — Charles Longuet, Marx's son-in-law, the Blanquist Édouard Vaillant, Leo Frankel, and some others who had been through the Commune. Finally, also from the General Council, there was the old group of Marx's co-workers — George Eccarius, Étienne Dupont, Friedrich Lessner, and Marx and Engels in person — the first full Congress either had attended, though Marx had taken part in the inaugural meetings. But there was a gap in the ranks of the old 'faithfuls'. Hermann Jung, the London-Swiss watchmaker, who had presided over many previous meetings as Marx's stout ally, had refused to come.

There was, indeed, already a rift in the old group. Marx's and Engels's tactics in trying to pack the Congress, the vindictiveness of their attacks on the Swiss recalcitrants, and, perhaps most of all, Marx's unqualified onslaughts on the British Trade Unionists who had forsaken the International, had antagonised both Jung and Eccarius ; and they were no longer prepared to follow Marx's lead. They did not like the Blanquists who had been brought on to the General Council ; and they were not prepared to see the International split by Marx's determination to get the leaders of the opposition, including Bakunin himself, formally expelled. Marx must have known well enough that such a policy would be the end of the International : it was bound to drive out the Spaniards and a good part of the Belgians, as well as most of the Swiss. As against this the Germans, nearly all strong advocates of parliamentary action, might be induced for the first time to play a real part ; but what would there be left for them to co-operate with, as there no longer existed any real movement in either Great Britain or France ? Marx, however, was fully determined on having his way, and on destroying the International rather than run any risk of letting it fall into his opponents' hands.

The Hague Congress had been meant to deal with a number of important issues of Socialist policy which had been referred for further consideration by the Federations at the Basle Congress of 1869. But when the time came no one had much attention to spare for anything except the great issue between the advocates of political action and the Anarchists. It was Marx versus Bakunin and, till that contest had been decided, little else. When it came to voting, there was a clear majority against the Anarchists and Federalists and for political action. It is interesting to see how the majority and minority on the main issues were made up. The figures cannot be taken as quite exact, as there were several divisions, and not every delegate voted.

	Majority	Minority
Germany . . .	10	—
Great Britain . . .	—	5
France	6	1
Belgium . . .	—	7
Switzerland . . .	2	2
Spain	1*	4
Hungary . . .	1	—
Bohemia . . .	1	—
Holland . . .	—	4
Denmark . . .	1	—
U.S.A. . . .	2	1
General Council . .	16	5
	40	29

* Marx's son-in-law, Lafargue.

Thus the General Council, made up largely of Marx's followers and of Blanquists, and the solid German group formed the bulk of the majority, while the Belgians and the dissident British were the chief elements in the minority. Switzerland was divided : Holland and Spain were with the dissidents, and so, of course, would the absent Italians have been had they sent a delegation. On the majority side, the Bohemian, the Hungarian, and the Dane, and, broadly, the delegates from the United States, represented non-existent movements, or nearly so ; and the French movement was dispersed and could not be really represented. It came very near to the Germans, including their exiles, plus the French Blanquists, outvoting the rest.

The Hague Congress began by passing a series of resolutions strengthening the powers of the General Council and, in effect, threatening with expulsion any group which opposed its political line. Then came the question of the future seat of the General Council, which had always sat in London. It was decided by a very narrow majority that London should no longer be the centre, and Engels thereupon proposed to transfer the seat of the General Council to New York. This startling proposal, which was entirely unexpected by most of those present, took the delegates aback, divided the majority, and put the minority into a dilemma. If Marx and his friends no longer wanted the International in London, where was it to go ? The Swiss, the Belgians, and the Dutch would have none of it ; for they were against the existence of any General Council with the powers the Congress had accorded to it. The Spaniards were in the same position ; and the laws of Germany would not have allowed the operation of an international organisation on German soil. France was obviously out of the question ; but the Blanquists were violently hostile to removing what they regarded as the central agency of the revolution out of Europe. In the end 30 delegates voted for New York ; 14 for London, though London did not want to continue ; 1 each for Brussels and Barcelona : 13 abstained.

It has sometimes been suggested that Marx and Engels really believed that the International could find a new basis for its operations in the United States and could be kept alive there until the time was ripe for its re-emergence in Europe. There had been from time to time hopeful accounts at the International's Congresses of the development of the American Labour movement ; and there had been some exchanges between the General Council and some of the Trade Union leaders in the United States. A single American, Andrew Carr Cameron (1834–90), editor of the Chicago *Workman's Advocate* and a leading member of the Eight Hours League and of the National Labor Union, had attended the Basle Congress of 1869 ; and there were three U.S.A. delegates at the Hague, two refugee Frenchmen and a German emigrant. But the International had never had any real hold in America, and was most unlikely to acquire any as the cast-off of Europe. F. A. Sorge (1827–1906), the German immigrant who had come from the United States to the Hague at Marx's urgent demand, and was being bullied by Marx into accepting the thankless office of General Secretary, was under no illusion about the prospects. It is beyond question that Marx and Engels wanted to transfer the General Council to New York, not for any good it was likely to do there, but in order to keep it out of the hands into which it was certain to fall if it remained in London. Hence the fury of the ex-Communards, who had reckoned on getting control now that the British Trade Unionists had gone away and the Anarchists been driven out.

Marx and Engels had, however, no power to put an end to the International, though they could deprive their opponents of a constitutional title to the succession. Outvoted at the Hague, the minority proceeded to reconstitute the International on the basis of complete decentralisation which they had favoured all along. Immediately after the Hague Congress the out-and-out Anarchists held a Congress at Zürich and decided, on Bakunin's motion, to found a new secret International of their own. From this gathering they went on to a public Congress at St.-Imier, called on the initiative of the Italians, and there took part in re-founding the I.W.M.A. as a free federation of autonomous national Federations. The St.-Imier Congress repudiated the decisions taken at the Hague, refused to recognise the Hague Congress as a valid meeting of the International, and claimed to be the true successor to the earlier Congresses held during the 1860s. In fact, it represented only the Italians, the Spaniards, and the Jura Swiss, with a sprinkling of French refugees.

These groups, however, soon established relations with the Belgians and the Dutch, who had formed a large part of the minority at the Hague ; and the St.-Imier Congress was followed by a number more, supported chiefly by the Swiss, the Belgians, the Spaniards, the Italians, and a number of refugee French groups. The earlier of these Congresses, up to 1874, still retained the support of one fraction of the British Federal Council, which split after the Hague Congress into two rival groups, both of negligible importance. In 1873 there were two rival International Congresses, both held at Geneva. But the Congress called by the New York General Council turned out pure farce. The General Council could not raise enough money to send any representative across the Atlantic ; and the organisation fell upon the shoulders of the unfortunate J. P. Becker, of Geneva. Marx and Engels, when they realised that the Congress was bound to be a failure, not only refused to attend it themselves but also discouraged their supporters, so that nobody at all went from London. There were no Belgians, Spaniards, or Italians — in fact, nobody at all except such Swiss and Germans in Switzerland as Becker could gather together and a single Austrian, by name Heinrich Oberwinder. Becker and Oberwinder between them manufactured credentials for about twenty delegates from alleged Sections of the International in German Switzerland, Germany, and Austria ; and this majority they used to vote down the French Genevese, who wished to remove the International's headquarters from New York to Geneva and to open negotiations with the seceders in the hope of reuniting the broken fragments. Thereafter, except in the United States, no more was heard of Marx's International. In America it lingered on for a few more years, to the accompaniment of violent internal disputes. Sorge resigned in 1874 ; and two or three years later it finally expired.

Meanwhile, the rival International was also gradually dwindling. It was not at the outset by any means wholly Anarchist. The British delegates, while they remained, were strong advocates of political action, and so were some of the Belgians and a few from other countries. In principle, what held the various groups together was a common insistence on the right of each national Federation to follow whatever policy it held best, without any control either by a General Council or even by vote of Congress. There was no General Council — only a Correspondence Bureau — and the debates held at the successive Congresses, even when they led to resolutions carried by a majority, had no binding force. In practice, the new International represented a number of different tendencies. The Spaniards and most of the Italians were sheer insurrectionists, the Spaniards still representing a considerable mass-movement engaged in actual revolutionary struggles, and the Italians ranging from fomenters of peasant risings in Sicily and the south to groups in some of the northern cities which were more concerned with forming Trade Unions and were showing signs of impending conversion to a belief in the possible value of non-revolutionary political action. The Swiss were a mixture of native Anarchists from the Jura Federation and of exiles from many countries — especially France, Italy, Russia, Germany, and Austria-Hungary. The majority of these exiles, except the Germans, were ardent revolutionaries who sided broadly with the Spaniards and Italians : the native Swiss leaders were theoretical Anarchists of a much less revolutionary temper — Federalists rather than insurrectionists, and often rather alarmed at the violence of the Spaniards and Italians. The Belgians and Dutch included Anarchist groups ; but the Belgians were for the most part inclined to follow the lead of César de Paepe, who stood for a middle-of-the-road attitude between the out-and-out Anarchists and the advocates of political action. The French were divided as well as scattered geographically : the Blanquists had withdrawn from both Internationals, and there was a growing tendency towards what was called 'Integralism', preached by Benoît Malon, which amounted to an assertion that all forms of activity were useful in their place and that, in particular, political action could be useful provided that it did not carry with it an abandonment of revolutionary purpose.

The discussions among representatives of these various tendencies at the successive Congresses of the new International came to turn largely — especially at the Geneva and Brussels meetings of 1873 and 1874 — on what may appear to be a purely verbal issue. In 1869 at Basle the International had embarked on a serious discussion of the organisation of the public services in the new social order that was to ensue on the workers' victory, and this discussion, in which César de Paepe was again the principal expositor, was resumed after the split. The big question facing the delegates was in effect what should be done in the case of industries and other services which clearly could not be organised on a small, local scale. It was a matter of general agreement that most forms of production would be taken over by workers' groups consisting of the actual producers in each single establishment and that these workers' Co-operatives would be under some sort of supervision by the local Commune of the district in which they were situated. It was also agreed that the local Commune would itself be responsible for the conduct of local public services, would own the land and probably the main capital installations, and would be

the foundation on which all larger structures of public administration and control would rest. Some thought of the Commune
as consisting of all the local inhabitants meeting together, and
delegating only limited powers to a council or group of officers
subject at any time to recall. Others tended to think of it rather
as itself a federation of the local producers' associations ; but
the difference was not felt to be vital, as both groups expected
every worker to play an active part in the Commune by direct
legislation or referendum as well as by choosing delegates and
giving them imperative instructions (the *mandat impératif*) and
recalling them at will.

It was further agreed that for a number of purposes, for
which the area of a single Commune was too small, the Communes would need to link up into Federations and to entrust
the conduct of the services in question to elected federal representatives. This seemed to be a fairly simple matter where
there was only a need for combined action by a few neighbour-
ing Communes — though even in such cases there was the
question whether the representatives would be entitled to bind
the Communes or would have to refer everything back for
communal consent. The real trouble arose over such things
as clearly needed unified control over quite large areas, up to —
or even beyond — the whole territory of a nation. There were
indeed two related problems at this level. In the first place,
most of the Anarchists were strongly anti-nationalist, and
looked forward to a complete disappearance of national frontiers and to a world administered by free local Communes
federated as much or as little as they chose without regard to
national frontiers. Secondly, there was a fear that, if a number
of the major services were allowed to be administered by a
single body operating over a large area, this body would turn
into a 'State' — that is, into a new power agency exercising
authority over the people and thus negating the freedom which
it was the revolution's purpose to ensure. To this objection
some, including de Paepe, answered by invoking the conception
of what the Germans called the *Volksstaat* — the People's
State — which would be not an authority over the people, like
the existing State, but a direct emanation of the people's will.

The notion of the 'People's State' could, however, be interpreted in different ways. Broadly speaking, the Germans

tended to understand by it a central authority based on the working class and expressive of the workers' collective will ; whereas the Belgians and the French, when they admitted it at all, conceived of it as a federal body deriving such authority as it should possess from the local Communes, out of which it was to be built up. The Anarchists of course objected strongly to the use of the word 'State', even with the prefix 'People's', to describe such a body, and insisted that no sort of *authority*, even in a federal form, must be allowed to survive into the new society. The middle party retorted that the body which was set to administer such national services as railways, main roads, and essential communications, such as posts and telegraphs, must be endowed with real power and could not possibly be required to remit every decision for ratification by each individual Commune, or be subject to the right of each Commune to contract out of a particular service. There would have, they pointed out, to be *some* central authority ; and they did not see the objection to calling this body a 'State', provided it was clearly understood to be a new sort of State, resting on the combined action of the local Communes and made up of communal delegates. But this middle attitude satisfied neither the Anarchists, for whom State and authority in all forms were the enemy, nor the Marxists, who wanted a workers' State armed with dictatorial powers to carry through the revolution and to destroy all forms of potential counter-revolutionary opposition. Nor of course did it satisfy the Blanquists, who on this issue were on the Marxists' side.

De Paepe and his, mainly Belgian, followers seceded from the old International and joined the Anarchists in the new one because they were opposed to Marx's policy of forcing upon the whole International both an admission of the need for political action and a General Council armed with a considerable amount of central authority over the National Federations — and also because they resented Marx's tactics against Bakunin and his followers. The narrowness of the Belgian franchise gave them no opportunity to run candidates for election to Parliament with any chance of success ; but many of them were disposed to think it very much their business to agitate for universal suffrage and for freedom in local government rather than turn their backs on the political struggle. The Walloons and Flemings had, however, a common dislike to a centralised State which would override their differences of culture and outlook ; but at the same time the high development of Belgian industries and services, such as transport, forced them to face the need for central agencies to control such enterprises on a national scale. They tended, therefore, to support the idea of a Federal State against the rival extremes of the centralised *Volksstaat* and the Anarchist conception of entirely self-governing local Communes. This situation led de Paepe to give much more careful and realistic thought than anyone else in the International to the question of the working structure of the new society ; but his realism did not gain him many followers outside his own country. It left him under the continual accusation of trimming between the rival factions : the Swiss, who were in some respects nearest to his point of view, were not face to face with the problems of developed industrialism to anything like the same extent.

In the light of what happened after 1872, it can be seen that the great debate between Marx and Bakunin at the Hague Congress ended, despite the formal decisions taken at the Hague, considerably more in favour of Bakunin than of Marx, as far as the elements which had made up the First International were concerned. After 1872 Marx had in effect hardly any following outside Germany ; and even in Germany his followers were contending fiercely for some years with the Lassallians, who sent delegates to the anti-authoritarian Brussels Congress of 1874. The following year the conflict inside Germany was ended in the main by the fusion of the Eisenach and Lassallian parties at the Gotha Congress, which left in being only a small Anarchist opposition, mainly in South Germany, headed by Johann Most. But the terms of the Gotha fusion were not at all to Marx's liking ; and with the Genevese and a section of the Belgians trying to recreate the International on a loosely federal basis, the French virtually out of action, the Spaniards and most of the Italians strongly hostile, and the British no longer interested, there was no foundation on which Marx could build any movement of his own. At the same time, though the Anarchists and Federalists were strong enough to keep a rather ineffective International together for some years longer, its foundations were being knocked away by the disruption of the revolutionary forces in Spain, by the gradual wearing out of the insurrectionary impulse over a large part of Italy, and by growing tension between the Anarchists and the middle groups which had been united with them in opposition to Marx. By 1877, when the anti-authoritarian International held its last Congress at Verviers, in Belgium, there was not much of a movement left for it to represent ; and the United Socialist Congress held that same year at Ghent, in the hope of building a new united International broad enough to include all shades of opinion, produced no practical results. In 1881 the Anarchists, this time with no attempt to bring in the middle parties, instituted a shadowy new International of their own ; but it had no connection with the growing main body of the Socialist movement, which was already turning, under German influence, to the formation of national Social Democratic Parties aiming at the conquest of political power. A new episode in the history of Socialism was beginning : the period of the First International was definitely over and done with.

The anti-authoritarian Congresses of the years after 1872, when they were not debating their several attitudes towards the State and political action, were very much concerned with two related problems — international industrial organisation and the general strike. The Belgians and Spaniards in particular, and also some of the French, tended to go back to the original conception of the International as a great federation of the workers across national frontiers for mutual aid in organisation and in trade disputes, for the prevention of blacklegging, and for the enforcement by concerted industrial action of such reforms as a shortening of the working day. Successive Congresses discussed plans of international Trade Union organisation, which were to rest on the double basis of local federations of all trades in a locality and of national and international federations of all the workers in a particular industry. The double form of organisation which was later to be characteristic of the French Confédération du Travail was already being advocated in these debates ; and the preference for industrial over craft Unions as the instruments for the conquest of economic power was already being clearly expressed. For the time being, except in Belgium, such plans could have no positive results. The only other countries far enough advanced to be in a position to act on them were Great Britain, where no impulse to such action existed, and the United States, which was too far away and too little in touch with European thought not to go its own way — as it did, first in the Knights of Labor and later in Daniel De Leon's successive attempts to build up a combined industrial and political movement on largely Marxist foundations.[1] The planners of the European International for the most part planted their schemes in barren ground ; but what they did subsequently influenced a good deal the development of Trade Unionism in France and in other Latin countries.

The idea of the general strike had obviously close connections with these projects of comprehensive industrial organisation. As we have seen, the general strike had been discussed earlier in the First International as a means of preventing or stopping war — and had been derided by Marx as an altogether visionary notion. In the 'seventies it was brought forward again, not mainly as a means of ending war, but rather as the form to be taken by the social revolution itself. Many of the Anarchists envisaged the world revolution as beginning with a general cessation of labour, paralysing *bourgeois* society and demonstrating plainly the workers' power. For it to be effective they needed a well-organised Trade Union movement animated by the spirit of proletarian brotherhood : hence their support of the plans for comprehensive Trade Union groupings, international as well as national. But most of the Anarchists did not expect the *bourgeois* State to fall simply as the result of a general cessation of labour. They expected the ruling classes to appeal to armed force in an endeavour to drive the strikers back to work : they expected the general strike to lead to civil war and open revolution. The 'Integralists', headed by Benoît Malon, retorted that the general strike and the ensuing revolution would be most likely to succeed if, in preparing for 'the day', the workers had also used their political power to penetrate into the *bourgeois* State so as to undermine its defences from within and make it harder for the reactionaries to use the machinery of State against the strikers. The Anarchists retorted that the use of parliamentary means would undermine the revolutionary will of the workers, and that the parliamentary

[1] See pages 365 ff.

representatives of the workers would certainly turn traitors when the time came.

The Anarchists have been spoken of in the foregoing paragraphs as if they had constituted a single united group, as on the whole, in relation to the issues I have been discussing, they actually did. But there were also conflicting trends among them. One group, which included Errico Malatesta and a good many of the Italians and Spaniards and some of the French, together with a considerable section of the Russian refugees, were, broadly, advocates of the complete destruction of existing society, by every available means, and were uninterested in any attempt to plan in advance the institutions of the new society, which they thought of vaguely as 'free communistic' or 'free socialistic', with strong emphasis on individual liberty. According to this school, the spontaneous and hitherto inhibited genius of the common people would easily settle the shape of the new society when the old order had been thoroughly demolished. But there were other Anarchists who put the main emphasis less on individual freedom than on the collective freedom of the small group, acting under the influence of the natural human impulses towards solidarity and mutual aid. This group, headed by Peter Kropotkin, came to be known as the Anarchist-Communists : it appeared first in the middle 'seventies in the discussions carried on by the Anarchists chiefly in the Jura Federation, which was the main support of the international Anarchist movement until it broke up in 1878. That year James Guillaume, the principal Swiss leader, retired from activity and went to live in Paris, leaving the movement in Switzerland chiefly in Kropotkin's hands. Bakunin had died in 1876, and had played no active part during the years after 1872.

Thus, well before 1880, the European upheaval in which the First International played its part had come finally to an end. The International was dead — the anti-authoritarian International as well as the Marxist, except that the Spanish Federation still maintained a shadowy existence. The attempt, at Ghent, to create a new inclusive Socialist International had led to no results, not only because the gulf between Anarchists and political Socialists was too wide to be bridged, but also because there was no sufficient impulse towards unity to induce common action even among relatively like-minded groups.

This eclipse of the international idea was largely due to the almost complete destruction of the French Socialist and work-ing-class movement, which up to 1871 had always held the central place in continental Socialist thought and action. After 1871 the strongest Socialist movement in Europe was the German, despite its division into two rival parties. But the German movement had for the time being almost no influence on opinion outside Germany. Before long it was to gain great influence ; indeed, German Social Democracy was destined to supply the new model for Socialist organisation over a large part of Europe. But this influence did not become important until after the Gotha Unity Congress of 1875 — or even then at once. In the 1870s, as in the 1850s, there were too many little groups, largely of exiles, busily holding inquests on their defeat and blaming one another for it, for any advance to be made towards a new form of unity. Blanquists and Marxists, Marxists and Anarchists, revolutionists and moderates slung brickbats to and fro. Of the protagonists Varlin and a number of others had perished in the disasters of the Paris Commune ; Bakunin was dead ; Marx was wrestling with the later volumes of *Das Kapital* and failing to make good progress with them in face of worsening health ; de Paepe was facing sharp differences of opinion in the Belgian movement ; Guillaume was getting sick of what seemed a fruitless struggle. The centres in which the International had been most active were in need of a rest, and were taking one, either compulsorily, as in France and Italy, or of their own accord.

In part the explanation of this decline is to be found in economic conditions. The middle 'seventies saw everywhere a sharp recession from the high economic activity of the pre-ceding years. The long period of falling prices which lasted nearly to the end of the century had set in : there was acute agricultural depression in many of the older countries, bringing with it industrial recession and unemployment. Trade Unions, which had been on the offensive from the late 'sixties to about 1874, found themselves reduced to postures of defence, where they were able to stand out at all. No doubt, in the long run, these very conditions had a good deal to do with the revival of Socialism in the 1880s ; but their immediate results were adverse, politically as well as economically. Only in Germany, where economic development was proceeding at a great rate after the unification of the Reich, were conditions favourable for a working-class advance — an advance soon to be met by Bismarck's Anti-Socialist Laws and reasserted in the astonishingly successful resistance to these laws by the unified German Social Democratic Party.

Before we come to consider the growth of Socialism in Germany, or the widespread European revival of the 1880s, it is necessary to describe in a more connected way than has been possible so far the ideas of the man who so nearly succeeded in wresting the control of the International from Karl Marx and in building it up on quite different foundations as the expression of a blend of Russian Nihilism, or near-Nihilism, with South European insurrectionary Anarchism. The method of treatment adopted in the chapters dealing with the International has not allowed Bakunin's fundamental social philosophy to be set out in any clear or comprehensive fashion. This task demands a chapter ; for, however chaotic Bakunin's writings and sayings may be, they do represent a definable attitude and, indeed, an intelligible structure of thought.

CHAPTER IX

BAKUNIN

MICHAEL BAKUNIN, the great antagonist of Marx in the First International and, if not the founder of modern Anarchism, at all events its outstanding leader when it was first shaping itself into an organised international movement, has been much written about but little read. Even from Mr. E. H. Carr's lengthy biography it is hardly possible to arrive at any clear notion of his ideas ; and practically none of his writings have been published in English, and very little of them is accessible in any modern edition available to those who cannot read Russian. His devoted admirer, James Guillaume, published in France in the early years of the present century a collected edition which brought together a good deal of his scattered writing ; but this and the preliminary volume issued by Max Nettlau in 1895 are hard to come by. Nettlau's monumental biography, never published, is to be had only in photographic copies in a few great libraries ; and the only edition of the main body of Bakunin's correspondence is in Russian.

Fortunately Bakunin's ideas were seldom abstruse, and it is fairly easy to present them in broad outline against the background of his life. Fortunately, too, Mr. Carr's biography exempts me from the need to discuss the events of his life in any detail. The essential facts, unlike the details, are simple, and soon told. Bakunin was born in 1814, four years before Marx. He was the son of an aristocratic Russian landowner of mildly liberal opinions, and was destined for the army. He attended the Artillery School, but was dismissed for negligence and transferred to an ordinary regiment, in which he served for a time in Poland. But at the age of 21 he deliberately got himself dismissed from the army on grounds of non-existent 'ill-health', escaping punishment for indiscipline only through family influence. He had already taken to philosophy and to more or less advanced opinions ; and he pressed urgently to be allowed to go to Germany, where he wanted in particular to study Hegelian philosophy — then the latest thing among the St. Petersburg intellectuals. After some years spent partly in study at Moscow — years during which he first became friendly with Belinski and then quarrelled with him — he at length, in 1840, got money from his father to pursue his studies abroad, and went to Berlin. There, and in Paris during the following years, he imbibed the ideas of the Young Hegelians and particularly of Feuerbach, and also came into direct touch with French ideas — particularly those of Proudhon, which were to become a major influence on him. He got to know both Marx and Proudhon, and impressed them both with the force of his turbulent personality. He took part in the movements of 1848 and the following years, attempting to bring into being a concerted movement of the Slav peoples against their oppressors — Russian, Austrian, and German, — but learning in the process a deep distrust of nationalism and of its leaders. Taking part in the Dresden insurrection of 1849, he was captured and sentenced to death by the Saxon Government, but was in the end handed over to the Austrians, who in turn surrendered him to the Russian Government. In Russia he was imprisoned for seven years in a fortress ; and less than two years of this period had elapsed when he wrote, for the Czar's own eyes, the celebrated confession which has been quoted so often against him since it was unearthed and published in 1921. In this confession Bakunin gave a full and accurate account of his doings as a revolutionary, except that he refused to include anything that might have incriminated any of his associates who were still within the reach of the Czar's Government. His tone was one of almost abject renunciation of his revolutionary principles, and at the same time of intense exaltation of the Slav peoples as against the Germans, for whom he expressed a deeply rooted hatred. This 'Pan-Slavism' squared well enough with Bakunin's previous attitude ; for he had been trying in 1848 to rouse the Slavs to revolt against the Austro-Hungarian Empire. Nor was there anything new in his appeal to the Czar to place himself at the head of a Pan-Slav movement of liberation. The only novel element was his repudiation of his revolutionary past in relation to Russia itself.

It will always remain a moot point how much discredit this

confession throws on Bakunin's sincerity as a revolutionary. Those who dislike him on other grounds will make the most of it : those who are disposed to like him will argue that it was no more than what he called it himself many years later — 'a big blunder' — and that no great weight should be attached to what a man writes in solitary confinement that looks like lasting for life, at any rate provided that he says nothing to incriminate anyone else. Personally, I come near to this second view : I cannot be at all sure how I should behave under similar circumstances, especially if I believed the cause for which I had contended to be lost and my own chance of aiding it to be quite gone. Still less can I blame so temperamental a person and one so given to self-explanation as Bakunin for feeling that he must write something for somebody to read and for preferring the Czar as reader to nobody at all. Bakunin's conduct was admittedly not heroic ; but I have no great liking for heroes, who are often perilously akin to fanatics. I do not defend the confession ; but neither do I feel disposed to hold it heavily against its author, whose subsequent conduct shows that his revolutionary faith was as sincere as it was apt to be, sometimes, misguided in its forms of expression and action. I suspect that Bakunin carried a guilty conscience about it for the rest of his life, and that this may have had something to do with the influence Nechaiev was able to exert over him.

The confession was written in the hope of securing, not the Czar's pardon, but the exchange of imprisonment in a fortress — then in Russia an unusual long-term punishment — for exile to Siberia. It was unavailing for that purpose, procuring him no more than permission to receive an occasional visit from his family. Between five and six years went by before his friends were able to secure his transfer to Siberia, where he was allowed to reside in Tomsk, supported by subsidies from his family in Russia. At Tomsk he fell in love with, and married, a local merchant's daughter ; but he was by no means prepared to settle down to a life of humdrum provincialism. Luckily for him, the Governor of Siberia, Muraviov, was his mother's cousin, and she pressed the Governor hard on his behalf. When Muraviov came to Tomsk and met Bakunin, the two struck up a friendship, and for a while Bakunin cherished the unfounded vision of Muraviov as the destined liberator of the

Slavs from the yoke of Austria and wrote enthusiastic letters to Herzen about his virtues. Muraviov, for his part, vainly asked the Czar's Government to pardon Bakunin and, when this was refused, allowed him and his wife to move to the Siberian capital, Irkutsk, where life was less dull and there was more hope of openings for the exile's talents. He was given a post at a comfortable salary in a new commercial company, founded with Muraviov's support, and was allowed to travel widely in Siberia on its behalf. But commerce was not to Bakunin's taste, and he soon ceased to carry out his duties. His salary, however, was still paid, thanks to his intimacy with the Governor; and when Muraviov retired in 1861 Bakunin's luck held, for the new Governor, Korsakov, was a cousin of his brother Paul's wife. Bakunin was, however, by this time set on making his escape, having come to the conclusion that he no longer stood any chance of being allowed to return to European Russia. Under pretence of a mercantile journey, from which he promised Korsakov to return, he borrowed enough money to finance his escape and managed to make his way to Japan, with the aid of papers provided by Korsakov for the purpose of his supposed mercantile proceedings. From Japan he took ship to the United States, and thence, after crossing the continent, to Europe. He reached London late in 1861, and there renewed his friendship with Alexander Herzen and Nicholas Ogarev, whom he had known in Russia; but in 1864, after certain fantastic adventures connected with an attempt to stir up a Polish rebellion, he decided to settle in Italy, where, with Naples as his chief centre of operations, he threw himself into the creation of a revolutionary movement based mainly on the discontented intellectuals and grossly exploited peasants of the former Kingdom of Naples and Sicily. At the same time he set to work to build up what he called an 'International Brotherhood' — a secret society of international revolutionaries which, as we have seen, had little real existence except as a circle of his many revolutionary friends. From Naples his influence spread into Central and Northern Italy; and when he moved from Italy and settled in Switzerland in 1867 he left a considerable, though chaotically organised, movement behind him. Its ramifications, indeed, already extended into Southern France and Catalonia; and through the missionary efforts of his friends, Giuseppe Fanelli and Charles Alerini, it was already beginning to get a foothold in other parts of Spain.

At this stage Bakunin, who had discussed his projects with Marx in London and was in touch with Marx as representing the International Working Men's Association, transferred his main attention to the newly founded League of Peace and Freedom, which, as we saw in a previous chapter, was organising an international Peace Congress to meet in Switzerland. We have seen how the I.W.M.A. first decided to give its full support to this body, and then proceeded to attach a number of conditions which the very mixed composition of the League rendered entirely unacceptable to most of its supporters. Bakunin and his friends in the League tried to bring that organisation over to the acceptance of a very advanced social programme, which included the abolition of inherited wealth and the emancipation of labour from capitalist exploitation. On this basis, Bakunin argued, there was no reason why the League and the I.W.M.A. should not work harmoniously together : on no other basis, he contended, was it of any use to work for peace, which could never be secured without a solution of the 'social problem' or while States resting on the exploitation of the majority of their peoples continued to exist. Defeated at the second Congress of the League of Peace and Freedom in 1868, Bakunin and his allies withdrew and formed, as we have seen, the Alliance of Socialist Democracy. Then followed the years of struggle for control of the International Working Men's Association between Marx and the followers of Bakunin. After the Hague Congress of 1872 Bakunin took the lead in forming a new secret Anarchist International ; but two years later he retired from political activity after the failure of the Bologna rising. He was in failing health, and in sore personal difficulties. In 1876 he died.

Bakunin was physically a giant, and of massive strength. His years of imprisonment after 1849 cost him the loss of all his teeth and did much to undermine his health ; but he remained capable of immense, though spasmodic, exertion. Wherever he went he exercised a volcanic force, and often a really remarkable fascination, on those with whom he associated : he was evidently a very difficult man to refuse, even when his requests were not easy to comply with. He was also in other respects a difficult man to associate with. Always short of money — indeed, having none except what he could get from his friends — he was a remorseless and insatiable borrower, not so much on account of the extravagance of his spending on himself as because he had no sense of economy, was very generous with the money he borrowed, and was usually in family difficulties which made awkward calls on his purse. When he got money he spent it at once, or gave it away, and went in search of new friends from whom he could borrow more, seldom, if ever, repaying anyone, but never quite running out of new suppliers. He lived much in other people's houses, greatly to their inconvenience, for he had no sense of either time or order, reduced any apartment he inhabited to chaos, and was apt to stay in bed all day and sit up all night, writing hard and consuming immense quantities of black coffee and tobacco. His correspondence was prodigious, and he was continually starting works which, begun as pamphlets, grew to the dimensions of large books and were usually abandoned in favour of something else long before they were finished. Most of Bakunin's works are unfinished ; and indeed there is no reason why they should ever have ended, for the more he wrote the more fresh subjects he opened up — till he got tired, and started to write something else embodying much the same essential ideas in a rather different setting. It was the same with the series of articles he agreed to write for various journals : they usually broke off in the middle, either because he had got tired of them, or because his attention had been called elsewhere. Bakunin certainly lived up to his anarchical principles : the attempt or two he made in his latter years to settle down to a more regular life came to grief almost before they were begun. Liberty he always proclaimed as the great principle of living ; and assuredly no one ever lived with more liberty on so little money that was his own.

Yet this most inconvenient man was evidently lovable, and inspired deep affection among his friends, who put up with a monstrous amount of discomfort at his hands. He had the aristocratic temperament in that form of it which renders its possessor totally unconscious of class-barriers, and as ready to live on an onion as to take luxury in its stride when luxury happens to come its way. He was eminently genial, almost incapable of taking offence, and utterly irresponsible. He was also a most loyal friend, ready to do anything for his intimates except repay the money he had borrowed from them, and very generous in praise of his opponents, if he regarded them as belonging fundamentally to the 'side' of the revolution — which was his passion. He spoke most generously of Marx's services to the cause, even when they were in sharp conflict and when Marx was reviling him and accusing him of all manner of crimes, besides those of which he was actually guilty. He praised Nechaiev's good qualities, even when Nechaiev had stolen his private papers and thrown him over after making all the use he could of the old man's patronage. He was indeed as incapable of meanness or malice as of ordinary *bourgeois* honesty in matters of money.

Bakunin's social theory began, and almost ended, with liberty. Against the claims of liberty nothing else in his view was worth any consideration at all. He attacked, remorselessly and without qualification, every institution that seemed to him to be inconsistent with liberty, and every sort of belief that ran counter to the recognition of liberty as the ultimate good. Yet he was very far from being an individualist, and he had the utmost scorn for the kinds of liberty that were preached by the *bourgeois* advocates of *laissez-faire*. He was, or believed himself to be, a Socialist as well as a libertarian, and no one has insisted more strongly than he on the evils of private property and of the competition of man with man. When he wrote about the nature of society he always laid emphasis on the immense impact of social environment on the individual, stressing fully as much as Durkheim the social origin and derivation of men's ideas of good and evil and the tremendous influence of habit on the development of human behaviour. True, he also insisted on the service done to humanity by those who were strong enough to revolt against the bonds of custom and opinion and thus to become social innovators whose example lifted men towards higher conceptions of freedom ; but he had no wish to do away with the influence of society on the individual, which he regarded as a natural fact. He distinguished sharply in this connection between society and the State. Society, he said, was natural to man : indeed it was common to man and to many kinds of animals, and must be accepted because it was part of the order of nature. The State, on the other hand, he regarded as essentially artificial — as an instrument created by some men for the exercise of power over others, either by force or by theocratic fraud. He made vehement attacks on Rousseau's conception of the social contract, both as historically untrue and as serving to justify the tyranny of man over man. Historically, he said, the entire notion was nonsensical, because it implied among men at an early stage of social development a form of utilitarian rationalistic individualism which was utterly out of relation to men as they actually were when States were first organised ; and he was equally hostile to the notion of an implied contract, which he denounced as a patent invention of would-be tyrants desirous of justifying their ascendancy. The adherents of the social contract doctrine, he contended, were plainly in the wrong because they represented men as living, prior to the institution of States, under conditions of unqualified egoistic self-assertion, unlimited by any conception of right or wrong. In truth, however, men had always lived in societies, and in these societies, quite apart from any statehood, notions of right and wrong had been present, in however rudimentary forms, from the very beginning. Man, he contended, was not in his basic nature the pure egoist the social contract theorists made him out to be : he had from the first both egoistic and social impulses as parts of his nature, as the animals had ; and the more developed conceptions of right and wrong which existed among civilised men had grown out of their primitive impulses and, far from being created or advanced by the State, had found in it their most determined enemy and perverter. The so-called 'democratic State' was hardly, if at all, better than others, in which the tyranny of man over man appeared more obviously : it served merely as the instrument through which a class of bureaucrats and politicians replaced the older types of exploiters as a ruling class oppressing the common man.

With this detestation of the State as an authoritarian weapon of tyranny went an equal hatred of Churches and indeed of the whole idea of God. In *Dieu et l'état* and in many other writings he assailed the notion of godhead with a vehemence fully as great as he made use of in attacking the State. In his view, the idea of a God was detestable both because it was fundamentally inconsistent with human freedom, and therefore quite inadmis-

sible, and because it ran counter to the notion of equality —
unless indeed it were to be an equality merely in slavery and
abjection. God, equally with the State, was for Bakunin the
very symbol of unfreedom and inequality ; and he accordingly
spoke of him in terms which to the believer seemed quite
appallingly blasphemous. But, violent though his language was,
his argument was on a high level of rationality. He thought
that the idea of God's existence arose out of a confusion of
thought, which he did his best to expose in a manner that has
something in common with that of the modern logical positivist
in face of similar verbal confusions. It was because men had
not understood nature that they had invoked the notion of God
to explain it, or rather to provide a false explanation verbally
plausible enough to pass muster until they had advanced to
knowledge — just as Joseph Priestley had invoked the notion
of *phlogiston* at an early stage in the growth of chemical science.

Bakunin did not deny that the religious impulse existed in
man and had performed a necessary function in the historical
development of humanity. But he hated priests and all the
mumbo-jumbo of religion as things which mankind should
have outgrown in view of the advance of scientific knowledge.
His account of the origins and development of religion was much
like Comte's : he regarded it as the embodiment of men's
primitive attempts to explain the phenomena of the world
around them by attributing to nature their own qualities of
will and activity ; and he saw such explanations as continually
giving way before the advance of knowledge, as men grew
more aware of regularities in the order of nature and became
more able to explain the working of the natural world in terms
of particular scientific hypotheses which 'worked' and could
therefore be treated as natural laws. Like Comte, he saw
humanity as passing through successive stages of fetishism and
polytheism to monotheism, and thus to the idea of a single order
operating throughout nature ; and, again like Comte, he saw
monotheism in its turn giving place to metaphysical explanations in which the notion of continual divine intervention found
no place, and metaphysics in its turn ceding ground to science
based on careful observation of the facts.

A good deal of this attitude had come to him first from
Feuerbach and from the materialists who diverged from

Hegelian Idealism. But he had complemented Feuerbach's conception of man as making God in his own image with Comte's conception of social evolution towards a 'positive' approach to human problems ; and he had also no doubt learnt much from his close friendship with the two Réclus brothers — Élisée and Elie — who were among the founders of modern human geography and anthropology and were among his close political associates in the 1860s and 1870s. With all these mentors he insisted that man was to be regarded as a part of nature and as governed by the same laws as ruled all other natural things. But he drew from this conception of man's status as part of the order of nature not a deterministic but a voluntaristic conclusion. Man, he asserted, was the maker of his own history, the more free the more he discovered the true laws of his own being and of the world around him ; influenced at every point by the conditions of living, not least by the economic conditions, but within the limiting circumstances of his environment and of his own nature making his own arrangements to bend the rules of physical nature to his will. Bakunin thus differed profoundly from Marx, because he laid great stress on the rôle of the individual innovator in the making of human history, and saw the course of history not as a predetermined process but as a long sequence of practical discoveries by man applied to the art of living. He admired Marx's account of the history of society, and largely agreed with Marx's diagnosis of the impending fall of capitalism before the advancing power of the working class. But he regarded the working class as the prospective victor over *bourgeois* society not because of the operations of historical necessity, but out of an abounding faith in its creative quality. Moreover, he envisaged this quality as present, not in the working class as a homogeneous mass or abstract totality, but in the separate individuals who composed the class ; and accordingly, where Marx emphasised the need for centralised control and disciplined class organisation, Bakunin put his faith in the spontaneous action of the individual workers and of such primary groups as their natural instincts for social co-operation would induce them to form as the need arose.

Bakunin, I have said, was deeply hostile to religion, though he recognised it as representing a stage of primitive thinking about the universe through which it had been unavoidable for mankind to pass. In the nineteenth century belief in God seemed to him to be a mere survival of the primitive, explicable only as the result of a deliberate imposition of priestcraft and its ally, the authoritarian State. The Church, he said again and again, is the State's younger brother (*cadet*), maintained by the State's rulers to do part of their dirty work, by impressing on men a belief in a world ruled by a supreme authority against which they have no right to rebel or to exercise their natural freedom. A God-ruled world, he exclaims, can of its very nature allow no room for human liberty. If it is man's duty to obey God, man is no longer his own master, and has no defence against the twin despotisms of King and priest, who command him in God's name to do what suits their book. If the universe is ruled by God it will seem natural for society to be ruled by a human monarch claiming divine sanction for his acts. Moreover, if in the universal order all things proceed from God's will — *de haut en bas* — it will seem natural for human societies to be similarly constructed from the top downwards, whereas all free societies — all societies in which men can enjoy freedom — must be built from the bottom upwards and must derive all their power from the active wills of the individuals they should exist to serve.

From this follows Bakunin's concept of 'Federalism', which he often couples with his slogans of 'Anti-statism' and 'Anti-theologism'. It is a case of 'the man versus the State', but not, as in Herbert Spencer, of the individual man as contrasted with society, but of the man in society, giving free expression to his natural sociality and will to co-operate freely with other men. This co-operation is natural, Bakunin argues, in the small groups in which men live together as neighbours ; and every legitimate form of larger social organisation must be made to rest firmly on these small natural groups. That is what Bakunin meant by 'Federalism' ; and he held that, if the basis were got right, men could safely federate into greater unities up to the vast federation of all humanity ; whereas if the State were made the basis of social organisation, its unnatural centralisation and authoritarian tendency would inevitably divide mankind into contending power groups, with war as the no less inevitable consequence.

As we have seen, this 'Federalist' conception of social

organisation usually set out from the local commune as the primary unit of collective action, and built up the larger structures on a basis of federation among the communes for common purposes, but in such a way that the final power should always rest with the communes and not with any independent authority superimposed upon them. In discussing the debates on the organisation of public services that took place at the Congresses of the First International, we have seen some of the difficulties that necessarily arise wherever economic development has advanced beyond the stage of self-subsistent village economy. Particularly in advanced industrial societies such questions as 'Who is to run the railways ?' have to be answered. The individual communes clearly cannot : nor can a federation of communes which has to refer back every decision to the judgment of the individual communes, or which leaves it open to any local commune to secede whenever it pleases. A possible answer is that the railwaymen, organised as a co-operative group, will take over the running of the railways in the new free society ; but this solution supposes both a form of workers' organisation extending across communal frontiers and authorised to take decisions affecting large areas and also either the complete independence of the railwaymen of any control in the general interest or a controlling body organised over a large enough area to make its control effective. The complete Anarchist-Communist can, of course, answer that these are unreal problems, because in the free society there will no longer be any conflict of interests or any need for controlling agencies, so that the railwaymen can safely be left to run the railways in the general service of the community. But even this answer involves a form of Syndicalist organisation of the railway workers in which decisions can be taken at a more than local level, and everything does not have to be referred back to each local group of railway workers. Of course, in practice, the Federalists did not deny that *some* authority would have to be delegated from the local communes to the federal agencies set up by them : they only refused to call it authority, and insisted on keeping it within the narrowest practicable limits. Where they put these limits depended very greatly on the economic structures of the societies in terms of whose problems they were accustomed to think. The less economically developed a society was the more insistent its Federalists were apt to be on the absoluteness of the local commune — that is, on its complete freedom to co-operate or not to co-operate with its neighbours in the conduct and control of common services.

Bakunin, being a Russian and thinking most, when not of Russia, of Italy — and of Southern Italy at that — belonged to the most extreme group of Federalists — the out-and-out Anarchists. Alexander Herzen, who was his friend, had always envisaged Socialism coming to Russia as the outcome not of a movement of the industrial proletariat but of a peasant revolution which would be able to build on the element of primitive communism in the structure of the Russian village economy — the *mir* ; and the *mir* appeared in early Russian Socialism as the equivalent of the commune in Western thought. Though Bakunin, like Herzen, was familiar with Western thought and had lived in Western cities, his mind always moved instinctively in the realm of a more primitive type of society. He was much more at home in Southern Italy than anywhere else in Western Europe ; and his ideas of social action were re-formed, after his long absence in prison and in Siberia, mainly while he was living in Naples. Even when he moved to Switzerland, which was economically much more advanced, he still found himself in a society that was intensely localised and, industrially, engaged in craft and domestic production with very little large-scale employment. He continued, then, to think of the problems of social reorganisation in terms of highly localised communities and, instinctively, in terms of peasants or rural labourers rather than of factory workers or miners or railway employees. The problem of co-ordinating the activities of local communes and of organising a few services over larger areas thus seemed to him a minor one, that could be dealt with easily if the fundamental structure of society were rightly organised on a basis of communal freedom. As against this, such thinkers as de Paepe, who shared his antagonism to the authoritarian State and his belief in the necessity of making the commune the basic agency of social action, were much more aware of the practical difficulties of applying such a policy to societies in which large-scale productive and business organisation had taken root.

The Federalists, when they had to face this kind of problem, sometimes fell back on the solution of 'direct legislation' — that is to say, they argued that communal independence could be limited by decisions taken by general referendum over larger areas, but in no other way. They rejected the view that a body of federal delegates from a number of communes could bind the communes they were supposed to represent, but accepted the right of the delegates to refer a question to the people, and of the people to arrive at a binding decision by a majority vote. But some Federalists — among them Bakunin — would have none of this. Such a doctrine appeared to them to amount to a readmission of the authoritarian principle by the back door. Their experiences of Napoleon III made them exceedingly suspicious of *plébiscites*; and they insisted, not only that no delegate could bind his constituents without their explicit consent, but also that no general assembly or body of voters had any right to bind a minority against its will. Carried to the extreme, this principle would have prevented even the local commune from taking any binding decisions by a majority vote ; but the extreme Anarchists did not recoil from this because they thought that in a neighbourhood group from which class-antagonisms had been banished it would always be possible to reach voluntary agreement of a sufficient proportion of those concerned to make it unnecessary to coerce the small minority that might refuse to fall in with the majority view. In order to understand this attitude it is necessary to realise that for the most part the extreme Anarchists, far from being individualists, were strong believers in the social nature of man and in the bonds of solidarity that held together men living in local communities under 'natural' conditions of social equality. The individualist brand of Anarchism, though it had its exponents in Europe, such as Max Stirner, was never strong except in the United States, where it grew up in a radically different social environment. The European Anarchists of the 1860s and 1870s — we shall come later to the peculiar developments of the movement in the 'eighties and 'nineties — were mostly *social* Anarchists, stressing most strongly that coercive institutions were unnecessary and harmful because man's essentially social nature enabled and entitled him to do without them. This was unquestionably Bakunin's point of view, as it was that of Kropotkin, who introduced the name 'Anarchist-

Communist' in order to make the position clear ; and it was also that of the creators of Anarcho-Syndicalism in Spain, Italy, and Southern France.

The thinkers who took this Social Anarchist standpoint differed considerably among themselves in the relative emphasis which they put on the local commune as the essential democratic agency of a free people and on producers' associations, which they nearly all regarded as the necessary means of carrying on economic enterprises in a free society. The more they thought in terms of industry, the more they stressed the functions of producers' associations : the more they thought in terms of peasant agricultural societies, the more they stressed the commune, which indeed they often regarded as itself a sort of producers' association for the use of the land in the common interest. Thus, at the one extreme, the commune came to be thought of, in big cities such as Lyons, as a federation of local producers' associations, while at the other extreme all the stress was laid on the commune as a unitary body assembling all its citizens for the taking of decisions by arriving at what Quakers call 'the sense of the meeting'.

Bakunin, if he ever considered the difficulties of organising a 'free' society under conditions of large-scale transport and production, swept them aside in the name of the one indefeasible principle of liberty. He was, indeed, very little concerned with anticipating the social structure of the future : his preoccupation was with the sweeping away of the dead lumber of past and present. Yet he hoped and expected much from the advance of scientific knowledge, and was no advocate of a return to the 'simple life'. It was merely that he conceived of the immediate task as essentially revolutionary and destructive and had no doubt of the capacity of the emancipated peoples to solve their problems when they arose. He insisted continually on the spontaneous and natural genius of the free man, and of free men associated in small groups — what are called to-day 'face to face' groups. He believed that in such groups the problem would be, not that of achieving a sufficient solidarity for common action, but that of preventing the solidarity from becoming so strong as to inhibit personal initiative. Formal coercion seems to him wantonly unnecessary because the influences of group custom and convention were so strong.

This solidarity he regarded not as a product of economic circumstances, but as a natural propensity which men share with the community-making species of the animal kingdom. It is a part, he kept saying, of man's *animality*, which the individual can never forsake, but can in some degree subject to his *humanity* — such subjection being the achievement of liberty.

Bakunin, when he is not fulminating against God and the State as the twin enemies of freedom, is indeed a most amiably idealistic writer — much as he would have resented the term. Regarding himself as an absolute materialist, and insisting that man must be regarded as simply a material being, he nevertheless endowed this being with the capacity to make the highest ideals for himself and for his fellows. These ideals, he affirmed, were not innate : there were no such things as innate ideas of any sort. Man was not God's creature, to have ideas or ideals implanted in him from without. He was, in one of Bakunin's favourite phrases, 'creator, not creature' — creator of his own ideas and values, not as an isolated individual, but in society. Bakunin's view of the nature of morality and of ideal values was essentially that they were products of social evolution, and that, as men advanced in knowledge and civilisation, their capacity for ideal-making increased. In this respect he was heir to the tradition of the great eighteenth-century enlightenment, and very far indeed from being the complete immoralist he has sometimes been misrepresented as having been, at any rate during his later years.

This taint of immoralism, as far as it was not simply mud thrown at him by his enemies, came to be attached to him largely because of his short-lived association with Nechaiev. The sentiment Nechaiev for a while aroused in him does indeed seem to have temporarily driven him out of his normal wits. Outside this connection Bakunin was often violent in phrase ; and he was of course prepared to support the most violent revolutionary methods against the Russian Government, or indeed against any Government he considered as showing its 'knouto-Germanic' qualities. Moreover, Bakunin took very seriously the idea, to be found in both Hegel and Saint-Simon, and particularly in Saint-Simon, of the division of history into epochs of construction and of destruction, and regarded himself as living towards the end of an epoch in which the task of destruction held the first place. He was thus on the side of Nechaiev in wishing to make a bonfire of the values as well as of the institutions of the society he lived in. He wanted to destroy not only its political structure and its economic arrangements but also the entire system of values that rested on the conception of inequality between man and man — the snobbery, the assumption of prescriptive rights reserved for the few, the unequal marriage system, and a great deal besides. But he wanted to engage in this task of wholesale destruction not as an immoral man emancipated from all ethical values, but, on the contrary, in the service of a superior 'natural' morality and in the spirit of the highest idealism : there was no tendency towards any form of Nihilism in most of his writings — much less towards the extreme form of nihilistic repudiation of all moral values in which Nechaiev exulted. To what extent Bakunin had a hand in the writing of the series of revolutionary pamphlets which were published under their joint aegis in 1869 will probably never be accurately known : it seems probable that he had some share even in the most violent of them — even in the celebrated *Revolutionary Catechism* itself. If so, they still remain out of tune with most of his other writings, both before and after this unfortunate connection. The likeliest view is that Bakunin was driven entirely off his balance by Nechaiev's flattery and by the story of the great young men's revolutionary movement in Russia that was looking to Bakunin for leadership, and that he allowed himself to endorse, and perhaps even to write, passages which ran counter to his entire philosophy. It is laid down in the *Catechism* that the true revolutionary 'despises and hates present-day social morality in all its forms and motivations. He regards as moral everything that forwards the triumph of the revolution.' . . . 'Every soft, enervating feeling of relationship, friendship, love, gratitude, even honour must be stifled in him by cold passion for the revolutionary cause.' Bakunin could not possibly have believed that, if he also believed, as he undoubtedly did, that morality was an evolutionary product of civilisation and that modern man, with all his subjection to evil institutions, was immensely ahead in this respect of the savage. No doubt men can believe inconsistent things, but hardly to such a point save at odd moments of mental aberration under some irresistibly powerful influence. Nechaiev did for a time have such an influence over Bakunin, though not for long ; and unfortunately the period of this influence coincided with a critical phase in Bakunin's contest with Marx in the International : so that Marx was induced to believe that Bakunin was an utter Nihilist as well as an enemy of the working-class cause.

There was, of course, plenty for Marx and Bakunin to quarrel about quite apart from Nechaiev's immoralism. Bakunin's conception of the free society, built from the small unit upwards to the larger federal groupings and resting on a basic human social solidarity, was deeply antagonistic to Marx's conception of organisation on a basis of economic class under the leadership of an advance-guard animated by a clear understanding of the historic mission of the proletariat. Marx, with his eyes fixed on the development of capitalist society in its most advanced forms, saw the coming struggle in terms of a conflict between highly centralised powers representing the class interests of capitalists and proletariat, and regarded every group that did not fit into this diagnosis as standing for a declining or obsolescent social form. Bakunin, on the other hand, thought of the revolution mainly as a ceaseless struggle between oppressors and oppressed, with the momentum of revolution located primarily in the groups of the downtrodden wherever they were found, and irrespective of their economic relation to the means of production. For Marx, the significant aspect of the contemporary class-struggle was the developing consciousness and organisation of the industrial workers, and particularly of those who were subject to the conditions of advanced large-scale capitalism. Bakunin, on the other hand, thought of the revolution much more in terms of the instinctive revolt of the most oppressed and downtrodden groups in society — the peasants in the relatively backward areas and the *lumpenproletariat* of such cities as Naples, in which modern industrialism had hardly taken root at all.

Moreover, Marx was in his very essence a rationalist belonging to a relatively advanced cultural tradition, with a deeply rooted scorn of barbarians, even when they were on the revolutionary side. Marx thought of the revolution as concerned primarily not merely with the destruction of the existing order, but with the construction of a more advanced social order in its stead ; and it seemed to him fantastic to suppose that this new order could be born among backward groups. He had a deep scorn of peasants and of Slav barbarians : the peasants, even in the advanced countries, were for him not capable of the creative power needed for revolutionary construction : they could only be drawn along in the wake of the class-conscious proletariat and be moulded by it, through collectivism, into modern men. It followed from this that Marx had no belief in the creative quality of any revolution originating in an economically backward country. He looked to the West to lead the way, and to the backward countries of Eastern and Southern Europe at most only to follow the lead of the more advanced nations. For Bakunin, on the other hand, the revolutionary impulse — the will to freedom — was a quality natural to men, and fully as likely to be found among peasants or among the *lumpenproletariat* of the cities of Italy or Spain as among the sophisticated industrial workers of England, or France, or Western Germany — indeed more likely, because these latter groups had been more infected with false ideas of democracy based on the acceptance of the State as a true expression of the national consciousness.

Bakunin, before his break with the League of Peace and Freedom, had persuaded the Central Committee of that body to adopt a programme which was meant to commit the League to an advanced social policy. This programme, presented to the League's second Congress, held at Berne in 1868, began by asserting the impossibility of separating the three aspects of the social problem — the questions of religion, of politics, and of economics. It then laid down the following three propositions :

   i. that religion, being a matter of individual conscience, should be eliminated from political institutions and also from public education, in order that the Churches may no longer be able to hamper the free development of society ;

  ii. that the United States of Europe can have no other organisation than that which rests on popular institutions having as their link federation, and as their principle the equality of individual rights, as well as the autonomy of the communes and provinces in the regulation of their respective concerns ;

 iii. that the present economic system stands in need of

radical change, if the purpose is to arrive at an equitable distribution of wealth, labour, leisure, education, these being an essential condition of the enfranchisement of the workers and of the abolition of the proletariat.

The third of these clauses was drawn up and proposed by Bakunin himself. The declaration ended with the words : 'The League protests against every attempt at social reform made by any sort of despotic power'.

When the middle-class adherents of the League of Peace and Freedom rejected these propositions and Bakunin and his friends broke away to establish the Alliance of Socialist Democracy, the Bakuninist programme was re-stated in much less temperate language. The programme of the Alliance began with the words 'The Alliance proclaims itself atheist : it stands for the abolition of cults, the substitution of science for faith, and of human for divine justice'. It then went on to declare for 'political, economic and social equalisation of classes and individuals of both sexes, beginning with the abolition of the right of inheritance, in order that in future each person's enjoyment shall be equal to his production, and that, in conformity with the decision of the last Workers' Congress at Brussels, the land, the instruments of production, and all other capital shall become the collective property of society as a whole, and shall thus be at the sole disposal of the workers, that is, of agricultural and industrial associations'. The programme of the Alliance then went on to declare in favour of 'equality of the means of development — that is to say, of maintenance, education and instruction at all levels of science, industry, and the arts' for all children of both sexes. Such equality, it was asserted, from being at the start only social and economic, would lead to greater natural equality among individuals by bringing about the disappearance of artificial inequalities resulting from wrong and unjust social organisation.

As a fourth proposition the Alliance laid down its repudiation of all political institutions except the republican, and its rejection of all political action save such as had 'as its direct and immediate object the triumph of the workers' cause against capital'. Fifthly, it went on to declare that 'all existing political and authoritarian States, reducing themselves more and more to the simple administrative functions of the public services, should disappear in the universal union of the free associations, both agricultural and industrial'. This 'universal association', it was proclaimed, was to be that of all the local associations *par la liberté*. 'The social question', it was declared, 'can find no real and definitive solution save on the basis of the international solidarity of the workers of all countries.' 'The Alliance repudiates all politics resting on so-called patriotism and rivalry between nations.'

There is an evident continuity of thought between these two proclamations, though the later, made after the final rift between Bakunin's group and the majority of the League of Peace and Freedom, is much the more challenging, and is notable as putting much greater emphasis on the rôle of the working class. The later formulation, however, pleased Marx no better than the earlier. He considered the putting of atheism in the forefront as bad tactics ; and he had only scorn for the notion of 'equalising' classes instead of abolishing them, and of putting the abolition of inheritance in the first place as an economic measure instead of seeking directly and immediately the entire abolition of private property in the means of production. Bakunin, as we have seen, readily gave way on the first of these points, by accepting 'abolition' instead of 'equalisation' of classes, but stuck to his guns on the question of inheritance, and on this issue was able to defeat Marx at the International Working Men's Congress of 1869.

The followers of Bakunin were, however, committed fully as much as the Marxists to the principle of collective ownership, the difference between them in this matter lying in their several views of the nature of the institutions through which the principle of collectivity would be carried into effect. The Bakuninists envisaged the coming United States of Europe as a federation, not of nations each possessing its own central government, but of free local communes each exercising full independence in the conduct of its affairs and grouped without regard to national frontiers ; whereas Marx thought in terms of a conquest of power by the working class in each country and of a federation of the national workers' States emanating from this conquest. This, in matters of immediate practice, was the unbridgeable gulf between the two conceptions of the coming revolution.

Of these two conceptions, one went — and still goes — with

the grain of modern society, and the other against it. For Marx, with his deterministic philosophy, to go against the grain was plain folly ; for his whole doctrine was an interpretation of historic tendencies regarded as irresistible and a summons to men to understand these tendencies and to work with, and not against, them. The advance of the powers of production, resting on the advance of man's mastery over his physical environment, carried with it the aggregation of men and things into greater and greater masses, and rendered the small neighbourhood group, such as the commune, more and more out of date as a basis for social action. The motive forces of social change, in Marx's view, were not such groups, resting on the natural solidarity of man as a gregarious animal, but vast economic classes, themselves the products of economic and scientific advance. Bakunin's entire approach seemed to Marx to be utterly unscientific and romantic and quite out of touch with contemporary realities — the dream of a barbarian grossly ignorant of the forces that were actually shaping the modern world.

There was something in this criticism — but not everything. The more the trend towards bigness and centralisation is accepted as a necessary consequence of the development and application of scientific knowledge, the more important it becomes to do what can be done to counteract the tendency for individual men and small groups to become engulfed in organisations too vast for ordinary men and women to be able to understand them, or for even the better equipped among them, if they do understand, to exercise any effective control. The 'Caesarism' of the two Napoleons showed the danger, though even Napoleon III was operating with forces that appear primitive beside the resources available to-day to anyone who can seize hold of the State and use it as an instrument for indoctrinating the people, as well as for more direct methods of coercion. Bakunin was right to be highly suspicious of the centralised, authoritarian State, even when it appeared as the democratic representative of the people or as the instrument of a hitherto exploited class. His 'federalist' solution was, indeed, open to many objections, most of which he never even attempted to meet. Any thinker who consistently maintains that freedom is not merely good but *the only* good is bound to find himself kicking continually against the pricks of sheer necessity, not only in his attempts to construct the model of a society on a completely 'free' basis, but equally in trying to bring such a society into being ; for, as Lenin once pertinently remarked, revolution is an exceedingly authoritative process, and an undirected revolutionary movement which relies entirely on the free initiative of the masses is bound to fail, or to break down even if it meets with success in its earlier stages. Bakunin of course knew this, and because he knew it, supported at the Basle Congress of 1869 the demand that the General Council of the International Working Men's Association should be given larger powers. He was ready to admit that the revolution would need strong direction, while it was actually engaged in its critical struggle ; but he could not admit that any element of authoritative power would be needed for the subsequent phase of revolutionary construction, or even for resisting counter-revolutionary attempts. Often though he stressed the strength of the influence of social habit and custom on most men, he seems to have supposed that the experience of revolution would mysteriously shake them free of their bondage and convert them suddenly into heroic initiators of new social behaviour. That, indeed, was part of the reason for his insistence on the need for a complete destruction of the old social structure as a preparation for building the new. No doubt he really expected that most men would remain, relatively to the leaders of the revolution, passive and unoriginal, and that the creative tasks of the revolution would fall on a minority of chosen spirits. But he also clearly believed that these chosen spirits would be able to draw the masses behind them into new ways of living, without needing to be armed with any special authority, or to accept any self-imposed common discipline. Therein he was clearly wrong ; but he was right in seeing the need, in the interest of individual and group freedom, to resist forms of 'democratic centralism' which tended to make ordinary people once more mere pawns in the game played by autocrats, or bureaucrats, without their real participation in the making of policy or the recognition of their right to go their own road, at any rate within fairly wide limits, and not to be badgered about.

Bakunin made an acute observation when he said that the political theorists who upheld the claims of the State, even on their own showing, made 'security, but never liberty' its essential gift to the people. The traditional form of the social contract doctrine, repeated by Rousseau, as he pointed out, found the origin of the State in the individuals' desire for security, which induced them to forgo a part of their 'natural liberty' with this end in view. But how, he asked, were those who gave up a part of their liberty to have any assurance of keeping the rest ? Rousseau himself, in what he said about the indivisibility of sovereignty, had shown that there could be no assurance. Merely to substitute 'popular' sovereignty for personal or oligarchical sovereignty could not alter its essential character. Security, of a sort, States might be able to provide — liberty never. And even the security they afforded was no real security, as long as the State could make, in peace and war, unlimited claims upon them.

This, like much else in Bakunin's writings, comes near to the language of individualism ; but, as we have seen, that was not at all what he meant. He was insistent on the need for collective ownership of property — and therein his Anarchism differed from that of the Proudhonists who, in the International, combated collective ownership in the name of the individual's right to enjoy the product of his own labour. Bakunin regarded the rewarding of the individual according to his works as no better than a transitional form of society still based on egoism : he wanted to go the full length of the formula 'From each according to his capacities : to each according to his needs'. Bakunin had indeed a strong admiration for Proudhon, and regarded him as the real founder of Anarchism and Federalism. Proudhon's teaching, he said, '*aboutit naturellement au fédéralisme*'. But he had none of Proudhon's suspicion of co-operative association as having in it the germ of bureaucracy and governmental authority. Regarding the village community, with its ancient traditions of collective organisation for the use of the land, as 'natural' to man — no less so than the life of the hive to the bees — he assumed co-operative rather than individual, or family, enterprise to be the natural expression of man's spontaneous social impulses, and accordingly good. Kropotkin, when he came to write of *Mutual Aid among Men and Animals* and to develop the more clearly articulated theory of Anarchist-Communism, found in Bakunin much on which to build, and relatively little to discard.

CHAPTER X

GERMAN SOCIALISM AFTER LASSALLE —
'CHRISTIAN SOCIALISTS' AND 'STATE
SOCIALISTS' — THE *KULTURKAMPF* AND
THE ANTI-SOCIALIST LAWS

LASSALLE'S career came to a sudden end in 1864, when his ambitious project of uniting the German working classes in a single comprehensive political association was hardly more than launched. He died, as we saw, in a duel, arising out of a ridiculous love-affair that had nothing to do either with his political activities or with his championship of the Countess Hatzfeldt. The movement which he had created had been so much his personal achievement that it would not have been at all surprising if it had fallen entirely to pieces at his death — the less so because his autocratic conduct of its affairs had already led to quarrels and secessions. Perhaps it would have collapsed entirely had there been in 1864 any alternative point of focus for the kind of working-class sentiment he had shown such skill in directing. But at the time of his death no such alternative existed. Wilhelm Liebknecht (1826–1900) had indeed returned to Germany in 1862 well primed by Marx with suspicions of Lassalle and with widely different ideas about German working-class policy ; but in 1864 Liebknecht had as yet no organised following. August Bebel (1840–1913), who was to be Liebknecht's principal colleague in founding the German Social Democratic Party, already had a following, at any rate in Saxony, and, young though he was, was becoming known over a much wider area. But Bebel's associations were with the Workmen's Educational Societies, which had formed in 1863 a federal League in opposition to Lassalle's movement and were working for the most part in alliance with the *bourgeois* Progressive parties and as supporters of the Co-operative projects of Schulze-Delitzsch. These Societies were not Socialist but Liberal-Progressive, and in 1864 Bebel himself was a very recent convert to Socialism, and had not yet brought over even his own local Workers' Educational Association to its support.

Lassalle had nominated his own successor to lead the General German Workers' Association. His nominee was Bernhard Becker (1826–82), who attempted to emulate Lassalle's auto-cratic methods, but soon found his colleagues unprepared to accept from him what they had allowed in Lassalle. Becker was displaced from the leadership and presently broke away and joined the rival camp of the Social Democrats. His task had not been made the easier by the Countess Hatzfeldt, who arrogated to herself as Lassalle's patroness the mission of holding the movement he had created true to his memory. When she too found the Association unwilling to do what she told it, she broke away with a small following and attempted to found a rival Association, which soon expired. The main body of the Lassallians, after two further aspirants to leadership had rapidly come and gone, accepted as leader the one really able man it could find, Johann Baptist von Schweitzer (1833–75). Schweitzer had been the founder and first editor, with Las-salle's approval, of the Berlin *Social Democrat*, which had begun to appear in 1864, shortly before Lassalle's death, and had been intended to include Marx and Engels among its collaborators, and to be the organ of the whole Socialist move-ment in Germany. Marx, however, had soon repudiated Schweitzer, whom he regarded as a secret ally of Bismarck ; and the *Social Democrat* had become to a great extent Schweit-zer's personal organ. There were two reasons why the General German Workers' Association was reluctant to accept him as leader — the notorious immorality of his private life and his aristocratic, Catholic origins. Jesuit-trained, he had been at the outset a supporter of Austrian against Prussian leadership, but had changed sides and had written a book, *Der Zeitgeist und das Christenthum* (1861), designed to prove that Christianity, in both its Catholic and its Protestant forms, was inseparably bound up with monarchy and inconsistent with the democratic spirit of the age. He was thus a highly controversial figure ; but in 1867 the General German Workers' Association at length accepted him as President, and in the same year he was elected to the Reichstag of the North German Confederation among the first Socialists to win seats in a German representative assembly.

From the beginning of the Lassallian movement Schweitzer, equally with Lassalle, had accepted the need for realising German unity under Prussian leadership, and had thus fallen foul of Marx and of his German follower, Liebknecht, who had come back to Germany in 1862 with the definite intention of attempting to build up a German Socialist movement on broadly Marxist lines. Wilhelm Liebknecht had taken part, as a young man, in the German Revolution of 1848, had escaped, after a spell in prison, to Switzerland, and had been expelled by the Swiss on suspicion of attempting to organise on Swiss territory a renewed revolutionary attempt. He had then settled in London, where he had become intimate with Marx and had lived as best he could by journalism. He returned to Germany to take up a position he had been offered on the *Norddeutsche Allgemeine Zeitung*, newly established by the former left-wing Republican, August Brass, as an organ of democratic opinion in Berlin. In this newspaper he was allowed to write strongly socialistic articles ; but he soon became convinced that Brass was in the pay of Bismarck, and that he was being made use of to attack the *bourgeois* Progressives in the interests of Prussian autocracy — that is to say, that Bismarck was trying to build up a sort of 'Conservative Socialism' with working-class support against the movement for constitutional reform. Liebknecht thereupon resigned his post, and before long became a member of Lassalle's General Workmen's Association, despite some misgivings about its tendency and doctrine. But soon after Lassalle's death he became convinced that the Association was going the same way as Brass's newspaper, and attacked the Lassallians as playing into Bismarck's hands. For these attacks he was served with a police order of expulsion from Prussia : he then settled in Leipzig, where the Saxon Government allowed more freedom of expression. At Leipzig he came into close touch with Bebel, and through him with the League of German Workers' Educational Societies which, as we saw, had been formed in 1863 in opposition to the Lassallian movement. Almost at once, Liebknecht succeeded in converting Bebel to Socialism ; and together in 1865 they persuaded the Workers' Societies of Saxony to adopt a Socialist programme. Three

years later the annual Congress of the whole League went over
to Socialism, and the minority which still favoured the Progressives seceded. But, as against this, a large group of seceders
from the Lassallian Association joined forces with the League to
found the following year at Eisenach the German Social Democratic Party.

Thus, over the ten years which followed the death of Lassalle there was a continuous struggle in Germany for the effective leadership of the growing working-class movement. Rapid
economic development and political unification both played
their parts in arousing the political and economic consciousness
of the industrial workers ; but there were two sharply contrast-
ing views about the policy to be adopted. It is not easy to state
shortly and simply the nature of the differences which in the
1860s already divided the Lassallians from the rival movement
which was growing up under the leadership of Liebknecht and
Bebel. Up to a point, indeed, they are fairly clear. Lassalle
and his successors directed their main attack against the *bourgeoisie* : they opposed the *bourgeois* demands for constitutional
government based on a limited franchise, insisted on the need
for manhood suffrage, and hoped by means of manhood suffrage
to convert the State into an instrument for the emancipation of
the workers from capitalist exploitation. They said relatively
little about the landlords, and did not pay any great attention to
peasant grievances. Nor did they attempt to work with the
petite bourgeoisie, who provided the main strength of the Progressive Parties in the various German States. Liebknecht and
Bebel, on the other hand, held that the right policy was to side
with the more progressive elements in the middle classes against
autocracy and aristocracy, in the belief that the workers' chance
of victory would come only after autocracy and landlordism had
been overthrown. This latter was, of course, the view of Marx
and Engels, which they had proclaimed in 1848 and had held
to steadily through the ensuing period of defeat. It was not,
however, a very easy policy to follow, in view of the strong
laissez-faire doctrine of a large section of the *bourgeoisie* and of
the extreme timidity of the Progressive Parties, above all in
Prussia. Nor could it be easy, in any case, to follow Marx's
precept that the workers should keep themselves strictly independent of the *bourgeois* parties, and at the same time support

them in their struggle against aristocracy and autocratic government.

There was, moreover, an additional complication. As we have seen, there existed in Germany a widespread desire for national unity, but no agreement either about the form which it ought to take or about the best means of working for it. One idea was that unity would have to be realised under Prussian leadership ; and this was plainly incompatible with the inclusion of Austria within the unified Reich. Another idea was that of a closer unity, of the kind which had been aimed at by the supporters of the Frankfurt Parliament of 1848, resting on constitutional, responsible government both for Germany as a whole (not necessarily excluding Austria) and for the constituent States. The adherents of the first of these conceptions were naturally most numerous in Prussia, and the opponents in the other German States : the second conception attracted liberal and progressive opinion, which saw in Prussian hegemony the danger of a powerful, warlike, autocratic Reich that would ride rough-shod over its subjects as well as over its neighbours. The Austro-Prussian War of 1866 destroyed the possibility of the inclusion of Austria in any reorganised German polity ; and the establishment the following year of the North German Con-federation, with the King of Prussia as its president, made the leadership of Prussia certain over most of Germany, especially as it was accompanied by the annexation of Hanover and Schleswig-Holstein by the victorious Prussians. The inclusion of the States of Southern Germany remained uncertain until the Prussian victory over France in 1870 and the annexation of Alsace-Lorraine put Prussia in a commanding position which was at once consolidated by the establishment of the unified German Reich.

Lassalle, as we have seen, had put the demand for manhood suffrage in the forefront of his programme and had used his Association to press this demand strongly on Bismarck, adjuring him at the same time to provide State funds for his proposed Co-operative Associations designed to compete with, and in due course to supplant, capitalist enterprise. Bismarck, in 1867, took Lassalle's advice about manhood suffrage, which was intro-duced for the assembly of the North German Confederation and extended four years later to the united Reich. Bismarck also toyed with Lassalle's idea of State aid to Co-operative Associations, but only on an insignificant scale. He did nothing to modify the highly undemocratic franchise in Prussia itself, or to introduce for the Confederation or the Reich any form of constitutional government that would make the ministry — the executive branch of government — responsible to the assembly. Moreover, the new Reichstag, as a legislative body, was made subject to the federal Bundesrat, which was in practice dominated by the Prussian Government. Thus, the concession of manhood suffrage by no means carried with it the power of the popularly elected Reichstag to control the State machine, even if a majority of its members wished to do so — and in practice there was no majority animated by such a wish. The Socialists, of either faction, could hope for the time being to win seats only in the major towns ; and in Germany as a whole the rural population was still in a large majority. Manhood suffrage, making possible the presence in the Reichstag of a growing body of Socialists and requiring for its effective exercise some freedom of political organisation and propaganda, did indeed mean a real advance ; but the new Constitution made the concession in such a way as positively to strengthen the hold of the Prussian autocracy over the whole of Germany. This hold was, moreover, made all the greater by the linking of the new Reich's establishment with the military victory over France and with the annexation of Alsace-Lorraine. The war was popular, and so was the annexation, and anyone who ventured to protest against either was unpopular and could be stamped on with impunity — the more so because Bismarck had cunningly lured Napoleon III into the appearance of being the aggressor. When the Paris Commune followed hard upon France's military disaster, it became still easier for Bismarck to turn and rend any opponent who could be accused of sympathising either with the Commune or with the International, which was supposed to have inspired it and had in fact rallied to its defence.

Up to the outbreak of the Franco-Prussian War in 1870 the struggle between the two factions of German Socialism went on with varying fortunes. The Liebknecht-Bebel faction, supported by Marx and Engels from abroad and encouraged by the International under Marx's influence, made steady progress in the local Workers' Societies which had formerly accepted the political leadership of the Progressives, and was also reinforced by repeated secessions from the ranks of the General German Workers' Association, culminating in the establishment of the Social Democratic Party at Eisenach in 1869. But the Lassallians, who had been losing ground until Schweitzer became President of their Association in 1867, then began to pick up again rapidly, largely because their advocacy of unification under Prussian leadership and their emphasis on manhood suffrage as a means of emancipation seemed to fit in closely with the actual course of events. The granting of manhood suffrage in the North German Confederation of 1867 reinforced hopes that Bismarck would give his support to the workers against the capitalists, and Schweitzer's election gave the Lassallians a vantage-point for their appeals.

Then came the war. Schweitzer and his followers, in accordance with their belief in Prussian leadership of the German nation, supported Bismarck against Napoleon III and voted for the war credits. On the other hand, Liebknecht, who had also been elected to the North German Reichstag in 1867, refused to vote for the war credits and took the lead in opposition to the annexation of Alsace-Lorraine. As soon as Napoleon III had been overthrown Liebknecht and his 'Eisenach' Party demanded an honourable peace with the French Republic and faced the unpopularity involved in opposing Bismarck in the hour of his triumph. In 1872, during the period of repression which followed the Paris Commune, Liebknecht was indicted for high treason and sentenced to two years in a fortress.

It soon became plain that the existence of two rival Socialist Parties in Germany was seriously hampering the growth of the movement. Moreover, Bismarck, after 1871, was no longer wooing the support of either. From the outbreak of the Paris Commune he had been violently denouncing every form of Social Democracy ; and Lassallians and Eisenachers were drawn together by a repression which affected both groups. In addition, the unification of Germany under Prussian leadership in 1871 had removed one great practical ground of difference. It became plain that, in order to fight the repression and to build up a strong electoral party, the Socialists needed to join forces. Schweitzer had been removed from the leadership of the Lassallians in 1871, under strong, though unjust, suspicion of being a secret agent of Bismarck ; and the General Association was losing ground, though it remained numerically stronger than the 'Eisenach' party. By 1874 both sections were ready to seek a basis for fusion, and in the following year they actually joined forces at the Gotha Unity Congress, forming a single German Social Democratic Workers' Party in which from the first the Eisenachers, though originally outnumbered, took the lead.

Liebknecht had opened up negotiations with the Lassallians without consulting Marx and Engels ; and the London exiles, when they saw the proposed terms of fusion, embodying a draft programme for the united party, were extremely angry. They were not against fusion, on proper terms ; but they argued that the Lassallian party was on the down grade and in a weak position, and that much better terms could have been secured if the Eisenachers had shown a determined front. Both Marx and Engels sent to their friends in Germany vigorous criticisms of the proposed new programme : Marx embodied his views in a long document, which he sent for private circulation among the Eisenach leaders. Liebknecht read it, and agreed with the few others who were allowed to see it that it should be suppressed. Bebel, and others who were suspected of being liable to be influenced by it, never saw it at all until it was published many years later by Engels in an attempt to influence the re-shaping of the programme which followed the repeal of the Anti-Socialist Laws in 1890. The contention of Liebknecht and of those who acted with him was that unity was essential and that the negotiations for it had already advanced too far for the issues raised by Marx and Engels to be reopened. Indeed, both Marx and Engels, however reluctantly, acquiesced in the suppression, seeing that publication of their views could not stop the programme from being adopted and could at most only provoke a fresh split.

Marx's memorandum, known since its publication by Engels as *Critique of the Gotha Programme*, raised afresh all the main differences which had divided him from Lassalle in the 1860s. He attacked, as involved in the phraseology of the programme, Lassalle's view of the 'iron law of wages', of the 'right to the whole product of labour', and of the character of the State and the proper attitude for a working-class party to take up in dealing with it. He began by attacking the sentence which declared 'Labour is the source of all wealth and culture and, since useful labour is possible only in society and through society, the entire proceeds of labour belong with equal rights to all members of society'. 'Labour', Marx wrote, 'is not the *source* of all wealth.' 'Nature' is just as much the source. Moreover, 'if useful labour is possible only in society and through society, the proceeds of labour belong to society and only so much will come to the individual worker as is not required to maintain society'. Marx next attacked a sentence which declared that 'in contemporary society, the means of labour are the monopoly of the capitalist class'. This, he said, was a distorted version of a sentence from the statutes of the International Working Men's Association — distorted because the Lassallians attacked only the capitalists and refrained from attacking the landlords as well.

Next came a sentence referring to communal ownership of the means of production as a means to 'the co-operative regulation of associated labour with an equitable distribution of the proceeds of labour'. What, Marx asked, is 'an equitable distribution'? If 'all the proceeds of labour belong with equal rights to all members of society' — including the non-producers — what becomes of the claim that each producer must receive the whole of the value he produces? From the total product a number of deductions have to be made before it is possible to arrive at the supply of goods available for consumption. These deductions include (1) whatever is needed for the replacement of means of production used up ; (2) a further allowance for the extension of future production ; (3) reserve or insurance funds to meet misadventures, or disturbances, due to natural events. These deductions 'can be determined by existing means and powers and partly by calculating probabilities, but are under no circumstances calculable by equity'. But, beyond these, further deductions have to be made to meet the costs of public administration and to provide for communal needs, such as schools, health services, and other public services, and also for the maintenance of the non-producers who are unable to work. Thus, only a part of the 'proceeds of labour' is left for distribution to the producers ;

but in a communistic society where public ownership of the means of production prevails the individual labourer no longer has any separate product of his own. He is merely a part of the total labour force of society. Evidently, then, the draft programme must be dealing, not with a fully established Communist society, but with a communistic society in a stage of transition, 'as it emerges from capitalist society'. In such a transitional economy the individual will receive, not the whole product of his labour, but the equivalent of the amount of labour he has contributed, less the necessary deductions, but not further diminished by the exactions of the now expropriated monopolists of land and capital resources. Accordingly, as the amounts of labour contributed by individuals to the common pool will be different, 'rights must be unequal instead of being equal'. Such defects, Marx argues, 'are unavoidable in the first phase of Communist society'. 'Right can never be higher than the economic structure and the cultural development of society conditioned by it.' In effect, what Marx is saying is that it is utopian nonsense to talk about 'equal rights' as coming into being with the establishment of a Communist society. Such 'equality' belongs only to 'a higher stage of Communist society, after the tyrannical subordination of individuals according to the distribution of labour and therewith also the distinction between manual and intellectual work have disappeared'. Only when 'all the sources of co-operative wealth are flowing more freely together with the all-round development of the individual, can the narrow, *bourgeois* horizon of rights be left behind' : only then will society inscribe on its banner 'From each according to his capacity : to each according to his need'.

This passage, later annotated with many side-linings and marks of approval by Lenin, has provided the main basis for the modern Communist theory of the distribution of incomes to the producers in the phase of society following directly upon the overthrow of capitalism. Marx went on to say 'how mischievous it is to fasten on our party again as dogmas ideas which at one time had some meaning, but have now become out-of-date nonsensical phraseology' — 'phraseology about "rights" and other nonsense of the democrats and French Socialists'. 'Rights', he is arguing, are really beside the point, and it is entirely wrong to put the main emphasis on distribution. For 'the distribution of the means of consumption at any time is simply a consequence of the distribution of the conditions of production' — *i.e.* of the ownership of the means of production. If these means are privately owned, the capitalist laws of distribution follow automatically : if they are publicly owned, a different law of distribution naturally applies. It is accordingly a retrograde step in theory to talk about equity in the distribution of incomes, instead of concentrating attention on altering the productive conditions which determine distribution as a matter of course.

Marx, throughout this passage, is following out the implications of 'scientific' Socialism. Socialism, he is arguing, is a scientifically demonstrable system with which notions of 'equity' have nothing to do. 'Equity', he is saying, is a legalistic concept which is strictly relative to the social system within which it is to be applied, and accordingly belongs to the 'superstructure'. The real determinant of notions of equity is the system of productive relations ; and therefore Socialists should direct their efforts to altering these relations in harmony with the movement of historical forces rather than attempt to amend the distribution of incomes by the light of rules which are out of harmony with the prevailing productive system. Marx does not mean that the workers ought not to struggle for higher wages and improved conditions under capitalism : on the contrary, he stresses the need for such a struggle. What he is arguing against is the illusion, as he regards it, that legal changes affecting the distribution of incomes can be effective against the 'laws' which determine the distribution of the product of industry as long as the means of production continue to be privately owned.

Marx turns next to a sentence in the draft Gotha Programme in which it is asserted that 'the liberation of labour must be the task of the working class, in opposition to which all other classes form merely a homogeneous reactionary mass'. The latter part of this sentence arouses his special ire. He denies emphatically that the capitalist *bourgeoisie* can properly be labelled as 'reactionary'. On the contrary, in its struggle against the feudal aristocracy and also against 'the intermediate classes which seek to defend social positions that are the creations of obsolete productive methods', the capitalist *bourgeoisie* must be counted as a revolutionary class. This *bourgeois* class is reactionary, not absolutely or in relation to the feudal classes and to the *petite bourgeoisie*, but only in relation to the proletariat, which is its destined supplanter. By way of contrast, the *petite bourgeoisie* of small traders, artisans, and comparatively well-to-do peasants is revolutionary only 'in view of its impending transference into the ranks of the proletariat' — that is, only to the extent to which it is driven, by the threat of extinction, to ally itself with the workers. Marx asks his German disciples the question, 'Did we tell the artisans, the small industrialists and the peasants at the last election, "You form merely part of a homogeneous reactionary mass against us together with the capitalist and feudal classes"?' On the contrary, he implies, the Social Democrats rightly wooed the *petit-bourgeois* classes for electoral support against the landowners and the great capitalists. The Lassallians, on the other hand, falsified the picture 'in order to put a good colour on his [Lassalle's] alliance with the absolutist and feudal rivals of the *bourgeoisie*'. Marx's way of stating his case is none too clear : but what he means is that the proletariat should help the *bourgeoisie*, great and little, as far as it is struggling against feudalism, and should woo the *petit-bourgeois* electors even though the 'democracy' for which they stand is tainted with the desire to defend obsolescent economic conditions. He is altogether opposed to any siding with the feudal classes or with autocratic government against the *bourgeois* constitutionalists.

The next question raised by Marx has to do with the question of internationalism. The sentence to which he takes objection is this : 'The working class takes action for its liberation in the first instance within the framework of the existing national State, and is conscious that the necessary result of its efforts, which are common to the workers of all civilised countries, will be the international brotherhood of nations'. Of course, Marx says, the workers have, in order to be able to fight at all, to organise at home as a class and to carry on the struggle within their own country ; but this relates to the 'form', and not to the 'content', of their struggle, and it is quite misleading to speak of them as working 'within the framework of the existing national State' — for the existing State itself has to act within an international framework of economic and political relations.

Capitalism is an international system ; and Bismarck as a statesman certainly did not make his name by acting 'within the national framework'. On the contrary, his greatness was built largely on his foreign policy. Moreover, what is this talk about 'brotherhood of nations' but the jargon of *bourgeois* pacifism as preached by the League of Peace and Freedom ? The international brotherhood that the Socialists ought to be proclaiming is that of the workers of all countries — not that of nations divided into conflicting classes. This need, Marx adds, is not done away with by the disruption of the International Working Men's Association, which was 'only a first attempt to create a central organ' for international working-class activity, and was 'no longer practicable in its first historic form after the fall of the Paris Commune'. Marx is here hitting out at the nationalistic attitude of the Lassallians towards the Franco-Prussian War and the annexation of Alsace-Lorraine. He is lamenting that the combined party is abandoning the working-class internationalism for which Liebknecht and other leaders had stood forth manfully in 1870 and 1871.

Then comes a section in which Marx attacks Lassalle's version of the 'iron law of wages'. If this law depends, as Lassalle said it did, on the Malthusian law of population, what is the sense of talking of abolishing it, as the Gotha Programme did, by abolishing the wage-system ? Marx states his own conception of the laws which regulate the price of labour-power under capitalism in terms of his now familiar distinction between paid and unpaid labour-time, without any reference to Malthus's doctrine, and reproaches his German followers for abandoning his analysis in favour of an erroneous and superseded notion of the *bourgeois* economists.

All this, however, is hardly more than skirmishing in comparison with the ensuing section of the *Critique*, in which Marx delivers a frontal attack on the Lassallian conception of the State and on Lassalle's proposals for emancipating the workers by means of State-aided Co-operative associations. These associations, the Programme says, are to be formed 'with State aid under the democratic control of the working people'. So, says Marx, the State, and not the working class, is to be the creator of the Co-operatives ; and Socialism is to come through the action of the State. How does this square with the belief that the workers' emancipation is the task of the workers themselves? Moreover, who are 'the working people' who are to exercise this 'democratic control' in a country in which the majority of 'workers' are not proletarians but peasants? Universal suffrage, in such a society, does not mean working-class control — far from it. Co-operative associations, Marx contends, are of value only in as far as they are 'independent creations of the workers, under tutelage neither of the government nor of the *bourgeoisie*'. A working class which asks the State to create its Co-operatives for it shows that it is 'neither in power nor yet ripe for power'.

What is this 'State' that is to do so much for the workers? The Programme speaks of it as the 'free State'; but what on earth does such a phrase mean? 'It is in no wise the aim of the workers . . . to free the State.' The State, in Germany as in Russia, is much too 'free' already. 'Freedom consists in converting the State from an organ controlling society into one completely controlled by society' — in other words, in restricting the State's freedom. The Programme, says Marx, 'shows how little it is penetrated by Socialist ideas in that it treats the State as an entity possessing its own intellectual, moral and independent foundations, instead of treating the existing (and any future) society as the foundation of the State (or of any future State)'. Existing States, says Marx, differ widely, but in the modern world they all 'stand on the foundations of *bourgeois* society' at different stages of its development. What Socialists have to consider is not existing States, but 'what changes the form of the State will undergo in Communist society'. In answering this question Marx puts forward these oft-quoted sentences:

> Between capitalist and Communist society lies a period of revolutionary transformation of the one into the other. To this corresponds a period of political transition during which the State can be nothing else than the revolutionary dictatorship of the proletariat.

Of all this, says Marx, the draft Gotha Programme has not a word to say. It merely recites 'the old familiar democratic litany' — universal suffrage, direct legislation, the plebiscite, a citizen army, and so on. Such demands, says Marx, 'have meaning only in a democratic Republic', and are meaningless in such a State as the 'Prusso-German Empire'. As the German Social Democrats did not dare — wisely, in Marx's view — to put forward the demand for such a Republic, the demands for universal suffrage, etc. could have no real significance. Marx was in effect arguing that there could be no way of peacefully remoulding such a 'police-guarded military despotism' as the German Reich, which could only be overthrown by revolution.

Marx made a number of further comments on particular points in the Programme, all in the same spirit ; but the details do not concern us here. The gist of his criticism was that the document agreed on by the two rival German Socialist parties made far too many concessions to the Lassallians, who would have had to accept fusion on much stiffer terms, and that these concessions gave away vital matters of principle, above all in relation to the attitude of Socialists to the existing Prusso-German State. In part, the criticism was directed against treating this particular State as if it were a 'democratic Republic' of the French, Swiss, or American type and ignoring its militaristic and feudal character, which it retained despite its 'embellishment with a parliamentary form of government' and the presence of some degree of *bourgeois* influence upon it. But, over and above this, Marx was saying that even when a democratic Republic has been brought into existence 'the class struggle has definitely to be fought to a finish in this final political form of *bourgeois* society'.

There has been much dispute among Marxian scholars about the meaning to be attached to Marx's reference to the 'dictatorship of the proletariat' in his *Critique of the Gotha Programme*. Lenin, when he was preparing to write *The State and Revolution* in 1917, annotated his copy of the *Critique* and also compared it with the text of the *Communist Manifesto* and with a letter written by Engels to Bebel while the Programme was under discussion. Engels, like Marx, had attacked especially the phraseology of the draft concerning the 'free State', and had written that 'it would be well to throw overboard all this chatter about the State, especially after the Commune, which was no longer a State in the proper sense of the word'. He had gone on to say that it had already been laid down in the *Communist Manifesto* that 'with the introduction of the Socialist order of society, the State will dissolve of itself, and disappear'. He then commented as follows :

> As the State is no more than a transitional phenomenon, of which use must be made in the revolutionary struggle for forcibly holding our antagonists in subjection, it is pure nonsense to talk about a 'Free People's State'. As long as the proletariat *needs* the State, it does so not in the interests of freedom, but for the purpose of holding its antagonists in subjection ; and as soon as it becomes possible to speak of 'freedom' the State, as such, ceases to exist.

Engels then proposed that in the Programme the word 'State' should be replaced throughout by 'Community' — a fine old German word, which corresponds to the French word '*Commune*'. Lenin, in commenting, noted that, whereas Engels proposed to drop the word 'State' from the Programme, Marx in his *Critique*, written more than a month later, retained the word in speaking of the period of transition. But, he said, there was no contradiction : they both meant the same. In capitalist society there is a 'State' 'in the proper sense of the word'. In the transition period there is still in a sense a 'State', but, like the Paris Commune, it is 'no longer a "State" in the proper sense of the word'. Finally, in Communist society, 'the "State" is not necessary : it withers away'. This seems a fair enough summary of what Marx and Engels clearly meant : what it does not tell is what form the 'dictatorship of the proletariat', foreshadowed by the Paris Commune, is to assume. Marx and Engels would undoubtedly have argued that the necessary forms would differ from case to case according to the circumstances under which the revolution occurred. They would have scouted the notion of laying down a fixed form, regardless of the character of the society in question or of the exigencies of the immediate situation. Thus, their idea of the 'dictatorship' cannot be held either to exclude universal suffrage or to require it : nor can it be regarded as including any particular view of the rôle of the Communist Party, beyond its general function of acting as the advance-guard of the whole proletariat, and not as a sect. The elaboration of the doctrine of dictatorship came later, and most of all from Lenin.

Despite Marx's and Engels's protests, the draft Programme was accepted with only minor modifications as the basis for the fusion of the two German Socialist parties ; and the united German Social Democratic Party came into formal existence in 1875. Although the Lassallians brought into it the larger number of members, the effective control fell practically from the outset into the hands of the Eisenach section. This happened largely because, from 1871 onwards, Bismarck and his Government had turned increasingly hostile to every kind of democratic Socialist movement and had thus made the Lassallian policy of working with the State against the rising *bourgeoisie* entirely impracticable. The situation in Germany was moreover complicated in the 1870s by the struggle in which Bismarck engaged with the Roman Catholic Church. The so-called *Kulturkampf* in Prussia began in 1871 with a measure restricting the political activities of the clergy — a retort to the opposition which many Catholics had put up to German unification under Prussian leadership. Then followed in 1872 measures for the exclusive State supervision of schools and for the banning of the Jesuit order. In 1873 came the 'May Laws' restricting the disciplinary powers of the Church over the faithful and excluding foreign clergy and even German clergy educated abroad. Many priests were gaoled, and many of the higher clergy driven from office. In 1874 the Prussian Government took power to expel offending clergy from the country, and in 1875 State subsidies to the Church were stopped and most of the religious orders dissolved. The struggle remained in full activity until about 1878, when the measures against the Church began to be gradually relaxed, as Bismarck needed allies for his protectionist policies against the liberals and for his attempts to destroy the growing power of Social Democracy.

Thus, in the 1870s, both the German Catholics and the Social Democrats found themselves ranged in opposition to the government of the newly established Reich, and under the necessity of appealing for support to the popular electorate which had been instituted for the Reichstag. But Catholics and Social Democrats were at the same time acutely hostile to each other, for the Social Democrats opposed the pretensions of the Church fully as much as Bismarck did, while the Catholics had to bid against the Social Democrats for the support of the working classes and the *petite bourgeoisie* in the predominantly Catholic areas, such as Bavaria and the Rhineland. There had indeed been a considerable Catholic Social movement — often called 'Christian Socialist' — in Germany from the early 'sixties. In 1863, in response to the challenge of Lassalle's crusade for a workers' party, Johann Döllinger (1799–1890) had urged German Catholics to take up the question of Socialism ; and in the following year this appeal had received powerful support from Wilhelm Emmanuel von Ketteler (1811–77), the aristocrat who had been a reforming member of the Frankfurt Assembly in 1848 and had become Bishop of Mainz two years later. Bishop von Ketteler published in 1864 a short book, *The Labour Question and Christianity*, in which he put forward advanced proposals for the improvement of working-class conditions and advocated action by the Catholic Church to establish Christian Co-operative societies independent of the State, to be financed with capital provided by the devout. In addition, von Ketteler favoured measures for the enforcement of fair wages and conditions and for security against unemployment and incapacity. He attacked strongly the abuses of capitalism and the immorality of the 'liberal' policy of *laissez-faire*, and demanded the moralisation of economic policy in accordance with Christian conceptions of justice and basic human rights. Von Ketteler was influenced greatly by Rodbertus, and also in some measure by the Christian Co-operative advocate, Victor Aimé Huber (1800–1869), to whose international activities on behalf of the Co-operative movement reference has been made already.

This 'Christian Socialist', or more properly 'Christian Social', movement continued to gather force during the 1860s. In addition to von Ketteler, its principal exponent was Canon Moufang (1817–90), also of Mainz, who wrote and preached extensively in its support. In 1868 a periodical, *Christian Social Letters*, began to appear ; and in 1869 a Conference of the German Catholic episcopate endorsed the movement. The Christian Socialists took over an organisation of Catholic journeymen's associations which had been started by the shoemaker-priest Adolph Kolping (1813–65) in the Rhineland as early as 1847, with the primary aim of restoring the life of the family, which was felt to be threatened by the growth of urbanisation and of factory employment. Kolping's local associations were presided over by priests and were active in both cultural and technical education. It was one of their cardinal tenets that moral must precede social regeneration. Kolping was a friend and supporter of von Ketteler ; and when the Catholics determined to organise a nation-wide movement, they took over his associations and also a number of similar associations which had been founded among the peasants, especially in Bavaria.

Thus, when the struggle between Bismarck and the Catholic Church began, the Catholics had already a strongly organised social movement behind them, and were able to put up a powerful resistance to the Government, while they carried on at the same time a continuous struggle against the 'materialist atheism' of the Socialist parties. Their social propaganda had also from the first an anti-Semitic streak, directed against the Jews who were prominent both among the liberal capitalists and among the Socialist leaders. Marx and Lassalle were of course both Jews. This anti-Semitism was, however, a good deal less virulent in the 'sixties than it became later : nor was it ever in Germany — as distinct from Austria — nearly so dominant among Catholics as among the Lutherans. Protestants were much later than Roman Catholics in launching a 'Christian Social' movement of their own in opposition to the Social Democrats ; but when they did, in the late 'seventies, it was both much more reactionary in politics and much more grossly anti-Semitic than the rival Catholic movement. Its leader, Pastor Adolf Stöcker (1835–1909), founded his Christian Social Labour Party only in 1878, and the following he enlisted came mainly from the lower middle classes in Prussia. His party was monarchist and strongly anti-liberal — in effect a mere adjunct of the Prussian court.

Von Ketteler, on the other hand, was a completely honest social reformer, though not of course a Socialist in any ordinary sense. He had begun, as we saw, by advocating a social movement under Church auspices entirely independent of the State ; but he seems to have realised the impracticability of his plan for Church-sponsored Co-operative Productive Societies, and in his later writings he became more and more an advocate of protective legislation in the interest of the workers. This later phase is best illustrated by his book, *Liberalism, Socialism, and Christianity*, published in 1871 just as the *Kulturkampf* was beginning. His work was followed up later by Frank Hitze (1851–1921) who in 1880 became general secretary of the Arbeiterwohl, the powerful Catholic welfare association, and leader of the Centre Party, which developed out of the Catholic Social movement. There was, however, a marked tendency for the main body of this movement to tend rightwards as soon as the *Kulturkampf* began to die down and the State turned its main attention to an attack on the Social Democratic Party.

In 1878 two attempts were made to assassinate the German Emperor Wilhelm. The Social Democrats had nothing to do with these attempts, which were the work of individual terrorists ; but Bismarck seized the occasion to institute a general persecution of the Socialists and to patch up a sort of truce with the Catholics. The Anti-Socialist Laws of 1878 and the following years drove the Social Democratic Party underground and forced it to conduct its organisation abroad, leaving its elected representatives in the Reichstag and in the lesser German legislatures to act as its agents in Germany itself. The Law of 1878 forbade the formation or continuance of any organisation which sought to subvert the existing State, or the social order, by advocacy of any form of Socialism, Social Democracy, or Communism. It thus decreed the dissolution of the Social Democratic Party and of all other Socialist bodies. The law made it impossible for the Social Democratic Party to hold any regular representative Congresses, and they were accordingly unable to revise the Programme which had been adopted at the Gotha Unity Congress of 1875 — though their candidates were of course able to put forward their own election programmes, and the party was able to achieve solid electoral successes despite the ban on its organisation. This explains why the Gotha Programme continued formally in force up to 1890, when the expiry of the Anti-Socialist Laws at length gave the opportunity for revising it. The Erfurt Programme, to which we shall come later, was then adopted in its place.

The Christian Social movement in Germany, during its heyday in the 1860s and 1870s, was waging war simultaneously on three fronts, with the major campaigns shifting from time to time from one front to another. In the predominantly Protestant States and in the Reich as a whole it was fighting against the extension of State power in such fields as education and freedom of speech and organisation, but was at the same time advocating social legislation in the interests of the workers. In the economic field it was fighting against *bourgeois* liberalism, which was for the most part addicted to free thought and rationalism as well as to *laissez-faire*. It was also fighting against the Social Democrats, who were its chief rivals for popular support in the Catholic industrial areas. Broadly speaking, it appeared in the 1860s mainly as the antagonist of capitalist liberalism, but did so largely because it was seeking for a means of rivalling Lassalle's Socialist appeal. In the 1870s, during the *Kulturkampf*, it was chiefly engaged in fighting Bismarck and opposing the power of the State, and found itself not seldom in alliance with the Socialists against autocratic government. In the 1880s, when the *Kulturkampf* was half over and the Socialists were the main victims of Government persecution, it became a balancing group between conservatives and liberals, and profited by the repression of the Socialists in its campaign to organise the Catholic workers. In the 1890s, when the Anti-Socialist Laws had ceased to operate, it moved still further to the right because of its growing struggle against Socialist influence, but continued to support social legislation as a necessary condition of keeping its hold on the Catholic workers.

At the same time, the doctrines of liberal capitalism and *laissez-faire* were under attack from yet another angle. The notion that the State should stand aside and allow capitalism to develop unchecked in the name of liberty and of economic law had always had to meet, in Germany, with powerful opposition from the philosophers who exalted the function of the State as the supreme exponent of the spirit of the people. Fichte, as well as Hegel, had been a powerful advocate of the claim of the State to regulate the whole life of the nation ; and the 'Young Hegelians' had been entirely hostile to the *laissez-faire* doctrines of the liberal economists. Nor had these doctrines gone unchallenged among the economists themselves. Friedrich List's *System of National Economy* (1841) had been a challenge to the classical economic doctrines, because of its insistence that it was the State's function to plan economic development in order to ensure that each country should make full use of its resources to realise its maximum potentiality for the production of wealth. Two years later, Wilhelm Roscher, the founder of the German

'Historical School' of economists, began the publication of the series of volumes in which he put forward his relativist view of economic laws, which he held to be valid only within the limits of particular economic systems and not absolutely. Bruno Hildebrand and Karl Knies followed up Roscher's method and doctrine during the next few years, with the broad effect of treating economics, not as a deductive science capable of yielding absolute precepts, but rather as an historical study to be closely related to law and politics. These writers, far from raising any objection of principle to State intervention in economic affairs, regarded it as right and proper for the State to lay down the conditions under which the business entrepreneur was to act. They were succeeded by a younger generation of economists — Gustav Schmoller, Adolf Held, Lujo Brentano, Christian Engel, Adolf Wagner, and others — who related their economic opinions much more directly to the growing challenge of Socialism. In 1872 this group called together at Eisenach — which had been the scene of the foundation of the Social Democratic Party three years before — a Congress of German Economists which pronounced in favour of a sort of 'State Socialism', though not, of course, of Social Democracy. The assembled economists, who included a high proportion of the holders of academic chairs in the subject in the German Universities, did not discuss who ought to control the State, but only how far the State, however controlled, ought to intervene in the regulation of economic affairs. They were agreed in attacking the whole conception of 'economic liberalism' and in attributing to liberal misdeeds the widespread grievances and discontents of the German workers. 'Social democracy', said Schmoller, the chief promoter of the movement, 'is a consequence of the sins of modern liberalism'; and in this spirit the Congress endorsed the demands for social legislation and for public planning of economic affairs. The name 'Professorial Socialists' (often translated 'Socialists of the Chair') which they readily accepted for themselves was the more significant because it came into use at a time when a sharp reaction had set in against Socialism after the suppression of the Paris Commune. Undoubtedly both the name and the Society for Social Politics which the group founded in 1873 helped the advance of Socialist opinion in Germany during the ensuing years, though most of the 'Professorial Socialists' had no connection at all with the Social Democratic movement, to which, politically, many of them were keenly opposed. 'Professorial Socialism' also helped to reinforce the criticisms of *laissez-faire* capitalism advanced by the Christian Socialists, and at the same time gave powerful intellectual backing to Bismarck's policies of compulsory social insurance, as well as to the protectionist trade policy which he adopted in 1880.

Meanwhile, the Christian Social movement was spreading from Germany into Austria. Its principal exponent there was Karl von Vogelsang (1818–90), who was born a German Protestant and became a member of the Prussian civil service, but was converted to Catholicism by von Ketteler and, removing to Austria in 1864, became the chief inspirer of the Austrian Christian Social Party. In *Vaterland*, the principal organ of the Austrian Catholic movement, and in his own journal, the *Monthly for Christian Social Reform*, he attacked the abuses of capitalism, which he regarded as a social disaster resulting from the revolt of the upper strata of modern society against Christianity. Violently anti-liberal and anti-Semite, von Vogelsang demanded a return to an orderly society regulated in accordance with Christian principle in a hierarchy of 'estates'. He called for a corporative organisation of industry in *Zünfte* (gilds, or corporations) regulated by, and functionally related to, a State founded on Christian principles. His corporations, which are the ancestors of the Corporative system of the Italian Fascists, were of course to include both masters and men, and were to transcend class antagonisms by uniting all classes in the service of the Christian community. For the handicrafts von Vogelsang advocated Co-operative organisation, and he also adumbrated a scheme of peasant Co-operation under the auspices of the Corporative State. His influence worked in with that of the German Protestant, Rudolf Meyer, who also settled in Austria, and whose book, *The Struggle for the Emancipation of the Fourth Estate* (1874–5), had a considerable influence on the development of the Austrian social movement. With these Corporative doctrines von Vogelsang — and the movement he inspired — combined a very strong dose of anti-Semitism, prompted, no doubt, by the leading position held by Jewish capitalism in Vienna and by the leading part played by Jews in the Viennese Socialist movement. The Christian Social movement in Austria, partly because of its anti-Semitic tendency, developed politically on much more reactionary lines than the parallel Catholic movement in Germany — or at any rate in most parts of Germany. In Bavaria, however, where Austrian influence was strong, the same tendencies appeared. The chief advocate of Christian Social policy in Bavaria was Georg Ratzinger (1844–99), who in 1881 published a general survey of the Christian Social movement. Ratzinger, though he attacked capitalism, was a strong defender of private property, which he considered should be held subject to moral rules laid down by the State. He also advocated a system of State-supervised Co-operative societies and, for private industry, co-partnership and sharing of profits. In general, however, Bavarian Catholicism tended to follow the Austrian lead.

The Christian Social movement in the German countries had its parallels elsewhere, especially in France and Belgium. In France, immediately after the defeat of the Paris Commune, Count Albert de Mun (1841–1914), with the collaboration of Maurice Maignon and René de La Tour du Pin Chambly, Marquis de la Charce (1834–1924), founded a society, called *Œuvre des Circles Catholiques d'Ouvriers*, with the purpose of restoring the unity of ancient France under a Christian monarchy, with a corporative organisation of industry under the patronage of the State. This movement began in strong hostility to the 'laicity' of the Third Republic. De Mun was its principal orator and organiser, and de La Tour du Pin, through his journal *Association Catholique*, its principal literary exponent. De Mun became a deputy in 1876 : he supported General Boulanger, and acquired a wide influence among the Catholic youth. Later, at the Pope's instance, he agreed to accept the Republic *de facto*. He supported the Papal Encyclical, *Rerum Novarum*, in 1891, and took a leading part as an anti-Dreyfusard in the famous *affaire*. De La Tour du Pin worked with de Mun until 1892, and then broke with him on the question of accepting the Republic, and became the leader of a section of the Christian Social movement which stood for the restoration of the Bourbons. Later he became a member of *Action Française*. Strongly anti-liberal, he was the nearest of the French Catholic Social writers to the standpoint of the Austrian group headed by von Vogelsang. He called himself a Christian Socialist: his best-known book, recording the progress of the movement and of his own ideas, is *Vers un ordre chrétien*, published in 1907. In Belgium the Christian Social approach was represented chiefly by Henry Xavier Charles Périn (1815–1905), who was Professor of Political Economy at Louvain from 1845, and attacked economic liberalism in his two main books, *La Richesse dans les sociétés chrétiennes* (1861) and *Les Lois de la société chrétienne* (1875). Périn was a strong opponent both of Social Democracy and of the 'State Socialism' of the German 'Professorial' school; and he also attacked the advocates of a Co-operative solution of the 'social question'. In his view the idea of Christian 'renunciation' was the necessary basis for a right economic order, which needed the control of a powerful Church as the guardian of its moral behaviour. His views came close at certain points to those of the followers of Le Play in France, such as Claudio Jannet (1844–94), whose *Le Socialisme d'état et la réforme sociale* (1889) similarly opposed the 'State Socialist' tendency among the academic critics of *laissez-faire*.

All the Christian Social writers of whom I have been speaking were, of course, opponents of the Social Democratic movement and, above all, of Marxism as a materialist system. Marx in his *Critique of the Gotha Programme* had told his German followers that their party 'ought to have taken the opportunity to state its conviction that *bourgeois* "freedom of conscience" [which was one of the demands put forward in the Programme] is neither more nor less than toleration of all sorts of religious freedom of conscience, and that its [the party's] aim is rather to set the conscience free from religious superstition'. Marxist Socialism was definitely an anti-religious creed, treating religious beliefs as mere parts of the ideological structures finally derived from the economic foundations of societies at particular stages of their development. Accordingly, the more Marxism became the accepted basis of Socialism as a political force, the more intense became the struggle between Christian Socialists and Social Democrats over the very foundations of social policy. But in the 'fifties and 'sixties Marxism was not yet, even in Germany, the dominant Socialist creed, and it was still possible for continental Catholics to express sympathy with

'Socialism' without incongruity with their religious beliefs—
though not of course without having the 'atheistical' tendencies
of many Socialists cast in their teeth. Bakunin and Marx, in
the struggles which destroyed the First International, were
agreed about religion, if about little else — though, even in
this, they disagreed about making it a central issue ; and Anarchism and French Republican Jacobinism, rather than Socialism
as such, were the political doctrines with which atheism was most
clearly associated in the popular consciousness. But as Marxist
Social Democracy made its great advances in the 1870s in Germany and spread from Germany to other countries, the Catholic
Church more and more regarded Social Democracy as its principal antagonist, and the 'Christian Socialism' of such men as
von Ketteler ceased to be tenable within the bounds of the
Catholic Church. Von Ketteler was among those who, in 1870,
opposed the acceptance of the new dogma of papal infallibility,
but bowed to the authority of the Church when the decision
had gone against them. When, therefore, in 1878 Leo XIII
issued his Encyclical *Quod Apostolici Muneris*, denouncing
Socialism, Communism, and Nihilism as creeds inconsistent
with true Christianity, all who accepted the Church's discipline
had to disavow Socialism and to re-name their doctrine if they
had professed to be 'Christian Socialists'. The Encyclical
referred in strong language to 'the deadly plague which is
tainting Society to its very core and bringing it to a state of
extreme peril'. 'We are alluding', Leo XIII continued, 'to
that sect of men who, under the motley and all but barbarous
terms and titles of Socialists, Communists, and Nihilists, are
spread abroad throughout the world and, bound intimately
together in baneful alliance, no longer look for strong support
in secret meetings held in darksome places, but, standing forth
openly and boldly in the light of day, strive to carry out the
purpose, long resolved upon, of uprooting the foundations of
civilised society at large.'

These words, appearing just as Bismarck was pushing
through his Anti-Socialist Laws in Germany, were influential
in bringing the active phase of the *Kulturkampf* to a close, and
in furthering a *rapprochement* between the German Empire and
the Catholic Church. They helped to unite these two hitherto
warring forces in a common offensive against Socialism in all

its forms. Correspondingly they helped, over most of continental Europe, to complete the identification of Socialist movements with hostility to organised religion, and to bring to an end the type of radical Christian doctrine of which Lamennais had been the most influential exponent. It looked for a time, in the 1880s, as if the same thing might happen in Great Britain, where the Social Democratic Federation took up the same militant attitude towards religion as the Marxist parties on the Continent. That this did not come about was due less to the efforts of Christian Socialists such as Stewart Headlam than to the eclipse of the British Social Democratic movement by the new movements which arose directly out of the London Dock Strike of 1889, the rise of the Miners' Federation, and the unexpected dissolution of the radical wing of the Liberal Party which followed the defection of its leader, Joseph Chamberlain, over the question of Irish Home Rule. These developments made possible the creation of a new British Socialist movement which was moved mainly by ethical impulses, and, even when it attacked the Churches, did so for the most part without feeling the need to break right away from every sort of religious belief, or to espouse a materialist philosophy in its place.

The distinctive kind of ethical Socialism which took root in Great Britain in the 1890s, and found expression in the Independent Labour Party under Keir Hardie's leadership, will be discussed in a subsequent volume of this work. The relevant point at this stage is that in Germany after 1878 the battle between Social Democracy and the Churches was joined in such a way as to impel the Socialists strongly towards the acceptance of the Marxist hostility to religion as a necessary element in the Socialist creed, and that from Germany this attitude spread to other countries as fast as they set about organising Social Democratic parties modelled upon the German party. The consequence was that the social rift between Socialists and those who continued to accept the established religions became very much wider than it had previously been : so that the Social Democrats tended, much more than the Socialists in Great Britain, to form a strongly coherent community within the wider society of the nation and to develop much more clannishness and isolation in affairs which had nothing directly to do with economics or politics. I am not suggesting that this came about through a one-sided self-isolation of the Socialists from the rest of the people : it was fully as much the consequence of the determined attempts of the Churches to keep their flocks from the contamination of association with the 'infidels'. But, whatever the relative strength of the forces at work, the isolation did happen, and its effects are very marked even to-day.

In France, of course, the rift between the religious and their opponents had existed for a long time before the 1870s. It was indeed a part of the revolutionary tradition. But up to the 1870s the creed most closely associated with irreligion in France had been, not Socialism, but rather Republican Jacobinism, and there had been ample room for Christian variants of the Socialist doctrine, as exemplified in the groups which followed such men as Buchez and inspired the English Christian Socialists from Ludlow and Maurice to Neale and Thomas Hughes. After the 'seventies this sort of Christian Socialism practically disappeared in France, giving place to forms of Christian Social activity which were directly and violently hostile to the Socialist parties of the Third Republic.

This chapter has ranged over a wide field and may appear to have brought together a number of matters which would have been better discussed apart. It has, however, been given its form advisedly and, I believe, for sufficient reasons. I found it impossible to deal with the development of the German Social Democratic Party from the death of Lassalle to the lapsing of the Anti-Socialist Laws without bringing in both the effects of the *Kulturkampf* and the changing phases of the Christian Social movement and also the peculiar type of 'Professorial Socialism' which developed as a sharp reaction against economic liberalism in a country bent on establishing and consolidating its national unity in the economic as well as in the political field. German Socialism took its peculiar shape under the influence of the peculiar development of German unity, as well as on the foundation of a specific cultural habit which based movements upon philosophies, rather than philosophies upon movements, and had hardly anything of the tentative empiricism of the British approach. A man or woman who joined the Independent Labour Party or the Fabian Society in Great Britain — or even the Social Democratic Federation — was not thereby cut off from social and cultural contacts with non-Socialists to anything like the same extent as the German — especially the middle-class German — who threw in his lot with Social Democracy. Indeed, for the German, Social Democracy was not so much a political creed as an entire culture, sharply separated both from the culture of the German *bourgeoisie* and from the rival culture which found its inspiration in the Catholic Church. Both Catholics and Social Democrats sought the allegiance of the whole man, in hostility to the no less exacting claims of the Prussian-dominated State. The effect was that both groups developed an intense cultural life of their own, in which the arts — especially music and literature — fell into place as essential elements of the common life of the party or faction. The strength of these cultural bonds stood the German Social Democrats in good stead during the period of repression, and enabled them to hold together through activities in the social field, despite the suppression of their political organisation. This helped them to maintain the contacts needed for their campaigning in the elections for the Reichstag and for other public bodies, in which they were still free to take part; for Bismarck was unable to persuade the Reichstag to destroy the freedom of elections or to remove the immunity enjoyed by public representatives and candidates. Speeches made in the Reichstag or in other public assemblies could still be freely reported in the newspapers; and socialistic journals, though subjected to heavy censorship in other respects, were still able to appear. The Social Democrats' own papers had to be printed abroad and smuggled into Germany; but there were, in Germany itself, newspapers friendly enough — or unfriendly enough to Bismarck — to give the Socialist parliamentarians quite a good show.

Thus German Socialism, thanks to its strong cultural basis, which was closely linked to Marxism, was able to weather the storm. Marx had indeed insisted, in the earlier years of the First International, on the need for building on actual movements rather than constructing a dogma into which movements were then required to fit. But when the actual movements took forms which he disliked, as they largely did in Spain and Italy, in Germany under Lassalle's influence, and in Great Britain as soon as the Trade Unions' most imme-

diate demands had been met, he was apt to forget his own
precepts and to become the grand inquisitor into heretical misdeeds. At the Gotha Congress of 1875 his own disciples in
Germany refused to follow his lead ; but, in spite of their
refusal, the German party in the main took the stamp he had
wished to impress upon it because, and as long as, it was driven
into the position of a persecuted sect. As soon as the persecution was lifted, in 1890, it discarded the programme of compromise which it had adopted against his advice, and adopted a
new programme which complied broadly with what he had
recommended. But no sooner had it done this, in the first
flush of its emancipation, than the old differences reappeared ;
and the party was plunged within a few years into the great
'Revisionist' controversy in which Eduard Bernstein and Karl
Kautsky were the theoretical protagonists. In the meantime,
however, Germany had replaced France as the predominant
influence on European Socialism, and a sort of Marxism had
become the common doctrine of most of the developing Socialist
parliamentary parties — at any rate in theory. Practice, on the
other hand, varied greatly from country to country, according
to the conditions within which the different parties had to act ;
and in Germany itself practice changed as soon as the limiting
conditions of the Anti-Socialist Laws were removed. After
1890 the revised programme of German Social Democracy
represented its reaction to a situation which had ceased to exist,
and accordingly the gulf between theory and practice rapidly
widened. In effect, the German party accepted in 1891 the
Marxism it had refused to swallow whole in 1875, not so much
because Marx or Engels had convinced it as because Bismarck
had : and when Bismarck's heavy hand was removed it soon
began to change its mind.

CHAPTER XI

MARX AND ENGELS — *DAS KAPITAL* AND *ANTI-DÜHRING*

THE defeat of the Paris Commune and the ensuing break-up of the First International left Marx and Engels to face, for the second time in their lives, the collapse of a widespread international movement on which they had built high hopes. In France Socialism had practically ceased to exist, and the Trade Union movement too had been almost wiped out. In Great Britain the Trade Union leaders, though they had not, as Marx alleged, 'sold themselves to Gladstone', were preoccupied with their own struggle with the law, and were in no mood to allow Marx to act in their name, or to listen to his advice. Spain and Italy were still in the throes of revolution, but were not at all disposed to look to Marx for guidance. In Belgium and Holland, Anarchist or near-Anarchist tendencies were uppermost for the time being. Switzerland was divided, as it had been throughout; but Marx had few links there, except with the veteran J. P. Becker. Only in Germany was there developing a Socialist party which professed to base its doctrine and policy on Marxian foundations, though already Marx was beginning to find followers in Russia and was being induced to change his attitude towards the Russians as he came to see that there was no prospect of early revolution in Western Europe and to conceive it as possible that the signal for the uprising of the West might have, after all, to come from the economically backward East, because there alone the conditions requisite for a successful social revolution appeared still to exist. During the years which immediately followed the Paris Commune the eyes of Marx and Engels were fixed mainly on Germany. Thereafter, when his German disciples had repudiated his advice at the Gotha Congress, and when, a few years later, the German Social Democratic Party fell under the axe-blow of Bismarck's Anti-Socialist Law, their eyes were turned more and more upon Russia, and they began to speculate more intently concerning the possibility that the endemic revolutionary unrest in the great Czarist empire might take a distinctive Socialist shape.

Marx had employed the years between the collapse of the revolutionary movements of 1848 and the foundation of the First International mainly in labouring upon his great work, through which he meant to give his 'Scientific Socialism' a final and magistral form. The first instalment of this work, much delayed by his ill-health and by the hard necessity of earning his daily bread, had been published in 1859 in German as *A Critique of Political Economy*, Volume I.[1] Subsequently he modified his plans, and, instead of producing further volumes of this work, decided to make a fresh start. But the first volume of his *magnum opus*, *Das Kapital*, appeared after many delays only in 1867, when the First International was already well launched on its course. No further volume was published in his lifetime. Volume II, *The Process of Capitalist Circulation*, was issued by Engels at Hamburg in 1885, two years after Marx's death. Volume III, *The Complete Process of Capitalist Production*, was similarly brought out by Engels only in 1894.

Thus, when the new Socialist movements based on Marx's teaching began to develop in the 1870s, first in Germany and then in other countries, the theoretical bible of Marxism was the first volume only of *Das Kapital*, bearing the sub-title *Capitalist Production*. This was the volume which Bakunin undertook to translate into Russian — with unfortunate consequences described in a previous chapter. A Russian translation, the first to appear in any foreign language, was published as early as 1872, and was not suppressed by the censorship : it enjoyed a substantial circulation, and did much to establish Marx's influence in revolutionary intellectual circles. The translator was Nikolai Danielson, better known by his pen-name, Nikolai-on. A French translation by J. Roy, which began to appear soon afterwards in parts, was completed in 1875 : it was revised by Marx himself. The first English translation, by Samuel Moore and Edward Aveling, edited by Engels, did not come out until 1887.

[1] *Zur Kritik der Politischen Oekonomie*, Berlin, 1859. No English translation appeared till 1909.

Of the later volumes of *Das Kapital* Volume II added little to the general structure of Marxist theory, though it is important for the detailed study of certain aspects of Marx's thought, notably in relation to his account of the 'contradictions of capitalism' and of the nature of commercial crises. It was left practically complete by the author. Volume III, on the other hand, added a great deal to what had been laid down in Volume I, and in particular threw much light on Marx's view of the relation between the highly abstract account of capitalist production given in the earlier chapters of Volume I and the actual processes of capitalist market economics. But it was not a finished product : it had to be put together by Engels from many manuscripts written over a long period, some of them before Volume I had taken final shape ; and it is, in effect, less a connected and coherent culmination to the whole work than a series of studies left at very different stages, and never fully co-ordinated into a unified whole. It has been much used both by Marxists and by opponents of Marxism during the past half-century ; but it came too late to make any contribution to the building up of the body of Marxist doctrine which became the theoretical foundation of the Social Democratic movement of the 1870s and 1880s, or to furnish ammunition to the earlier critics who set out to destroy Marxism from the standpoint of the orthodox schools of Political Economy. During the years when the great theoretical warfare between Marxists and anti-Marxists was being waged, to the accompaniment of the rise of Social Democracy as a political force, Marxism meant, for most of the participants on both sides, what was embodied in the *Communist Manifesto* and in the opening volume of *Das Kapital*, and not much besides. *The Critique of Political Economy* was almost unknown outside Germany : *The Poverty of Philosophy*, originally written in French, was not translated into German until 1885, and appeared in English only in 1900. Even the *Communist Manifesto* was not reprinted in German until 1872, or in English until 1886. A Russian translation, by Bakunin, was published by Herzen in *Kolokol* in the early 'sixties ; and a second, with a specially written preface by Marx, was published in 1882.

In the first volume of the present work an attempt has been made, setting out from the *Communist Manifesto*, to present a summary account of the Marxian doctrine as it stood in the minds of its authors at the time of the European Revolutions of 1848. In this account the stress was laid mainly on the Materialist Conception of History and on the views of Marx and Engels on contemporary politics, and no attempt was made to discuss their formulation of a new economic theory — or rather a theory of the economic basis of capitalist production. In the present volume a little has been said on this subject in connection with Marx's dissent from the economic theories of Lassalle ; and the Marxian theory of the State has come up for discussion both in the same chapter and in the account of the fusion of the two German Socialist parties in 1875. It is now necessary to give a fuller account of the economic doctrines formulated in the *Critique of Political Economy* and in the first volume of *Das Kapital* in order to relate Marxism, in the final form given to it by its main author in his lifetime, to the Social Democratic movements which professedly based themselves upon it in the seventies and eighties of the nineteenth century.

Das Kapital is in many respects a forbidding book. Its most readable chapters, embodying Marx's account of the development of the capitalist system from the seventeenth century to the middle of the nineteenth, come late, after the nine massive chapters in which Marx expounds his theory of value and of surplus value. These earlier chapters are not only difficult in themselves, but also couched in a form derived from the classical Economics of the early nineteenth century, and not easy to master without a knowledge of Ricardian terminology. They are, in addition, much affected by their author's Hegelian upbringing, and highly abstract in their method — in sharp contrast with the refreshing realism and concreteness of the historical chapters which follow them. These qualities, however, did not prevent them from becoming the basis for an entire system of Socialist Economic Theory which had less and less in common with orthodox Political Economy as the latter, discarding the Ricardian approach to the study of value, turned increasingly away from the concepts employed by the classical school. Orthodox economists directed themselves more and more towards a consideration of the working of the price mechanism, and ceased, in particular, to make any use of the distinction between 'use value' and 'exchange value' on which

Marx so largely built. Marxian Economics thus came to develop as a system and as a way of approach to Economics entirely different from the orthodox Economics of the later nineteenth century, with a terminology entirely its own — or rather derived from a classical Political Economy which the later orthodox economists regarded as obsolete. The 'value' Marx was talking about was something essentially different from 'value' as conceived by Jevons or Marshall, or by Walras or Menger or any exponent of the theory of final or marginal utility. So wide was the divergence that it was almost impossible for Marxists to argue with orthodox economists without getting at cross-purposes, and simply reiterating their rival theories without attempting to meet — or even to see — each other's case.

The explanation of this divergence is simple. The orthodox economists after Mill took the capitalist system as given and were concerned only to examine its working; whereas Marx was setting out to attack it, to demonstrate its historical relativity, and to lay his finger on the inherent 'contradictions' that would inevitably bring about its destruction. In the eyes of the orthodox economists the essential task of Political Economy — or of Economics, as they came more and more to prefer calling it — was to analyse the market process, taking for granted the private ownership of the means of production, their operation for private profit, and the availability of a body of workers whose services could be hired for a wage. They did not, indeed, study the market process just as they found it, in all the complexity of its actual working as influenced by many non-economic factors — or rather they did so only incidentally. They preferred, in presenting their general thesis, to make simplifying assumptions, such as the existence of unlimited competition — save in exceptional cases which they dealt with separately — and the transferability of capital or of labour from one employment to another without regard to its specific character. Monopoly they treated as an exception ; unemployment as an outcome of friction ; international trade as a special case of the division of labour. Of course, in practice they were defending the system as well as explaining how it worked ; but their defence took the form of assuming the market economy based on private ownership to be a natural phenomenon and of seeking to show that, given such an economy, the highest production would be secured by allowing it to operate in accordance with its own 'natural' laws, and that any attempt by the State or by any external agency to interfere with the working of these laws would necessarily reduce production and therewith reduce the size of the 'cake' that could be put at the consumers' disposal. The distribution of this cake among the owners of the factors of production — including labour — they represented as necessarily governed by the laws of the market — in the last resort, by the consumers' preparedness to buy and by the competition of the producers to attract demand, or in offering their services in production on competitive terms.

In this kind of Economics the central subject of study was price, including the prices not only of all sorts of finished goods, but also of land, of labour, and of capital in the form of money or credit. Every factor of production, as well as every kind of goods, had its price, determined by the higgling of the market in which it was bought and sold. The essential task of the economist was to study and analyse this complex structure of prices and to formulate the laws of its working. 'Value', if the word was retained at all, meant only price stripped of its denomination in terms of a particular kind of money : there ceased to be any such thing as that 'exchange value' which the classical economists had regarded as essentially distinct from the constantly varying prices at which things were actually bought and sold.

For Ricardo exchange value, as distinct from market price, had stood for the amount of human labour that had gone into the making of a commodity. Market price would continually deviate from this value, but would also continually tend to return to it ; and under conditions of equilibrium between supply and demand, price and value would necessarily coincide. Ricardo did not invent this theory that the exchange value of a thing was determined by the amount of human labour incorporated in it : he took it over from a long line of predecessors. He did, however, make it the central doctrine of his new formulation of Economic Theory, and in doing so furnished his anticapitalist critics with an argument on which they immediately seized. Ricardo, indeed, had treated labour rather as the *measure* than as the *source* of values ; but the distinction was not very clear, and his critics had promptly identified the two. If the value of a thing depended on the labour incorporated in it, they argued, clearly the labourer had a right to receive back in exchange for his labour the full value he had contributed — to wit, the whole value of the product. Anything short of this meant that his labour was being exploited in the interests of those who had contributed nothing to the value. This was the labour theory of value in the form in which, as we saw in the first volume of this work, it was put forward by the early anti-capitalist critics of Ricardian doctrine. Marx rejected this view in its individualistic form, in which it required that each labourer should receive the full value of his product. He did so on the ground that, in capitalist production, the individual labourer could not be said to have a specific product : he was only a contributor to an essentially *social* process of production. Accordingly, the claim to the whole product could be significant under capitalist conditions only if it were advanced on behalf, not of the individual labourer, but of the labouring class as a whole. Exploitation existed, as the earlier critics of Ricardo had said it did ; but it was in its essence exploitation not of one individual by another, but of class by class.

To this point we must come back. What concerns us for the time being is that the classical economists held a theory of exchange value, as something distinct from market price, and as determined, wholly or mainly, by the amounts of labour, direct or indirect, incorporated in the various commodities that were placed on the market. In other words, they treated exchange value as depending entirely on the conditions of production, and as unaffected by the fluctuations of market demand ; whereas they recognised that market prices were settled by the interaction of the forces of supply and demand, and believed that these prices oscillated continually round exchange values, with a continual tendency to return to the latter whenever the forces of supply and demand were evenly balanced.

By the time of John Stuart Mill, whose *Principles of Political Economy* first appeared in 1848, orthodox economic doctrine had moved considerably away from the Ricardian position — in Marx's view, greatly for the worse. For the conception of the 'amount of labour' incorporated in a commodity the post-Ricardians had increasingly substituted the conception of what the labour actually cost, or tended to cost when supply and demand were in balance. This view had been explicitly rejected by Ricardo, who had held that exchange value was unaffected by the wages paid, as distinct from the amount of labour embodied, and had backed up his assertion by saying that if all wages were doubled or halved, this would not mean that the exchange values of products were similarly doubled or halved, because exchange value was essentially a ratio between quantities of goods exchanged, and not an absolute magnitude. Ricardo did indeed assume that relative wages would tend to correspond to the relative amounts of labour expended, and would deviate from this correspondence only under the influence of temporary market fluctuations. His successors therefore argued that 'normal wage' could be regarded as corresponding to 'value' or to 'normal price' of an amount of labour. Taking the normal wages cost, instead of the 'amount of labour', as a determinant of value made it possible for them to bring into the reckoning other 'costs' besides that of labour, so as to arrive at a conception of the 'values', or 'normal prices', of commodities as determined by what John Stuart Mill called their 'prices of production', including costs of capital-use and of managerial services as well as costs of labour.

Marx, as we shall see, accepted a view nearly akin to Mill's when he came, in his third volume, to discuss the actual working of the price system under capitalism and its function in redistributing 'surplus value' in such a way as to equalise the returns accruing to competing capitalists. But he insisted that this fixing of prices by the higgling of the competitive market had nothing to do with the determination of exchange values ; and he habitually denounced as 'vulgar economists' those who thought it had and discarded the Ricardian view that exchange values depended on the amounts of labour incorporated in the goods produced. But John Stuart Mill, though he by no means held that the 'value' of a commodity was settled exclusively by the amount of labour incorporated in it, did continue to believe that 'exchange value', which he equated with 'normal price' stripped of its specific monetary form, was determined exclusively from the side of production and that the state of demand came in only as a cause of deviation from this value or 'normal price'. After Mill, however, orthodox Economics took an entirely different turn. The whole concept of exchange value, as distinct from price, was gradually discarded, and study was concentrated on actual market prices, which were regarded as the outcome of demand factors operating as stimulants to production by entrepreneurs — the entrepreneur being guided by his costs of production in deciding how much to produce in response to any given expectation of market demand.

The new orthodox Economics also got away from the classical distinction between two kinds of value — 'value in use' and 'value in exchange'. This distinction was based on the evident fact that the prices charged for things were not proportionate to their usefulness. A very useful thing might be very cheap, if it cost little effort to produce. Accordingly, it seemed that the explanation of prices and values must be sought in some property of commodities entirely apart from their usefulness. A thing, it was said, must have 'use value' — *i.e.* must be of some use — in order to rank at all as a commodity ; but its value, or its price, would not depend on *how* useful it was. This distinction between 'use value' and 'exchange value' led to the search for some common property in commodities, other than their usefulness, that caused them to have different prices ; and, when usefulness was excluded as a cause, the explanation could be sought only in the conditions under which commodities were produced, and the most obvious common factor was that all, or nearly all, commodities had cost labour of one kind or another.

The new doctrine of 'final utility', or 'marginal utility' as it came to be called, removed the barrier in the way of regarding usefulness as a factor influencing price. What affected price, it was explained, was not the usefulness of a commodity in any absolute sense, but only the utility of the final 'dose' bought by the 'marginal' consumer, whose willingness to pay so much, and no more, determined the price at which, in a fully competitive market, all the other 'doses' of the same commodity would have to be sold. The relevant factor was not the 'utility' of a loaf of bread as such, but that of the 'final' loaf successfully disposed of in the market. Of course, it had also to be recognised that the number of loaves offered for sale would be affected by the price they were expected to fetch, and that producers would do their best to produce only as many loaves as they could expect to sell at a profit. How many these would be, in relation to any given condition of demand, would depend on the costs of production — but, again, not on the cost of producing a loaf as such — for this would vary from baker to baker, and also according to the number each baker produced — but on the cost of producing the 'final' loaf needed to bring supply into equilibrium with demand at a price yielding the 'final' baker a reasonable return.

This 'marginalist' theory of prices, though subject to numerous qualifications, has long been an accepted tenet of orthodox Economics. It was indeed pretty generally accepted in Marx's own lifetime. Jevons published his *Theory of Political Economy*, in which the new doctrine was fully expounded, in 1871 ; and on the Continent Léon Walras and Anton Menger almost simultaneously announced practically identical theories. Marx, however, had worked out his economic theories well before this supersession of the Ricardian theory by the new orthodoxy. The latest writer by whom he was substantially affected was John Stuart Mill, who still clung to the older basic conception of the theory of value ; and his later writings show almost no sign that he had been influenced at all by the later developments of orthodox theory. The entire theoretical system expounded in *Das Kapital* sets out from the starting-point of Ricardian economics, and rests on a complete acceptance of the sharp distinction between 'use value' and 'exchange value', and of the equally sharp distinction between 'exchange value' and market price. Moreover, Marxian Economics has kept ever since the shape thus given to it, and has continued to use a set of concepts and a terminology derived from elements in early classical Economics which were superseded in other quarters more than eighty years ago.

Of course, neither Marx nor Ricardo, in asserting that the value of a commodity corresponded to the 'amount of labour' embodied in it, fell into the absurdity of supposing that if one man took twice as long as another to make an identical thing, he produced twice the value. Only 'necessary labour-time' was creative of value ; and 'necessary labour-time' meant primarily the time it would take an 'ordinary' workman to perform a given task, using the prevailing technical methods. The assumption that, at any given stage in the development of productive techniques, there would be such a normal, necessary time for the 'ordinary' workman was made without question, though of course Marx was well aware that output would differ from man to man and from factory to factory in accordance with differences, not only in skill, industry, and managerial efficiency, but also in the mechanical aids available to the worker. Some men, and some factories, would be more productive than others ; but Marx, together with other economists of his day, accepted the idea of a 'normal' — which he sometimes called an 'average' — output as determining the 'necessary labour-time', and therewith the 'value' of the product.

The phrase 'necessary labour-time' was, however, sometimes used by Marx in an essentially different sense. As we have seen, he laid down that a thing could not rank as a commodity at all unless it possessed 'use value', and was therefore (unless it could be had without limit for nothing) marketable so as to meet a human want. On this basis, Marx sometimes spoke of commodities produced in excess of market demand as having no 'value', despite the labour embodied in them, and of this labour as not being 'necessary labour'. This was in reality a recognition that demand conditions entered into the creation of values, not merely in the sense that 'use value' must be present in every commodity, but also in a quantitative sense. There was in this conception of 'necessary labour-time' the germ of a marginalist theory ; but it was neither developed nor recognised by Marx for what it was. Save in a few isolated passages, he meant by 'necessary labour-time' the time it would take an ordinary worker to make a thing, irrespective of the conditions of demand. His entire theory remained within the framework of the 'classical' conception of value ; and, as far as he was conscious of the later developments of orthodox theory, he dismissed them as mere 'vulgar Economics' which were limited to the superficial phenomena of capitalism and stopped short of penetrating beneath the appearances to the fundamental reality.

This, of course, does not prove Marx wrong ; for his purpose was not, like that of the modern orthodox economists, to study the workings of the price system : it was to expose capitalism as a system of class-exploitation. For this purpose there may be a use for such concepts as 'exchange value', distinguished from price, and for a study of the conditions of production in abstraction from those of market demand. But whereas it is clear nowadays that what Marx has to say about 'value' and 'surplus value' is entirely unrelated to the prices at which commodities are actually bought and sold, this neither was nor could be so apparent to his readers when the first volume of *Das Kapital* was published : nor is there in that volume anything to indicate that Marx himself was conscious of the gulf. Only in the posthumous third volume, which was not published until 1894, is it made plain that commodities are not in fact sold, and have no tendency to be sold, at prices corresponding to their values as Marx defines them. And even the chapters dealing with this question in Volume III reflect, in the account they give of the actual process of price determination, the views of John Stuart Mill rather than those of any later economist.

Marx, then, in *Das Kapital*, is using the concepts and the terminology of Ricardian Economics for his own purpose — that of exposing capitalism as a system of class-exploitation. He begins, as we have seen, with a sharp distinction between 'use values' and 'exchange values'. Each commodity has a specific use, and must have this in order to be a commodity at all — for the essence of being a commodity is that a thing shall be intended for sale, and no one can be expected to buy utterly useless things. That said, 'use value' in effect drops out of the discussion — though as we shall see it comes back at certain points later on. The concern of Marxism, as of classical Economics, is with 'exchange values' — that is, with the ratios of exchange between one kind of commodity and another. There must, Marx argues, be some property common to all commodities which makes possible the establishment of rates of exchange between them ; and this, he says, can be nothing else than that they are all products of human labour. This was not a specifically Marxian view : it was simply a reassertion of the Ricardian doctrine. So was the further assertion that, accordingly, the exchange values of different things depend on the relative amounts of labour incorporated in them.

Marxism, as a specific doctrine, begins only when the further concept of 'surplus value' is introduced. If the value of a thing corresponds to the amount of labour it embodies, why does not the labourer receive the whole product — or rather, why is not the entire product available for distribution among the labourers who have produced it ? Marx answers that the reason lies in the labourer being himself treated under capitalism as a commodity, and accordingly receiving no more than the equivalent of the amount of labour that has been used up in producing him — that is, than his subsistence, including the means of maintaining the supply of labourers by propagating his kind, and including also the equivalent of any special costs that have gone in equipping him with a particular kind of skill. Labour, like other commodities, is bought and sold in a competitive market on terms that depend on the conditions of its production. This does not mean that the labourer's actual wage is tied to a fixed level of subsistence — that was one of the issues on which Marx fell foul of Lassalle — for the higgling of the market may raise wages above or depress them below the labourer's cost of production. But, by and large, labour — or rather, in Marx's phrase, 'labour power' — tends to be bought and sold at an 'exchange value' which is essentially different from the exchange value of what the labourer produces ; and the difference between the value of 'labour power' and the value of the product constitutes what Marx calls 'surplus value'.

It should be explained at this point that Marx speaks throughout in terms, not of the product of any particular worker, or even of any particular kind of worker, but of what he terms 'abstract undifferentiated human labour'. Just as there is a property common to all commodities (in the ordinary sense) that enables them to be reduced to a common standard of value, so there is a common property in all labour. 'Abstract human labour' is not exactly unskilled labour, though coming near to it. Sometimes Marx calls it 'average labour' ; but more often he regards it as corresponding to the type of nearly unskilled labour which he thinks of as typical of the developing factory system and as destined more and more, with the advance of mechanisation, to supersede special kinds of skill. In the developed industrial areas, he says, most labour is already of this kind ; and he evidently expects the process to continue as capitalism expands further. All other forms of actual labour, he holds, can be measured in standard units of 'abstract labour', an hour's skilled labour counting as a multiple of an hour's labour of the simpler sort. Regarded in this manner, the whole labour force can be treated as a homogeneous mass of 'labour power' offered for sale in the labour market, and bought at a wage-level normally corresponding to the costs of its subsistence and of maintaining the supply. Trade Unions can affect wages, either by enabling particular groups of workers to get more than they could by individual bargaining, or by preventing the capitalist class from beating down the conventional subsistence level. For this level is not absolutely fixed — indeed, Marx thinks of it as tending to fall as the concentrated power of capitalism beats harder upon the workers in its efforts to escape from the 'contradictions' of capitalistic enterprise.

'Surplus value', then, is the difference between the cost of any given quantity of 'labour power' of this abstract sort, and the value of what this lump of labour produces. The reason why the capitalists are thus able to buy 'labour power' for less than the equivalent of its product lie in their possession of a monopolistic ownership of the means of production. In the historical chapters of Volume I Marx sets out to explain how this monopolistic position was established and developed. It arose, he says, out of the private ownership of land and was developed in its early stages mainly by means of the accumulated profits of mercantile and financial enterprise. Its other side was the increasing divorce of the working masses from the soil through enclosures and evictions, so that they lost all ownership or control of the means of production — a process which created a growing proletariat compelled to live by the sale of its labour power. The monopoly of ownership enabled the landowning and capitalist classes to appropriate to themselves all the benefits resulting from the advance in the powers of production — or, as Marx calls them in another passage, the economic gains of social co-operation — that is, of large-scale and mechanised enterprise. The capitalist law of wages, instead of making the workers participants in the increased output resulting from technical advance, holds the workers' share down to their cost of production, or near it, so that with the growth of productivity this share tends continually to decrease, and the amount of surplus value to expand. The workers, Marx explains, fight against this tendency towards greater and greater exploitation by struggling to reduce the standard hours of labour ; and they can achieve some success in this — witness the Ten Hours Act of 1847, which he never tired of citing. But the capitalists respond to these attempts to limit their appropriation of surplus value by driving the machines faster, so as to add to the intensity of the labour process. Marx, using his concept of 'abstract labour', treats such intensification as the crowding of more than an hour's such labour into an hour by the clock, and distinguishes it from increases in productivity brought about by improved techniques without imposing on the worker a heavier hourly task.

Under the general term 'surplus value' Marx grouped together every element in the receipts from the sale of commodities that did not pass to the labourer in the form of wages. He thus treated rent, interest, and profits — the classical trinity — as constituting parts of a single fund accruing to the possessing classes. In Volume I these two parts of value — what was paid out in wages, and surplus value — were left in simple contrast, as if the entire surplus value accrued to the owning classes for their own enjoyment or for investment in additional means of production. In his later volumes Marx refined on that thesis, mainly by drawing a distinction between productive and unproductive labour. In Marx's view only labour engaged in extractive or manufacturing industry, or in transporting goods from place to place, could create value. All other labour — clerical and administrative labour, all labour employed in distribution, as distinct from transport, in financial operations, or in personal services — was unproductive, and its cost had to be met out of surplus value. What accrued as spendable incomes to the owning classes was the total surplus value less the costs involved in its realisation, the latter including all the costs of bookkeeping, administration, distribution, and finance. This distinction, however, was not understood in Marx's lifetime : nor does it greatly affect his general view.

In correspondence with the division of all 'value' into 'wage' and 'surplus', Marx distinguished between two kinds of capital — 'constant' and 'variable'. 'Variable' capital is simply the sum paid out by the capitalists in wages to productive labour : 'constant' capital is all the rest. This distinction has nothing to do with that between 'fixed' and 'circulating' capital, used by orthodox economists and also occasionally by Marx. It is directly related to his belief that only labour — or rather some kinds of labour — can create value. Thus, he argues that whatever accrues to the capitalists as 'surplus value' must be derived exclusively from the part of their capital which they lay out on the purchase of productive labour, and that all other capital can do no more than transfer to the finished product the value of the productive labour already stored up in the buildings, instruments, or materials it is used to buy. Its value remains 'constant', whereas the value of capital spent on buying productive labour is 'variable' because the labour creates more value than the labourers receive back in wages. Accordingly, in Marx's system, all profits, all interest, and all rent have their source in the buying of labour power for less than the value it produces.

In reply to this view, as enunciated in Volume I, Marx's critics accused him of being absurd. If he were right, they said, it would pay employers to use as much labour and as little machinery as possible, because the more labour they used the more surplus value would they get. But it was evident that, in general, the greatest gains accrued to the capitalists who made the greatest use of machinery as a means of superseding labour or of replacing skilled by unskilled workers at a lower wage. Marx's answer to this argument was not fully presented until Volume III was published. He there drew a sharp distinction between the amount of surplus value that accrued to a capitalist in the first instance and the amount which the working of the capitalist system allowed him to keep for himself. The former, he contended, was derived solely from the 'variable' part of the capital ; but the profits realised by each individual capitalist would tend to be reduced to equality by the higgling of the competitive market, and this equal rate would necessarily be reckoned on the total capital used in the business, and not on the 'variable' capital alone. Thus the profits of the individual businesses depended, not on the amounts of surplus value they were able to extract, but on the conditions of the competitive struggle. It might well happen that a firm with a high ratio of 'variable' to 'constant' capital, and therefore with a high rate of 'surplus value', would be driven out of the market by a more highly mechanised firm, with a higher ratio of 'constant' capital. But Marx did not regard this as in any way affecting the validity of his theory.

I doubt if anyone reading only the first volume of *Das Kapital* could have known that this was what Marx meant, and I doubt if he himself fully realised the implications of his theory when he first advanced it. It is, however, not difficult to see why he regarded as unimportant the attacks which were made on it because of this apparent flying in the face of what was common knowledge. In reading *Das Kapital* it is necessary always to bear in mind the highly 'socialised' nature of his entire approach. As we have seen, he begins by reducing all the specifically different kinds of commodities — different in respect of their 'use values' — to a common category of lumps of exchange value. He then treats labour in the same way, reducing all the specific forms of labour to units of an un-differentiated mass of 'abstract labour'. Similarly, he treats all the individual capitalists as simply units in a single ex-ploiting capitalist class. This done, he proceeds to study, not the conditions governing the prices of particular com-modities or kinds of labour, nor the returns accruing to indi-vidual capitalists, but the general conditions of the division of the product of capitalist enterprise into wages of productive labour on the one hand and 'surplus value' on the other. He formulates no particular theory of wage differentials, or of profits, or interest, or rent. With such matters he is hardly concerned : what does concern him is the general class-relation-ship between possessing classes and workers, each treated as a sum of homogeneous units.

Thus he is no more dealing with the profit accruing to a particular capitalist than with the wage received by a particular worker, or group of workers. Indeed, in his treatment of wages, he is concerned to argue that the apparent differences between time-workers and piece-workers are not fundamental, and that all wages have a common, underlying character. Marx wishes to stress throughout the homogeneity, the fundamental solidarity, of the class, and to present a picture not so much of capitalism as it is, with many conflicting factions at work in every area, as of a quintessential capitalism in which every part of the system is carried to its logical conclusion and is seen operating *simpliciter*, according to the law of its own nature. This process of abstraction from the complexities of the real world is no less, and no more, legitimate in the form in which

Marx uses it than in the similar abstract constructions of the orthodox economists, the valid difference being that, whereas. the latter reduce everything to an atomism of individual market relations, Marx, at the other extreme, collectivises everything, and offers the model of an economic world in which abstract capital and abstract labour are the protagonists in a struggle for mastery.

What Marx was giving an account of, in his general theory of surplus value, was, then, not the exploitation of particular workers by particular capitalists, but the exploitation of the working class as a whole. But he did not, and could not, confine his analysis entirely to the global relations of the capitalist class and the workers ; for he needed to render an account of the processes by which surplus value was extracted, and this led him to examine the conditions of exploitation as they were affected by the different 'compositions of capital' in different businesses or at different times. By the 'composition of capital' Marx meant simply the proportion of the total capital of a business used in paying the wages of productive labour — 'variable' capital — to the capital used in other ways — 'constant capital'. He saw that, if he was right in holding that the 'variable' capital was the only source of surplus value, there would be a tendency for the *rate* of surplus value in relation to total capital to fall as workers, or skilled workers, were increasingly replaced by machines. If, however, mechanisation increased the productivity of labour, the *amount* of surplus value would tend to rise as fewer hours of labour were required to cover the workers' subsistence needs. The capitalist would thus be compensated for the fall in the proportion of his total capital yielding surplus value by a rise in the 'rate of exploitation' — that is, in the proportion of the workers' product surplus to the cost of labour power. Thus the advance of mechanisation would give back, on account of rising productivity, what it threatened to take away by increasing the proportion of 'constant' to 'variable' capital.

Marx, following up a notorious statement made by Nassau Senior in opposing the reduction of hours, in which Senior had asserted that the capitalist's profit was made out of the product of the 'last hour', expressed his conception of the exploitation of the workers in terms of a distinction between 'paid' and 'unpaid' hours of labour. The 'paid' hours were those during which the workers produced the equivalent of their subsistence wages : the 'unpaid' hours were those during which they continued to work beyond this limit, creating surplus value for which they received no return. As productivity rose, the number of 'paid' hours fell ; and the number of 'unpaid' hours increased unless the workers were able to win a reduction in the total length of the working day. If they did win such a reduction the hours no longer worked were lopped off the surplus value accruing to the capitalists, and the capitalists' only expedient was to increase the intensity of the work required during each working hour. The capitalists, faced with a continuous tendency towards greater mechanisation, which they could not resist without being worsted in the competitive struggle for profit, had to alter the 'composition' of capital in such a way as to render the 'constant' capital a larger proportion of the total. This benefited them, despite the narrowing of the proportion from which surplus value could be drawn, because of the great increase in total production which resulted from it, and because of the reduction it made possible in the 'paid' labour time. But mechanisation also required a greatly enlarged total capital, which was provided out of the surplus value which was not used for the consumption of the capitalist class ; and in this situation, despite the increase in the total mass of surplus value, the *rate* of profit, measured on total capital, had, Marx thought, a tendency to fall — a tendency accentuated by any success in reducing the total length of the working day.

The whole of this complicated argument took its shape from Marx's initial assumption that, because value could be created only by labour, only capital used in paying productive labour could generate surplus value. But it was necessary to admit, as an obvious fact, that the profits reaped by particular capitalists were derived from the difference between their total costs of production and the sums realised from the sale of their output, and that in this connection the 'composition' of the capital of any particular business was without relevance except through its effect on unit costs. This being so, the entire concept of surplus value would have been left in the air if Marx had been talking about the same problems as the orthodox economists ; and these economists, seeing this, dismissed his whole system as nonsensical, because quite unrelated to the facts of the market. But neither Marx nor his followers were in any way moved by the numerous refutations of Marxism in which this argument was employed. The whole Marxist set of concepts was accepted as the theoretical foundation of the Social Democratic movement which developed in the 'seventies and 'eighties, first in Germany and then in other countries. It became a faith, as well as an economic theory ; and, as it rested on certain fundamental affirmations which could be neither proved nor disproved by comparing them with the actual phenomena of the capitalist market, the Marxists and the orthodox economists for the most part went their several ways, denouncing each other's basic assumptions, but unable to come to grips in argument because they were talking about essentially different things.

The assertion that labour is the sole source and measure of value would be subject to verification or disproof, at any rate in part, if 'value', as used in this connection, had any relation to market price such as Ricardo supposed it to possess. It is simply untrue that the amount of labour incorporated in a commodity is the sole determinant of its market price, or even of a 'normal price' at which it tends to be sold when supply and demand are in balance. For one thing, the 'amount of labour' is a highly abstract concept — for no one has ever satisfactorily explained how different kinds of labour can be reduced to units of 'abstract, undifferentiated labour' without begging the question by taking the actual wage differences between one kind of labour and another as a basis for the measurement. For another thing, as Ricardo himself recognised, the period over which capital has to be locked up in the process of production affects the price at which a commodity can be sold without loss — or rather, it does so in any system in which interest has to be paid on the capital employed or investment in the means of production is made for the purpose of profit. That is to say, the time factor in payment for the use of money or capital resources affects selling prices under any form of capitalist enterprise. Thirdly, the costs of production are only one factor in determining the prices at which commodities are sold ; and the costs relevant in this connection are not all the costs, but only the costs incurred at or near the 'margin' of production.

None of these facts, however, can be adduced in disproof of a theory of 'values' which has no connection at all with the prices at which things are bought and sold. There is no way of either proving or disproving the contention that labour is the only source of 'value' if 'value' means simply that of which labour is the source. 'Value', in this sense, cannot be measured. Indeed, Marx himself denies that under developed capitalist conditions any labourer has a measurable product of his own ; and presumably this applies to groups of workers employed in particular establishments or industries as well as to the individual workmen. There is, in effect, according to Marx, only a single great mass of value generated by productive labour as a whole, and incapable of being broken up so as to assign definite parts of it to particular producing units.

The entire gigantic construction of the Marxian theory of value turns out, then, to be neither more nor less than a set of variations on the general theme that the labouring class is exploited because a part of the product of industry accrues to non-workers, who are able to appropriate this part by virtue of their monopoly of ownership of the means of production — a monopoly which allows them to deny the workers access to the means of life except on terms which will yield a return to the owning classes. It did not need Marx's Economics to enable such a theory of class-exploitation to be formulated ; and in sober truth Marx added nothing to it except a number of complications which arose mainly out of his attempt to hitch his theory of surplus value on to the Ricardian value theory that he found accepted by the capitalist economists of his own day — or rather of the period during which he was working out his own doctrine. The whole Marxian theory of value, stripped of its Ricardian trappings and of the complications into which Marx was led by his attempt to refine upon the conclusions of his anti-capitalist predecessors, amounts to the very simple assertion that under capitalism the owning classes appropriate a part of the product of industry and agriculture without working for it, and that this involves the exploitation of the subject labour class. Perhaps to this should be added the assertion that as productivity increases, the owning classes are able to appropriate a growing proportion of the total output, because the proportion needed to provide for the workers' subsistence and reproduction is reduced.

But though the gigantic superstructure of the Marxian theory of value really adds nothing to these simple assertions, that does not mean that it failed to serve Marx's purpose. On the contrary, it was highly effective. It gave the leaders of the working class in the countries to which its influence extended a sense of having reason as well as justice on their side. It seemed to fulfil a vital part of Marx's requirement that Socialism should be formulated, not as an utopian aspiration, but as a scientific doctrine. It provided a formidable logically constructed system which was proof against any arguments that could be brought against it by anyone who rejected its basic assumptions ; and it successfully obscured the fact that these assumptions themselves were neither proved nor capable of proof or objective verification such as scientific method ordinarily requires. It served, indeed, as a powerful stimulus to belief and to action, and in this pragmatic sense it was as 'true' as it needed to be for the purpose in view. I am not suggesting in the least that Marx was conscious that at bottom his whole theoretical system of Economics rested on belief and not upon scientific demonstration : plainly, he believed in his own system and put it forward in entire good faith, quite unaware that its claim to be 'scientific' was really bogus, and that it was not even a usable hypothesis that could be tested by the facts, but a call to action based on unproven belief.

To call such a theoretical structure 'scientific' is really an entire misnomer. It is in truth a gigantic metaphysical construction, quite unrelated to any statement or hypothesis that can be tested or verified. There is no way in which it is possible to check or verify the statement that the values of commodities depend on the amounts of labour incorporated in them unless these 'values' can be measured by some other test. If the prices of commodities bear no settled relation to their 'values', the whole structure of values is removed from the sphere of actual exchanges and subsists only in a metaphysical vacuum. Neither Marx nor his critics saw this at the time when his doctrine was advanced because most economists did then suppose that there was a real phenomenon of 'normal price', corresponding to normal value, at which things tended to be bought and sold under conditions of equilibrium between the forces of supply and demand. Marx's 'value' stemmed from this classical conception of 'exchange value' equalling 'normal price'. But this conception did not fit Marx's analysis, because he was not prepared to regard all forms of labour as 'productive', and was concerned in particular to deny that stored labour (constant capital) could give rise to 'surplus value'. Accordingly he found himself forced, when he came to face the question in Volume III, to cut the values of commodities entirely away from their selling prices. This left his theory of value out of all contact with anything that could be measured empirically : it involved postulating 'value' as a theoretically measurable, but practically quite unmeasurable entity. Such a conception can no doubt be regarded — as it has been by successive generations of Marxists — as making sense ; but such sense as it makes is certainly not the sense of 'science' in any now recognised use of that most unprecise term. Marx, in the final form of his theory of value, was talking metaphysics and not science ; and it is a curious paradox that this least scientific — because least verifiable — part of his social theory should have attracted, and should continue to attract, so many natural scientists who would put up with nothing at all analogous to it in the practice of their own disciplines.

Professor Tawney, I think, once spoke of Marx as 'the last of the schoolmen'. Unfortunately, he was by no means the last ; but the thrust goes home. Was it also Professor Tawney who said that he did not need the theory of surplus value to tell him that the capitalists exploited the workers ? Yet that, in effect, was what the theory did proclaim — that, and nothing besides. At the time when Marx formulated it, however, as a refinement on the earlier theories of Thomas Hodgskin, John Francis Bray, and a number of other 'Ricardian' Socialists, it seemed to do much more than this, because it accepted as a starting-point what orthodox economists were then saying about 'value', and proceeded on this basis to demonstrate the exploitation of labour out of their very mouths.

But, of course, *Das Kapital* — I mean Volume I — contains very much besides the theory of value elaborated in the opening chapters. These chapters themselves cover a great many matters besides the formulation of the theory of surplus value. For example, Chapter 4, 'The General Formula for Capital', embodies Marx's attempt to define the characteristic structure of capitalist production in the light of its historical development. 'The modern history of capital', Marx says at the beginning of this chapter, 'dates from the creation in the sixteenth century of a world-embracing commerce and a world-embracing market. . . . As a matter of history, capital, as opposed to landed property, invariably takes at first the form of money : it appears as money-wealth, as the capital of the merchant and of the usurer.' He then goes on to say that this characteristic persists in the developed capitalist system, in the sense that all *new* capital continues to come into existence as money, which is then transformed into real capital when it is used to buy productive assets. From this characterisation of the working of capitalism he derives his 'general formula' — M—C—M. For the pre-capitalist individual or family producer, the process of production for exchange begins with the making of a saleable commodity, which is then turned into money, the money being thereafter used to buy some different commodity, or commodities, which the producer needs. Thus, says Marx, the formula for pre-capitalist production for the market is C—M—C (Commodity—Money—Commodity). As against this, the capitalist entrepreneur begins with a stock of money which he uses to employ labour in making commodities, the latter being thereafter sold for money : the formula is inverted, and becomes M—C—M. There could, however, be no point in going through the process of production if at the end the capitalist merely got back the money he had originally laid out. He would not set the wheels in motion unless he expected to get back more than he had laid out. Accordingly, the working of capitalism depends on the final 'M' in this formula standing for a larger sum of money than the 'M' with which the process began. The true general formula for capital is M—C—M', when M' stands for M + ΔM — that is, for an increment which represents the capitalist's gain.

I have cited this rather elaborate formulation because Marxists make frequent use of it. The essence of what Marx is saying is that the rise of capitalism transforms production from a single process of exchange of commodity for commodity, with money serving merely as a convenient medium of exchange, into a complex process in which the commodities produced cease to be ends and become mere means to money-making. Thus, the capitalist as such is not concerned primarily with producing either directly to satisfy his own needs or to procure the means of satisfying his own needs by exchange. He is essentially a money-maker, for whom production is worth while only if it brings in a money profit. This appears most plainly in the case of the merchant, the earliest form of typical capitalist. The merchant begins with a stock of money : he lays this out on goods, which he then seeks to sell for more than they cost him. In the system of industrial capitalism the process is more complicated, because the industrialist appears primarily as an owner of physical productive resources — buildings, machinery, and materials — which he uses for the production of commodities with the aid of hired labour. But the underlying situation is still the same. The capitalist begins with money, which he lays out partly on physical productive resources and partly on hired labour. His aim is to regain, over a period, not only the money he has laid out, but also an increment, which is his profit. In some cases, however, the owner of money, instead of laying it out in these ways, lends it at interest, again with the object of getting back more than he lent. In these cases the commodity disappears altogether from the process, and the general formula for interest-bearing capital is simply M—M′— that is, from Money to More Money, without any intermediate term.

Marx is here answering those who argue that the intervention of the capitalist in no significant way alters the simple exchange relation expressed in the formula C—M—C. Orthodox economists have often begun their exposition with an account of the process of exchange as it occurs in a street market in a country town. Producers arrive and lay out their wares, which they sell one to another, using money as a convenient means of exchanging goods for goods. Each participant, under normal conditions, reaps an advantage from the exchange, in the sense that at the end of the day he has got what is of more use to him than what he has sold in exchange for it. There need, however, have been in such a case no gain in terms of money values by anyone — or rather, such gains and the corresponding losses will have been accidental, due to faulty judgment or temporary glut or scarcity of particular products, or the like. Orthodox economists who began with the description of such a market usually went on to say that the great competitive market of capitalism followed the same law, giving each participant, apart from accident, not only a fair equivalent for what he had to sell, but also a real gain in the utility, or use value, which he acquired. As against this, Marx argued that the great capitalist market is operated on a totally different principle, because each seller is aiming, not at a gain in use value, but at a money gain, and this gain must be realised at someone else's expense.

At whose, then ? Marx begins by demolishing the view that the capitalists' gains are derived from selling their wares for more than they are worth. If this were so, he says, they would to a great extent only be cheating one another ; for every transaction would involve a loss as well as a gain. Commodities, he says, are on the whole, and apart from temporary higglings of the market, sold for what they are worth. The capitalists' gains, save in special cases of monopoly, come not from overcharging the buyers, but from some quite different source. This source is their ability, because of their monopoly control of the means of production, to buy 'labour power' at its commodity value, and to appropriate the difference between the value of 'labour power' and the value produced by labour. So we find ourselves back again, by another route, at the theory of surplus value of which we have already taken account.

The essential difference between the simple country-town exchange market and the great market of capitalism is that in the former the individual producer first produces what he can with his own and his family's labour and then gets what he can in exchange for it, whereas in the latter production is not embarked upon at all, or labour employed, unless the capitalist sees a prospect of making a profit. It cannot pay the individual producer to refrain from producing, nor has he any control over what his produce will fetch in terms either of money or of other goods he needs. But it may very well pay the capitalist to refrain for a time from producing at all, or to cut down his production, when the market fails to offer him a sufficiently profitable prospect. Therefore, says Marx, the capitalist mode of production leads straight to unemployment, to intermittent employment and insecurity, and to recurrent crises which lay whole economies prostrate and compel the workers to go without goods they could make for mutual exchange did not the capitalist monopoly of access to the means of production bar the way.

Marx, however, was not an 'under-consumptionist'. He did not attribute the instability of capitalist production to capitalist restrictionism in face of a limited consumers' market. He scouted the notion that the maintenance of higher wage-levels could prevent business crises by increasing the consuming power of the mass of the people. He did indeed count among the final 'contradictions of capitalism' its tendency to expand the means of production beyond the absorptive power of the consumers' market, and he did look to socialised production to overcome this contradiction and to remove the limits on the expansion of productive power. But he also argued against those who regarded low wages as the cause of crises that, in fact, crises usually broke out when wages were exceptionally high; and he was emphatic that no redistribution of the product in the interest of the workers, even if it were possible, could prevent the recurrence of crises as long as the capitalist system remained in being. The real cause of crises he believed to lie in the inherent tendency of capital to accumulate on a vaster and vaster scale. This tendency towards accumulation he regarded as an inescapable part of the capitalist system, with its continual drive towards money-making. The extraction of a large share in the product as 'surplus value' by the possessing classes meant, in his view, that these classes would be in perpetual search of profitable openings for the use of the money they did not wish to spend on personal consumption. Technical progress would provide an outlet for part of this accumulation in the provision of improved instruments of production. These would result in changes in the 'composition' of capital, reducing the proportion of 'variable' to 'constant' capital and therewith displacing labour in favour of more and more complex machines. But this process would carry with it an expansion in the scale and in the total amount of production, because the new machines would be profitable only if more was produced with their aid. Moreover, even if the new machines steadily displaced older machines, by driving their owners out of the competitive market, only investment on an ever-increasing scale, involving a rapid expansion of total productive power, would suffice to absorb the funds for which the capitalists were seeking profitable uses. Accordingly, Marx argued, there was endemic in capitalism a tendency to expand productive resources faster than the market for their products could possibly expand ; and this was bound to bring about crises whenever the market was glutted with the output of the new or improved factories. The great commercial crises which recurred at intervals of about ten years were attributed by Marx chiefly to this cause. When a crisis occurred, the effect was to drive a great many existing productive enterprises into bankruptcy, and painfully to restore the balance by removing their output from the market. This achieved, the whole process started over again. In his second volume Marx went into much fuller detail about the sequence of events from crisis to recovery and thence to renewed crisis, attempting to relate the duration of the 'cycle' to the period required for the new capital instruments brought into being during the period of revival to make their full impact on the market. This, however, was only a secondary aspect of his theory : the essential element in it was that capitalism, by its very nature as a system based on the exploitation of 'labour-power', had a necessary tendency to accumulate capital resources faster than the market could absorb their products.

Of course, Marx also pointed out that the consequences of this tendency could be held in check by the finding of additional markets, and adduced this as the main reason for the capitalist insistence on exports and on the opening up to trade of the less developed parts of the world, in which the surplus products of the advanced countries could be either sold in exchange for foodstuffs or materials or invested with a view to future returns. He held that this had been happening in his own day in such a fashion as to enable the capitalism of the advanced countries to stave off the doom that would otherwise have overtaken it. But all this part of his doctrine, including the entire question of the relation of advanced capitalism to Economic Imperialism, was developed so much further after his death — especially by Lenin — that it would be anachronistic to discuss it all fully here.

It will be seen that Marx, far from stressing the restrictionist aspects of capitalism, was insistent on its essentially expansionist character. He regarded it as incapable of survival except under conditions which would allow it to expand at an ever-increasing rate. This, indeed, followed from his view that wages were held down to a level dependent on the labourer's 'cost of production', and that increasing productivity was therefore bound to mean that the labourer would receive a diminishing fraction of the total product. Even if the rate of profit measured on the total capital must tend to fall with increasing mechanisation, he saw the total *mass* of surplus value as tending to grow at a faster and faster rate, the efforts of the workers to reduce the hours of unpaid labour being quite inadequate to prevent this, though they might succeed in reducing the hours of labour enough to check the tendency in some degree.

Marx was always vehement against those who argued that Trade Unions were powerless in face of any 'iron law' regulating the distribution of the product. But he was well aware that their power had narrow limits, for two main reasons : first, because advancing capitalism was continually substituting machines for workers, and thus throwing large numbers out of work ; and, secondly, because whenever a crisis occurred one effect of it was to undermine Trade Union power and to enable the capitalists to take back at any rate a part of any concessions they had been forced to make while the level of employment was high. Marx laid great stress on the necessary tendency of capitalism to build up a 'reserve army' of workers, which it could employ when trade was good and throw aside as soon as a slump occurred. He saw how these reserve workers were drawn from the countryside to the industrial areas in times of high employment, and how they served to prevent wages from rising as fast as productive power increased. At the same time, he saw how rising population in the industrialised countries both provided the capitalists with more labour-power to exploit and prevented the growth of any effective 'monopoly' of labour.

In *Das Kapital*, the analysis of the working of contemporary capitalism preceded the historical chapters, in which Marx traced and illustrated the phases of its growth. These historical chapters, which occupy much more than half the volume, form the unquestionably masterly part of Marx's work. Whatever criticisms can be advanced against his formulation of the theory of value and surplus value, on the ground that this part of his doctrine rests on the quicksands of an obsolete Ricardian dogma, no one to-day can question that the historical part of Volume I has accomplished a far-reaching transformation in historical approach and method, or that the account Marx gives of the growth of capitalist society is in all its essential features broadly correct. Needless to say, later research has thrown much additional light on the social and economic history of the Western world over the centuries which Marx rapidly traversed in these chapters ; but it was he who, above anyone else, gave the impetus to these researches, and their general effect has been to consolidate, rather than to supersede, the conclusions at which he arrived.

I do not propose, in the present volume, to attempt to summarise what is itself a masterly summary of the history of Western Capitalism up to the early part of the nineteenth century. The distinction Marx drew between the Merchant Capitalism of the opening phases and the Industrial Capitalism which was superimposed on it in the age of the great inventions is now generally accepted ; and so is the analysis of the increasing part played by finance as an independent business power, with the hints Marx threw out, to be developed by later writers, of the coming of an age of Finance Capitalism with the growing concentration and centralisation of economic power.

Nothing analogous to much in these chapters could have been written at any earlier period. Like Engels before him, Marx made great use of the mass of official information about economic and social affairs that was poured out in ever-increasing volume in Great Britain during the second quarter of the nineteenth century, and especially after the Reform Act of 1832. Marx and Engels owed much to such men as Edwin Chadwick, who combined with a belief in the virtues of 'free, capitalist enterprise' a matchless zeal in exposing its defects. The working of capitalism could not have been convincingly and realistically described without the aid of these officially vouched - for first - hand accounts from Factory Inspectors, Mines Inspectors, Commissioners of many kinds, and painstaking Civil Servants who made it their task to collect and record the facts. But it was Marx who, above all other students, used these indispensable materials to found, if not a new subject, at any rate a new way of handling an old subject and thus giving it an immensely wider significance. Of course, Marx's inspiration to do this — and Engels's before him — came from their conception of history. In the historical chapters of *Das Kapital* Marx was consciously applying his Materialist Conception of History to the study of the rise of capitalism in the West, and was writing, not a specialised economic history as a supplement to the general history of the period he covered, but a fundamental history on which future general histories would need to be based. He was taking the economic factor as the unifying element in the development of the Western countries since the Renaissance and the Reformation, and was showing by example how this factor had been primary in settling the course of evolution in the West as a whole. Even those who refuse to accept the Materialist Conception of History as a valid guide to the entire development of the human race can hardly deny that, for the period and for the area with which Marx was dealing, the use of this conception threw a great new light on the course of events, or that his contribution was, in this respect, supremely important. For this purpose, at any rate, the Materialist Conception of History triumphantly *worked* — not so as to explain every event, or so as to exclude the operation of other causes, but as providing the indispensable key to an otherwise often unintelligible sequence of historical changes which were transforming the lives of men. On this score alone, *Das Kapital* must rank as one of the very great books of the nineteenth century ; and it is perhaps fair to suggest that its masterly handling of the historical forces has contributed to gain an undue acceptance for the much more questionable chapters in which Marx worked out his theoretical exposition of economic doctrine.

The later volumes of *Das Kapital*, to which so far incidental reference has been made only when this was necessary in order to elucidate the meaning of Volume I, are of very much less significance. Indeed, the most that can be said for them is that they elaborate Marx's fundamental theory at a number of points, without adding to it anything of really primary importance. Marx's failure to publish either of them in his lifetime has usually been attributed to ill-health ; and this may indeed have been the cause. But the second volume was in draft and at an advanced stage of revision not long after the first appeared ; and it is hardly fanciful to suggest that its non-appearance may have been due in part to Marx's dissatisfaction with it, and to his fear of an anti-climax. As for the third volume, which is of much greater importance than the second, it is, as we have seen already, less a finished book than a great gathering of material from the mass of manuscripts, written at widely separated dates, which Engels inherited at his friend's death.

The first part of Volume III, in which Marx discusses the relation between 'surplus value' and profit, and therewith between 'values' and prices, does indeed constitute a finished piece of work, and one which is a necessary complement to Volume I. In subsequent sections the discussions on interest-bearing capital and on land-rent are interesting in themselves and provide important secondary elaborations of Marx's central doctrines. But as the volume proceeds, to a length of well over a thousand pages, the reader gradually becomes aware that it is leading up to no conclusions, and is, in effect, petering out rather than coming to an end. In particular, the vitally important chapter on economic classes is left as a mere beginning, with the problems hardly posed, and no approach to a solution. Volume I, with all its limitations and shortcomings, is a living book with a shape and a clear purpose clearly expressed. Volume II is a vast excursus on a particular aspect, embodying an important study of the causes of economic crises. Volume III is a torso, with the head missing.

It can never be known to what extent Marx's failure to bring his general scheme to a successful conclusion was the outcome not only of the author's ill-health and of the troubles that beset him despite Engels's unfailing generosity, but also of a weakness inherent from the beginning in his entire plan of work. Marx, when he began writing *Das Kapital*, could not have known, unless he had hit on the discovery for himself, that capitalist Economics were to take well before he had finished a turn away from the classical theories which he, in common with most of his contemporaries, took for granted as giving a broadly correct description of how capitalism worked and of the laws governing the production and distribution of wealth under capitalistic conditions. He could not have known that his system would come to be, not, as he had intended, a critique of the accepted orthodoxy leading to radically different conclusions, but a structure divorced from all contact with the Political Economy of capitalism, in the new shape given to it by the English and Austrian exponents of the notion of marginal utility. He could not have known that what he wrote down as statements of unquestioned truths, common to himself and to his opponents, would come, because of their abandonment by the orthodox, to appear as distinctively Marxian notions — as happened in the case of the labour theory of value. Marxian Economics, as distinct from Marxian Economic History, came, as orthodox Economics took a new turn, to be really a period piece. But Marx, having formulated his general theory in terms taken over from the Ricardians, found himself quite unable to adapt it to the subsequent developments of orthodox theory, or to take any account of these developments within the framework he had made for his writing. Because of this, he was scornful of the developments in orthodox theory that he was unable to fit into his scheme ; and he simply ignored them.

There was, however, more than this in Marx's failure to develop his system into a finished structure. It does really seem as if, after observing with the greatest acuteness the development of capitalism up to the middle of the nineteenth century, he ceased thereafter to make any realistic appraisal of the actual movement of events. Thus, he continued to reckon on the continuing erosion of the *petite bourgeoisie*, as standing for obsolescent methods of small-scale production, without ever making allowance for the importance of the new *petite bourgeoisie* that was being created by the advance of large-scale industry with its increasing host of managerial and administrative employees. In *Theories of Surplus Value* we find him criticising Ricardo for failing to take note of 'the steady growth of the middle classes standing between the workers on the one hand and the capitalists and landlords on the other' and pointing out that the growth of these classes 'enhances the security and power of the upper ten thousand'. But he describes these growing elements in society as 'for the most part supported directly from revenues which fall as a burden on the labour base' of the social structure. That is to say, he regards them, not as positive contributors to production, but solely as extractors of surplus value. This, of course, squares with his refusal to assign any value-creating quality to the labour of the active capitalist; but this very refusal blinds him to the importance of the development of a new middle class consisting not only of shareholders or rentiers, but also to a great extent of active supervisory workers, technicians and managers in the service of large-scale industry. He continued, too, to predict the progressive disappearance of skilled labour without ever seeing to what an extent new forms of skill, based on advanced machine techniques, were arising to take the place of the old. He continued to speak of the 'increasing misery' of the proletariat even when standards of living were manifestly getting better for the majority of the workers; and he continued to predict the increasing supersession of the petty capitalist when the development of the joint-stock company was already creating a new host of small investors whose stake was in large-scale production of the most advanced kind.

This amounts to saying that Marx stopped thinking fundamentally about the development of capitalism when he had finished writing Volume I of *Das Kapital*, and that his later economic writings are rather excrescences on what he had then written than products of any direct study of subsequent events. *Das Kapital* as a whole in effect refers to the capitalist system as it had developed up to about the middle of the nineteenth century, and for the most part ignores what happened to it during the latter part of its author's own life. To this point we shall have to come back when the time comes to consider the great 'revisionist' controversy stirred up by Eduard Bernstein in the 1890s, and again when we have to deal with the development of Marxism in Russia during the present century. For the present we are concerned with the contribution which *Das Kapital* made to the Marxist revival of the 1870s and 1880s, after the First International had melted away in the reactionary heat generated by the Paris Commune. What Marx contributed at this stage was an impressive — not to say a massive — reformulation and rationalisation of a large body of earlier Socialist economic theory, together with a startlingly new and cogent presentation of the economic and social history of capitalism, which added greatly to the prestige of the general theory of historical evolution on which it was based.

Marx's last years, after the collapse of the International, were a period of increasing ill-health which interfered seriously with his work, despite the relief from financial troubles afforded to him by the generous help of Engels. Unable to bring the later volumes of *Das Kapital* to a satisfactory completion, he worked away energetically, whenever he could, amassing fresh knowledge, especially about Russia and South-Eastern Europe. He learnt Serbian as well as Russian, and took a deep interest in the Turkish question. The success of his book in Russian intellectual circles led him to concentrate a great deal of his attention on Russia, to which his hopes of early revolution had been transferred after it had become evident that no speedy uprising was to be looked for in the West. Among Marx's latest writings was the preface which he wrote for a new Russian translation of the *Communist Manifesto*, made by Vera Zasulich, and published in Geneva in 1882. Marx there raised the question whether, as most of the leaders of Russian Socialism claimed, what was left of the system of peasant communism in the Russian villages could be used as the foundation for a new Socialist structure, so that Russia would not need to pass through all the stages of capitalistic development that had been traversed in Western Europe. His answer, though hesitant, was very different from that which he would have made at any earlier period. He began by insisting on the immensity of the changes that had come about in Russia since 1848, when the *Manifesto* had not deemed it necessary even to refer to that country in describing the outlook and policy of the proletariat in the various parts of Europe. In 1848 the European reactionaries had proclaimed the Czar as their chief and had relied on his aid to save them from proletarian revolution. But now (in 1882), says Marx, the Czar, at Gatchina, is the prisoner of the revolution, sheltering from the assassins who menace his life ; and 'Russia constitutes the advance-guard of the European revolutionary movement'. Marx then referred to the feverish speed with which capitalism was developing in Russia, including a rapid growth of capitalistic forms of landed property, and observed that, side by side with these innovations, 'the peasants possess in common more than half the land'.

A question accordingly arises. Can Russian peasant communism, can this already much-disintegrated form of the primitive common ownership of the land, be transformed directly into a higher communistic form of landed property ? Or will it have first to undergo the same process of dissolution as appears in the historical evolution of the West ?

The only possible answer that can be made at the present time is this. If the Russian revolution becomes the signal for a working-class revolution in the West, so that the two revolutions complement each other, the existing communal property in Russia can become the starting point for a communistic evolution.

These oft-quoted sentences were taken at the time as implying Marx's support of the Narodnik thesis discussed in a previous chapter, and as an endorsement both of the policy of concentrating in Russian revolutionary activity mainly on the peasants, and even of the revolutionary terrorism which, in Marx's words, had made the Czar 'the prisoner of the revolution'. Only after Marx's death was the battle sharply joined in Russia between his followers and the Narodniks, and Russian Socialism split between the westernising Social Democrats and the much larger movement which rested on the efforts of the intellectuals to stir up revolutionary feeling among the peasant masses.

Marx's wife, to whom he was very deeply attached, died of cancer in the year in which this preface appeared, and Marx himself had a serious illness from which he never really rallied. He died the following year, leaving Engels to carry on his work for another dozen years.

It has often been made a matter for argument how far Engels was merely Marx's friend and faithful disciple, or how far he played a significant part in the making of what is everywhere known as Marxism. Engels himself always attributed the leadership to Marx, and credited him with the main share in the authorship of their common doctrine. In the field of theoretical Economics this is evidently true, even though Engels, in 1843, had written the long article which furnished Marx with his first impetus towards the study and criticism of classical economic theory. Marx, and not Engels, constructed out of materials drawn from Adam Smith and Ricardo and from their earlier anti-capitalist critics, the vast system of Socialist economic theory which takes up the greater part of the three volumes of *Das Kapital*. Marx, too, seems to have been mainly responsible for working out the Materialist Conception of History on the basis of his earlier Hegelian studies of social evolution ; but in this field it is much more difficult to assign the two men their respective shares, because they were living and working daily together during a large part of the time when this part of their joint theory was taking shape. On the whole, we must take Engels's word for it that the major contribution came from Marx ; but at the least Engels's share was considerable, as the works which they wrote together while they were clearing their minds plainly reveal. It was, however, always Marx who gave the doctrine in this part of the field its final shape. After 1848 Engels had unquestionably a large share in the works in which they sought to apply their historical conceptions to the analysis of the forces which led to the defeat of the European revolutionary movement ; and in this field of politico-economic criticism Engels's contribution has to be reckoned as fully equal to that of Marx. Indeed, in dealing with contemporary developments the two were plainly on an equality, as their correspondence is amply enough to show.

Military matters had a fascination for Engels, and Marx always deferred to him in this respect. But the principal field in which the undoubted leadership lay with Engels was that of the physical sciences and of the application to them of the dialectical method. Marx himself, after his general theory had taken shape in his mind, wrote hardly anything about method, except in the retrospective introduction to the *Critique of Political Economy*, where he was explaining how he had arrived at his way of approach to social and economic questions. Engels, on the other hand, wrote largely on the subject, both in the series of articles republished in book form as *Anti-Dühring* and elsewhere — particularly in the unfinished work issued as *Dialectics of Nature* long after his death. No great attention was paid to his writings on this theme while he was alive : indeed, the latter part of *Anti-Dühring* was relegated from the main part of the Leipzig *Vorwaerts* to a scientific supplement, after the earlier articles had been subject to much criticism inside the German Social Democratic Party, largely on the ground that they were above the heads of most of the paper's readers and of too little general interest to deserve the space they occupied. Engels's writings on the Dialectic and on its relation to the physical sciences came into favour only at a much later date — mainly after the Russian Revolution of 1917 had set the victorious Bolsheviks the problem of making an entirely new society on Marxian foundations, and had raised in an immediate and practical way the problem of the theoretical basis of the new order over the entire field of human knowledge. Outside Russia too the rapid pace of scientific advance, above all in the arts of war, and the increasingly powerful impact of science on every aspect of social life had set scientists to philosophising more and more actively — though not always deeply — about the relation of physical science to the entire structure of human thought and institutions ; and it was natural that scientists who turned to Socialism should wish to discover a philosophy of science that would fit in with their Socialist convictions. Marxism had a particular attraction for many natural scientists because it professed to stand for the application of scientific method to the social field ; and many scientists who encountered Marxism first as an economic or political doctrine went on to enquire into its applicability to the natural sciences themselves. Engels's long-neglected scientific writings then came into fashion, bringing back with them the Dialectic, which in the West had receded far into the background of Socialist thinking, where it had not been discarded altogether.

Only a part of *Anti-Dühring* is directly concerned with natural science, or with the Dialectic in relation to it. The book includes a long section on Political Economy, to which Marx contributed a chapter, and also a substantial section dealing with the history and theory of Socialism. The economic section is a very readable introduction to Marxian economic theory, and includes an important chapter in which Engels replies to Dühring's assertion that political, and not economic, factors are the main moving forces in history ; and the section on Socialism contains an excellent simple summary of the Materialist Conception. The references to natural science come mainly in the opening chapters, in which Engels is first delivering a frontal attack on Dühring's philosophy, which was a blend of metaphysics and positivism, with strong Hegelian influences imperfectly digested. They recur in the chapters in which Engels is answering Dühring's attack on Marx's use of dialectical method and phraseology.

In effect, what Engels is arguing throughout these chapters is that natural science is necessarily dialectical because it is concerned with the study, not of static objects regarded as independent one of another, but of motions and interactions. When things are studied as static and independent of other things, contradictions are excluded, precisely because this kind of study is dealing with abstractions. As soon as things are considered under the aspect of force and motion, and as influencing and influenced by other things, or rather by other forces and motions, what Engels calls 'contradictions' are found at every turn ; for everything is in process of becoming what it was not. Moreover, both the natural sciences and mathematics furnish examples of 'contradictions' on which men have based successful manipulation of the forces of nature. Engels argues that the entire calculus, which is the root of higher mathematics and of mathematical physics, rests on the contradiction that a very small quantity of a thing — a quantity so small as to be negligible — equals no quantity at all. He also contends that chemical classification furnishes examples in which the basis of qualitative differences is found to be quantitative ; for quite different substances are found to differ only in the number of atoms of different sorts of which they are made up, without any variation in the proportions. The dialectically boiling kettle is invoked, as it has been so often, in support of the view that qualitative differences can be reduced by analysis to differences of quantity — and so on.

Of course, Engels made no claim that either he and Marx, or Hegel, had invented dialectical method. On the contrary, he insisted that, in thinking about reality, as distinct from abstractions, the natural, common-sense way was to think dialectically, because that mode of thought was imposed on men by the real forces with which they needed to deal. His claim for Marx and himself was that, setting out from real things rather than from abstractions, they had successfully applied the dialectical method to the study of history and of society, and had broken away from 'metaphysical' ways of treating these subjects. The Dialectic they applied was, of course, 'materialistic' — by which Engels meant primarily that they began with the things themselves, and not with ideas about them, as Hegel and all the idealists had done. But it was not 'materialistic' in the older sense of the term, in which matter and mind were contrasted as two different substances, but a materialism in which this dualism was got rid of, and mind, as distinct from the 'idea', was regarded as a part of nature, and as governed by nature's laws. The meaning of this kind of 'materialism' was discussed in the first volume of this work, in connection with the Materialist Conception of History ; and there is no need to traverse the ground over again. What concerns us here is that Engels, in invoking the dialectical method, professes to derive it from things and not to fix it upon things. It is not, he says, a free creation of anyone's mind : it is what the observer can see for himself, if he is not blinded by idealism, and can prove for himself by manipulating the forces of nature in accordance with the laws he discovers with its aid. 'Dialectics', Engels declares, 'is nothing more than the science of the general laws of motion and development of nature, human society, and thought.'

The use to which Engels proceeds to put his dialectical method in relation to social studies is best illustrated by the three chapters in which he replies to Dühring's assertion of the primacy of political factors in the shaping of human history. This assertion, Engels says, appears on analysis to mean that the clue to historical development is to be found in the exercise of force by some men for the oppression of others. Force, says Engels, is never more than a means : the aim in using force is economic advantage. Take the case of slavery. Captives made in war were killed, and not enslaved, until a situation developed in which there was an economic advantage in enslaving them for purposes of productive labour. Slavery was once a necessary means to the development of the powers of production. 'We should never forget that our entire economic, political and intellectual development has as its presupposition a state of affairs in which slavery was as necessary as it was universally recognised. . . . When we examine these questions, we are forced to say — however contradictory and heretical it may sound — that the introduction of slavery under the conditions of that time was a great step forward.'

Engels is here arguing against those Socialists, including Eugen Dühring, who tried to establish the case for Socialism on a basis of absolute values. There are no such values, he maintains : all values are relative to conditions of time and place. Not only slavery, but also in turn serfdom and wage-labour, were great advances in their day. Similarly the destruction of primitive communal ownership of land was a great advance, because it was the means to making agriculture more productive. Far from being forced by an oppressive ruling class on the cultivators of the land, it came into being through the perception of the cultivators themselves that they could better their position by escaping from the trammels of primitive collectivism. Engels holds that it is an entirely false view that political conquerors, native or foreign, have forced reactionary economic systems on their reluctant subjects. Or rather, this has happened only by way of exception.

The rôle played in history by force as contrasted with economic development is now clear. In the first place, all political power is originally based on an economic, social function, and increases in proportion as the members of society, through the dissolution of the primitive community, become transformed into private producers, and thus come to be more and more separated from the administrators of the general functions of society. Secondly, after the political force has made itself independent in relation to society, and has transformed itself from society's servant into its master, it can work in either of two directions. Either it works in the sense and direction of the regular economic movement — in which case no conflict arises between them, the economic development being only accelerated : or, (political) force works against economic development — in which case, as a rule, with but few exceptions, force succumbs to it. These few exceptions are isolated cases of conquest, in which barbarian conquerors have exterminated or driven out the population of a country and have laid waste or allowed to go to ruin productive powers which they did not know how to use.

Ordinarily, Engels argues, this is by no means what happens. In the internal growth of societies, political power usually follows and rests upon economic function ; and in most cases of conquest from outside, where an economically less advanced people conquers one more advanced, the victors are forced to take over the more developed methods of the vanquished. The economic powers usually get their way : they provide the sole *general* clue to the understanding of human history through all its successive stages.

This, of course, implies that capitalism too was an advance on what went before it, and fulfilled in its day a beneficent function in enlarging the means of living. This indeed is explicitly stated, and is an essential part of the Marxist doctrine. If Marx and Engels attack capitalism, they do so not because they regard it as inherently evil, however fiercely they denounce its oppression, but because it is obsolete, or rapidly becoming so, and is turning into a fetter upon the further development of the powers of production. This attitude, Engels emphasises, is simply part of their general attitude to man and nature. In the realm of knowledge absolute truth is unattainable : all 'truths' are only the best possible approximations at a particular stage in the evolution of man's knowledge. They are what came later to be called 'pragmatic' truths : they are of value because, however imperfectly, they enable men to handle natural forces, including man himself, for their advantage in better living. They all involve, because of their imperfection, an element of 'contradiction' ; but fortunately they can be revised and improved, each generation building on the achievements of its predecessors.

When Engels (and similarly when Marx) expresses scorn for Socialists who profess to base their systems on absolute ethical principles and denounce the entire past history of mankind for failing to come up to their ideals, what is meant is that every time and place has its own best practicable way of handling current problems, and the only real solutions are such imperfect solutions as contemporary conditions allow. Engels, however, believed — and of course this is also true of Marx — that the advance of technical productivity had already, and for the first time in history, reached a point at which it had become unnecessary for class-oppression to continue. At length, they believed, it had become possible to produce enough to satisfy the needs of all men, if the fetters imposed on production by capitalist monopoly were removed. To this extent, they were themselves 'utopians' ; but they were so, not as advocates of universal, absolute rights or claims, but because they over-estimated the extent of the advance in production that the scientific revolution had made immediately practicable.

Their relativism explains their hostility, which comes out in *Anti-Dühring* as well as in Marx's *Critique of the Gotha Pro-*

gramme, to 'equality' as a Socialist slogan. Obviously, says Engels, men are not equal : obviously they are unequal in their productive powers. The only sense in which it is reasonable to demand equality for them is that in which equality means the absence of artificial discrimination. Class constitutes such a discrimination, and should therefore be swept away now that it is no longer needed for the organisation of production, and has indeed become an obstacle to it. Moreover, differences in remuneration can be narrowed when the training of men for skilled tasks becomes a social function, paid for by the society and not by the individual ; for when this is the case the trained man loses his claim to receive a higher return on account of the higher productivity that is the result of his training. But even this does not involve equality ; for men differ in capacity and industry as well as in acquired skills.

All this part of Engels's writing, ignored at the time, was taken up with avidity, as we have seen, when the Russians had to face the actual problems of building a new society on a foundation of collective ownership and control. There will be more to be said about it when, in a later volume of the present work, the Communist interpretation of Marxism comes to be discussed. We shall then see Engels coming into his own as the nearly equal partner of Marx in the creation of 'Scientific Socialism'. In his own day, however, he appeared rather as Marx's follower and interpreter than as the original thinker he was ; and of course his own self-effacing attitude, wherever Marx was concerned, helped to reinforce this view of his work.

Finally, we must ask, what manner of men were these two great twin brothers, who, for good or ill, swept aside all the earlier Socialisms, and imposed their own conception on by far the greater part of the Socialism of the later nineteenth and of the present century ? That they were arrogant, and ungenerous to rival theorists, is evident both from their public writings and from their intimate correspondence. Believing themselves to have discovered a clue to the understanding of human history and therewith to the guidance of mankind in the contemporary struggle, they were exceedingly scornful of well-meaning thinkers who appeared to them to be in a hopeless metaphysical muddle, or to be animated by mere goodwill without any understanding of the forces by which social development was actually shaped. They were, moreover, very ready to throw charges of disingenuousness at anyone who ventured to criticise their work ; and they had a habit of invective in the course of argument that belonged to the German tradition and had become by the nineteenth century largely alien to British, and even to French, ways of expression in scholarly controversy, though it was taken over, and carried much further, by their Russian disciples. Marx, in particular, had in some degree the characteristic infirmity of the exile — a persistent *malaise* which aggravated the effects of poverty and ill-health. Through all his years of residence in London, and with all his study of English conditions, he never came any nearer to an understanding, much less to an acceptance, of the modes of British thought and action. He came much nearer to understanding the French, but not to liking them. He remained a German of the Germans, eternally convinced that German thought was the only really profound thought, and that it was the mission of Germany — of a regenerated, Socialist Germany — to take the lead in the coming Socialist revolution. Engels approached much more nearly than Marx ever did to understanding the English ; for he had to do business with them, as well as to live in their midst, and he had, besides, a much more extravert temperament. But, when it was a matter of defending Marx against anyone who ventured to criticise or oppose him, Engels could easily outdo his friend in vituperation, and was quite as ready to impute either crass stupidity or ignoble motives.

Marx was by temperament a scholar. He had a real shrinking from self-advertisement, and from any publicity for his personality, as distinct from his ideas. He was torn in twain when Engels tried to act as his publicity manager ; for he was as eager to secure recognition for his work as unwilling to have any parade made of his personal affairs. Engels had much the thicker skin and the greater resiliency. He was a healthy animal, whereas Marx, though powerfully built, was seldom well and often seriously ill. Marx, passionately attached to his wife and family, bore poverty ill on this account : Engels, immensely generous, had no money troubles to contend with, though he had for many years to put up with the irksomeness of uncongenial employment.

The two, with all their dissimilarity, formed a remarkable partnership. Engels did much to direct Marx's studies towards realism, and away from abstractions masquerading as higher values. It was Engels who showed Marx the way both to build a new Socialist Political Economy on the foundations of classical Economics and to use English blue-books to illuminate their common theory of economic and social development. It is certain that without Engels's encouragement — even apart from its financial aspects — Marx could never have written *Das Kapital* or made the impact which he did make on the Socialist movement of his day.

Engels, however, was a lively, rather than a profound, thinker. He was full of ideas ; but he could be wildly wrong, as he was when he asserted that in the Franco-Prussian War 'the weapons used have reached such a stage of perfection that further progress which would have any revolutionising influence is no longer possible . . .' and that 'all further improvements are more or less unimportant for field warfare' (*Anti-Dühring*). He jumped easily to conclusions, and swallowed notions whole without troubling to investigate them very closely. While Marx lived, he was much more Marxist than his colleague : only after Marx's death did he begin to think for himself about matters in which he had been accustomed to defer to his colleague's judgment, so as to allow, for example, much more influence of a secondary sort to non-economic factors in the shaping of history and, in practical matters, to accommodate his ideas to the actual development of German Social Democracy despite its evident divergence from the pattern which he and Marx had wished to impose on it at the time of the Gotha Programme. Engels had a large fund of enthusiasm, and much less sense of the difficulty of straight thinking than his more scholarly associate.

For both Marx and Engels the conception of Socialism as science — social science — was of over-mastering importance. Scornful though they were of Auguste Comte, they shared to the full his view, derived from Saint-Simon, that the essential task of the nineteenth century was to apply the scientific method, which had achieved such wonders in the physical realm, to human society, and to construct a 'science of society' that would put the finishing touch to the 'encyclopaedia of the sciences', and render unnecessary any sort of metaphysical philosophy by driving *a priori* thought from its last stronghold. Like Comte again, they saw history as the furnisher of the material for the making of this last and highest science. But they regarded Comte as a charlatan because his 'social science' rested on psychological foundations rather than on a realistic study of economic development, and because his conception of the rôles of 'order' and 'progress' appeared to them to be based on a false antithesis. They were essentially revolutionaries : Comte emphatically was not. Where he saw social solidarity they saw the conflict of classes as the clue to the understanding of contemporary social events and to the interpretation of men's past.

In Marxism, the 'class' replaced the Hegelian 'Idea' as the master-clue to historical understanding. Marx and Engels found their essential conceptions at a time when the outstanding function of current economic development appeared to be the destruction of the individual craft producer and his replacement by a mass of almost unskilled factory operatives who could be treated as mere undifferentiated units of the commodity, labour-power. The early factory system had everywhere this character : it was a means of superseding individual skill and of cheapening production by converting the worker into an appendage of the power-driven machine. For the capitalists of the Industrial Revolution the chief virtue of power-driven machinery was that it made possible the highly productive employment of almost unskilled labour. Marx, generalising on the basis of what he saw and what he read in the blue-books about the rising factory system, anticipated that the further advance of capitalism would carry this dehumanising process to much greater lengths, until it had reduced all the wage-earners to an undifferentiated mass of abstract labour-power. Long before he died — indeed, long before *Das Kapital* was published — this had become a seriously incorrect picture of what was happening in the most advanced industrial areas, especially in engineering and in the industries making capital goods. But Marx, after the 1840s, never made any first-hand study of changing industrial conditions in Great Britain ; and what he had concluded from his earlier investigations, made at Engels's prompting, continued for some time longer to hold good to a great extent for the countries which took to mechanical production well after Great Britain.

Consequently, Marx was never induced to reconsider his original conclusions concerning the developing tendencies of capitalist production as they affected the workers ; and he continued to think of the working class primarily in terms of the unskilled factory workers as a depersonalised mass standing in opposition to an equally depersonalised mass of concentrated capital. This caused him seriously to misunderstand what was happening to the British Trade Unions with whose leaders' aid he tried to build the First International. He saw their craft unionism as a reactionary manifestation, whereas it was really the reflection of a change in the character of production and foreshadowed an increasing differentiation of skills and occupations rather than the reduction of the entire proletariat to a homogeneous class of victims of increasing misery. Engels, with his greater knowledge of industry, should have been able to put him right about this, but never did : indeed, while Marx lived, he showed no greater awareness than his friend of the new forces that were being generated by the technical changes that were making the metal trades, rather than the textiles, the leaders in capitalistic development.

These defects of vision, however, far from hindering the acceptance of Marxism, positively made it easier, not in Great Britain, but in the countries which had still to catch up on Great Britain's lead. Most of all did they make Marxism fit the mental requirements of the industrial workers in the areas which were invaded by highly developed capitalist enterprise without passing through the intermediate stages through which British industrialism had passed. Marxism fitted well the conditions of Germany in the 1870s and 1880s ; and it fitted even better the small but highly mechanised industrial section of the Russian economy right up to 1917. These differences partly explain why Marxism, in becoming the gospel of the major part of continental Socialism, failed to make any similar impact on Great Britain.

Marxism, then, was a powerful and impressive analysis of the conditions of capitalist production at a particular phase of its development ; and it had some claim to be regarded as 'scientific' to the extent to which it was based on the study of

the actual working of capitalism up to the middle of the nineteenth century. But as soon as Marx stopped writing economic
and social history and wrote instead theoretical Economics, he
ceased to behave as a scientist studying facts and started spin-
ning theories out of his own head in a highly unscientific and
indeed metaphysical manner. The entire construction of the
classical Economics of Ricardo and his immediate successors
was based on deductions from abstract statements : it was a
logical construct which owed its plausibility to an apparent
resemblance to the facts of the market economy, but was not
founded on any induction from these facts, or verifiable by
reference to them. Marx took over this deductively based
system lock, stock, and barrel, without any apparent perception
of its essentially unscientific character. He then proceeded to
superimpose upon it, in the guise of a 'critical' evaluation, a
further structure of a deductive sort, which turned out to be
even less open to any process of verification by reference to
actual events. Whether Marx's theoretical Economics were
true or untrue may be a moot point. Internally coherent they
may have been : logically correct they may have been as deductions from the original set of assumptions ; but 'scientific', in
any proper use of the word, they most certainly were not.

CHAPTER XII

ANARCHISTS AND ANARCHIST-COMMUNISTS — KROPOTKIN

I N the eleventh edition of the *Encyclopaedia Britannica*, published in 1910, the article on Anarchism was written by Prince Peter Kropotkin, who became, after Bakunin's death, the leading theorist of what came to be known as 'Anarchist-Communism'. Kropotkin gave an account of Anarchism as a social doctrine and of its historical development, and touched in passing on the question of violence and its connection with the Anarchist movement. The general public, he said, was under the impression that violence was the essence of Anarchism, but this was far from being the case. Acts of violence by Anarchists were retaliations against violence directed against them by Governments which themselves rested on violence. 'Violence is resorted to by all parties in proportion as their open action is obstructed by repression, and exceptional laws render them outlaws.' In this last phrase Kropotkin was of course alluding to the exceptional laws which, from 1878 onwards, were enacted in Germany and in many other countries, not only against Anarchists, but against every sort of movement that was deemed to disseminate revolutionary ideas.

To Kropotkin's article the editor of the *Encyclopaedia* appended a long footnote. In this, an account was given of the long series of 'Anarchist outrages' which, beginning in 1878, created in the 1880s a widespread scare among the Governments and police departments of the Western world. 'Propaganda by deed', as the use of assassination as a political weapon came to be called, was of course no new thing in 1878. It had been endemic in Russia since Alexander II, after beginning his reign as a reformer by the freeing of the serfs, had reverted to reaction and repression, and had embarked in the middle 'sixties on a determined attempt to uproot the radical groups among the

Russian intellectuals. The long series of attempts on the Czar's life made during this period had begun with Kara-kozov's in 1866, and had been accompanied by attacks on leading reactionary officials. In the years 1877 and 1878 a new wave of intensified repression was met by a series of terrorist acts which were to culminate in 1881, despite the return to a milder policy, in the death of the Czar.

Outside Russia, though acts of violence had been common in both Spain and Italy, the political assassination of crowned heads and police chiefs had not played any important part. This new development — new, that is, to Western Europe — set in from 1878, when attempts were made almost simultaneously to kill the German Kaiser, Wilhelm I, the Spanish King, Alfonso XII, and King Humbert of Italy. These attempts enabled Bismarck to induce the Reichstag to pass the Anti-Socialist Law he had been demanding from it for some years ; and they were also the occasion of the Papal Encyclical — *Quod Apostolici Muneris* — directed against Anarchism and Socialism at the end of the year.

The editor of the *Encyclopaedia Britannica* explained in his note that he had appended an account of 'Anarchist outrages' to Kropotkin's article 'for convenience in stating the facts under the heading where a reader would expect to find them' — though he said also that 'the general public view which regards Anarchist doctrines indiscriminately is to that extent a confusion of terms' — meaning by 'to that extent' that 'philosophic Anarchists would repudiate the connection'.

The number of Anarchists who had any part in the activities that, from 1878 onwards, gave the entire movement so bad a name was always very small. Most of the Russians who attempted to kill a Czar or a leading repressive official were not Anarchists but Narodniks — that is to say, revolutionaries in bitter revolt against Czarist oppression and believers in some sort of agrarian Socialism to be developed by means of a peasant revolt. They were followers of Peter Lavrov or of the exiled Chernyshevsky, rather than of Nechaiev or of Bakunin. In the West, outside Spain and Italy, the assassins, even when they were members of Anarchist bodies, acted entirely as individuals, or at most a few together. If, in Spain and Italy, larger groups were involved in the killings, this was to be attributed much less to Anarchism than to traditions which went back a long way into the history of both these countries.

'Anarchism', in the sense that came to be commonly given to the word in the 1880s — that is, Anarchism as 'propaganda by the deed', with assassination as its principal method — was never the creed of any large numbers. But the Anarchists who were not killers were not prepared wholly to dissociate themselves from those who were. One reason for this was that, in common with many who were not Anarchists, they regarded the killings in Russia as fully justifiable retaliations for the sufferings inflicted both on the mass of the Russian people and on anyone who took their part against the Czarist police system ; and it was difficult for those who defended assassination in one country to be wholly against it elsewhere. A second reason was that many Anarchists who would never have resorted to killing were prepared to justify it theoretically as a means of protesting against the entire authoritarian system — that is of meeting the force of the State with the only means of resistance available to the oppressed. This indeed was Kropotkin's own attitude, though in practice he was strongly opposed to the policy of 'propaganda by deed' in Western countries as far more likely to aggravate than to relieve the repression.

From 1878 onwards the 'Anarchist crime wave' continued to gather force. In that year, in Russia, Vera Zasulich (1851–1919), later prominent in the Socialist movement, shot at Trepov, the reactionary chief of the Czarist police, and was acquitted because of her victim's unpopularity. The two attempts on the life of Wilhelm I of Germany were both made by men who had some connection with the Anarchist wing of Socialism. Emil Heinrich Max Hoedel, who tried first, was a Saxon tinsmith who had become a vendor of left-wing journals. Karl Eduard Nobiling, who followed him three weeks later, was an intellectual of upper-class origin from Posen. But both men appear to have acted entirely alone, without any organised backing. Juan Oliver Moncasi, who tried to kill Alfonso XII a few months later, was a working cooper : he too seems to have acted alone. It is uncertain whether Otero y González, who made a similar attempt the following year, had any political connections : at any rate none were traced to him. Giovanni Passamente, who attempted to kill Humbert of Italy, was a professed Internationalist — a cook by trade ; but no complicity of the Italian Section of the International could be discovered.

In Russia, on the other hand, the terrorist movement was a highly organised affair. It was not for the most part specifically Anarchist, though there were Anarchists in its ranks. It sprang out of the revolutionary traditions of the Narodniks, and was influenced fully as much by Chernyskevsky as by Bakunin. It can be said to have had its direct origins in the society Zemlya i Volya (Land and Freedom¹), founded in 1862. This body issued a proclamation affirming the right to revolution and calling for a constituent assembly to lay down a new constitution for a free Russian society. Many similar manifestoes were issued in the early 1860s as the disillusionment following on the emancipation of the serfs gained ground, and as repression descended again on Russia after the Polish revolt. There were sporadic peasant risings, usually known as the movement of the Buntars (*bunt* means rising, *putsch*, *émeute*) in the 1860s ; and these were savagely crushed and the revolutionary movement for the time almost destroyed, though Nechaiev and other agitators carried on their propaganda in a small way, especially among the students.

Then, in the early 1870s, came the widespread and mainly spontaneous movement to 'go among the people', to live with them, at once educating them and learning from them, in order to prepare the way for revolutionary change, whether or not this change would need to be achieved by violence. This movement towards the people, which reached its height in 1872 and 1873, was met by mass arrests, imprisonments, and deportations to Siberia, and was destroyed within a few years. Its fate drove over to ideas of revolutionary terrorism many who had previously shrunk from such methods. At first, the effect was manifested in single-handed attempts at the killing of particularly obnoxious Czarist officials. These culminated in Vera Zasulich's acquittal after she had attempted to kill Trepov in 1878. Thereafter, prisoners implicated in such affairs were not given the benefit of trial by jury.

Before this, in 1877, Zemlya i Volya had been revived. It was not at the outset a terrorist body, though it did not exclude assassination by way of reprisal for the execution of 'agitators'.

¹ Or 'Land and Will'. *Volya* in Russian means both will and freedom.

But in the following year it split into two rival groups. One section, Cherny Peredyel (Black Earth Distribution), devoted itself mainly to propaganda among the peasants in favour of radical land redistribution, without charges for compensation to landowners. This group, of which G. V. Plekhanov was a member, held aloof from terrorist activity, though it did not condemn it absolutely in all cases. The other section, much smaller and bound together by a much more rigid discipline, formed Narodnaya Volya (People's Will or People's Freedom) and, taking its stand on the ferocity with which all attempts at any sort of propaganda were repressed, set out to retaliate by a campaign of terror, with the supreme purpose of killing Alexander II, whom its members had come to regard as the head and forefront of the reaction.

Of this new movement Andrei Ivanovich Zhelyabov (1850–1881) soon became the outstanding leader, with Sophie Perovskaya (1854–81), an aristocrat who had joined the movement but had at first adhered to Cherny Peredyel, as his principal co-leader. Zhelyabov was himself the son of serfs ; but he had received a higher education, and had got into trouble for mildly revolutionary activities in his student days. He was not an Anarchist, but an advocate of a Constituent Assembly, to be achieved by revolution if other means failed. The repression drove him to the extreme left ; and he took over the leadership of the group from Alexander Mihailov (1857–83), its chief inspirer. In Kiev, where the movement was strong, the outstanding figure was Valerian Osinski (1853–79), who was caught and executed before Narodnaya Volya had reached the peak of its activity. Mihailov too was arrested and imprisoned in 1880 — he died in prison three years later — and had no part in the final stage of Narodnaya Volya's brief, sensational campaign.

Narodnaya Volya was controlled by an Executive Committee under Zhelyabov's direction — the celebrated 'Executive Committee' whose proclamations resounded throughout Europe from the moment when it announced its firm intention to kill the Czar as a reprisal for his betrayal of the liberal principles he had once appeared to express. From 1878 onwards the Executive Committee was continuously engaged in organising attempts to kill Alexander, and it received the credit for other attempts that were not of its devising. Neither Alexander Soloviev (1846–79), the school teacher who shot at the Czar and was executed in 1879, nor the joiner Stepan Khalturin (1857–82), who the following year managed to blow up the dining-room in the Winter Palace and only missed killing the Czar by a sheer accident, acted under the orders of the Executive Committee of Narodnaya Volya. Khalturin, indeed, appears to have acted alone, as a reprisal for the breaking-up of the Northern Workers' Union which he had organised in 1878. He escaped detection, but was caught and executed in 1882 after taking part in the killing of Strelnikov at Odessa.

Narodnaya Volya was the only one among the terrorist groups which concentrated attention on itself by its expressed intention of killing Alexander II, and by its repeated attempts to carry this determination into effect. It was directly responsible for at least four attempts before its final success in 1881. Among these was the attempt of Leo Hartmann (1850–1913), Sophie Perovskaya, and others to blow up the railway carriage in which the Czar was returning to St. Petersburg from South Russia. The explosion blew up a baggage wagon in the royal train. Hartmann, a Russian of German origin and a member of the 'Executive Committee', escaped abroad and settled in France. The Russian Government applied for his extradition ; but the French Government — that of Freycinet — refused to give him up, though it later expelled him from French territory. This was a European *cause célèbre*. Hartmann went to London, where he got to know Marx and Engels, and acted as a sort of emissary of Narodnaya Volya — or of what was left of it — abroad. He never returned to Russia.

The Hartmann episode, organised by Zhelyabov's group, preceded Khalturin's attempt. During the same year, 1879, there were other killings of unpopular Czarist governors and officials, followed by numerous arrests, imprisonments, and deportations to Siberia, and by a number of executions. Then, early in 1881, after an interval during which Narodnaya Volya postponed action for fear of doing the prisoners harm at their trials, came the culminating attempt which resulted in Alexander's death. There were in fact two attempts — one, which failed because the route was changed at the last moment, to blow up the Czar's carriage by means of a bomb put in place by tunnelling under a road along which he was expected to pass ; the other, which succeeded, to kill him with grenades thrown by individual revolutionaries as he passed. Zhelyabov personally organised the latter attempt, but was arrested the day before it was due to be made. Sophie Perovskaya took his place at the head of the organisation ; and two bombs were thrown in rapid succession, one, which missed, by Nikolai Rysakov (1862–81), a young workman who had been personally enlisted by Zhelyabov, and the second, which killed both the thrower and the Czar, by another worker, Ignatie Grinevitski (1856–81), who was also active in the Workers' Section of Narodnaya Volya.

Rysakov, arrested on the spot, and another of the group, a young metal-worker named Timothy Mihailov, made revelations about their fellow-conspirators in the hope of saving their own lives, and the police were able to arrest nearly all the active leaders of Narodnaya Volya who were still at large. Zhelyabov, already in prison before the event, insisted on taking his full share of the responsibility and on being tried with the others who were directly involved in the assassination ; and he, Sophie Perovskaya, Rysakov, Timothy Mihailov, and Nikolai Kibalchich, who had prepared the explosives, were publicly hanged after a summary trial without jury. Incidentally, this Kibalchich left behind him the plans for a jet-propelled aeroplane, which, unearthed by the Bolsheviks from the police archives, cause him to be proclaimed to-day in the Soviet Union as the real pioneer of jet-propulsion. He was a quite eminent technician, who worked secretly for the terrorists while pursuing an apparently blameless career.

The assassination of Alexander II was the theme of an exulting proclamation issued by the remaining members of the Executive Committee of Narodnaya Volya. But actually the organisation was almost broken up by the arrest of its leaders, one after another, as a consequence of the revelations of Rysakov and others. Its Workers' Section, and also the quite important section it had been able to form in the fighting forces under the naval officer Nikolai Sukhanov (1853–82), were almost completely destroyed ; and the efforts of Vera Figner (1852–194?) to revive it were ended by her arrest in 1884. With most of the others who escaped execution, she received a life sentence.

Many died in prison ; she was one of the few leaders of Narodnaya Volya who survived to be released by the revolution of 1905.[1]

In the same year, 1881, as saw the death of Alexander II, President Garfield was assassinated in the United States ; but his killer, despite attempts to establish a connection, had no associations with any Anarchist or terrorist movement. After the assassination of Alexander, Narodnaya Volya announced its responsibility for the killing, and threatened further action unless the new Czar, Alexander III, mended his ways. This he was far from doing. Before the death of Alexander II, his chief minister, Count Loris-Melikov, had been doing his best to persuade him to agree to moderate measures of administrative and constitutional reform ; but Alexander III was much more reactionary than his father, and a fresh wave of repression was unloosed. In London the German Anarchist, Johann Most, published in his journal, *Freiheit*, an article justifying the killing of Alexander II, and was sent to prison for sixteen months ; at the end of his sentence he emigrated to the United States and there re-started *Freiheit* and took a leading part in the American Anarchist movement. Most had a stormy career behind him before he started *Freiheit* in London in 1880. Born in Germany, he had worked as a bookbinder in Switzerland and then in Austria, where he had been sentenced in 1869 for high treason, but had been deported after an amnesty. Returning to Germany, he had praised the Paris Commune — which had cost him a further prison sentence. He had edited the *Freie Presse*, first at Chemnitz, in Saxony, where he supported a metal-workers' strike, and subsequently in Berlin. In 1874 he had been elected to the Reichstag as a Social Democrat, but had turned Anarchist and lost his seat in 1878.

Most's article about the killing of Alexander II appeared in 1881. The same year an International Anarchist Congress was held in London ; and it was widely believed thereafter that this gathering had established a new secret International, to replace the defunct International Working Men's Association, and that this half-imaginary body was the directing

---

[1] The Narodnik movement will be dealt with more fully in the next volume, in connection with the development of the Social Revolutionary Party in Russia.

power behind the various manifestations of 'propaganda by deed'. In fact the London Congress, which was attended by delegates from France, Belgium, Switzerland, Italy, Spain, Germany, Austria, and the United States, displayed differences of tendency much too wide for the creation of any effective central directing agency — even apart from the fact that to set up such a body would have been altogether inconsistent with the autonomist views of most of the participants.

'Propaganda by deed' had indeed been approved in principle by an Anarchist Congress held in Switzerland, at La Chaux-de-Fonds, in 1879 ; but those who upheld it, including Kropotkin, did so for the most part as justified under the conditions existing in Russia, as an answer to extreme repression, or on theoretical grounds of Anarchist principle, rather than as a policy to be recommended for general adoption.

In 1882 the question took on a new aspect, when the French Government embarked on a round of arrests of Anarchist leaders. In order to understand the situation of French Anarchism in the 1880s, however, it is necessary to begin by saying something of the general condition of the French working-class movement during the years after the fall of the Paris Commune. For a time the movement almost ceased to exist. Every kind of workers' society that could be suspected of any militant purpose was broken up : a law of 1872 made membership of any sort of international body a punishable offence. Local *chambres syndicales* — associations of workers in a particular trade — maintained a precarious existence only by disclaiming all militant intentions and declaring their support of conciliation and of united action with the *chambres patronales*. In 1872 an attempt was made to form in Paris a federation of the local *chambres syndicales*, under the name of *Cercle d'Union Ouvrière* ; but this body was at once dissolved by the police. The Government set up a committee of enquiry into labour conditions, which sat until 1875 and received evidence from many employers' bodies, but none from the workers. In 1873 private subscriptions made it possible to send a workers' delegation to the Vienna International Exhibition ; but the Government refused to help. Not until 1876 were the first steps taken towards re-creating a national movement. In that year a National Labour Congress was held in Paris, organised by moderates who were careful to keep it on lines acceptable to the liberals. Its tone was in fact mainly mutualist and Co-operative : it declared against class-struggles and for a policy of collaboration between employers and workers. Its one advanced resolution called for the putting forward of workers as parliamentary and municipal candidates. Its leaders, Charles Edmé Chabert (1818– ?), a former member of the International, and Jean Joseph Barberet (1838–1920), were not Socialists, but moderate reformers : Barberet subsequently became the leading civil service expert on labour questions.

This Congress met with a mixed reception from the Socialists. Édouard Vaillant and the Blanquists as a group attacked it violently, as an attempt to betray the workers. But Jules Guesde (1845–1922), soon to become the outstanding leader of the French Socialist movement, defended it as a modest beginning of Trade Union revival. Guesde, who had been associated up to this point with the Anarchist wing of the International, and had been exiled for supporting the Paris Commune in a journal he had edited at Montpellier, resumed about this time his propagandist work in France ; and his new journal, *Égalité*, became the pioneer of the reviving Socialist movement.

In 1877 a small secret Congress of French 'anti-author-itarians' met in Switzerland, at La Chaux-de-Fonds, and re-founded the French Section of the International Working Men's Association as a Section of the anti-Marxist International. The principal inspirer of this activity was Paul Brousse (1854–1912), subsequently the leader of the French Possibilist Socialist Party ; and he also started a journal, *L'Avant-Garde*, as the organ of the movement. Louis-Jean Pindy, who had been active in the Paris I.W.M.A. and in the Commune, and had escaped to Switzerland, became Corresponding Secretary of the new Section, with the mission of maintaining contacts with the underground groups in France. When a second Labour Congress was held at Lyons in 1878, there were a few Socialist delegates, but the main body still consisted of mutualist moderates, and a motion in favour of collectivism was heavily defeated. During that year an International Exhibition was being held in Paris, and it was decided to convene an International Labour Congress to meet there, in order to establish contacts with the various workers' delegations from other countries. The

Government, however, vetoed the meeting, and most of the French organising committee accepted the ban. Not so Guesde and the group that had already gathered round *Égalité*. This group decided to hold the Congress despite the prohibition : the first meeting was broken up by the police, and Guesde and the other leaders were sent to prison. From prison they managed to issue a manifesto calling for a Socialist revival, and there was an immediate and widespread response. The following year Auguste Blanqui, who was still in prison, was elected deputy for Bordeaux. The Government invalidated the election, but ordered his release and allowed him to stand again ; but his refusal to compromise with the Radicals who had voted for him on the previous occasion lost him the seat. Nevertheless the tide was flowing strongly, since the defeat of Marshal Macmahon's attempt to destroy the Republic had appeared to render the Republican form of government at length secure. There was a readiness to relax the repression practised against the workers, and in 1879 the long-sought amnesty for those who had taken part in the Commune was at length voted. The following year the Communard prisoners came back from New Caledonia — those who were still alive — and Communard exiles flocked back from Switzerland, England, and other countries in which they had taken refuge, many of them to resume their old activities in the working-class and Socialist movements.

Already, in 1879, the National Labour Congress held at Marseilles had shown an immense change of attitude. It was attended not only by numerous Trade Union delegates, but also by Socialist and Anarchist delegates from a variety of newly founded societies. Its tone was predominantly collectivist : it passed resolutions in favour not only of the public ownership of the means of production, but also of the establishment of a workers' party. Jules Guesde dominated the proceedings : out of the Congress arose a Fédération des Ouvriers Socialistes de France, which in 1882 developed into the Parti Ouvrier, the first of the modern French Socialist parties.

Guesde had by this time greatly changed his views. In founding *Égalité* he had sought the collaboration of Wilhelm Liebknecht as well as of César de Paepe, and by 1880 he had come fully under the influence of Marxian ideas. In that year he visited Marx in London and consulted him about the status and programme of the new party — just as Hyndman, in Great Britain, did only a year later. In France, Guesde collaborated closely with Marx's son-in-law, Paul Lafargue ; and when a Congress met in Paris in 1880 to approve the statutes and programme of the new party, they were faced with, and endorsed, a draft which was theoretically Marxist and based in respect of organisation mainly on the German Social Democratic Party. Guesde, however, did not carry with him the whole movement out of which his party had arisen. At the Havre Labour Congress of 1880 both the Mutualists and the Anarchists broke away. The Mutualists formed a rival Union des Chambres Syndicales de France, which soon collapsed : the Anarchists also set about creating a separate organisation.

Even within Guesde's new Federation a sharp dispute soon set in. Guesde's policy, based on that of German Social Democracy, required a centralised, disciplined party strictly independent of alliances with the *bourgeois* parties, and therewith an attempt to subordinate the Trade Unions to the party's leadership. This policy ran counter, in France, to a strong sentiment in favour of Trade Union independence of party control, and also to a wish, on the part of many Socialists, to join forces with the left wing of *bourgeois* Radicalism in opposition to the preponderant power of the Conservatives. In particular, many Socialists saw little hope of winning either parliamentary or municipal contests without Radical support, and were desirous of a policy which would admit the need for a united left Republican front in elections. In 1881 Paul Brousse, a former Communard exile, put himself at the head of a demand for what he called *possibilisme* — that is, for taking such chances as offered to secure practical advances towards Socialism, by the promotion of social legislation and of progressive municipal policies. The advocates of Trade Union autonomy within the Guesdist Federation joined hands with the Broussists, and in 1882 there was a split. The 'Possibilists' established a Fédération des Travailleurs Socialistes as a rival to the Guesdist Parti Ouvrier.

During these years Trade Unionism was growing fast, and many federal bodies were being set up, both as federations of local *syndicats* in the same trade or industry and as local federations of the *syndicats* of the various trades. Legally, the Trade

Unions had still no assured status ; but in practice a considerable degree of toleration was accorded, and there were no longer serious obstacles in their way. Legal recognition of the right to combine followed in 1884, though serious battles had still to be fought before it was extended to cover public employees. But before this there had been an outbreak of strikes, especially in the mining and metal industries, where the workers' organisations were most militant, and Anarchist influences were said to be great.

The principal centre of these disturbances was the area round Lyons, which had resumed its old militancy. In 1881 there was founded at Lyons a journal, *Le Droit social*, which became the principal organ of French Anarchism. The following year a big strike took place at Montceau-les-Mines, provoked by extremely reactionary management, and during the strike a number of acts of violence were committed. The Government, regarding the Lyons Anarchists as responsible for these acts, decided to take strong action against the growing Anarchist movement. A large number of Anarchist journalists and propagandists were arrested — among them Kropotkin, who had recently moved across the frontier from Switzerland and was collaborating with the group which had founded *Le Droit social*. Others arrested included the French Anarchists Émile Gautier, Toussaint Bordat, and Joseph Bernard. They were all charged with violation of the law of 1872 by becoming members of an Anarchist International that was alleged to have been established at the London Congress of 1881, and they were all condemned, despite the absence of any real evidence that such a body had any existence. Another Anarchist, Antoine Cyvoct, who had fled from Lyons to Brussels, was arrested there and handed over to the French by the Belgian Government. He was accused of having been responsible for a bomb outrage in Lyons in 1882, and was condemned to death despite the lack of any evidence that he had been concerned in the affair. Later, he was pardoned by President Grévy. Soon after his arrest a big Paris demonstration of unemployed workers, headed by Émile Pouget and by the former Communard Louise Michel, both active Anarchists, broke into some bakers' shops, and Louise Michel distributed the bread taken from them among the unemployed workers. She and

Pouget were gaoled as an outcome of this affair, and many other Anarchists were sentenced in Paris and in the other big industrial towns. Most of them remained in prison until 1886, when they were released by President Grévy. In that year there were further Anarchist disturbances, and the movement of 'propaganda by deed' took a fresh lease of life in the 1890s.

During the 1880s, despite the repression, the French Anarchists produced not only a large number of journals advocating militant policies, but also a considerable literature of a theoretical kind. The principal French Anarchist writers of this decade included Émile Gautier, whose first important book, *Le Darwinisme social*, appeared in 1880, and was followed by a journal, *L'Anarchie*, in which much of his writing appeared. Gautier was a lawyer and a noted writer whose speeches did much to stimulate the Anarchist tendencies in the Trade Unions. An even greater influence was Jean Grave, whose book, *La Société au lendemain de la révolution*, was published in 1882. Grave had originally been a shoemaker, but had become a compositor, and later a journalist. He had worked for *Le Révolté* at Geneva under Kropotkin, and stood, much more than Gautier, for Anarchist-Communism rather than for Anarchism pure and simple. Charles Malato, whose *Philosophie de l'anarchisme* appeared in 1889, was another leading figure in the formulation of Anarchist theory. To these must be added Louise Michel, who issued her Memoirs in 1886, and her chief book, *Le Monde nouveau*, in 1888. Émile Pouget, who later became a leading theorist of French Syndicalism, though active in the 1880s, did not become an outstanding figure till the 'nineties, when his journal, *Le Père Peinard*, gained a considerable popular circulation.

In the 1880s Syndicalism had still to emerge as a clearly defined doctrine, and in the circles hostile to parliamentary action Anarchism and Anarchist-Communism held the field. After the legalising statute of 1884 Trade Unions grew fast, and in 1886 a national Trade Union Congress at Lyons set up a Fédération Nationale de Syndicats which at once became the arena for a struggle between the rival tendencies. At the next Congress, in 1887, the *syndicats* declared in favour of collective ownership of the means of production, and also began to discuss the question of the general strike, which was to play so important a part in the theory of Syndicalism at a later stage. The following year the general strike, as a means of social transformation, was accepted in principle ; and this decision was endorsed in subsequent years. The Congress of 1888, reacting against the attempts of the rival Socialist groups and parties to bring the *syndicats* under political control, also adopted a resolution declaring that they should be wholly independent of political parties. But, despite this decision, during the next few years the Fédération de Syndicats fell more and more under Guesdist influence and became little more than an appendage of the Parti Ouvrier. This helped the growth of a rival movement, which began to take shape towards the end of the 1880s, for the establishment of local federations, usually called Bourses du Travail,[1] designed to act both as labour exchanges under Trade Union control and as Trades Councils, with a wide range of propagandist, organising, and educational activities. The Paris Bourse du Travail, established in 1888, took the lead ; and in 1892 a Federation of Bourses was set up as a rival to the Federation of Syndicats, and soon became the rallying-point for all Trade Unionists who stood for a revolutionary industrial policy to be carried on in entire independence of the contending Socialist factions. Fernand Pelloutier (1867–1901), who had been a follower of Guesde, soon became the leading figure in the new movement ; and the Anarchist-Communists, headed by Pouget and Paul Delesalle (1870–1948), joined forces with him to create the French Syndicalist movement which reached its height in the first decade of the twentieth century. These developments will be studied in their place, but they fall for the most part beyond the period covered in this volume. It has been necessary to mention them here because they arose directly out of the struggles between Guesdists, Possibilists, and Anarchist-Communists for the control of the developing Trade Union movement of the 1880s.

Outside France Anarchism continued throughout the 1880s on its divided course. In Spain, and especially in Catalonia, Bakuninist Anarchism began to develop into Anarcho-Syndicalism, which first appeared as a defined tendency at a National

---

[1] The movement for forming Bourses du Travail had actually begun in Belgium in the 1870s. They had been already advocated by César de Paepe in 1868.

Workers' Congress in 1882. In Italy there was a growing rift between north and south. We have seen how, in the 'seventies, the Lombard Federation broke away from the Bakuninists to found a new Section of the International on lines nearer to Marxism, and how in 1879 Andrea Costa, hitherto active on the Anarchist side, went over to Marxian Socialism and became the creator of an Italian Socialist Party. Social Democracy, however, gained no foothold in the south or in Sicily, and little in Central Italy. In these areas Anarchism retained its appeal, and Errico Malatesta built up a large following. Thus divided into rival factions, the Italian working-class movement was unable to make much headway. In 1882 a number of Socialist groups, mainly in the north, joined forces to fight the elections ; and three years later these groups amalgamated to form a national Socialist Party. But progress was slow, and it was not until 1892 that a reorganised party took shape, on the model of the Marxian Social Democratic Parties of Western Europe.

In Germany Anarchism never took much hold ; but one effect of Bismarck's Anti-Socialist Laws was to give it a temporary following when the Socialist movement was driven underground. After Johann Most and Wilhelm Hasselmann had left the country, German Anarchism lacked leaders, and the Germans made no significant contribution to Anarchist theory. But in 1883 Anarchism won notoriety in Germany on account of the attempt of a small group of printers to blow up the Kaiser on the occasion of a great patriotic celebration of German unity. The conspirators, whose leader was a compositor named Reinsdorf, laid a charge of explosives under the road along which the royal family was due to pass ; but the charge was never exploded, possibly because the conspirators took fright at the last moment. Reinsdorf and two others were executed, and Bismarck used the opportunity to strengthen his repressive laws with a special measure against the possession of dynamite or other explosives. About the same time there were similar dynamite plots in Austria, followed by special measures against Anarchists and Socialists and the deportation of many foreigners from the Austrian dominions. *Die Zukunft*, the chief Socialist newspaper, was suppressed, and the leading Socialists were expelled from Vienna. One Anarchist, by name

Stellmacher, found guilty of murder, was executed, and many others were imprisoned for varying terms.

The remaining country in which an Anarchist scare developed in the 1880s was the United States. A number of Anarchists, as well as many Socialists, had taken refuge there during the 1870s, and more followed, especially from Germany, when Bismarck's Anti-Socialist Law came into force. American Anarchism had a native tradition of its own, going back to Josiah Warren (1799–1874). Warren had been an Owenite, and had taken part in the New Harmony experiment, which had convinced him that even Owen's type of community involved a form of coercion that was destructive of the individual's claims. Re-acting against common ownership, he worked out a theory of cost-price exchange based on labour-time, evidently derived from Owen but also foreshadowing some of Proudhon's ideas of equitable contract as the foundation of a good society. Warren first opened a store, at which he put his system into practice, and issued labour notes rather like those which Owen issued at his Labour Exchanges. In 1846 he expounded his ideas in his *True Civilisation*, and a little later he founded a community in Ohio on a basis of strictly individualistic enter-prise. Lysander Spooner (1808–87) was another pioneer of the extreme individualistic school. Warren's principal follower, Stephen Pearl Andrews (1812–86), further developed the ideas of individualistic Anarchism in his *Constitution of Government in the Sovereignty of the Individual* (1851). The chief successor of Warren and Andrews was Benjamin R. Tucker (1854– ?), who founded his *Radical Review* in 1878 and his better-known journal, *Liberty*, in 1881. His principal work, *Instead of a Book*, in which he attacked Socialism and Communism from the individualistic standpoint, appeared in 1893.

This native American Anarchism had nothing in common either with European Anarchist-Communism in its various forms or with the 'Anarchism' of the dynamiters. As Anar-chists from Europe arrived in the United States, conflict soon developed between them and the native Anarchists such as Andrews and Tucker. The Proudhonists, who found an American exponent in W. A. Greene of Boston, provided a sort of bridge between the individualistic and the Socialistic schools of Anarchism in the United States ; but they were not numer-

ous. At Anarchist Congresses held at Albany in 1878 and at
Alleghany City in 1879 there were violent disputes, and the
revolutionary element broke away under the leadership of
Michael Schwab of Chicago, an emigrant from Germany. In
1883 an Anarchist Congress, held at Pittsburg, drew up a programme which combined a revolutionary demand for the
abolition of class-rule with advocacy both of Co-operative production and of a system of equal exchanges on a non-profit
basis — a mixture of the ideas of Warren and Proudhon with
those of European Anarchist-Communism. This programme,
with an appeal to the workers to organise for its realisation, was
issued at Chicago under the auspices of German, Czech,
French, and English-speaking Anarchist groups. Chicago was
at this period the centre of acute disturbances arising out of the
workers' movement for the eight hours' day and the disputes
over the rights of organisation at the McCormick Harvester
plant ; and there were numerous clashes between the workers
and the police, who behaved with great violence as strike-
breakers. In 1886 August Spies, one of the Anarchist leaders,
called a meeting in the Haymarket to protest against the action
of the police, who broke it up despite its peaceful character,
vouched for by the Mayor. In the struggle following the police
charge, a bomb was thrown, and a number of policemen were
among those killed and wounded. Mass arrests of leading
Anarchists followed : and four, Albert Parsons, George Engel,
August Spies, and Adolph Fischer, were executed, and many
more, including Michael Schwab, given long prison sentences.
At the trial it was never proved that any of the arrested men
had had anything to do with the bomb-throwing, or had
approved of it ; but their admitted revolutionary faith was
taken as evidence of their guilt. The miscarriage of justice led
to strong and persistent protests, and six years after the trial,
in 1893, Governor Altgeld granted the survivors an uncon-
ditional pardon.

The affair of the Chicago Anarchists created an immense
stir, not only in the United States, but in Europe as well.
Socialists everywhere denounced the action of Judge Gary, who
had presided at the trial, and demanded the release of the
surviving prisoners. In the United States, however, despite
Altgeld's action, the effect of the affair was to destroy the tolera-

tion that had previously been extended to the preaching of revolutionary ideas, and to break up many of the more extreme groups among the refugees from Europe. Moreover, everywhere the Chicago episode, following on the Anarchist outrages in Western Europe, made the main Socialist organisations more than ever determined to shake off all connection with the Anarchists, and helped to bring about the definitive exclusion of the Anarchist societies from the growing international Socialist movement.

During the late 'eighties 'propaganda by deed' appeared to be on the decline, except in Russia, Italy, and Spain, where it continued sporadically every year. In 1887 three separate attempts were made to kill Alexander III, and bombs were exploded in the Cortes and in the Finance Ministry at Madrid. In France, especially, the 'nineties were a period of many crimes by individuals professing Anarchist opinions, and the authorities and a large part of the public became convinced that these must be the work of some central Anarchist organisation, secretly organised with large resources coming from some unknown source. There is in fact not the smallest evidence to support this view, and all the circumstances brought to light in the numerous trials of Anarchists discredit it.

The men who were responsible for the outrages of the 1890s — François Auguste Ravachol, Auguste Vaillant, Émile Henri, Santo Geronimo Caserio, and the rest — were all shown to have acted either quite alone or with only a very few confederates, and all the attempts to implicate such Anarchist leaders as Jean Grave, Sébastien Faure, and Émile Pouget only made it clear that they were entirely innocent of any part in the crimes. The assassins did not belong to any one type — unless being at cross purposes with the world be regarded as constituting a type. They ranged from sheer criminals, such as Ravachol, whose earlier murders were entirely without political motive, to solitary fanatics, such as Auguste Vaillant — who had, by the way, no connection at all with Édouard Vaillant, the Blanquist leader. A number of them were of very mean intelligence ; for example, Santo Geronimo Caserio, the young Italian workman who assassinated President Sadi Carnot at Lyons in 1894. Some of them were definitely members of Anarchist groups ; but the Anarchists were divided into a great many tiny groups, with little connection between them. The main fact that emerges from a study of the numerous bomb-throwers and other assassins who struck terror into the hearts of the French *bourgeoisie* in the 1890s is that the motive prompting most of them was revenge, not so much for wrongs suffered personally, as for the persecutions inflicted by Governments and for the sentences passed on earlier assassins. It is hardly open to doubt that the extreme vindictiveness with which a succession of French Governments tried to suppress Anarchism and to implicate the many in the crimes of the few, far from destroying the movement, helped to keep it alive.

If there had been, as these Governments and their police advisers supposed, a central Anarchist body directing the individual acts, wholesale suppression, involving the innocent with the guilty, might have been effective. As there was no such central body, each execution and each round of arrests and imprisonments of more suspects, often after farcical trials, merely stirred up a few more partly demented individuals to attempt vengeance. Moreover, the readiness with which reactionary politicians, such as Dupuy and Casimir-Perier, identified Anarchism with any form of working-class militancy and aided even the most reactionary employers against strikers in the name of law and order, created for the Anarchists — even for those guilty of senseless criminal acts — an amount of sympathy they would certainly not have received had the authorities behaved less hysterically. The hysteria was not confined to France : it showed itself in one country after another, and was industriously fanned by sensational newspapers. It culminated in 1898 in the International Conference of Governments, held at Rome, for the purpose of concerting means of combating the Anarchist danger, especially by the suppression of Anarchist groups and newspapers, and by the enacting of special laws for the summary punishment not merely of 'propagandists by deed', but of anyone openly professing Anarchist opinions. If nothing much came of this Conference the main reasons were, first, that many countries had already passed drastic exceptional laws ; and secondly, that after about 1900 the 'Anarchist crime wave' began definitely to recede.

Why were the 1880s and 1890s marked by this strange emergence of criminal Anarchism in a number of Western countries, and above all in France ? It has been argued that one cause was the invention of dynamite by Alfred Nobel in 1868 — or rather the diffusion of the knowledge of easy means of handling it and its extended use in industry, which made it not very difficult to procure. But a high proportion of the Western Anarchists did not use dynamite — though of course some did. There were as many stabbings and shootings as bomb-throwings. Some reactionaries suggested that the trouble in France was due to the amnesty granted to the Communards and to the increased freedom to form political associations after 1880 ; but the movement had actually begun in 1878, before the Communards came back, and hardly any ex-Communards played any part in it. Louise Michel came nearest ; but she was no assassin. Her closest approach to crime was looting a baker's shop to feed the unemployed.

These explanations will not do. It is much more likely that, in the West, Anarchist 'propaganda by deed' was an incidental accompaniment of a much greater social movement with which it had only a psychological connection. Over all Western Europe, in the 1880s and 1890s, the social conscience was being widely stirred, and the modern Socialist and democratic movements were taking shape. Among most of those who felt these stirrings, the solution was found in activity in the growing Socialist parties, Trade Unions, and social reform societies, ranging from the most revolutionary to the most moderate. But there were a few who could find no satisfaction in these bodies, and were driven by a sense of wrong and of Government oppression into a state of sheer revolt against society. Such persons tended, in the 1880s and 1890s, to profess Anarchist opinions, though their Anarchism had only a little in common with that of such men as Kropotkin or Réclus. In the twentieth century they would have become Fascists or Nazis ; and some of them got as near to this as they could by joining the special anti-Anarchist police after a spell of Anarchist activity. In all, they were few ; but they were able to create a sensation and to bring off not a few *coups* because they were few and isolated and therefore difficult to catch except in the act. Their activity began to die down in the new century not so much because the police became better at tracking them down — though this may have been the case — as because Governments became less repressive and furnished them with less excuse and — what was even more important — with less sympathy. For, as Socialism and Trade Unionism became stronger and better organised and achieved a more fully recognised position in society, there were fewer workers whose hands were against the entire social order and who were willing to regard all its enemies as their friends. This may not be the whole explanation of the decline of Anarchist violence, but it certainly comes nearer to it than any other that has yet been offered. In France in particular Anarchist violence died down as Syndicalism took shape and diverted the currents of anti-State opinion into more constructive channels. Syndicalism, as it were, sublimated the impulses of 'propaganda by deed', and, in taking over many of the ideas of the Anarchist thinkers, discarded the sheerly insane elements. These had never led more than a tiny minority of Anarchists into deeds of violence ; but it had been difficult for the theoretical Anarchists to refrain from defending them against the repression which hit at both groups alike.

Some may think that too much space has been given to the discussion of forms of Anarchism which have almost no connection with the development of Socialist thought. But these manifestations of political crime did have a considerable importance for Socialists in general as well as for the Anarchists, who had to bear the chief blame for them in the public mind. A great many Anarchists — including some of the criminals — called themselves Socialists or Collectivists as well as Anarchists. Despite Marx's ferocious campaign against Bakunin, Anarchism continued in the 1880s to be commonly regarded as a form of Socialism ; and continental Social Democrats were always trying to emphasise their sharp differences from Anarchism in all its forms. This was, however, much less true of Great Britain than of the continental West. In Great Britain murderous Anarchism never existed on any substantial scale. Only Irishmen, who were certainly not Anarchists, used the bomb as a political weapon. In the only case in Great Britain of Anarchists making bombs — that of the Walsall Anarchists of 1892 — the bombs were intended for foreign use. The bomb explosion in Greenwich Park in 1894 was unintentional ; and the man who was carrying it and was killed by it was a French Anarchist without British political connections. It too was presumably meant for export. There were in Great Britain a number of Anarchist refugees from the Continent, and it was often alleged, especially after most other countries had passed special anti-Anarchist laws and had expelled their Anarchist refugees — that London was the real centre of the secret International to which the outrages were attributed. There is, however, little to support any such view ; and in any case Anarchism in Great Britain was a theoretical attitude rather than a form of militant action. These conditions made the struggle between Anarchists and Socialists less fierce than it was elsewhere ; and, as we shall see, there was no sharp separation between the two movements in the 1880s. Anarchists took part in the Social Democratic Federation and even in the Fabian Society, and, on a larger scale, in William Morris's Socialist League — from which, in the end, they succeeded in driving Morris out, only to destroy the League itself as a consequence of their victory. This episode, however, is best left over till we come to discuss the record of British Socialism in the 1880s.

We can now turn to the more general development of Anarchism as a social theory, and to the movements in which this theory found expression after the collapse of the First International and the sharp break between Marxian Social Democracy and the anti-authoritarian tendencies represented in various forms by the Swiss, Belgian, Spanish, and Italian opponents of centralisation and of the State. Anarchism as a philosophic doctrine sets out from a root-and-branch opposition to all forms of society which rest on the basis of coercive authority. Anarchism, as an ideal, means a free society from which the coercive elements have disappeared. But hostility to the existence of any kind of coercive authority is compatible with widely different positive views. The Anarchists, very broadly, fall into two main groups — the individualists, who want as far as possible to do without social organisation, as well as without the State ; and the collectivists, or Anarchist-Communists, who combine opposition to the State as a coercive agency with a strong belief in the virtues of non-coercive association and co-operation. Not all Anarchists fall neatly into this classification. Godwin and Proudhon, whose views were discussed in the first volume of this work, both lie somewhere between the two extremes. But most of the thinkers who have espoused Anarchism — with or without the name — can be assigned with fair accuracy to the one group or the other. Bakunin, Kropotkin, Réclus, Jean Grave, and Émile Pouget belong to the communistic, or collectivistic, part of the movement. Max Stirner, among the Germans, and Benjamin Tucker and most of the native American Anarchists, belong to the individualistic part.

With the individualistic kind of Anarchism this book is not concerned, except when it enters into conflict with the other kind. It has manifestly nothing to do with Socialism. On the other hand, collectivist Anarchism — or Anarchist-Communism, as it was to be called later — came into being definitely as a form of Socialism ; and we have already needed to follow the struggles between it and authoritarian Socialism in the First International. The purpose of the remainder of the present chapter is mainly to trace what happened to the development of this second sort of Anarchism after the International had finally collapsed, and in particular to discuss Anarchist-Communism as it developed in the hands of Prince Peter Kropotkin in the 1880s and 1890s. We shall, however, stop short in this volume of the theoretical aspects of the re-emergence of Anarchist-Communism as Syndicalism or Anarcho-Syndicalism in the working-class movements of the Latin countries at the beginning of the twentieth century.

As we saw in discussing Bakunin's doctrines, the socialistic form of Anarchism rests on a sharp distinction between 'natural' and 'unnatural' forms of association and collective action. The socialistic Anarchists insist that society is natural to man, and lay the greatest stress on the propensity of men, at all stages of social development, to work together in a friendly way in pursuance of common objectives. The title of one of Kropotkin's best-known works brings out very clearly the fundamental belief on which this kind of Anarchism rests. The book is called *Mutual Aid*, and it sets out to show that such aid is characteristic, not only of savages and barbarians as well as of civilised men, but also of many animals. It belongs, Kropotkin is urging, to the animal kingdom and to man as a member of that kingdom : it is not a product of civilisation, but a fundamental quality of the life of gregarious creatures. Kropotkin, in this book, was concerned to attack the notion, widely accepted as

'Darwinian', that the realm of nature was one of sheer struggle for individual survival, in which only the 'fittest' could survive. He did not, of course, deny the existence of such a struggle ; but he insisted that it was only one aspect of nature, and that everywhere the opposite principle of 'mutual aid' was also to be found at work.

This 'natural' propensity to co-operate, the Anarchist-Communists argued, operated most strongly and directly in small, face-to-face groups — above all in the family and in the clan as an enlarged family. But as the scale of social living increased, and as the division of labour advanced, it operated also among the members of the diverse social groups into which society became organised, and between groups as well as within them. The opposing tendency towards antagonism within and between groups was traced, above all, to the development of private property — as it had been earlier by Rousseau in his *Discourse on the Origin of Inequality* — and to the emergence of class-divisions resting on property relations. Accordingly, the socialistic Anarchists, equally with the Marxists and the Utopian Socialists, stood for the abolition of private property and for collective ownership of the means of production. They differed from the Marxists, not on this issue, but concerning the character of the 'collectivity' in which the ownership should be vested. The Marxists thought of the 'collective' as a large-scale entity — as large at least as the nation : the Anarchists thought of it as the 'people' on the spot — the small, neighbourhood group which used the means of production in a co-operative way for the satisfaction of the needs of its members. 'Collectivism', as Bakunin and his followers used the word, had reference to the local, face-to-face group of co-operating producers and consumers : it had nothing in common with the later usage, in which the word came to mean 'State Socialism' — ownership by the great 'collective' which was represented by the democratised State. The 'State', according to the Anarchists, as an essentially coercive body — which Marx too considered it to be — could not represent the people, with their natural propensity towards 'mutual aid'. It was an authority superimposed on the 'people' — not a natural emanation of the popular will to co-operate.

The socialistic Anarchists, then, were in search of a kind of society that would be built upon a basis of natural co-operative-ness, and, in being so, would stimulate, instead of repressing, men's natural propensity to 'mutual aid'. They believed that, if the face-to-face groups could be organised in such a way as to eliminate economic antagonisms, it would be easy to extend the same principle of action over wider areas without resorting to any sort of coercive authority. This they hoped to achieve by substituting for the State, organised from above, the method of free federation, through which the small local or functional units would group themselves at need for common action. Thus, the various producing groups within a single local com-munity would come together to form the local commune ; and the local communes would group themselves over larger or smaller areas for particular common purposes, such as the conduct of common services. We have seen how de Paepe and others attempted in the reports presented to the Congresses of the International to draw up plans for the conduct of the public services in accordance with this principle. De Paepe, indeed, was never completely an Anarchist ; but in the controversies between the Marxists and the Anarchists he came much nearer to the Bakuninist than to the Marxist position, and, when the split came, he and his Belgian followers continued to work with the Anarchists in the anti-Marxist International. The Belgians, however, were never so entirely Anarchist as the Jura Swiss or the Italians and Spaniards. It was in the Jura Federation, and among the Russian and other exiles who had followed Bakunin's leadership in Geneva, that the gospel of Anarchist Communism was fully worked out — chiefly by Kropotkin and Élisée Réclus — in the later 'seventies. *Le Révolté*, conducted mainly by Kropotkin and Réclus at Geneva from 1879 and transferred to Paris in 1885, became the principal organ of the movement.[1]

After 1871 French Switzerland became more than ever the centre of anti-authoritarian Socialist thought. In France, for the time being, every form of organised Socialist activity was proscribed, and even Trade Unionism was reduced to entire impotence, though it never quite ceased to exist. In Germany the Eisenachers and the Lassallians, up to 1875, fought each

[1] In 1887 the title was changed to *La Révolte*, and it continued to appear under this name until 1894. It was succeeded in 1895 by Jean Grave's *Les Temps nouveaux*, which lasted until August 1914.

other as well as Bismarck ; and the latter coquetted at times with the Anarchists, with whom they shared a belief in the need to develop Co-operative production. But both Marxists and Lassallians were firm believers in political action, which the Anarchists and Anarchist-Communists rejected ; and after the fusion of the two German parties in 1875 German Social Democracy was more and more dominated by Marxist ideas and preoccupied with the struggle to establish its political position. Certain groups, headed by Wilhelm Hasselmann and Johann Most, took an Anarchist line ; but in 1880 both Hasselmann and Most were expelled from the party and driven abroad. Most, as we have seen, went first to London, where he founded *Freiheit* as an Anarchist organ in 1880, and then two years later to the United States, whither Hasselmann had preceded him. Both carried on their Anarchist propaganda in America ; but in Germany they had no successors of note.

With the French out of action and the Germans developing their movement on essentially national lines within the framework of the new constitution of the German Reich, Switzerland, as the home of a host of refugees, especially from France and Russia, became for a time the centre of revolutionary ferment in Western Europe, though there were also important groups in London, which was especially a point of focus for exiled Blanquists. But as the wave of anti-Anarchist feeling rose higher in the 1880s, the Swiss Government found itself subject to increasing pressure from the greater European powers to take action against the refugees who used it as a convenient centre for hatching revolutionary plots. When the Anti-Socialist Laws were put into force in Germany the German Social Democrats were compelled to transfer a large part of their organisation abroad, and Switzerland was the obvious choice. Thence they directed the work of the party and sent forth their newspaper, *The Social Democrat*, edited by Eduard Bernstein, and their pamphlets for circulation in Germany. Austrian Socialists expelled from Vienna, and Hungarian and Czech Socialists, also operated from Swiss territory ; and Switzerland also continued to harbour large groups of Russian exiles and of Italians, as well as Frenchmen who had made their escapes after the fall of the Paris Commune. On the whole, the Swiss rejected the increasing pressure that was put upon them both to surrender refugees who were 'wanted' in their own countries and to prevent the refugee groups from continuing their work ; but they did considerably stiffen their attitude towards those who could be labelled 'Anarchists' and accused of any form of incitement to violence.

Consequently, when the Communards were amnestied and returned to France, a number of refugees from other countries, including Kropotkin, soon followed them, and, in the 1880s, France became the principal centre of theoretical as well as of 'practical' Anarchism. The French Government, however, as we have seen, speedily took measures against the Anarchists, and imprisoned not only those who actually resorted to violent acts, but also a number of the leading theorists of Anarchism, such as Gautier and Louise Michel, and with them Kropotkin, who, on his release in 1886, transferred his headquarters to London.

Prince Peter Alexeivich Kropotkin (1842–1921) is unquestionably the leading figure in the development of Anarchist-Communism as a social doctrine. Born into the highest circle of Russian aristocracy, he was educated in the Corps of Pages directly attached to the Czar, with the prospect of a military career before him in one of the most aristocratic regiments. As a youth he shared the enthusiasm which greeted Alexander II's accession and his decision to emancipate the serfs. He was often in personal attendance on the new Czar, and soon became conscious of the strange mixture of idealism and autocratic assumption in Alexander's character, and also of the fear which constantly haunted him — a fear which had in it nothing of personal cowardice, but nevertheless drove him into the arms of the reactionaries at every hint of opposition or resistance to oppression. Kropotkin shared the deep disillusion which spread through the Russian intelligentsia when the emancipation was largely nullified by the burdens imposed on the serfs for compensation to the landowners and by the ferocious suppression of every manifestation of discontent. When the time came for him to leave the Corps of Pages and to choose his regiment, he chose, not one of the crack regiments that would have led to a high official career, but a Siberian Cossack regiment which involved burying himself in a remote province and forfeiting his chances of social success. He had several

motives for this choice. In part, it was a voluntary renunciation of a career which repelled him ; but it had also a positive side. Count Muriakov, the Governor-General of East Siberia who had recently annexed the Amur region, was an advanced reformer, and had done much to purge the administration of corrupt and reactionary officials. If there was one place where a Russian could serve the Czarist régime without becoming an instrument of reaction, East Siberia seemed, in 1862, to be that place. But, in addition to this, there was a further attraction. Kropotkin's studies at the Page's School had been primarily mathematical and scientific, and his bent was most of all towards geographical, geological, and ethnological research. East Siberia was from both these standpoints an unrecorded country ; and he hoped to be able to work in these fields. In this he was, in fact, highly successful : he travelled over a large part of Siberia and even into Chinese Manchuria making observations, and his work laid the foundations of scientific study of the lands and peoples of the Russian Far East. His reports were later written up while he was in prison in Russia and published by the Russian Geographical Society, of which he had earlier been offered the secretaryship. Still later, he used more of his materials in his work for Élisée Réclus' great *General Geography*. Kropotkin was in fact as eminent in geology as he became later in the realm of social thought.

Kropotkin remained in Siberia, on military service, but mainly engaged in his work of scientific survey, until the end of 1866. But he became more and more averse from serving the Czar as reaction gained the upper hand in Russia and as its effects spread to Siberia. He was, moreover, outraged by the brutal suppression of the Polish revolt, some of whose exiled victims came under his authority. At length he decided to throw up his position and, despite his father's disapproval, to enrol himself as a student at St. Petersburg University in order to complete his mathematical and scientific qualifications. For the next five years he was first a student and then engaged in geographical and geological research and in writing up part of his account of Siberia for the Geographical Society. Then, in 1872, came his first visit to Western Europe, where he stayed mainly in Switzerland, first at Zürich and then at Geneva and in the Jura. He there came into touch with the International, first through Marx's Russian supporter, Utin. But almost at once he threw in his lot with the rival group which followed Bakunin. The two men never met ; but Kropotkin made friends with Joukovsky, and joined the Bakuninist Section of the International at Geneva just at the time when the great dispute which split the movement and destroyed its Marxist Section was at its height. He returned to Russia with a mass of Socialist and Anarchist literature, which he successfully smuggled across the frontier, and with his faith in 'free collectivism' fully formed. Back in Russia he found the repression at its height and threw himself into the revolutionary struggle as an advocate of propaganda to win over the peasants and workers as against Zhelyabov's policy of revolutionary terror carried on by small groups of intellectuals out of contact with the masses. He soon got himself into trouble. One after another the members of his circle were arrested, and in 1874 he found himself a prisoner in the fortress of St. Peter and St. Paul. He had, however, influential friends, especially among the scientists ; and after a time he was allowed books and papers in order to continue his scientific work for the Geographical Society. His health broke down after two years waiting for trial. He was badly ill when, in 1876, he was removed to a different prison to await trial, and later to the prison hospital. Thence, with the help of friends, he contrived to make his escape and, after hiding for a time in St. Petersburg, got away across Finland into Sweden with a false passport, and thence to England.

At this time Kropotkin had every intention of returning to Russia to resume his revolutionary work. In fact, he never returned there until after the Revolution of 1917, when he went home to spend his last years and to die in disillusion — for he retained his Anarchism and his hatred of centralised authority to the end. Arriving in Western Europe he was almost at once caught up in the Anarchist movement. In London he stayed only for a few months, supporting himself mainly by writing reviews and notes on scientific matters for *Nature*, then edited by J. Scott Keltie. He did not feel at all at home in England, where he knew nobody and was appalled at the absence of revolutionary or Socialist feeling among both workers and intellectuals. He got into touch with the friends he had made in Switzerland on his previous visit to the West — especially with James Guillaume, with whom he had formed a strong friendship. In 1877 he left England and settled at La Chaux-de-Fonds, becoming a member of the Jura Federation, which was carrying on the Bakuninist wing of the First International. Bakunin had died the previous year. There Kropotkin soon made a new close friend — Jacques Élisée Réclus (1830–1905), who had taken part in the Paris Commune and was at the centre of a group of Communards including Louis-Jean Pindy, Paul Brousse, Gustave Lefrançais, and Benoît Malon. There too were a number of Italian Internationalists, headed by Carlo Cafiero and Errico Malatesta, as well as a number of Russians, Spaniards, and other refugees of Anarchist, or near-Anarchist, opinions.

Kropotkin formed a strong attachment for the Jura Swiss, and a deep admiration for their liberty-loving way of life. He saw in their combination of domestic industry — especially watch-making — with work on their own land a kind of life of which he strongly approved. He wanted, of course, to rid them of the merchants and middlemen who oppressed them, and he believed that, if they were set free from capitalist impositions, they would be able to prosper abundantly in their small communities. His experience of living among them did much to influence his economic and social ideas, and references to their way of life are frequent in his writings — especially in *Fields, Factories and Workshops* — though, as we shall see, he was no opponent of machinery, or even of large-scale production in its proper place. What he came to hold most deeply was that the good life for man depended on the industrial worker not being cut off from the land and not being forced to spend his entire life at a single occupation, however skilled — much less at unskilled factory work. He admired the fight the Jura watch-makers were putting up against the competition of factory-made products, and their preference for going short to giving up their freedom. They were able to hold out, he argued, because they had kept the land, and were therefore able to maintain themselves in times of trade depression. He recognised, however, that in many trades the handicraftsmen were fighting a losing battle against the machine ; and part of his problem, in constructing his social philosophy, was to find a solution of this difficulty.

To that question we shall come back. For the time being

Kropotkin was too busy with the affairs of the dying International to work his theories out in any comprehensive form. He attended some of the later Congresses of the anti-Marxist International, and also the abortive Socialist Unity Congress held at Ghent in 1877. There he narrowly escaped arrest by the Belgian police, who would probably have handed him over to the Russians. He got away to London, and worked for a time in the British Museum ; but he soon left for France, where, though the amnesty to the Communards had not yet been enacted, relaxation of the repression had already opened the way to a renewal of Socialist and Anarchist propaganda. He collaborated in Paris with Jules Guesde, who had not yet gone over to Marxism, in starting small Socialist clubs and societies, but was soon in danger of arrest on account of his connection with the International. In 1878 he returned to Switzerland, and there, in co-operation with Élisée Réclus, the Savoyard F. Dumartheray, and the Genevese clerk Herzig, started an Anarchist journal, *Le Révolté*, which soon became the principal organ of the Anarchist-Communist movement. The paper had a hard struggle. It was started without funds and after the first few issues was unable to find a printer — upon which its promoters managed to buy a modest plant on credit, and took to printing it themselves. It began at a difficult time, early in 1879, when the hue and cry against the Anarchists was mounting towards its height after the outbreak of 'propaganda by deed' during the previous year. But it managed to survive, and in it appeared much of Kropotkin's best writing. Kropotkin continued to conduct it in Switzerland until, after the assassination of Alexander II in 1881, he was expelled from that country under pressure from the Czarist Government. Just before his expulsion he had attended the London Anarchist Congress of 1881, where he had opposed the policy of 'propaganda by deed' as inexpedient. This, however, was not known publicly, and as he defended the killing of the Czar in his paper, he was credited with opinions which he was far from holding. To justify killing the Czar in Russia, where there was no other way of protest against the bitter persecution of liberal opinions, was a quite different thing from favouring any general policy of assassination or bomb-throwing ; and to such a policy Kropotkin never subscribed.

Expelled from Switzerland, Kropotkin moved across the border to Thonon, in France. He soon established contacts with the rapidly developing workers' movement of the Lyons region, in which Anarchist influences were strong. But he was threatened with assassination by Czarist agents, and in 1881 he moved to London, where he remained for about a year. Again he was repelled, as Herzen had been before him, by the temper of English society. He visited Radical clubs, making speeches about conditions in Russia, and he met Hyndman, who had recently published *England for All* and started the Democratic Federation. He also addressed, in broken English, the annual gala of the Durham Miners; but he made no friends, and at the end of a year decided to move back to France, despite the danger of arrest. Back in France, he resumed his contacts with the Lyons workers, and continued to edit *Le Révolté*, which was still published in Switzerland. A severe economic crisis in the Lyons silk industry was causing widespread distress, and the workers broke out into revolt, of which the Anarchists put themselves at the head. Kropotkin's part in the movement led to his arrest, with Émile Gautier and others, in 1882, and to his imprisonment under the law of 1872 which made membership of the International a crime. He was charged with having helped to form a new Anarchist International at the London Congress of 1881; and, as we have seen, this body was credited by Governments and reactionaries with the central direction of every sort of Anarchist violence all over Europe. Kropotkin could have escaped; but he preferred to face his trial, and, unlike those who were tried with him, refused to appeal against his sentence. He remained in prison in France until President Grévy released the Anarchist prisoners in 1886. He then left France and settled down in England, which was his home until his return to Russia near the end of his life. He was greatly struck by the change in the climate of English opinion since his sojourn there in 1881-2. He now found a lively Socialist movement in being, with a struggle in full swing between the Marxists of Hyndman's Social Democratic Federation and the libertarians of William Morris's Socialist League; and he also found a ferment of social ideas among the younger intellectuals. He soon made friends, and settled down happily to pass the rest of his active life in writing the series of books on which his fame rests. Some of these were written in French — his *Great French Revolution* (1893), on which he had been at work intermittently for many years, and *The Conquest of Bread* (1892), his first major exposition of his Anarchist-Communist gospel. His *Memoirs of a Revolutionist* (1902), from which much of the foregoing narrative has been taken, also appeared first in French. But he soon learnt to write in English, contributing many articles to English periodicals, and also publishing numerous pamphlets. *Fields, Factories and Workshops* (1898) and *Mutual Aid* (1902), his two most popular books, both made their first appearance in English.

His pamphlets are legion. Many of them appeared first in *Le Révolté* or in other periodicals, or were issued from the press at which *Le Révolté* was printed. Most of them reappeared in many editions, and in a number of languages. Most often reprinted, under varying titles, has been *An Appeal to the Young* (*Aux jeunes gens*), which came out first at Geneva in 1881. In England many of them were issued from the press of *Freedom*, the Anarchist-Communist journal which he helped to found in 1886.

Kropotkin, as we have seen, received a scientific training; and this deeply influenced his thought. Though he was bitterly opposed to capitalist industrialism and an ardent advocate of the independent small producer, he was by no means hostile to machinery or to the use of science to increase productive power. He professed himself quite unable to agree with William Morris's hostility to mechanised industry, though he agreed with him in so much besides. He wanted to liberate mankind from the burden of overwork and looked to technological advance to provide the means. He always argued, however, that the scientists would never use their skill to diminish the burden of human labour as long as they themselves had no direct experience of manual work. The great discoveries of the past, he contended, had come not from scientists in the laboratory but from actual working people, who could make and operate the machines they devised. The professional technicians and scientists had only taken these discoveries made by practical men and improved upon them ; and unless the divorce between science and practice could be ended he prophesied that invention would dry up, or where it continued, would fail to take the human factor into account. He also believed that large-scale production, except in the making of intermediate standardised products, was not really economical, and that its advance had been due largely to the cheapness of unskilled labour. When such labour could no longer be exploited he held that it would be found more economical, as well as much better from the standpoint of human happiness, to produce most finished products in relatively small establishments, or even in small workshops ; and he put great hopes on the advent of electric power as a means of distributing the power needed for industry over wide areas, in such a way as to make possible both the decentralisation of industry into the countryside and the successful competition of the small workshop with the mass-producing factory. Where the workshop could not hold its own, he favoured factories using large-scale power equipment ; but he wanted to see these transferred to villages, and the workers in them enabled to combine industrial with agricultural pursuits. No worker, he contended, should practise only a single trade. He believed, with Fourier, that happiness depended on variety as well as choice of occupation ; and he also shared Fourier's belief in the pleasantness of labour, rightly carried on, and above all in the human satisfaction to be derived from intensive agricultural work in producing food of high quality. He made much study of advances in intensive cultivation, and was convinced that even the most populous countries could feed their populations from the produce of their own land if they adopted the right methods.

Kropotkin's belief in the combination of industry and agriculture led him to oppose strongly the *laissez-faire* policies which had made such countries as Great Britain dependent on imported foodstuffs for the means of life ; and he also wanted countries to become much more nearly self-supporting, in respect of manufactures as well as of food, because he believed the search for wider markets and the competition of the industrial countries as exporters to be both an important cause of wars and a factor making for intensified capitalist exploitation. He asserted, and was much criticised for asserting, that world commerce was destined to shrink as one country after another developed its own manufacturing industries and excluded the products of the exporting countries. He urged Great Britain to realise that its manufacturing domination was bound to end, and to take steps, by increasing its agricultural production and diversifying its manufactures to meet the needs of the home market, to prevent the disaster that would otherwise overtake it when its exports fell into decline.

Kropotkin also took the view — most unfashionable in his day — that there was no real evidence of mass-production driving the arts of small-scale production out of existence. He emphasised both the tenacity with which the small-scale producers were holding out in France and Germany, and the extent to which new forms of small-scale production were springing up to replace those which were superseded by factory methods — including the tendency of large-scale industries to call for the services of small firms in making auxiliary components and subsidiary products. On these grounds he denied Marx's doctrine of increasing capitalist concentration and of the supersession of skill as leading to the reduction of the 'labour army' to an undifferentiated mass of 'labour-power'. He admitted that these tendencies were at work under capitalism, but asserted that there were equally powerful forces making the opposite way, and that these latter would prevail as soon as the workers took matters into their own hands.

In all this he was deeply influenced by what he had seen both in Siberia and in Switzerland, and in the areas of France — Lyons and the French Jura — that he knew best. No doubt, to a large extent, the wish was father to the belief ; for Kropotkin wanted the 'small men' to survive and the factories, run as workers' Co-operatives, to be kept as small as the technical conditions of efficient production allowed. It was part of his fundamental philosophy that men lived most happily in smallish groups, and that in such groups they could best develop their innate propensities towards mutual aid and democratic ways of life. He laid great stress on the distinction, discussed at the beginning of this chapter, between 'natural' and 'unnatural' forms of social structure, and on the idea that the large society could operate on a basis of freedom only if it rested on a foundation of self-organising small communities.

Such small communities, he believed, given common ownership and control of the means of production and a 'reintegration'—a favourite word of his—of life through the co-ordination of industry with agriculture, could manage without any sort of coercive authority. They would be held together by the bond of their co-operative effort to supply themselves with the means of good living ; and the spirit of co-operation, thus established in the basic social units, would readily extend itself to the management of such common affairs as needed to be organised over larger areas. This view was, of course, much too simple ; and Kropotkin came no nearer than other Anarchists to confronting the real difficulties in the way. Like most Anarchists, he put great emphasis on the influence of education in preparing men rightly or wrongly for the arts of life. He was strongly critical of contemporary practices in both general and technical education. In general education he held that an immense amount of time was wasted by trying to teach children out of books, or by rote, instead of letting them learn by actual doing and making ; and technical education, he held, was for the most part either perverted into training young people for particular routine employments instead of equipping them with a wider craft sense which they could apply in many different fields, or misdirected to the production of managers and supervisors as slave-drivers of exploited workers in mass-producing establishments. He cited instances in which, despite the bad environment of capitalism, better methods were followed in the teaching of small groups of technicians ; and his chief praise was accorded wherever he found two conditions satisfied —a stress on the teaching of mathematics and basic science rather than of particular techniques, and a wide opportunity to make things for actual use.

The reader of Kropotkin's writings is struck again and again by the contrast between the essential reasonableness, and even moderation, of what he says about such matters as these, and the intransigeance of his more purely political writings. Even in these, he has little of the bitterness that is characteristic of much Anarchist literature. Even when he was most indignant or furious, he remained an essentially lovable person, and there was in him not the smallest trace of that streak of insanity that is continually showing itself in Bakunin's work. Bakunin managed to be dictatorial as well as the enemy of dictation : Kropotkin had no wish to dictate to anybody. He did really believe in freedom, and regarded coercion as an unnecessary result of wrong social institutions.

It was never quite clear why he supposed that, in view of men's natural propensity to mutual aid, the world had come to be so dominated by coercive government and the competitive struggle of man with man, or why he deemed it possible that these evils should be done away with, so as not to return. The nearest he came to offering an explanation was when, echoing many earlier Socialists, he said that always, up to the nineteenth century, productive power had been too small to allow everyone the means of good living, but that already men had in their hands the means to universal abundance, if they would but set out to provide, as neighbours, for their common needs instead of chasing round the world for markets and for products they could well make at home. In this we even now see that he was much too optimistic ; for even if the world has knowledge enough, in the twentieth century, of the means to create plenty for all, we are well aware that this plenty cannot be made actual without a vast investment in the development of the backward countries and a vast programme of fundamental education in the arts of civilisation. But this over-optimism was not peculiar to Kropotkin : it was the common faith of most of the nineteenth-century Socialists, and a vital driving force in impelling them as propagandists. They blamed capitalism for scarcity : we can see to-day that abolishing capitalism, though it may be a necessary condition of the advance towards universal prosperity, cannot by itself bring about the great works of construction that are needed or turn the ignorant into producers capable of understanding and practising modern scientifically based techniques.

Kropotkin's Anarchism, or rather Anarchist-Communism, stands at the opposite pole from the extreme individualist Anarchism with which it is often confused. The very basis of Kropotkin's faith is a belief in natural co-operativeness — in 'mutual aid' as a natural human quality more potent than egoism or the will to power. He always lays the main emphasis on this 'natural' force that is only waiting to be released from the trammels of the coercive authority which prevents it from working freely, but can never suppress it altogether. It follows from this that the main task of the social reformer, in the true sense of the word, is destructive, and that, when the necessary destruction has been brought about, men can be safely left to undertake the task of constructing the new society in accordance with their natural co-operative impulses. It is therefore both unnecessary and wrong to devise constitutions for the coming society, or even to predict, save in the most general terms, how it will be organised. The task for the present is to destroy : creation is the function not of utopian projectors but of the people themselves when they have been set free.

Such a gospel is manifestly open to widely different interpretations in terms of the actual policy to be followed. The work of destruction can be regarded either as primarily a matter of changing men's minds so as to undermine their acceptance of coercive authority as 'natural', or as essentially requiring destructive activity directed against every sort of actual agency of coercion. It can lead to bomb-throwing, or to the stirring up of insurrection, or to anti-authoritarian propaganda, or to the writing of philosophical treatises about freedom. Or, of course, it can result in minglings of these several methods in very different proportions in the activities of particular Anarchists. Moreover, the Anarchist has to decide for himself at what point, if any, social organisation ceases to be coercive and comes to stand for the principle of free association. The most individualistic Anarchists in effect deny that there is any such point, and regard all forms of association with mistrust, if not with positive hostility. As we have seen, there is in Godwin, and also in Proudhon in some of his moods, a strong element of this mistrust. The Anarchist-Communist, on the other hand, is a believer in free association, as contrasted with coercive organisation, and has therefore to try to find the dividing line. This, however, cannot in the nature of the case be at all easy to find. The Anarchists, in general, are opposed not only to States and Governments — that is, to political authority — but also to other kinds of authority that repress human freedom and spontaneity. They are against economic as much as against political authority ; and they are also against religious authority, as embodied in Churches, and against any kind of moral authority that coerces men even in informal ways — for example, through the oppressive influence of traditional taboos and customs. Up to a point, they are all in agreement in identifying the institutions it is requisite to destroy. These include all States and

Governments, all Churches — and the Catholic Church in particular — the entire system of capitalism (but not necessarily private ownership), and all forms of class or racial privilege. But they get at loggerheads about private property. Most of them seek its abolition, at any rate in the case of all major means of production, including the land. But some — the individualists — regard a system of private property, purged of all monopolistic elements, as the very foundation-stone of human liberty, while others, wishing to establish collective ownership of the major means of production, are set on leaving the small producer in assured control of the instruments he can personally use, and on vesting as many more as possible in fairly small Co-operatives of associated individuals. This is Proudhon's attitude. Most of the Anarchist-Communists are against leaving *ownership* of means of production to either individuals or such Co-operatives, on the ground that only the community as a whole has a title to own such things ; but the Anarchist-Communists themselves fall into a difficulty when they attempt to define the body in which collective ownership is to be vested. Most often, they assign this rôle to the local Commune, consisting of the whole body of citizens directly assembled. But some of them feel that this comes too near to turning the Commune into a new kind of coercive authority, and hold that, in the new society, the very conception of ownership will disappear. Kropotkin, for example, distinguishes between two stages in the coming revolutionary society — collectivism and Communism. Collectivism, he says, is a transitional stage, during which the conception of ownership will survive and will take the form of ownership by the Communes, locally or through free federations. But this stage will pass : as society moves to the full acceptance of the principle 'From each according to his abilities, to each according to his needs', the entire notion of ownership will wither away, and only then will true Communism come into being. This, it will be seen, bears some resemblance, though with an important difference, to the Marxian conception of the 'withering away' of the State. The difference is that the Anarchists insist that the State must be destroyed at once, and that only the notion of ownership will be subject to the gradual 'withering'.

This is not the only difficulty. Even more important in

practice was the question of the attitude to be taken by Anarchists towards the economic institutions created by the workers themselves — Co-operative Societies and other 'mutual' bodies, and Trade Unions. Most of them, except the individualists, have laid stress on the importance of Producers' Co-operation as a means of organising production in the coming society. But they have been strongly critical of Consumers' Co-operation, as involving exploitation of the producers by the consumers and the retention of the capitalist form of interest on capital and profits distributed as 'dividends'; and they have also been well aware of the danger of Producers' Co-operatives developing into profit-seeking agencies controlled by particular groups of workers. They have mostly tried to meet these dangers by insisting that distribution should be undertaken by the Communes themselves, and that the Producers' Co-operatives in the various trades should be mere sections of the Communes, acting as the agents of the whole local community. But some of them have seen that this involves a danger of the Communes becoming coercive authorities, giving orders to the producers' groups, and the only answer has seemed to be that, in a naturally organised society, no question involving coercion would in fact arise.

The problem of Trade Unionism became, much more than that of the Co-operatives, a dividing line in Anarchist-Communist thought. One school, of which Jean Grave (1854–1939) was a leading exponent, did not regard the Trade Union as having any part to play in the structure of the coming society as the body out of which would spring workers' Co-operatives for the control of industry. He wrote, in his book *Terre libre* :

I do not see society divided into co-operatives. I do not believe in groups concerned exclusively with production. In my view, the needs of consumption will be the moving factors in inducing individuals to group themselves for ensuring the satisfaction of their wants, either by producing for themselves, or by an exchange of services entirely disconnected from any measure of value. Exchange of services, be it noted, not of commodities.

Grave had worked with Kropotkin on *Le Révolté* ; and this view was also in the main Kropotkin's. It did not, of course, exclude making use of Trade Unions as instruments in the revolutionary struggle. But it denied that they would either have any rôle in a free society or be transformed into associations for the control and management of industry. This was the dividing line between the Anarchist-Communists proper and the Anarcho-Syndicalists who became the creators of revolutionary Syndicalism. While one section of the Anarchists went over to Syndicalism, another, basing its ideas on Kropotkin and Grave, held aloof from what they regarded as surrender of the principle of economic liberty into the hands of authoritative Trade Unions.

Grave, however, was definitely an Anarchist-Communist, rather than an Anarchist pure and simple. He believed, with Kropotkin, in the basic importance of mutual aid and of free association. Other Anarchists, even if they rejected individualist Anarchism and insisted on the need for communal ownership of the means of production, were much more suspicious of association. For example, the Italian Anarchist-Communist Errico Malatesta (1853–1932), who spent a life of incessant revolutionary propaganda in Europe and America, wrote in *Le Réveil* in 1906 as follows :

> The only way of deciding what are matters of collective interest and what collectivity should determine them, the only way of destroying antagonisms, of establishing agreement between opposing interests, and of reconciling the liberty of each with the liberty of all, is free agreement by consent among those who feel the usefulness and the necessity of such agreement. . . . Our belief is that the only way of emancipation and of progress is that all shall have the liberty and the means of advocating and putting into practice their ideas — that is to say, anarchy. Thus, the more advanced minorities will persuade and draw after them the more backward by the force of reason and example.

To one who held such opinions, the Trade Union, or any agency for the control of industry based upon it, was evidently suspect as a potential means of coercion of the 'more advanced' by the 'more backward' members.

This passage from Malatesta brings out an element which was of great importance in the thought of a number of the Anarchists of the late nineteenth century. Well aware that they were only a tiny minority and that the main body of the people — and of the workers — did not share their flaming indignation against existing society or their passionate belief in liberty, they had to ask themselves the question whether they could hope to bring the masses over to their point of view, or whether they were bound to remain a chosen few acting in the real interests of an apathetic, or even hostile, majority. Those who became Anarcho-Syndicalists, on the whole, believed that, by acting *sur le terrain de classe*, they could inspire the main body of the workers, not indeed with their own faith, but with a sufficient *élan révolutionnaire* to create a mass-movement. But there were others who had no such belief, and held that the revolution was bound to be the work of a 'conscious minority' acting without the support of the main body of the oppressed, or even in face of its hostility. This view, in its extreme form, led to 'propaganda by deed', as an instrument of revolutionary terrorism. In a less extreme form it coincided with Blanqui's faith in the efficacy of a small revolutionary *élite*, which would draw the masses after it in the course of the revolution, but would have to make the revolution itself without their help. But the Blanquists were authoritarians, whereas the Anarchists who agreed with them on this point were libertarians, opposed to any sort of dictatorship. They had accordingly to emphasise the need for the revolutionary few to use every opportunity to act upon the mass by taking advantage of particular grievances, sufferings, and discontents to stir up *émeutes* with the purpose of undermining the authority of the State and of every other coercive institution of the existing system. This was Malatesta's general attitude ; and it was shared by a number of the French Anarchists, such as Émile Gautier, Charles Malato, and Sébastien Faure.

This notion of '*la minorité consciente*' has played a considerable part in French revolutionary thought ever since the revolutionaries discovered that universal suffrage, far from necessarily favouring Radical policies, could be used as a powerful weapon on the other side. This lesson was first driven home by Napoleon III after 1848 ; and it was confirmed after the disaster of 1870, when the constituencies returned a majority of anti-Republicans to be the makers of the new Constitution. The domination of '*les ruraux*' in the 1870s, the pitiless slaughter of the Communards, and the repressive régime that followed, made representative democracy appear to be the tool of reaction, and sent men's thoughts back to the years after 1848 and to what Proudhon had said about the illusions of political representation. Nor could it be overlooked that Bismarck had deliberately chosen manhood suffrage as the system of election to the new German Reichstag or, later, that a Reichstag thus elected had approved the Anti-Socialist Laws. It might be true, as Bakunin and Kropotkin answered, that on the morrow of the revolution men, set free from the shackles of authority, would suddenly learn to act co-operatively and to manage their affairs in a spirit of fraternal equality. But it was only too plain that they did not behave so now, and that they could not be expected to do so in the near future unless the revolution had first set them free.

Accordingly many of the Anarchists, even while they were doing their best to stir the masses to action, felt and expressed their scorn of mass stupidity, and used this stupidity as an argument against the political Socialists, who based their hopes on a wide franchise and on winning the votes of fools. Since the majority had voted repeatedly for the reactionary candidates, or for *bourgeois* candidates who were really no less reactionary than the open opponents of the Republic, was it not foolish to hope for success from parliamentary methods ? The advocacy of abstention from voting extended beyond the ranks of the Anarchists to many who saw political action as futile until the mass of the workers had suffered a change of heart, or been enlightened by propaganda. Going out to catch votes, it was urged, emasculated the candidate who had to woo the stupid, the short-sighted, and the self-interested ; and, in destroying the purity of the candidate's Socialism, it also destroyed that of the party under whose auspices he fought. The abstentionists were always in a minority in working-class congresses ; but, though they could not carry their own policies, they had not a little influence in persuading the Trade Unions that they had better, as organised bodies, hold aloof from political parties and contests, and rely on their own strength to carry on the struggle for emancipation in the industrial field, where they could fight ʻ*sur le terrain de classe*ʼ, and not get involved in campaigns which had to be directed to winning votes irrespective of the class to which the voters belonged. This attitude was to play a vital part in the development of revolutionary

Syndicalism, which, without forbidding its adherents to vote, put its entire emphasis on 'direct action' and held political representation in contempt as a means of advancing to the new social system.

The Anarchists had also, of course, a theoretical case against representative government — not only because it was 'government', to which they objected on principle, but also because they denied that, in a political sense, one man could represent another. It might be possible, they said, for a delegate to represent a group of individuals in relation to a definite issue or form of activity ; but even so he would need to be carefully instructed and always subject to recall. Political representation, however, was something quite different from such delegation for a particular purpose : it implied that the representative had authority to act for his constituents on any issue that might come up, and to substitute his will for theirs. It was, in effect, a thoroughly authoritarian conception with which the good Anarchist could have nothing to do.

Proudhon had written, in a letter of 1861, 'Can you possibly believe that a man who advances ahead of his age can both be right and remain popular ? Please understand, my friend, that the most backward thing in existence, the most retrograde element in every country, is the mass — is what you call democracy.' This sentiment was often echoed in Anarchist writings. Malatesta wrote in *L'Anarchie* : 'It is certain that in the purest state of society, in which the great majority of men, beaten down by poverty and brutalised by superstition, lie abjectly prostrate, the destiny of mankind depends on the activity of a relatively small number of individuals'.

Nevertheless, even those who uttered such sentiments for the most part had faith in the creative capacity of the people after the revolution, and were content that the liberated masses should shape their future in their own way — aided, of course, by the advice of the wiser among them, but in no wise coerced. Those who emphasised most the need for utter destruction of the existing order were the least concerned to foresee or to plan what would come afterwards. Malatesta at the International Congress of the Bakuninists in 1876 spoke as follows :

How will society be organised ? We do not and we cannot know. No doubt, we too have busied ourselves with projects of social reorganisation, but we attach to them only a very relative importance. They are bound to be wrong, perhaps entirely fantastic. . . . Above all else, our task is to destroy, to destroy every obstacle that now stands in the way of the free development of social law, and also to prevent the reconstruction of these obstacles, no matter in what form, or the creation of new ones. It will be for the free and fertile functioning of the natural laws of society to accomplish the destinies of mankind.

The Anarchists, then, did not believe that the freedom they demanded for men would include a freedom to flout the 'laws of nature'. They thought of these laws, under conditions of human freedom, as *determining* the course of human history. To this extent they were Anarchists because they did not believe in an anarchical world. Equally with the Marxists, many of them believed their doctrine to be 'scientific' and in tune with the march of science, and held the coming of Anarchism to be inevitable under the law of nature. This applies more to the Anarchist-Communists than to the more individualistic types, until at the other extreme we meet that kind of *laissez-faire* Anarchism which rests on a no less emphatic faith in the 'natural law' of the 'free market'. Truly, in the nineteenth century science cast a long shadow.

CHAPTER XIII

AMERICAN SOCIALISM IN THE SECOND HALF OF THE NINETEENTH CENTURY— HENRY GEORGE AND DANIEL DE LEON

THE American continent has never produced a Socialist thinker of major rank. Henry George, who came nearest to creating a movement in some respects analogous to European Socialism, was never a Socialist in any full sense and became less socialistic as he was compelled to ask himself how socialistic he really was. Edward Bellamy, who wrote a popular Socialist utopia and for a time inspired a party of his own, was not an original thinker but only a populariser of other men's ideas. Daniel De Leon has to be considered because of the very high tribute paid to him by Lenin, but hardly stands up to the test. Eugene Debs, the biggest personal force in American Socialism, was a leader and organiser rather than a theorist. In the first half of the nineteenth century, Albert Brisbane, the leader and inspirer of the American Fourierists, was a considerable person, but only in the second rank. So was Robert Owen's collaborator, William Maclure ; and Owen's son, Robert Dale Owen, and his co-worker, Frances Wright, made important contacts with the nascent working-class movements. Josiah Warren, with his Proudhon-like theory of equitable exchanges, belongs to Anarchism and to the long line of American monetary reformers rather than to Socialism.

American Socialism is, indeed, peculiarly difficult to write about because it is so largely an imported doctrine, though there were always in it native elements as well. Every wave of immigration from Europe brought with it an assortment of European Socialists ; and each great setback to Socialism in Europe carried across the Atlantic its special contingent of political refugees. Most of the political exiles who stayed in Europe hoped to return to their own countries and remained unassimilated in the countries to which they had fled. As against this, a high proportion of the exiles who went to the United States settled there for good and became American citizens, with an interest in the politics of their adopted country. This, however, did not mean that they ceased to be German, or French, or Italian, or to consort largely with companions from their own countries of origin ; for whereas in Great Britain or in Switzerland the exiles were isolated small groups or individuals, in the United States each active politician among the refugees could find whole communities of his own countrymen who had come to America not for political but for economic reasons, and were open to be influenced by propaganda carried on in their own languages and largely in terms of European ideas, merely modified to fit the American environment. In London or Geneva the refugees were all leaders deprived of their former followers, but still trying to influence them from exile. In the United States the refugees could gather round them little groups of disciples from their own countries, and had to face the problem both of welding these diverse groups together and of establishing relations with the workers who had grown up under American conditions and with the leaders of working-class and Radical movements of a distinctively American kind.

During the first half of the nineteenth century, as we saw in the first volume of this work, the outstanding influences were those of Fourier and Owen, whose ideas of community-making were adaptable to the conditions of a largely unsettled country in which new communities were continually being established, with or without a theoretical basis, on virgin soil. These conditions also suited the types of theory which laid emphasis on the monetary factor in social justice ; for communities breaking new ground were in constant danger of becoming the prey of fraudulent financiers and bankers and often suffered from an absolute shortage of cash for financing their production and exchanges. That was why not only Josiah Warren's exchange banks but also many later projects of 'free money' caught hold, and continued to be influential right through the century — in the 'Greenback' Labor Party of the 1870s and in William Jennings Bryan's celebrated presidential campaign of 1896. Most of these monetary plans, however, had little or nothing to do with Socialism ; and I do not propose to discuss them, save quite incidentally, in this chapter.

After the period of Fourierist and of Owenite influence had passed its peak, community-making on a socialistic basis went on for some time in the United States. Cabet and his followers established Icaria in Texas in 1848 and moved two years later to Nauvoo, the old Mormon centre in Illinois. Cabet left the settlement in 1856; and after his death that year it had several moves, the last American Icaria coming to an end only in 1895. Considérant, Fourier's principal French follower, working with Albert Brisbane, set up a phalanstery in Texas in 1852 ; but it soon came to grief. He remained in America, however, till 1869, and was concerned in the later developments of American Fourierism. These two ventures — Cabet's and Considérant's — must be regarded as the first repercussions on the United States of the European Revolutions of 1848 ; but the defeat of these revolutions sent to America not only community-makers but also other kinds of Socialist refugees, including Germans who had been connected with Marx and with the Communist League. The most important of this group was Marx's friend and correspondent, Joseph Weydemeyer (1818–66), who became the first active exponent of Marxism in the United States. In 1853 he established in New York the American Workers' Alliance, with a largely German following, and published, in German, a short-lived Socialist journal, *Die Reform*. The exiles for the most part threw themselves into the anti-slavery movement, and in the 1860s many of them fought for the North in the Civil War, which had a great effect in assimilating them as Americans, and also for a time interrupted the development of Socialist propaganda. At its end, the American Labor movement began to take a new shape. Ira Steward (1831–83), a mechanic of English birth, became the inspirer throughout the Northern States of a widespread agitation for the eight hours' day. Eight Hours Leagues, based on the craft Unions, which were already numerous, were set up in the principal towns, and for the first time a considerable Labour movement began to appear. Steward advocated the eight hours' day not merely as a means of lightening the burden of labour but also as the starting-point for a complete transformation of the industrial system. He believed that its effect would be to force up wages and, in doing so, not only to stimulate greatly increased production through higher mechanisation, but also to make it possible for the workers to accumulate capital and with its aid to become their own masters and destroy the capitalist system. Steward's agitation resulted in the enactment of eight hours' laws for public employees in New York, Wisconsin, and other States, and also in the establishment of a number of Bureaux of Labor Statistics to study industrial conditions. He worked with the American Marxists and joined with a group of them in trying to establish an International Labor Union after the collapse of the American Section of the First International.

To the same period belongs the National Labor Union, founded at Baltimore in 1866 under the leadership of William H. Sylvis (1828–69), who had already established the International Molders' Union. The National Labor Union began by demanding the eight hours' day; but it soon concentrated its main attention on the attempt to establish Producers' Co-operatives and on programmes of monetary reform in the interests of small producers as well as of wage-earners. It proclaimed international objectives and got into touch with the I.W.M.A. in London. A. C. Cameron, one of its active leaders and editor of *The Workingman's Advocate*, attended the I.W.M.A. Congress at Basle in 1869; and the following year the National Labor Union declared its adherence 'to the principles of the International Workmen's Association' and expressed the intention of joining it. But the N.L.U. never carried out this intention: it was indeed already beginning to disintegrate. Sylvis, the real driving force behind it, had died in 1869; and thereafter it became more and more preoccupied with monetary reform. It survived to run an independent candidate for the Presidency in 1872, but then broke up, most of its leaders passing over into the Greenback Labor Party, which ran Peter Cooper for the Presidency in 1876.

These two movements were forging ahead rapidly when, in 1867, Marx's follower, Friedrich Adolf Sorge (1827–1906), set up in New York the General German Working Men's Association, which two years later joined the First International. Sorge had taken part in the Baden Revolution of 1849 and, after being expelled from Switzerland and Belgium, had settled in the United States in 1852. In America he opposed Wilhelm Weitling and by 1867 had become the leading figure in the New York Communist Club. After the Civil War he was for a time chiefly active in the free thought movement; but by 1867 he deemed the time ripe for a revival of Marxism. When the First International's headquarters were transferred to the United States in 1872 he reluctantly became its secretary, resigning two years later in face of the quarrels which were rending its American Section asunder. After its collapse he became convinced that the first necessity was to build up a strong Trade Union movement, and he was one of the advisers of Samuel Gompers in the establishment of the American Federation of Labor. By profession a music-teacher, he stood mainly aloof from politics after the 1870s, but retained his Marxist faith and wrote with considerable penetration about American labour conditions and policy.

The National Labor Union having disappointed the I.W.M.A.'s hopes, the American Section of the International was based largely on immigrant groups, each with its own language section, and was prey to all the conflicts which beset European Socialism in the 'seventies. The defeat of the Paris Commune and the ensuing repression in Europe sent a fresh wave of exiles to the United States; and Marxists, Blanquists, Bakuninists, Proudhonists, and all the other groups fought out their battles over again in the country of their adoption. Largely on this account they made little impact on the main body of American workers, who were soon to respond to a quite different kind of leadership.

For a time, however, it seemed as if some sort of American Socialist Party might emerge from the efforts of the exiles. In 1869 a group of followers of Lassalle had established in Chicago a Universal German Workmen's Association; and out of this body developed, in 1874, an Illinois Labor Party which gained a substantial following. It rested on an attempt to promote united action between urban workers and farmers. The same year a Social Democratic Workmen's Party of North America was founded in New York by the Marxists; and two years later these two parties and what was left of the groups attached to the First International amalgamated to form the Working Men's Party of the United States, with Philip van Patten as secretary. This body turned, in 1877, into the Socialist Labor Party, which, as we shall see, became under De Leon's leadership the leading Socialist body of the United States during the final decades of the century. At the outset it was mainly a grouping of a number of national Sections, with Germans pre-ponderating. Its formation was partly a consequence of the fusion in Germany of the Marxists and Lassallians in 1875 ; and its programme clearly reflected that of the First Inter-national in its Marxist days. 'The industrial emancipation of labor,' it proclaimed, 'which must be achieved by the working classes themselves, independent of all political parties but their own, is . . . the great end to which every political movement should be subordinated as a means.'

At the outset the new party decided to run no candidates, but to build up its strength first among the workers. But it soon changed its mind, and local Sections put up candidates in a number of States and won some victories. In the meantime, however, there had been a breach with the Trade Unions, on which it had been hoped to exert a large influence. The Trade Unionists who had joined in creating the party wanted it to devote its main attention to industrial affairs rather than to political propaganda ; but at the Convention of 1877 they were voted down and the party decided to concentrate mainly on the work of Socialist education.

This breach was largely the outcome of the rapid spread of Trade Unionism and of farmers' movements during the late 'sixties and early 'seventies. Already the hopes of converting the farmers to Socialism were being reduced by the emergence of the separate farmers' movement known as the Grange, under the leadership of Oliver H. Kelly. The Grange, founded in 1866, failed to attract any large following until the depression which followed the commercial crisis of 1873. It then spread at a great pace in the South and Middle West, and became an important factor in the politics of a number of States on account of its pressure for the regulation of railroad rates and for other measures in the interest of the farming community. It also organised a large number of Co-operative societies of various kinds — for marketing, for the collective buying of farm requi-sites, and for the production of agricultural machinery — but most of these ventures came to disaster in face of the continued depression of agricultural prices. By the end of the 1870s the Grange had lost most of its members. It survived mainly in those States which had been least affected by the depression ;

for in these areas it had developed mainly as a social agency, without going into politics or embarking on extensive Co-operative schemes. When it revived in the 1890s it was no longer a political force, and its strength was chiefly in the Northern States, in which it had been relatively unimportant in its earlier days. It still exists, and carries on substantial social activities in farming areas, as well as a certain amount of Co-operative work.

While the farmers were flocking into the Granger movement, American Trade Unionism was also developing along new lines. In 1869, as the aftermath of a strike of Philadelphia garment workers, Uriah Smith Stephens (1821–82) founded a secret society to which he gave the name of the Noble Order of the Knights of Labor. His leading helpers in this enterprise were an Irish clothiers' cutter named J. L. Wright and an English Owenite gold-beater named Frederick Turner ; and these two drew up the elaborate ritual with which the Knights conducted their proceedings. It had much in common both with Free-masonry and with the rituals that had been used in British craft Unions during the early part of the century. Stephens, the founder, had been trained for the ministry, but had become a tailor, and had been active in a number of local craft Unions. Realising their ineffectiveness in face of the growing power of capitalism, he conceived the idea of a secret order, of which all who were most alive in the workers' movements would become individual members, drawing the masses after them. The Order of the Knights of Labor was never a federation of separate Trade Unions : it was a single society enrolling only individual members, and in practice its success was greatest in those trades and industries in which craft Unionism was weak or non-existent — in the mines, on the railways, and in the factories employing a high proportion of less skilled labour. Stephens held that 'the physical, intellectual, and moral condition of mankind is governed entirely by the conditions that surround the productive toiler, and make the progress of a people or indicate, unerringly, the downfall of a nation'. This, he said, held good 'in every age and in every country' ; and he called for an inclusive workers' movement based on the promotion of the workers' common interests through the rational exploitation of the means of production. Stephens was hardly a Socialist, though he was prepared to co-operate with Socialists and actually took their side in the struggles which later rent the Knights of Labor asunder. He had much in common with Ira Steward, in believing that the raising of wage standards was the clue to social reorganisation ; but he put his trust in direct industrial action rather than in legislation to achieve his industrial ends. He was associated after 1878 with the Greenback Labor Party, to which reference has been made already.

The Knights of Labor did not become of much importance for some years after the great commercial crisis of 1873. They played a minor part in the great strikes of miners and railroad workers in 1877. In 1878 they ceased to be a secret order, and denounced craft Unions, deciding to organise themselves into departments on a basis of industry. The following year Stephens was succeeded in the leadership by Terence Vincent Powderly (1849–1924), an immigrant from Ireland, who thereafter dominated the organisation, but had to fight a series of internal battles before he established his ascendancy. Powderly, though he shared Stephens's belief in 'inclusive unionism' — that is, in the 'One Big Union' — was hostile to aggressive strike action and favoured conciliation and the establishment of orderly forms of collective bargaining. He was also more of a 'politician' than Stephens, in the sense of putting greater emphasis on the use of the organisation as a 'pressure group' acting on Congress and on the State Governments. But most American employers, in the large-scale industries, were not at all prepared to recognise Trade Unionism or to enter into collective agreements ; and despite Powderly's wish to follow pacific policies the Knights were again and again forced into strike action and brought into conflict with State and Federal Governments, when use was made of soldiers or militia as strike-breakers or when the law was invoked against Trade Union activity.

From the 'seventies to the middle 'eighties the Knights of Labor were the foremost Trade Union organisation in the United States. Then their influence rapidly declined, partly as a consequence of serious defeat in a big railroad strike and partly because of the wave of reaction which spread over the United States after the affair of the Chicago Anarchists, discussed in the previous chapter. Powderly and his principal lieutenants, in the hope of maintaining their respectability, took a violent line in support of the execution of Albert Parsons and his fellow-Anarchists, despite the want of any real evidence of their responsibility for the Haymarket bomb-throwing. There were secessions on the left in protest against this attitude, as well as on the right among those who had been scared by the Chicago affair and its repercussions on public opinion. Moreover, there had already begun a strong movement towards the establishment of centrally organised national Unions in particular trades and industries ; and many of the groups in the Knights were in rebellion against the centralised direction of policy on which it was based. Samuel Gompers (1850-1924) was already in the field, organising the new federal Trade Unionism that was about to take shape in the American Federation of Labor. Faced with more and more secessions, the Knights turned for a time to politics. In 1893 Daniel De Leon attempted to capture the organisation, and Powderly was ousted from the leadership; but the attempt failed, the De Leonites seceded, and the Knights collapsed.

We have run ahead of our story in carrying the account of the Knights of Labor through to the end. We must now go back to the 1870s — to the consequences of the crisis of 1873 on the political Labor movement. While the Socialists in the Eastern States and in Illinois were joining forces in the body which became the Socialist Labor Party, a rival movement was growing up chiefly in the West, Middle West, and South, with currency reform as its principal immediate objective. This began as the 'Greenback' movement in the late 'sixties, with an attack on the bankers and financiers who first bought up the Civil War 'greenback' notes at a heavy discount and then secured legislation which enabled them to recover the full value. It developed into a demand for a new system of paper currency, free from control by the financiers, which would hold up farm prices and ensure adequate credits for the producers. Making headway first among the farmers, the movement spread to the industrial workers whose wages were being reduced or who had been thrown out of work during the depression ; and in 1878 a Greenback Labor Convention at Toledo, Ohio, organised a combined movement of farmers and workers to put up Greenback candidates for Congress and for the Presidency. The new movement polled over a million votes, and got 14 of its supporters returned to Congress. It lasted on through the 1880s, but gradually lost its strength as, in one State after another, its supporters were absorbed into the Democratic Party. But for a time it secured considerable successes, and prevented the growth of any effective Socialist movement, especially in the Western States.

The Greenback Labor movement was at its height when, in 1879, Henry George published *Progress and Poverty*, and achieved an immense and immediate popular success. Henry George (1839–97) had been born in Philadelphia, but had moved West and had become in California a moderately successful editor and newspaper proprietor. *Progress and Poverty* was not his first work. He had expressed much the same ideas in *Our Land and Land Policy* as early as 1871, without attracting much notice, and had been writing steadily in his papers ever since. But *Progress and Poverty* appeared at a moment when, in both America and Europe, public opinion was ready to receive it ; and its style and use of biblical quotations went home to the hearts of a great many bewildered and discontented people who wanted to know why the advance of capitalism brought with it so many evils and so great an instability in economic affairs.

The most curious thing about *Progress and Poverty* is that, though it made an enormous impact on opinion on both sides of the Atlantic, there was nothing at all new in what its author had to say. Not merely had the land monopoly been subject to attack for a whole century (since the writings of Ogilvie and Wallace) and to vehement attack for the best part of a century (since those of Thomas Spence and Tom Paine) : George's remedy of a tax on land value through the socialisation of rent had been part of Spence's 'Plan' and had been worked out in detail in the 1850s by the Scottish land reformer, Patrick Edward Dove (1815–73), in his *Elements of Political Science* (1854), which formed the second part of his main work on *The Science of Politics*. Dove had demanded that the State should buy out the landlords, meeting the cost by taxing them as well, and should thereafter let out the land to the highest bidders. He had based his case on the historical argument that private property in land, whatever its justification at earlier periods of history, had become an abuse and a restraint on production under modern conditions, when there was no longer any free land open to the individual for tillage without payment to a proprietor; and, like George, he had argued his case on the basis of the Ricardian theory of rent as a surplus accruing to the landowner without any service on his part, as a consequence of increasing population and demand. Few, however, had read Dove, even in Great Britain, and hardly anyone in the United States; and George himself was probably quite unaware that he had been anticipated. Indeed, he evidently worked out his opinions for himself with little reference to any previous writer — or even to such contemporary movements as the Land Tenure Reform Association in Great Britain, in which, as we shall see, John Stuart Mill played a leading part.

Henry George's main argument was simple. Conditions in the United States had made him aware both of the rapid rise of urban land values as towns grew up in newly settled districts and of the rising tendency of agricultural rents as free land suitable for farming became harder and harder to find. It was manifest in America, as it had been much sooner in the more thickly settled countries of the Old World, that economic development and rising population brought the owners of land a great unearned increment in values and enabled them to levy an ever-increasing toll on producers and house-occupiers of every sort. Was it not evident, he asked, that such a system was both grossly contrary to natural justice and highly restrictive in its effects? It enabled the owners of land not only to exact a toll for its use, but also to swell their returns by holding land out of use in order to constitute an artificial scarcity. The remedy, he held, was simple. God had given the land to the people as a common possession: let them remove it from those who had wrongly usurped its ownership. The best way of doing this was not for the people to till the land in common — George believed strongly in individual enterprise — but for the State to levy on every parcel of land an annual tax equal to the economic rent — that is, to its unimproved value, as distinct from any value added to it by the application of capital or labour, but including the value derived from its situation and advantages of proximity to markets, as well as from its natural fertility. George held that such taxation could best be introduced by stages, so as to avoid hardship; but he was opposed, unlike Dove, to the payment of any compensation to the owners, whose incomes would fall gradually to zero if they were mere absentee owners (unless they were providers of capital assets as well as of land) or, where they used the land themselves, to the value of the labour and capital they bestowed on it.

Henry George drew no distinction between labour and capital. He regarded the owners of both these factors of production as equally entitled to a return, and grouped them together as the victims of exploitation by the land monopolists. He argued that, if economic rent accrued to the State as representing the whole people, there would be no need for any other taxes — hence the name 'Single Tax', which he used later in describing his proposal. But, over and above this relief from taxation, which would benefit all the producers, further advantages would accrue. Land would always be available to those who could make the most productive use of it and would therefore be prepared to offer the highest rent. No more land would be held out of use because its owner preferred to enjoy it unproductively, or to wait until he could exact a higher rent or selling price. The restrictions which landlordism put on production would be lifted, and all barriers in the way of maximum productivity would be removed. It will be seen that George had a thorough faith in the benefits of a competitive economy, and that he was far from wishing the State to take any hand in organising or controlling production. Indeed, he came out later, in his *Protection or Free Trade?* (1886), as a complete advocate of free trade on the basis of the most orthodox *laissez-faire* doctrine.

Henry George had, however, a sincere concern for the well-being of the workers, as he made plain in his books *Social Problems* (1883) and *The Condition of Labour* (1891) — the latter a reply to the famous Papal Encyclical on the same theme; and both in the United States and in his lecturing tours in Great Britain he appeared, until well on in the 1880s, as the ally of the workers in their struggle against exploitation. By capitalists as well as by landowners he was denounced on both sides of the Atlantic as a subverter, guilty of attacking the 'rights of property' and aiming at the entire uprooting of social order. His wholehearted belief in the virtues of private enterprise was ignored, or went unnoticed ; and he consorted with Socialists and Radicals who tried in vain to convince him that what he said about land ownership was equally true, in developed societies, about the ownership of capital resources. Moreover, in his earlier days, he was not only regarded as an advocate of land nationalisation, but was quite ready to accept the label. Only in the late 'eighties did he take to describing his remedy as the 'Single Tax', or seek to distinguish himself from the socialistic advocates of nationalisation of the land.

It seems best to leave the discussion of Henry George's activities and influence in Great Britain to the next chapter, in which we shall be dealing with the developments of British Socialism in the 1880s. There is no doubt about the importance of the part his book played in these developments, or that the British Socialists were able to use his ideas as a most convenient starting-point for their own propaganda. But what George did in Great Britain had no effect on his influence in America, though his support of Irish claims in his book on *The Irish Land Question* (1881) did help to win him support in Irish-American circles. His main influence, in the United States as well as elsewhere, rested on his power to put his simple case against landlordism in ethical terms, based on a democratic interpretation of Christian teaching, that aroused a sympathetic response among a great many of those who felt themselves to be the victims of economic injustice, whether they were workers or farmers or shopkeepers or small entrepreneurs of any kind. Indeed, his converts included a sprinkling of rich men — industrialists or commercial entrepreneurs who had no reason to love landlords or financial speculators and were attracted by the notion — as old as Saint-Simon — of an alliance of the productive elements in society against the 'non-producers', the idle who contributed nothing, but benefited by every advance in productivity due to the activities of others and of society as a whole.

It was in California that Henry George worked out his ideas and first offered them to the world. But he chose New York, rather than San Francisco, as the centre from which he could best spread his gospel ; and in 1880 he took up his headquarters there and began to campaign for its acceptance. In 1886 the New York Central Labor Union and the De Leonite Socialist Labor Party united in urging him to become a candidate for the mayoralty of New York ; and in the ensuing campaign he came near to being elected as the candidate of the United Labor Party. But one effect of the campaign was to clarify George's position as an opponent of Socialism. He was prepared to go a certain distance to meet the Socialists — for example, in advocating the nationalisation of railroads and other public services which needed to be carried on as monopolies ; but beyond this he would not go, and in 1887 the United Labor Party which had sponsored his candidature broke in pieces, expelling the Socialists who had supported him in the election, but destroying itself in the process.

Daniel De Leon (1852–1914) had been among George's supporters in the campaign of 1886. When the break came, he associated himself for a time with Edward Bellamy (1850–98), whose Socialist utopia, *Looking Backward*, appeared in 1887. Bellamy was a novelist and journalist who worked out his social ideas without contact with the working-class movement, but became the inspirer of a number of clubs, which went by the name 'Nationalist', because of Bellamy's advocacy of national-isation as the basis of an equalitarian society. Next to *Looking Backward*, his best-known work is the pamphlet *The Parable of the Water Tank*, which has been often reprinted. He followed up *Looking Backward* with a second utopian story, *Equality* (1897), and before that edited in succession *The Nationalist* (1889–91) and *The New Nation* (1891–4). During these years he commanded a considerable following ; but his movement gradually died away. De Leon, its most influential supporter, deserted it in 1890 for the Socialist Labor Party ; and thereafter its following was mainly middle-class. Most of its supporters passed over into the People's Party, which nominated General Weaver in the presidential election of 1892 and subsequently merged into the Democratic Party during W. J. Bryan's campaign of 1896. A section of the Populists, however, refused to merge with the Democrats, and fought with a candidate of their own, Warton Barker, in the presidential election of 1900. They polled only a few votes, and the party then virtually disappeared.

Edward Bellamy's gospel was one of complete economic equality, based on a complete system of State Socialism. Fully accepting the need for highly mechanised large-scale produc-

374

tion, he advocated comprehensive State ownership and planning as the basis of economic activity, and argued that labour should be organised as an 'industrial army' for the common service of the whole people. 'The idea of an industrial army for maintaining the community, precisely as the military army protects it, suggested the advisability of seeing if a plan which was found to work so well for purposes of destruction might not be profitably applied to the business of production, now in shocking confusion.' William Morris, reviewing *Looking Backward* in the *Commonweal*, expressed his entire revulsion in face of the servile conception of the status of labour in Bellamy's utopia ; but the book had a very large sale in Great Britain and in the United States, and was translated into many languages. It stands for the most extreme form of State Socialism ; but its advocacy of complete economic equality gave it an appeal to many Socialists, especially to middle-class Socialists who regarded Socialism primarily as an ethical rather than an economic gospel.

During the same period the Danish-American Socialist, Lawrence Gronlund (1848–99), had a considerable influence. His best-known work, *The Co-operative Commonwealth* (1884), was translated into many languages and was edited, for its English edition, by Bernard Shaw. But Gronlund, unlike Bellamy, never became the leader of a movement. His ethical Socialism made its contribution to many of the Socialist groups of the 1880s and 1890s, but did not become identified with any particular sect.

In 1890 a new recruit, Daniel De Leon, joined the Socialist Labor Party, of which he soon became the leader. Born in Curaçao, De Leon came to the United States in his early twenties, and became a lecturer on international law at Columbia University. After supporting Henry George in New York in 1886 and thereafter joining the Knights of Labor and Bellamy's Nationalist movement, he became, in 1891, editor of *The People*, the S.L.P.'s organ, and therein developed his distinctive Socialist ideas, which won him the high praise of Lenin at a later period. In the S.L.P. he became the advocate of a renewed attempt to organise the Trade Union movement under Socialist leadership, in rivalry with the American Federation of Labor, which was taking the place previously occupied by the Knights of Labor. In 1895, in pursuance of this policy, he persuaded the S.L.P. to launch the Trades and Labor Alliance as a federation of Trade Unions and Socialist bodies with an advanced Socialist programme, based on a militant conception of Industrial Unionism. De Leon was a strong opponent of reformist Socialism, and regarded a militant class organisation of the workers as the necessary instrument for the overthrow of capitalism. Accepting Marx's view of the State as essentially an organ of class coercion, he favoured political action solely as a convenient means of agitation and not as a method of securing useful reforms within the capitalist system. Basing his doctrine on the Materialist Conception of History, he emphasised the economic character of political institutions and the need for their supersession by a new kind of social organisation based on the industrial working-class movement. In his numerous pamphlets and booklets he presented an uncompromising version of left-wing Marxism which was in sharp contrast to the policies actually followed by the European Social Democratic Parties ; and he conducted relentless war against the type of Trade Unionism represented by Samuel Gompers and the American Federation of Labor, which set out to exact the best possible terms from capitalism without attempting to overthrow it. In his best-known pamphlet, *Two Pages from Roman History* (1903), he invoked the Gracchi in support of his proletarian conception of class-warfare. In *Socialism and Anarchism* (1901) he opposed the Anarchist view which repudiated political action, but insisted that such action should always be regarded solely as a form of revolutionary propaganda. In *What Means This Strike?* (1898) he emphasised the rôle of the strike as a preparation for revolutionary action, rather than a means of improving the workers' lot under capitalism ; and in *The Burning Question of Trade Unionism* (1904) he preached the gospel of revolutionary Industrial Unionism which he carried into the Industrial Workers of the World, founded the following year. De Leon, in face of the commanding position that came to be occupied by the American Federation of Labor, was the leading advocate in the 1890s of the policy of 'dual unionism' — which meant that revolutionary Trade Unionists should join and endeavour to capture the reformist Unions as well as establish a militant Trade Union movement of their own.

For a time, after 1895, the De Leonites controlled the Central Labor Federation of New York ; but this body seceded from the Trades and Labor Alliance in 1898, and thereafter De Leonite influence in the Trade Union movement gradually waned, except among certain sections of the miners and among immigrant workers in the mass-production industries. In 1899 troubles inside the Socialist Labor Party itself came to a head. A considerable section of the membership, led by Morris Hillquit and Henry Slobodin, seceded and formed a separate organisation, which developed into the American Socialist Party, with a programme closely in line with that of the Social Democratic Parties of Western Europe. The De Leonites, left in control of the Socialist Labor Party, at their Convention in 1900 eliminated all immediate demands from the party programme, and proclaimed an out-and-out revolutionary policy. At the presidential election of that year they polled fewer than 35,000 votes, in opposition to Eugene Victor Debs (1855–1926), the nominee of the Social Democrats, who received nearly 100,000. Thereafter the De Leonites' fortunes merged with those of the Industrial Unionist movement, until dissension over political action caused a further rift, and the Industrial Workers of the World became divided into two warring factions, the one, with its headquarters at Detroit, still under De Leonite leadership, and the other, and larger, centred at Chicago and led by William D. Haywood (1869–1928) on the basis of a complete repudiation of politics as an instrument of the working-class struggle. These developments, however, go a long way beyond the period covered in this volume. They will be discussed in their place, when we come to consider the growth of Industrial Unionism and Syndicalism in the twentieth century. We shall then see also how the De Leonite movement, while it was declining in the United States, threw off in Great Britain offshoots which went to the making of left-wing Socialism, especially on the Clyde, and supplied a high proportion of the first leaders of British Communism after the World War of 1914–18.

After 1886, when the De Leonites supported Henry George in his campaign for the mayoralty of New York, the United Labor Party which had conducted this campaign fell to pieces. Henry George became more consciously anti-Socialist, and his followers either merged politically with the radical wing of the Democratic Party or organised themselves, outside parties, in propagandist bodies for the promotion of 'Single Tax' ideas. 'Single Taxers', indeed, emphasised more and more their divergence from Socialism, both in the United States and in Great Britain ; and the individualistic aspects of George's doctrine were brought out more and more clearly, especially in connection with his uncompromising defence of free trade and his hostility to State regulation of economic affairs. Although American Socialism, measured by the size of its voting support in presidential and congressional elections, continued for a time to advance, it became once more a doctrine acceptable mainly to immigrants of European origin, and ceased to have any close connection with popular discontents arising out of specifically American conditions, or to make alliances with 'popular' movements appealing to farmers and small entrepreneurs as well as to wage-workers. Only in a few States, above all in Wisconsin, with its large German population, did the movement manage to preserve a wide enough appeal to give it substantial electoral successes. But the history of American Socialism as it developed after the foundation of the Social Democracy Party of America in 1898, under Debs's leadership, must be left for consideration in the next volume of this history.

CHAPTER XIV

THE REVIVAL OF BRITISH SOCIALISM — WILLIAM MORRIS

I T is often said that Socialism died out in Great Britain between the last Chartist Conference in 1858 and the foundation of the Democratic Federation in 1881. This is not quite true, even if the term 'Socialism' is used in a restricted sense, so as to exclude the Christian Socialists. There were Socialists throughout this time, apart from the foreign refugees whose clubs existed over the whole period after the 1840s and were strongly reinforced in the 1870s after the fall of the Paris Commune. These clubs had at all times a few British members, and some links with British groups interested in internationalism. Moreover, there were always old Chartists, some of whom certainly regarded themselves as Socialists or Communists, even if they did not habitually use the name. A number of them reappeared in the Democratic Federation in the 1880s — for example, the shoemaker Charles Murray; and more were active in the 'sixties and 'seventies. Robert Hartwell, who led the London Working Men's Association in 1866, was an old Chartist. There were also Owenites : Lloyd Jones lived until 1886, and was active in Trade Union and Co-operative affairs till near his end. Then there were the men who formed the British Section of the International Working Men's Association in the early 'seventies, such as John Hales. Hales carried on after the disappearance of the International, and represented the London Commonwealth Club at the Ghent Socialist Unity Congress of 1877.

Nevertheless, it is true that between the late 'fifties, when Ernest Jones at last gave up his attempt to carry on Chartism as a Socialist agitation, and the early 'eighties there was in Great Britain no Socialist movement, either Marxist or Owenite or of any other sort. The Christian Socialists were active in the late 'sixties and early 'seventies ; but they had almost ceased to call themselves by that name, and had thrown in their lot with the Co-operative movement, which they tried hard, without lasting success, to turn in the direction of Producers' Co-operation. There was a revival of this kind of activity in the 'eighties and 'nineties, especially under the leadership of Thomas Blandford (1861–99), who was Secretary of the Co-operative Productive Federation from 1893 ; but Blandford was not regarded as a Socialist, and the revived movement never used the name. George Jacob Holyoake (1817–1906), the veteran Secularist and Co-operator, was a strong opponent of the new Socialism of the 1880s, though he remained an ardent advocate of Co-operative Production. After the rise of the Rochdale Pioneers, despite the efforts of the Christian Socialists, the Co-operative movement took shape definitely as a movement of consumers, and turned its back on Owenite Socialism. This insistence on consumers' control need not, of course, have prevented it from being Socialist in its aspirations. But in fact it was not : it was strongly voluntarist, and hostile to State intervention. Claiming to be 'a State within the State', it was opposed — or rather the great majority of its leaders were — to such ideas as that of nationalisation ; and, if it still paid lip-service to the ideal of a 'Co-operative Commonwealth' that was to arise some day in the distant future, in practice it settled down to work within the conditions of the capitalist system, with interest on share capital and 'dividend on purchases' as its outstanding methods. The almost complete conversion of the Co-operative movement to this conception of consumers' control and voluntarism as the basis of membership was mainly due to the degree in which these methods fitted the conditions of the time and enabled the movement to spread and prosper ; but something was also due to the forceful personality of John Thomas Whitehead Mitchell (1828–95), who was the almost undisputed leader of Consumers' Co-operation in the second half of the nineteenth century. Mitchell believed fiercely and combatively in both consumers' control and voluntarism, and in carrying on Co-operation as a business movement with no nonsense. He fought to extend Co-operative Production — not Producers' Co-operation — under the control of the federated Consumers' Societies ; and he was victorious all along the line against Holyoake and Edward Vansittart Neale, the Christian Socialist who gave his life to the Co-operative movement as Secretary of the Co-operative Union. Neale and Holyoake and a few others — for example, Edward Owen Greening (1836–1923), who lived on to take part in the Guild Socialist movement in the next century — held to the older Co-operative ideas, at least to the extent of wishing the workers employed in the Co-operative factories to enjoy a measure of self-government. Dr. Henry Travis (1807–84), formerly secretary to Owen's Queenwood Community, and also Owen's literary executor, tried to keep Owenite Socialism alive in his books, *The Co-operative System of Society* (1871) and *English Socialism* (1880) ; but he had no following. Mitchell swept such idealists aside ; and there was never any doubt that he had the support of the vast majority of the active committee-men from the local Consumers' Societies.

Co-operation, then, had cut its Socialist connections at any rate by the 1860s, when the great Wholesale Societies were founded and the consumers' movement settled down to its career of solid business success. Trade Unionism cannot be quite so easily characterised ; for it was much less uniform. But there was certainly no prominent Trade Union leader between 1860 and 1880 who thought of calling himself a Socialist ; and this holds good of the men who took part in the First International under Marx's leadership. There were, no doubt, a few active Trade Unionists who were conscious Socialists ; but they were foreigners who had settled in Great Britain — J. G. Eccarius (1818–89), the German tailor who was Secretary of the International and parted company with Marx during the dispute which wrecked it in 1872 ; Adam Weiler, the German cabinet-maker who was active in the Eight Hours League and moved Socialist resolutions at the Trades Union Congress ; and a few more. Some of the Englishmen were no doubt sympathetic to Socialism — for example, the Carpenters' leader, Robert Applegarth (1834–1924), who stayed in the International longer than most — but they regarded it as a foreign movement, not as a gospel at all applicable to the Great Britain of the 1870s.

The nearest approach to a Socialist body of any substance was the Land and Labour League, about which Marx wrote enthusiastically in some of his letters at the end of the 1860s.

This body, which had J. G. Eccarius and the engineer Martin J. Boon as its joint secretaries and John Weston as its treasurer, was founded in 1869 under the influence of the group that was collaborating with Marx on the General Council of the International Working Men's Association ; and Marx had high hopes of its prospects. Cowell Stepney, Thomas Mottershead, and a number of other active 'Internationalists' were on its Council ; and at first it seems to have received a good deal of Trade Union support. Its programme, drawn up by a committee of forty delegates from working-class bodies in London, began with an outright demand for land nationalisation. This was followed by eight further points — Home Colonisation ; National, Secular, Gratuitous, and Compulsory Education ; Suppression of Private Banks of Issue — the State only to issue Paper Money ; a direct and progressive Property Tax, in lieu of all other taxes ; liquidation of the National Debt ; Abolition of the Standing Army ; Reduction in the Hours of Labour ; and Equal Electoral Rights, with Payment of Members. The programme was reminiscent of both Owenism and Chartism. Drafted at a time of serious unemployment, it proposed to settle the unemployed on the nationalised land, and to use the army, before its final disbandment, as a 'pioneer force to weed, drain and level the wastes for cultivation'. For a time, it looked as if the Land and Labour League might become a powerful propagandist organisation. But the medicine it recommended soon proved to be too strong for most of the Trade Union leaders with whom Marx was attempting to work ; and some of them soon gave their support to the much less radical Land Tenure Reform Association, founded in 1870, largely under the influence of John Stuart Mill. The supporters of this body included, with Trade Unionists such as George Odger, Lucraft and Cremer, a number of Radical politicians and economists of note — among them Charles Dilke, Peter Taylor, John Morley, and Professors Henry Fawcett, J. E. Cairnes, and James Thorold Rogers, the economic historian. There was a sharp contest between the protagonists of the two bodies ; and when Marx lost his hold on the Trade Union leaders in 1871 the Land and Labour League ceased to count for much, and gradually faded away.

The Land Tenure Reform Association agreed with the Land

and Labour League that the unearned increment which appeared in land values belonged properly to society as a whole as its creator, and that the landlord had no right to it. Its promoters were prepared to tax away this increment ; but they would not go to the length of nationalisation. Their plan was mainly one of leasehold enfranchisement and of settling more workers on the land as proprietors of their holdings. John Stuart Mill, though he had become, in a theoretical sense, increasingly sympathetic to Socialism in his later years, was by no means prepared to support the anti-capitalist proposals of the Land and Labour League, which denounced landlords, usurers, and industrial exploiters in unmeasured terms and gave its manifesto an almost revolutionary tone. In practice, he was still seeking to reform capitalism rather than to overthrow it. His earlier views, in his discussion of the Utopian Socialists in the successive editions of his *Principles of Political Economy*, have been discussed in the previous volume of this work. His later views were not a little influenced by his stepdaughter, Helen Taylor (1831–1907), who became an active member of the Social Democratic Federation.

There was, of course, nothing new in the Land and Labour League's advocacy of making the land the property of the whole society. Forms of land nationalisation had been explicitly advocated by Thomas Spence [1] before the end of the eighteenth century, by Bronterre O'Brien's National Reform League in the 1840s, and Patrick Dove had published his 'Single Tax' doctrines in the 1850s. The Land Tenure Reform Association held much less forthright views than any of these, at any rate about immediate policy. There was, however, in the 'sixties and 'seventies, a still living tradition of hostility to landlordism, which was continually reinforced by the Irish struggle against rack-renting and absentee owners. Anti-landlord propaganda played a large part in the Fenian movement, led by O'Donovan Rossa, which ran its course during the same years as the First International ; and the same theme was taken up by Michael Davitt (1846–1906) on his release from prison in 1877.

Two years later Davitt founded the Irish Land League, and developed it on the basis of a demand for land nationalisation, as against the traditional demand for peasant proprietorship.

[1] Hyndman reprinted Spence's pamphlet in 1882.

Davitt's movement had large repercussions on opinion in Great Britain, where an English Land League, to which Hyndman belonged, was founded in its support. The same year as saw the birth of the Democratic Federation, with land nationalisation as one of its demands, the Land Nationalisation Society was founded, mainly by the efforts of the well-known scientist Alfred Russel Wallace (1823–1913), whose book *Land Nationalisation* appeared in 1882. There was also an active movement among the Scottish crofters, organised by a Scottish Land and Labour League, which merged into the Social Democratic Federation soon after its establishment but seceded with the Socialist Leaguers in 1884, and survived to become a constituent of the Scottish Labour Party in 1888. Dr. G. B. Clark (1846–1930), who had been connected with the British Council of the International and was a crofters' M.P. from 1885 to 1900, and Robert Bontine Cunninghame Graham, later active in the Scottish Labour Party and in the Social Democratic Federation and also Radical M.P. from 1886 to 1892, were among its leading promoters.

Thus, the movement against landlordism was in full swing in Ireland and already active in Great Britain before Henry George's *Progress and Poverty* became known on this side of the Atlantic. Wallace in particular seems to have developed his plan of land nationalisation quite independently of Henry George; and it would almost certainly have figured in the programme of the Democratic Federation if *Progress and Poverty* had never been written. There was, however, an indirect connection, through Ireland. Michael Davitt, who had worked out his ideas during his years in gaol — where he was badly maltreated — visited America soon after his release, and there met Henry George shortly before the book appeared. George's doctrines undoubtedly impressed him, and he became an eager populariser of George's ideas and was probably responsible for George's visit to Ireland in 1882. Davitt, however, while he welcomed George as an ally, was definitely a land nationaliser and a Socialist, and by no means accepted George's views on the virtues of free trade and *laissez-faire*. Wallace too was a Socialist as well as an advocate of land nationalisation, though he took little part in any organised Socialist movement.

In the 1870s, apart from the agitation for land reform, four further groups demand notice as representative of Radical tendencies which helped to prepare the ground for the revival of Socialism. They were widely different. Two were numerically small, but important on account of the personal qualities of their leading supporters. These were Positivism, of which Professor Beesly and Frederic Harrison (1831–1923) were the principal exponents, and the new Christian Socialist movement led by the Rev. Stewart Headlam. The other two were popular movements, with a wide following among Radical workers — the Birmingham Radicals, led by Joseph Chamberlain and closely allied with the London Radicals who followed Charles Dilke, and the Republican Radical Secularists, who looked for leadership to Charles Bradlaugh. None of these movements, except Stewart Headlam's, accepted Socialism — of which, indeed, Bradlaugh proclaimed himself the sturdy opponent. Nevertheless they all contributed in their several ways to the Socialist revival which took place in Great Britain during the 1880s.

Edward Spencer Beesly (1831–1915), Professor of History at University College, London, and translator of Auguste Comte's *Positive Polity*, was a thoroughgoing Radical in strong sympathy with the working-class movement, which he was always ready to help. He presided over the meeting at which the First International was set up, as he did later over the celebrated debate between Hyndman and Henry George on the issue 'Single Tax versus Socialism', and over many other meetings at which controversial working-class issues were discussed. He contributed to George Potter's *Beehive*, and helped the Trade Unions, with Frederic Harrison, in the great legal struggles between 1867 and 1875. He was on the side of every advanced movement that needed support, and never hesitated to speak out his mind. But he was a convinced Comtist, and, as such, a disbeliever in Socialism. For Comte's political theory involved a dualism of State and Church — not the Church of the theologians, but the Positivist Church of Humanity — a dualism in which a new priesthood was, not indeed to govern the world as a temporal power, but to control all education and to act as the unifying force in directing the human race towards 'scientific' government. Beesly could always say, when he presided over a debate at which Socialists and Anti-Socialists tore each other's ideas to pieces, that he disagreed with both the disputants. But that did not prevent him, or his ally Harrison, from doing splendid service to the Trade Unions in their hour of need : nor did it prevent Beesly from being on very friendly terms with Hyndman and other leaders of the new Socialist movement.

Stewart Duckworth Headlam (1847–1924), on the other hand, was a Socialist, and threw himself actively into the new Socialist agitation, first in the Social Democratic Federation and later in the Fabian Society. A High Churchman, holding an East End curacy in London, in a district — Bethnal Green — where the influence of Bradlaugh was strong, Headlam took the field against the Secularists with a vigorous exposition of Christian Social doctrine largely derived from the Christian Socialists of the 1850s, but much more militantly expressed. In 1877 he founded the Guild of St. Matthew, a society made up of Church of England priests and active laymen with a definitely Socialist outlook. When Henry George's *Progress and Poverty* appeared, he welcomed it eagerly, but went beyond it in applying its doctrine to capital as well as to land. Headlam's work, at first confined to London, took the form of attending Secularist and Republican meetings and, while endorsing or going beyond the social demands of the promoters, calling upon them to recognise Christ as their true leader in a crusade against poverty and oppression. Headlam wrote many pamphlets ; but he was not a theorist so much as a practical 'gospeller', who gave the impetus to a considerable group of Socialist parsons, mostly High Anglicans, during the later years of the century. As at the time of Maurice and his group, Christian Socialism made little appeal to Low Church evangelicals : it found a response among those who were later called 'Anglo-Catholics' on the one hand, and on the other among some of the 'modernists'. The strong 'other-worldliness' of the evangelicals and the strong individualism of some of the Nonconformist groups stood in its way.

Positivism and Christian Socialism were both small movements, confined almost entirely to intellectuals. For the popular movements which helped to prepare the way for the Socialist revival we must turn to the Radicalism of Joseph Chamberlain and Charles Dilke, and to the atheistical Republican Radicalism of Charles Bradlaugh, with whom, for a time, Annie Besant worked in close co-operation.

Joseph Chamberlain (1836–1914) retired from business with a fortune in 1874, and devoted himself wholly to politics. He was already well known not only in Birmingham, where he had been elected to the Town Council as a Radical in 1869, but also as chairman of the National Education League, the Church's arch-enemy in the struggle for control of the schools. In 1873 he had become Mayor of Birmingham, a town of great Radical traditions ; and at the head of a Radical majority he carried through during the next few years an extensive programme of municipal reform. Gas and water were municipalised, a beginning was made with clearing the slums, and a model sanitary administration was introduced. In 1875 Chamberlain convened at Birmingham a Municipal Sanitary Conference, which was the real beginning of the movement later known as 'municipal' or 'gas and water' Socialism. The following year he was elected to Parliament ; and the year after that he set to work to organise, with Francis Schnadhorst (1840–1900), the National Liberal Federation, a body designed to bring the local Liberal and Radical Associations over to Radicalism and to unite them in a campaign against the Whig elements in the party. This was the body which organised the Liberal electoral victory of 1880 ; and one effect of its work was to carry Chamberlain into the Cabinet as President of the Board of Trade, with Sir Charles Dilke (1843–1911) first as Under-Secretary for Foreign Affairs and thereafter, from 1882, as President of the Local Government Board. Chamberlain and Dilke were the prime movers in the legislation which, in 1884 and 1885, liberalised the county franchise and redistributed parliamentary seats so as to give greater weight to the big towns and mining districts.

The foundation of the Democratic Federation thus coincided with a marked Liberal move to the left ; and during the first half of the 'eighties the Socialists had a hard battle to fight against the Chamberlainite Radicals. Chamberlain's policy had, however, another aspect : he was a strong imperialist, and was unable to stomach the idea of Irish self-government in any form in which it might threaten imperial unity. The Liberal victory of 1880 coincided in time with the emergence of Michael

Davitt's Land League, supported in its earlier stages by Parnell, who had become Nationalist leader in 1878. Faced with Davitt's 'No Rent' campaign, the Liberal Government resorted to intensified coercion ; and this brought them into sharp conflict with a large body of British Radical opinion. Chamberlain's share in it lost him a good deal of his Radical support ; and, as we shall see, the Democratic Federation, in its first years, gave pride of place to the Irish question. When Gladstone became convinced that Irish Home Rule was the only possible solution, Chamberlain and Dilke resigned from the Government, and set out to organise their following on the basis of a policy of intensified Radicalism at home, and imperial unity as the keynote of external policy. Chamberlain's 'Unauthorised Programme' of 1885 was his bid to win over the Liberal Party and to check the rise of Socialism as a separate political force. But this 'Home Radicalism' was offered to the electors as the running mate of Irish coercion and imperialistic development.

In the 'Unauthorised Programme', Chamberlain and Dilke bid high. The Programme appropriated a large part of the case made by the Socialists and by Henry George ; but instead of nationalisation or the 'Single Tax', the means of remedying the injustice done to the many by the loss of their shares in the common heritage was to be the payment by the rich of a 'ransom' in the form of high taxation. Out of the proceeds of this 'ransom', the whole people were to receive the benefits of free education, improved housing, more social services — the *insignia* of what is now called the 'Welfare State'. Farmers were to get security of tenure, fair rent courts, and fuller compensation for improvements ; the agricultural labourer was to be given the chance of getting a small farm of his own ('three acres and a cow') ; there were to be powers of compulsory land purchase for public use, and so on. In addition, the Church was to be disestablished, plural voting was to be done away with, and payment of M.P.s was to be introduced. Of Chamberlain's earlier Radical proposals, the only ingredient now missing was Republicanism, which was hardly a suitable policy for an imperialist statesman. But even in 1885 Chamberlain made it clear that the monarch should be no more than a figurehead of Empire, and would interfere at peril of her crown with the march of Radical democracy.

In advocating this challenging Programme — challenging, that is, to his own party — Chamberlain explicitly referred to Socialism, which, he said, ought to be regarded as 'not a stigma, but a modern tendency pressing for recognition'. He added that 'the path of legislative progress in England has been for years, and must continue to be, distinctly socialistic'.

This Programme, it must be kept in mind, was published in 1885, two years after the Democratic Federation had adopted a fully Socialist programme, and at a point when the electorate had just been greatly enlarged (from under three to nearly five millions in Great Britain, excluding Ireland). In Ireland, the extended county franchise had made a present of a large number of seats to the Nationalist Party ; in the Scottish Highlands it had made possible the founding of a considerable crofters' movement ; while in England, though strengthening Conservative control of the rural constituencies, it had also stimulated a considerable agitation for land reform by the English Land Restoration League and other bodies.

Of course, the 'Unauthorised Programme' did not mean that Chamberlain had been converted to Socialism. He remained, not only a vigorous imperialist, but also a strong believer in private enterprise. But in this latter respect Henry George and many of the land reformers shared his views. Chamberlain's social gospel was much more closely akin to Henry George's than to Marx's ; but, because of his imperialism — or at least largely because of it — he differed from George in disbelieving in *laissez-faire*. He wanted a State that would intervene actively as the ally of capitalist enterprise — not merely stand aside, and keep the ring. It was this capitalist activism that impelled him, ten years later, to take office in a Conservative Government and to become the leader of a campaign for imperial economic unity.

After the issue of the 'Unauthorised Programme', Chamberlain did not at once break with the Liberals. He took office in Gladstone's new Cabinet as President of the Local Government Board ; but he resigned again almost at once, when Gladstone produced his Home Rule Bill. Thereafter, for nine years, he headed a separate Liberal Unionist Party, which moved more and more towards the Conservatives. In the meantime Charles Dilke, who did not follow his colleague's move towards Toryism, had been temporarily removed from the political scene in 1885, in consequence of a divorce case. The great attempt to convert the Liberal Party to advanced Radicalism had definitely failed ; and the crusade had left behind it a large body of Radicals who did not know what to do next. Liberalism and Chamberlainism having both failed them, they were half-ready for a new gospel. Then, and not till then, were conditions in Great Britain really ripe for the growth of a Socialist movement — provided Socialism could be presented to them in such a form as to enable them to regard it as the fulfilment of their Liberal-Radical ideas.

In 1881, when Henry Mayers Hyndman (1842-1921) took the lead in establishing the Democratic Federation, the conditions were not ripe for a Socialist movement as a parliamentary force ; and this fact, as we shall see, largely explains the subsequent history of the movement he began. Opposition to Irish coercion was indeed a good cry ; and so was land reform. But neither provided a sufficient foundation for a political movement capable of offering an effective challenge either to Liberalism as a whole or to the Chamberlainite Radical version of it. As long as there was a powerful Radical left wing at work within the Liberal Party, with some prospect of bringing the party over to the Chamberlainite home policy, there was little inducement for Trade Union leaders or their active followers to rally to the Socialist cause, or even to form an independent Labour political movement. That chance came only when Chamberlainism and Gladstonian Liberalism had definitely parted company, and when supporters of Chamberlain found themselves forced to swallow his imperialism as well as his policy of social reform.

1886 was thus the critical date ; and from this point really began the current of opinion which swept Marxian Socialism into a backwater and carried the major elements of the British working-class left into the New Unionism of 1889 and the independent Labour representation movement of the 1890s. Up to 1886, the Socialists were working against the current : after 1886, for a variety of reasons to which we shall come later, the British Marxists failed to swim with it, and lost their chance.

Before we come to the Socialist developments of the 1880s we have still to consider the last of the four prevailing forces which contributed to its development. This force was the Radical Republican movement which looked for leadership to Charles Bradlaugh (1833–91) and was based on active hostility to religion as well as to aristocratic privilege. Rationalism and Secularism, as doctrines associated with advanced political and social opinions, had a long history before Bradlaugh's day. From Paine's Deism to Richard Carlile's Secularist Republicanism, thence to Robert Owen's Rational Religion and to the Secularism of George Jacob Holyoake, which developed out of it, there had been a succession of anti-theological Radical movements, often associated with Republicanism, which had appealed especially to a considerable section of the skilled craftsmen in the older, handworking crafts, and, under their leadership, to a part of the urban proletariat in the industrial areas. These movements had not always been 'extremist' : the Owenites certainly were not. But they had tended to be social outcasts in the eminently religious environment of nineteenth-century Britain ; and their followers tended to associate with the foreign Socialist exiles, most of whom shared their anti-ecclesiastical attitude. Radical Republicanism, however, on its Secularist side, had developed, after the Chartist days, largely into an individualist libertarian movement strongly hostile to collective regulation, and akin in this respect more to individualistic Anarchism than to Socialism, though most of its adherents stopped short of this extreme.

Bradlaugh was definitely an individualistic Radical, but not an Anarchist. His rebellion against the society of his day began with religious doubts, forcibly expressed at the age of 15, when he was clerk to a coal merchant. At 16 he was forced to leave home, and found shelter among Secularists, including the widow of Richard Carlile. He then tried to combine propaganda with business as a coal merchant, but failed and, at the age of 17, enlisted in the army. Three years later his family bought his discharge and he became clerk to a solicitor in London. He soon shifted to another firm, but while in this employment gained a wide knowledge of the law, which he later put to effective use. Meanwhile he had resumed his anti-religious propaganda, using the name 'Iconoclast' in order not to lose his job. In 1858 he extended his speaking to the provinces, and soon became well known for riotous meetings and conflicts with the police. His vigorous and effective oratory speedily gained him a substantial following in many of the towns he visited, and he came to be regarded as the natural leader of a Republican Party which was also militantly atheistic. In 1860 a group of Sheffield free-thinking Radicals founded the *National Reformer* ; and two years later Bradlaugh acquired this journal, which became an influential organ of the extreme left. He was active, as a member of the National Reform League, in the working-class agitation which preceded the Reform Act of 1867. In 1866 he organised the National Secular Society, of which he became president ; and this body became the main agency for his movement, though he was also active in the Malthusian League. In 1870 he went as a delegate from the English Radicals to the Spanish Republicans ; and the following year he tried to mediate between the Paris Commune and the National Assembly, but was not allowed to enter France. Before this, in 1868, he had unsuccessfully contested Northampton in the election that followed the Reform Act. He stood again twice, without success, in 1874 ; but on his fourth attempt, in 1880, he was elected as the colleague of the middle-class Radical, Henry Labouchere, who founded *Truth*. Refusing to take the oath, and demanding the right to affirm instead, he was refused his seat by the House of Commons, but was later allowed by it to affirm 'at his own risk'. He then took his seat, and voted ; but his right to do this was challenged in the courts, and he was unseated. Attempting to continue to sit in spite of this ruling, he was expelled from the House by force. He then, in 1881, stood again for election, and was again returned. The House of Commons again expelled him. The following year he presented himself once more to the electors of Northampton, and was once more returned. He then went to the House, and attempted to administer the oath to himself. The House of Commons yet again excluded him. By this time he was involved in a number of legal actions arising out of the contest, and was in danger of bankruptcy, which would have confirmed his exclusion. But he fought on, presenting himself yet again at the bar of the House, and being again forcibly removed. In 1883 a Bill to allow affirmation in place of taking the oath failed by only two votes to pass the House. In 1884 Bradlaugh was yet again elected at Northampton, but made no attempt to take his seat until the following year, when the House excluded him once more. He was returned, still in company with Labouchere, in 1885, and was at length allowed to take his seat when Parliament met at the beginning of 1886. That year he was re-elected for the last time, and continued to represent Northampton till his death in 1891.

All through these years of struggle Bradlaugh had been engaged in a number of other crusades, especially on behalf of the freedom of the press. He fought fiercely against the blasphemy laws and against the restrictions on birth-control propaganda ; and he was also a great upholder of the right of public meeting. In these struggles he was closely associated, from 1874 to 1887, with Annie Besant (1847–1933), who finally broke with him on account of his hostility to Socialism and went over to the Socialist side. He was also, in and out of Parliament, a leading defender of Indian Nationalist claims — and in this too Annie Besant was his active co-worker. After he had been allowed to take his seat, he succeeded in carrying a number of important legal reforms, including the right of affirmation, which was at last legally sanctioned in 1888.

Bradlaugh's hostility to Socialism was a great thorn in the side of British Socialists during the 1880s. His propaganda appealed to those sections of the working class that would have been most likely to espouse the Socialist cause if no other, equally Radical, had offered itself ; and his prolonged struggle with the House of Commons earned him a great deal of sympathy, and added weight to his opinions. His death in 1891 was a factor on the side of Socialism ; for many of his followers thereafter rallied to one or another of the Socialist bodies. But his movement itself must also be regarded, despite his opposition to Socialism, as having helped to prepare the way for it ; for his iconoclasm and his attacks on the reactionary attitude of the Nonconformist sects, as well as of the Established Church, contributed to the breakaway from *bourgeois* Nonconformist political leadership which was a necessity for the growth of a powerful independent working-class political movement.

Bradlaugh's anti-Socialism rested largely on his opposition to the Marxism of the Social Democratic Federation. He was by temperament a libertarian, with a strong mistrust of authority, even when it purported to be the authority of the workers as a class. If he had lived well into the 'nineties, he might possibly have found himself less in opposition to the New Socialism which developed after the rise of the New Unionism of 1889. But it is unlikely that he would ever have become a Socialist, of any sort. He was too deeply concerned with asserting the rights of the individual to go his own way to have much attention to spare for any other cause. He had, however, at any rate one cause in common with the Socialists — the defence of free speech and of the right of public meeting and demonstration. As we shall see, his followers played an active part in the struggle for the right to hold meetings in Trafalgar Square during the 1880s — the Law and Liberty League, formed in 1887, was largely made up of the Republican followers of Bradlaugh and Charles Dilke, who shared between them the main influence in the left-wing Radical Clubs in the London area.

There is one further movement, or rather attempt to create a movement, that must be mentioned before we come to Hyndman and the Democratic Federation of 1881. In 1879 the veteran John Sketchley (1822–190?) published at Birmingham a booklet, *Principles of Social Democracy*, in which he called for the establishment in Great Britain of a Social Democratic Party on the German model. He followed this up with an attempt to form a Midland Social Democratic Party as a nucleus for the larger body ; but nothing came of the venture, which either petered out or was soon absorbed into the national movement launched under Hyndman's leadership. Sketchley thereafter worked for a while as organiser for the Democratic Federation in the Midlands, and was active later as a Socialist in Hull. But his work was soon forgotten, and he played no leading part.

We can now, with this background in mind, consider what H. M. Hyndman had in view in founding the Democratic Federation. His plan, as he described it to Karl Marx at the outset, was to bring about a revival of the Chartist agitation ; and his hopes were centred on the Radical Clubs and on their discontent with the policy of the Liberal Government, especially in the matter of its coercive policy in Ireland. Hyndman was not seeking, at this stage, to set up a definitely Socialist body. His aim was rather to stimulate a mass-movement of working-class discontent, using as his principal agencies the Radical Working Men's Clubs which existed in large numbers in the working-class areas — especially in London — and had been stirred to life by Chamberlain's Radical propaganda. In London Dilke had a very powerful influence in these clubs, and so had Bradlaugh. Hyndman hoped to break them away both from the Radical wing of the Liberal Party and from the Secularists, and to weld them together into a movement resembling Chartism, but with a better defined social programme. Hyndman, indeed, was still barely launched on his career as a Socialist : he had only just been converted to Socialism by reading, in French, Karl Marx's *Capital*, given to him by an unorthodox friend, H. A. Butler-Johnstone, who had been M.P. for Canterbury, first as a Tory, and later as an Independent, from 1862 to 1878. He read the book on shipboard, in 1880, on his way to the United States ; and in America he read *Progress and Poverty*, which had come out the previous year. The two between them converted him, not to Henry Georgism, but to Marxian Social-ism, which he continued to profess ardently for the rest of his life. On his return, he made Marx's acquaintance and visited him often to discuss his plans. Marx was discouraging about the prospects of a Chartist revival ; but Hyndman went ahead undeterred. He wrote a small book, *England for All*, in which he referred with approval to Marx's doctrine, but omitted to mention him by name, while expressing the hope that *Capital* would soon be made available in English. This omission roused the ire of Engels, who disliked Hyndman and objected to his friendship with Marx ; and Engels induced Marx to break with him. Why Hyndman failed to mention Marx's name has never been made quite clear. Marx stated in a letter to Sorge that Hyndman had told him he did not want to prejudice the success of his plans by associating them at the outset with the leader of the First International and the defender of the Paris Commune — and perhaps this may have weighed with him. But this is not a very satisfactory explanation ; for his references to a 'German thinker' were bound to be known as referring to Marx, and, if he had really wanted to keep Marx's name out of his propaganda, he would hardly have mentioned him at all, even in this guise. Whatever the explanation, the consequence was that the British Socialist revival started without Marx's blessing, and that Hyndman's movement was hampered by Engels's active hostility after Marx's death in 1883.

Hyndman, then, was a recent convert to Socialism when he set out on his attempt to revive the Chartist agitation. What he was trying to do was to seduce the Radical Clubs, first in London and then elsewhere, from their allegiance to the Chamberlainites or the Bradlaughites, and to create a new working-class party which he hoped to bring over in time to his new-found Socialist faith. The Radical opposition to Irish coercion and the widespread Radical support for Davitt's Irish Land League furnished the immediate occasion. Among those who took part in the preliminary private meetings held to consider Hyndman's project were Butler-Johnstone, already mentioned, E. S. Beesly, Joseph Cowen, the well-known Radical M.P. for Newcastle-on-Tyne, and J. Lord, who was secretary of the Rose Street Democratic Club — a principal gathering-place of foreign Socialist exiles, which had started a British section in 1880. At the first meeting held to consider his plan, the chair was taken by Joseph Cowen, who had been the leader of the Northern Reform Union in 1867, and had supported the northern miners in many of their struggles and showed his Radicalism in international as well as in home affairs. Cowen, however, soon dropped out, and Hyndman himself presided over the later meetings. Most of the Radical Clubs failed to come in : the influences of Dilke and of Bradlaugh were still too strong. But the Democratic Federation was started in a small way, and its first important act was to send a delegation to Ireland at the invitation of Davitt's Land League. The delegation came back with a scarifying report on the conditions of dire poverty and repression prevailing in Ireland ; and the Federation, acting in alliance with an English auxiliary of the Land League, on which Hyndman also served, held a series of open-air meetings in Hyde Park to protest against the Government's policy and sent out speakers to address the Radical Clubs, mainly on the same theme. Some progress was being made with these efforts when, in May 1882, Lord Frederick Cavendish and F. H. Burke were assassinated in Phoenix Park, Dublin. The assassinations caused a wave of anti-Irish feeling in Great Britain. Already a manifesto — the 'Tyrone Manifesto', issued by the Democratic Federation against the Liberal Government — had caused the withdrawal of many of the Radical Clubs ; and after the Phoenix Park affair there were further secessions. The Federation, however, stood to its guns, denouncing the new measures of coercion which the Government introduced, and arguing that the acts of violence in Ireland were the inescapable answer to misgovernment and repression.

These developments were fatal to the success of Hyndman's original plan — if indeed there had ever been any prospect of its success. Instead of a federation based on the Radical Clubs of London, he created only a small society of persons who either had no connection with Liberalism or were prepared to break with it entirely, and were ready to espouse not merely Radical but actually revolutionary opinions and to approve of the use of force as a political weapon. Among those who naturally felt no difficulty in endorsing such an attitude were many of the foreign refugees, who readily transferred their faith in revolution in their own countries to British conditions. These supporters were for the most part already Socialists of one sort or another ; and their influence helped to turn the Federation into a definitely Socialist body. In its original programme, land nationalisation, already advocated by Davitt, was the only definitely socialistic plank. But in a declaration of principles adopted by its Conference in 1882 it denounced 'the landlord and capitalist parties' as the enemies of the workers, and declared that 'those whose labour makes the wealth of these islands must rely on themselves alone'. It went on to say that 'it is the aim of the Democratic Federation to afford the means for organising the workers of Great Britain and Ireland, so that they may be in a position to secure those interests of the mass of the people which are now persistently sacrificed to the greed and selfishness of the well-to-do'. The following year it came out with an explicit declaration for Socialism, embodied in a pamphlet, *Socialism Made Plain*, which had a widish circulation. The public ownership of capital, as well as of land, was demanded : the monopolistic element in the private ownership of the means of industrial production was denounced as fully as much a source of exploitation as the land monopoly. 'So long as the means of production, either of raw materials or manufactured goods, are a monopoly of a class, so long must the labourers on the farm, in the mine, or in the factory sell themselves for a bare subsistence wage.

. . . The creation of wealth is already a social business, where each is forced to co-operate with his neighbour ; it is high time that exchange of the produce should be social too, and removed from the control of individual greed and individual profit.'

In January 1883, while this transition from radicalism to Socialism was still in progress, the celebrated poet and artist-craftsman William Morris joined the Democratic Federation ; and for the next two years he and Hyndman worked together as its best-known leaders. They were both prominent in the work of transforming the Federation into a definitely Socialist body, and in supporting the change of name to Social Democratic Federation in 1884. Morris's conversion to Socialism was, indeed, as thoroughgoing as Hyndman's, though not quite so sudden — for he had been a sort of Socialist for some time before, though he had taken no part in Socialist agitation. From the beginning of 1883 he threw himself with determination into the struggle, though he had little taste for it. Indeed, he soon stood well to the left of Hyndman because he was not at all a politician and was deeply distrustful of political tactics and compromises. For a time, however, the two managed to work closely together. They wrote in collaboration a long pamphlet entitled *A Summary of the Principles of Socialism*, and both played a large part in the establishment of *Justice* as the organ of the movement. That was in 1884, the year of the Reform Act which enfranchised the workers in the county constituencies and also extended the suffrage in the towns. It was also the year in which the number of the unemployed began to shoot up towards the peak total reached in 1886. But the Social Democratic Federation was already too deeply preoccupied with internal disputes to be able to give much thought to anything except its own affairs.

As we have seen, the Democratic Federation had at the outset no clearly defined programme and consisted of very heterogeneous elements. Even when most of the Radicals who were not prepared to sever connection with Liberalism had dropped away, there remained wide enough differences to prevent the 'Socialists' from settling down amicably together. In 1884 there were in the S.D.F. at least five main groups, each with a strong personality at its head. First, there was Hyndman's own close following, most of whom thought in terms of making a political party on the model of the German Social Democratic Party and regarded Socialism as essentially a matter of political action. Secondly, there was a group of Trade Unionists, also politically minded, but less influenced by Marxism : this group agreed with the Hyndmanites in denouncing the Liberal-Labour Trade Union leaders and was already feeling its way towards a New Unionism which would bring in the less skilled workers to break the monopoly of the skilled crafts. It differed from the Hyndmanites mainly in paying more attention to industrial questions, and in realising that the industrial movement could not be subordinated to the political, as it had been in Germany. John Burns (1858–1943), who was also active in London Radical municipal politics, was the outstanding figure in this group. The third group, based mainly on certain Radical clubs and societies in East London — especially the Stratford Radical Club — was deeply influenced by Anarchism. Its leader, Joseph Lane, had been active in East London throughout the 1870s, mainly in connection with the old Chartists, Charles and J. F. Murray, in the Manhood Suffrage Association and also in close touch with the foreign Anarchist groups. Lane had formed in the East End, almost simultaneously with the foundation of the Democratic Federation, a body called the Labour Emancipation League, which had become very active in open-air propaganda and had set up a number of branches. Until 1884 the L.E.L. remained separate from the Democratic Federation ; but during the previous year it had taken part in discussions intended to bring about unification of the left-wing societies, and a joint Socialist Manifesto had been issued in the names of the Federation, the L.E.L., and the various foreign Socialist groups in London, announcing their intention to continue the work of the defunct International. The L.E.L. thereafter, without sacrificing its identity, agreed to affiliate to the Democratic Federation provided that the Federation became openly and completely Socialist ; and the Federation not only changed its name, but also adopted most of the L.E.L.'s programme, including the statement of its object as 'the establishment of a free condition of society based on the principle of political equality, with equal social rights for all, and the complete emancipation of labour'. There were the seeds of trouble in this phrasing ; for the words 'a free condition of society' were closely associated with the propaganda of Anarchism, and in fact the group controlling the L.E.L. consisted largely of Anarchists and Anarchist-Communists, who were in sharp disagreement with Hyndman's political Marxism.

The fourth group in the S.D.F. in 1884, if it can be called a group, consisted of a number of individuals, mostly intellectuals, who had become converts to Socialism, but had not yet clearly defined their point of view. Among them were a number of the group which was engaged simultaneously in setting up the Fabian Society; and they also included converts from Radicalism, such as William Morris and Ernest Belfort Bax (1854–1926), who were learning their Socialism as they went along — Bax chiefly from Germany: he became a frequent writer on German Socialism. Many of this group had been brought over by reading *Progress and Poverty*, and by seeing that its arguments applied as much, under British conditions, to capital as to land; but few of them, except Bax, knew anything of Marxism or of Anarchism, and they were often rather ·at sea in listening to the vigorous disputations of the rival schools of thought. Finally, in Scotland a considerable agitation was developing among the crofters, largely influenced by the propaganda of Henry George and the Irish Land League; and this group formed in 1884 a Scottish Land and Labour League, loosely affiliated to the S.D.F.

The exact causes of the split which, at the end of 1884, rent the Social Democratic Federation in twain have been much disputed, largely because the issues were manifold and never clearly defined. Whatever they were, in December 1884 a majority of the S.D.F.'s Executive, headed by William Morris, resigned and decided to form a new society, which took the name of Socialist League. The seceders resigned, rather than use their majority to claim from a Conference of the Federation the right to the name and the control. They did this on Morris's advice; for he thought it preferable not to engage in a wrangle for the control of the organisation under the eyes of the press, which would have made the most of it to discredit Socialism, and he also wished to be rid of a number of prominent members of the S.D.F. whose good faith he mistrusted, and hoped to make a new start with a group of colleagues animated by principles more akin to his own. The actual charges which the seceders flung at Hyndman and his followers were those of dictatorial and undemocratic control of the Federation's affairs and of 'political opportunism'. These charges had more than one foundation ; but the first arose in part out of a dispute concerning the newly founded Scottish Land and Labour League. Andreas Scheu (1844–1927), a refugee from Austria and a member of the S.D.F. Executive, had endorsed the decision that the Scots, instead of becoming an ordinary Section of the Federation, should become loosely affiliated in the same way as the Labour Emancipation League. Hyndman, who thought in terms of a centralised and disciplined party, objected strongly to such arrangements, and denounced Scheu for his action. He also accused Scheu and another member of the Executive, W. J. Clarke, of being Anarchists, and demanded their expulsion.

This seems to have been the immediate cause of the trouble, which involved the L.E.L. as well as the Scots. But in the background there was also a further cause of dispute. The Anarchists and Anarchist-Communists in the S.D.F. were hostile to parliamentary action in any circumstances, whereas the Hyndmanites were definitely setting out to establish a political party with parliamentary ambitions. Between these two groups was a third, which without opposing political action on principle, considered that the time was not ripe for it, and that the Socialists would only make their cause ridiculous if they put up candidates without a great deal of preliminary educational work to convert the active section of the working class to Socialism. The majority which voted against Hyndman on the Executive was made up of this group, supported by the Anarchists and Anarchist-Communists and, paradoxically enough, by Engels also from outside. For Engels, as we have seen, intensely distrusted Hyndman, despite his endorsement of Marxism, and regarded him as a political careerist who was trying to use Socialism for his own purposes.

Many years later, William Morris is said to have come to the conclusion that he had been wrong in 1884 in suspecting Hyndman's motives and in leaving the S.D.F. That was after he had been through a disillusioning experience in trying to work with the Anarchists in the Socialist League, and had been actually thrust out by them from the editorship of *The Commonweal*, the journal established by the League in 1885 with his money, and dependent thereafter mainly on his financial and literary support. Morris is said (by Hyndman) to have admitted his mistake in a speech made in support of Hyndman, but there is no record of his actual words. I suppose, if Hyndman's report is correct, he meant three things — that he had wrongly suspected Hyndman's integrity ; that he and his supporters ought to have stayed in the S.D.F. and fought the issue out ; and that he had allowed himself to be too much influenced by the Anarchists and near-Anarchists, whom he had got to know better in later years.

At all events, the split occurred ; and from the beginning of 1885 there were three rival Socialist organisations in the field, not counting either the Anarchists proper, who had their own organisation — the Allied Anarchists — or the Anarchist-Communists, who soon formed a group round the journal *Freedom*, which they started with Kropotkin's help in 1886. These three were the S.D.F., led by Hyndman, but with John Burns increasingly active ; the Socialist League, with William Morris as reluctant leader, and with the Labour Emancipation League, which had seceded from the S.D.F., as a tumultuous ally ; and the Fabian Society, which had been formed in 1884, but was still only feeling its way, and was not widely known. Side by side with these three were the Land Nationalisation Society, with Alfred Russel Wallace as president ; the Land Restoration League, originally set up in 1883 as the Land Reform Union, which followed Henry George's gospel and had close personal connections with the small Christian Socialist groups ; the Scottish Land and Labour League, which became an independent Scottish Section of the Socialist League, and a number of lesser bodies which arose and disappeared one after another. There was indeed a considerable ferment of ideas on the left, especially among the intellectuals. But for the time being the big Trade Unions were hardly stirred at all, and most of their leaders still put their faith in the Radical wing of the Liberal Party.

Chamberlain's Unauthorised Manifesto appeared almost at the same moment as that of the Socialist League announcing its formation ; and at the end of the same year the first General Election held on the newly extended franchise brought to the

House of Commons a substantial group of Liberal-Labour M.P.s — mostly miners. The election also sent the S.D.F. into the field, with John Burns, who polled quite well at Nottingham, and with two candidates in London, who fared almost unbelievably ill. These latter became the subject of angry recrimination. They were both undoubtedly financed by 'Tory gold', given to the S.D.F. in the hope of splitting the Liberal vote. The money seems actually to have come to the S.D.F. through Henry Hyde Champion (1859–1928), then one of its leading supporters, and to have been supplied to him through the Tory journalist, Maltman Barry, who had at one time been connected with the First International. The S.D.F. Executive did not officially know, but must have been well aware, whence the money came. As it was engaged in an attempt to detach the workers from the Liberal Party, it could have had no scruples about endangering Liberal seats ; and it could fairly argue that 'Tory gold' was no worse than the 'Liberal gold' which helped to finance some of the 'Lib-Labs'. But that was a mere *tu quoque*, not likely to appeal to the Trade Unions or to those Socialists who did draw a distinction between Liberal-Radicals and Tories, and had attachments to the Liberal left. This was the position of the Fabians, who roundly denounced the S.D.F.'s action. Most of the Fabians who had joined the S.D.F. withdrew and transferred their main energies to building up the Fabian Society as an independent force. In 1885 the Society was still a tiny group of forty members, and had published nothing of importance. Its coming into the open as a policy-making body dates from the report on *Government Organisation of Unemployed Labour*, which it issued the following year, when the trade depression was at its worst.[1]

The Socialist League also denounced the S.D.F.'s action, though it had no preference for Liberals as against Tories. The League, as we have seen, consisted partly of out-and-out opponents of parliamentary action and partly of Socialists who held that the time was not yet ripe for it. Very possibly the question of 'Tory gold', or something like it, may have come up during the discussions about fighting parliamentary contests that had

---

[1] The Fabian Society will be more fully discussed in the next volume of this work, as its main importance came later, and it is best dealt with in connection with Keir Hardie's Independent Labour Party.

been going on before the split. The seceders, in their Manifesto, spoke of 'electioneering alliances' as among Hyndman's crimes ; but it is not clear whether this referred to alliances with Tories or Liberals.

It has usually been held that the 'Tory gold' scandal did the S.D.F. a great deal of harm. But what really did the harm was the revelation of the S.D.F.'s weakness, even in a largely working-class constituency such as Kennington, where its candidate polled only 32 votes, against 3351 for the Tory and 2991 for the Liberal. The 'Tory gold' affair no doubt provided the anti-Socialists with a handy additional argument ; but the S.D.F. was already so deeply embroiled with the Lib-Labs that relations could hardly have been worsened. The Fabian and other middle-class secessions were of importance, because the individuals concerned were of high capacity and transferred their energies to rival movements — the Fabian Society and, later, the movement for independent Labour representation which led up to the establishment of the Independent Labour Party in 1893. But for the time being the S.D.F. gained from its successes in other fields a good deal more than it had lost through its electoral fiasco. Throughout 1885 the numbers unemployed had continued to mount ; and the S.D.F., largely thanks to John Burns, managed to put itself effectively at the head of the unemployed agitation, especially in London. At the same time — and no doubt in close connection with the growth of demonstrations by and on behalf of the unemployed — a struggle began in London and in some of the provincial towns over the right of public meeting and procession ; and in this field too the S.D.F. was able to play a considerable, though not in its own person the leading, part.

The basis of the S.D.F.'s agitation on behalf of the unemployed was the demand, long familiar in continental Socialism, for the 'right to work'. The Government, it was urged, was under an obligation to ensure access to the means of production for every citizen and to establish public works to employ those whom capitalist industry rejected. In this campaign particular stress was usually laid on the demand for 'Home Colonisation' — which went back to Robert Owen's proposals first made at the end of the Napoleonic Wars. The Government, it was urged, should take the land that was lying unproductive out of the hands of its private owners and should settle the unemployed upon it in Co-operative Colonies, in which the fullest use should be made of modern productive techniques. This demand linked up conveniently with the land agitation that was being carried on by the Land Restoration League, the Land Nationalisation Society, and a number of other bodies. But the S.D.F. of course wanted the State to enter industry as well as agriculture, and often echoed Kropotkin's proposals for a 'reintegration' of the two in new settlements whose inhabitants would combine agricultural with manufacturing production. Work was the first demand ; but with it went the insistence that the State, if it failed to provide work for the unemployed, should give them maintenance at a fair standard of living. Most members of the S.D.F., however intent they were on projects of Home Colonisation, were also convinced that the prevention of recurrent large-scale unemployment was impossible as long as capitalism continued to exist. Hyndman and his followers laid great stress on Marx's conception of the 'reserve army of labour' as a necessity of capitalist industry both for ensuring the supply of workers in times of boom and for keeping wages low because of the competition to find jobs. Accordingly they combined propaganda for socialisation, of industry as well as of land, with their demands on the existing State for work or maintenance. Their agitation took the form of demonstrations and processions to demand immediate relief, as well as longer-term measures ; and one of the most effective of their methods was to lead unemployed processions to the churches on Sundays. This particular campaign, organised mainly by John Burns, culminated at the beginning of 1887 in a great procession to St. Paul's Cathedral, followed by open-air addresses outside the Cathedral to express disapproval of what the preacher had told his audience about the necessity for the coexistence of the rich and the poor.

It is interesting to observe the attitude which the Fabian Society, still only feeling its way, took up towards this agitation. The Society appointed a committee, with Sidney Webb, Frank Podmore, and Hubert Bland as its leading members, to draw up a report on the whole question of public provision of work for the unemployed ; and this report, drafted mainly by Webb and Podmore, makes very curious reading to-day. The authors evidently regarded as nonsensical the entire idea of Home Colonies ; and they also scouted the notion that any cure could be looked for from the institution of public works. Government-employed labour, they announced, was notoriously inefficient, because the Government could not coerce or sweat its employees as a private employer could. Public works could be even tolerably efficient only when they were of a kind that could be performed mainly by quite unskilled labour, without the need for much capital equipment. Within these limits the report recommended certain action, including the establishment of a national corps of navvies for heavy unskilled work and, rather surprisingly, the State cultivation of tobacco on unused land. It also recommended that gas and water services, railways and canals, and the distribution of alcoholic drinks should be carried on under public ownership, but made no further proposals for nationalisation. To these recommendations it added, still more surprisingly, an endorsement of compulsory military service as a means both of reducing unemployment and of training the workers in the idea of public service. True, in publishing the report the Fabian Society prefixed to it a statement that all the proposals contained in it were to be regarded as mere palliatives, designed to deal with the unemployment problem within the conditions of the existing economic system ; and the phrasing of this statement suggests that some members of the Society may have felt a good deal of doubt concerning the report. But it was issued, and was actually Sidney Webb's first piece of writing for the Society.

As trade revived from 1887 onwards, the unemployed agitation died down and gave place to the struggle for improved wages and conditions out of which the 'New Unionism' emerged. But the battle for free speech continued, with the Socialists acting in this matter in alliance with the followers of Charles Bradlaugh and with the main body of working-class Radicals. The trouble began with what is known as the 'Dod Street Affair' of 1885. Dod Street, in Limehouse, was an old pitch for outdoor meetings, which had been held there without police interference for a number of years ; but in 1885, faced with the rising unemployed agitation, the police tried to put a stop to the meetings and arrested a succession of speakers. The Socialists and the Radical Clubs thereupon organised a series

of mass processions and demonstrations, converging on Dod
Street ; and the police gave way. The centre of trouble was
then transferred to Trafalgar Square, also an old rendezvous
for demonstrations of many kinds. In 1886 a small group of
Trade Unionists, in opposition to the official Trade Union
leadership, but with Tory backing, had organised a 'Fair Trade'
movement to demand the exclusion of foreign manufactures as
a means of curing unemployment ; and the Socialists were at
one with the Radicals in their vigorous opposition to this group.
The Irish Societies in London were also very active, protesting
against the Government's policy of coercion ; and all these
groups — Socialists, Radicals, Irishmen, and 'Fair Traders' —
regarded Trafalgar Square as the best place for mass demonstrations, particularly because of its nearness to the Houses
of Parliament and to Whitehall. In February 1886 the 'Fair
Traders' announced their intention to hold a demonstration in
the Square, and the S.D.F. and their unemployed allies thereupon decided to hold a counter-demonstration at the same time
and place. Rival processions therefore converged on Trafalgar
Square, and rival meetings were held without serious incident.
The question then arose how to get the crowds away from the
Square without clashes; and the Socialists, apparently after
discussion with the police, decided to march in procession to
Hyde Park, leaving the 'Fair Traders' to take another route.
On the way to Hyde Park many windows were broken in Pall
Mall clubs, from which insults are said to have been hurled at
the crowd ; and, tempers having been roused, shops were
looted in St. James's Street and in Piccadilly, mainly after the
Socialist procession had already passed by. The real responsibility for the lootings was never fixed : it seems to have been a
spontaneous outburst of hooliganism, and certainly the S.D.F.
leaders had nothing to do with it. But the effects were considerable. The Mansion House Fund for relief of the unemployed shot up suddenly ; the London Commissioner of Police
resigned and was replaced by a soldier — Sir Charles Warren —
who announced his intention of putting down demonstrations
with a firm hand ; and a number of the S.D.F. leaders, including Hyndman, Burns, and Champion, were put on trial for
incitement to riot. Their acquittal by the jury, after a speech
by Burns subsequently reprinted as a pamphlet, with the title

The Man with the Red Flag, was a singular triumph for the
S.D.F. ; but it did not deter Sir Charles Warren from continuing his policy of 'firmness'. Meetings in and processions
to Trafalgar Square were banned, but continued to be held in
defiance of the police ; and at one of these a demonstrator, by
name Alfred Linnell, was killed. William Morris wrote his
'Death Song' — one of the series of *Chants for Socialists* of
which the first had appeared in *Justice* before the split.

In these struggles the Bradlaughites also played their part,
organising for the purpose a Law and Liberty League in which
Annie Besant was the most active worker. But by 1887 Annie
Besant's long collaboration with Bradlaugh had been brought
to an end. At first she had shared his opposition to Socialism ;
but she was converted by the Socialists' arguments and for a
time joined the S.D.F. Leaving Bradlaugh's *National Reformer*,
of which she had been joint editor, she started a paper of her
own, *The Link*, and endeavoured to unite the Socialist and
Radical bodies in the struggle for freedom of speech and meeting. Out of her work arose, quite unexpectedly, the strike of
the match-girls at Bryant & May's in 1888. A deputation from
these girls visited her at the office of *The Link* and, announcing
their intention to strike, asked her to take up their grievances.
She responded by helping to organise the strike and to enlist
public support, and thus struck the first open blow for the
'New Unionism' which, to the discomfiture of the S.D.F., soon
pushed their Marxian Socialism into the background and prepared the way for the 'New Socialism' of the Independent
Labour Party. Annie Besant herself, meanwhile, had left the
S.D.F. and transferred her activity to the Fabian Society. She
was one of the Fabian essayists of 1889, but was soon, by yet
another transition, to leave active work for the Socialist movement for Theosophy and for Indian Nationalism.

The 'New Unionism' and the 'New Socialism' which
developed side by side with it fall outside the scope of the
present volume. They will be considered in the next volume
of this work, which will carry on the story of Socialist thought
from the late 'eighties to the Soviet Revolution of 1917. It
remains, then, in this chapter only to consider the ideas which
lay behind the Socialist movements of the 1880s — with the
exception of the Fabian Society, which became important only

after 1889, when *Fabian Essays* appeared. This means that in the present chapter we have mainly to deal with three men — Hyndman, as the leader of the Social Democratic Federation, John Burns, as the principal Socialist organiser of the unemployed and the leader of the Socialist wing in the Trade Unions before Keir Hardie, and William Morris, who alone of the three made any substantial original contribution to Socialist thought. As much as is relevant of the record of the Socialist League after the split will arise in connection with William Morris's relations with it.

Hyndman was in a way a most unfortunate man. Had he begun his Socialist career ten years later than he did, after the New Unionism had made its appearance, he could hardly have been as contemptuous of Trade Unions and of industrial action generally as he showed himself from the beginning. He would hardly have come to like them, for his mind had a very strong parliamentary bent ; but he would have realised their importance, and would have found men with whom he could collaborate in bringing the Trade Unionists over to Socialism — men who would have influenced him as well as helped him. He might have succeeded in the 1890s in achieving what was impossible in the 1880s — indeed as long as there was any hope of the Liberal Party swallowing Chamberlain's and Dilke's Radical medicine — the creation of a revived Chartist movement as the basis for an independent Socialist Party. Such a party could hardly have been Marxist : religious feeling was too strong among the majority of Trade Unionists for the acceptance of Marxist materialism to be possible ; but it could have been set up — as the Independent Labour Party actually was — on a basis that would not have prevented a Marxist from leading it, provided he had been prepared to refrain from ramming the less acceptable parts of Marx down his followers' throats. In 1881 Hyndman would certainly have been ready to do this : indeed, it was what he had in mind. He was not, at that stage, a doctrinaire : he may even have been too much of an opportunist. But when the Radical workers he had hoped to attract did not come, or fell away, he was left at the head of an essentially sectarian movement, in which he had no colleagues, except John Burns, who were able to stand up to him. Presently Burns fell away, having done his best by his organisation of the unemployed to give the S.D.F. a real working-class backing, but having found in the New Unionism a field in which he could play a much more effective and un-hampered part. Hyndman was left cock of the walk in the S.D.F. ; but he had not much of a dunghill to crow from. The secession of the Socialist League and the withdrawal of the Fabians had left him with a group of second-rate colleagues, mostly very honest and excellent people in their way, but minority-minded, and compelled to fight a battle on two fronts — against the Radicals and against their fellow-Socialists of other brands. The split reinforced their sectarianism : it caused them to cling close to political Marxism of the German Social Democratic type, and to persist in believing that the British Socialist Party ought to be organised on the German model, despite the great difference in the conditions under which it had to work — by which I mean both the very different system of government and the different temper of the people. Neither Liberal nor Conservative Governments ever obliged the S.D.F. by passing an Anti-Socialist Law, or even by engaging in any considerable degree of repression — for in the Trafalgar Square struggle it was the Government that in the end gave way.

Under these circumstances, Hyndman's naturally dic-tatorial temper met with too few obstacles, and his mind hardened into a literal Marxism which was wholly unlike Marx. Marx, in the 1860s, had done his best to take the Trade Union leaders as he found them, though later the Paris Com-mune and the quarrel with the Bakuninites wrecked his efforts. Hyndman did nothing but scold the Trade Unions, as well as the Radicals, for not being what they were not.

The consequence was that Hyndman and with him the S.D.F. developed a peculiarly arid version of the Marxist gospel, with the main emphasis placed on the theory of value and almost none on the historical aspects of Marx's teaching. The good recruit to the S.D.F. had to master the Marxist economic terminology, which he then threw about to the bewilderment of those who could be got to listen to him. Above all, in discarding the ethical for the 'scientific' appeal, the British Marxists cut themselves off from the powerful ethical impulses that were stirring workers and intellectuals

alike, and stamped themselves indelibly as the exponents of a
foreign gospel. To criticise them on this ground is not to say
that Marx's economics were wrong — though I think they
were : it is simply to say that their way of approach entirely
failed to fit the mood of the people they had to win over in
order to make their movement a national force. There was of
course a small minority to which their appeal did go home ;
but the great social forces which were developing in the Great
Britain of their day they failed entirely to understand — partly
at any rate because they had started too soon for success, and
had soon come to attribute their lack of success to the stupidity
of the masses rather than to their own self-righteousness.

Hyndman wrote a good deal, and wrote most of it well, as
far as style and presentation were concerned. But he was not
an original thinker, and he added nothing of substance to what
he had learnt from Marx. His best book on Socialism is *The
Historical Basis of Socialism in Great Britain* : his *Commercial
Crises of the Nineteenth Century* is superficial. He was a competent debater : the pamphlet reports of his public debates
with Henry George and with Charles Bradlaugh had a wide
sale, and in the debate with George he scored heavily in giving
his opponent's arguments a Socialist twist. But nature meant
him to be a politician rather than a writer, and he never got
half a chance of doing what he really wanted to do. He would
most likely have been a good parliamentary leader, if he had
ever been able to get into Parliament and find a party to lead.
As matters were, he spent an ineffective lifetime being faithful
to his conception of Socialism, but finding no real scope for his
abilities in the leadership of a sect which was not strong enough
to return even a single member to Parliament. His one period
of happy activity came to him only during the first World War,
when he worked energetically and sensibly on the War Workers'
Emergency Committee as the colleague of Labour men whom
he had been fighting most of his life. But the war of 1914 also
completed the breach between him and his old organisation,
the S.D.F., which had by that time been metamorphosed into
the British Socialist Party and was soon to provide the nucleus
for the Communist Party of Great Britain. An ardent supporter
of the war, he was disavowed by the majority of his followers,
and seceded from the B.S.P. to form a new National Socialist

Party, which thereafter resumed the old name, Social Democratic Federation, but never acquired any strength or importance. His career of unrewarded faithfulness to his conception
of Socialism is answer enough to the charge of self-seeking that
was often brought against him in the 1880s. He was not a
self-seeker ; but he was a man who ardently wanted power and
had a strong tendency to order others about. These qualities
may be valuable in success : in defeat they are disastrous.
Hyndman's career is a record, not so much of an 'adventurous
life' — to quote the title of his autobiography — as of abilities
run to waste largely, though not entirely, through no fault of
his own.

Next to Hyndman, the outstanding figure in the S.D.F.
after the split was John Burns, 'The Man with the Red Flag'
as it pleased him in those days to be called. Burns had no
pretensions at all to be a thinker : he was essentially a speaker
and an organiser with an immense talent for getting himself,
and any movement he took part in, into the news. A skilled
engineer and a member of the old-fashioned craft Union, the
Amalgamated Society of Engineers, he had none of the exclusive
craft spirit, and was happiest when he could put himself at the
head of a body of unskilled workers, who were both more easily
moved by his eloquence and more responsive to leadership.
Burns had an entirely real feeling for the 'bottom dog', and a
real eloquence in expressing it. He had the art of dramatising
himself as a leader, and of making his hearers feel that he was
at one with them. Egotistic and ambitious, vainglorious in
success and a bad colleague because he always wanted his own
way, he served admirably, by his faults as well as his virtues,
certain needs of his time. It was he who made the unemployed
into a movement of which capitalism had to take notice ; and
it was he who, scenting from afar the possibilities and the significance of the Dock Strike of 1889, rushed in, though he
had nothing to do with it, and constituted himself its leader,
with excellent results for the strikers. It is practically certain
that, but for Burns's leadership, the dockers would have been
beaten ; for only he could have held them together long enough
to enable aid to reach them from sympathisers in England and
in Australia, and probably no one else could have prevented
the strike from being broken by violence, followed by police

intervention and the destruction of the improvised organisation that had been set up after the stoppage began. Burns, with his conspicuous white straw-hat, meant to make him readily visible, seemed to have the art of being promptly on the spot wherever trouble threatened, and of dealing with it in such a way as to prevent disorder. He was a magnificent strike leader for unskilled workers : he knew how to talk to them, and how to invest himself with a magical quality of representativeness in their eyes. He would never have done for a Trade Union leader ; for he would have been hopeless at the humdrum daily tasks of administration, and would never have been able to work as one of a team. But in the situations of 1886 and 1889 he was entirely in his element, and thereafter he was a national figure.

Burns in the 1880s was an ardent Socialist ; but his Socialism had no backing of theory, or even of solid thought. He was at bottom, as his later career showed, much more a Radical than a Socialist. After 1889 he did good work in the field of London government on the new London County Council ; and in 1892 he was elected to Parliament for Battersea, where he built up a local empire that was all his own. But in Parliament he would not work with Keir Hardie, who offered to accept his leadership. Though he had fallen right out of sympathy with the doctrinaire Socialism of the S.D.F., he refused to come to terms with the new Independent Labour political movement which had been partly called into existence by his own work in stimulating the New Unionism of 1889. He preferred to plough a lonely furrow, or to bide his time in the hope of a revived Radicalism that could use the Liberal Party as its instrument. That refusal to throw in his lot with the new Labour movement brought him back in the long run to the Liberalism he had denounced so fervently in his early days. But there was something in him that survived the experience of being a Liberal Cabinet Minister and becoming deeply offensive to most of his old friends while he was at the Local Government Board. That something — a deep-laid Radical internationalism — led him to resign his office in 1914 rather than approve of British participation in the first World War. Right or wrong, he then showed his fundamental honesty ; for he had assuredly nothing to gain. He simply retired into private life, dividing his time between his passion for London's history and the pleasure he derived from boasting about his own past to a circle of listeners at the National Liberal Club. Egotism and honesty are not inconsistent qualities : that he showed. But Burns's egotism was continuously on view : his honesty was less apparent. Nevertheless he served his purpose, and has his niche in Socialist history as the protagonist of that uprising of the less skilled workers which he led to the first victory, and then refused to follow on its further course.

William Morris (1834–96) was a very different person from either Burns or Hyndman ; for he had no egotism at all and no taste — he had even a keen distaste — for leadership. Morris did not want to join the Democratic Federation, or to found the Socialist League. He did not really want to take any part in politics : he had plenty of other things — things he felt he was better at — waiting to be done. Throughout his period of Socialist activity, his conscience drove him remorselessly on. He wore himself out with speaking in the open air — for which he was quite unfitted — and in little lecture-rooms all over the country, talking to audiences which had for the most part, as he knew, hardly any understanding of what he was trying to say. He sat through endless committee meetings and conferences, at which quarrels were always occurring about what seemed to him to be mostly trivialities, unworthy of serious attention. Naturally hot-tempered and impatient, he schooled himself to play the part of peace-maker — usually in vain. He did all this, after his first burst of enthusiasm, with a growing sense of futility and of the certainty of failure in the short run, though he had no doubt about the coming of Socialism some time in the future.

After the split Morris toiled away for the Socialist League as he had toiled during the two previous years for the Federation. But the League always remained small, and was never united by any clear community of purpose. It was strongest in London, but there the Anarchist element was always considerable, and always a source of trouble. Its next greatest stronghold was in Yorkshire, which in the main followed the seceders, whereas Lancashire stayed mainly with the S.D.F. It was also fairly strong in Glasgow and in the parts of Scotland where the Scottish Land and Labour League had a hold. It had a following on the North-East Coast ; but both Scotland and the North-East went their own ways, without paying much attention to directions from London. Norwich was another substantial centre, and there were scattered groups in a number of other places. But there was never a national movement of any real significance ; and *The Commonweal*, which Morris edited much against the grain, as well as paid for, never had much of a circulation, despite its literary excellence. Morris had nothing of the journalist in him ; and though some of his articles were of high quality, these were probably the least read by the persons for whom they were meant.

The League, because of its small membership and its lack of funds, had to be conducted by an executive drawn mainly from its London members ; and as these dwindled the Anarchists got more and more control, until they finally ousted Morris from the editorship of *The Commonweal*, and yet expected him to go on paying for it. By the end of 1890 he was clear of the Socialist League — what was left of it — and deeply disillusioned by his experience. Withdrawing with a small group of faithful followers, he formed the Hammersmith Socialist Society out of the League's Hammersmith branch, and for a while the meetings went on in the long room which he had placed at its disposal at Kelmscott House. But the Hammersmith Socialist Society was never more than an affirmation of unaltered faith in Socialism. It had no real function, and it gradually died away. Meanwhile what was left of the Socialist League staggered on till it was absorbed into Kropotkin's Freedom Group in 1895.

What were the issues between Morris, who often seemed to be more than half an Anarchist himself, and the Anarchists who ended by driving him out of the League ? It needs to be remembered that during the years of the League's existence Anarchism was passing through the phase of 'propaganda by deed', recorded in a previous chapter. There was throughout the 1880s a great newspaper outcry against the Anarchists and a great stirring of opinion against them ; for though only a few resorted to bomb-throwing or assassination, outside Russia, and not many in the West even approved of such methods, a great many more felt called upon publicly to defend the bomb-throwers when they were caught by capitalist justice, and only a few Anarchists were prepared to repudiate them openly. Morris never felt any sympathy for dynamiters, except perhaps in Russia, and did not feel called upon to defend their doings, though he did rally to the cause of Anarchists whom he believed to have been unjustly condemned — the Chicago Martyrs, for example — and did protest strongly when Governments and public opinion made the bomb-throwings a reason for attacks on free speech or on the right to advocate revolutionary ideas. The Anarchists with whom he most sympathised intellectually were the Anarchist-Communists, who grouped themselves round Kropotkin and Mrs. Charlotte Wilson (who for a long time was both an Anarchist and a Fabian). But the Anarchists with whom he had to deal in the League — Frank Kitz, David Nicoll, C. W. Mowbray, and the rest — did not belong to this group, which held aloof. The League Anarchists were of the school rather of Johann Most, and included a good number of German exiles : their two strongholds were the old Rose Street International Club, mentioned earlier in this chapter, and the East End group which followed Joseph Lane and the Labour Emancipation League. The majority of these groups were advocates of revolutionary violence, though not necessarily of assassination. They were demanding a root-and-branch destruction of existing social institutions, to clear the ground for a new construction about which they refused to speculate in advance. Morris, revolutionary though he was, found this destructiveness altogether repellent. He agreed that civilisation was rotten at the core, and that its institutions needed a thorough uprooting. But he did not believe that the work could be well done in a destructive mood, or without a vision and an understanding of the new society that was to replace the old. In his view, the essential work that needed doing was educational : the first task was to find and train a sufficient corps of constructively minded Socialists, who would be able gradually to leaven the lump of soulless labour which capitalism had brought into being. He regarded both premature violence and premature playing at politics with aversion, because he did not believe that the new world could be built as it should be either by rioting with no clear purpose or by parliamentary compromise. As the parliamentarians formed by far the largest group among both intellectuals and workers who were coming over to some sort of Socialism, his opposition to them threw him into association with the extremists on the other side, with whom he agreed no better. He therefore became more and more isolated, though respected by almost everyone. His Socialism was not indeed of a kind that could be popular ; for it proceeded from one question which he was continually asking himself. That question was 'How should I feel if I had to live the sort of life most men are compelled to live in order to earn their bread ?' His answer was not only, or even mainly, that most of the workers were wretchedly poor : it was that they were forced to spend their lives in work from which they could hope to get neither pleasure nor satisfaction. No pleasure, for the work was mostly drudgery, in which a man could feel no pride : no satisfaction, because it was done for a profit-seeking master, with only the cash nexus uniting the working team. Morris, in effect, was attributing to all men — or, shall we say, felt that he ought in justice to attribute to all men — what he himself felt. He had great pleasure in his work — so much that he could never rest. Why should other men be denied such pleasure ? He worked, not for a master, but in the service of his ideals. Why should not other men be able to do the same ? He knew perfectly well that most people did not feel as he did about these matters ; but he attributed their failure to do so to the long servitude to which they had been subjected, and believed that in a well-ordered society, freed from profit-making and exploitation, that was how most men would feel. To think anything else would have seemed to him unjust, because it would have involved a denial of what he believed to be the fundamentally natural human values and of the ideal of social equality.

During the years of his association with the Socialist League, Morris's views about politics underwent a gradual change, as he reacted more and more against his Anarchist associates. But this deeply rooted belief that in a properly constituted society all normal men could and should feel as he did remained with him to the end. Right up to 1890, when he was on the eve of his break with the League, he was still expressing his entire disbelief in the value of parliamentary action as a means to Socialism. He would admit no more than that 'in the last act of the Revolution the Socialists may be obliged to use the form of Parliament in order to cripple the resistance of the reactionists by making it formally illegal'; but that, he said, could only come 'when the Socialists are strong enough to capture the Parliament in order to put an end to it'. In the meantime, he denied that it would be possible to 'jockey Parliament into Socialism'. Indeed, he held that attempts to do so would result only in 'dishing' the Socialists, who would find themselves being used by the Parliament instead of using it. Socialists, he said, instead of involving themselves in the parliamentary game, should get on with their proper tasks of education — of increasing 'discontent with the vile slavery of to-day', and of showing the discontented 'that they can themselves destroy their slavery'. He asked of those who regarded this as a policy of despair, 'Is it nothing to point out to them what lies beyond the period of struggle ?'

Nevertheless, during the last years of Morris's life, his attitude to politics underwent a gradual change. Continuing to dislike parliamentarianism as much as ever, and as convinced as ever that the British Socialist movement was taking a wrong turn, he saw the way things were going as the 'New Socialism' of the Fabians and the Independent Labour Party pushed the S.D.F. and the Anarchists aside and began to build up a political movement more closely related to the actual claims and interests of the workers enrolled in the new Unions of the gasworkers, dockers, and other less skilled groups. He came to believe, if not that Socialism, as he understood it, could be established by constitutional means, at all events that there was no alternative to going through a phase in which the attempt would be made. The only sort of 'Socialism' that could arise in this way, he considered, was State Socialism, or, to use his own phrase, 'collectivist bureaucracy'. This he saw, not as a desirable system, but as perhaps a necessary transitional stage that would prepare men for 'the revolution', and might be, in the circumstances, preferable to immediate revolutionism of a merely destructive kind. But he envisaged this bastard 'Socialism', not as fulfilling any part of his ideal, but as something against which men would revolt when they felt its consequences. The only real change in his attitude was that he became ready to admit that the building up of a strong political movement based on the Trade Unions, even if it used parliamentary means, might help to educate the workers for the real tasks of 'the revolution'. Mere reformist parliamentarianism of the 'Lib-Lab' type he regarded with abhorrence right to the end.

This Morrisite Socialism has much in common, not with Anarchism pure and simple, but with Anarchist-Communism. Morris's utopia, depicted in *News from Nowhere*, is a society from which governmental institutions will have totally disappeared, and such organisation as survives will arise out of the spontaneous activities of free groups. That was what Kropotkin also believed, as Godwin had believed it before him. But Morris differed from Kropotkin in not being prepared to destroy the State until men were ready for a way of life that would make it unnecessary. His zeal for education was not for formal education at all — in that he greatly disbelieved, because he held that it indoctrinated the people in false values. The education he wanted was education in the arts and faith of comradely living ; and he was always revolted by the preaching of hatred which seemed to be erected into an end in itself. Like Lenin, he wanted the State to 'wither away' and rejected the Anarchist view that men should simply pull it down without putting anything in its place to guide them through the transition to a classless society. Quite unlike Lenin, he rested his hopes of this 'withering away' on a change in the minds of men — of enough men to guide the mass towards the spirit of free association, not after, but before the revolution.

It has often been said that Morris's Socialism arose out of his art, and out of his revolt against the degradation of the arts under capitalism. But this is only half true. It arose also out of a deep passion for fellowship and social equality — the passion he expressed in John Ball's Sermon at the Cross in *A Dream of John Ball*. This desire for fellowship was as deeply rooted in him as his passion for creative craftsmanship. Indeed, the two were inseparable in his mind ; for he could not conceive of a man living a good life of fellowship without being a craftsman, in the sense of getting a positive pleasure out of his daily work. Kropotkin, who partly agreed with him about this, differed from him in understanding that real craft pleasure could be got from the manipulation and tending of great complicated machines as well as from the handicrafts ; but he too believed that, for happiness, most men needed to work in manageably small groups, in which they could see the effect of their own efforts and get a sense of worth-while achievement. Morris, on the other hand, acutely disliked, not machines, but machines that depersonalised the product, and hated the whole trend towards mass-production as necessarily turning some workers — probably the great majority — into mere adjuncts to machines they could not even set up for themselves. But Kropotkin, as a man of science by both temperament and training, could not oppose technical progress based on science : he could only try to prove that individual and small-scale production, rightly organised and supplied with power, could beat the mass-production factory at its own game. Morris, as a practitioner of many crafts, and no scientist at all — unless it be science to be profoundly learned about many materials and processes — could and did deny the reality of technological progress and insist that most mass-produced goods were, and were bound to be, shoddy and unpleasing because of the very conditions under which they were made.

He could not, indeed, have held any other view, on the basis of his fundamental beliefs. The reign of fellowship and equality appeared to him to be quite irreconcilable with any state of affairs in which the designer and the executant were two separate persons, with no human bond between them. He wanted each man to be free to design as well as to execute, because only by doing both could he truly express his personality in his product, and thus achieve the integrated satisfaction of creative work. Everything made, Morris held, ought to be 'a joy to the maker and a joy to the user' : it ought to be beautiful as well as useful, and to communicate to the user the pleasure which its maker had taken in producing it. As he grew more disillusioned about the near future, he came to say that there would have to be more machinery before there could be less — meaning that men would have to pass through a State Socialist phase of large-scale production on their way to a society in which they would demand both better work and better products. But he always regarded this transitional stage with aversion, because it would leave man the producer the slave of the machine, even if it provided man the consumer with a larger supply of inferior goods.

John Ruskin (1819–1900) had, of course, said most of this

before Morris said it ; and Ruskin's influence on Morris's thinking was profound. *Unto This Last* (1862) had proclaimed the equalitarian part of Morris's gospel, in opposition to the egoism of current economic doctrines ; and the famous chapter on 'Gothic Architecture' in *Stones of Venice* had proclaimed the need for a reintegration of design and execution as the necessary basis for a restoration of the popular arts and of artistic feeling among the people. Morris took these doctrines over from Ruskin, passed them through the test of his own experience, and made them the foundation of a revolutionary Socialist gospel, of which Ruskin had stopped short. *Fors Clavigera*, in which Ruskin preached to such working men as would listen to him, was an appeal mainly to voluntary individual effort, not to the creation of a Socialist movement accepting class-struggle as its necessary method. But the basic ideas about fellowship and the good life were the same.

Morris's conversion to revolutionary Socialism, at a time when Socialism of any sort had been almost forgotten in Great Britain, shocked and offended many of his admirers who had been prepared to accept his artistic gospel until he translated it into terms of class-action, and grafted a sort of Marxism upon it. It was one thing to rail against the commercialism which had befouled the arts and to make beautiful things by old, forgotten processes for the few who could afford to buy them. It was quite another to proclaim the entire doom of modern civilisation, and to associate with a destructive rabble which lacked all sense of beauty and of the higher values. In the main, Morris admitted the lack. He spoke often in his private letters of the deep degradation into which the British working class had fallen, of their ignorance and lack of desire for beauty, or even for excellence of any sort. But, unlike most of his artistic followers, he attributed the shortcomings of the common people not to human nature but to commercialism as rooted in the capitalist system and ineradicable except by a complete change in the social and economic order. Deeply as he loved his work, he hated the conditions under which most of his pretty things had to be made merely as toys for wealthy purchasers, without whom he could not have done it at all ; and he was prepared to see it all swept away, in the faith that men, in getting a new start, would recover their natural bent for artistry — which he saw as universal among primitive peoples, and therefore as 'natural'. Morris belonged to the long line of reformers of manners whose final appeal is to a 'nature' which they contrast with 'civilisation'. In him this 'naturalism' proceeded from the requirements of his own nature, in which the creative artistic impulse was over-mastering. He could not have seen — it would have felt like treason in him to admit — that most men neither had nor ever would have this tremendous will to create, or even that their creativeness might take non-artistic forms. For him art was life and life was art — or nothing worth-while at all.

Yet, even if he mistook his own impulses for the natural man's, there was substance in his doctrine. There is a prodigious pleasure in the sense of successful creation, and most men are capable of experiencing this pleasure. For most of them, however, the creation that yields this rich harvest of delight is not, in the modern world, artistic in any ordinary sense of the word. It can arise out of many kinds of activity — from building a business or running a society to cultivating one's garden or being good at a game. I know well that it can arise out of intellectual effort which has no artistic quality ; and it can arise too, especially I think for women, out of the creation of good personal relations or the good handling of a difficult personal problem. The free society need not have, even as its ideal, the making of everyone into an artist-craftsman : what it must seek is to give everyone the opportunity of finding scope for the exercise of creative qualities for the benefit of the society — or at least not to its detriment.

But there is more than this to be said ; for was not Morris correct in holding that the daily compulsion of work in which no pleasure can be found deadens the human spirit, and drives men away from creativeness into the search for merely passive satisfactions ? I think he was right, and that this is an essential part of his contribution to Socialist thought.

Both as writer and as practitioner of many crafts, Morris has been rated very differently, living and dead. It has often been said that he did too many things well to do any of them supremely well, and that all his work is in the last analysis mere craftsmanship rather than the product of the artistic imagination. But this judgment rests on a flat denial of what he most deeply believed — that the artist should be, not someone set apart from the common man, but the skilled exponent of a traditional craft deeply rooted in the life of the people, and responsive to their needs. That he could not be such a craftsman in a world given over to commercialism he admitted : that his own work was not rooted in the present life of the people he ruefully admitted too. But he was trying, in everything he did, to recapture the lost tradition of the old arts and crafts — from architecture downwards — that had been of vital significance in the lives of common men in the mediaeval towns, if not in the countryside. His mediaevalism rested on this idea, long before he had seen any connection between art and Socialism. But his Socialism arose out of the same attitude that inspired one of his earliest prose writings — *The Story of an Unknown Church* — written in his student days. He there described a mediaeval mason-carver, carving away at the decoration of a church, with a deep satisfaction derived from the sense of a personal creative contribution to a collective effort. That same sense of the good life as service through personal creation and comradely co-operation runs through all his work.

Of Morris's Socialist writings the most popular has been, and still is, *News from Nowhere*, his utopia. He said explicitly that it was not a prediction, but a description of the kind of society in which he would feel most at home. Reviewing Edward Bellamy's *Looking Backward*, which repelled him with its picture of a completely planned social order in which he felt there would be no scope for the things he valued most, he said that a man who wrote an utopia should write down his personal vision of the good society rather than attempt to forecast the future. That is what he did in *News from Nowhere* ; and what emerged was above all his delight in simple friendliness, and his belief that the good society could rest on no other foundation, widely though it might diverge in other respects from his personal vision of it. This same gospel of friendship and fellowship runs through *A Dream of John Ball*, the most beautifully written of all his works. It appears again in his long, unfinished revolutionary poem, *The Pilgrims of Hope*, which was published first in *The Commonweal*, and was never revised as he had meant it to be. The same spirit is present in his pamphlets, especially in *Why I am a Socialist* and *A Factory as it Might Be* — and in his books of collected addresses, *Signs of Change* and *Hopes and Fears for Art*. He deeply wanted to live in a friendly world, and to get away from all the bickerings and hatreds that made his work for Socialism so uncongenial. He was entirely lacking in the will to power : he never wanted to lead, only to help. This itself meant that he could not lead well. Quarrels hurt him too much, and he could not ride roughshod over the veriest fool until he had lost his temper ; and when he had lost it he suffered afterwards from such remorse that he often undid his own good work. Such men may not be very good at making the kingdom of heaven, but they are of it. And that is much ; for even if they fail to make movements in their own day, their record survives, and helps to keep the cause sweet.

CHAPTER XV

SOCIALISM IN THE EARLY 1890s.
CONCLUSION

IN 1891, after Bismarck's fall from office and the repeal of the Anti-Socialist Laws, the German Social Democratic Party met at Erfurt to formulate a new programme. During the years of repression no full conference of the party had been possible, and the programme adopted at Gotha in 1875, on the occasion of the fusion of the Marxist and Lassallian parties, had remained unaltered. But by 1891 the Lassallians had virtually ceased to exist ; and the new programme was meant to expunge the Lassallian elements in the compromise of 1875, to which Marx had objected so strongly, and to embody a complete acceptance of Marxism. The following year Karl Kautsky, entrusted by the party with the task of producing a textbook for party members explaining and amplifying the programme, published his book *The Workers' Programme*, which became thereafter the authoritative exposition of Marxism not only in Germany, but in the many other countries in which Social Democratic Parties had been founded on the German model. It is therefore worth-while to study the Erfurt Programme, and Kautsky's glosses upon it, with some care ; for they contain the clearest statement of the policies for which the Social Democratic Parties of Europe professed to stand during the whole ensuing period up to 1914.

By the time the Erfurt Programme was adopted, Social Democratic Parties, professing the Marxist gospel, had come into existence in quite a number of countries. Pablo Iglesias (1850–1925) had established a Spanish Social Democratic Party in 1879, and a Danish Party had come into being the same year. Jules Guesde's Parti Ouvrier in France had taken definite shape by 1882 ; and Hyndman's Democratic Federation had adopted a Socialist programme in 1883, and had become the Social Democratic Federation in 1884. In 1883

G. V. Plekhanov (1857–1918) and P. B. Axelrod (1850–1928) had founded in Russia the Emancipation of Labour group which formed the nucleus of the Russian Social Democratic Party. The Norwegian Social Democratic Party began in 1887, the Austrian and the Swiss in 1888, and the Swedish in 1889. In Italy the situation was still confused : the Labour Party formed in 1885, which included anarchistic as well as Socialist groups, was dissolved by the Government the following year, and its successor, a Labour Party with a definitely Marxist programme, was not fully constituted until 1892. In Holland Ferdinand Domela Nieuwenhuis (1846–1919) had formed a Socialist Party in 1878, but had thereafter gone over to Anarchism. A split had followed ; and a new body, the Social Democratic League, had been established on a Marxist basis in 1889. Polish and Finnish parties were in course of formation, though they did not take definite shape until 1892.

In Belgium, as we shall see, Marxism had not had matters all its own way. The Belgian Labour Party, which was fully constituted in 1885 under César de Paepe's influence, stood for a somewhat different conception of Socialism from that of the definitely Marxist parties and also rested on a different relation to the Trade Unions and Co-operative Societies with which it was organically connected. It preserved some of the characteristic features of de Paepe's reports to the International, and was much less 'State Socialist' than the parties founded on the German model. But the differences were no longer wide enough to prevent close collaboration between it and the Social Democratic Parties of a more definitely Marxist complexion.

Even outside Belgium, of course, the Marxists did not have things all their own way. As we have seen, there were sharp divisions in France between the Guesdists, who followed the Marxian model, and the Possibilists led by Paul Brousse ; and the Blanquists also kept their own organisation, while Benoît Malon (1841–93) was gathering round him the group of intellectuals who later became the Independent Socialists. In Spain and in Italy the Marxists were only one section, in sharp conflict with rival groups ; and there were similar divisions in Holland, Switzerland, and even Denmark. Poland too, and of course Russia, were battlefields for rival tendencies ; and in Great Britain, though the Socialist League was petering out, the Social Democratic Federation was being challenged both by the Fabians and by the Independent Labour movement which was soon, in 1893, to take formal shape in Keir Hardie's Independent Labour Party. In the United States, the Socialist Labor Party, which Daniel De Leon joined in 1890, was coming to stand for a left-wing Marxism that was to result in a split and to the formation of a more orthodox Social Democratic Party in 1900.

Marxism, however, as interpreted by the German Social Democratic Party, was unquestionably the main force in the world Socialist movement in 1891. The success with which the German Social Democrats had held out against the Anti-Socialist Laws and had pursued their election campaigns in spite of them had given their party an enormous prestige. As the first Socialist Party to become organised on a really national scale and to win victories by appealing to a democratic electorate, it became the model for many other countries, and its ideas encountered serious resistance only in the Latin countries, in Great Britain, and in Eastern Europe, where Narodnik and similar movements still exercised a preponderant influence. In such countries as Czarist Russia (including Russian Poland), where the political conditions made parliamentary activities impossible, the Socialist groups and parties necessarily maintained an underground revolutionary character ; but in the West it had come by 1891 to be the rule for the major Socialist Parties to fight elections and to accept the conditions which parliamentary campaigning required, by combining with their Socialist aspirations the advocacy of immediate reforms, such as were thought likely to appeal to a wide electorate and were capable of being carried out within the capitalist system. The Erfurt Programme of 1891, for example, contained besides its general exposition of Socialist objectives a section embodying immediate demands not only for the reform of the political structure, but also for the extension of social services and for legislation to protect the workers' rights and interests under capitalism. There were in all the parties groups which denounced the inclusion of these 'palliatives' and maintained that elections should be fought only on a full Socialist platform and with the purpose of converting the workers to Socialism rather than winning seats or promoting reforms ; but in practice the exigencies of parliamentary electioneering made it necessary for the Socialist Parties to press for immediate reforms in advance of the full conquest of power by the workers. It was impracticable for a Socialist Party, without inviting defeat, to adhere to the principle that constructive work could begin only after the 'revolution', or even after the Socialists had won a majority in Parliament.

Nevertheless, the Social Democratic Parties, while they demanded immediate reforms, were still trying, in the 1890s, to keep these demands subordinate to the advocacy of Socialism itself. Paul Brousse's Possibilism, which stressed the importance of reforms within capitalism, was definitely unorthodox doctrine. German Revisionism, advocated by Eduard Bernstein (1850–1932), was not clearly formulated till the late 'nineties, when it aroused a prodigious controversy both in Germany and elsewhere. In 1892 Karl Kautsky (1854–1938), in the preface to his book expounding the Erfurt Programme, was still thanking Bernstein for his help, without any indication of differences between them.

Let us, then, see what the Erfurt Programme, which had so great an influence on European Socialism during the 1890s, actually had to say. It began with a statement, based on the *Communist Manifesto* of 1848, about the historical tendency of capitalism. The tendency towards capitalist concentration and the crushing out of small businesses by the great combines was strongly emphasised, and it was asserted no less strongly that the same tendency was at work in the countryside, crushing out the small farmer and replacing him by capitalist large-scale farming. It was stated unequivocally that 'Ever greater grows the number of proletarians, ever more enormous the army of surplus workers, ever sharper the opposition between exploiters and exploited, ever bitterer the class-war between *bourgeoisie* and proletariat, which divides modern society into two hostile camps, and is the common hall-mark of all industrial countries'.

This was undiluted Marxism of 1848, reiterated more than forty years later. 'The economic development of *bourgeois* society', the Programme began, 'leads by natural necessity to the downfall of small industry, the foundation of which is formed by the worker's private ownership of his means of production. It separates the worker from his means of production, and converts him into a propertyless proletarian, while the means of production become the monopoly of a relatively small number of capitalists and large landowners.' Kautsky, in the later editions of his book expounding the Programme, had to agree that the available statistics did not bear this out in the case of the landowners, and that peasant ownership appeared to be advancing rather than losing ground. But he held this to be a temporary deviation from the trend, and he continued to assert the correctness of the diagnosis as far as industry was concerned. Bernstein, in his revisionist writings, denied this, arguing that small business was changing its field and character rather than absolutely or relatively losing ground ; but Kautsky, and the main body of the Social Democratic leaders, stuck to their guns. It was indeed true in Germany, which had been a great centre of small-scale artisan production, that the individual craftsmen were losing out to the factories, and that the most spectacular growth was in the heavy industries of the Ruhr, Silesia, and parts of Saxony. In Germany small-scale industry was being superseded, in 1890, at a great rate, and large-scale industry was growing fast. Moreover, German industrial development had not yet reached the stage at which the creation of a new *petite bourgeoisie*, based on modern methods of production, was advancing so fast as to reveal itself as a powerful counter-tendency, nor had Trade Unions in the large-scale industries yet achieved any strong organisation or bargaining power.

It was therefore possible for the draftsmen of the Programme to go on to assert, still in the manner of 1848, that despite 'a gigantic growth in the productivity of human labour . . . all the advantages of this transformation are monopolised by capitalists and large landowners', and that there was 'a growing increase in the insecurity of existence, of misery, oppression, enslavement, debasement and exploitation' for the proletarians and the *petite bourgeoisie* alike. The Socialists in Great Britain were saying much the same things, though there it was very much plainer than in Germany that for a considerable section of the workers there had been since 1850 an almost continuous rise in real wages, confirmed by the figures of consumption per head of a number of basic commodities. For Germany in 1890 there were not many figures available ; but what there were showed real wages rising fairly fast, largely of course, since about 1875, on account of falling prices rather than increasing money rates. The Socialists' answer to those who brought out these trends in criticism of their case was that the improvement had been confined to limited groups of skilled workers, that the unskilled, whose number was continually growing, had had no share in it, and that unemployment was getting worse as crises increased in severity and duration. The memory of the great depression was still very much alive, and worse was believed to be on the way.

The remedy for this situation put forward in the Erfurt Programme was socialisation. All the Lassallian demands for State action to develop Co-operative Production were expunged. 'Only the transformation of capitalistic private ownership of the means of production — the land, the mines, raw materials, tools, machines, and means of transport — into social owner-ship, and the transformation of production of commodities for sale into socialist production administered for and by society, can bring about that large-scale industry and the steadily increasing productive capacity of social labour shall be changed from a source of misery and oppression for the hitherto ex-ploited classes into a source of the highest welfare.'

The Programme went on to declare that the change to public ownership and the transformation of society would emancipate not only the proletariat, but the entire oppressed human race. It could, however, only be the work of the workers themselves, because 'all the other classes, despite their mutually conflicting interests, take their stand on the basis of private ownership of the means of production'. It then asserted the necessarily political character of the working-class struggle, on the ground that 'the working class cannot successfully carry on its economic battles or develop its economic organisation without political rights'. 'It cannot achieve the passing of the means of production into community-ownership without winning political power.'

This was a clear assertion, in the Marxist manner, of the necessity of political action, directed against both Anarchists and those who wished to give primacy to the Trade Union struggle. But it was also ambiguous ; for it did not say whether the workers' political action was to be revolutionary or parliamentary, or, if both, how the two were to be related. Marx, in 1848 and later in the First International, had upheld the need for parliamentary action, but had regarded it merely as a means to strengthen the workers for the revolutionary struggle. He had asserted the positive value of such measures as the Ten Hours Act and the Acts making for parliamentary reform. But he had treated such action as merely preparatory to the revolution which would establish the new society — though in his dealings with the British Trade Unionists and Reformers he had kept this aspect of his teaching well in the background, and had indeed expressed the opinion that the revolution *might* possibly be achieved without violence in the special conditions of Great Britain and the United States. The Erfurt Programme, on the other hand, contained no hint of violent revolution. It went on to demand, as immediate reforms, universal equal direct suffrage for both men and women, the ballot, proportional representation, biennial Parliaments, direct legislation through initiative and referendum, provincial and local self-government by elected representatives, and a number of other reforms in the system of government. These, it is true, were all labelled as 'immediate demands', and were coupled with many other proposals for social and economic legislation. It can be argued that the absence from the Programme of any mention of extra-legal action was purely tactical — for any such mention might have provoked a renewal of repressive measures against the party. It is of course true that this might have happened had the Social Democrats openly proclaimed revolutionary intentions ; and I am not suggesting that they had consciously renounced their revolutionary creed. But the entire tone of the new Programme was that of a party with a Socialist ideal towards which it proposed to advance by means of far-reaching reforms, to be achieved by constitutional action ; and that was how the party did in fact develop, despite its repudiation of Bernstein's 'revisionist' proposals a decade later. Let us say that the Erfurt Programme, in emphasising the need for political action by the working class, left the long-run method of action undefined, but clearly contemplated in the short run the exclusive use of parliamentary methods, and that there was no hint of any sort of proletarian dictatorship as contemplated at any stage.

From the general declaration of the need for political action the Programme went on to an emphatic assertion of internationalism. 'The interests of the working class are the same in all countries with capitalist methods of production. With the expansion of world transport and of production for the world market the condition of the workers in any one country becomes continually more dependent on that of the workers in other countries. . . . The Social Democratic Party of Germany feels and proclaims itself *one* with the class-conscious workers of all other countries.'

Next, the Programme declares that the aim is a classless society, and that the party is setting out to end 'every kind of exploitation and oppression, whether it be directed against a class, a party, a sex, or a race'.

Thus ends the declaratory part of the Erfurt Programme. The remainder is taken up with the list of immediate demands, from which the specifically political demands have been cited already. High among these comes the claim for full freedom of speech, assembly and organisation. The others include, in the social field, compulsory and secular education for all, a free medical service, the abolition of all laws prejudicial to women, the recognition that religion is entirely a private matter and that churches should be left to manage their own affairs quite apart from the State, the popular election of judges, legal reform and abolition of the death penalty, and, last but not least, 'education of all to be capable of bearing arms : an armed nation in place of a standing army : decision on war and peace by the people's representatives : settlement of all international disputes by arbitration'.

Next come the demands for tax reform — graduated taxes on incomes and property, abolition of all indirect taxes, and 'a tax on inheritance, graduated according to the size of the inheritance and the degree of kinship'. Then follow the demands for industrial legislation — the eight hours' day, prohibition of child labour and of night work, the Saturday half-holiday and the free Sunday, the abolition of truck, factory inspection and the enforcement of better hygiene, repeal of special laws which put agricultural workers and personal servants in a status of inferiority, freedom of combination, a general system of workmen's insurance, with workers' participation in the administration, and a number of more special demands which it is unnecessary to cite.

All this amounts to a full programme of political, economic, and social reform, to be furthered by parliamentary means. It should be observed that no proposal for socialisation appears among the immediate measures. The socialisation of land or capital was evidently regarded as belonging to a later stage, following the workers' acquisition of political power. Whether it would come into a later series of demands for parliamentary action, or would be altogether postponed till after 'the revolution', was not said. It was, however, made sufficiently clear that socialisation, when it did come, would mean 'production administered for and through society', which at least strongly suggested State management. There was no suggestion of 'workers' control' through Co-operatives or specially constituted corporations.

If we turn for enlightenment on this matter to Kautsky's commentary, we shall find but little. Kautsky devotes many pages, first to an exposure of the futility of proposals to transform the economic structure of society by means of voluntary Co-operation, and then to an exposition of the inevitability of larger and larger units for the control of production. He says that the area of the State as a whole is the least that can be taken as adequate, and that even this may be in some respects too small. He describes with enthusiasm the necessary tendency for the control of production to become wholly a function of the State, transformed into the democratic agent of the whole people; and he asserts the need for State ownership and administration of all the essential means of production. Then comes the chapter in which he turns to consider the organisation of the future society in which this change to public ownership will have taken place. In effect, what this chapter says is that it is impossible to predict how industry or any kind of production will be administered in the society of the future, beyond saying that it will be collective and unified under State control. Any attempt to predict in such a matter is dismissed as 'utopian'; and it is categorically stated that the Social Democratic Party has no attitude or programme in this respect. Kautsky considers that it may be legitimate for individual Socialists to speculate about the future organisation of industry, and to put forward their notions, not as predictions, but as contributions to discussion. But he emphatically repudiates the idea that the party, as a party, should pronounce at all on the question. The reader is left, then, with the impression of a strong bias towards large-scale organisation and planning of industry on at the least a national basis, with the State as the director of industrial policy, but with no further guidance about the probable forms of organisation, and none at all on the part to be played by the workers in the control of the several industries in which they are engaged.

At the same time Kautsky, while emphasising the need for international as well as national planning of industry, shares Kropotkin's opinion that under a Socialist system international trade will be of less extent than under capitalism. He bases this view on the anticipation that production will be planned with a view to consumption rather than to the sale of the product, and that, whereas capitalism is driven further and further afield in search of markets to absorb its increasing output, Socialism will give first place to production for the supply of the needs of the consumers in each country, and will tend to exchange only for the purpose of procuring supplies that cannot be produced at home. Production for collective consumption was, he says, the hall-mark both of primitive communism and of most pre-capitalist forms of economic organisation ; and he looks forward to the reappearance of this 'co-operative' system in a society set free from capitalist merchanting and profit-seeking imperialist expansion.

Such, then, is the Erfurt Programme which the German Social Democrats, believing themselves faithful Marxists, drew up on the morrow of their recovery of freedom of propaganda with the repeal of the Anti-Socialist Laws. They had Engels's advice in drawing up their Programme, and his enthusiastic endorsement of their policy when it had been prepared. In 1895, in almost his last work, a long introduction to a new edition of Marx's *Class Struggles in France*, Engels wrote of the German Social Democratic Party and its two million voters as 'the most numerous, most compact mass, the decisive shock-force of the international proletarian army'. He wrote enthusiastically of the excellent use the party had made of universal suffrage, and looked forward hopefully to the time when it would be supported not merely by a quarter, but by a clear majority, of the electors. In the same passage he laid stress on the great changes that had come about since 1848 in the possibilities of successful insurrection. All these changes, he said, had been in favour of the military, and against the rebels, so that popular risings no longer stood, save under most exceptional circumstances, any chance at all of success. He said also that the German Social Democrats had shown in practice that larger use than had seemed possible in 1848 could be made of the institutions of capitalist constitutional government to further the workers' cause ; and he asserted that the repeal of the Anti-Socialist Laws had shown the impotence of autocracy and force to suppress a movement truly resting on working-class support. He had indeed appeared, in the published version of his introduction, to be abandoning altogether the idea that Socialism would have to be achieved by revolutionary action.

This, however, Engels had not done. After explaining how the development of military service had loaded the dice against insurrections, he had gone on to write as follows :

> Does this mean that in the future the street fight will play no further rôle ? Certainly not. It means only that since 1848 the conditions have become far more unfavourable for civil fighting, and far more favourable for the military. A future street fight can therefore be victorious only when this unfavourable situation is counteracted by other factors. Accordingly, it will occur less often in the beginning of a great revolution than in its further progress, and will have to be carried out with greater force.

This passage, and some others which there is no need to quote, were cut out of Engels's introduction by the German editors, who held that they might damage the Social Democratic Party. Engels continued to think of Socialism as requiring a revolutionary uprising at some stage, but had also come round to the view that it was right for the time being to put the emphasis on constitutional political action. The editors who censored his article may have done so for purely tactical reasons ; but I think they also disliked what he said on other grounds. Even in 1890 the German Social Democratic Party was well on the way to becoming a party of constitutional political action.

Indeed, it would probably have taken that road much earlier but for its period of outlawry under the Anti-Socialist Laws. In 1891 its leaders congratulated themselves on having expunged the Lassallian phrases from their new programme. They had indeed got rid of the phrases, but not of the underlying ideas. The State, as it appeared in the Erfurt Programme, was given all, and more than all, the attributes to which Marx had taken violent objection in the Gotha Programme of 1875. And Kautsky, the official interpreter of the Erfurt Programme, went much further still, and produced what was essentially a textbook of State Socialist doctrine.

It is interesting and instructive to compare this new programme of German Social Democracy with the programme drawn up only two years later by the Belgian Labour Party. This party had been established in 1885 by Eduard Anseele, Louis Bertrand, and César de Paepe, the leading Belgian theorist, who died in 1890. In 1893, the year in which the Programme was drawn up, the Belgians, after a series of political general strikes, at length secured a reform of the very narrow franchise. The new system was manhood suffrage, combined with wide opportunities for plural voting. The election which followed the reform sent thirty Socialists to the Chamber of Deputies, where there had been none before. The Belgian Labour Party was therefore facing a quite new situation, in which for the first time it had the means of making effective use of parliamentary action. Under the influence of the new conditions, it was emerging from the semi-Anarchism that had been thrust on it by the denial of the vote and was turning itself into an election-fighting party with an immediate programme as well as a set of longer-run objectives. Its Brussels Programme, like the German Erfurt Programme, began with a Declaration of Principles and then went on to set out a number of immediate demands for reform. But there were very large differences between the two documents. These appeared less in the declarations of principles than in the immediate proposals ; but there was even in the two declarations a difference of approach. Both demanded common ownership of the means of production ; but the Belgians, using the phrase 'collective appropriation' to describe their aims, asserted as its purpose the 'securing for every human being the greatest possible sense of freedom and well-being', and made mention of the right of 'individuals or groups' to enjoy the common heritage. What these phrases meant will come out more clearly when we discuss the party's immediate demands.

Again, whereas the Germans had put all the emphasis on political action, the Belgians took a different line. 'Socialism must pursue simultaneously the economic, moral and political emancipation of the proletariat. Nevertheless the economic point of view must be paramount, for the concentration of capital in the hands of a single class forms the basis of all the other forms of domination.' It should be noted that Belgian capitalism showed a very advanced form of concentration for the time, and that the Belgian capitalists, aided by the Government, had fought the Trade Unions with singular ferocity. Belgium was essentially a capitalist- and financier-ridden rather than a landlord-ridden society. The enemies of the Belgian workers were mainly *bourgeois*, not feudal landowners or militarists.

A further difference in the two approaches was that the Belgians gave morals an explicit rôle in the process of social transformation. They proclaimed that the transformation of capitalism into 'collectivism' must necessarily be accompanied by 'a correlative transformation in morals, by the development of altruistic feelings and the practice of solidarity'. Marx would have scorned such an appeal to altruism as *petit-bourgeois* nonsense, altogether out of place in any statement of 'Scientific Socialism'. The Belgians did not agree. From the days of Colins, through those of Désiré Brismée and César de Paepe, moral reformation and the idea of human solidarity, or brotherhood, had played a large part in the propaganda of Socialism among the Belgian people.

Finally, the Belgian Declaration of Principles laid down that 'the workers, in their struggle against the capitalist class, must fight by every means in their power, and particularly by political action, by the development of free associations, and by the unceasing propaganda of Socialist principles'. This insistence on 'free association', as on a par with political action, gives the Belgian Programme a distinctive character.

We come now to the more immediate demands — though

the word 'immediate' is not used by the Belgians, who call their second part their 'Programme', in contrast with the 'Declaration' that precedes it. On the political side, there is only one distinctive difference. The Belgians, like the Germans, demand universal suffrage, including both sexes, proportional representation, direct legislation, and local and regional self-government. But they also call for the 'creation of Legislative Councils, representing the different functions of society — industry, commerce, agriculture, education, etc. — such Councils to be autonomous within the limits of their competence and except for the veto of Parliament ; such Councils to be federated for the study and defence of their common interests'. In a later section, the Programme deals specifically with a proposed 'Superior Council of Education', to be elected by the School Committees — which in turn are to be chosen by universal suffrage ; and in its economic section it calls for 'Administration of the public services by special autonomous Commissions, under the control of the State'. It further demands the 'creation of committees elected by the workmen and *employés* of the public services to discuss with the central administration the conditions of the remuneration and organisation of labour'. In another section, it calls for 'intervention of trade associations in the fixing of rates of wages and in the general regulation of industry' ; and in yet another it demands for Trade Unions the right to tender for the collective execution of public works.

Finally, the Belgian Programme, unlike the German, has something to say about the future conduct of public services — that is, of those to be operated on a local or regional basis. The passage runs as follows :

(*a*) The Commune, or a federation of Communes composing one centre of population, is to operate the means of transport — tramways, omnibuses, cabs, local railways, etc.

(*b*) The Commune, or federation of Communes, is to operate directly the services of general interest at present worked under concessions by companies — lighting, water-supply, markets, highways, heating, security, health.

It should be explained that in Belgium the unit of local administration is, and was, the local Commune, but that the larger towns were divided into several separate Communes. 'Federation of Communes' in (*a*) refers to cases of such division, whereas in (*b*) it has a wider meaning.

It is evident that the Belgian approach to the problem of the control of industry differs a great deal from the German and that its characteristic features go back to the projects, studied in a previous chapter, which César de Paepe put before the Congresses of the International both before and after the Hague split. The Belgian Labour Party of 1892 had lost all trace of Anarchism : it was as set as the German on the conquest of political power. But its conception of society was much less centralist, and it was not prepared either to heap powers in the State as a necessary consequence of the growth of large-scale industrialism or to say merely that the structure of the coming society could not be determined in advance and was not a matter on which Socialists should express any collective opinion. The Belgians wanted as much local control, or decentralisation, as possible : they wanted some sort of functional bodies for the control of industries and services which require nation-wide administration. They were alive to the problem of 'workers' control', at any rate to the extent of demanding not only consultation but also some sort of participation. They emphasised the rôle of the local Commune rather than that of the State ; and they laid stress, as the Germans did not, on individual and group liberty, as well as on the emancipation of the workers as a class. These are very important differences ; and no less important is the appeal to moral impulses, as well as to economic necessity. The Belgian approach was definitely not Marxist, though it took in some of Marx's doctrines. It was derived rather from the 'federalist' than from the authoritarian tendency in the International.

I have left unmentioned many points on which there are no significant differences between the two Programmes. Both are internationalist ; both stand for sex equality and for a classless society, as well as for collective ownership. Both demand separation of Church and State, universal secular education, freedom of speech, writing and assembly, judicial reform, Trade Union liberty, a general scheme of social insurance, progressive taxation and abolition of indirect taxes, prohibition of children's employment, and a number of other particular reforms. The

439

Belgians did not go so far as the Germans in respect of inheritance, demanding only the suppression of intestate succession
except in the case of near kin. The Belgians were also cautious
about the land question. They demanded nationalisation of
forests and development of common lands, but beyond this
only 'the progressive taking over of the land by the State or the
Communes'. But, unlike the Germans, they declared openly
for the establishment of a Republic.

In these two Programmes, then, we have two different
attitudes towards the situation created by the emergent possibility of appealing to a wide electorate and of building up a
political party not primarily as a revolutionary force but as a
body accepting the conditions of electioneering and of participation in parliamentary government. The one attitude is highly
centralist, and fits in with the trend towards unification of the
German Reich and the breaking down of the separation of its
component States. The other is hostile to centralisation, and
fits the conditions of a society in which the Flemish and the
Walloon elements could not settle down happily together, at
any rate without a wide provincial autonomy. But there is
more in the divergences than a mere difference of national
situation, important though that factor undoubtedly was.
The Belgian approach is much more libertarian than the
German, and recognises much more the need for diversity of
organisation — for some sort of functional structure as well
as for local freedom, and for considering the workers, not only
as a single class, but also as individuals and in their various
groups.

In the next volume of this history we shall have to consider
how these and other tendencies in the new 'social democracy'
that was taking shape in the 1890s worked themselves out in
the parties and politics of the Second International. That
successor to the First International actually began in 1889,
when two rival International Socialist Congresses met in Paris,
the one sponsored by the Guesdists, the French followers of
Marx, and the other by the French Possibilists, led by Paul
Brousse — with the British Marxists of the S.D.F. paradoxically attending the Possibilist gathering, and the British moderate Socialists the Marxian. The account of these Congresses
must, however, be left over to the next volume, as they need to

be considered in connection with what followed them rather than with what led up to them.

It remains, in bringing this second volume to a close, only to stress the length of the distance travelled in Socialist thought and practice between 1850 and 1890. In 1848, although Marx and Engels were calling on the working class to take control of a social revolution deemed to be imminent all over Europe, nowhere save in France was this even remotely possible ; and even in France it was possible only in Paris, and events soon showed that success was impracticable even there. After the defeats of 1848 and the following years — defeats of *bourgeois* rather than of proletarian revolution — there ensued a period of fully a dozen years during which the working-class movements of most European countries were in eclipse, at any rate politically and to a great extent economically as well. Then came the rapid resurgence of the 1860s — a resurgence of which the First International was a symptom and a consequence even more than a cause. That movement was wrecked by the Franco-Prussian War, of which the Paris Commune was only a secondary effect — for if Napoleon III's empire had been overthrown by revolution without war, as it might well have been, the revolution would have taken, not a proletarian, but a *bourgeois* Republican form. The events of 1870 and 1871 destroyed the French working-class movement for the time being ; and in so doing they transferred the leadership of West European Socialism from France to Germany, ideologically as well as in practice. Despite the Anti-Socialist Laws, the German Social Democratic Party became the representative of the outstanding Socialist movement of Europe, and a model for imitation in many other countries. It had rivals — the Anarchist-Communists, the French Blanquists and, later, the Possibilists, the Belgians guided by de Paepe, and the Italians and Spaniards, who acted on their own, without much connection with what went on in other countries. But German Marxism came to be the one coherent international force in the labour world ; and its leaders in Germany, rather than Marx or, later, Engels from outside, necessarily had its shaping in their hands. While Bismarck was in power and the Anti-Socialist Laws were in force, these leaders were too busy fighting their day-to-day battles for survival to give much thought to programme-making, and the repression from which they suffered necessarily indisposed them to become 'constitutionalists'. But no sooner was the repression removed by Bismarck's fall than they were called upon to face the consequences of their success in standing up under it. After an initial setback, they had succeeded in rebuilding their party, despite its outlawry, as a powerful political force ; and the repression itself had attracted to their candidates a growing mass of support, not only from the working class, but also from the discontented in other classes. After 1890, they had to choose between losing the moderates by continuing to behave as an out-and-out revolutionary workers' party and adapting their tactics in order to retain and increase, under the changed conditions, the *petit-bourgeois* and peasant backing they had secured as Bismarck's most formidable antagonists. They attempted to have matters both ways by reaffirming their full loyalty to Marxism as a long-run policy, but at the same time adopting an immediate programme suitable for propaganda among the *petite bourgeoisie*. But in both long-run objectives and immediate demands they showed themselves essentially centralists ; and they could do this with advantage to their propaganda because centralism ranged them on the side of Reich unity not only against separatist tendencies, but also against Prussia, with its utterly undemocratic electoral system in sharp contrast to the manhood suffrage in force in Reichstag elections.

Meanwhile in Great Britain the new Socialism had been making only a slow and shaky start. It was bad luck for Hyndman that he fell foul of Marx, not because Marx mattered in Great Britain, but because his — and still more Engels's — hostility cost the Social Democratic Federation the loss of international recognition, and especially the countenance of the German Social Democratic Party, which it was trying to emulate. Moreover, in Great Britain the struggle between Social Democrats and Anarchists, or Federalists, had not been fought out in the 1860s and 1870s, and had still to be faced in the 1880s, when it took shape in the contest between the S.D.F. and the Socialist League. This contest was one factor in holding back the growth of Socialism in Great Britain until the situation had been basically changed by the rise of the New Unionism : so that broadly Socialist ideas first found their way to the main body of the workers in Trade Union rather than in political guise — with the important consequence that, whereas in most countries the Socialist Parties had a large influence in shaping the Trade Union movement, in Great Britain the Trade Unions shaped the political movement into the form of a Labour Party based mainly on Trade Union affiliations and dominated in its Conferences by the Trade Union vote.

In France events took yet another turn ; for there Social Democracy based on Marxism had to face, not a working class ignorant of Socialist ideas, but one which had been exposed to rival Socialist doctrines and appeals throughout the nineteenth century. In France the Marxists could appear only as one among a number of Socialist groups, with the Blanquists active long before they were heard of, and the tradition of Babeuf and the Conspiracy of the Equals linking them to the great Revolution of 1789. Though in the 1870s French Socialism, with its leaders scattered in prison or in exile, had almost ceased to exist as an organised movement, the Socialist tradition remained alive in the minds of a great many workers ; and when the revival came, the old divisions came back with it. Proudhonism reasserted itself through the reorganised Trade Unions, taking the new form of a demand for a proletarian unity which seemed unattainable in the political field, but might nevertheless be secured *sur le terrain de classe* — that is, industrially — by means of Trade Unions unattached to any of the rival Socialist groups and parties. Against this rock Jules Guesde's attempts to turn the Trade Unions into subordinate allies of the Parti Ouvrier broke vainly, whereas in Germany a similar tactic succeeded very well. The anti-Marxism of many of the French Internationalists reasserted itself in the *syndicalisme révolutionnaire* of Fernand Pelloutier's Fédération des Bourses du Travail and, later, of the Confédération Générale du Travail. French Socialism never became fully Marxist, and French Trade Unionism never accepted either a Marxian, or any rival, lead towards parliamentary politics.

Italy and Spain too remained disputed territories, which were battlegrounds between Marxian Social Democrats and various brands of Syndicalism and Anarchism. In the United States, Daniel De Leon became the apostle of a deviant Marxism, which rejected palliatives altogether and, forfeiting any chances it might have had of electoral success, prepared the way for the pure industrialism of the Industrial Workers of the World — an American variant of Syndicalism. In Russia, Marxism took root among the industrial workers in the few, but large, mass-producing factories, but could make no headway in the villages against the Narodniks and their Social Revolutionary successors, and could consequently achieve little till Czarism itself began, in 1905, to break under the strain of defeat in war — a breakdown which became complete under the much severer strain of the years after 1914. Developing under conditions entirely different from those of the parliamentary West, though much more like those of the West in the first half of the nineteenth century, Russian Marxism took a turn entirely unlike that of German Social Democracy after 1890. The Mensheviks indeed based their attitudes and policies, as nearly as circumstances allowed, on Social Democracy in its developing German form ; but the Bolsheviks, under Lenin's guidance, went back for their inspiration to the *Communist Manifesto* and became the founders of modern Communism, developing Marx's ideas on the rôle of the Party and of dictatorship into a comprehensive doctrine of total revolution. The seeds of this new interpretation of Marxism were being sown before 1890 — the point at which this book ends ; but they did not sprout till later, and to attempt to discuss them now would be out of place.

SELECT BIBLIOGRAPHY

GENERAL REFERENCES

BENOÎT MALON's *Histoire du socialisme* is not a good book, but it contains a great deal of information not easily to be found elsewhere. It is in five volumes : the first (1882) covers the period up to Babeuf ; the second (1883) deals with French Socialism from 1789 to 1878 ; the third (1884) covers Great Britain, Germany, and Russia; the fourth (1885) covers Belgium, Italy, Switzerland, Spain, Portugal, Poland, Serbia, Roumania, Austria-Hungary, Denmark, Norway, and Sweden ; the fifth (n.d.) deals with the First International, the United States, and Anarchist Socialism. H. W. Laidler's *Social-Economic Movements* (1944), originally published in 1927 as *A History of Socialist Thought*, is sketchy, but handy for dates and elementary facts. See also his *Socialism in Thought and Action* (1920). Sir Alexander Gray's *The Socialist Tradition: Moses to Lenin* (1946) is slight, but amusing. E. Dolléans, *Histoire du mouvement ouvrier* (vol. i [1830–71], 1936 ; vol. ii [1871–1936], 1939), deals mainly with France and Great Britain. Max Beer's *Allgemeine Geschichte des Sozialismus und der sozialen Kämpfe* (revised 1929), translated in five volumes as *Socialism and Social Struggles* (1922–5), is useful : vol. 5 is the relevant part. Élie Halévy's *Histoire du socialisme européen* (1948), prepared for publication from his lecture notes, is good but slight. See also G. Adler, *Geschichte des Sozialismus und Kommunismus* (1899) ; K. Diehl, *Über Sozialismus, Kommunismus und Anarchismus* (1911) ; H. Denis, *Histoire des systèmes économiques et socialistes* (2 vols., 1904–7) ; A. C. A. Compère-Morel (ed.), *Encyclopédie socialiste, syndicale et co-opérative de l'Internationale ouvrière* (8 vols., 1912–13) ; the same writer's *Grand Dictionnaire socialiste* (1924) ; W. D. P. Bliss, *Handbook of Socialism* (1895) and (ed.) *Encyclopaedia of Social Reform* (1895) ; W. Sombart, *Socialism and the Social Movement* (1896 ; English translation of revised edition, 1909) ; V. Pareto, *Les Systèmes socialistes* (2 vols., 1902–3); A. Schaeffle, *The Quintessence of Socialism* (1877 ; English translation, 1888) and *The Impossibility of Social Democracy* (English translation, 1892) ; P. Leroy-Beaulieu, *Collectivism* (English translation, 1908) ; R. Flint, *Socialism* (1894) ; T. Kirkup, *History of Socialism* (1892 ; revised by E. R. Pease, 1913) ; J. Rae, *Contemporary Socialism* (1884) ; E. de Laveleye, *The Socialism of To-day* (English translation, with an account of Socialism in England, by G. H. Orpen, 1884).

445

CHAPTER I

For the situation in Europe after 1848, reference should be made to the works in which Marx and Engels analysed the developments in Germany and France — *Revolution and Counter-revolution in Germany* (mainly by Engels), written in 1851 as a series of articles for the *New York Daily Tribune*, and first published in book form in 1896 ; *The Class-struggles in France, 1848–50*, written in 1850 for the *Neue Rheinische Zeitung*, published in book form in German in 1895, and in English in 1924 (in the U.S.A.), and in England in a new translation in 1934 ; and *The Eighteenth Brumaire of Napoleon Bonaparte*, first published in German in 1852 in J. Weydemeyer's *Die Revolution* (New York), reprinted in Hamburg in 1869, and translated into English by Daniel De Leon and published in New York in 1898. Of this last there have been two later English translations, issued in 1926 and 1935. Marx's book on the trial of the Cologne leaders of the Communist League, *Materialen, Erklärungen und Schriften zum Kölner Kommunistenprozess, 1851–2*, appeared in two editions, at Basle and at Boston, in 1853. There is a French, but no English, translation. The revised German edition of 1885 contains an important historical introduction by Engels, and also an epilogue written by Marx in 1875. Marx's *Address to the Communist League* (1850) can be found in most selections from his works — *e.g.* in Emile Burns's *Handbook of Marxism* (1935). Reference should also be made to the *Marx-Engels Correspondence*, which is available for part of this period in French as well as in German. A few letters are in the English selection, *The Correspondence of Marx and Engels* (1934).

See also *Démocraties et capitalisme, 1848–60*, by C. H. Poutras, in the *Peuples et civilisations* series ; J. P. Plamenatz, *The Revolutionary Movement in France, 1815–71* (1952) ; H. A. L. Fisher, *The Republican Tradition in Europe* (1911) ; E. Dolléans, *Histoire du mouvement ouvrier*, vol. i (1936) ; F. Mehring, *Geschichte der deutschen Sozialdemokratie* (1897–8 ; revised edition, 1922).

For the decline of Chartism see the works given in the bibliography to Volume I of this work — especially G. D. H. Cole, *Chartist Portraits* (1941) ; P. W. Slosson, *The Decline of Chartism* (1916) ; S. Maccoby, *English Radicalism, 1832–1852* (1935), and the succeeding volume, covering the years from 1853 to 1886 ; T. Rothstein, *From Chartism to Labourism* (1929) ; and John Saville's volume of edited selections, *Ernest Jones, Chartist* (1952).

For the English Christian Socialists see C. E. Raven, *Christian Socialism, 1848–1854* (1920) ; Benjamin Jones, *Co-operative Production* (2 vols., 1894) ; and other works mentioned in the bibliography given in Volume I of this work. For continental Christian Social movements see F. S. Nitti, *Catholic Socialism* (1895) ; P. T. Moon, *The Labor Problem and the Catholic Social Movement in France* (1921) ; and the further references given under Chapter X.

SELECT BIBLIOGRAPHY

For Leclaire see Charles Robert's life, *Biographie d'un homme utile* (1878) ; Leclaire's own pamphlet, *De la misère et des moyens à employer pour la faire cesser* (1850) ; and J. Gaumont, *Histoire générale de la coopération en France* (1923-4). For Godin see Aneurin Williams's translation of D. F. Prudhommeaux's *Twenty-eight Years of Co-partnership at Guise* (revised 1908) ; H. Honegger's *Godin und das Familistère von Guise* (1919) ; C. R. Fay, *Co-operation at Home and Abroad*, vol. i (1908) ; and among Godin's own works *Solutions sociales* (1871); *La Richesse au service du peuple* (1874); *Le Gouvernement* (1883); and *Mutualité sociale et association du capital et du travail* (1891), translated as *The Association of Capital with Labor* (New York, 1881).

CHAPTER II

For von Ketteler see the works listed in the book list for Chapter X. For German Christian Socialism in a wider sense see, in addition to Nitti's book, there mentioned, the books by E. de Laveleye and John Rae, mentioned in the General section of this bibliography.

For Rodbertus see E. C. K. Gonner, *The Social Philosophy of Rodbertus* (1899) ; H. Dietzel, *Karl Rodbertus* (2 vols., 1886-8) ; E. G. Jentsch, *Rodbertus* (1899) ; G. Adler, *Rodbertus, der Begründer des wissenschaftlichen Socialismus* (1884) ; and of Rodbertus's own works, *Sociale Briefe an von Kirchmann* (1850-51), translated as *Over-production and Crises* (1898) ; and *Neue Briefe über Grundrente, Rentenprinzip und sociale Frage* (ed. R. Michels, 1926).

For Marlo see E. Allix, *L'Œuvre économique de Karl Marlo* (1898) ; W. E. Biermann, *Karl Georg Winkelblech* (1909) ; A. E. F. Schaeffle, *Kapitalismus und Socialismus* (1870) ; J. Rae, *Contemporary Socialism* (1884) ; and Marlo's principal work, *Untersuchungen über die Organisation der Arbeit* (3 vols., 1848-59). There is also a volume of Marlo's *Nachlass*, edited by W. E. Biermann (Leipzig, 1911).

CHAPTER III

As I do not read Russian, I can provide only a most inadequate bibliography for this chapter out of my own knowledge. For Pestel, Pugachov, and the Decembrists generally, as well as for the later thinkers, see T. G. Masaryk, *The Spirit of Russia* (original, 1913 ; translated 1919) ; I. M. Lubin, *Zur Charakteristik und zur Quellenanalyse von Pestels 'Russkaja Pravda'* (1930) ; Benoît Malon, *Histoire du socialisme*, vol. iii (1884) ; M. N. Pokrovsky, *Brief History of Russia* (English translation, 1933) ; Richard Hare, *Pioneers of Russian Social Thought* (1951). For Belinsky and his group see V. G. Belinsky, *Select Philosophical Works* (published in English in U.S.S.R., 1948); Masaryk *op. cit.* and Hare *op. cit.*, and also P. Miliukov, *Le Mouvement intellectuel russe* (French translation, 1918); and D. S. Mirsky, *History of Russian Literature* (1927). These works are also useful for the rest of the chapter.

For Herzen see especially his diaries, published in English as *My Past and Thoughts* (1924–7). His other writings are not for the most part available in English, but some of them are in French or German. Some indeed were written originally in German. In English there is only his *Letter to Michelet on the Russian People and Socialism* (1855). This was first published in French (shorter version, 1851 ; full version, 1852). In French there are his *Letters from Italy and France* (1871 — originally published in German in 1850) ; *From the Other Shore* (1870 — originally printed privately in Russian, first published in German in 1850) ; *La Russie* (1849) ; *Lettre d'un Russe à Mazzini* (1850 — in Italian, 1849) ; *Du développement des idées révolutionnaires en Russie* (1851). His novel, *Who is to Blame?*, originally published serially in Russia (1845–7) and in book form in 1847, is available in French in the *Gazette du Nord* (1859). There is no English version.

For Herzen's life see E. H. Carr, *The Romantic Exiles* (1933), and R. Labry, *Alexandre Ivanovic Herzen* (in French, 1928).

For Chernyshevsky see G. V. Plekhanov, *N. G. Tschernischewsky* (Stuttgart, 1894) ; Y. Steklov, *N. Tschernischewsky, ein Lebensbild* (1913) ; and, of his own writings, his *Select Philosophical Essays* (U.S.S.R., in English, 1953); *L'Économie politique jugée par la science* (French translation, Brussels, 1874) ; *La Possession communale du sol* (translated with a brief biography, Paris, 1903); and *Lettres sans adresse* (on the abolition of serfdom — Liège, 1874).

For Peter Lavrov see his *Historical Letters* (in German, 1901 ; in French, 1903). Most of his writings are available only in Russian : the most important are *An Essay on the History of Modern Thought* (Geneva, 1888–94), *The Problems of Historical Understanding* (Moscow, 1898), and *Principal Periods in the History of Thought* (Moscow, 1903). For an account of his sociological doctrines see J. F. Hecker, *Russian Sociology* (1915), and T. G. Masaryk's *The Spirit of Russia* (English translation, 1919). The French and German editions of the *Historical Letters* both have useful introductions, by M. Goldsmith and C. Rappoport respectively.

CHAPTER IV

The only good account of early Belgian Socialism that I know of is in Louis Bertrand, *Histoire de la démocratie et du socialisme en Belgique depuis 1830* (2 vols., 1906–7), which is very difficult to find. It should be read with the same author's *Histoire de la coopération en Belgique* (2 vols., 1903), and with his *La Belgique en 1866* (1880) and *La Belgique économique, sociale et financière de 1830 à 1900*. Consult also his *Souvenirs d'un meneur socialiste* (1927). The smaller *Histoire du socialisme en Belgique*, by J. Destrée and E. Vandervelde (1898), does not cover the early period. There are two chapters, dealing respectively with Colins and with Kats, De Keyser, and others, in vols. ii and iv of B. Malon's *Histoire du socialisme*.

The principal works of Colins are *Socialisme rationnel* (3 vols., 1851) ; *Qu'est-ce que la science sociale?* (4 vols., 1851–4) ; *De la justice dans la science, hors l'Église et hors la Révolution* (3 vols., 1860), and *La Science sociale* (15 vols., 1857–96), edited by Agathon de Potter. For an outline of his ideas see A. Hugentobler, *L'Extinction du pauperisme* (1867). See also G. Parent, *Le Socialisme de Colins* (1912).

The writings of Jacob Kats are mostly in Flemish : they include many plays, popular almanacs, and poems. His most important works, *Werk en kapitaal* (1872) and *Het boek des volks* (1840), are available only in Flemish. In French there is *La Situation de l'ouvrier* (1864). There is a Life, in Flemish, by Julius Kuypers (1930).

De Keyser's chief work, *Het natuer in regt* (1854), is available only in Flemish. In French there is only *L'Enfant de la Révolution* (1830).

For Louis de Potter see the Life by E. V. Turenhoudt (Brussels, 1946), which has a full bibliography. His writings include *De la révolution à faire d'après l'expérience des révolutions avortées* (Paris, 1831) ; *Révolution belge: souvenirs personnels* (2 vols., Brussels, 1839) ; *Études sociales* (2 vols., Brussels, 1841–3) ; *A.B.C. de la science sociale* (Brussels, 1848) ; *Les Belges de 1830 et la Belgique en 1850* (Brussels, 1850) ; *Catéchisme sociale* (Brussels, 1850) ; *Dictionnaire rationnel* (Brussels, 1852) ; and his posthumous *Souvenirs* (1900).

For Agathon de Potter see especially his *M. Poulin et le socialisme rationnel* (1875) and his *Économie sociale* (2 vols., 1874).

CHAPTER V

The standard edition of Lassalle's writings is that of E. Bernstein, *Gesammelte Reden und Schriften* (12 vols., Berlin, 1919–20), supplemented by that of Gustav Mayer, *Nachgelassene Briefe und Schriften* (6 vols., Stuttgart, 1921–5), and by the same editor's *Bismarck und Lassalle, ihr Briefwechsel und ihre Gespräche* (Berlin, 1928). See also *Ferdinand Lassalles Briefe an Georg Herwegh*, edited by M. Herwegh (Zürich, 1896) ; *Briefe an Hans von Bülow von Ferdinand Lassalle* (Dresden, 1893) ; and *Intime Briefe F. Lassalles an Eltern und Schwester*, edited by E. Bernstein (Berlin, 1905).

Very little of Lassalle has been translated into English. There are translations of his *Open Letter to the National Labor Association of Germany*, by J. Ehrmann and F. Bader (New York, n.d.) ; of *The Working Man's Programme*, by Edward Peters (New York, n.d.), and of part of his *Herr Bastiat Schultze von Delitsch*, under the title *What is Capital?*, by F. Keddell (New York, 1900). His address, *Science and the Working Man*, was translated by Thorstein Veblen (New York, n.d.).

Works on Lassalle in English include E. Bernstein's *Ferdinand*

Lassalle as a Social Reformer (in German, 1892; in English, 1893);
G. Brandes, *Ferdinand Lassalle* (1911); W. H. Dawson, *German
Socialism and Ferdinand Lassalle* (1888); and David Footman, *The
Primrose Path* (1946). See also Bertrand Russell, *German Social
Democracy* (1896).

See also H. Oncken, *Lassalle : eine politische Biographie* (1912);
E. Bernstein, *Ferdinand Lassalle, eine Würdigung des Lehrers und
Kämpfers* (1919).

For the Lassallians see Bernhard Becker, *Geschichte der Arbeiter-
Agitation Ferdinand Lassalles* (1874); E. Thier, *Rodbertus, Lassalle,
Adolph Wagner* (1930). See also F. Mehring's *Life of Karl Marx*
(in English, 1936); the *Marx-Engels Correspondence*, and Mehring's
Geschichte, already cited.

CHAPTER VI

By far the best history of the International Working Men's Association, despite its strong partisanship, is that of Bakunin's Swiss
follower, James Guillaume — *L'Internationale, documents et souvenirs,
1864–1878* (4 vols., Paris, 1905–10). Guillaume reprints a great many
documents and articles and provides the only approach to a consecutive
record of the proceedings at the successive Congresses and Conferences, both before and after the split of 1872. He is, of course,
strongly hostile to Marx, and his account needs correction at many
points. But no other work is nearly so comprehensive, or can serve
as a foundation for the study of the International's affairs. Indeed,
some of the Congresses and Conferences are nowhere else reported —
or at least I have been unable to find reports. The Congress Reports
known to me are as follows : Geneva, 1866, in French (by the Pole,
Card); Brussels, 1868, in French ; Basle, 1869, in English (issued in
London). I can find no separately published Reports of the Inaugural
Conference of 1864, of the Lausanne Congress of 1867, or of the Hague
Congress of 1872. Nor is there known to me any full record of the
London Conferences of 1865 and 1871. For the period after the split
there are Reports, in French, of the Le Locle Congress of 1874, the
Verviers Congress of 1875, and the Berne Congress of 1876, and also
of the Ghent Socialist Unity Congress of 1877 — this last privately
printed and apparently never issued to the public. For other Congresses and Conferences, Guillaume's book is usually the most important source ; and he also gives a good account of many of the Congresses
of the Jura Federation and other Anarchist or near-Anarchist groups.

The other contemporary accounts of the First International include
E. Villetard, *Histoire de l'Internationale* (Paris, 1872 ; American
translation, *History of the International*, New Haven, 1874) ; Eichhoff,
Die internationale Arbeiterassociation (Berlin, 1868), and the three
works of O. Testut, *L'Association internationale de travailleurs* (Lyons,

1870), *Le Livre bleu de l'Internationale* (Paris, 1871), and *L'Internationale et le jacobinisme au ban de l'Europe* (Paris, 1872). None of these is of much value, except that Testut reproduces a number of documents which are useful for detailed study of the fortunes of the International in France. Another first-hand work, of greater value, is Paul Brousse, *Le Marxisme dans l'Internationale* (Paris, 1882).

To these must be added the two pamphlets published by the Marxists in the course of the quarrel with Bakunin — *Les Prétendues Scissions dans l'Internationale* (Geneva, 1872) and *L'Alliance de la démocratie socialiste et l'association internationale des travailleurs* (1873). The latter, written by Marx and Engels, was also published in English. Consult also *Mémoire adressé par la fédération jurassienne de l'association internationale des travailleurs à toutes les fédérations de l'Internationale* (Sonvillier, Switzerland, 1873). There is also useful material in the published reports of the police proceedings against the French Section of the International — *Procès de l'association internationale des travailleurs. Première et Deuxième Commissions du bureau de Paris* (Paris, June 1870) and the *Troisième Procès* (Paris, July 1870). See also *Les Séances officielles de l'Internationale à Paris pendant le siège et pendant la Commune* (Paris, 1872).

Of later histories, the earliest is Vera Zasulich, *Sketch of the History of the International* (1889), which is available in several languages. The fullest, written from a strict Marxist-Communist standpoint, is Y. M. Stekloff's *History of the First International* (in Russian, 1918 ; English translation, London, 1928) : this covers the Anarchist International after 1872 as well as the earlier history. There is a short account in R. W. Postgate, *The Workers' International* (London, 1920), which deals also with the Second International and with the beginnings of the Third. Another account is that of G. Jaeckh, *Die Internationale* (Leipzig, 1904 ; English translation, *The International, a Sketch*, the same year). Other works to be consulted include B. Malon's *Histoire du socialisme*, vol. v ; R. Meyer, *Der Emancipationskampf des vierten Standes* (Berlin, 1874) ; M. de Preaudau, *Michel Bakunin: le collectivisme dans l'Internationale* (Paris, 1912) ; and E. H. Carr, *Michael Bakunin* (London, 1937). The *Correspondence* of Marx and Engels and F. Mehring's *Life of Karl Marx* should also be consulted.

CHAPTER VII

There is an enormous literature dealing with the Paris Commune. Marx's manifesto written for the I.W.M.A. in its support and published as *The Civil War in France* (1871) is a key document. The standard history by an eye-witness is that of P. O. Lissagaray, *Histoire de la Commune de 1871* (Brussels, 1876 ; English translation by Eleanor Marx Aveling, London, 1886 ; revised and annotated French edition, edited by A. Dunois, Paris, 1929). Another useful contemporary account is P. Lanjalley and P. Corriez, *Histoire de la révolution du 18ᵉ mars* (1871). Among hostile accounts written at the time the most significant are J. Claretie, *Histoire de la révolution de 1870–71* (5 vols., Paris, 1874–6), and M. Du Camp, *Les Convulsions de Paris* (4 vols., Paris, 1878). See also J. Simon, *Le Gouvernement de M. Thiers* (Paris, 1878). Of more recent accounts the fullest in English is F. Jellinek, *The Paris Commune of 1871* (London, 1937), which contains a good bibliography (London, 1937). In French, E. Lepelletier's four-volume study, *Histoire de la Commune de 1871* (Paris, 1911–13), is valuable for reprints of documents as well as for its detailed narrative. The volume in Jean Jaurès's *Histoire socialiste* (vol. xi), written by Louis Dubreuil, *Histoire de la Commune* (Paris, 1908), is a competent piece of work. So are the two books by G. Bourgin, *Histoire de la Commune* (1925) and *Les Premières Journées de la Commune* (Paris, 1928). G. Laronze, *Histoire de la Commune de 1871* (1928), incorporates material, especially from legal sources, not used by previous writers ; while E. S. Mason, *The Paris Commune* (New York, 1930), makes full use of Blanquist manuscript sources. G. Weill, *Histoire du mouvement social en France, 1852–1902* (1904 ; revised 1924), contains an excellent section on the background. A collection of V. I. Lenin's writings on the Commune appeared in English, under the title *The Paris Commune*, in 1933. See also his comments in *The State and Revolution* (1917). For an Anarchist view see P. Kropotkin, *The Paris Commune* (1891), and, for a somewhat similar view, E. Belfort Bax, V. Dave, and William Morris, *A Short Account of the Paris Commune* (1886).

The following may be mentioned among a large number of contemporary memoirs : Jean Allemane, *Mémoires d'un communard* (Paris, n.d.) ; C. Beslay, *Mes Souvenirs* (1873) and *La Vérité sur la Commune* (1877) ; G. Cluseret, *Mémoires* (1877–8) ; G. da Costa, *La Commune vécue* (3 vols., 1903–5) ; G. Flourens, *Paris livrée* (1871) ; J. Guesde, *Çà et là* (1914) ; F. Jourde, *Souvenirs d'un membre de la Commune* (1877) ; G. Lefrançais, *Souvenirs d'un révolutionnaire* (1902) ; B. Malon, *La Troisième Défaite du prolétariat français* (1871) ; Louis Michel, *La Commune* (1898) ; L. N. Rossel, *Papiers posthumes* (1871) ; Jules Vallès, *L'Insurgé* (1886) ; P. Vésinier, *Comment a péri la Commune?* (1892) ; M. Vuillaume, *Mes Cahiers rouges au temps de la Commune* (10 vols., 1908–14). See also Victor Hugo's *L'Année terrible* (1872) ; L. Halévy, *Notes et souvenirs, 1871–2* (1888) ; and E. A. Vizetelly, *My Adventures in the Commune* (1914).

The *Journal Officiel* of the Commune, containing decrees and short reports of meetings, was reprinted in one volume (Paris, 1879). There are also a number of collections of official documents, listed by F. Jellinek, *op. cit.*

Of biographical studies of Communards the following deserve mention : M. Dommanget, *Eugène Varlin* (1926) ; E. Faillet, *Biographie de Varlin* (1885) ; C. Prolès, *Les Hommes de la Révolution* (1898).

SELECT BIBLIOGRAPHY

CHAPTER VIII

Most of the references for this chapter have been given already under Chapter VI. James Guillaume's *L'Internationale* remains the principal source. For conditions in Belgium see the works of L. Bertrand cited in the bibliography under Chapter IV. For César de Paepe see the short biography of him by Louis Bertrand (Brussels, 1909), the same writer's *Histoire de la démocratie et du socialisme en Belgique depuis 1830* (2 vols., 1906–7), and B. Malon's *Histoire du socialisme*, vol. iv. De Paepe contributed largely to the sections of Malon's work dealing with Belgium, Holland, and Great Britain. His writings have never been collected : many of the most important remain scattered in the journals in which they originally appeared. The most ambitious of these is his *Cours d'économie sociale*, published in *l'Économie sociale* in 1875 and 1876. His *Objet de la science économique* appeared serially in *La Société nouvelle* between 1888 and 1890. His numerous reports written for the First International include the following : *Rapport sur la coopération, le crédit mutuel et le travail des femmes* (Lausanne, 1867) ; *Mémoires sur la propriété terrienne* (Brussels, 1868 ; Basle, 1869) ; *Essai sur l'organisation des services publics* (Brussels, 1874 — translated into several languages, including English). Other works include *Examen de quelques questions sociales* (Brussels, 1866) — his first publication ; numerous articles in the *Tribune du peuple* (1861–9) and in other periodicals ; and a number of occasional pamphlets and addresses.

For the activities of the Bakuninist Sections of the International the principal source is Guillaume, supplemented by Benoît Malon, and by E. H. Carr's *Michael Bakunin* (1937). See also the references given under Chapter IX. For Switzerland see also J. Langhard, *Die anarchistische Bewegung in der Schweiz*, and P. Kropotkin, *Memoirs of a Revolutionist* (1906). For Italy see also R. Michels, *Il proletariato e la borghesia nel movimento socialista italiano* (1908) and *Storia critica del movimento socialista italiano* (1926); A. Angiolini and E. Ciacchi, *Socialismo e socialisti in Italia* (1920) ; L. Valiani, *Storia del movimento socialista*, vol. i (1951); and Benedetto Croce, *History of Italy from 1871 to 1915* (English translation, 1929). For Spain, G. Brenan, *The Spanish Labyrinth* (1943).

For Nechaiev and for Utin see Guillaume and Carr, and also the *Marx-Engels Correspondence* (in German — only selection in English). For France after the Commune see E. Dolléans, *Histoire du mouvement ouvrier*, vol. ii (1939) ; G. Weill, *Histoire du mouvement social en France, 1852–1924* (1924) ; P. Louis, *Histoire du socialisme en France* (revised 1950) ; vol. xi of J. Jaurès's *Histoire socialiste*, 1908 ; A. Zévaès, *De la semaine sanglante au Congrès de Marseille* (1911). For the Blanquists see C. da Costa, *Les Blanquistes* (1912).

For Germany see the references given under Chapter X. For Great Britain, Max Beer, *History of British Socialism*, vol. ii (revised

1929) ; T. Rothstein, *From Chartism to Labourism* (1929) ; and again the *Marx-Engels Correspondence.*

For the International in the United States see M. Hillquit, *History of Socialism in the United States* (revised 1910) ; J. R. Commons and associates, *History of Labor in the United States* (4 vols., 1918–19) ; and D. G. Egbert and S. Persons (editors), *Socialism and American Life* (2 vols., Princeton, 1952).

CHAPTER IX

Bakunin's complete works, including his letters, are available only in Russian editions. His more important writings can be read in French, in the six-volume edition edited by M. Nettlau (vol. 1) and J. Guillaume (vols. 2-6) (Paris, 1895–1913). In English is *God and the State*, translated by the American Anarchist, B. R. Tucker (1883).

The most satisfactory recent study of Bakunin is Benoît P. Hepner's *Bakounine et le panslavisme révolutionnaire* (1950).

The best Life available is E. H. Carr, *Michael Bakunin* (1937). Max Nettlau's massive biography (3 vols. in German, 1896–1900) exists only in a number of duplicated copies deposited in leading libraries, including the British Museum. Nettlau's great collection of Bakunin MSS. and other materials is in the library of the International Institute for Social History at Amsterdam. There is also a long biography by Y. M. Stekloff (4 vols., in Russian, 1934–6). K. J. Kenafick's *Michael Bakunin and Karl Marx* (Melbourne, 1948), based largely on Guillaume, is strongly partisan.

There is a great deal about Bakunin in Guillaume's *L'Internationale*. Reference should also be made to the *Marx-Engels Correspondence*.

CHAPTER X

For German Social Democracy after Lassalle's death see Bertrand Russell, *German Social Democracy* (1896) ; R. T. Ely, *French and German Socialism in Modern Times* (1883) ; A. Rosenberg, *The Origins of the German Republic* (English translation, 1931) and *Democracy and Socialism* (English translation, 1939) ; W. H. Dawson, *The Evolution of Modern Germany* (1908) ; August Bebel, *My Life* (3 vols., in German, 1911, abridged English version of vols. 1 and 2, 1912) ; F. Mehring, *Geschichte der deutschen Sozialdemokratie* (4 vols., revised 1922) ; S. Neumann, *Die deutschen Parteien* (1932) ; R. Lipinski, *Die Sozialdemokratie* (2 vols., 1927–8) ; E. Milhaud, *La Démocratie socialiste allemande* (1903) ; Kurt Eisner, *Wilhelm Liebknecht, sein Leben und Werken* (1906) ; B. Becker, *Geschichte der Arbeiter-Agitation Ferdinand Lassalles* (1874) ; R. Rocker, *Johann Most* (1924) ; W. Sombart, *Socialism and the Social Movement* (English translation, 1909) ; F. Mehring, *Life of Karl Marx* (English translation, 1936); the *Marx-Engels Correspondence*; G. Mayer, *Friedrich Engels* (1934, abridged English version, 1936) and the same writer's *Johann Baptist von Schweitzer und die Sozialdemokratie* (1909). For German Christian Socialism see J. Rae, *Contemporary Socialism* (1884); E. de Laveleye, *Socialism To-day* (English translation, 1884); F. S. Nitti, *Catholic Socialism* (English translation, 1895); G. Metlake, *Christian Social Reform* (1912). For von Ketteler see his *Freiheit, Autorität und Kirche* (1862); *Die Arbeiterfrage und das Christenthum* (1864); *Deutschland nach dem Kriege von 1866* (1867); *Liberalismus, Socialismus und Christenthum* (1871); *Predigten* (2 vols., 1878); *Ausgewählte Schriften*, edited by J. Mumbauer, with a biographical introduction (3 vols., 1924), and for comment O. Pfülf, *Bischof Ketteler* (3 vols., 1899); F. Vigener, *Ketteler, ein deutsches Bischofsleben des 19. Jahrhunderts* (1924); T. Brauer, *Ketteler der deutsche Bischof und Sozialreformer* (1927); M. M. Neuefeind, *Bischof Ketteler und die soziale Frage seiner Zeit* (1927). For F. Hitze see his *Die soziale Frage* (1877); *Kapital und Arbeit* (1881); *Die Arbeiterfrage* (1899); and *Zur Würdigung der deutschen Arbeiter Sozialpolitik* (1913); and also F. Müller, *Franz Hitze und sein Werk* (1928).

For Vogelsang see his *Gesammelte Aufsätze über Socialpolitik* (1885–6), and *Vogelsang: extraits de ses œuvres* (2 vols., in French, 1905); and also J. Schwalber, *Vogelsang und die moderne christlich-soziale Politik* (1927). See also Rudolph Meyer, *The Struggle for the Emancipation of the Fourth Estate* (2 vols., 1874–5); G. Ratzinger, *Die Volkswirthschaft in ihren sittlichen Grundlagen* (1881, enlarged 1895).

For de Mun see his *Discours et écrits divers* (7 vols., 1888–1904); *Combats d'hier et d'aujourd'hui* (6 vols., 1910–16); and *Ma Vocation sociale* (1908). See also V. Giraud, *Un Grand Français: Albert de Mun* (1918); J. Piou, *Le Comte Albert de Mun* (1925); and P. T. Moon, *The Labor Problem and the Social Catholic Movement in France* (New York, 1921). For Périn see his *La Richesse dans les sociétés chrétiennes* (1861) and *Les Lois de la société chrétienne* (1875).

For the relevant Papal Encyclicals see *The Pope and the People: Select Letters and Addresses on Social Questions* (1902; revised edition, 1943). The separate Encyclicals can also be had in pamphlet form.

For the 'State Socialists' see J. Rae, *Contemporary Socialism* (1884); C. Gide and C. Rist, *History of Economic Doctrines* (English translation, 1915); R. Goldscheid, *Staatssozialismus oder Staatskapitalismus* (1917).

CHAPTER XI

For the earlier writings of Marx and Engels see the works listed in the bibliographies to the relevant chapters of Volume I. There is a bibliography in Mehring's *Karl Marx* and a more recent one in H. C. Desroches and C. Hubert, *La Signification du marxisme* (1948).

Marx's *Zur Kritik der politischen Okonomie*, described as 'Volume I', first appeared in 1859. Kautsky's edition of 1907 includes the 'General Introduction' from Marx's MSS. An English translation by I. N. Stone, including this introduction, appeared in 1909 as *A Contribution to the Critique of Political Economy*.

The first volume of *Das Kapital*, dealing with *Capitalist Production*, was published in German in 1867 : a revised edition appeared in 1872–3, and a third edition, corrected by Engels from Marx's MSS., in 1883. A fourth edition, also supervised by Engels, was published in 1890. A French translation by J. Roy, corrected by Marx, came out in 1875, and an English translation, from the third German edition, in 1887 (in 2 vols.). It was entitled *Capital: a Critical Analysis of Capitalist Production*, and the translation was by Samuel Moore and Edward Aveling : it was edited by Engels. A different translation by Ernst Untermann, from the second edition, appeared in Chicago in 1906, and a third, by Eden and Cedar Paul, from the fourth edition in London in 1928. A separate translation of the first nine chapters, under the title *The Theory of Value*, appeared in London in 1890.

The second volume, dealing with *The Process of Capitalist Circulation*, was issued in German by Engels in 1885. It was translated into English by Ernst Untermann, and published in America and England in 1907. The third volume, *The Complete Process of Capitalist Production*, was edited by Engels and published in German in 1894. An English translation, by Untermann, appeared in Chicago in 1909. Marx's studies of the work of his predecessors, *Theorien über den Mehrwert*, were edited by Kautsky and published in three volumes between 1905 and 1910. A French translation, in eight volumes, appeared in 1924–5, and a volume of selections, edited by G. A. Bonner and Emile Burns, was published in English in 1953.

There have been many abridgements of *Capital*. The best known, in English, are Edward Aveling's *The Student's Marx* (1891); Karl Kautsky's *The Economic Doctrines of Karl Marx* (English translation, 1925); and Julian Borchardt's *The People's Marx* (English translation, 1921). There are also extensive extracts in E. Burns, *A Handbook of Marxism* (1935).

The four volumes edited by F. Mehring under the title *Aus dem literarischen Nachlass von Karl Marx, Friedrich Engels und Ferdinand Lassalle* (1902) are important chiefly for Marx's and Engels's earlier writings.

Marx's Address to the First International on *Value, Price and Profit* was first published in English in 1865. The pamphlet on Wage Labour and Capital (*Lohnarbeit und Kapital*) first appeared as a series of articles in the *Neue Rheinische Zeitung* in 1849 : an English translation, by J. L. Joynes, was issued in 1885. There have been several subsequent translations.

Engels's *Umrisse zu einer Kritik der Nationalökonomie* appeared in 1844 in the *Deutsch-französische Jahrbücher* edited by Ruge and Marx. His *Herrn Eugen Dührings Umwälzung der Wissenschaft*, containing sections by Marx, was published in 1878, and first translated, as *Landmarks of Scientific Socialism*, by A. Lewis (Chicago, 1907). A new translation, by Emile Burns, entitled *Herr Eugen Dühring's Revolution in Science* [*Anti-Dühring*], appeared in the 1930s, but bears no date. Engels's *Dialectics of Nature*, left unfinished at his death and unpublished until the 1930s, was issued in an English translation by C. P. Dutt in 1940.

The literature of Marxism is much too vast to allow mention to be made here of more than a very few works dealing particularly with Marxist economics. Among these are E. von Böhm-Bawerk, *Karl Marx and the Close of his System* (1896 ; English translation, 1898) ; G. D. H. Cole, *The Meaning of Marxism* (1948) ; Joan Robinson, *An Essay on Marxian Economics* (1942) ; D. Ryazonov, *Marx and Engels* (English translation, 1927) ; S. Hook, *Towards the Understanding of Karl Marx* (1933).

CHAPTER XII

There is a dearth of general books on Anarchism in English. There are translations of P. Eltzbacher's *Anarchism* (Berlin, 1900 ; English translation, 1908) and of E. V. Zenker's *Anarchism* (1895 ; English translation, 1897). E. A. Vizetelly's *The Anarchists* (1911) deals mainly with the 'Anarchists by the deed' from 1877 onwards, and is of no use for Anarchist theory. The standard histories in German are Max Nettlau's *Die Vorfrühling der Anarchie* (1925) and *Der Anarchismus von Proudhon zu Kropotkin* (1927). See also his extensive *Bibliographie de l'anarchie* (Brussels, 1897) and his papers in the International Institute for Social History at Amsterdam. Other works include K. Diehl, *Uber Sozialismus, Kommunismus und Anarchismus* (Jena, 1911) ; G. Adler, *Geschichte des Sozialismus und Kommunismus* (1899) ; R. Stammler, *Die Theorie des Anarchismus* (1894) ; J. Garin, *L'Anarchie et les anarchistes* (1885) ; F. Dubois, *Le Péril anarchiste* (1885) ; G. V. Plekhanov, *Socialism and Anarchism* (1894 ; translated by Eleanor Marx Aveling, 1908); B. Malon, *Histoire du socialisme*, vol. v, ch. 31 (1885) ; A. Naquet, *L'Anarchisme et le collectivisme* (1904).

See also J. Maitron, *Histoire du mouvement anarchiste en France, 1880–1914* (1951) ; L. Levine, *Syndicalism in France* (1914) ; E. Dolléans, *Histoire du mouvement ouvrier*, vol. ii (1939) ; P. Louis, *Histoire du socialisme en France* (revised 1950) ; E. Yaroslavsky, *History of Anarchism in Russia* (n.d.) ; P. F. Brissenden, *The I.W.W.: a Study of American Syndicalism* (1918) ; New York State, Joint Legislative Committee Investigating Seditious Activities, *Revolutionary*

Radicalism (4 vols., Albany, 1920) ; J. R. Commons and associates, *History of Labor in the United States* (2 vols., 1918) ; J. Langhard, *Die anarchistische Bewegung in der Schweitz* (1903).

For Godwin and Proudhon see the references given in the bibliography to Volume I of this work.

For Bakunin see under Chapter IX of this volume.

For Zhelyabov and the Russian terrorists of the 1870s and 1880s see David Footman's *Red Prelude* (1944), which includes a Life of Zhelyabov and a useful biographical index. Footman used a typescript work by A. I. S. Branfoot, *A Critical Study of the Narodnik Movement* (1926), deposited in the London University Library. He also refers to K. Zilliacus, *The Russian Revolutionary Movement* (English translation, 1905), which I have not seen, and to George Kennan's *Siberia and the Exile System* (1891). S. Stepniak's *Underground Russia* (1882), *Russia under the Czars* (1885), and *The Career of a Nihilist* (1889), should also be consulted.

For American Anarchism see also Josiah Warren, *Equitable Commerce* (1846) and *True Civilisation* (*c.* 1850 — in parts) ; Lysander Spooner, *Poverty : its Illegal Causes and Legal Cure* (1846) and *An Essay on the Trial by Jury* (1852) ; S. P. Andrews, *Constitution of Government in the Sovereignty of the Individual* (1851) and *The Science of Society* (1853) ; B. R. Tucker, *Instead of a Book* (1893). For a commentary on these writers see E. M. Schuster, *Native American Anarchism* (1932), and W. Bailie, *Josiah Warren* (1906). See also A. Spies, *Autobiography* (1887) ; A. Spies and A. R. Parsons, *The Great Anarchist Trial* (report of speeches, 1886) ; A. R. Parsons, *Anarchism, Its Philosophy and Scientific Basis* (1887) ; H. David, *The History of the Haymarket Affair* (1936) ; L. E. Parsons, *Life of Albert R. Parsons* (second edition, 1903) ; J. Most, *Die freie Gesellschaft* (1884) ; *Kriegswissenschaft* (1888), and *Memorien* (2 vols., 1903–5) ; R. Rocker, *Johann Most, das Leben eines Rebellen* (1924) ; W. D. P. Bliss, *Encyclopaedia of Social Reform* (revised 1908) — *s.v.* Chicago Anarchists ; the report of *The Trial of the Chicago Anarchists*, by D. D. Lum (1886), and pamphlet reports of the speeches made at the trial, collected in L. E. Parsons, *The Famous Speeches of the Eight Chicago Anarchists* (1886).

For Kropotkin see his *Memoirs of a Revolutionist* (English translation, 1906) ; *The Conquest of Bread* (1892 ; English translation, 1913) ; *Mutual Aid* (1902) ; *Fields, Factories and Workshops* (1899) ; *The Great French Revolution* (1909) ; *Modern Science and Anarchism* (1903) ; *Ideals and Realities in Russian Literature* (1905) ; *In Russian and French Prisons* (1887); *The State : its Part in History* (1898) ; *Revolutionary Pamphlets*, edited by R. N. Baldwin (1927) ; and numerous separate pamphlets, issued in many editions. Among these are *An Appeal to the Young* (1881) ; *The Place of Anarchism in Socialist Evolution* (1887) ; *The Commune of Paris* ; *War* ; *Anarchist Communism, its Basis and Principles* ; *The Wage System* (1889) ; *Expro-*

priation; *The State : its Historic Rôle* (1893); *Anarchism, its Philo-sophy and Ideal* (1896); *Law and Authority* (1882); *Wars and Capitalism*; *Anarchist Morality* (1891); *Revolutionary Government*; *Agriculture* (1893). I have given the dates of first publication where I know them. See also Kropotkin's article on 'Anarchism' in the *Encyclopaedia Britannica* (1910 edition).

There is much information in J. Guillaume's *L'Internationale*. See also the files of *Le Révolté* (1879–87), *La Révolte* (1887–94), and *Les Temps nouveaux* (Jean Grave, 1895–1914). See also E. Pouget's journal, *Le Père Peinard*, which began in 1889.

For the French Anarchists see also Jean Grave, *L'Anarchie, son but, ses moyens* (1899); *La Société au lendemain de la Révolution* (1882); *La Société mourante et l'anarchie* (1893); *L'Individu et la société* (1897); *La Société future* (1895); *Les Adventures de Nono* (1901); *Réformes-Révolution* (1910); Émile Gautier, *Le Darwinisme social* (1880); S. Faure, *La Douleur universelle* (1895); C. Malato, *Philo-sophie de l'anarchie* (1889); *Révolution chrétienne et révolution sociale* (1891); *De la Commune à l'anarchie* (? 1894); *L'Homme nouveau* (1898); J. H. Mackay, *Anarchistes: mœurs du jour* (1892); A. Hamon, *Psychologie de l'anarchiste-socialiste* (1895); *Socialisme et anarchisme* (1905); J. Guesde, *Çà et là* (1914) and articles in *Égalité* (founded 1877).

For Élisée Réclus see his *Correspondance* (3 vols., Paris, 1911–25); *L'Évolution, la révolution, et l'idéal anarchiste* (1898); and numerous pamphlets, in various languages.

For Malatesta see many pamphlets, including *A Talk about Anarchist Communism*; *Anarchy*; *Entre paysans*; *Au café — dia-logues sur le socialisme anarchiste* (1902). See also the collected *Pro-paganda socialista fra contadini* (1884); *La politica parlamentare nel movimento socialista* (1890); *Il nostro programma* (1903); and see also M. Nettlau's *Errico Malatesta* (1922, in Italian).

CHAPTER XIII

For a full bibliography of American Socialism see vol. 2 of D. D. Egbert and S. Persons, *Socialism and American Life* (1952). For general history of American Socialism see M. Hillquit, *History of Socialism in the United States* (1903); L. Symes and T. Clement, *Rebel America* (1934); C. A. Madison, *Critics and Crusaders* (1947); J. Macy, *Socialism in America* (1916); J. R. Commons and associates, *History of Labor in the United States* (4 vols., 1918–35); and *A Docu-mentary History of American Industrial Society* (10 vols., 1910–11); P. S. Foner, *History of the Labor Movement in the United States to the Founding of the American Federation of Labor* (1947); N. J. Ware, *The Labor Movement in the United States, 1860–1895* (1929); A. Bimba, *History of the American Working Class* (1927); J. Oneal,

The Workers in American History (1910 — latest edition, 1927) ; F. E. Haynes, *Social Politics in the United States* (1924) ; P. K. Crosser, *Ideologies and American Labor* (1941).

Among biographies see J. C. Sylvis, *The Life, Speeches, Labors and Essays of William H. Sylvis* (1872) ; C. Todes, *William H. Sylvis and the National Labor Union* (1942) ; K. Obermann, *Joseph Weydemeyer* (1947) ; A. E. Morgan, *Edward Bellamy* (1944) and *The Philosophy of Edward Bellamy* (1945) ; J. R. Buchanan, *The Story of a Labor Agitator* (1903) ; A. Sotheran, *Horace Greeley and other Pioneers of American Socialism* (1915).

More specialised works include W. F. Kamman, *Socialism in German American Literature* (1917) ; B. D. Wolfe, *Marx and America* (1934) ; H. Schlüter, *Die Anfänge der deutschen Arbeiterbewegung in America* (1907) and *Die Internationale in Amerika* (1918) ; R. T. Ely, *The Labor Movement in America* (1890) ; E. and E. M. Aveling, *The Working-Class Movement in America* (1888) ; W. J. Kerby, *Le Socialisme aux États-Unis* (1897) ; C. H. Vail, *Modern Socialism* (1897) ; L. Gronlund, *The Co-operative Commonwealth* (1884) and *Our Destiny* (1891) ; N. Fine, *Labor and Farmer Parties in the United States, 1828–1928* (1928).

For De Leon see the collected edition of his *Speeches and Editorials* (2 vols., n.d.) ; *As to Politics* (reprinted articles, 1935) ; *What Means This Strike?* (1898) ; *Reform or Revolution* (1899) ; *Socialism versus Anarchism* (1901) ; *The Burning Question of Trade Unionism* (1904) ; *Principles of Industrial Unionism* (1905) ; *Socialist Reconstruction of Society* (1905) ; *Two Pages from Roman History* (1908), etc. See also the symposium *Daniel De Leon, the Man and his Work* (1919).

For the Knights of Labor see their *Proceedings* (1878–1913) and *Journal* (1880–1918) ; T. V. Powderly, *Thirty Years of Labor* (1889). For U. S. Stephens see G. E. McNeill, *The Labor Movement* (1887), and N. J. Ware, *op. cit.*

For Henry George's works see *Our Land and Land Policy* (1871) ; *Progress and Poverty* (1879) ; *The Irish Land Question* (1881) ; *Social Problems* (1883) ; *Protection or Free Trade?* (1886) ; *The Condition of Labor* (1891) ; *A Perplexed Philosopher* (1892) — all included in his *Complete Works* (8 vols., 1906–11). See also H. George, jr., *Life of Henry George* (2 vols., 1911) ; L. F. Post, *The Prophet of San Francisco* (1930) ; A. N. Young, *History of the Single Tax Movement in the United States* (1916) ; and for Henry George in England, H. M. Hyndman's *Record of an Adventurous Life* (1911), and articles by E. P. Lawrence in the American *Journal of Economics and Sociology* (July and October 1951).

For Edward Bellamy see his two Socialist novels, *Looking Backward* (1887) and *Equality* (1897), and also, among his pamphlets, *The Parable of the Water Tank* (n.d.), *Plutocracy or Nationalism, which?* (1889), and *The Programme of the Nationalists* (1894).

SELECT BIBLIOGRAPHY

CHAPTER XIV

For the period between the decline of Chartism and the Socialist revival of the 1880s see F. E. Gillespie, *Labour and Politics in England, 1850–1867* (1927) ; T. Rothstein, *From Chartism to Labourism* (1929) ; A. W. Humphrey, *History of Labour Representation* (1912) and *Robert Applegarth* (1915) ; G. D. H. Cole, *British Working-Class Politics, 1832–1914* (1941) and *The Common People* (with R. W. Postgate, revised 1946) ; H. B. Bonner, *Life of Charles Bradlaugh* (1894) ; F. W. Soutter, *Fights for Freedom* (1925) and *Recollections of a Labour Pioneer* (1923) ; M. Beer, *History of British Socialism* (1920 ; revised 1929) ; J. Clayton, *The Rise and Decline of Socialism in Great Britain* (1926). H. M. Pelling's *The Origins of the Labour Party* (1954) appeared after this book was finished ; but I read it in typescript before passing my final proofs.

For the Social Democratic Federation see H. W. Lee and E. Archbold, *Social Democracy in Britain* (1935) ; H. M. Hyndman, *The Record of an Adventurous Life* (1911) and *Further Reminiscences* (1912) ; F. J. Gould, *H. M. Hyndman, Prophet of Democracy* (1928) ; R. T. Hyndman, *The Last Years of H. M. Hyndman* (1923) ; W. Kent, *John Burns: Labour's Lost Leader* (1950) ; G. D. H. Cole, *John Burns* (1943) ; J. Burgess, *John Burns: the Rise and Progress of a Right Honourable* (1911) ; Edward Carpenter, *My Days and Dreams* (1916) ; E. Belfort Bax, *Reflections and Reminiscences* (1918).

Hyndman's principal writings include *England for All* (1881) ; *The Historical Basis of Socialism* (1883); *Commercial Crises of the Nineteenth Century* (1892) ; *Economics of Socialism* (1896) ; *The Future of Democracy* (1915) ; *The Awakening of Asia* (1919) ; *The Evolution of Revolution* (1920). See also H. M. Hyndman and William Morris, *A Summary of the Principles of Socialism* (1884), and the report of Hyndman's debate with C. Bradlaugh, *Will Socialism benefit the English People?* (1884). See also various pamphlets of Hyndman, issued by the S.D.F. — e.g. *Socialism and Slavery* (1884), and the reports of the S.D.F. and the files of *Justice* and *The Social Democrat*.

For the Socialist League see the files of *The Commonweal*; the *Manifesto of the Socialist League*, annotated by W. Morris and E. B. Bax (1885) ; *Socialist League Address to Trades' Unions* (1885); *For Whom Shall We Vote?* (1885) ; T. Binning, *Organised Labour: the Duty of Trades' Unions in relation to Socialism* (1886).

For William Morris see *Life*, by J. W. Mackail (1899) ; Aymer Vallance, *William Morris, his Art, his Writings, and his Public Life* (1897) ; J. Bruce Glasier, *William Morris and the Early Days of the Socialist Movement* (1921) ; H. V. Wiles, *William Morris of Walthamstow* (1951) ; *The Letters of William Morris*, edited by Philip Henderson (1950) ; and the Introduction by May Morris to the twenty-four volumes and to the two supplementary volumes of the *Collected*

Works (1910–15 ; supplementary volumes, 1936). Among Morris's own writings see especially *News from Nowhere* (1891) ; *A Dream of John Ball* (1888) ; *The Pilgrims of Hope* (from *The Commonweal*, 1886) ; *Signs of Change* (1888) ; *Hopes and Fears for Art* (1882) ; *Architecture, Industry and Wealth* (1902) ; *Essays and Lectures on Art and Socialism* (1947) ; *Socialism, its Growth and Outcome*, with E. Belfort Bax (1893) ; *Gothic Architecture* (1893). Of the pamphlets the following deserve mention : *Under an Elm Tree* (1891) ; *Useful Work versus Useless Toil* (1886) ; *How I Became a Socialist* (1896) ; *Monopoly: or How Labour is Robbed* (1890) ; *True and False Society* (1888) ; *A Short Account of the Commune of Paris*, with E. B. Bax and Victor Dave (1886) ; *The Decorative Arts* (n.d.) ; *Art, Labour and Socialism* (1884) ; *Communism* (1903) ; *Chants for Socialists* (1884–5) ; *The Tables Turned, or Nupkins Awakened* (1887).

See also E. Belfort Bax, *The Religion of Socialism* (1886) ; *The Ethics of Socialism* (1889) ; *Outlooks from the New Standpoint* (1891) ; *Outspoken Essays on Social Subjects* (1897) ; *Essays in Socialism* (1906) ; *The Last Episode of the French Revolution* (1911) ; *Reminiscences and Reflections* (1918) ; Edward Carpenter, *Towards Democracy* (1883 ; completed 1905) ; *Civilisation, its Cause and Cure* (1889) ; *My Days and Dreams* (1916).

For the Fabians see E. R. Pease, *History of the Fabian Society* (1916 ; revised 1925) ; W. Knight (ed.), *Memorials of Thomas Davidson, the Wandering Scholar* (1907) ; Bernard Shaw, *The Early History of the Fabian Society* (1892), *Essays in Fabian Socialism* (1932), and (ed.) *Fabian Essays in Socialism* (1889 ; and see Prefaces to later editions — most recent, 1948) ; Margaret Cole, *Beatrice Webb* (1945) and (ed.) *The Webbs and their Work* (1949) ; M. A. Hamilton, *Sidney and Beatrice Webb* (1933) ; Beatrice Webb, *My Apprenticeship* (1926) and *Our Partnership* (1948). See also the files of *The Practical Socialist*, edited by T. Bolas (1886–7), and the bound volumes of *Fabian Tracts*. The Fabian Society's published Annual Reports begin in 1889, and *Fabian News* in 1891.

For Annie Besant see her *Autobiography* (1893), and *Lives* by G. Williams (*The Passionate Pilgrim*, 1932) and G. West (1927), as well as numerous pamphlets and the files of *The National Reformer*, *The Link*, and *Our Corner*. For Bradlaugh see his *Autobiography* (1873), the biography by Hypatia Bradlaugh Bonner (1894) and the centenary volume, *Charles Bradlaugh, Champion of Liberty* (1933), and also his *Labour and Law* (1891), *The National Reformer*, and many pamphlets. For Chamberlain's Radicalism see the *Unauthorised Programme* (1885) and *Life*, by J. L. Garvin (1932–4). For Dilke see G. M. Tuckwell and S. Gwynn, *Memoirs of Sir Charles Dilke* (1917).

Book references for Keir Hardie and Robert Blatchford will be given in Volume III.

SELECT BIBLIOGRAPHY

CHAPTER XV

For the Programmes of the German Social Democratic Party (1891) and the Belgian Labour Party (1893) see R. C. K. Ensor, *Modern Socialism as Set Forth by Socialists* (1903 ; revised 1910). For Kautsky see the files of *Die neue Zeit* from 1883 ; *The Workers' Programme* (1892).

INDEX OF NAMES

Abbe, Ernst, 11
Abeele, Van den, 70
Abreu, Joaquín, 186
Alerini, Charles, 187, 217
Alexander I, 33
Alexander II, 32, 38, 39, 42, 49, 53, 315, 319 ff., 342, 346
Alexander III, 322, 333
Alfonso XII, King of Spain, 189, 316, 317
Allemane, Jean, 152, 154, 452
Allix, Jules, 149 f., 157
Altgeld, J. P., 332
Amadeus of Savoy, King of Spain, 189
Andrews, S. P., 331, 458
Anseele, Eduard, 70, 436
Applegarth, Robert, xi, 129, 162, 381
Assi, A.-A., 152, 153
Aveling, Edward, 268, 456, 460
Avicella, Ordax, 186
Avrial, Auguste, 172
Axelrod, P. B., 426

Baader, F. X. von, 34
Babeuf, Gracchus, 26, 54, 179, 443
Babick, 172
Bacon, Francis, 59
Bakunin, Michael, xi, 36, 41, 45, 47, 50, 52, 54, 68, 85, 100, 102, 109, 114, 116 ff., 129, 130 ff., 179, 181 ff., 187, 190 ff., 202, 207, 210, 211, 212, 213 ff., 262, 269, 315, 316, 318, 336, 338, 339, 344, 351, 358, 451, 453, 454
Barberet, J. J., 324
Barbès, Armand, 38
Barcía, Roque, 186
Barker, Warton, 374
Barry, Maltman, 403
Bastelica, André, 105, 187, 197
Bax, E. Belfort, xi, 400, 452, 461, 462
Bazaine, Marshal, 143, 156
Bebel, August, xi, 86, 129, 142, 176, 177, 237 f., 239 f., 454
Becker, Bernhard, 86, 238, 450, 454

Becker, Hermann, 71
Becker, J. P., 98, 100, 101, 125, 191, 203, 267
Beesly, E. S., 385 f., 396
Belgiojoso, Princess of, 179
Belinsky, V. G., xi, 34, 36 f., 48, 214, 447 f.
Bellamy, Edward, xi, 361, 374 f., 423, 460
Bentham, Jeremy, 48
Bernard, Joseph, 327
Bernstein, Eduard, xi, 266, 300, 341, 428, 429, 431, 449
Bertrand, Louis, 70, 436, 448, 453
Besant, Annie, 393, 408, 462
Beslay, Charles, 148, 149, 452
Bignami, Enrico, 179, 181
Bismarck, Otto Eduard Leopold, 16, 30, 84, 85, 119, 145, 147, 176 f., 238 ff., 253 ff., 256 f., 259, 262, 265, 266, 267, 330, 341, 425, 441 f.
Blanc, Louis, 15, 48, 67, 78, 79, 96, 110, 113, 144, 161
Bland, Hubert, 405
Blandford, Thomas, 380
Blanqui, L. A., xi, 38, 54, 90, 117, 118, 135 f., 140, 143, 151, 152, 155, 161, 325, 357, 441
Bobczynski, 98
Böhmert, Viktor, 10
Bonald, L. G. A., 34
Boon, Martin J., 382
Bordat, Toussaint, 327
Borde, Frédéric, 66
Boulanger, General, 135, 260
Bovia, Giovanni, 181
Bradlaugh, Charles, 385, 391 ff., 406, 408, 411, 461, 462
Brailsford, H. N., vii
Brass, August, 239
Bray, J. F., 21, 32, 289
Brentano, Lujo, 258
Bright, John, 5, 113
Brisbane, Albert, 363
Brismée, Désiré, 437
Brousse, Paul, xi, 156, 324, 326, 345, 426, 428, 440, 451

465

Brunel, A. M., 150 f., 159
Bryan, W. J., 362, 374
Buchez, P. J. B., 264
Büchner, Ludwig, 48
Buonarroti, P. M., 151, 179
Burke, F. H., 396
Burns, John, xi, 399, 402, 403, 404, 405, 407 f., 409 f., 412 ff., 461
Butler-Johnstone, H. A., 395, 396

Cabet, Étienne, 9, 26, 32, 57, 186, 363
Cafiero, Carlo, 179, 183, 345
Cairnes, J. E., 382
Cámara, Sixto, 186
Camélinat, Rémy Zéphirin, 152, 153
Cameron, A. C., 201, 364
Campini, Leopoldo, 179
Caporusso, Stefano, 183
Carlile, Richard, 391
Carlyle, Thomas, 29
Carnot, President Sadi, 333
Carr, E. H., 40, 213, 453, 454
Carter, James, 109, 162
Caserio, Santo Geronimo, 333
Casimir-Perier, A., 334
Catherine II, 33
Cavaignac, General, 38, 58, 66
Cavendish, Lord Frederick, 396
Chaädaev, Peter, 34
Chabert, C. E., 324
Chamberlain, Joseph, 263, 385, 386, 387 ff., 402 f., 409, 462
Champion, H. H., xi, 403, 407 f.
Champseix, Léodile, 153
Chernyshevsky, N. G., xi, 37, 46, 48 ff., 51, 54, 316, 318, 448
Clark, G. B., 384
Clarke, W. J., 401
Clément, J. B., 152
Clément, Victor, 171
Cluseret, G. P., 150, 159, 452
Cohn, James, 197
Coleridge, S. T., 29
Colins, Baron J. H. de, xi, 57 ff., 67 f., 69, 70, 99, 437, 449
Comte, A., 57, 62, 66, 221, 222, 311 f., 385
Considérant, Victor, 9, 10, 363
Cooper, Peter, 364
Cooper, William, xi
Costa, Andrea, 183, 185, 330
Coullery, Pierre, 99, 100, 125, 129, 191
Courbet, Gustave, 150
Cowen, Joseph, 396

Cremer, W. R., 98, 109, 113, 382
Cyvoct, Antoine, 327

Da Costa, Charles, Eugène, and Gaston, 172
Danielson, Nikolai, 268
Darboy, Archbishop, 156, 160
Davitt, Michael, 383 f., 384, 388, 396, 397
De La Tour du Pin, René, 260
De Leon, Daniel, xi, 209, 361, 365, 369, 373, 374, 375 ff., 427, 443, 446, 460
De Paepe, C., xi, 49, 64, 66, 98, 99 f., 109, 111 f., 115, 125, 126, 129, 130, 197, 204, 206 f., 211, 225, 325, 329, 340, 426, 436, 437, 439, 441, 453
Debs, E. V., xi, 361, 377, 378
Delaporte, 66
Delesalle, Paul, 329
Delescluze, L. C., xi, 144, 149, 150
Descamps, 172
Descartes, René, 59
Dietzgen, Joseph, xi
Dilke, Sir Charles, 382, 385, 386, 387, 388, 389 f., 394, 395, 396, 409, 462
Dobrolubov, N. A., 48
Döllinger, Johann, 254
Dombrowski, Jaroslaw, 152, 159
Dostoievsky, Feodor, 50
Dove, Patrick E., 370 f., 372, 383
Dreyfus, Alfred, 135, 260
Dühring, Eugen, xi, 303 ff., 457
Dumartheray, F., 346
Dupleix, François, 98, 100, 101
Dupont, Clovis, 172
Dupont, E., 90, 91, 98, 109, 199
Dupuy, C. A., 334
Durkheim, Émile, 219
Duval, E. V., 152, 154, 159

Eccarius, J. G., 90, 95, 98, 108, 109, 125, 129, 130, 131, 162, 197, 199, 381, 382
Engel, Christian, 258
Engel, George, 332
Engels, Friedrich, xi, 1 ff., 12, 14, 15, 18, 21, 72 f., 75, 92, 142, 179, 187, 193, 197, 199, 201, 202 f., 238, 240, 244, 251 f., 266, 267 ff., 296, 298, 301, 302 ff., 320, 395, 401, 434 ff., 441, 446, 451, 455 ff.
Eudes, Émile, 152, 155

INDEX OF NAMES

Fanelli, Giuseppe, 124, 181, 187, 217
Farga-Pellicer, Rafael, 187
Faure, Sébastien, 333, 357, 459
Fava, Angelo, 179
Fawcett, Henry, 382
Fazy, James, 113
Ferrari, Giuseppe, 179
Ferré, Théophile, 152, 155 f., 160
Feuerbach, Ludwig, 36, 48, 214, 221 f.
Fichte, J. G., 15, 16 f., 257
Figner, Vera, 321
Fischer, Adolph, 332
Flourens, Gustave, 151, 452
Fourier, Charles, 9, 10, 15, 32, 46, 49 f., 57, 96, 179, 186, 349, 361, 362, 363
Frankel, Leo, 152, 154, 158, 160, 168, 197, 199
Freycinet, C. L. de S. de, 320
Fribourg, E. C., 90, 98
Friscia, Saverio, 181, 182

Gambetta, Léon, 151
Gambon, C. F., 144, 161
Gambuzzi, Carlo, 181
Garfield, President J. A., 322
Garibaldi, Giuseppe, 89, 90, 113, 114, 178, 180, 181, 183
Garrido, Fernando, 186 f.
Gary, Judge, 332
Gautier, Émile, 327, 328, 342, 347, 357, 459
George, Henry, xi, 361, 370 ff., 375, 377, 384, 385, 386, 388, 389, 395, 400, 402, 411, 460
Gerhard, H., 70
Gladstone, W. E., 162, 267, 388, 389
Gnocchi-Viani, Osvaldo, 185
Godin, J. B. A., 10, 447
Godwin, William, 337, 419
Gogol, N. V., 37
Gompers, Samuel, 365, 369, 376
Goupil, É. A., 172
Graham, R. B. Cunninghame, xi, 384
Grave, Jean, 328, 333, 338, 340, 355, 356, 459
Greene, W. A., 331
Greening, E. O., 381
Grévy, President Jules, 327, 328, 347
Grinevitski, Ignatie, 321
Gronlund, Lawrence, 375, 460
Grousset, Paschal, 172

Guesde, Jules, xi, 151, 156, 324 ff., 329, 346, 425, 426, 440, 443, 452, 459
Guillaume, James, xi, 100 f., 116, 125, 153, 191, 192, 193, 210, 211, 345, 450, 453, 454, 459

Hales, John, 162, 197, 379
Hardie, J. Keir, xi, 263, 403, 409, 413, 427
Harrison, Frederic, 385, 386
Hartmann, Leo, 320
Hartwell, Robert, 379
Hasselmann, Wilhelm, 330, 341
Hatzfeldt, Countess, 73 ff., 237, 238
Haxthausen, August von, 43 f.
Haywood, W. D., 377
Headlam, Stewart D., 263, 385, 386
Hegel, G. W. F., 15, 17, 34 f., 76 f., 228, 257, 305
Held, Adolf, 258
Henri, Émile, 333
Herder, J. G., 34
Herwegh, Georg, 40
Herzen, Alexander, xi, 33, 34, 36, 37 ff., 49, 50 ff., 56, 113, 216, 225, 269, 347, 448
Herzen, Nathalie, 38, 40
Herzig, 346
Hess, Moses, 125
Hildebrand, Bruno, 28, 258
Hillquit, Morris, 377, 454, 459
Hitze, Frank, 256, 455
Hodgskin, Thomas, 289
Hoedel, E. H. M., 317
Holyoake, G. J., 8, 380, 381, 391
Howell, George, 98, 162
Huber, V. A., 8, 254
Hugentobler, A., 64, 66, 449
Hughes, Thomas, 264
Hugo, Victor, 113, 144, 452
Humbert, King of Italy, 316, 317
Hyndman, H. M., xi, 326, 347, 383, 384, 385, 390, 394 ff., 401 f., 404 f., 407 f., 409 ff., 414, 425, 442, 460, 461

Iglesias, Pablo, 425
Isabella, Queen of Spain, 186, 189

Jannet, Claudio, 261
Jaurès, Jean, xi, 453
Jevons, W. S., 271, 276
Johannard, Jules, 171
Jones, Ernest, 5, 379, 446
Jones, Lloyd, 379

Joukovsky, Nicholas, 124, 344
Jourde, François, 152, 154, 158, 160, 452
Jung, Hermann, 90, 98, 109, 129, 162, 197, 199

Karakozov, 316
Kats, F. J., 67, 69, 70, 99, 449
Kautsky, Karl, xi, 266, 425, 428 f., 433 f., 436, 456, 463
Kelly, Oliver H., 366
Keltie, J. Scott, 344
Ketteler, Bishop W. E. von, xi, 9, 15, 254 ff., 259, 262, 447, 455
Keyser, Napoléon de, 67 f., 69, 70, 99, 449
Khalturin, Stepan, 320
Kibalchich, Nikolai, 321
Kirchmann, von, 21
Kitz, Frank, 416
Knies, Karl, 28, 258
Kolping, Adolph, 254 f.
Korsakov, Governor, 216
Kropotkin, Prince Peter, xi, 153, 156, 210, 226, 236, 315 f., 317, 323, 327, 328, 335, 338 f., 340, 342 ff., 358, 402, 415, 416, 419, 434, 452, 453, 458 f.

Labouchere, Henry, 392, 393
Lafargue, Paul, 187, 188, 190, 326
Lamennais, Félicité, 15, 172, 263
Lane, Joseph, 399, 416
Lassalle, Ferdinand, xi, 21, 24, 30, 71 ff., 95 ff., 99, 110, 119, 176, 237 ff., 249, 254, 255, 257, 264, 265, 279, 365, 430, 449 f., 456
Laveleye, Émile de, 25, 445, 447, 455
Lavrov, P. L., xi, 53 ff., 316, 448
Le Play, M. F., 261
Leclaire, E. J., 10, 447
Ledru-Rollin, A. P. A., 149
Lefrançais, Gustave, 150, 345, 452
Lemonnier, Charles, 113
Lenin, Nikolai, 41 f., 52, 166, 172, 235, 246, 251, 294, 361, 419, 452
Leo, André, 153
Leo XIII, 262
Lessner, Friedrich, 98, 129, 199
Liebknecht, Wilhelm, xi, 71, 86, 97, 98, 129, 142, 176, 177, 237, 239, 240 ff., 249 f., 325, 454
Limousin, Charles, 90, 98
Linnell, Alfred, 407
Lissagaray, P. O., 152, 451
List, Friedrich, 257

Lo Savio, Nicolo, 181
Longuet, Charles, 151, 199
Lord, J., 396
Lorenzo, Anselmo, 189
Loris-Melikov, Count M. T., 322
Louis-Philippe, 38
Lucraft, Benjamin, 125, 129, 162, 382
Ludlow, J. M., 264

Maclure, William, 361
Macmahon, Marshal M. E. P. M. de, 325
Magallan, Sarro, 187
Maignon, Maurice, 260
Maine, Sir Henry, 44
Maistre, Joseph de, 34
Malatesta, Errico, xi, 185, 210, 330, 345, 356, 357, 359 f., 459
Malato, Charles, 328, 357, 459
Malon, Benoit, xi, 45, 105, 144, 152, 153 f., 161, 185, 204, 209, 345, 426, 445, 447, 452, 453, 457
Malthus, T. R., 27, 80, 249, 382
Mann, Tom, xi
Margall. See Pi y Margall
Marlo, Karl, xi, 16, 20, 25 ff., 30, 447
Marmocci, Constantino, 179
Marsal y Anglosa, A., 187
Marselau, N. A., 189
Marshall, Alfred, 271
Marx, Jenny, 302
Marx, Karl, xi, 1 ff., 11 f., 14, 18, 21, 24, 29, 41 f., 45, 51, 52, 53, 68, 69, 71 ff., 90 ff., 114, 116 ff., 128, 130 ff., 141, 142, 151, 154, 160, 162 ff., 172, 174, 176 f., 178 ff., 181, 185 ff., 190 ff., 207 ff., 211 f., 214, 217, 219, 222, 230 ff., 237 ff., 244 ff., 255, 261 f., 265 f., 267 ff., 308 ff., 320, 326, 336, 339, 350, 381, 382, 389, 394 f., 405, 410 f., 431, 434, 436, 439, 441, 442, 444, 446, 450, 451, 454 f., 455 ff.
Maurer, G. L. von, 44
Maurice, F. D., 264, 386
Mazzini, Giuseppe, 89 f., 119, 178, 179, 180, 183
Menger, Anton, 271, 276
Meredith, George, 86
Mesa, José, 189
Meyendorf, Baroness, 73
Meyer, Rudolf, 259, 451, 455
Michel, Louise, 151, 327 f., 328, 335, 342, 452

Mihailov, Alexander, 319
Mihailov, Timothy, 321
Mikhailovsky, Nikolai, 56
Mill, J. S., 48, 113, 271, 273 f.,
　278, 371, 382, 383
Minghetti, Marco, 179
Miot, Jules, 172
Mitchell, J. T. W., 380, 381
Moncasi, Juan Oliver, 317
Monturiol, Narciso, 186
Moore, Samuel, 268, 456
Morley, John, 382
Morris, William, xi, 337, 347, 348,
　375, 398, 400, 401 f., 408, 409,
　414 ff., 452, 461 f.
Most, Johann, xi, 120, 207, 322,
　330, 341, 416, 454, 458
Mottershead, Thomas, 162, 197, 382
Moufang, Christopher, 16, 254
Mowbray, C. W., 416
Mroczowski, Valery, 124
Mun, Count Albert de, 260, 455
Munts, José, 186
Muraviev, Nikite, 33
Muraviov, Nikolai, 215 f.
Muriakov, Count, 343
Murray, Charles, 379, 399
Murray, J. F., 399

Nabruzzi, Giuseppe, 183
Napoleon I, 33, 57, 58, 66, 135, 234
Napoleon II, 58, 66
Napoleon III, 9, 58, 66, 69, 72, 88,
　106, 113, 134 ff., 177, 226, 234,
　242 f., 357, 441
Neale, E. Vansittart, 8, 264, 380 f.
Nechaiev, Sergei, xi, 42, 47, 50,
　194 ff., 219, 228 ff., 316, 318, 453
Nettlau, Max, 213, 454, 457, 459
Nicholas I, 32, 33, 35, 38 f., 214 ff.
Nicoll, David, 416
Nieuwenhuis, F. Domela, 426
Nikolai-on, 268
Nobel, Alfred, 335
Nobiling, K. E., 317
Nothjung, Peter, 3

Oberwinder, Heinrich, 203
O'Brien, Bronterre, 383
Odger, George, 98, 109, 162, 382
Ogarev, Nathalie, 40
Ogarev, Nicholas, 38, 216
Ogilvie, William, 370
O'Mahony, John, 93
Osinski, Valerian, 319
Otero y González, 317

Owen, Robert, 22, 32, 57, 80, 96,
　97, 186, 331, 361, 362, 381, 391,
　404
Owen, Robert Dale, 361

Paepe, César de. See De Paepe
Paine, Tom, 370, 391
Parnell, C. S., 388
Parsons, Albert, 332, 369, 458
Passamente, Giovanni, 317 f.
Patten, Philip van, 365
Pelling, H. M., vii, 461
Pelloutier, Fernand, 329, 443
Périn, H. X. C., 261, 455
Perovskaya, Sophie, 54, 319 ff.
Perret, Henri, 197
Pestel, P. I., 33, 447
Petrashevsky, 50
Pi y Margall, Francisco, 189
Pillot, Y. Y., 172
Pindy, L.-J., 152, 153, 324, 345
Pisacane, Carlo, 180
Pisarev, D. I., 46, 47
Plekhanov, G. V., xi, 319, 426, 448,
　457
Podmore, Frank, 405
Potter, Agathon de, 66, 449
Potter, George, 385
Potter, Louis de, 58, 66, 449
Pottier, Eugène, 171
Pouget, Émile, 327 f., 328, 329, 333,
　338, 459
Powderly, Terence, xi, 368 f., 460
Priestley, Joseph, 221
Prim, General Juan, 189
Protot, Eugène, 152, 155
Proudhon, P. J., xi, 11 f., 15, 21, 91,
　93, 94 f., 97, 108, 134, 138, 141,
　149, 151, 167, 181, 186, 214, 236,
　331, 332, 337, 354, 358, 359, 443
Pugachov, Emilion, 33, 447
Pyat, Félix, 144, 149, 161

Quinet, Edgar, 113

Rae, John, 25
Ranc, Arthur, 151
Ranvier, Gabriel, 150
Ratzinger, Georg, 260
Ravachol, F. A., 333
Réclus, Élie, 222
Réclus, Élisée, xi, 124, 156, 222, 335,
　338, 340, 345, 346, 459
Reinsdorf, 330
Rey, Aristide, 124

Ricardo, David, 80, 272 ff., 276, 286 f., 299, 302, 314
Richard, Albert, 105, 124
Rigault, Raoul, 152, 155 f., 160, 173
Robert, Charles, 10, 447
Rochat, Charles, 197
Rochefort, Henri, 135, 144, 153, 157
Rodbertus, Karl, xi, 16, 19, 20 ff., 28, 29, 30 f., 78, 80, 447
Rogers, J. E. Thorold, 382
Roscher, Wilhelm, 28, 30, 257 f.
Rossa, O'Donovan, 383
Rossel, Nathaniel, 152, 156, 159, 452
Rossi, Gabrielo, 179
Rousseau, J.-J., 236, 339
Roy, J., 268, 456
Ruskin, John, xi, 29, 420 f.
Rysakov, Nikolai, 321

Saint-Simon, Comte Henri, 15, 30, 57, 62, 66, 179, 228, 311, 373
Salvochea, Fermín, 187
Sand, George, 149
Schaeffle, A. E. F., 20, 445, 447
Schaffer, Karl, 3, 4, 98
Schelling, F. W. J., 34
Scheu, Andreas, 401
Schmoller, Gustav, 258
Schulze-Delitzsch, Hermann, 9, 24, 78, 79 ff., 83, 96, 237
Schwab, Michael, 332
Schweitzer, J. B. von, xi, 86, 238 f., 243 f.
Schwitzguébel, Adhemar, 191
Senior, Nassau, 284
Sentiñon, Gaspar, 187
Serraillier, Auguste, 171, 197
Shaw, G. Bernard, xi, 375, 462
Sketchley, John, 394
Slobodin, Henry, 377
Smith, Adam, 302
Soloviev, Alexander, 320
Sorge, F. A., xi, 199, 201 ff., 364, 395
Southey, Robert, 29
Spence, Thomas, 62, 370, 383
Spencer, Herbert, 223
Spies, August, 332, 458
Spooner, Lysander, 331, 458
Stalin, Joseph, 51
Stampa, Gaspare, 180, 181, 182
Stein, Laurenz von, 15
Stellmacher, 331
Stephens, James, 93
Stephens, Uriah, xi, 367 f., 460

Stepney, Cowell, 129, 162, 382
Steward, Ira, 363 f., 368
Stirner, Max, 47, 226, 338
Stöcker, Adolf, 16, 255
Strelnikov, 320
Sukhanov, Nikolai, 321
Sylvis, W. H., xi, 354, 460

Tanari, Sebastiano, 181, 182
Tawney, R. H., 289
Taylor, Helen, 383
Taylor, Peter, 382
Theisz, Albert, 152, 153
Thiers, Adolphe, 143, 145, 146 ff., 158, 161, 165, 170, 173
Thompson, William, 21
Tikhomirov, Leo, 54
Tkachev, Peter, 54
Tocqueville, Alexis de, 42
Todt, Rudolph, 16
Tolain, H. L., 90, 94, 98, 105, 107, 115, 116, 125, 129, 133, 138, 139, 140, 141, 144, 161
Travis, Henry, 381
Trepov, police chief, 317, 318
Tridon, Gustave, 152, 155
Trivulzio, Christine, 179
Trombetti, Domenico, 183
Tucci, Alberto, 124, 181
Tucker, B. R., 331, 338, 458
Turgenev, Ivan, 47
Turgenev, N. I., 33 f.
Turner, Frederick, 367
Tvertinov, A., 49

Utin, Nicholas, 196 f., 344

Vaillant, Auguste, 333
Vaillant, Édouard, 152, 155, 158, 197, 199, 324, 333
Vallès, Jules, 151, 452
Varlin, E. V., xi, 90, 98, 105, 107, 116, 125, 129, 133, 139 f., 141, 152 f., 154, 158, 160, 161, 168, 211, 452
Vermorel, Auguste, 152, 156
Vésinier, Paul, 171, 452
Vogelsang, Karl von, 259 f., 261, 455

Wagner, Adolf, 258
Wallace, A. Russel, 384, 402
Wallace, Robert, 370
Walras, Léon, 271, 276
Walton, Alfred, 109, 162
Warren, Sir Charles, 407 f.

Warren, Josiah, xi, 331, 332, 361, 362, 458
Weaver, General, 374
Webb, Beatrice, xi, 462
Webb, Sidney, xi, 405 f., 462
Weiler, Adam, 381
Weitling, Wilhelm, 364
Weston, John, 95, 382
Weydemeyer, Joseph, 71, 363, 446, 460
Wilhelm I, German Emperor, 256; 316, 317, 330
Willich, August, 3, 4, 71

Wilson, Charlotte, 416
Winkelblech, K. G. *See* Marlo, Karl
Wolff, Major Luigi, 90, 98, 99, 178
Wright, Frances, 361
Wright, J. L., 367
Wroblewski, Walery, 151 f., 159

Zabicki, Anton, 197
Zasulich, Vera, 301, 317, 318
Zhelyabov, A. I., xi, 54, 319 ff., 344, 458

INDEX

Abstentionism, 358
Action Française, 260
Administration of public services, 164, 204 f., 438
Agriculture under Socialism, 27, 126. *See also* Peasants
Alliance of Socialist Democracy, 121 f., 124 f., 131, 132, 182, 184, 190, 191, 196, 217, 232
Alsace-Lorraine, 142, 241, 242, 243, 249
America. *See* United States
American Civil War, 3, 89, 91, 114, 150, 363, 364, 369
American Federation of Labor, 365, 369, 375, 376
American Socialist Party, 377 ff.
American Workers' Alliance, 363
Anarchism, vi, 102, 109, 113, 120, 128, 140, 151, 166 f., 178 ff., 183, 185, 188 ff., 198 ff., 209 ff., 217 ff., 267, 315 ff., 368 f., 400, 401, 414 ff., 426, 439, 442, 443, 457 f. *See also under countries*; Individualist, 331 f., 337 f., 352, 353 f., 360
Anarchist-Communism, vi, 210, 224, 227, 315 ff., 332, 337 ff., 342 ff., 400, 401, 416, 419, 458 f.
Anarchist Congress (1881), 322, 327, 347
Anarchist International, 208, 217, 322 f., 327, 333 f., 337, 347. *See also* International Working Men's Association, Anarchist
Anarchist violence, 315 ff., 333 ff., 346, 357, 415 f.
Anarchists, Allied, 402
Anarcho-Syndicalism, 227, 329 f., 338, 357
Anglo-Catholicism, 386
Anti-Dühring, 303 ff., 308, 311
Anti-Semitism, 74, 255, 259 f.
Anti-Socialist Laws, 212, 244, 256, 257, 262, 264 f., 266, 267, 316, 330, 331, 341, 358, 410, 425, 427, 434, 435, 441
Apprenticeship, 7

Arbitration, industrial, 128; international, 432
Artisans, 429
Artists, Committee of Revolutionary, 150
Arts, social significance of, 37, 67
Atheism, 232, 233. *See also* Religion *and* Secularism
Australia, 412
Austria, Anarchism in, 330 f.
Austria, Christian Social movement in, 259 f.
Austria, Socialism in, 25, 176, 203, 330 f., 341
Austria and Lombardy, 73
Austria-Hungary, 175, 176, 177, 204, 214
Austro-Prussian War, 241
Autocracy, 61 f., 66

Baden, 364
Balkans, Socialism in, 190
Bank of France, 152, 154, 158
Banks. *See* Credit
Barcelona, 186, 187, 188, 189, 190, 201
Battersea, 413
Bavaria, 255, 260
Beehive, The, 385
Belgian Labour Party, 436 ff., 463
Belgian Revolution (1830), 67, 69
Belgium, Anarchism in, 120, 267, 340, 439
Belgium, Socialism in, vi, 57 ff., 93, 99 f., 108, 120, 125 f., 133, 175, 192, 197, 200 f., 202, 204, 206 f., 208, 211, 267, 340, 426, 436 ff., 448 f.
Berlin, 99
Bethnal Green, 386
Birmingham, 385, 387
Birth-control, 393
Blanquists, 54, 90, 106, 117 f., 135, 136, 137, 140, 147, 150 ff., 155 f., 160, 166, 170, 172, 178, 197, 198, 199, 200, 204, 206, 211, 324, 325, 341, 357, 365, 426, 443
Blasphemy laws, 393
Bohemia, 199, 200

473

Bologna rising (1874), 184, 217
Bourgeoisie, Socialist attitudes to, 72,
85 f., 97, 118, 136 f., 165, 177,
185 f., 190, 222, 240 f., 247 f., 253,
326, 428 ff.
Bourgeoisie, petite, 2, 5, 55, 68, 82, 83,
124, 130, 165, 240, 248, 299, 429,
437, 442
Bourses du Travail, 329
British Socialist Party, 411
Brussels, 69, 135. For Congresses
see under I.W.M.A.
Bryant & May, 408
Budapest, 154
Bulgaria, 176
Buntars, 318
Bureaucracy, 417

Caesarism, 234
California, 370, 373
Capital (Marx), 83, 194, 195 f., 211,
268 ff., 276 ff., 289 ff., 302, 311,
312, 395, 456
Capital, accumulation of, 22, 27,
293 f.; concentration of, 350;
constant and variable, 282 f., 284;
finance, 290 f., 296; Marx's
account of, 290 ff., 296 f.
Capitalism. See Bourgeoisie and In-
dustrialisation
Capitalism, contradictions of. See
Contradictions; Merchant, 290 f.,
296
Carlists, 189
Cartagena, 189
Catalonia, 121, 186, 187, 216, 329
Catholic Church, Roman, 9, 16, 34,
262, 354. See also Papal En-
cyclicals and Christian Social
movements; on Socialism, 262
Central Revolutionary Committee,
Blanquist, 155
Centralisation. See Decentralisation
Centralism, 117 ff., 166, 168, 222,
234 ff., 326, 401, 440, 442
Chambres Syndicales, 137 f., 144,
153, 323 f., 326
Chartism, 5, 89, 106, 379, 391, 395,
396, 446
Cherny Peredyel, 319
Chicago Anarchists, 332 f., 368 f.,
416
Chicago Industrial Workers of the
World, 377
Child labour, 432, 439
Christian Social movements, in Aus-

tria, 259 f., 454; in Belgium, 261;
in France, 260 f., 264, 454; in Ger-
many, 9, 11, 16, 253 ff., 447, 454 f.
Christian Socialism, vi, 23, 26; in
Great Britain, 7 f., 11, 80, 264,
379 f., 385, 386, 402, 446
Church and State, 432, 439. See also
Kulturkampf
Church of Humanity, 385
Citizen army, 280, 432
Civil Society (Hegel), 17
Civil War in France, The, 162 ff., 172
Class structure under capitalism, 25,
29
Class struggle, 24, 83, 93, 96, 101,
107, 140, 164 ff., 174, 178, 222,
226, 230, 234, 247 f., 277, 280, 309,
312 ff., 357, 358, 376, 428 f., 430 f.,
437, 443
Classless society, 432
Collectivisation. See Socialisation
Collectivism, 339, 354
Cologne, 3 f.
Cologne Communist trials, 4, 71
Commonweal, The, 415, 423
Commune, as basic social institution,
46, 48 ff., 62, 64, 67 f., 120, 130,
140, 146 ff., 163 ff., 167, 170, 180,
204 ff., 224, 227 f., 233, 252, 301 f.,
307, 340, 354, 438 f.
Communism, Anarchist. See Anar-
chist-Communism; Bakunin on,
123; modern, 51, 52, 246, 377;
pre-Marxian, 26, 46, 379. See also
Cabet and Icaria
Communist League, 1 ff.
Communist Manifesto, 12, 14, 18, 45,
76, 80, 92, 175, 251, 269, 301, 428,
444
Confédération Générale du Travail,
169, 208, 443
Conquest, its rôle in history, 307
Conscience, freedom of, 261
Conscious minority, 357 f., 359
Conscription, 406
Contradictions, dialectical, 305, 308;
of capitalism, 82, 269, 271, 280, 293
Control of industry, 355 f., 433 f.,
438 ff.
Co-operation, 24, 79, 186, 188, 254,
355; Consumers', 96, 110, 127,
355, 380 f. See also Rochdale
Pioneers; in Europe, 8 f.; in
France, 8, 9; in Germany, 8, 78;
in Great Britain, 7 f., 88, 380; in
United States, 366, 447; Pro-

ducers', 7 f., 9, 11, 18, 24, 48, 62, 68, 78, 81, 83, 91, 94 ff., 97, 108, 110, 112, 120, 126 f., 140, 158, 168, 204 f., 224, 241 f., 249 f., 259, 332, 341, 355 f., 364, 380 f.
Co-operative Colonies, 405
Co-operative movement, agricultural, 130, 366 ; Christian, 254, 255
Co-operative Productive Federation, 380
Co-operative Union, 381
Co-operative Wholesale Societies, 381
Co-partnership, 11, 260
Cotton operatives, 6
Credit, 23, 24, 28, 95, 96, 128, 364, 369 ; gratuitous, 94, 99, 108, 110, 126, 134, 139 ; Banks, 62, 80, 94, 97, 108, 110, 112, 126, 127, 134, 139, 167, 362
Crimean War, 114
Crises, economic, 2, 5, 82, 102, 128, 211, 269, 293 f., 411
Critique of Political Economy, 4, 71, 72, 73, 83, 268, 269, 270, 308, 456
Crofters, Highland, 384, 389, 400

Darwinism, 339
'Days of June', 38, 66, 135, 174
Decembrists, 32 ff., 36, 44, 64
Decentralisation, 46, 49, 68, 140, 193, 202, 204 ff., 222, 337, 438, 439, 440. *See also* Federalism
Democratic Federation. *See* Social Democratic Federation
Democratic Party (U.S.A.), 370, 374, 378
Democratic Socialism. *See* Social Democracy
Denmark, Socialism in, 199, 200 f., 425, 426
Determinism, 52, 55, 59, 222, 234, 360
Detroit, 377
Dialectic, Marxist, 304 ff.
Dialectics of Nature, 303
Dictatorship, 82 ; of the proletariat, 117, 136, 140 f., 148, 166, 172, 250 ff., 357, 431
Direct legislation, 226, 250, 438
Disestablishment, 388
Distribution, laws of, 245 ff. *See also* Wages
Distributive trades, 355
Division of labour, 49 f.
Dock strike, London (1889), 263, 412

Dod Street affair, 406
Dresden, 214
Dreyfus case, 135
Durham Miners' Gala, 347
Dynamite, 335

Economic Imperialism, 294
Education, social function of, 61 f., 63, 67, 111, 351 ; Socialist attitudes to, 108, 128, 158, 382, 416, 439 ; technical, 351
Education League, National, 387
Eight hours' day, 108, 364, 432
Eight Hours League (U.K.), 381
Eight Hours Leagues (U.S.A.), 363 f.
Eisenachers. *See under* German Social Democratic Party
Electricity, social effects of, 349
Emancipation of Labour Group, 426
Encyclopaedia Britannica, 315 f.
Engineers, Amalgamated Society of, 6, 412
Equality, 26, 94, 123, 124, 136, 232, 246, 309, 358, 399, 420
Erfurt Programme, 425 ff., 431 ff., 436, 463
Ethical Socialism, 263, 410 f.
Europe, United States of, 231, 233
Evangelicals, 386
Exiles, Socialist, after 1848, 1 ff., 90, 93, 98, 99, 114, 133, 148, 179, 379 ; after Paris Commune, 148 ff., 161 f., 174, 190, 191, 197, 202, 341, 345, 365, 379, 396, 397 ; in U.S.A., 201, 322, 361 f., 363, 365

Fabian Society, 264, 337, 386, 400, 402, 403, 404, 405 f., 408 f., 410, 427, 462
Factory legislation, 81, 119, 174, 432. *See also* Ten Hours Act
Factory system, 15, 312. *See also* Industrialisation
Fair Traders, 407
Familistère of Guise, 10
Family, Socialist views on, 64, 94, 111, 339
Farming, State, 130
Fascio Operaio, 183
Fascism, 259, 335
Federalism, 68, 117, 140, 167, 170, 184, 204 ff., 340, 439
Fellowship, 420, 423
Fenians, 92 f., 132, 174, 383
Feudal Socialism, 18

Feudalism, 16, 19, 97, 186, 223 ff., 234 f., 247
Finance capitalism, 290 f., 296
Finland, 344, 426
Fonctionnaires, 164
Food imports, 5
Force, its rôle in history, 307
Foreign trade, 249 f., 434
Fors Clavigera, 421
Fourierism, 9 f., 46, 79, 96, 179, 186, 361, 362, 363
France, Anarchism in, 120, 140, 151, 323, 324 ff., 333, 334, 340, 346, 347, 355, 443, 457, 459
France, Socialism in, v, vi, 11 f., 57, 66, 75 f., 101, 120, 122, 128, 133, 161, 192, 197, 199, 200, 211, 216, 267, 323 ff., 426, 443
France, Trade Unions in. *See under* Trade Unions
Franco-Prussian War, 87, 102, 133, 142, 177, 192, 242 f., 249, 311, 441
Frankfurt Parliament, 241
Fraternal Democrats, 89
Free Thought movement, 365
Free Trade, 378, 384
Freedom, 402
Freedom. *See* Liberty
Freedom Group, 415
Freedom of speech, 432, 439
Freemasons, 367
French Assembly (1871), 144 ff., 169, 170 f., 172, 357
French Revolution (1789), 25 f., 33, 37, 135, 443 ; (1830), 58 ; (1848), 38, 58, 66, 135

General strike, 122, 128, 208 f., 209
General strikes in Belgium, 436
Geneva, 98, 100, 107, 121 f., 124, 131, 182, 190, 191, 194, 196, 197, 340, 343, 362
Geneva Propaganda Section, 190 f., 344
German Centre Party, 256
German Constitution (1870), 240
German Eisenach Party, v, 86, 129, 132, 142, 177, 207, 243, 340, 454 f.
German Progressive Party, 85 f., 97, 99, 119, 176 f., 237 f., 239, 240 f., 243
German Revolution of 1848, 14, 73, 85
German Social Democratic Party, 212, 237, 244, 253 f., 256, 257,

264 ff., 303, 341, 399, 425, 427 ff., 441 f., 442, 454 f., 463
German Workers' Educational Societies, 237, 238, 239 f.
German Working Men's Association, General, 24, 81, 95 f., 98, 238 ff., 243 f.
Germany, Anarchism in, 330, 337, 341
Germany, economic development of, 429 f.
Germany, Socialism in, vi, 11, 13, 14 ff., 71 ff., 98 f., 163, 176 f., 197, 198 f., 200 f., 207 f., 211, 212, 237 ff., 267, 310, 330, 341, 425 ff.
Germany, unification of, 84, 87, 176 f., 212, 240, 241, 330, 440, 442
Ghent, 69
Ghent Unity Congress, 208, 346
Glasgow, 414
God and the State, 117
Gotha Congress and Programme (1875), 207, 211, 244 ff., 256, 261 266, 267, 425, 436
Gradualism, 52
Granger movement, 366 f.
Great Britain, Anarchism in, 322, 336, 337, 401, 414 ff., 442
Great Britain, economic development of, 4 f.
Great Britain, Socialism in, vi, 57, 200, 379 ff., 461 f.
Great Britain, Trade Unions in. *See under* Trade Unions
Greece, 190
Greenback Party, 362, 364, 368, 369 ff.
Greenwich Park, 336
Guild of St. Matthew, 386
Guild Socialism, 381
Guilds, 27, 259

Habit, social influence of, 235
Hamburg, 1
Hammersmith Socialist Society, 415
Havana, 58
Hegelianism, 15 ff., 34 f., 36 ff., 76 ff., 83, 214, 222, 228, 270, 303, 304, 305, 312
Hegelians, Young, 15 f., 36, 214
Highlands, Scottish. *See* Crofters
Historical School, 28 f., 30, 258
History, theories of, 23, 24, 25 f., 52 ff., 59 f., 77, 221 f., 228 f., 270, 297, 304, 306 ff., 311. *See also* Materialist Conception of History

Holland, Anarchism in, 267, 426
Holland, Socialism in, 69, 70, 109, 192, 199, 200 f., 202, 204, 267, 426
Holy Alliance, 33
Home Colonisation, 382, 404, 405, 406
Hornby v. Close, 105
Hours of labour, 22, 108, 128. *See also* Eight hours' day *and* Ten Hours Act
Hungary, Socialism in, 154, 176, 199, 200
Hungry 'Forties, 175
Hyde Park, 407

Icaria, 32, 363
Idealism, 47, 52, 76, 222, 228, 305. *See also* Hegelianism
Illinois Labour Party, 365, 369
Imperialism, 389. *See also* Economic Imperialism
Incentives, 63. *See also* Pleasure in work
Increasing misery, theory of, 82, 300
Independent Labour Party, 263, 264, 403, 404, 408, 413, 427
Independent Socialists (France), 426
Indian nationalism, 393, 408
Individualism, 17, 47, 53, 55, 56, 210, 222, 223, 226, 227 f., 236, 331 f., 378, 421
Industrial and Provident Societies Acts, 7
Industrial armies, 65, 375, 382
Industrial Revolution, 312. *See also* Industrialisation
Industrial Unionism, 376, 377
Industrial Workers of the World, 377, 444
Industrialisation, 4 ff., 18 ff., 25, 42 ff., 62, 68 f., 91, 99 f., 139 f., 174, 185 f., 207, 225, 312, 348 ff.
Inheritance, 63, 76 f., 123, 124, 130 f., 233, 432, 440
Insurance, social, 27 f., 259, 432
Insurrection, effects of modern techniques on, 435
Integral Socialism, 185, 209
Interest, theory of, 298
International, Anarchist. *See* Anarchist International
International, Second, vi, 103, 440
International Association, Chartist, 89

International Labor Union, 364
International Revolutionary Brotherhood, 121, 182
International Trade, 249 f., 434
International Trade Unionism, 208, 209
International Working Men's Association, v, vi, 3, 7, 11, 12, 52, 66, 71, 81, 88 ff., 137 ff., 152 ff., 162, 163, 166, 171 f., 173, 176 ff., 217, 224, 230, 242, 245, 249, 265, 267, 300, 313, 337, 338, 340, 343, 364, 365, 379, 381 f., 384, 385, 395, 403, 431, 439, 441, 450 f., 453 f. ; British Federal Council, 197 f., 198, 202, 379, 384. Congresses and Conferences : 1864 (London), 98 f., 100, 101, 105, 138 ; 1865 (London), 99, 103 f. ; 1866 (Geneva), 101, 105 f., 181 ; 1867 (Lausanne), 99, 109 f., 114 ff., 181 ; 1868 (Brussels), 99, 122, 125 ff., 162, 187 ; 1869 (Berne), 129 ff., 141 f., 162, 183, 187, 233, 235, 364 ; 1871 (London), 189, 196, 198 ; 1872 (The Hague), 150, 162, 174 ff., 183, 184, 192, 198 ff., 200, 201, 204, 207, 217, 439 ; 1873 (Geneva), 202 f. General Council, 104, 125, 129, 131 f., 190, 191, 192, 193, 196, 198, 199, 200, 201 f., 202 f., 206, 382 ; Inaugural Address, 94 ; Preamble and Rules, 101 f., 105 ff., 245. Sections, Federations, and Delegations : Austria, 129, 203 ; Belgium, 70, 98, 99, 103, 109, 125 f., 127, 128, 129, 133, 192, 197, 198, 200, 201, 202, 206, 379, 439 ; Bohemia, 199, 200 ; Denmark, 197, 200 ; France, 90 f., 94, 101, 105, 106 f., 108, 109, 116, 125, 128, 129, 130, 133, 137 ff., 152 ff., 171 f., 192, 197, 199, 200, 242 ; Geneva, 124, 131, 190 f., 203 ; Geneva Propaganda Section, 190 f., 344 ; Germany, 109, 125, 129, 132, 133, 197, 198 f., 200, 203 ; Great Britain, 88, 90, 98, 101, 104, 106, 109, 125, 129, 133, 162, 197 f., 199, 200, 313, 381, 385, 403. *See also* British Federal Council *above* ; Holland, 70, 199, 200, 201, 202 ; Hungary, 199, 200 ; Italy, 109, 120, 125, 129, 133, 178, 181 ff., 202 ; Jura, 184, 191 f., 202, 204, 210, 340, 345 ;

Spain, 125, 126, 129, 133, 187 ff., 197, 198, 200, 202 ; Switzerland, 98, 100 f., 106, 107 f., 109, 112, 125, 129, 190 ff., 198, 200, 201, 203. *See also* Geneva *and* Jura *above* ; U.S.A., 129, 199, 200, 201 f., 364, 365, 454. Anti-Authoritarian, 204 ff., 340, 346, 453 f. Congresses : 1872 (St.-Imier), 150, 202 ; 1873 (Geneva), 204 ; 1874 (Brussels and Le Locle), 204, 207 ; 1876 (Berne), 359 ; 1877 (Verviers), 208
Internationalism, 84, 248 f., 439
Investment, foreign, 5
Ireland, 91, 132, 336, 368, 388, 390, 394, 396 f.
Irish Home Rule, 263, 388, 389
Irish Land League, 383 f., 388, 396, 400
Irish land question, 373, 383 f., 390
Irish Nationalist Party, 389
Irkutsk, 216
Italy, Anarchism in, 179 ff., 185, 330, 333, 356
Italy, Mazzinist organisations in, 89 f., 99, 119 f., 178, 183, 184
Italy, Socialism in, vi, 102 f., 119 f., 122, 129, 133, 163, 175, 178 ff., 182 f., 197, 202, 203, 208, 216, 330, 426, 443
Italy, Trade Unions in, 180
Italy, unification of, 180

Jacobinism, 136 f., 140 f., 143, 147, 149, 160, 170, 264
Japan, 216
Jena, 11
Jet-propulsion, 321
Jews. *See* Anti-Semitism
Jews in Prussia, 74
Jews in Vienna, 259 f.
Joint-stock companies, 300
Jura, Socialism in, 100, 107, 125, 343 ff., 350
Jura, watch-making in. *See* Watch-making
Jura Federation. *See under* International Working Men's Association

Kapital, Das. See Capital
Kelmscott House, 415
Kiev, 319
Knights of Labor, 367 ff., 375
Kolkhoz, the, 51

Kolokol, 33, 38 ff., 42, 269
Kulturkampf, 253, 255 ff., 262, 264

Labour, obligatory, 27
Labour Emancipation League (G.B.), 399 f., 401, 402, 416 ; (Russia), 426
Labour Exchanges, 331
Labour Party, British, 443
Labour Representation League, 197
Labour theory of value. *See* Value
Labour-time, necessary, 277
Laissez-faire, 167, 219, 240, 254, 389. *See also* Liberalism, economic
Land and Labour League, 95, 381 ff.
Land League, English, 384 ; Irish, 383 f., 388, 396, 400
Land monopoly, 370 ff.
Land nationalisation, 62, 67 f., 95, 111 f., 126, 129 f., 132, 168, 180, 370 ff., 382 ff., 397, 440
Land Nationalisation Society, 384, 402, 405
Land purchase, 388
Land Restoration League, 389, 402, 405
Land taxation, 370 ff., 382, 383, 388
Land Tenure Reform Association, 371, 382 f.
Landlordism, 19, 44, 248, 383. *See also* Feudalism
Lassallians, v, 21, 71 ff., 86, 99, 108, 119, 120, 129, 142, 176 f., 207, 238 ff., 243 f., 251, 253, 340 f., 365, 366, 425, 430, 436, 449 f.
Law and Liberty League, 394, 408
Law reform, 393, 432, 439
Le Creusot, 134, 153
League of Peace and Freedom, 113 ff., 118, 119, 122 ff., 125, 132, 165, 182, 187, 217, 231 ff., 249
Liberal and Radical Associations, 387. *See also* Radical Clubs
Liberal Federation, National, 387
Liberal Party, British, 263, 387 ff., 395, 403
Liberal-Labourism, vi, 399, 403, 419
Liberalism, economic, 15, 17 ff., 26, 28 f., 30, 85, 98, 257 ff. *See also* Laissez-faire
Liberty, 219 ff., 233 ff., 355 ff., 393 f., 440. *See also* Anarchism *and* Federalism
Local government reform, 387, 438. *See also* Commune

Lombardy, 73, 179, 185
London building dispute (1859), 6
London Commonwealth Club, 379
London County Council, 413
London Trades Council, 6, 89, 98, 104
London Working Men's Association, 379
Looking Backward, 374 f., 423
Lumpenproletariat, 230, 231
Lyons, 105, 134, 141, 154, 177, 187, 190, 327, 328, 333, 347

Madrid, 187, 188, 333
Malthusian League, 392
Malthusianism, 80, 81, 249
Manchester, 4
Manchester School, 15
Manchuria, 343
Mandat impératif, 166, 205
Manhood suffrage, 5, 18, 24, 33, 67, 78 f., 82, 84, 104, 136, 138, 148, 165 f., 240, 241, 242, 243, 250, 357, 358, 436, 438
'Manifesto of the Sixty', 138
Marriage, control of, 27, 64
Marseilles, 105, 134, 141, 177, 187, 190, 197, 325
Marxism, v, vi, 1 ff., 12 f., 21, 36, 37, 86 f., 267 ff., 427 ff., 455 ff. *See also* Marx, Karl
Marxism, in Great Britain, 390 ff., 401, 409 ff. ; in Russia, 267, 268, 301 f., 444 ; in U.S.A., 363 ff., 443
Mass-production, 350, 420
Master and Servant Acts, 93, 104, 119, 174
Match-girls' strike, 408
Materialism, 48, 59, 221 f., 305 f., 408
Materialist Conception of History, 297, 303, 306, 311, 376
Mechanisation, 25, 282, 284, 293 f., 345, 348, 363. *See also* Mass-production
Mensheviks, 444
Merchant capitalism, 290 f., 296
Metz, 143
Middle classes, 68 f., 299 ff. *See also Bourgeoisie*
Milan, 181, 182, 185
Miners' Federation of Great Britain, 263
Miners' National Union, 6
Mir, the, 43 f., 225

Monopoly, 26, 82, 117, 271, 280, 308, 397, 429
Montceau-les-Mines, 327
Municipalisation, 387, 406
Mutual Aid, 338 f., 348, 352
Mutualism, 11 f., 94, 326. *See also* Proudhonism

Nabat, 54
Naples, 120, 181 f., 216, 230
Narodnaya Volya, 54, 319 ff.
Narodniks, 42, 48, 49, 50, 53 ff., 56, 302, 316, 318, 427, 444
National Labor Union (U.S.A.), 201, 364, 365
National Socialist Party (G.B.), 411
Nationalism, 19, 35, 84, 119, 178, 205, 214, 393
Nationalist Clubs (U.S.A.), 374, 375
Nauvoo, 363
New Harmony, 331
New Rhenish Review, 1 f., 71
New Unionism, 390, 394, 399, 406, 408, 410, 442 f.
New York, 201, 202, 365, 373 f., 377
New York Communist Club, 364
News from Nowhere, 419, 423
Nihilism, 46 ff., 50, 196, 212, 229, 230, 262
Nonconformists, 386, 393
North German Confederation, 18, 84, 142, 238, 241
Northampton, 392
Northern Reform Union, 396
Northern Workers' Union (Russia), 320
Norway, 25, 426
Norwich, 415
Nottingham, 403

'One Big Union', 368
Organisation of labour, 79, 96
Owenism, 8, 11, 22, 80, 95, 97, 361, 362, 379, 381, 391, 404

Pall Mall, 407
Panpolism, 26
Pan-Slavism, 35 f., 214
Papal Encyclicals, 260, 262, 316
Parable of the Water Tank, 374
Paris, 3, 38, 103, 105, 134, 137, 161, 177, 441
Paris, siege of, 143, 169 f.
Paris Commune, v, 105, 133, 134 ff., 146 ff., 174, 188, 196, 197 f., 211,

242, 249, 252, 258, 267, 300, 322, 324, 325, 357, 392, 410, 441, 451 f. ; leaders of, 148 ff.
Paris National Guard, 144 ff., 150, 154, 157 f., 159 f., 169, 171
Parliamentarianism, 42, 45, 51, 209, 358, 416 ff., 432. *See also* Political action
Parti Ouvrier Français, 151, 156, 325 f., 329, 425, 426, 440, 443
Patriotism, 233
Payment of M.P.s, 382, 388
Peace Congresses, International, 113 ff.
Peasant proprietorship, 383, 429
Peasants, rôle of, 43 f., 49 f., 112, 130, 165, 167, 225, 227, 250, 301 f.
People's Party (U.S.A.), 374
Phalanstères, 50
Phoenix Park, 396
Pleasure in work, 417, 419 ff.
Plebiscites, 226
Poland, Socialism in, 175 f., 216, 426, 427
Polish exiles in Switzerland, 190
Polish Revolt (1863), 33, 39, 42, 343
Political action, 101 f., 107, 108, 112 f., 307, 358, 366, 401 f., 403 f., 430 f. *See also* Parliamentarianism
Population problem, 27
Populists (U.S.A.), 374
Portugal, 9, 57
Positivism, 222, 385 f. *See also* Comte, Auguste
Possibilist Party (France), 154, 156, 324, 326, 426, 428, 440
Press, freedom of, 393
Productivity, 287, 295, 309, 352, 429, 430
Professorial Socialism. *See* Socialism of the Chair
Profit-sharing, 10 f., 260
Progress and Poverty, 370 ff., 384, 386, 395, 400
Propaganda by deed. *See* Anarchist violence
Property, 46, 61, 139, 233. *See also* Inheritance *and* Socialisation
Property, taxes on, 63, 382
Proportional Representation, 438
Protection, 27, 259, 349 f., 372
Protestantism, 16
Proudhonism, 11 f., 90 f., 93 f., 96, 97, 105, 108, 110, 111 f., 116, 123, 126, 132, 134, 138 ff., 152, 158,

167 f., 181, 186, 214, 236, 331, 337, 359, 361, 365, 443
Prussia, 3, 15, 17, 20, 41, 72 f., 84, 85 ff., 142, 176 f., 239, 241, 242 f., 253, 442
Public meeting, right of, 393, 394, 404, 406 ff., 432
Public works, 406, 438

Quod Apostolici Muneris, 262, 316

Radical Clubs, 394 f., 396, 397, 399, 406 f.
Radicalism, vi, 37, 89, 106 f., 115, 123 f., 135, 141, 171, 186, 385, 386 ff., 390 ff., 398, 400, 406, 410, 413
Railway nationalisation, 112, 126, 224, 374, 438
Rational Socialism, 57 ff.
Rationalism, 37, 230, 391
Reform Act (1867), 83, 93, 109, 132 f., 164, 174, 177, 392 ; (1884), 398
Reform League, National, 6, 89, 104, 106, 109, 197, 383, 392
Refugees. *See* Exiles
Regionalism, 189, 438. *See also* Federalism
Reintegration of labour, 351, 405
Religion, Bakunin's view of, 220 f., 222 f., 228, 231, 232, 262 ; Marx's view of, 264, 432 ; Natural, 68 ; social origin of, 59 f., 221
Rent, Henry George on, 371 ; Marx on, 298
Representative government, 359. *See also* Parliamentarianism
Republicanism, 136, 232, 250 f., 326, 386, 388, 390 f., 394, 440
Rerum Novarum, 260
Revisionism, 266, 300, 429, 431
Revolution, permanent, 2
Revolutionary Brotherhood, 121, 182
Revolutionary Catechism, 195, 229
Revolutionary Committee (Nechaiev), 194 f.
Revolutionism and Reformism, vi, 12 f., 29, 61, 68, 91 f., 135, 192 ff., 209 f., 219 ff., 358 ff., 397, 416 ff., 421 f., 431, 435 f.
Revolutions of 1848, 1 ff., 38, 71, 73, 89, 180, 192, 239, 270, 301, 363, 441
Rhineland, 1, 84, 99, 254
Right to work, 79, 404
Rights of Man, 26, 77 f., 246 f.

Rochdale Pioneers, 7, 8, 187, 380
Rome Anti-Anarchist Congress
   (1898), 334
Rose Street Club, 396, 416
Rouen, 134
Ruhr, 429
Russia, Anarchism in, 315 ff., 333
Russia, Marx's views on, 267, 301 f.
Russia, Socialism in, vi, 9, 32 ff.,
   51 f., 194 ff., 267 f., 301, 302,
   317 ff., 426, 427, 444, 447 f.
Russian Revolution (1917), vi, 304,
   344, 408
Russians in Switzerland, 190, 341

Saint-Simonianism, 30, 57, 179,
   228, 373
Saturday half-holiday, 432
Saxony, 237, 239, 429
Schleswig-Holstein, 241
Science, social impact of, 304
Scientific Socialism, 247, 267, 288,
   303 ff., 309, 311 ff., 360, 410 f.
Scotland, Socialism in, 415
Scottish crofters. See Crofters
Scottish Labour Party, 384
Scottish Land and Labour League,
   384, 400, 401, 402, 414
Secularism, 380, 385, 386, 391 ff.
Sedan, 143
Semaine sanglante, la, 157
Serfdom, 307
Serfs, emancipation of, 33, 34, 39 f.,
   44, 49, 342
Sheffield outrages, 105
Siberia, 215 f., 342 f.
Sicily, 181, 203, 330
Silesia, 429
Single Tax, 372 f., 378, 383, 385, 388.
   See also Land taxation
Sittlichkeit, 34
Sixty ', ' Manifesto of the, 138
Slavery, 307
Slavophils, 34 ff., 40, 44
Small holdings, 388
Social contract, 220
Social Democracy, growth of, 12, 31,
   208, 269, 286, 330, 376, 394, 410,
   425 ff., 443 f.
Social Democracy Party (U.S.A.),
   377, 378
Social Democratic Federation, 263,
   264, 337, 347, 379, 383, 384, 386,
   388, 389, 390, 393, 394 ff., 407 ff.,
   414, 425, 426, 440, 442, 461
Social Democratic Party (Germany).

See German Social Democratic
   Party
Social Democratic Party of North
   America, 365
Social science, 60, 65 f.
Socialisation, 23, 27, 28, 30, 57, 62,
   65, 67, 94, 95, 112, 126, 139, 168,
   180, 204 ff., 224, 309, 339 f., 354,
   397 f., 405, 430, 432 f., 436 f.
Socialism. See also Social Demo-
   cracy and under countries; Brad-
   laugh on, 393; Chamberlain on,
   389; Christian. See Christian
   Socialism; ethical, 263, 410 f.;
   Guild, 381; Integral, 185, 209;
   of the Chair, 16, 28, 258; Owenite.
   See Owenism; Rational, 57 ff.;
   Scientific. See Scientific Socialism; State, 20, 24, 28, 117, 258,
   261, 339, 426, 455; Utopian. See
   Utopianism
Socialist Labor Party (U.S.A.), 365,
   369, 373 f., 375 ff., 427
Socialist Labour Party (G.B.), 377
Socialist League, 337, 347, 400 ff.,
   409, 414 ff., 426, 442, 461 f.
Spain, Anarchism in, 128, 188 ff.,
   329 f., 333
Spain, Socialism in, vi, 9, 57, 102,
   109, 121, 122, 133, 163, 175,
   186 ff., 197, 198, 200 f., 202, 203,
   207 f., 208, 210, 329 f., 425, 426,
   443
Spanish Revolution (1868), 128, 186,
   189, 392
Stalinism, 51
Standing army, abolition of, 382, 432
State, theory of, 15 ff., 34 f., 37,
   45 f., 63 f., 79, 82 f., 97, 111 f.,
   117 f., 148, 162 ff., 165 ff., 205 ff.,
   209 f., 219 ff., 232 f., 248, 249 ff.,
   257, 270, 339, 353 f., 376
State, Welfare, 30, 388
State Capitalism, 30
State intervention, 23, 27, 28 f.
State Socialism. See Socialism,
   State
Strike, general. See General strike
Strikes, theory of, 376
Strikes in 1860s, 102, 103, 108, 109,
   128
Surplus value, 277 ff., 298, 299. See
   also Value
Sweden, Socialism in, 426
Switzerland, Anarchism in, 100 f.,
   120, 323, 340, 345

Switzerland, Socialism in, vi, 57, 66, 98, 100 f., 107 f., 120, 121, 124 f., 128, 133, 163, 176, 182, 190, 198, 200 f., 203, 207, 210, 239, 267, 340, 341, 346, 426
Syndicalism, 90, 113, 120, 166 f., 224, 328 f., 336, 338, 356, 359, 377, 443 f.

Taxation, 63, 67, 68, 432 f., 439. *See also* Inheritance, Land taxation, *and* Single Tax
Ten Hours Act, 6, 81, 91, 95, 281, 431
Terrorism, 54, 156, 316 ff., 458
Theosophy, 408
Tomsk, 215
'Tory gold', 403 f.
Trade Unionism, international, 208, 209
Trade Unions, vi, 9, 81, 91, 102 f., 127 f., 132, 167 f., 174, 211, 355 f., 429, 437 ; and politics, 358 ; and wages, 21, 23, 81, 295 ; in France, 88, 90, 105, 106 f., 134 f., 137 ff., 151, 152, 209, 323 ff. ; in Great Britain, 5 ff., 9, 11, 83, 88, 90, 93, 101, 104 f., 106, 109, 119, 133, 162 f., 174 f., 197 f., 199, 313, 381, 385, 390, 402, 406 f., 408, 431, 443 ; in Italy, 180 ; in U.S.A., 363 ff., 367 ff., 376 f.
Trades and Labor Alliance, 376
Trades Councils, 104. *See also* London Trades Council
Trades Union Congress, British, 6, 104, 162, 197, 381
Trafalgar Square, 407, 410
Truck, 432
Turin, 185
Turkey, 175, 176

Unauthorised Programme (Chamberlain), 388 ff., 402
Under-consumption, 293
Unemployed demonstrations, 405, 410
Unemployment, 211, 292, 295, 327, 382, 398, 404 ff.
Unified Socialist Party (France), 155

United Kingdom Alliance of Organised Trades, 128
United Labor Party (New York), 373, 374
United States, Anarchism in, 322, 331 ff., 337, 341, 368 f., 458
United States, Socialism in, vi, 1, 9, 32, 199, 200 ff., 209, 361 ff., 427, 443 f., 459 f.
Universal Peace Union, 114
Universal Suffrage. *See* Manhood Suffrage
Unto This Last, 421
Use value, 275, 278, 283
Utilitarianism, 37, 48, 220
Utility, marginal, 271, 275 f.
Utopianism, 38, 57, 59, 339, 383

Value, labour theory of, 21 f., 83, 245, 272 ff., 331 ; in relation to price, 270 f., 273 ff., 288 f., 292 f.
Values, absolute and relative, 306 f., 308 f.
Vienna, 176, 259 f.
Volksgeist, 77 f., 84
Volksstaat, 117, 205 ff.
Vpered, 53

Wages, theories of, 21, 22, 23 f., 72, 80 ff., 96, 97, 244 f., 249, 279 ff., 283, 295, 363, 397
Walsall Anarchists, 336
War Emergency Workers' National Committee, 411
Watch-making in Jura, 100, 345
Welfare State, 30, 388
Wisconsin, 378
Women, emancipation of, 432, 439
Women's employment, 94
Women's Suffrage, 94
Workers' control, 438, 439. *See also* Control of industry
Working Men's Party of the United States, 365 f.

Yorkshire, 414

Zeiss works, Jena, 11
Zemlya i Volya, 318 ff.
Zünfte, 27, 259

END OF VOL. II

PRINTED BY LOWE AND BRYDONE (PRINTERS) LTD., LONDON